711

PEACE FOR OUR TIME

£1-50

Roger Parkinson

PEACE FOR OUR TIME

Munich to Dunkirk – the inside story

Rupert Hart-Davis : London

Granada Publishing Limited
First published in Great Britain 1971 by Rupert Hart-Davis Ltd
3 Upper James Street London W1R 4BP

Copyright © 1971 by Roger Parkinson

ISBN 0 246 64098 7

Printed in Great Britain by
Northumberland Press Limited
Gateshead

Contents

vi

Maps

Some Major Figures Involved

AMERY, Leopold: Colonial Office Under-Secretary, 1919; First Lord of the Admiralty, 1922; Colonial Secretary, 1924-1929, including Dominions Secretary from 1925; Secretary for India and Burma, 1940.

ANDERSON, Sir John, 1st Viscount Waverley: Permanent Under-Secretary at Home Office, 1922-1932; Home Secretary and Minister of Home Security, 1939-1940; Lord President of the Council, 1940.

ASHTON-GWATKIN, Frank: attached to Runciman Mission, 1938; seconded to Ministry of Economic Warfare, September 1939.

ATTOLICO, Bernado: Italian Ambassador to Berlin.

BECK, Colonel Jósef: Polish Foreign Minister.

BENES, Edward: successor to Masaryk as President of Czechoslovakia, 1935; resigned 1938.

BILLOTTE, General G. H. G.: French Army Group commander, 1939, 1940.

BONNET, Georges; French Ambassador to US, 1937; Foreign Minister, 1938.

BRAUCHITSCH, General Walther von: Commander-in-Chief of the German Army.

BRIDGES, Sir Edward: Secretary to the British Cabinet and War Cabinet.

BROWN, Ernest: Minister of Labour, appointed 1937.

BURCKHARDT, Dr Carl: League of Nations Commissioner for Danzig.

BURGIN, Leslie: Minister of Transport, 1937; Minister without Portfolio, 1939; Minister of Supply, July 1939.

CADOGAN, Sir Alexander: Permanent Under-Secretary of State at the Foreign Office, appointed 1 January 1938.

CAMPBELL, Sir Ronald: transferred to Embassy at Belgrade, August 1935; Ambassador at Paris from 1 November 1939.

CHATFIELD, Alfred, 1st Baron: First Sea Lord and Chief of Naval Staff, 1933-1938; Minister for Co-ordination of Defence from 2 January 1939 to 1940.

CIANO, Count Galeazzo: Italian Minister of Propaganda, 1935; Foreign Minister 1936-1943; son-in-law of Mussolini.

CLARK, Sir Noel: British Chargé at Rome, 1938, 1939.

CLIVE, Sir Robert Henry: Ambassador at Brussels from July 1933; retired December 1939.

COLVILLE, Ian: succeeded Walter Elliot as Secretary of State for Scotland, May 1938.

COOPER, Sir Alfred Duff, 1st Viscount Norwich: Secretary of State for War, 1935-1937; First Lord of the Admiralty, resigned 1938; Minister of Information 1940-1942; Ambassador to France, 1944-1947.

CORBIN, Charles: French Ambassador to London.

COULONDRE, Robert: French Ambassador, Berlin, in succession to François-Poncet.

DALADIER, Édouard: French War Minister, 1936; Premier, 1938; resigned May 1940.

DILL, General Sir John: BEF Corps Commander; Chief of the Imperial General Staff, 1940; head of Joint Staff Mission to Washington until his death in 1943.

EDEN, Sir (Robert) Anthony: Foreign Under-Secretary, 1931; Lord Privy Seal, 1934; Foreign Secretary, 1936, resigned 1938; Dominions Secretary, 1939; War Secretary, May 1940; Foreign Secretary, December 1940.

ELLIOT, Walter: Secretary of State for Scotland, 1936-1938; Minister of Health 1938-1940.

FORSTER, Albert: Gauleiter of Danzig.

FRANÇOIS-PONCET, André: French Ambassador at Berlin, replaced by Coulondre, December 1938.

GAMELIN, Maurice Gustave: Chief of General Staff, French Army, 1935, replaced by Weygand, 1940.

GEORGES, General Alphonse-Joseph: French Army Commander, North-East.

GOEBBELS, Joseph: Head of Nazi Ministry of Public Enlightenment and Propaganda from 1933.

GÖRING, Hermann Wilhelm: entered Nazi Government 1933; posts included Reich Commissioner for Air.

GORT, John Standish, Field-Marshal, Viscount: Commander-in-Chief British Field Force, 1939-1940.

GREENWOOD, Arthur: Deputy Leader of the British Labour Party, 1935; Minister without Portfolio, 1940.

HACHA, Emil: President of Czechoslovakia, 1938, following Benes's resignation; puppet President of German protectorate 1939-1945.

HAILSHAM, Douglas McGarel Hogg, 1st Viscount: Attorney-General 1922-1924, 1924-1928; Lord Chancellor 1928-1929; War Secretary 1931-1935; Lord President of the Council, March 1938.

HALDER, General Franz: Chief of Staff, German Army.

HALIFAX, Edward, 1st Earl of: Viceroy of India, 1926-1931; Foreign Secretary 1938-1940; Ambassador to US, 1941-1946.

HANKEY, Maurice Paschal, 1st Baron: Secretary of Cabinet and Committee of Imperial Defence, 1912-1938; Clerk of Privy Council, 1923-1938; Minister without Portfolio, 1939; Chancellor of Duchy of Lancaster, 1940.

HENDERSON, Sir Nevile Meyrick: Ambassador at Berlin from April 1937

HENLEIN, Konrad: Sudeten-German leader; Gauleiter 1938; Civil Commissioner for Bohemia, 1939.

HESS, Rudolf: Deputy Nazi leader, 1934; appointed Hitler's successor-designate after Göring, 1939.

HOARE, Sir Reginald Hervey: Ambassador at Bucharest from February 1935

HOARE, Sir Samuel John, 1st Viscount Templewood: Air Secretary, 1922-1929; Secretary of State for India, 1931-1935; Foreign Secretary 1935, resigning over his part in the abortive Hoare-Laval Pact; First Lord, 1936; Home Secretary, 1937-1939; Ambassador on Special Mission to Madrid, 1940.

HORE-BELISHA, Leslie: Minister of Transport, 1934; Secretary of State for War, 1937-1940.

INSKIP, Sir Thomas, 1st Viscount: Minister for Co-ordination of Defence, 1936-1939, 2 January; Lord Chancellor, 1939; Leader of House of Lords, 1940.

IRONSIDE, Sir (William) Edmund: Chief of the Imperial General Staff; Field-Marshal, 1940 and Commander of Home Defence Forces, succeeded as CIGS by Sir John Dill.

KEITEL, Wilhelm: Chief of Supreme Command of German Armed Forces, 1938.

KENNARD, Sir Howard William: Ambassador at Warsaw from January 1935; Embassy removed to Angers (France), November 1939.

KENNEDY, Joseph Patrick: US Ambassador at London.

KIRKPATRICK, Ivone Augustine: Chargé at Berlin, 1936, 1937 until 14 December 1938; transferred to Foreign Office, Whitehall.

LÉGER, Alexis: Permanent Secretary-General French Foreign Office (Quai d'Orsay); replaced May 1940 by Charles Roux.

LINDSAY, Sir Ronald Charles: British Ambassador at Washington from 1930; retired 17 October 1939.

LIPSKI, Jósef: Polish Ambassador at Berlin.

LITVINOV, Maxim: Bolshevist Ambassador to London, 1917-1918; Commissar for Foreign Affairs, 1930-May 1939.

MACDONALD, Malcolm: Colonial Secretary, 1935; 1938-1940; Minister of Health, 1940-1941.

MAISKY, Ivan: Soviet Ambassador to London, 1932-1943.

MALLET, Victor Alex: Ambassador to Stockholm from 16 January 1940.

MASON-MACFARLANE, Lieut-Colonel Frank Noel: Military Attaché at Berlin and Copenhagen from 13 December 1937.

MAUGHAM, Lord: Lord Chancellor, 1938, 1939.

MOLOTOV, Vyacheslav Mikhailovich: Chairman of Council of People's Commissars 1930-1941; Foreign Minister, in succession to Litvinov, from May 1939 to 1949.

MORRISON, Herbert Stanley: Minister of Supply, 1940; Home Secretary, 1940.

MORRISON, William Shepherd: Minister of Agriculture and Fisheries, 1936-1939; of Food, 1939-1940; Postmaster-General, 1940.

NEWALL, Sir Cyril: Chief of Air Staff, 1937-1940; Marshal of RAF, 1940; Governor-General of New Zealand, 1941.

NEWTON, Sir Basil Cochrane: Ambassador at Prague from March 1937: Ambassador at Baghdad from 3 May 1939.

PERTH, Lord: Ambassador at Rome from October 1933; retired 29 May 1939; Director-General at Ministry of Information, 1939.

PHIPPS, Sir Eric Clare: Ambassador at Paris from April 1937; retired 5 November 1939.

PLUNKETT-ERNLE-ERLE-DRAX, Admiral the Hon. Sir R. A. R.: Head of British Mission to Moscow, August 1939.

POUND, Sir (Alfred) Dudley: Commander-in-Chief Royal Navy Mediterranean, 1936-1939; First Sea Lord, 1939-1943.

RAEDER, Admiral Erich: Chief of the German Naval Staff.

REYNAUD, Paul: replaced Daladier as French Premier, 21 March 1940.

RIBBENTROP, Joachim von: ex-wine merchant; German Ambassador at London, 1936-1938; Foreign Minister.

RUNCIMAN, Walter, Viscount: head of British mission to Czechoslovakia, August 1938; former President of Board of Trade; later Lord President of the Council.

RYAN, Sir Andrew: Consul-General, Durazzo, from October 1936; retired 30 September 1939.

SCHMIDT, Dr Paul: Hitler's interpreter.

SCHULENBURG, Count Friedrich Werner von der: German Ambassador at Moscow.

SEEDS, Sir William: Ambassador at Moscow from 19 January 1939.

SHEPHERD, Edward Henry: Consul-General at Danzig from November 1937; appointed Consul-General at Amsterdam, 16 October 1939.

SIMON, Sir John Allsebrook: Attorney-General, 1913-1915; Home Secretary, 1915-1916, resigning in opposition to conscription; Foreign Secretary under MacDonald's coalition, 1931; Home Secretary, 1935-1937; Chancellor of Exchequer, 1937-1940.

SINCLAIR, Sir Archibald, 1st Viscount Thurso: Leader of British Liberal Party, 1935; Secretary of State for Air, May 1940-1945.

STANHOPE, James Richard, 7th Earl: First Lord of the Admiralty, 1938-1939; Lord President of the Council, 1939-1940.

STANLEY, Oliver: Minister of Transport, 1933-1934; Minister of Labour, 1934-1935; President of Board of Education, 1935-1937; of Board of Trade, 1937-1940; Secretary of State for War, December 1940; Colonial Secretary, 1942.

STRANG, William: Head of British Foreign Office East European Department; promoted to an Acting Assistant Under-Secretary of State, 11 September 1939.

VANSITTART, Sir Robert Gilbert: Permanent Under-Secretary of State for Foreign Affairs from 1930; Chief Diplomatic Adviser to Chamberlain's Government from 1 January 1938; retired 1941.

WATERLOW, Sir Sydney Philip: Ambassador at Athens from November 1933; retired 29 June 1939.

WEIZSÄCKER, Baron Ernst von: German State Secretary.

WELLES, Sumner: US Under-Secretary of State; President Roosevelt's envoy to Europe, 1938.

WILSON, Sir Horace: Chief Industrial Adviser to the Government; Chamberlain's close friend and adviser.

WINTERTON, Lord: Chancellor of the Duchy of Lancaster; 'Father' of the House of Commons.

ZETLAND, Marquess of: British Secretary of State for India and Burma.

Abbreviations

BEF   British Expeditionary Force

CID   Committee for Imperial Defence

CIGS   Chief of the Imperial General Staff

FPC   Foreign Policy Committee

HMG   His Majesty's Government

MCC   Military Coordination Committee

OKW   *Oberkommando der Wehrmacht* (Armed Forces High Command)

EUROPE

after World War One

Iceland

FAROES

Bergen

Scapa
Flow

Stavanger

Egersund

London

Wilhelmshaven

Neth.

Lille

Belg.

Valenciennes

Namur

Godesburg

Givet

Saarbrucken

Paris

Maginot
Line

Karlsruhe

France

Strasbourg

Basle

Switz.

Portugal

Spain

●Madrid

Introduction

Both opponents and supporters of Neville Chamberlain can use the Cabinet Papers, now released from security restrictions, to strengthen previous beliefs. Plenty of material shows Chamberlain stubborn, vain, short-sighted and blinkered; equally, plenty shows him sincere, determined, concerned and wise. The few who condemned Chamberlain at the time of Munich, will find their past opinions confirmed; likewise, the many who applauded his efforts to prolong peace will find no reason now to change their minds.

But for those with an open mind in those terrible months, or those born since who can be more objective, the Papers reveal a man often indecisive and wavering, often stubborn, grossly mistaken, yet often wise, a man who clutched too long on the flickering, fading shadow of peace because he hated war, and because he thought his country unwilling and unprepared to face it. He opposed a man evil indeed but also suffering from doubts and indecision. And his Cabinet members changed their minds, argued, became confused and panicked, acted in fact as humans usually do in time of crisis.

I have attempted to provide narration rather than presumptuous judgement. I have also relied on information available to Chamberlain and his Cabinet at the time, apart from introducing parallel secret discussions in Germany and Rome to reveal simultaneous lines of thought. Above all, I have tried to avoid easy comparisons based on hindsight, such as whether Britain would have done better to fight Germany in late 1938 or late 1939 – a comparison impossible for Chamberlain and therefore irrelevant. To ease the narrative, I have taken the liberty of reverting the Cabinet Minutes to direct speech wherever possible.

My most fervent thanks go, as always, to Betty, an indispensable wife and partner. I also gratefully acknowledge the help of the Public Records Office staff, in leading me through the documentary maze; the staff of the London Library; the Editor of *The Scotsman*, in giving me time to write this book; and permission granted by the Controller of Her Majesty's Stationery Office for the quotations from *Documents on British Foreign Policy* (Series 3, vols. II-VII), which are Crown copyright. These quotations are fully detailed in the source lists at the end of the book. I also express my gratitude for the help obtained from memoirs and previous works on this period; quotations have especially been taken from the following books, which are also detailed in the source lists and in the bibliography. Churchill, *The Gathering Storm;* Feiling, *Life of Neville Chamberlain;* Minney, *The Private Papers of Hore-Belisha;* Henderson, *Failure of a Mission;* Halifax, *Fullness of Days;* Ismay, *Memoirs;* Hoare, *Nine Troubled Years;* Nicolson, *Diaries and Letters* (1930-1939 and 1939-1945); Kirkpatrick, *The Inner Circle;* Eden, *The Reckoning;* Bryant, *Turn of the Tide.*

1

Black Wednesday

Discussion, like peace, had ended; and the massive table stood cleared of papers in the dark and empty Cabinet Room, 10 Downing Street. Nine times in the last eleven days the Cabinet had assembled there. In nearby Whitehall waited a sad and silent crowd; fresh flowers had been placed against the Cenotaph to honour the heroes of the Great War; and all in the crowd feared the next Great War would erupt in a few hours' time, twenty years after the first had finished. Conflict was inevitable now; and when war came an immediate, devastating aerial bombardment would be brought on Britain's capital, from which few would survive. This the crowd believed. No adequate defence existed against German bombers; experts had told them so.

Five hundred yards away the narrow benches of the House of Commons were packed. Like the crowd outside, members were silent, waiting. They were mourners at a funeral; peace was dead, no man had done more than the Right Honourable Neville Chamberlain to keep it alive, and now they had gathered to hear him bury it. As he had said on the radio the evening before: 'How horrible, fantastic, incredible it is that we should be digging trenches and trying on gas-masks here because of a quarrel in a far-away country between people of whom we know nothing! ... I would not hesitate to pay even a third visit to Germany if I thought it would do any good.... I am myself a man of peace to the depths of my soul. Armed conflict between nations is a nightmare to me.'[1]

The Prime Minister entered the Chamber immediately after the Speaker's preliminary announcement. His thin face was pinched and tired; he had been up until 2 o'clock that morning preparing this speech. For Chamberlain the moment meant terrible failure; he wrote to his sister a few days later: 'I only know that, as the hours went by, events seemed to be closing in and driving us to the edge of the abyss with a horrifying certainty and rapidity. Only Annie knows what I went through in those agonizing hours, when hope seemed almost extinguished.... For me, I confess that it seemed only too possible that

I

all the prayers of all the peoples of the world, including Germany herself, might break against the fanatical obstinacy of one man.'[2]

Chamberlain started his speech, hardly reading from his notes, his voice carefully calm, his words measured. The Commons clock showed almost ten to three. All knew the story of the tragedy he had to recite; only the ending had still to be stated.

Herr Hitler's ultimatum that the Czechs should bow to his territorial demands had expired 50 minutes before, at 2 o'clock this very afternoon, 28 September 1938, 'Black Wednesday'. The Führer had pledged to take that country by force on 1 October if this acquiescence was not forthcoming. Now he would do so; his mobile divisions were making final preparations; and Britain had declared that if German tanks pushed into Czechoslovakia 'the immediate result must be that France will be bound to come to her assistance and Great Britain and Russia will certainly stand by France'. Hence the inevitability of war. Thirty-eight million gas-masks had been issued; a State of Emergency declared by Order in Council; trenches were being hurriedly dug; cellars and basements requisitioned for air raid shelters. Territorial Army units had been commanded to assemble, and the British Fleet had mobilized. Royal Navy warships now steamed ready on the high seas or waited at anchor at bleak Scapa Flow.

The Prime Minister recounted the events of the last few weeks and days. He described how both Britain and France had rejected Hitler's final terms; he confessed to the failure of appeasement. Churchill sat hunched, huge and still at the end of one row, Attlee sat opposite Chamberlain, his feet on the table. The 20 members of the Cabinet sat in a line on the Government front bench, or, like Lord Halifax, the Foreign Secretary, listened from the crowded Peers' Gallery. The Prime Minister continued, occasionally taking off his pince-nez with finger and thumb and glancing up at the ceiling. Tension increased as Chamberlain said he had made a last attempt to preserve peace: he had sent a message to Mussolini, asking him to appeal to Hitler. 'In reply to my message I was informed that instructions had been sent ... that Mussolini hoped Herr Hitler would see his way to postpone action. ... In response, Herr Hitler has agreed to postpone mobilization for 24 hours.' But it seemed that at the most the opening of hostilities had been delayed; the end would be just the same.

The clock showed twelve minutes to four. At that moment a note was sent down from Halifax in the Peers' Gallery. The scrap of paper passed from hand to hand along the Government front bench, Chamberlain oblivious to the message as it approached him. The paper reached Sir Samuel Hoare, the Home Secretary, then Sir John Simon, the Chancellor of the Exchequer, who glanced at it and hurriedly passed it up to the Prime Minister. Chamberlain stopped his speech; the House waited in silence while he readjusted his pince-nez and read.

Suddenly Chamberlain raised his head. 'That is not all. I have something further to say to the House yet.' His voice louder now, he continued amidst the murmuring: 'I have been informed by Herr Hitler that he invites me to meet him tomorrow morning. He has also invited Sr. Mussolini and M. Daladier. Sr. Mussolini has accepted, and I have no doubt M. Daladier will also accept. I need not say what my answer will be.... I am sure that the House will be ready to release me now to go and see what I can make of this last effort.' For one moment the House stayed still; then Members broke into a frenzy of relief; they shouted and they cheered, they rose to applaud the man who had saved London, Britain, Europe. 'Thank God for the Prime Minister,' cried Conservatives. 'Stand up, you brute!' hissed an irate MP to the National Labour member, Harold Nicolson. Amid almost hysterical tumult, crowded by his fervent supporters, sat Chamberlain, small like a sparrow and smiling with satisfaction. Appeasement had worked after all. Briefly his face changed when Churchill said: 'I congratulate you on your fortune. You were very lucky.' But the shadow soon passed: frail peace had been revived. As he wrote to his sister: 'I dare say Annie has told you, or will tell you, of the birth of the last desperate snatch at the last tuft on the very verge of the precipice. That the news of the deliverance should come to me in the very act of closing my speech in the House, was a piece of drama that no work of fiction ever surpassed.'[3]

Early next morning he told the excited crowd at Croydon airport that he hoped he might soon quote: 'Out of this nettle, Danger, we pluck this flower, Safety.' When someone suggested an even better phrase, Disraeli's – 'peace for our time' – he impatiently dismissed it as far too fanciful. The 69-year-old Prime Minister of Great Britain strode briskly over the concrete to his waiting aeroplane, a small, vulnerable figure armed solely with a swinging umbrella. His destination was Munich.

Anschluss and After

The immediate origins of the Munich Conference lay in a scheme the Prime Minister had revealed to his startled Cabinet exactly two weeks before. Leslie Hore-Belisha, Secretary of State for War, scribbled in his diary: 'It came as a bombshell.'[1] But the main causes of the conference form a central thread in the tangle of diplomatic, political and military manoeuvrings in spring and summer 1938, when fears multiplied, statesmen panicked or retreated into dogma, mistake reacted on mistake.

Six months before, Chamberlain had held a farewell lunch at 10 Downing Street in honour of the German Ambassador, Joachim von Ribbentrop, departing to become Foreign Minister. About 16 people were present; the occasion had been polite, even cordial; conversation ranged from uncontroversial diplomatic items to grouse shooting in Scotland. Half-way through the meal a Foreign Office messenger brought a message to Sir Alexander Cadogan, who read the note then walked round to Halifax, who showed it to Chamberlain. The three of them left the room with Ribbentrop. Chamberlain had been informed that at the very moment he and the guests had been wishing Ribbentrop well, Hitler was invading Austria. Tanks were grinding down the roads towards Vienna. The German takeover of Austria – *Anschluss* – was being put into practice, as Ribbentrop must have known it would be that day, despite his feigned surprise. The meal continued in icy coldness.

Yet in London the event had been expected. Even Anthony Eden, who had resigned as Foreign Secretary three weeks before on 20 February, had told Ribbentrop: 'People in England recognized that a closer connection between Germany and Austria would have to come about sometime.' And Chamberlain and his Cabinet, however much they might deplore Hitler's method, could still fit *Anschluss* into the belief that Germany had been wronged by the Versailles Treaty of 1919, by which the victors of the Great War had imposed their dictatorial will upon the vanquished.

Sir Nevile Henderson, British Ambassador at Berlin and Chamberlain's prime apostle of appeasement, wrote: 'I believed that there was no real prospect of stability either in Germany or in Europe generally until the grievances arising out of the Versailles Treaty – which had created Hitler – had been rectified so far as the Germans were concerned. This done, I trusted that Hitler and the reasons for his existence and the methods of his régime, would disappear. But in the meantime I thought that the right policy was to carry conciliation to its utmost point.'[2] The Versailles Treaty had splintered the old Austro-Hungarian Empire and had erected an artificial barrier between Austria and Germany. It had left too many pretexts for future quarrels: the Baltic port of Danzig, which was claimed by Germany and Poland, and given to Poland under the control of the League of Nations with the artificial status of a 'Free City'; the port of Memel which, like Danzig, had a German population, but seized by Lithuania in 1923; Teschen, in Czechoslovakia, claimed by Poland; and the whole issue of minorities trapped by the Treaty boundaries in new, alien nations – especially the Sudeten Germans in Czechoslovakia.

Back in 1934 and 1935, Nazi Germany was to Chamberlain 'the bully of Europe', and the threat of military action was 'the only thing Germans understand'. In May 1938, after the Austrian takeover, Hitler was still 'utterly untrustworthy and dishonest'.[3] On 14 March, two days after *Anschluss*, 'After what has happened no one anywhere will feel any confidence as to what Herr Hitler will do next.'[4] And yet, after meeting him on 19 September, Chamberlain wrote, 'In spite of the hardness and ruthlessness I thought I saw in his face, I got the impression that here was a man who could be relied upon when he had given his word.'[5] By autumn 1938, appeasement seemed to Chamberlain not only the best policy, but the only policy; and he adhered to it with characteristic stubbornness. His inflexible manner was accentuated by aloofness. 'You can't know Mr Chamberlain until you have been with him for five years,' his chauffeur claimed. He never let himself go; even when matters were troubling him deeply, he merely seemed colder and further away. His speech became more dry, more pedantic – he used more double negatives. He had few friends and preferred the solitude of Chequers to London dinner parties: the remote Prime Minister found excitement in a 'magnificent specimen of houndstongue' at his country retreat. He would return unwillingly to London after a few snatched hours in the woods and fields of the Chilterns.

The Cabinet fully realized that after Austria, Hitler's next target would be Czechoslovakia. The Minutes for the meeting on Saturday, 12 March, when German forces were still advancing into Austria, show this realization and the belief that only limited scope existed for British action. 'The Prime Minister said that although there was probably not very much that could be done, he had thought that the Cabinet should meet.' *Anschluss* 'made international appeasement much more difficult'. There was concern that Czechoslovakia was now threatened, but this concern must be kept as quiet as possible. Chamberlain 'warned the Cabinet against giving the impression that [Britain] was faced with the prospect of war within a few weeks.'[6]

Militarily, Czechoslovakia's defences had been outflanked; economically, she could now be more easily strangled. Czechoslovakia, together with Yugoslavia and Roumania, had been created after the Great War from the Austrian Empire's shattered remains. She epitomized everything Hitler loathed most; so too did the Czechs, the *Untermenschen*, the subhumans – except, of course, the Sudeten. These *Auslandsdeutschen*, Germans in exile, must be brought into the Reich. The British Foreign Office and Cabinet watched with apprehension as the Sudeten reacted. *Anschluss*, cabled the British Consul at Liberec, 'has set in motion an avalanche of national feeling amongst the Sudeten Germans'. The British Military Attaché remarked, 'Nazism has gone to their heads like wine.... Nothing short of incorporation in the German Reich will satisfy the majority of people.'[7] The Cabinet also learned that Konrad Henlein had consolidated his leadership over the extremist *Sudetendeutsche Heimalfront*, the SHF.

The Cabinet appreciated that France was in a difficult position. In 1925 she had guaranteed the Czech and Polish frontiers. But political upheavals in Paris complicated attempts to learn what the French intended. The day before *Anschluss* the Chautemps government fell; Leon Blum's administration lasted only four weeks; then Edouard Daladier, War Minister since 1936, formed another government. Paris was paralysed when Czechoslovakia was suddenly threatened. Even when Daladier took control on 10 April, France still hesitated to declare support. Georges Bonnet, now Foreign Minister, believed Czechoslovakia already 'a doomed nation'.

But at the Cabinet meeting on 14 March, Chamberlain warned against Britain taking too firm a stand over Austria. Halifax agreed 'in a dislike of threats that could not be carried out. I think, however, that if the Government wants to get public opinion behind them they must show that they are not afraid to tell the Dictators what they think'. Chamberlain agreed, provided that 'the condemnation is confined to method and the shock to public opinion, and does not indicate that events are leading to war'.

But in the Commons debate that day, Churchill spoke out. In a newspaper article four days later, he called for a defence agreement between Britain, France, and 'the Powers of the second rank in Europe'. But Churchill was not a Minister – according to Chamberlain, 'if I take him into the Cabinet, he will dominate it. He won't give others a chance of even talking'. Chamberlain opposed this idea of collective

6

security. He wrote to his sister after the article: 'To be badgered and pressed to come out and give a clear, decided, bold and unmistakable lead, show "ordinary courage", and all the rest of the twaddle, is calculated to vex the man who has to take the responsibility of the consequences. As a matter of fact, the plan of the "Grand Alliance", as Winston calls it, had occurred to me long before he mentioned it. ... It is a very attractive idea, indeed there is almost everything to be said for it until you come to examine its practicability.... You have only to look at the map to see that nothing that France or we could do could possibly save Czechoslovakia.'[8]

Nevertheless, hard facts had still to be faced, and Chamberlain, in a Commons speech on 24 March, admitted there now existed a 'profound disturbance of international confidence'. What were Britain's obligations? She was bound, Chamberlain said, by the 1925 Treaty of Locarno to go to the defence of France and Belgium against unprovoked attack. Legally this did not extend to helping France if she implemented her treaty with Czechoslovakia, but 'where peace and war are concerned, legal obligations are not alone involved and if war broke out, it would be unlikely to be confined to those who have assumed such obligations. It would be quite impossible to say where it might end and what Governments might not become involved.... This is especially true in the case of two countries with long association like Great Britain and France.' As a result, measures must now be taken to increase production, particularly for RAF and anti-aircraft defence. 'Full and rapid equipment of the nation for self-defence must be the primary aim.'

But Cabinet meetings preceding this speech reveal the limits of those armament plans. Chamberlain firmly ruled out conscription, and although rearmament occupied a good deal of Cabinet time, his were the views which prevailed: 'We should speed up our existing plans for rearmament – which would be far more useful than to announce new plans.'[9] Minutes for these important meetings show the lines of thought leading to the 24 March speech. On 22 March, for example, the Cabinet had before them a Chiefs of Staff Sub-Committee report, 'the dominant conclusion of which was that no pressure which this country and its possible allies could exercise would suffice to prevent the defeat of Czechoslovakia'. Halifax said 'I myself and, I think, the Prime Minister also, began our examination with some sympathy towards the idea of a guarantee [to Czechoslovakia]. Clearly, however, a decision cannot be reached without some knowledge of the military position.... The Report is an extremely melancholy one, but no Government could afford to overlook it.' Halifax felt 'he was not in a position to recommend a policy involving a risk of war.... We should endeavour to induce the Government of Czechoslovakia to apply themselves to producing a direct settlement with the Sudeten-*Deutsch*'. He added: 'The policy is likely to prove unpalatable to the French.'[10]

The Cabinet meetings in those days after *Anschluss* saw the emphasis first placed on a policy which was to be increasingly followed by Chamberlain. It entailed diplomatic pressure plus appeasement, plus a strictly restrained attitude towards commitments, plus primarily defensive rearmament measures. During the coming months he was to be preoccupied with balancing these various factors. He would refer foreign policy matters to an inner Committee of the Cabinet, chaired by himself. Service Ministers were not invited to its meetings: the emphasis was to be on appeasement, not rearmament. The Foreign Policy Committee (FPC) had 31 meetings between 16 June 1938 and 25 August 1939, and was usually attended by 10 or 11 Ministers. Increasingly however, and especially after Munich, Chamberlain came to rely upon the 'Inner Cabinet' – the Foreign Secretary, the Chancellor of the Exchequer and the Home Secretary. The 'Big Four' met on frequent, largely unrecorded occasions, and initiated important policy changes. And, at times of peak anxiety, Chamberlain would dispense even with this small group and would consult only his Foreign Secretary.

Chamberlain has been criticized for acting outside the Cabinet. But his accusers have been unduly harsh. Granted there were occasions when important moves were made without Cabinet consultation, notably the request on 13 September for an interview with Hitler, the decision on 18 September to guarantee Czechoslovakia, and, in March 1939, an important shift in attitude towards the Soviet Union. But these occasions were exceptions, and some were genuinely due to urgency. As for the FPC, while excluding Service Ministers might have been a mistake, Chamberlain could claim they were represented by his Minister for Coordination of Defence, who was included; and the Committee was a means of speeding decision – the forerunner in fact of the present Defence and Overseas Policy Committee. Moreover, few Prime Ministers have served without an innermost group of confidants such as the 'Big Four' – Churchill was to sometimes take decisions with even fewer advisers and, indeed, undertook important steps on his own initiative when he was merely First Lord.

Stanley Baldwin, Chamberlain's predecessor, had taken little share in Foreign Policy, preferring instead to leave Anthony Eden with a free hand. Chamberlain, when he took office on 28 May 1937, rapidly revealed his different attitude; he had strong views about foreign affairs and intended to see them implemented. His ideas on conciliation clashed with Eden's preference for sterner action, so Eden eventually went. Chamberlain was relieved. But Churchill, when he heard of the resignation, lay awake 'consumed by emotions of sorrow and fear. There seemed one strong young figure standing up against long, dismal, drawling tides of drift and surrender, of wrong measurements and feeble impulses.... Now he has gone. I watched the daylight slowly creep through the windows and saw before me in mental gaze the vision of Death.'[11]

Halifax, who replaced Eden, seemed more sympathetic. Yet he wrote: 'It was with great reluctance that I agreed to accept the post.' He realized 'how thankless in present circumstances the work of any Foreign Secretary was bound to be'.[12] He was to serve Chamberlain well whatever his personal beliefs.

Before Halifax took office Sir Robert Vansittart, official head of the Foreign Office and hostile to the Nazis, had been in effect replaced by Sir Alexander Cadogan: Sir Robert had been re-appointed 'Chief Diplomatic Adviser' which, although represented as promotion, gave him less influence. Chamberlain relied on Cadogan, and even more on Sir Horace Wilson who, when Chamberlain had been Chancellor, had rendered him sterling service. Wilson was now installed as the Prime Minister's principal official adviser.

So, at the head of his small team, Chamberlain directed Britain's foreign policy during those critical months of 1938, declaring increasingly that to rely on collective security, which had dragged nations to war in 1914, was to be trussed to a corpse, to partake in alliances was to be dangerously committed, and yet to believe in isolation was to believe in a dream. Instead, he claimed, Mussolini must be edged away from Hitler, some good must be found in the Führer, and appeals to this good must bring about peace. Every man had his human side, said Chamberlain; whole peoples did not wish war. He sought with desperation to find that streak of virtue in the Führer's character; the search became a mission, appeasement a crusade. The British parliamentary opposition, with its policy of arms for Spain, sanctions against Japan, alliance with Russia, 'standing up' to dictators, was fundamentally and dangerously mistaken. Such a policy could only lead to conflict, and Britain was ill-prepared for war.

Even Churchill admitted at a private party on 16 March 1938: 'We stand to lose everything by failing to take strong action – and yet if we take strong action London will be a shambles in half an hour.'[13] This ghastly dilemma lay behind Chamberlain's conviction that Britain must stay out of conflict, that she must rearm only for defence, not for Continental expeditions. If Hitler believed Britain busy improving her offensive, rather than defensive, powers, it might make him aggressive. Chamberlain wrote soon after taking office: 'I believe the double policy of rearmament and better relations with Germany and Italy will carry us safely through the danger period, if only the Foreign Office will play up.'[14] He spoke his mind most freely in his beloved Birmingham, and there, in April 1938, he declared that he hated the thought of the hard-won savings of the British people being used to construct weapons of war, but 'we have no alternative but to go on with it'. And yet, he went on, 'do not forget we are all members of the human race, and subject to the like passions and affections, and fears and desires. There must be something in common between us if only we can find it, and perhaps by our very aloofness from the rest of Europe we may have some special part to play as conciliator and mediator.' He wanted to 'make gentle the life of the world'.[15] He was convinced that the British public were vehemently opposed to war, that the Czechs would anyway not benefit from intervention, and, perhaps most important, that Britain was unprepared. This last of course could not be stated publicly.

In 1938, a story circulated Berlin: 'The English have so many aeroplanes that the sky is black with them, those of France are so numerous that they obscure the sun. But when Hermann Göring presses the button, birds themselves have to walk.' It was certainly accepted, both in Germany and Britain, that the Luftwaffe was a terrible striking weapon. German bombs would destroy London. So, until London and Britain could be better defended, until the British people were materially and mentally ready for war, until all chances of peace had gone, appeasement must be accepted – even if this meant risking Czechoslovakia. Even if it meant humiliation, subterfuge, carrying self-interest to astonishing, even shabby extremes.

Dedication to appeasement often meant ignoring facets of the international situation not relevant to that policy. Dependence on it meant ignoring an alternative until too late. Emphasis on peace meant hindered rearmament: extensive military preparations would dislocate the peacetime economy. Increasing military strength above a restricted level might arouse Hitler's wrath. And the stronger the current against Chamberlain, the more desperate and stubborn he became. Meanwhile, though Hitler did not work to a long-term timetable, events in 1938 moved almost inexorably towards conflict.

The main consequence of Chamberlain's policy was Britain's failure ever to gain the initiative. Appeasement, and its aftermath, meant that Chamberlain and his Cabinet were always one step behind Hitler; even when each waited to see what the other would do, Chamberlain waited longer – until he knew the Führer's intentions he could not know how he might be appeased. And leaving the initiative to such an opportunist was fatal. Linked with this failing was another. In their hurry to keep up behind Hitler, Chamberlain and his Cabinet had time only to see immediate problems, never the long-term situation. Thus, Munich settled the Sudeten problem, but not the overall Czech situation. The alleged ultimatum to Roumania forced Chamberlain to jump into a hasty alliance with Poland, but he had had no time to develop the capability to carry out this commitment. Always Hitler had the initiative – until Dunkirk. Only then, when defeat removed the remaining legacies of appeasement, could a fresh start be made.

On 28 March 1938, the Sudeten extremist, Konrad Henlein, secretly met Hitler, Ribbentrop and Hess. Henlein summarized his view as follows: 'We [the Sudeten] must always demand so much that we can never be satisfied.' The Führer approved.[16] Six weeks after *Anschluss*, on 21 April, Hitler held a military conference. Attending was General Keitel, head of the *Oberkommando der Wehrmacht* (OKW) which had taken over the work of the War Ministry early that year. The meeting was designed to update the anti-Czechoslovakia military programme. Keitel preferred 'lightning-swift action as the result of an incident'.[17] And only three days later, Henlein put into practice the programme agreed by Hitler on 28 March. Assembling after the Easter recess, the British Cabinet heard that after a demonstration at Karlsbad, Henlein had made eight loud demands, including transformation of Czechoslovakia into a 'state of nationalities' and 'full liberty for the Germans to demonstrate their adhesion to Germanism'. Edward Benes, the unfortunate Czech President, was convinced that to meet these demands would mean the end of Czechoslovakian independence. Britain on the other hand urged him to concede. Henderson was among those who insisted that the Sudeten claims were morally well founded; at the same time, Sir Eric Phipps, Ambassador at Paris, stressed the weaknesses of France. So at the subsequent Cabinet meetings Chamberlain held even more emphatically that Britain must not tie herself to France and become involved. Efforts to meet the Sudeten demands were not only necessary, but also morally proper – Chamberlain's convenient mixture of expediency and justification.

Chamberlain could express these views when Daladier and Bonnet flew to London on 28 April for two days of urgent talks. And Britain refused to agree to provide even two army divisions specifically for a Continental War: Britain and France could not save Czechoslovakia alone; Polish help would be 'uncertain'; the Russians were unreliable. This last view was at that time accepted dogma at the Foreign Office; only nine days before, Britain's Ambassador at Moscow had reported: 'The Soviet Union must be counted out of European politics.'[18] So although 'it made [Chamberlain's] blood boil to see Germany ... increasing her domination over free people', one could only believe Hitler would be satisfied once the Sudeten claims had been met. Initially, Daladier objected: 'War could only be avoided if Great Britain and France made their determination quite clear to maintain the peace of Europe.' The talks adjourned for lunch, a 'gloomy' affair. But eventually a compromise was reached: the Czechs would be urged to make concessions, but if these failed, Britain would warn Hitler 'of the dangers of which they were aware, namely, that France would be compelled to intervene ... and that HM Government would not guarantee that they would not do the same'.[19]

Yet Hitler was in fact more wary about taking the offensive against the Czechs than the Cabinet believed. On 20 May, Keitel gave the Führer the draft of a military directive, based upon Hitler's previous instructions for 'Operation Green' – the code name for actions against Czechoslovakia. The introduction to this document revealed Hitler's caution: 'It is not my intention to smash Czechoslovakia by military action in the immediate future without provocation.'[20] He had no definite plan worked out; he was apprehensive over possible French and British intervention; his army was not fully ready – military defects brought to light in the *Anschluss* operation had not yet been completely rectified.

But on this same day, the Czechs made a show of strength: reservists were recalled and frontier posts manned. The British Cabinet reacted with alarm. On 21 May the French reaffirmed their support to the Czechs, and the British Cabinet, due to their half-commitment, had to approve a personal message from Halifax to Ribbentrop warning that Britain should not be counted on to stand aside.[21] Support also came from the Russians, and by next day Sunday, 22 May, hostilities seemed imminent. But Hitler was still unready. So, on Sunday, a council was hastily called in Berlin, and the Czech Ambassador was assured that Germany had no aggressive intentions. The crisis cooled. Britain and France dropped their short-lived stern attitude.

The events of the weekend, especially those on 21 May, had two important consequences; the first was Hitler's intense rage, his 'brainstorm' as Henderson termed it, at the jubilation of those who declared he had been deterred by vigorous and united opposition. Still violently angry on 28 May, he abruptly summoned a conference at the Chancellory, virulently threatened the Czechs, and on 30 May struck out the opening sentence to 'Operation Green', to substitute: 'It is my unalterable decision to smash Czechoslovakia by military action in the near future ...'[22] The second result added feeling in London against the Czech leaders who had brought the situation about. Successive Cabinet meetings stressed the urgency of concessions. The Czechs must be brought under tight control and, as Henderson told the German State Secretary, Weizsäcker, Britain and France warned Prague on 1 June, that they would abandon her if she would not listen to reason; in August Henderson followed this with more: 'Britain would not think of risking even one sailor or airman for Czechoslovakia.'[23] Hitler was delighted; this was tantamount to encouragement.

Summer of 1938 came, and the British Parliament went into recess. Chamberlain slipped up to Scotland to rest. The people enjoyed the sunshine and most of them hardly thought about little-known, faraway Czechoslovakia. But while the British tanned themselves on

12

the beaches of Bognor and Brighton, across the water in Europe tension steadily increased in Embassy buildings at Berlin, Prague, Paris and Rome. The Czechs were proving remarkably stubborn; and even when Benes seemed flexible, Sudeten demands outpaced him, as Hitler and Henlein intended they should. So, on 26 July, Chamberlain announced the mission to Prague of Lord Runciman, former President of the Board of Trade and allegedly expert at settling industrial disputes. This appointment, he said, was 'in response to a request from the Government of Czechoslovakia' – in fact reluctantly made. And Runciman saw the difficulties; he confided to Halifax: 'You're setting me adrift in a small boat in mid-Atlantic.' Chamberlain emphasized that he would be acting on his own responsibility, 'not in any sense as an arbitrator, but as an investigator and mediator, and not under instructions from His Majesty's or any other Government'. Runciman was to find Benes a tougher negotiator than any industrial chief.

The following day, an incredible telegram arrived from Henderson at Berlin. 'I do not envy Lord Runciman the difficult and thankless job which he is undertaking. The Czechs are a pig-headed race and Benes not the least pig-headed among them.... War would doubtless serve the purpose of all the Jews, communists and doctrinaires in the world for whom Nazism is anathema, but it would be a terrible risk for Germany herself.... That this is not apparent to Hitler I cannot believe. I hate the excessive nationalism of Nazism myself, but the remedy of war would be worse than the disease.... If it comes, it will not be Hitler or the mass of Germans who have sought it, this year at any rate. They will be, of course, blamed for it. Unjustly, in my opinion.' Two points had to be borne in mind, Henderson told Halifax: the first was that as long as the Germans trusted the British and had 'confidence in the sincerity and impartiality of our effort, the battle is not lost'. But this led to the second: 'We shall have at long last to put our foot down very firmly and say to Benes "You must".'[24] These two points represented the bones of appeasement in the third quarter of 1938.

Many in the German Reichswehr were as apprehensive as Henderson. Plotters against Hitler, notably Admiral Canaris, became more active; and in mid-August an attempt was made to stir Britain to more vigorous opposition. General Edwald von Kleist slipped into London and arranged to see Vansittart and Churchill, though Henderson had warned 'it would be unwise for him to be received in official circles'.[25] After his meeting, Sir Robert told Halifax that according to Kleist war was a 'complete certainty' unless Britain took a firmer stand. Kleist appeared 'very incredulous that we should not be more exactly informed as to Hitler's timetable, but when I questioned him again he said: "After 27 September it will be too late." ' Churchill went so far as to present Kleist with a letter to take back with him: 'I am sure that the crossing of the frontier of Czechoslovakia by German armies or aviation in force will bring about renewal of the World War. I am as certain as I was at the end of July 1914, that England will march with France.'[26] Yet even this went no further than the official line. Churchill in any case lacked authority. Virtually all he did was to contribute to the case against Kleist, who was executed in 1945; the letter was discovered by the Gestapo.[27] Chamberlain thought 'we must discount a good deal of what [Kleist] says. Nevertheless, I confess to some feeling of uneasiness and I don't feel sure that we ought not to do something.' One measure would be to 'send for Henderson and take care everyone knew it'.

The Nazi rally at Nuremberg was less than two weeks away. Colonel F. N. Mason-MacFarlane, Military Attaché in Berlin, cabled on 24 August: 'The idea is widely prevalent that unless Lord Runciman produces a basis for negotiations satisfactory to the Germans, prior to the *Partei Tag* [Party Day], Herr Hitler will decide and declare at Nuremberg that he cannot delay any more and that direct action must ensue.'[28] Final plans were indeed being drawn up at the headquarters of the OKW and OKH [Army High Command], aimed at making the forces ready for action by 1 October. Colonel Jodl prepared an urgent paper for the Führer on 24 August. But the same day, and the next, saw favourable talks between Czech and Sudeten representatives. Runciman, who had sent back a Mr Ashton-Gwatkin to report, was asked by Halifax whether he would agree to making a direct personal approach to Hitler to explain the improved situation.[29] But Runciman was against extending his activities 'beyond the frontiers of Czechoslovakia'.[30]

In response to Kleist's warning, Henderson flew to London on 28 August 'for consultations', accompanied by considerable publicity as intended. He had long talks with Chamberlain and Halifax, and attended a special Cabinet meeting – Parliament was still in recess – before returning to Berlin on the last day of the month. Halifax told the Cabinet: 'The only deterrent which would be likely to be effective would be an announcement that if Germany invaded Czechoslovakia we should declare war upon her.' He thought this might well prove effective, but on the other hand, first, it might divide public opinion; secondly, Czechoslovakia would still be overrun; and thirdly, she would anyway not survive a war in her present form. 'It might, therefore, be said that there was not much use in fighting a war for an object which one could not secure.' Granted, dictators had to be stopped from taking what they want by force. 'But I ask myself whether it is justifiable to fight a certain war now in order to forestall a possible war later ... the two lines which we should pursue are, first, to keep Germany guessing as to what our intentions are, and secondly, to do all that we can to forward the success of Lord Runciman.' This had one major drawback. Everyone was trying to keep everyone else guessing – Germans, French, Italians, Czechs, Russians and British.

But the Cabinet thoroughly approved of Halifax's statement; Chamberlain described it as 'masterful'.

Besides Halifax's three reasons against taking a firm line, military unreadiness provided a fourth. The Air Secretary, Sir Kingsley Wood, looked with 'great apprehension at the prospect of war at the present time'. Leslie Hore-Belisha agreed; he wrote in his diary that night: 'I am alarmed at what it means for the Army. All we could do at the outset would be to provide a force of two divisions which would be inadequately equipped for any offensive operations.... Our rearmament programme is behind on what is necessary for our own defence, and we have concentrated on the Navy and Air. We cannot at present put an army into the field large enough to have any decisive effect.'

These would be the factors behind Chamberlain's flight to Munich. But on 30 August not all Ministers were convinced. Walter Elliot, Minister of Health, felt uneasily 'it is desirable to make some show of force'. Oliver Stanley, President of the Board of Trade, feared that if war came and France became involved, Britain would not intervene, though this 'might be the last chance of standing up against German aggression'. Strongest opposition came from Duff Cooper, First Lord of the Admiralty. He wanted to show Britain 'thinking of the possibility of using force', and proposed British warships should make a demonstrative Fleet movement.

But these misgivings had no effect. Indeed, the Prime Minister summed up: 'the Cabinet is unanimous in the view that we should not utter a threat to Hitler that if he goes into Czechoslovakia we should declare war upon him.... It is of the utmost importance that this decision should be kept secret. I ask Ministers to bear this in mind in private conversations.' Then he added, as a closing remark, 'There remains the hypothetical case that, in spite of all our efforts to bring about a settlement, Herr Hitler might brush everything aside and have recourse to force. What we should do in that event cannot be decided today.' So there was to be no warning. Hitler was to be kept guessing over British intentions. And if he guessed wrong and invaded, Britain herself had not planned what she should do.[31]

A disturbing telegram from Runciman reached Halifax later that day. 'The position is most difficult. Benes has made his contribution in a long nine-page memorandum covered with bolt holes and qualifications – no use for publication. What I want is a well condensed quarto page of the Sudeten Karlsbad points amalgamated with the seven points to which B has already agreed.... The signs of bad government accumulate day by day and at any moment Hitler may find an excuse for crossing the frontier in order to maintain order.... I have not been able to take a day off for their wonderful partridge shooting, alas.'[32] Next day, Halifax answered: 'If, as your telegram seems to suggest, Benes is playing fast and loose, is it not a case for taking drastic action?' In view of the urgency Benes should be told that he must publish the seven points *at once*, as the definite and unalterable basis of all future negotiation, and that if he will not publish them as his own unforced offer, you will publish them forthwith'.[33] But Runciman returned: 'Publication of seven points at present time would be disastrous.'[34] He amplified this next day, 1 September; the seven points had been superseded by Benes's last memorandum, which in turn, the Sudeten leader, Kundt, considered insufficient. Runciman saw 'definite disadvantages in my publishing, as opposed to producing, a scheme of my own. It would mean nailing my colours (and of course, in the eyes of the world, the colours of HMG) to the mast.'[35]

Halifax had cabled Sir Basil Newton, British Ambassador at Prague on 31 August: 'German military preparations ... make it essential that the Czechoslovak Government should agree with the Sudeten Germans without delay.'[36] This was more true than he knew. A few hours earlier Hitler had scrawled his signature to Jodl's plan for staging an incident to provoke war. Despite the misgivings of the German commander in the West about holding back the French, and Hitler's own doubts on Mussolini's support, the target date for 'Operation Green' was set for the end of September.[37]

The Soviet Ambassador's large official black car drove through the Kent countryside that Friday, and drew up outside Chartwell, Winston Churchill's home. Ivan Maisky had asked to see Churchill, a private person, because, 'the Soviet Government preferred this channel to a direct offer to the Foreign Office, which might have encountered a rebuff.' That day the French Chargé d'Affaires in Moscow had seen Litvinov, the Soviet Foreign Minister, and asked what Russia would do if the Germans attacked Czechoslovakia. 'The Russians had resolved to fulfil their obligations,' Litvinov said, and he advised invoking the League of Nations Council. In addition, he thought, Russia, France and Czechoslovakia should hold immediate staff conversations, and France, Russia and Britain should issue a joint declaration.[38] At last, one of the powers was prepared to state her position. Churchill sent Halifax an account of the talk; small chance existed that he or his Prime Minister would act. Newton saw Benes in Prague on Saturday, 3 September, and told him, in effect, that Britain would support Henlein rather than go to war; 'the Czech Government should go forthwith and unreservedly to the limit of coercion, which limit ought not to stop short of the eight Karlsbad points.'[39]

As Newton pushed desperately in Prague, Hitler was holding a top military conference at his mountain retreat, the Berghof. On the agenda were final arrangements for the conquest of Czechoslovakia. X-day was to be fixed for noon, 27 September.[40]

Then, on 4 September, came a dramatic change in the Prague climate. Perhaps as a result of Newton's strict line, or of the news of a visit Henlein had just made to Hitler, or perhaps as a subtle negotiating twist, Benes invited the Sudeten leaders to the Hradschin Palace and virtually offered them all they wanted. It seemed a complete surrender; and it will never be known whether Benes perhaps guessed his offer would be rejected. Runciman cabled Halifax on 7 September: 'Position is still very delicate.... This basis represents ... in fact a real self-government. If Sudetens accept it, I should say that the way is at last clear to an agreement.'[41]

But that day, just before Runciman's telegram arrived, a delegation of Sudeten Germans arrived at Mährisch-Ostrau to investigate conditions, and claimed a riot had taken place, that a Sudeten German Deputy had been insulted and beaten up by a Czech policeman. The Sudeten German party was then of course 'not in a position to proceed with negotiations until the Mährisch-Ostrau incidents have been liquidated'. British Embassy officials subsequently investigated the 'riot', and concluded: the disturbance had been staged; the Deputy had not been beaten; he was actually assaulting a Czech at the time of the 'beating'; if he had been beaten, he would have got 'no more than he deserved'.[42]

But rights and wrongs were irrelevant. From now on there had to be a succession of incidents – pretexts for keeping the issue alive. And according to Hitler's plan, an 'incident' would be used to start the German war machine lumbering forward.

Already, on 6 September, Nazis were assembling for the annual Nuremberg rally, where, on 12 September, Hitler would speak. Henderson went to Nuremberg that night, 'where I shall be out of touch as I am informed that for security's sake I can take no cypher with me in the train, in which I shall live.... It is no exaggeration to say that the world is awaiting with anxiety the message which Hitler has to deliver ...the anxiety is no less great in Germany than elsewhere.... I do wish it might be possible to get at any rate *The Times*, Camrose, Beaverbrook Press, etc. to write up Hitler as the apostle of Peace. It will be terribly short-sighted if this is not done.'[43] Already feeling very ill from a sickness which was to put him out of action for a vital four months, Henderson only meant to stay 36 hours at the rally; in fact he stayed five days, cooped in the diplomatic train, writing important despatches on flimsy blank pages ripped from cheap detective novels because he had forgotten to bring paper.

The Times leader of 7 September must have pleased him. While not calling Hitler 'the apostle of Peace', it went beyond any of Hitler's or Henlein's demands. The Czech Government, it said, should consider 'making Czechoslovakia a more homogeneous state by the cession of that fringe of alien population who are contiguous to the nation to which they are united by race'. 'Things look black, even very black, I am afraid,' wrote Eden. *The Times* bloomer may be a loosening of the stone that sets off the avalanche. No one can tell.'[44] This leader seemed to reinforce Hitler's belief that Britain would not fight over Czechoslovakia, a belief he stressed at a military conference on 9 September. At this meeting, attended by Keitel, Brauchitsch and Halder, Hitler loudly berated the army, which was still uneasy, for timidity and inefficiency. X-Day was fixed for 30 September, preceded by a Sudeten rising.

Without consulting the Cabinet, Halifax and Chamberlain decided that the latest reports warranted a reversal of part of the Cabinet's conclusions of 30 August: Hitler should be warned. Henderson was instructed on 9 September to give Ribbentrop a message for Hitler, that the British Government believed France would intervene if the Czechs asked for help; and 'the sequence of events must result in a general conflict from which Great Britain could not stand aside.'[45]

But Sir Nevile, still at Nuremberg, objected strongly to the official warning. It might, he thought, result in another 'brainstorm'. 'If we say too much now, it may just upset the apple-cart. *I have made the British position as clear as daylight to people who count.* I cannot do more here. It is essential to keep cool as the atmosphere is electric.'[46] He repeated this the same day in a letter to Halifax. 'The form of Hitler's genius is on the borderline of madness. He may already have stepped over the edge.... A second 21 May would push him over.'[47]

Nazis at Nuremberg were activated by a diatribe by Göring on 10 September: 'A petty segment of Europe is harassing the human race,' yelled the man whom Sir Nevile considered the 'most sympathetic' of the Nazi leaders. 'This miserable pygmy race is oppressing a cultured people, and behind it [is] Moscow and the eternal mask of the Jew devil....' In contrast, a speech broadcast by Benes that evening was quiet and reasonable. 'Let us all preserve calmness ... but let us be optimistic, and, above all, let us not forget that faith and goodwill will move mountains.'

On Sunday, a determined and defensive Chamberlain wrote: 'I fully realize that, if eventually things go wrong ... there will be many, including Winston, who will say that the British Government must bear the responsibility, and that if only they had had the courage to tell Hitler now that, if he used force, we should at once declare war, that could have stopped him.' But this would have meant passing the decision for peace or war into the hands of a ruler of another country, 'and a lunatic at that'. Besides, Chamberlain drew from a book he was reading on George Canning: 'you should never menace unless you are in a position to carry out your threats.'[48]

The French were angling for last minute support, should they have to intervene. Phipps reported from Paris that Bonnet had asked, as a friend, this direct question: 'We are going to march – will you march with us?' Halifax, anxious to avoid commitment, passed him this reply: 'While His Majesty's Government would never allow the security of France to be threatened, they are unable to make precise statements of the character of their future action or the time at which it would be taken, in circumstances that they cannot at present foresee.'[49]

Still without a firm promise of support, the French leaders now asked Gamelin's military advice. He proposed an attack on Germany in the Saar area, where a battle would be fought, 'initially a modern version of the Somme'. So Daladier now faced a daunting prospect.[50] Militarily, the vision was horrible; Russia might help, but Britain was prevaricating; and only three days before, Roosevelt had declared that it was totally incorrect to link the United States with France and Britain in an alliance against Hitler.

Chamberlain's Cabinet met at 11 a.m. on Monday, 12 September, and heard of the warning which Henderson was to have given to Hitler, but in fact had kept. Hitler, Halifax said, 'is possibly, or even probably, mad. He might have taken a definite decision to attack Czechoslovakia. ... If Herr Hitler has made up his mind to attack, it is probable that nothing which we can do would stop him. There is a body of opinion which thinks that he can be stopped by a direct ultimatum. This is, however, at the best a very doubtful view.' So Halifax had altered his 30 August view. Now action must not be taken by Britain which would involve Hitler in what he could regard as a 'public humiliation'.[51]

The hours before Hitler's address slipped by. Henderson had left Nuremberg to be at his Embassy should the speech mean war. In Prague, the streets were dark and gloomy; a steady, cold, drenching drizzle was falling. In London that evening, Chamberlain sat by a large wireless set at 10 Downing Street. In Nuremberg the arc lamps shed a cold light on thousands of faces; a searchlight picked up the small erect figure of the Führer on the high rostrum; the roaring 'Sieg Heil! Sieg Heil! Sieg Heil!' subsided; Hitler began to speak. 'You will understand, my comrades, that a Great Power cannot for a second time suffer such an infamous encroachment upon its rights....' At each deliberate pause Sieg Heil bayed again to the black sky. The Sudeten, shouted Hitler, were 'tortured creatures'. The situation was like that in Palestine, but with one important difference. 'The poor Arabs are defenceless and deserted. The Germans in Czechoslovakia are neither defenceless nor deserted. And people should take notice of that fact....'[52]

Almost immediately after the diatribe, riots flared in Sudetenland. Newton cabled during the night: 'Situation at Eger and Karlsbad has become ugly. Huge crowds assembled after Nuremberg speech last night and police have used fire [-arms?]. Military have also been called out. Official sources say so far six dead.'[53]

But Hitler's secret deadline had not yet arrived. His speech, despite the attack on Czechoslovakia and Benes, and the incitement to the Sudeten, carefully avoided the far limit. As the Czechs noted with relief, he did not demand the Sudetenland outright. Yet in Prague, German bombers were expected almost at any moment. Newton cabled to Halifax on the deteriorating situation. 'Martial law is being proclaimed in two or three of the affected districts.'[54] Rifle shots continued around the wet Sudeten streets; sudden explosions tore the heavy, dark sky; casualties mounted. In Paris, the French Cabinet met on the thirteenth, almost throughout the day, but remained divided over whether the obligations to Czechoslovakia should be honoured. Bonnet was stricken with eleventh-hour panic. Phipps rang Halifax at 1.25 p.m.: 'M. Bonnet has just telephoned to say that in view of the grave incidents in Czechoslovakia ... it is most urgent for Lord Runciman to issue without delay a declaration stating that he is about to propose a plan calculated to bridge over differences.' But Runciman replied: 'Publication of our plan would be of no use in present circumstances. Immediate problem is one of law and order.'[55]

As fighting continued in the Sudetenland, and as dusk fell in London, British Service Ministers and Chiefs of Staff met to discuss precautionary measures. 'Feeling is against any premature action,' noted Hore-Belisha in his diary.[56] Chamberlain was anxious to avoid increasing tension; in particular, he was not prepared to mobilize the Fleet without consulting the full Cabinet.[57] At 7.10 p.m. Halifax received another call from Phipps. 'I saw the Minister for Foreign Affairs this afternoon. Bonnet was very upset and said peace must be preserved at any price, as neither France nor Great Britain was ready for war.... M. Bonnet's collapse seems to me so sudden and so extraordinary that I am asking for an interview with M. Daladier.'[58] French firmness had melted away. The attempt to call Hitler's bluff had apparently failed. Yet now it could be too late; the French might have to fight – with little hope of victory – and Britain would be pulled in too.

Sir Eric telephoned again at 8.30 p.m. to describe his meeting with Daladier. 'I was careful not to give away M. Bonnet, for, if they are of different opinions, this might have led to a Cabinet crisis with deplorable results.' But Daladier's attitude was similar. 'I finally asked point blank whether he adhered to policy expounded to me by him on 8 September. He replied, but with evident lack of enthusiasm, that if Germans used force French would be obliged also.... M. Daladier of today was quite a different one to the M. Daladier of 8 September, and tone and language were very different indeed. I fear the French have been bluffing....'[59]

One hour and 40 minutes later a telegram arrived from Sir Eric.

20

'Following is a very urgent message that M. Daladier has dictated to me and begged me to send immediately to the Prime Minister. "Things are moving very rapidly and in such a grave manner that they risk getting out of control almost at once.... Entry of German troops into Czechoslovakia must at all costs be prevented. If not France will be faced with her obligations.... To avoid this I propose two things: (1) Lord Runciman to make known his plan publicly and immediately. (2) Can he also bring the two parties together in his presence? Should above procedure not be sufficient I propose (3) An immediate proposal to Hitler for a meeting of the Three Powers."' With the French leaders in their present state of mind, the confrontation with Hitler could only have resulted in surrender. Daladier finished his message: 'Do you agree to my above proposals, or would you suggest any others?'[60] Chamberlain had indeed an idea. Time had now come for his last effort to keep the peace. The plan he had been considering for a fort-night must be put into operation. With a touch of cloak and dagger, he titled his scheme 'Plan Z'. He would have to inform the Cabinet; but first, late on 13 September, Chamberlain sent an urgent message to the Führer.

'God is good to me!' exclaimed the atheist Adolf Hitler when he read it.

3

Munich

The Cabinet met at 10 Downing Street at 11 a.m. on Wednesday, 14 September. 'International Affairs' modestly headed the agenda, but the meeting had barely begun before Chamberlain made his 'bombshell' announcement. As Churchill later wrote, he had 'been communing with himself'.[1] He revealed the plan 'which has occurred to me as one which might yet be put into practice at a moment's notice, and which would have some chance at the eleventh hour of preserving peace'. Henderson, he continued, believed that if Hitler 'has decided to invade Czechoslovakia, this new idea might cause him to cancel that intention'. Surprise was the vital element, and as no hint must leak out, he had thought it better to postpone mentioning it to the last moment.

'The plan is that, as soon as it becomes clear that a solution can be reached in no other way, I myself should go to Germany to see Herr Hitler.' Originally he had intended not to tell Hitler until the journey had actually started. 'This procedure, however ... would expose me to a rebuff; Herr Hitler might say that he had a cold and could not see me.' The telegram asking Hitler's consent had therefore been sent the previous evening, via Henderson. It had read: 'In view of increasingly critical situation, I propose to come over at once to see you with a view to trying to find a peaceful solution. ... I propose to come across by air and am ready to start tomorrow.'[2] The Cabinet therefore had to agree to steps already taken. Success for Plan Z also depended on accurate timing, Chamberlain said. 'Up to yesterday afternoon, 13 September, I had it in mind that this plan should be put into effect probably towards the end of this week. Yesterday afternoon, however, events started to move rapidly and there was a succession of "incidents" in the Sudeten areas.' Also, the previous afternoon Phipps had sent a 'remarkable communication': Bonnet 'seemed thoroughly cowed'. He had therefore been forced to act; 'unless Plan Z is put into effect quickly, it cannot be adopted at all.'

According to the Minutes 'The Prime Minister hoped that the idea would appeal to the Hitlerian mentality. Herr Hitler liked to see Heads of State and it might be agreeable to his vanity that the British Prime Minister should take so unprecedented a step.' He thought the 'right course is to open by an appeal to Herr Hitler on the grounds that he has a great chance of obtaining fame for himself by making peace in Europe'. The Cabinet discussed the best reply if Hitler demanded a plebiscite in the Sudetenland. Chamberlain thought the demand should not be totally rejected. 'The only answer which I can find is one which I am most unwilling to contemplate, namely, that this country should join in guaranteeing the integrity of the rest of Czechoslovakia. This would be a new liability, and I realize that we could not save Czechoslovakia if Germany decided to overrun it. The value of the guarantee would lie in its deterrent effect.' Finally, he referred to a statement of Göring's to Henderson 'that if once the present difficulty was settled, we in this country would be surprised at the moderation of the German demands'.[3]

So Chamberlain was at the start of the path to Munich. The plan had been born in his mind at least as early as 25 August, when he had discussed with Ashton-Gwatkin 'the proposal that some eminent person should be sent to see Hitler'.[4] Runciman had been asked, but had refused. Privately, Chamberlain had begun to consider himself; he had confided first in Halifax and Henderson, and wrote to his sister on 3 September: 'Is it not horrible to think that the fate of hundreds of millions depends on one man, and he is half mad? I keep racking my brains to try and devise some means of averting a catastrophe, if it should seem to be upon us. I thought of one so unconventional and daring that it rather took Halifax's breath away. But since Henderson thought it might save the situation at the eleventh hour, I haven't abandoned it, though I hope all the time that it won't be necessary to try it.'[5] Chamberlain had summoned Simon and Cadogan to the Cabinet Room on 8 September, and told them of the plan. Halifax, who was also there, suggested Vansittart should know, and he too was called in. He strongly urged the Prime Minister to abandon the idea. 'Neville Chamberlain put his elbows on the Cabinet table and his head between his hands and never said a word.'[6] Two days later, Hoare was also included. 'I told him that he was taking a great political risk ...'.[7] Chamberlain had no time to consult the Cabinet; nor were the French informed, except by Halifax's tantalizing telegram – sent after the message to Hitler – that 'the Prime Minister is exploring tonight another possibility of direct action in Berlin, on which he should hope to be in a position to inform you fully tomorrow.'[8]

Hitler replied early in the afternoon. He would be 'absolutely at the disposal of the Prime Minister' and hoped a meeting might be arranged the following day.[9] Chamberlain felt an immense surge of relief; and

23

fondly believed Hitler's reaction perhaps indicated some good in the man after all. 'Afterwards I heard from Hitler himself,' he told his sister, 'and it was confirmed by others who were with him, that he was struck all of a heap, and exclaimed "I can't possibly let a man of his age come all this way; I must go to London." Of course, when he considered it further he saw that wouldn't do.... But it shows a side of Hitler that would surprise many people in this country.'[10] Extra newspaper editions suddenly appeared in the darkening Prague streets; banner headlines announced Chamberlain's proposed mission. Newsboys shouted: 'Extra! Extra! Read how the mighty head of the British Empire goes begging to Hitler!'[11] Czechs viewed British intentions with increasing suspicion.

Few first flights can have been so celebrated as Chamberlain's that Thursday morning, 15 September 1938. He left London soon after dawn to world-wide acclamation. *Le Matin* described 'a man of 69 making his first aeroplane flight ... to see if he can banish the frightful nightmare which hangs over us and save humanity.' In Berlin, according to Henderson, 'the news ... came last night as a bombshell and was greeted by the public with enormous relief and satisfaction.' And Mussolini commented to his Foreign Minister, Count Ciano: 'There will not be war. But this is the liquidation of English prestige.'[12]

Konrad Henlein was also travelling to see Hitler. He planned to establish himself in Bavaria, from where he and his *Freikorps* followers could launch terrorist raids across the frontier; Henlein believed he had every chance of firm support from Hitler.

The Prime Minister and Sir Horace Wilson arrived at Munich airport soon after noon, earlier than anticipated. They were met by rolling drums, Ribbentrop, and Henderson, most apprehensive about Chamberlain's condition after his first flight; 'I'm tough and wiry,' he was assured. They drove to the station through the rain, and took Hitler's special train for Berchtesgaden. 'All the way up there were people at the crossings, the stations, and at the windows of the houses, all "heiling" and saluting,' wrote Chamberlain.

As the train rattled towards the mountains, the German radio in Czechoslovakia was broadcasting an ominous proclamation by Henlein. Addressed to *'Meine Volksgenossen'*, the statement declared that in 1919 the Sudeten Germans had been denied the right of self-determination which had been formerly promised to them and had been forced against their will into the Czech state. All attempts to reach an honourable settlement had failed. 'We wish to live as free German men! We wish for peace and work again in our homes! We wish to go home to the Reich.'[13]

A few minutes after 4 p.m. Chamberlain and his party arrived at Berchtesgaden. Accommodation had been hurriedly arranged at a hotel, and half an hour later the group left in a fleet of cars for the

24

20 minute drive up the mountain to the Berghof, Hitler's retreat. Hills and peaks were shrouded in mist; the atmosphere was clammy; rain splattered on the windows. The Führer, with Keitel and others of his entourage, was waiting to receive Chamberlain half-way down the steps leading to the house. Chamberlain later described his first impression: the Führer was 'bareheaded and dressed in a khaki-coloured coat of broadcloth with a red armlet and a swastika on it, and the military cross on his breast. He wore black trousers, such as we wear in the evening, and black patent-leather lace-up shoes. His hair is brown, not black, his eyes blue, his expression rather disagreeable, especially in repose, and altogether he looks entirely undistinguished. You would never notice him in a crowd and would take him for the house painter he once was.'[14]

They walked along the bare passage to the huge reception room, for tea. Conversation was desultory; Hitler, said Chamberlain, 'seemed very shy, and his features did not relax while I endeavoured small talk'. Twenty minutes later he abruptly asked what procedure Chamberlain proposed for the discussions. To the intense annoyance of Ribbentrop who had hoped to be included, Chamberlain preferred a *tête-à-tête*. Henderson claimed he had suggested this to Chamberlain, to exclude the Nazi Foreign Minister, whose 'interventions were never helpful and often the reverse'.[15] Unfortunate consequences were to result.

Chamberlain, Hitler and Dr Paul Schmidt, the interpreter, walked upstairs, through a long room amply decorated with paintings of nudes, to Hitler's study. His room was almost monastic in its austerity, with only a small stove, three chairs, a sofa, and a small table with two bottles of mineral water – which Hitler overlooked to share with his guest. Here, just seven months before, the Chancellor of Austria had been forced to sign away his country's independence; he was now incarcerated in a cramped room at the Vienna Hotel Metropole, made to clean his SS guards' latrines with his face towel. Hitler and Chamberlain talked for three hours. Downstairs, Henderson and Wilson waited in the reception room, where a constant stream of German press despatches arrived concerning incidents in the Sudetenland. A report claimed 40 Germans killed by the Czechs; an official British observer later amended this to one casualty. The Prime Minister intended the talks should begin in an exploratory fashion: he suggested they 'might perhaps usefully devote this afternoon to a clarification of each other's points of view ... leaving, perhaps, the Czechoslovakia problem till tomorrow.' But Hitler stressed 'there was a question which was very urgent and could not wait.... According to today's information 300 Sudeten Germans had been killed and many more injured and that produced a situation which demanded instant solution, so that it would be better if we started at once on it.' So Chamberlain was pressed into having to take an immediate, perhaps premature, decision. He had no detailed brief; he would have no time to prepare his answer.

First the Führer gave his version of events. 'For the most part H spoke quietly and in low tones,' Chamberlain wrote. 'I did not see any trace of insanity, but occasionally he became very excited and poured out his indignation against the Czechs in a torrent of words, so that several times I had to stop him and ask that I might have a chance to hear what he was talking about. I soon saw that the situation was much more critical than I had anticipated.' The pressure for a quick decision was maintained. 'I knew that his troops and tanks and guns and planes were ready to pounce, and only awaiting his word, and it was clear that rapid decisions must be taken if the situation was to be saved ... He said that he had from his youth been obsessed with the racial theory and he felt that Germans were one.' He admitted some Germans could not possibly be brought into the Reich, but the Sudeten on the Czech frontiers could – 'they wanted to, and he was determined that they should come in'. Sudeten secession marked the limit of his claims: 'he was out for racial unity and he did not want a lot of Czechs, all he wanted were Sudeten Germans'.

Hitler refused to go into details. 'All this seems to be academic; I want to get down to realities.' According to Chamberlain, Hitler said at this time: 'I am determined to settle it and settle it soon and I am prepared to risk a world war rather than allow this to drag on.' Reacting either in fear or in genuine protest, Chamberlain interrupted: 'If the Führer is determined to settle this matter by force without waiting even for a discussion between ourselves to take place, what did he let me come here for? I have wasted my time ...'. But Hitler had made his point. Exactly the right amount of pressure had been applied: now followed the final manipulation: 'Well, if the British Government are prepared to accept the idea of secession in principle and to say so, there might be a chance then to have a talk. If you tell me that the British Government cannot accept the principle of secession, then I agree it is of no use to proceed with our conversations.'

Chamberlain was cornered and must have known it. It was not enough to reply that he would go and consult his Cabinet; he had to leave his word as hostage. 'I said that I was not in a position to give such an assurance on behalf of the British Government who had not authorized me to say anything of the kind, and moreover I could not possibly make such a declaration without consulting the French Government and Lord Runciman. But I could give him my personal opinion, which was that on principle I had nothing to say against the separation of the Sudeten Germans from the rest of Czechoslovakia ...' In the official German records of the talks, using Dr Schmidt's notes, Chamberlain's statement appears even more definite: '[Chamberlain] could state personally that he admitted the principle of the separation of the Sudeten areas. The difficulty appeared to him to lie in the practical execution of these principles. He wished, therefore, to return to England in order to report to the Government and to obtain their approval of his personal attitude.'[16]

The Prime Minister returned to London the following morning, Friday, 16 September. Also returning was Runciman, recalled for consultations. Chamberlain and his emissary met at Downing Street in the evening, and Runciman began to alter his report to include the Berchtesgaden proposals. The report was not made official until 28 September – by then further drastically altered to bring it in line with events. As a result, Runciman's report went even beyond the 'practicalities' discussed at Berchtesgaden: he recommended handing over predominantly 'German' areas in the Sudetenland without even a plebiscite.

So far the Czechs themselves had been told nothing. Nor would they be, officially, until the Anglo-French proposals were presented three days later. Preservation of peace came before diplomatic niceties. Chamberlain was perhaps fortified by the lines penned in his honour by the Poet Laureate, John Masefield, and published in Friday's issue of *The Times*:

> *As Priam to Achilles for his son,*
> *So you, into the night, divinely led,*
> *To ask that young men's bodies, not yet dead,*
> *Be given from the battle not begun.*

Berchtesgaden, not Munich, represents the pinnacle of appeasement. Events which followed were echoes of that first confrontation when the ex-house-painter decisively out-manoeuvred the Birmingham screw-manufacturer's son; it was at Hitler's mountain retreat that Chamberlain committed himself, in principle, to the handover of Sudetenland. The words 'in principle' might have been Chamberlain's escape clause, but they also let Hitler avoid 'academic' details at that time. The Prime Minister, once committed, was hobbled; now Hitler could make his detailed demands, which would have to be accepted as long as they were within the unspecified framework of the Berchtesgaden agreement. Months of appeasement had pushed Chamberlain into an inferior position at Berchtesgaden, a position made vastly worse by the French collapse of the last few days. Hitler deliberately forced the pace; the appeasement policy could not be changed in a moment; Britain was unfit for the only alternative, war, the French even more so.

So Chamberlain's agreement 'in principle' was not given on the grounds of justice, to revert the wrongs of Versailles; nor to prevent further Czech disintegration – by then the riots were firmly under control. It was simply to preserve peace. Chamberlain was to tell the Commons, 'my visit alone prevented an invasion', but he might equally have said 'my visit was only to prevent an invasion'. Peace had to be kept, at almost any price. Subsequent events merely set this price.

A note of desperation crept into Chamberlain's statement to the Cabinet. He had to justify himself; reason had to be found for the agreement stronger than merely peace at a price unknown. Chamberlain stressed three factors at the 17 September meeting. He claimed Sudetenland was all Hitler wanted; Hitler could be trusted (this was new); and he himself had established relations which would be useful in future. The Cabinet had to rely on Chamberlain's version of the talks. Ribbentrop, excluded from the talks, had peevishly refused to allow him an official transcript. He had nothing to refresh his memory but brief notes jotted down afterwards.

First, the Cabinet heard a statement from Runciman, who had failed to bring the parties together, and felt Czechoslovakia could not remain as she was. Runciman's remarks made an excellent introduction for Chamberlain. The Prime Minister began by explaining how he attached great importance to the 'dramatic side of the visit', since 'we are dealing with an individual and a new technique of diplomacy relying on personal contacts is required.... I saw no signs of insanity, but many of excitement. Occasionally Herr Hitler lost the thread of what he was saying and would go off into a tirade. It is impossible not to be impressed with the power of the man. He is extremely determined; he had thought out what he wanted and he meant to get it, and he would not brook opposition beyond a certain point. Further, and this is a point of considerable importance, I formed the opinion that Herr Hitler's objectives are strictly limited.' He stressed Hitler's assurance that 'he did not wish to include the Czechs into the Reich. When he had included the Sudeten Germans in the Reich he would be satisfied. He referred to his Treaties with Belgium and Holland. The only other place which he mentioned was Memel, which he said he was prepared to leave, provided the Lithuanians stood by the Statute of Memel.... The impression left on me was that Herr Hitler meant what he said.... My view is that Herr Hitler was telling the truth.' Duff Cooper noted in his diary that the Prime Minister also described Hitler to the Cabinet as the 'commonest little dog you ever saw'. Chamberlain came close to admitting he had been confined to listening to, and then agreeing with, Hitler's demands. 'There was no opportunity for me to put smaller points, or to try and impose conditions, or to get Herr Hitler to accept alternative solutions which seemed reasonable over here but which would not have been accepted in the atmosphere prevailing at Berchtesgaden.'

He finished by stressing the value of the personal relationship which had been formed. 'Herr Hitler's manner was definitely different when we left his study. He stopped half way down the stairs and lamented the fact that the bad weather made it impossible for him to take me to see the view from the top of the mountain ... he hoped this might be possible on some other occasion.... Information from other sources has been to the effect that the Führer has been most favourably impressed. This is of the utmost importance, since the future conduct of these negotiations depends mainly upon personal contacts.' One last point had to be emphasized: the necessity for speed. As Chamberlain said: 'A discussion in Parliament at the present time would result in wrecking very delicate negotiations.... Parliament will be summoned as soon as that course will be helpful. In effect, Parliament will be informed of the decision of His Majesty's Government after it has been taken.'[17]

During this statement, Halifax had received a telegram from Phipps: the French were restive: 'I understand from quarters close to M. Daladier that there is considerable heart-burning that French Government have not yet been given any indication by His Majesty's Government of what occurred at Berchtesgaden.' As the French would be the first to have to support Czechoslovakia if Germany invaded, this was understandable. So the Cabinet agreed to ask the French leaders over as soon as possible, and the meeting adjourned from 1.30 p.m. till 3 p.m. Back at the Foreign Office, Halifax sent the invitation. During the break, some members were uneasy as they thought over Chamberlain's words. How would Sudetenland be transferred to the Reich? If there were to be self-determination, how could this work? How could Nazi pressure be avoided? What areas would be selected? If there were voting, who would be eligible? Hore-Belisha jotted down some comments in his War Office study. 'We must have a clear foreknowledge of the problems raised by self-determination and of the terms of the principle.... Hitler says that he is attached to the principle of race. Ethnologists affirm that in Bohemia it is impossible to tell who are Czechs and who are German by race.... Surely it has never been intended to give a reply to Hitler without giving the Czechs an opportunity of adequate consideration.... The more I reflect on the transfer of territories, the more I feel we are bereaving Czechoslovakia of its power to exist....'[18]

Others felt a similar disquiet, notably Duff Cooper; and the afternoon Cabinet session promised to be lively. So it was. Ministers clearly recognized that either the transfer proposals would be accepted, or there would be war. A long, involved, sometimes heated discussion therefore took place on whether Czechoslovakia was worth fighting over. Chamberlain made his own view perfectly clear. 'If at any time we were convinced that some vital British interest was at stake, then, of course, we should have to go through with it; but we should have to be very fully satisfied that this was the case.... The alternatives today are not between abject surrender and war. Acceptance of the principle of self-determination is not an abject surrender.' Duff Cooper and others were unconvinced; and in the absence of unanimity the Minutes could only tactfully state that 'while the Cabinet was in general agreement with the views expressed by the Prime Minister, it was undesirable to record any conclusion until discussions with the French Government had taken place.' These would start at 11 a.m. the following day, 17 September.[19]

Chamberlain was awakened early to meet the French at Croydon. He had an exhausting day ahead; and it began with news of a message which had called Halifax from his bed soon after 2 a.m. The Czechs had decided to mobilize. They would however delay until they heard from London and Paris.[20] So, still without calling the Czechs in, ten British and seven French representatives sat down to talk. On the French side sat Daladier, squat and square, his peasant face flushed red, the ex-artillery soldier; white-faced Bonnet, sensitive, nervous and always alert; Alexis Léger, yellow-complexioned, silent and sphinx-like. Chamberlain opened with a brisk account of the Berchtesgaden talks, and then asked for the French views. Neither side wished to give an opinion first and tossed the question to and fro across the table. The French, the Cabinet were told next day, had said 'the Prime Minister's account was of great interest, and they were anxious to hear the views of the British Government, who had by now had some days to deliberate over the position.' This barb failed to bring a firm response. Chamberlain replied that 'since the French were bound by Treaty obligations, and we were not, he thought that it was for the French to express their views first.... The French representatives in turn had found some means of passing the ball back into our court and so matters continued during the whole morning. Just before lunch, however, M. Daladier said that the real question at issue was what we could do in order to ensure peace.'

Chamberlain who commented 'the darkest hour was before lunch', told the Cabinet that talks had improved during the meal. Meanwhile, as the British and French Ministers ate their cold meat and pickles, Hitler was having an extremely busy day. Instructions were being issued to cover the launching of attacks for five German armies, totalling 36 divisions, three of them armoured.[21] This force would strike over the border into Czechoslovakia on X-day, less than a fortnight away.

Talks resumed at 3.30 p.m. next day. Immediately, Chamberlain stressed: 'There must clearly be some cession of territorial area to the Reich. But it would be very difficult for us to carve up Czechoslovakia, unless the Czechoslovak Government themselves were prepared to admit the necessity for frontier rectifications.' He therefore suggested they consider the possibility of some arrangements specifically for the Sudeten areas. But Daladier thought it essential to consult the Czech Government. France, he said, was firmly against a plebiscite; if 'friendly pressure were brought to bear on Prague' it might be possible to persuade the Czechs to agree to 'giving up some portion of Sudeten territory.' But 'they could hardly bring pressure to bear on the Czechoslovak Government to agree to the cession of part of their present territory, unless they could assure them of some sort of international guarantee of what remained.' And Germany must be a party to the guarantee agreement.

Chamberlain hesitated; Halifax, typically, displayed legalistic caution: if there were guarantees, he would like to see 'associated with them some undertaking on the part of the Czech Government that in issues involving peace and war they should accept the advice of His Majesty's Government, and that if they did not accept this advice His Majesty's Government would then be automatically absolved of their guarantee.' There was a break while Chamberlain considered the question. Then, when the meeting resumed, he agreed that, in view of the great changes contemplated in the positions of Czechoslovakia and France, 'they must give the assurances for which the French Government had asked.'[22]

In that quarter-hour break, Chamberlain, without consulting the full Cabinet, had abruptly reversed Britain's policy of avoiding commitments, especially those in the East. He considered the guarantee an evil necessary for Anglo-French accord, and Czech agreement to the Sudeten handover. Risks of immediate war would be reduced, but at the risk of increased likelihood of British involvement later. In the short-term, the guarantee was part of the appeasement policy; but in the long-term, it implied the contrary – British willingness to oppose Hitler by force, even when not directly threatened.

At 10.30 that night the Anglo-French delegates met again, to discuss and agree on the communication to the Czechs. Chamberlain wanted this despatched immediately, but Daladier, unlike Chamberlain apparently, required his Cabinet's approval first. The Prime Minister warned: 'Time is going by and delay might be extremely dangerous. We should be running a very big risk if I am compelled to postpone my meeting with Herr Hitler beyond Wednesday, 21 September.... The British Ministers have also taken decisions without consulting their colleagues.' He was 'frankly afraid' of delay in Paris and 'would like to know whether there was any doubt about the nature of the final French reply'. Daladier said he would insist upon a definite 'yes' or 'no' decision from his Council, and to speed matters he suggested the agreed draft should be cabled to Prague to be presented at lunch-time the next day, following a telephone call.[23] So, at 2.45 in the cold morning of Monday, 19 September, Halifax sent Newton the message: 'We [France and Britain] are both convinced that, after recent events, the point has now been reached where the further maintenance within the boundaries of the new Czechoslovak State of the district mainly inhabited by Sudeten-*Deutsch* cannot in fact continue any longer....'

They hoped 'some international body including the Czech representative' could arrange the transfer, which would probably have to include areas with over 50 per cent of German inhabitants and Britain and France 'would be prepared, as a contribution to the pacification of Europe, to join in an international guarantee of the new boundaries of the Czechoslovak State against unprovoked aggression'.[24]

Nor, despite the extra time now available, was the British Cabinet consulted. A meeting was held at 11 a.m. on Monday, but Chamberlain explained everything that had been done, that the French had now approved, and British and French Ambassadors at Prague had been instructed to deliver the proposal to Benes. The Cabinet could only endorse Chamberlain's *fait accompli*. 'Most of us disliked the idea,' claimed Hore-Belisha in his diary, 'but in the end there didn't seem to be any alternative. . . . The proposed guarantee filled me with apprehension.'[25]

Reports of an Anglo-French decision to support Hitler's demands had already leaked in Berlin and Prague. And German newspaper headlines screamed: WOMEN AND CHILDREN MOWED DOWN BY CZECH ARMOURED CARS ... BLOODY REGIME – NEW CZECH MURDERS OF GERMANS.[26] In Prague an atmosphere of numbed shock prevailed. And when Newton eventually saw Benes at 2 p.m. he found him 'greatly moved and agitated'. Benes initially refused even to discuss the matter because his Government had not been consulted; the harassed Newton stressed the urgency of a decision and, according to his report to Halifax that night, 'speaking with self-control but with bitterness [Benes] showed that he felt that, after all the efforts which he and his Government had made, they were being abandoned. I pointed out to him that at least he was being offered a new and important guarantee by His Majesty's Government.'[27] Impatient and fearful, London and Paris could only wait for the Czech decision, which could mean peace or war. Yet Chamberlain, remarkably calm and optimistic, wrote to his sister: 'I have still many anxious days before me, but the most gnawing anxiety is gone, for I feel that I have nothing to reproach myself with, and that on the contrary up to now things are going the way I want.'[28] Churchill was less complacent. 'The British and French Cabinets at this time presented a front of two overripe melons crushed together, whereas what was needed was a gleam of steel.'[29] All day on Tuesday, 20 September, the wait continued; Chamberlain's visit to Hitler had to be postponed from Wednesday until lunch-time Thursday. Clashes increased on the Czech border between police and Henlein's rampaging *Freikorps*. Henlein now tried to create more trouble by urging the separatist Slovak People's Party to claim Slovak autonomy. In the effort to keep tension taut, Hitler saw the Hungarian Prime Minister and Foreign Minister, and almost ordered them to demand the return of Czechoslovak districts claimed by Budapest. There was a 'danger of the Czechs sub-mitting to every demand'.[30]

Then, at 9.35 p.m. on the 20th, Newton telephoned the Czech reply. Prague had rejected the proposals. He transmitted the main points from a statement read to him by the Czech Foreign Minister, Dr Krofta. The Czechs were convinced the Franco-British document could not bring peace – the State would be mutilated; the Czechs complained of the lack of consultation; Krofta 'begged for a reconsideration'.[31] Chamberlain's appeasement seemed to have failed, but an hour later, Newton telephoned again. The official Czech reply, he had been secretly informed, should not be considered the last word. 'If I can deliver a kind of ultimatum to President Benes, on Wednesday, he and his Government will feel able to bow to *force majeure*.'[32] Newton's informant was none other than Milan Hodza, the Czech Prime Minister.[33]

Immediate pressure was applied in London, Paris and Prague. Phipps telephoned at 12.20 a.m.: 'Minister for Foreign Affairs tells me he has instructed French Minister at Prague to make immediate representation to M. Benes.'[34] Indeed, unknown to Phipps, Bonnet had gone even further; abandoning all pretence of honouring commit-ments, he had ordered his Ambassador to point out that if Czecho-slovakia opposed Hitler, she would do so alone. Bonnet's devious excuse for this abrogation was that it enabled Benes to step down.[35]

Halifax hurried to 10 Downing Street for an urgent *tête-à-tête*. And at 1.20 Newton was told: 'You should at once join with your French colleague in pointing out to Czech Government that their reply in no way meets the crucial situation.... Anglo-French proposals remain in our view the only chance of avoiding immediate German attack.'[36] The exhausted, miserable Benes was called from his couch, and he promised his Government's final reply by mid-day. But at 7.30 a.m. Newton telephoned through a communication from Dr Hodza's Private Secre-tary: 'I am speaking on behalf of President of the Council Dr Hodza, who asks me to convey to you following personal and preliminary information: The Government's reply is affirmative.'[37] In the chill light of morning Newton felt some pity for the wretched Benes. 'If final reply of Czechoslovak Government is favourable, I would suggest, whether by public statement or otherwise, something should be done without delay to express appreciation of the far-sighted patriotism, moral courage and wisdom of the Czech Government and people.' Newton added: 'I think it is very important not only to sweeten the pill for M. Benes and his Government personally, but also to help them in every possible way to convince their public.'[38] Isolated voices pro-tested stridently Czechoslovakia's fate. 'The partition of Czechoslovakia under pressure from England and France,' declared Churchill in a press statement, 'amounts to the complete surrender of the Western Democracies to the Nazi threat of force.' Not only Czechoslovakia was menaced, but the freedom and the democracy of all nations.[39] Russia's representative at the League of Nations, Maxim Litvinov, told the Assembly that the Soviet Union had been approached by Czechoslovakia on Monday; his country would stand by her obligations, he said.

But now it was too late. At 6.45 p.m. Chamberlain announced to his Cabinet a further message from Prague. Newton had been given a declaration by Krofta: 'Under pressure of urgent insistence ... Czechoslovakia Government sadly accept French and British proposals ... Czechoslovak Government accept them as a whole, emphasizing principle of guarantee as formulated and on supposition that the two Governments will not tolerate a German invasion of Czechoslovak territory....'[40] Although expected, this news brought immense relief to most Ministers. Chamberlain was loudly congratulated. But a difficult problem had still to be solved: the definition of the guarantee to truncated Czechoslovakia. The Prime Minister said two main questions had to be considered. 'First, should the guarantee be joint or several? Second, which Powers should be guarantors? In regard to the first question, examination only strengthened the case against a several guarantee. Every nation except ourselves might run out and leave us to bear the burden.... The guarantee is against "unprovoked aggression". Who is to determine whether a particular case constituted "unprovoked aggression"?' Other Ministers shared his apprehension. 'It was felt that the right plan was to have a joint guarantee, and to provide for a meeting of the guarantors to decide in any particular case whether "unprovoked aggression" had taken place.' Either to include Germany among the guarantors, or to exclude her completely, was considered unwise: she would therefore be invited to sign a separate non-aggression pact with Czechoslovakia. The joint guarantors would be France, Britain and Russia. 'Germany might think that some slur was put upon her by failure to include her as a guarantor', but fortunately 'there was almost certainly no prospect of persuading Germany to sign a document which was also signed by Russia'.

Another question remained: what if Hitler brought up the issue of other minorities in Czechoslovakia? A long discussion led nowhere; and already there were ominous signs that Poland and Hungary might snatch pickings from Czech territory. The view expressed by Hoare served to end this debate; the minority issue 'would be a test of Hitler's sincerity'.[41] Chamberlain was wished good luck for his second 'adventure' to see Hitler. Prospects for peace seemed to have improved immeasurably.

But the situation deteriorated drastically during Wednesday night. Sudeten *Freikorps* groups had slipped across the frontier in the dark and had occupied Asch.[42] An anxious Halifax instructed Henderson next morning, 22 September, to urge the German Government to prevent further incursions. Yet, despite alarms, Chamberlain glowed optimistically as his aircraft droned through the German sky. As he told Parliament later, he 'expected that when I got back to Godesberg I had only to discuss quietly with [Hitler] the proposals that I had brought with me'. Far less confident, of course, was Churchill. While Chamberlain was driving from Cologne airport to Godesberg, a group of politicians were assembling in his flat. Churchill said he had just returned from Downing Street; the Cabinet, he believed, had at last taken a firm stand. He had been informed – incorrectly – that Chamberlain was to present four demands: that Hitler should order early demobilization; that the transfer of the Sudeten territories should be undertaken gradually through an international commission; that there should be 'no nonsense' about Polish or Hungarian claims; and that a firm guarantee should be implemented for the rest of Czechoslovakia. Hitler would never accept such terms; Churchill, standing by the elegant fireplace, whisky and soda in hand, declared: 'In that case Chamberlain will return tonight and we shall have war.' Someone suggested it would be dangerous for Chamberlain to be still in German territory; Churchill growled: 'Even the Germans would not be so stupid as to deprive us of our beloved Prime Minister.'[43]

By now, Chamberlain was crossing the Rhine from the Petersburg Hotel, Königswinter, to meet Hitler at his favourite inn at Godesberg. The autumn evening was glorious and as the ferry throbbed gently through the glistening water, hundreds of sightseers lined the banks, reminding Henderson of Oxford and Cambridge boat race day. Over Godesberg fluttered the Swastika and the Union Jack, side by side. Observers judged Hitler either very nervous, or very angry. He had ugly black rings under his eyes and when he walked his dainty steps would suddenly be checked by a neurotic twitch. Gossips said Hitler had been having nervous crises lately, during which he would fling himself on the floor and gnaw the carpet.[44]

The telephone interrupted discussion at Churchill's flat. Jan Masaryk, the Czech Ambassador, told him the Germans had occupied Asch and that Hodza, the Prime Minister, had resigned. Soon afterwards Attlee telephoned to pledge Labour support for any action Churchill and his group might decide to take. The meeting at 11 Morpeth Mansions then decided that if Chamberlain came back with 'peace with honour', or if he broke off talks with Hitler, they would stand by him. But if he returned with 'peace with dishonour', they would vote against him. Further talks were adjourned to await information on the Godesberg encounter; Harold Nicolson wrote in his diary: 'We all feel it is terrifying that a man like Chamberlain should be exposed to such terrors and temptations.... I walk back feeling we are very near to war. When war comes it will be a terrible shock to the country. The bombing of London by itself will provoke panic and perhaps riots.'[45] Churchill's group was small, but influential. Yet Chamberlain had powerful support too. General Sir Edmund Ironside, future Chief of the Imperial General Staff, wrote on that same day: 'Chamberlain is of course right. We have not the means of defending ourselves and he knows it.... We cannot expose ourselves now to a German attack. We simply commit suicide if we do.'[46]

Meanwhile, Halifax, increasingly disturbed by the telegrams from Prague and Paris, could stand the waiting no longer. At 5.15 he telephoned Phipps with an urgent message for Léger. 'We have no information of progress of talks at Godesberg,' the message began, 'but we are much disturbed by reports of incursions of *Sudetendeutsch* organizations over border.' And, 'we should be glad to know if, in consequence of [the new events], you would now think it right to withdraw advice to Prague not to mobilize.'[47] An hour and a quarter later, Phipps replied: 'M. Léger considers that advice to Prague not to mobilize should certainly be withdrawn. He is advising French Government in this sense.'[48]

Yet London and Paris had still to hear the tragic outcome of the Godesberg talks. At 10.10 p.m. Halifax told Sir Eric Phipps: 'News from Godesberg is not very clear, but Prime Minister has issued statement urging necessity of all parties refraining from action of any kind that might interfere with progress of conversations.'[49] Not until 10.30 p.m. did Chamberlain telephone to say that 'his interview with Herr Hitler had been most unsatisfactory',[50] and only during the night did details arrive of the disastrous three-hour confrontation in the boardroom of the Godesberg Hotel – the same inn from which Hitler had launched his 1934 bloodbath to rid himself of rivals. Chamberlain described his shock when, after informing Hitler that the Czechs had accepted the German proposals, the Führer had declared, after a slight pause: *'Es tut mir fürchtbar leid, aber das geht nicht mehr'* – 'I am extremely sorry but that will no longer do,' and had pushed back his chair, folded his arms, crossed his legs, and scowled.

Hitler dragged up the issue of the other minority groups in Czechoslovakia – the 'test of Hitler's sincerity'. The Sudetenland problem must be settled definitely and completely by 1 October. No time was to be allowed for self-determination, the principle which had been accepted at the Berchtesgaden meeting. Instead, Hitler stressed, 'the fundamental fact was that neither the Sudetens, nor the Slovaks, nor the Poles, nor the Hungarians wanted to remain in Czechoslovakia, and the Czechs were attempting to thwart them by force.' Chamberlain protested, 'he had induced his colleagues, the French, and the Czechs, to agree to the idea of self-determination, in fact he had got exactly what the Führer wanted and without the expenditure of a drop of blood. In doing so he had been obliged to take his political life into

36

his hands.' Only one possibility existed, said Hitler. 'A frontier line must be drawn at once.' The Czechs must withdraw from this line and the area must be occupied by Germany immediately. He proposed a border along the language frontier, but if the Czechs objected, then he would agree to a plebiscite – but the territory would still be occupied by German troops at once. The plebiscite would be held 'everywhere' and would be based on the 1918 situation, 'that is to say, the Germans who had since left the territory would be entitled to vote and the Czechs who had since been planted there would not...'. 'The decisive element is speed,' Hitler added, 'because whilst we are sitting here we are at the mercy of events and an irreparable incident could occur at any moment.'

The two agreed to examine the map which Hitler had had prepared; they went downstairs where they were joined by Ribbentrop, Wilson and Henderson. Chamberlain told the Cabinet two days later: 'I was relieved to notice that the area on this map did not appear too different from the 50 per cent area marked on the maps which had been examined here.' The Cabinet Minutes for 24 September continue: 'The Prime Minister said that the conversations were continually interrupted by messages brought in at opportune moments reporting fresh outrages, which generally proved to be quite false.' Chamberlain tried to persuade Hitler to control the Sudetens 'whilst we took similar action at Prague'. Hitler replied that he would do his best, 'but it is an intolerable strain on my nerves to hold my hand in view of the constant Czech provocation, when I know that I could at any moment rout the Czechs with one armoured battalion.' The two adjourned until the following morning.[51]

Back in his hotel Chamberlain sifted through Hitler's frightening statements. A telephone call came through from Whitehall, where Ministers were anxious for news. Chamberlain disposed of them as briefly as he could. At midnight he sat down to write the Führer a letter, to make the British position clear. Typically, however, he avoided stating categorically what Britain would do in the event of a German invasion. 'I do not think you have realized the impossibility of my agreeing to put forward any plan unless I have reason to suppose it will be considered by public opinion in my country, in France, and indeed in the world generally, as carrying out the principles agreed upon in an orderly fashion and freedom [sic] from threat of force.' Immediate German occupation 'would be condemned as an unnecessary display of force'. He suggested the Sudeten Germans themselves should be entrusted with maintaining law and order. Early next day, 23 September, the letter was sent over to Hitler's camp. The morning meeting was cancelled and a reply was expected before lunch. Chamberlain and Henderson paced the wide balcony along the hotel; they had a long wait – no reply came from Hitler until mid-afternoon. 'Our cars were standing idle at the door,' wrote Ivone Kirkpatrick, 'and the crowd of bewildered spectators were anxiously wondering why Achilles was still sitting in his tent.... We sat down to a rather grim lunch. Mr Chamberlain discussed the theatre and spoke of his early days in Birmingham.'[52]

During those hours, Halifax in London pressed for more vigorous action, and in doing so revealed for the first time a significant divergence of opinion between himself and his Prime Minister. Henderson had told him during the night that the Czechs must still be urged not to mobilize; since then had come reports of more troop movements, press stories of the Godesberg negotiations breaking down, and no sign of renewed contact between Chamberlain and Hitler. At 1.40 in the afternoon Halifax therefore telephoned the Prime Minister. 'In the light of your information and ours we are profoundly disturbed ... and we feel that this decision [to urge the Czechs not to mobilize] must now be reversed. We propose to make necessary communication in this sense at 3 p.m. today.'[53] Twenty minutes later Henderson sent a hurried reply: 'We expect reply to this morning's letter at any moment, and think you should wait a little longer before making this communication....'[54]

At 3.35 p.m. Hitler's answer came. The Führer merely repeated all he had said the previous night; Chamberlain told the Cabinet the following day: 'The tone was not as courteous, or considerate, as one would wish, but it was worth remembering that Germans are apt to express themselves curtly.'[55] Chamberlain's first reaction was to agree with Halifax's decision to lift the ban on Czech mobilization. War was brought closer than ever; and Britain was still unprepared. An increasingly apprehensive Halifax contacted him again. 'If you are anticipating a breakdown in your negotiations will you consider whether some Cabinet action, authorizing further precautionary steps, should not be taken forthwith.'[56] Before replying Chamberlain asked Hitler to set down his demands in an official memorandum, and give an assurance that Czechoslovakia would not be attacked while the negotiations continued. Dr Schmidt had hinted to a member of the Prime Minister's staff that the Führer may not have understood properly the original proposals discussed at Berchtesgaden. Chamberlain now wanted to explore the possibility of a temporary compromise, involving some immediate and limited territorial cession. Henderson and Wilson were instructed to deliver this letter. Ribbentrop refused them entrance to Hitler's room, but told them the Führer would agree to Chamberlain's memorandum. Chamberlain would see Hitler at about 10.00 that night, and study the German document before returning to London.

He crossed the Rhine at 10.30. The Führer was waiting for him on the waterside steps and took Chamberlain, who was pleased to find him far more cordial than before, into the hotel lounge. But as the two leaders made conversation Henderson and Wilson were hurriedly reading the memorandum; they found it 'was an outrageous document, expressed in the most peremptory terms, and demanding that the evacuation of the Sudeten German area by Czech troops and police should start on Monday, 26 September, to be completed a day or two later'. Chamberlain thereupon said, that if this was the nature of the memorandum, there was nothing for me to do and I had half-risen from my chair to leave.[57]

But Hitler did not want a complete breakdown yet and Chamberlain was persuaded to stay. Talks, often heated, continued. The Prime Minister received another serious setback. Kirkpatrick, who was acting as secretary at the meeting, said in his official report: 'A message was brought in to Herr von Ribbentrop, who announced in a portentous tone that M. Benes had ordered general mobilization.' 'In that case things are settled,' declared Hitler. Chamberlain, flustered but determined asked why: 'Mobilization is a precaution, but not necessarily an offensive measure. There is mobilization on the other side too.' Hitler said the Czech move clearly indicated that Prague did not intend to cede territory. Chamberlain asked: 'Who mobilized first?' 'The Czechs,' Hitler replied. 'On the contrary,' retorted Chamberlain, 'Germany mobilized first – she had called up reservists and moved troops to the frontier.' Hitler shouted: 'When mobilization is ordered here you'll see the difference between the peace and war strength of the German Army.' Appropriate military measures now had to be taken to meet Czech mobilization, he added, and the Prime Minister said there was no point in further discussion.

Once again he was persuaded to stay. The time limit, as set forth in the German document, he declared, would produce 'a deplorable effect on public opinion in England and probably elsewhere. The Memorandum is an ultimatum.' He tossed the paper on to the table in front of him. 'It has the word "Memorandum" on the top,' replied Hitler. 'I am more impressed by the contents than by the title,' Chamberlain retorted. Dr Schmidt translated the paper orally into English and when he came to the words 'The following demands are made by the German Government', Chamberlain interrupted: 'We are ostensibly negotiating a peaceful settlement and the German Government is putting forward demands.' Hitler said he had no objection to substituting 'proposal'. Chamberlain agreed that 'no time should be lost in carrying the memorandum into effect' should the Czechs accept it, and said he would do his best to see that the transfer was carried out 'in a reasonable time' – adding that he felt he had a 'certain responsibility' over this. Hitler asked: 'What exactly do you regard as a reasonable time?' 'I cannot say now what would be a reasonable time,' replied

Chamberlain, 'but I mean a reasonable time, and Herr Hitler can safely trust my sincerity.'

A number of other minor alterations were made to the memorandum. 'You're the only man to whom I've ever made a concession,' said Hitler. Instead of insisting that Czech evacuation should take place between 26 and 28 September, he substituted 1 October as the 'one single date'. Chamberlain was apparently grateful: Dr Schmidt reported him as saying that 'he fully appreciated the Führer's consideration on the point'. And yet 1 October had been Hitler's X-Day for many weeks.[58]

Chamberlain asked for a further 'concession'. Could the German troops' occupation be confined to territory with a considerable German preponderance, say, for example, 80 per cent? Hitler claimed he himself had raised this possibility that very morning with his military advisers and had been told that such a partial occupation was technically impossible. The Prime Minister said he would submit the proposals to the Czechs and when discussions broke up at 1.30 a.m., Hitler emphasized that the Czech problem was his last territorial demand in Europe, which Chamberlain apparently believed. 'Chamberlain bid a hearty farewell to the Führer,' recorded Schmidt. 'He said he had the feeling that a relationship of confidence had grown up between himself and the Führer.'

Back over the chilly waters of the Rhine and walking into his hotel, Chamberlain was asked by a journalist: 'Is the position hopeless?' 'I would not like to say that,' he replied. 'It's up to the Czechs now.'[59] As a result of enterprise and courage shown by Colonel Mason-MacFarlane, the German Memorandum was in Czech hands before dawn on Saturday, 24 September. The Colonel flew back to Berlin, motored to the Czech frontier, then walked two kilometres in the dark through barbed wire positions, at considerable risk of being shot by either side.[60]

After a few hours of much needed sleep, the Prime Minister flew back to London later on Saturday morning; Hitler returned to Berlin in the afternoon. The British diplomats from the Berlin Embassy had to wait at Cologne for the next train. 'We filled in the time by paying a visit to the cathedral,' wrote Kirkpatrick. 'Henderson, who was depressed by our experiences at Godesberg, knelt in the knave and prayed for peace.'[61] Meanwhile, the French Ministerial Council found itself unable to decide what action to take; Russia again showed a firmer attitude. The Soviets would fight, declared Litvinov, if France decided to honour her commitment. He suggested a meeting of the three Powers, together with Roumania and any other reliable small Power. 'This would show the Germans that we mean business.'[62] As before, the Russian proposal was ignored.

The Cabinet gathered for a crucial meeting at 5.30 that evening, to decide whether to advise the Czechs to accept or reject Hitler's latest demands – whether to continue the search for peace or to risk immediate outbreak of war. Two hours before they met, the Prime Minister talked with his closest colleagues, Simon, Halifax and Hoare, and Chamberlain expressed himself 'satisfied that Herr Hitler would not go back on his word'.

He opened the 5.30 Cabinet meeting with a remarkable assessment. 'On the first day at Godesberg I had felt indignant that ... Herr Hitler was ... pressing new demands on me. After further conversation ... however, I modified my view on this point. In order to understand people's actions it is necessary to appreciate their motives and to see how their minds work.... Herr Hitler has a narrow mind and is violently prejudiced on certain subjects. But he would not deliberately deceive a man whom he respects and with whom he has been in negotiation, and I'm sure Herr Hitler now feels some respect for me.'

Some members of the Cabinet, notably Duff Cooper and Hore-Belisha, listened with increasing astonishment as Chamberlain went on: 'When Herr Hitler announces that he means to do something, it is certain that he will do it. In the present instance Herr Hitler has said that if the principle of self-determination is accepted, he will carry it out. I think he is doing so, although he has odd views as to the proper way of giving effect to that principle. I don't believe that Herr Hitler thought he was departing in any way from the spirit of what he agreed to at Berchtesgaden.' Hitler had told him no more territorial demands would be made; and had also said 'if the present question can be settled peacefully, it might be a turning point in Anglo-German relations.' Eagerly, Chamberlain added: 'It would be a great tragedy if we lost this opportunity. A peaceful settlement of Europe depended upon an Anglo-German understanding.... I have now established an influence over Hitler, and he trusts me and is willing to work with me.... I hope, therefore, that the Cabinet will examine very carefully the differences between the proposals made last Sunday and the present proposals, and will consider whether those differences justify us going to war.' He said that on his return to London he had flown up the Thames and had imagined a German bomber flying the same course. 'I asked myself what degree of protection we could afford to the thousands of homes which I saw stretched out below me. And I felt that we are in no position to justify waging a war today in order to prevent a war hereafter.' Chamberlain came closest to the truth when he commented: 'I hope ... that my colleagues will not think that I am making any attempts to disguise the fact that, if we now possessed a superior force to Germany, we should probably be considering these proposals in a very different spirit. But we must look facts in the face.'

The first fact to be faced was the urgent need for a decision on Britain's attitude should the French go to war. Chamberlain proposed a method of giving his Cabinet a few extra hours before committing the country. If the Czechs refused Hitler's demands, and 'if the French decided to back Czechoslovakia, the next point would be to ascertain what action they proposed to take.' In other words, the Cabinet need not reach a conclusion until the French had.

But the Prime Minister then met greater opposition than he ever had before in the Cabinet Room. Duff Cooper declared: 'I fear ... unless we act promptly, intervention might come too late to be effective. Herr Hitler still doesn't believe this country will, in any circumstances, go to war.... As regards the promises which Herr Hitler made to the Prime Minister, I don't feel confidence can be placed in them.' Order general mobilization now, he urged. 'This would make our position clear to the German Government and might yet result in deterring them from war. Hore-Belisha thought, 'We should not be forgiven if some sudden attack was made on this country and we had failed to take the necessary steps to put ourselves in a proper state of protection.' Walter Elliot agreed. But Chamberlain, anxious to steer discussion back to general policy, ruled that defence measures be considered the next day. Faced with the prospect of a disastrous split, he played for time. The debate reverted to less controversial points. Duff Cooper asked if the inclusion of France, Russia and Britain in a joint guarantee had been discussed at Godesberg. Chamberlain replied: 'Russia was not mentioned.'

The Cabinet agreed the French should be asked their opinion. Chamberlain was encouraged by the message which had just arrived from Phipps: 'All that is best in France is against war, *almost* at any price – hence the really deep and pathetic gratitude shown to our Prime Minister....'[63] Daladier and Bonnet were asked to come over the following afternoon.[64] Thirty minutes later a cable went to Prague. 'Prime Minister hopes that any reply of Czechoslovak Government to German Memorandum may be transmitted through him. If Czechoslovak Government was able and desired to send a special representative to London to discuss matters we should be very happy to receive him, preferably on Monday [26 September].'[65] So the French and British leaders each relied on the other to give an opinion first; and the unfortunate Czechs were not to be called in until Anglo-French consultations had been concluded.

Duff Cooper had left the Cabinet Room as unconvinced as ever. 'Personally, I believe that Hitler has cast a spell over Neville.... After all Hitler's achievement is not due to his intellectual attainments, not to his oratorical powers, but to the extraordinary influence which he seems to be able to exercise over his fellow creatures.... I believe that Neville is under that influence at the present time. "It all depends," he said, "on whether we can trust Hitler." "Trust him for what?" I asked.'

The Cabinet would meet again at 10.30 the following morning. Hore-Belisha went home to 'clear my mind in readiness for tomorrow's meeting'. He jotted down notes on the points he wished to make. 'In my judgement we have incurred a moral obligation to the Czechs and we are no longer the free agents we were before the matter started.... It is quite clear that Hitler only understands one argument and that is the argument he has been displaying – a display of force.... No one is more conscious than I am of our present deficiencies. Chiefs of Staff view – to take offensive against Germany now would be like "a man attacking a tiger before he has loaded his gun". But life is only worth living for certain things....'[66] Also troubled was Halifax, Chamberlain's main instrument for putting appeasement into practice. Vansittart, too, was convinced the Government had 'drifted too fast and too far'.[67]

The Cabinet meeting on Sunday morning, 25 September, opened with preliminary remarks by Halifax: Daladier and Bonnet would be flying to London for discussions at about 5 p.m.; Halifax also said Eden had told him he hoped, if Hitler's proposals were as stated in the newspapers, Britain would reject them. No news had been received yet from Prague. He then told a silent Cabinet that in effect he now opposed the Prime Minister. His face expressionless, Chamberlain listened to his carefully chosen words. 'I have found my opinion changing somewhat in the last day or so.... Yesterday I felt that the difference between acceptance of the principle of last Sunday's proposal and the scheme now put forward a week later for its application, did not invoke a new acceptance of principle. I am not quite sure, however, that I still hold that view.... I cannot rid my mind of the fact that Herr Hitler has given us nothing and that he is dictating terms, just as though he had won a war but without having had to fight.' Consequently, he said slowly and sadly, 'I do not feel it would be right to put pressure on Czechoslovakia to accept. We should lay the case before them.' He fully realized and fully accepted the implications. 'If they reject it, I imagine that the French will join in, and if France goes in, we should join with them.' There was a slight pause; the Cabinet remained silent; then Halifax spoke again: 'I have worked most closely with the Prime Minister throughout the long crisis. I am not quite sure that our minds are still altogether as one. Nevertheless, I thought it right to express my own hesitation with complete frankness.'

As Halifax finished the Cabinet noisily revealed just how split it was. First to speak was Lord Hailsham, Lord President of the Council. He agreed with Halifax. Lord Stanhope and Lord Maugham both believed the Czechs should be persuaded to accept. Lord Winterton said the proposals should be immediately rejected by Britain. Sir Thomas Inskip was typically more cautious: the full facts should be given to the Czechs, and Prague should be warned – which 'would need delicate handling' – that French help to Czechoslovakia should not be assured. Sir Kingsley Wood, Air Secretary, supported Chamberlain: the terms should be accepted, albeit with 'intense disgust'.

Halifax briefly interrupted the succession of opinions to announce that Masaryk, the Czech Ambassador, wanted to deliver an urgent message after the meeting. Then the flow continued. Duff Cooper, predictably, declared 'We should now tell the Czech Government that we regard the terms as intolerable and that, if they refuse the ultimatum presented to them, we would stand by them and that we hoped France would do the same.' The Prime Minister sat silent, with his pince-nez resting upon the papers in front of him, as one by one his Ministers took sides. Oliver Stanley believed the proposals should be rejected. Malcolm MacDonald was vague: pressure could not be brought on the Czechs, but they should be given the full facts.

To Lord De La Warr, appeasement was finished. But the Marquess of Zetland believed war might bring an even worse régime in Germany. 'Many of those who are clamouring for us to take a stronger attitude with Germany would adopt a different view when a world war had been in progress a month or so.'

Ministers in opposition were disappointed with Sir John Simon: he believed that the facts should be given objectively, and Britain should indicate she would be prepared to give a guarantee, but, that 'we should not say that, if they reject these proposed terms we should come to their aid'. Leslie Burgin thought the Czechs should be told to accept the terms and that, if they rejected them 'they should not look to us for certain support'. Walter Elliot agreed with Halifax. Leslie Hore-Belisha said the Czechs should be told that 'we took the view Czechoslovakia would be justified in refusing to accept these proposals'. With nothing decided and some Ministers still to speak, the meeting adjourned until 3.00 p.m. It seemed that of the 17 who had so far given opinions, eight were generally against continuing the present British policy of appeasement; eight supported the Prime Minister; one, Colville, had declined to commit himself. The Cabinet was indeed sliced down the centre.[68]

Britain's elderly Prime Minister was living and working under almost intolerable strain; the pressures of the international situation were now supplemented by the fears of a collapse of his domestic political support; and of course political upheaval at home could only further weaken Britain's state of preparedness. In Berlin, by contrast, the atmosphere seemed almost calm. The weather that autumn Sunday was summer-like; Berliners crowded the parks and lakes to enjoy the sunshine. Paris was undecided, like London; in Prague there was fear. In Venice, the dapper Count Ciano, Italian Foreign Minister, met Prince Philip of Hesse, Hitler's emissary, and took him to see Mussolini; Hesse told the Duce the destruction of Czechoslovakia would begin not later than 1 October.[69]

Strangely, the spate of diplomatic messages dwindled during the day. Everyone seemed to be waiting. Ministers filed into the Cabinet Room punctually at 3.00. The meeting was surprisingly short. Halifax opened: a special conference of the French Council would delay the arrival of Daladier and Bonnet, and he and Chamberlain had therefore arranged to see the Czech Ambassador at about 5.00 to receive his 'urgent message'.

The round of opinions continued. Sir Samuel Hoare believed the Czechs should be allowed to speak for themselves. Conflict should be avoided for as long as possible; 'the longer the delay, the stronger our position will become. I also think that consideration should be given to the question whether, if war broke out, it might not be in the interests not merely of ourselves but of our allies, that we should delay joining in.' Clearly Chamberlain had a strong supporter there. But the next speaker, W. S. Morrison found great difficulty in 'pressing the Czechs to accept the ultimatum'. Finally Ernest Brown said Britain should accept the terms and should persuade the Czechs to do the same.

The Prime Minister had a total of ten supporters; eight appeared to be against him, while two had declined to show clearly what they thought. Chamberlain spoke, knowing he must prevent the Cabinet from splintering. He appealed for loyalty and for unity. 'We are faced with a critical situation.... It is important that the Cabinet should present a uniform front.' He manoeuvred for a compromise; it was not up to Britain to accept, or reject, Hitler's terms. 'We are only acting as an intermediary. The final responsibility for acceptance or rejection lies with the Czech Government.' Ignoring his attitude – and behaviour – till now, Chamberlain conveniently claimed 'there is no pressure we can exert except in the literal sense'. Britain, he implied, was removed from further responsibility; much of the argument was rendered irrelevant.

But even Chamberlain could not hide Britain completely in the shadows. 'If France goes to war, it is almost inevitable that we ourselves will be involved.' This placed Britain in an embarrassing position. 'We cannot therefore say to the Czechs that if they rejected these proposals we would remain completely aloof, since that might not be the case.' He relied once again on negative action. 'Firstly, we should not say that if the proposals were rejected we undertook to declare war on Germany; secondly, equally, we should not say that if the proposals were rejected we would in no circumstances declare war on Germany; thirdly, we should put before the representatives of the French and Czechoslovak Government the full facts of the situation, as we saw them, in their true light.'

To agree would be to accept that Britain's position should remain unstated and that when Britain presented the 'full facts as we saw them in their true light' this would mean the facts as Chamberlain interpreted them and in the light in which he saw them. Yet any Minister rejecting Chamberlain's compromise proposals would almost inevitably have to resign, and the consequences would be critical, not only from a personal but also from a national and international point of view. Dissenting Ministers had to consider whether they would help the Czechs more – and help halt Hitler – by staying or by leaving the Cabinet. Adroitly Chamberlain now made it more difficult for those Ministers disagreeing with him to push themselves forward, and easier for those who merely felt uneasy to remain silent: he eased discussion back to safe administrative matters; any rebel Minister would therefore have to interrupt him. He hurriedly suggested that the talks with the French should be divided in two, with a Cabinet meeting in the interval before an Anglo-French decision was reached. For the third time that day, the Cabinet adjourned. Chamberlain's adept handling had won him a victory: the further dissenting Ministers went with him, the more difficult it would be for them to justify coming out in opposition.[70]

Soon after the Cabinet had dispersed, Masaryk was ushered into Chamberlain's room. He read a prepared document: 'My Government has now studied the document and the map. It is a *de facto* ultimatum of the sort usually presented to a vanquished nation, and not a proposition to a Sovereign State which has shown the greatest possible readiness to make sacrifices for the appeasement of Europe.' Chamberlain and Halifax listened with increasing dismay. 'My Government is amazed with the contents of the memorandum. The proposals go far beyond what we agreed to in the so-called Anglo-French plan. They deprive us of every safeguard for our national existence.... My Government wish me to declare in all solemnity that Herr Hitler's demands in their present form are absolutely and unconditionally unacceptable to my Government. Against these new and cruel demands my Government feel bound to make their utmost resistance and we shall do so, God helping. The nation of St Wenceslas, John Hus and Thomas Masaryk will not be a nation of slaves. We rely upon the two great Western democracies, whose wishes we have followed much against our own judgement, to stand by us in our hour of trial.' He handed the official Note to Chamberlain and abruptly left. No more could be said. The Czechs had made plain their complete rejection of Hitler's terms – and the British and French leaders had not even had time to work out their joint policy.[71]

At 9.35 p.m. Chamberlain opened Anglo-French discussions with his account of the Godesberg events. Daladier made a clear and apparently uncompromising statement of France's attitude: his Council had refused to recognize Hitler's right to take Sudetenland by force and had refused to agree to Hitler's demand for a plebiscite in those areas which had an obvious Czech majority. 'We are confronted with a plan of Herr Hitler and his régime, not so much to take over three and a half million Germans as to destroy Czechoslovakia by force, enslaving her, and afterwards realizing the domination of Europe, which is his object.' Chamberlain described the subsequent dialogue when he addressed the Cabinet meeting during the adjournment at 11.40 p.m.:

Prime Minister: What do you propose to do next?
Daladier: I propose that it should be suggested to Herr Hitler that he should return to the plan agreed upon last Sunday.
Prime Minister: What will happen if Herr Hitler refuses?
Daladier: I suppose that everyone will do his duty. I have no proposals to make.
Prime Minister: Herr Hitler told me that his Memorandum constituted his last word, and that if he could not reach a peaceful settlement he would impose on Czechoslovakia a frontier based on strategic considerations.
Daladier: In that case Germany will be guilty of an unprovoked aggression.
Prime Minister: Would France then declare war?
Daladier: France would fulfil her obligations of assistance.

The French refused to be more specific. 'M. Daladier said he could not discuss technical questions, but France's future action would depend upon many things.' Chamberlain pressed him further. 'Finally, M. Daladier said it would be ridiculous to mobilize a large force of men and to leave them doing nothing. The German fortifications opposite the Maginot Line were not as yet very solid, and he thought that France could try a land offensive, after a period of concentration. Likewise, it would of course be possible to use the French Air Force against certain military and industrial centres in Germany.' Daladier wondered whether this really was Hitler's last word. If so, at least 'we should send for the Czechs and hear what they had to say before they were sacrificed'.

Finally, he put three questions to the British. Did they accept Herr Hitler's plan? Did the British Government intend to press the plan on the Czech Government? Did the British think that no action should be taken by the French? Chamberlain said he replied as follows: firstly, 'it was for the Czechs and not for this country or France to accept or reject Herr Hitler's proposals'; secondly, 'we had received a message from the Czech Government which did not represent their complete reply – it was clear, however, that the nature of the interim reply was an unqualified refusal. In any case we were not in a position

47

to put pressure on the Czechs.' Thirdly, he was not sure it was for His Majesty's Government to tell the French what they should do, but clearly whatever decision the French Government arrived at might affect Britain; 'it was important to know what France intended to do'. Gamelin, the French Chief of Staff, should be invited to visit London the following day for consultations. Daladier agreed. The Anglo-French conference then decided to adjourn for 30 minutes to allow the British Cabinet to meet. At this meeting Chamberlain claimed: 'I think it is significant that never once did the French put the question: "If we go to war with Germany will you come in too?"'

Duff Cooper again proved hostile. 'The British Ministers appear to have contested the French point of view on every point and to have allowed it to appear that they disagreed with the French Government's suggestions, without making any positive contribution themselves.' The Prime Minister merely replied that he could not accept this criticism, and continued, 'I have a further suggestion ... It is now clear that the Czechoslovak Government have decided to reject Herr Hitler's proposals, and it is necessary to consider transmitting the refusal to Herr Hitler. As matters stand, Herr Hitler will march into Czechoslovakia, and we should then have to see what France would do. I am unwilling to leave unexplored any possible chance of avoiding war. Therefore I suggest that, basing myself on the personal conversations I have had with Herr Hitler, I should write a personal letter ... saying that I have received intimation that the Prague Government are likely to reject [his] proposals and making one last appeal to him.' This appeal would take the form of a suggestion for a Joint Commission to consider how the proposals already accepted by the Czechs could be put into effect, in an orderly manner, as quickly as possible, and without shocking public opinion. Chamberlain would send this letter by special emissary – Sir Horace Wilson. And Sir Horace would have a further, more important, task. 'I think it is out of the question for me to make a further visit to the Führer. If the letter fails to secure any response from Herr Hitler, Sir Horace Wilson should be authorized to give a personal message from me to the effect that if this appeal was refused, France would go to war and if that happened, it seemed certain that we should be drawn in.' Some element of bluff might exist in Hitler's attitude, and this proposal would give him a possible escape route. Duff Cooper wanted the warning made stronger. 'We should say definitely to Herr Hitler that, if this appeal was rejected, the Czechs would fight and the French would come to their aid and we should come in on their side too.' Chamberlain retorted: 'I am quite clear that this should not be said in my letter. To do so would rule out all chance of acceptance of this appeal.'

Banking on this last chance, Chamberlain's fertile mind had apparently come up with the ideal compromise to merge 'doves' and 'hawks'

48

in his Cabinet. He had been pushed into stronger action than he would have wished, by both the Czech rejection and the French stand; but the plan seemed to unify his Cabinet. No more voices were raised in opposition.[72] The British and French representatives assembled again at 12.35, but only for a few moments. They decided to close the Anglo-French talks for the night. The Czechs, in response to Halifax's appeal, would not 'at this stage' publish the Note handed to Chamberlain.[73] But the British and French had still to agree before Prague made her announcement; and time was limited.

Early on Monday morning, 26 September, Chamberlain sent Wilson, and the letter, to Hitler. The letter described the Czech rejection of Hitler's demands, and suggested that German and Czech representatives should meet. Hitler himself had said the only differences lay in the method of carrying out an agreed principle. 'Surely the tragic consequence of a conflict ought not to be incurred over a difference of method.'[74] Henderson arranged to see Hitler with Wilson at 5.00 that afternoon. So, when the British and French Ministers met once more something definite had been arranged for them to agree. 'M. Daladier expressed himself entirely in agreement with the Prime Minister's initiative.' Chamberlain said Hitler was to make a speech that evening, which 'no doubt ... would reveal his final intentions'.[75] Daladier's agreement with Chamberlain's initiative was a shift in the French position; Chamberlain, at a Cabinet meeting immediately afterwards, attributed this to an early morning meeting alone with Daladier, who, speaking more freely than at a formal conference, said 'frankly, he did not feel that he had expressed himself well on the previous evening.... If Germany attacked Czechoslovakia and hostilities ensued, the French intended to go to war and to commence hostilities with Germany within five days.'[76]

At last, a clear French statement had been made. And leaders of both countries seemed now to act with a new-found courage. Chamberlain revealed to the Cabinet that his instructions to Wilson had gone even beyond those agreed at the previous meeting; if Sir Horace could get no satisfaction, Hitler would be told that Britain should 'feel obliged to support France'. Nor, apparently, did Chamberlain believe the conference proposal *would* meet with success; he placed 'no particular hopes on this last appeal'. Nor on an appeal to Britain, Germany, France, Czechoslovakia, Poland and Hungary made that morning by President Roosevelt. Adopting the new spirit, the whole Cabinet 'approved the action taken by the Prime Minister'.

Chamberlain read to the Cabinet a statement from Churchill, urging that Parliament should now be summoned; he himself agreed, and suggested either Tuesday or Wednesday. Hitler's speech that evening would probably indicate whether immediate full mobilization was necessary and following a suggestion from Simon, the Cabinet agreed that the Prime Minister, with the Lord President of the Council, should arrange for this if necessary, without summoning the Cabinet.

Chamberlain described the military position detailed to him by Gamelin that morning. The French intended to enter the war and launch an attack within about five days; objectives in the German line had already been selected. France was well aware that she would suffer heavily from air attacks. Gamelin thought the Czech army 'would give a good account of themselves'.[77] The Cabinet dispersed and the new air of resolution spread in both Paris and London. Phipps reported 'Opinion has undergone a complete change since Hitler's last demands have become known.'[78] In London, Churchill had an interview with Chamberlain and Halifax. 'Lord Halifax and I were at one,' he wrote in his memoirs, 'and I certainly thought the Prime Minister was in full accord.' The three drafted a strong communiqué which was later issued to the press: 'If, in spite of the efforts made by the British Prime Minister, a German attack is made upon Czechoslovakia, the immediate result must be that France will be bound to come to her assistance, and Great Britain and Russia will certainly stand by France.'[79] The announcement, the firmest so far, indicated the lengths to which Chamberlain now felt he was being pushed, and with what speed. Although Russia was included in the statement, she had not even been consulted yet.

Churchill was buoyant. Returning to his flat he found a group waiting for him, including Harold Macmillan, Robert Boothby, Archibald Sinclair, Leo Amery, Selwyn Lloyd and Harold Nicolson. 'Winston bursts in,' wrote Nicolson in his diary. 'He says that the Cabinet were in a blue funk last night and that Simon was urging further retreat. But the younger people revolted and the Simon faction began to lose ground. Then came the French, all brave and solid this time, plus Gamelin who restored confidence. In the end the Cabinet were all united in feeling how brave, how strong, how resolute they had always been.... Winston gathers that the memorandum or letter which Horace Wilson is to give Hitler is not in the least a retreat. It is merely an attempt to save Hitler's face if he wants to climb down.' Another discussion was taking place at that moment, between Gamelin and Inskip, plus the three British service ministers. Gamelin this time gave a depressing picture of Czechoslovakia's ability to withstand a German invasion. Asked how long Czechoslovakia would hold out against Germany, he replied: 'Were I a politician and not a soldier I would be able to give a figure, but as it is I am only prepared to say she could hold out certainly for a few weeks, but perhaps not for a few months.'[80]

At 5.00 that Monday afternoon Wilson and Henderson saw Hitler at the Reich Chancellery. In three hours the Führer was scheduled to speak at the *Sportpalast*. And the British met with a terrifying reception. Schmidt wrote a shocked note afterwards: 'For the first and only time in my presence, Hitler completely lost his head.'[81] 'Gazed at him in fascination,' recounted Ivone Kirkpatrick. 'During one of his many tirades I was unable to take my eyes off him and my pencil remained poised above the paper. Sir Horace Wilson noticed this and whispered: "Are you getting everything down? It's frightfully important." I whispered back: "I'm not likely to forget a word." Nor did I.'[82] Not until 7.20 p.m. did Chamberlain hear the first details from Sir Horace. 'Very violent hour,' his message began. 'He is clearly determined to make great passionate speech tonight and was most impatient.' At one point Hitler had made as if to walk out and 'was only with difficulty persuaded to listen to any more and then only with insane interruptions'.[83] Later Sir Horace added 'in view of intense emotion and frequent references to tonight's speech it seemed better not to deliver special message and I am to see him again tomorrow morning'. So the firm declaration was still unmade.[84]

Kirkpatrick later supplied a full official record of the stormy conversation. Sir Horace had handed Hitler the written message from Chamberlain and said how shocked British public opinion had been by the terms of Germany's Godesberg memorandum. 'Herr Hitler interrupted to say that in that event it was no use talking any more.' Sir Horace persisted – 'Herr Hitler interrupted to vociferate in staccato accents that the problem must be solved forthwith without any further delay' – Sir Horace said the Prime Minister fully appreciated this but the difficulty lay in the procedure – 'Herr Hitler made gestures and exclamations of disgust and impatience.' Sir Horace insisted that Schmidt should read a translation of Chamberlain's letter; when the interpreter came to the words 'the Czechoslovak Government ... regard as wholly unacceptable the proposal ...' Herr Hitler jumped from his chair and made to leave the room, muttering that it was no use talking further and that the time for action had come. 'Sir Horace Wilson endeavoured to pacify Herr Hitler and to continue his remarks, but he was interrupted once more by the Chancellor. Herr Hitler declared that it was not a question of giving Germany something in theory, but of boggling and delaying the moment ... in practice. Germany was being treated like niggers; one would not dare to treat even the Turks like that. "On 1 October I shall have Czechoslovakia where I want her." If France and England decided to strike, let them strike. He did not care a farthing.' At one point he declared he must have an affirmative reply from the Czechs within two days, 'that was to say by Wednesday'. Henderson asked: 'Midnight Wednesday?' Hitler replied: 'No, by 2 p.m.' As the confrontation concluded, Hitler repeated 'come what might, by negotiation or by force, Sudeten German territory would be in German military occupation on 1 October.'[85] Chamberlain had hardly had time to digest the preliminary information on the Chancellery interview before Hitler's *Sportpalast* speech began. And it was more explosive and venomous than any he had made. The Führer flung insult after insult, and each was devoured by the screeching mob. 'This state began with a single lie, and the father of this lie was named Benes.' Benes and his henchman had set out to destroy the German minority; the Germans were being persecuted, shot as traitors if they refused to fire upon their fellow Germans; Benes had put his country at the service of the Bolsheviks as an advanced air base from which to blast the Fatherland; the daily number of refugees, claimed Hitler, had risen to 214,000. 'Whole stretches of country are depopulated, villages burned down, attempts made to smoke out the Germans with grenades and gas. Herr Benes, however, sits in Prague and is convinced "Nothing can happen to me: in the end England and France stand behind me...." And now, my countrymen, I believe that the time has come when one must mince matters no more.' The Nazi crowd yelled in frenzy. 'Now two men stand arrayed one against the other: there is Herr Benes and here am I.' His voice sounded even more hysterical through the massive loudspeakers. 'We are two men of different make-up. In the great struggle of the peoples, while Herr Benes was sneaking about through the world, I, as a decent German soldier, did my duty. And now today I stand over against this man as a soldier of my people.' The crowd roared approval. 'My patience is at an end.... The decision now lies in his hands. Peace or War.... I have never been a coward. Now I go before my people as its first soldier. And behind me – this world should know – there marches a different people from that of 1918.' The Führer spat out a challenge: 'We are determined! Now, let Benes make his choice!'[86]

Hitler sat down, hair plastered to his pale forehead with sweat. Goebbels jumped to his feet. 'One thing is sure – 1918 will never be repeated!' he yelled. Hitler leaped to his feet again, pounded his hand on the table, shouted '*Ja!*' and slumped again exhausted into his chair.[87] Chamberlain could only despair. London and the rest of Britain were preparing for conflict. Workmen were digging trenches in the smooth turf of Green Park by Buckingham Palace; posters were being pasted on to buildings – 'City of Westminster: Air Raid Precautions. Gas Masks Notice....' The Royal Navy was being partially mobilized; at the War Office orders were being issued by telephone and telegrams to all Territorials of Coast Defence Units and the 1st and 2nd Anti-aircraft Divisions.

The Times next day meekly described Hitler's outburst as a 'rather offensive statement of a perfectly reasonable case'. But few readers could have agreed. And at 10 a.m. Chamberlain signalled to Wilson in Berlin. 'After violent attack on Benes we feel it is useless to ask the Czech Government to approach Germans with a fresh offer.' But later in the morning Sir Horace was also told that a press statement would be issued that as Hitler apparently had no faith in the Czechs carrying out their promise of a Sudetenland handover, Britain would see they did. The British Government, said Chamberlain, felt 'morally responsible'. He apparently hoped to switch back from being a mere link between Hitler and Benes, to bringing pressure on Prague.[88] Yet at noon Wilson saw Hitler once more, to deliver the Prime Minister's personal warning of Britain's position should hostilities start – the warning which he had avoided giving the previous evening. Two alternatives were left, he said. 'If the Czechs accepted the memorandum, well and good. If they rejected it, the question arose, where would the conflict end?' Hitler interrupted to shout that the first end would be the total destruction of Czechoslovakia. Sir Horace declared the French would feel obliged to fulfil their treaty obligations if the Germans attacked Czechoslovakia. 'If the forces of France become actively engaged in hostilities against Germany ... the British Government would feel obliged to support her.' This meant, Hitler replied, that if France attacked Germany, Great Britain was under an obligation to attack Germany also. 'He could only take note of this communication.'[89] Chamberlain's warning to Hitler was plain and strong; but, according to Schmidt's official notes, Wilson weakened it as he left the room, 'I shall try to make these Czechs sensible,' he said. Almost before he had walked down the wide Chancellery steps, Hitler called for his Adjutant and flung the waiting German war machine into action; he ordered assault units to be ready 'to begin action against "Green" on 30 September'.[90]

Chamberlain's tide of determination was ebbing. Perhaps after all he had been relying upon his last appeal to Hitler. Now came a short signal from Rome, which later had important consequences. Lord Perth, Britain's Ambassador, suggested: 'It might possibly be helpful if I were authorized to convey officially and immediately to Count Ciano ... the hope that Sr. Mussolini would use his influence.'[91]

Prague was remarkably calm, despite Chamberlain's grim message to Benes, 'Information His Majesty's Government now have from Berlin makes it clear that German forces will have orders to cross Czechoslovak frontier almost immediately, unless by 2 p.m. tomorrow Czechoslovak Government have accepted German terms.... Nothing that any other Power can do will prevent this fate for your own country and people, and this remains true whatever may be the ultimate issue of a possible world war.'[92] The Prime Minister had by now come almost full circle, and applied pressure he had ruled out only two days before. And, ironically, Hitler was also having last minute doubts; Schmidt believed the Führer was hesitating to take 'the extreme steps'. Hitler had been informed by the German Military Attaché in Paris that the French 'partial mobilization' would probably result in the deployment of 65 divisions within the first six days, and Germany had only 12 with which to face them; Hitler knew Britain to be making military preparations; Prague was calm and defiant; his Generals were apprehensive; the German people were generally apathetic.

These considerations were before the Führer as he replied to Chamberlain during Tuesday evening; and his letter was more reasonable than previous ones. German objectives were strictly limited, he stressed. The immediate occupation by German contingents was no more than a security measure, and would only extend to the specified line. 'The final delimitation of the frontier would take place in accordance with the procedure which I have already described ... the British and, if necessary, the French, Governments can guarantee the quick fulfilment of my proposal. ... I am even ready to give formal guarantee for the remainder of Czechoslovakia.' Hitler's letter, in marked contrast to the language of his *Sportpalast* speech, concluded: 'I must leave it to your judgement whether, in view of these facts, you consider that you should continue your effort, for which I should like to take this opportunity of once more sincerely thanking you, to spoil such manoeuvres and bring the Government in Prague to reason at the very last hour.'[93] Transmitted by Henderson, this reached the Foreign Office at 8.40 p.m. Forty minutes later the Cabinet assembled, for what would be the last meeting before the Munich Agreement. Chamberlain began by assessing the latest situation. Contrary to usual practice he, and not the Foreign Secretary, described the most recent reports; and all of them served to stress the stupidity of going to war at that particular time. The Prime Minister said Henderson believed that 'unless at this eleventh hour we advised Czechoslovakia to make the best terms she could with Berlin, we should be exposing Czechoslovakia to the fate of Abyssinia.' Chamberlain had seen Mason-MacFarlane, just returned from Czechoslovakia. The Colonel had found the morale of the country very poor, and believed the people would offer only feeble resistance. More than this, the Dominion High Commissioners had all visited Downing Street that afternoon, and all thought further pressure should be put on the Czechs. Wilson described his two interviews with Hitler. 'It is clear we have to deal with a firm conviction on Herr Hitler's part that Dr Benes is a twister who would never implement his promises but would continue to prevaricate.'

Duff Cooper maintained: 'If we waited until there was complete unanimity with the Dominion Governments on issues of peace and war in Europe, it would mean we should never go to war.' He regretted that Wilson had not delivered the special, verbal warning from Chamberlain to Hitler before the latter's *Sportpalast* speech. 'Public opinion in Germany still doubted whether we would come into the war, and I think that we have, in fact, given some justification for this doubt.' As for the latest ideas, they 'really amounted to a proposal that, at the eleventh hour, after having seen the French Ministers, we should

54

urge Czechoslovakia to a policy of surrender. It is no use urging this course on Czechoslovakia unless we also tell her that, unless she adopts it, we would refuse to come to her help.... This course is quite unjustified and I cannot be associated with it.'

But Chamberlain had discussed Hitler's offer with 'the three colleagues who are in constant consultation with me,' presumably Halifax, Hoare and either Simon or Wilson. 'We thought this offer was perhaps the last opportunity for avoiding war, and that it was not right we should decide against its adoption, without putting all the facts before the Cabinet and leaving them to judge for themselves.' Only now did Halifax make a contribution. And the reason for his silence was immediately obvious: he still strongly disagreed with putting pressure on the Czechs. 'It amounts to a complete capitulation to Germany.... I do not feel that it is right to do more than place before M. Benes an objective account of the position.... I feel that there is a much greater difference between the Franco-British proposals and the German Memorandum than one of time, method and degree. We cannot press the Czech Government to do what we believe to be wrong.' Chamberlain said Halifax had given powerful and perhaps convincing reasons. 'If this is the general view of my colleagues I am prepared to leave it at that.' There was no need even to ask opinions, Chamberlain clearly had insufficient support.

But Ministers, apart from the select few, did not know and never would be officially informed that a new plan had in fact been proposed to Hitler. At 6.45 p.m., Halifax, presumably with some reluctance, had instructed Henderson to put forward an important new suggestion. This involved a revised time-table for the Sudeten handover; it envisaged German troops occupying the territories of Egerland and Asch, outside the Czech fortified line, on 1 October. There should be a meeting of German and Czech plenipotentiaries with a British representative at some Sudetenland town on 3 October. On the latter date an International Boundary Commission should meet, consisting of German, Czech and British members, and if possible observers and members of the British Legion should arrive to assist in maintaining order. On 10 October German troops would enter zones where the plenipotentiaries had completed arrangements.[94] While the Cabinet meeting was taking place in London, Henderson was seeking an interview with Weizsäcker. A meeting was arranged for 11 p.m. that night.

Meanwhile, Chamberlain had another weapon for the Cabinet meeting – Hitler's reply to the letter given to him by Wilson. He read it, and Hitler's more reasonable tone was immediately obvious. Consequently it was agreed that 'the letter might be found on examination to afford some ground on which a further proposal for a peaceful settlement could be based'. Once again though Chamberlain was checked by his Ministers, who 'thought, however, that the letter, which was obviously phrased very carefully, would require examination before any final conclusion could be expressed upon it'.

This struggle continued between Chamberlain and the majority of his Cabinet. He mentioned the speech he was scheduled to give in the Commons next day. 'I do not propose to commit myself to any statement to the effect that, if Germany invaded Czechoslovakia, we should at once go to war with Germany.' But the Cabinet insisted he 'should base himself on the position that, if in fulfilment of her obligations to Czechoslovakia the forces of France became engaged in active hostilities against Germany we should feel obliged to support them'. Chamberlain refused to concede more to the 'hawks'. He demanded, and the Cabinet had to agree, that the speech should also be based 'on the theme that he was working for peace to the last possible moment'. Then, right at the finish of this peculiar see-saw session, he announced an important measure of defiance; during the afternoon he had agreed with Duff Cooper that naval mobilization should proceed. Yet still convinced that more efforts should be made for peace, he signalled to Perth in Rome to carry out his idea, and ask Ciano to persuade Mussolini to use his influence with Hitler.

He sat up late to prepare his speech. At 1.45 in the morning a depressing message arrived from Henderson; not long before midnight he had seen Weizsäcker to present the suggestion for a revised transfer timetable. The plan would be handed to Hitler, but Weizsäcker did not believe he would, or even could, take it into consideration.[95] Chamberlain could do no more. At 2.00 a.m., exactly 12 hours before the German ultimatum to Czechoslovakia would expire, he went wearily to bed.

'Black Wednesday', 28 September, dawned. Hospitals were emptied of all patients who could possibly be moved, ready for casualties; school children evacuees crammed the platforms of the main line stations. War had almost come; German bombers would soon arrive. In Europe refugees streamed in panic from likely battlefields on the Czech-German border; Parisians quit their beloved city; Berliners knew little, but feared the worst. Events followed in quick succession, all apparently heading direct to conflict. Yet there were two parallel paths, one led to war – the other to Munich.

11.5 a.m. Mussolini ordered his Ambassador at Berlin, Attolico, to ask Hitler to delay 24 hours. Attolico rushed from his Embassy, but failed to find his car. His chauffeur hailed a taxi instead.

11.10 a.m. Henderson reported that the French Ambassador, François-Poncet, had told him of intended new proposals from Paris. These went even further than Britain's the previous night. France was to suggest the Germans should take the whole of Egerland.[96]

11.15 a.m. François-Poncet saw Hitler, and immediately noticed a remarkable change in him: he seemed strained, nervous, even unsure of himself – and apparently impressed by the latest French proposals.

11.20 a.m. The Admiralty ordered the mobilization of the British Fleet.

11.30 a.m. A breathless Attolico reached the Chancellery with Mussolini's message. The Führer left François-Poncet in order to see him. 'I have an urgent message for you,' shouted Attolico still some yards down the corridor. And it was then, according to Schmidt, that the Führer declared: 'Tell the Duce that I accept his proposal.' Schmidt noticed Hitler spoke in a tone of obvious relief. Also at 11.30 a.m. two messages from Chamberlain left the Foreign Office; the first was for Henderson. 'You should seek immediate interview with German Chancellor and deliver to him the following personal message: "After reading your letter I feel certain that you can get all essentials without war and without delay."' This important and astonishing statement was made despite the Cabinet's decision that Hitler's letter 'would require examination before any final conclusion could be expressed upon it'. The message continued: 'I am ready to come to Berlin myself at once to discuss arrangements for transfer with you and representatives of Czech Government, together with representatives of France and Italy if you desire. I feel convinced we can reach agreement in a week.... However much you distrust Prague Government's intentions, you cannot doubt power of British and French Governments to see that promises are carried out fairly and fully and forthwith.'[96]

Chamberlain's second message was for Mussolini. It tied in neatly with the step Mussolini had already taken. 'I have today addressed last appeal to Herr Hitler to abstain from force to settle Sudeten problem.... I have offered myself to go at once to Berlin.... I trust Your Excellency will inform German Chancellor that you are willing to be represented and urge him to agree to my proposal which will keep all our peoples out of war. I have already guaranteed that Czech promises shall be caried out.'[97]

11.45 a.m. Hitler returned to François-Poncet, who had been waiting while he spoke to Attolico, and told him 'my friend' Mussolini had asked him to delay events.

Noon. One telephone call was being made from Rome to London; another from Berlin to Rome: Perth reported Mussolini's search for a 24 hour postponement of Hitler's advance; Attolico reported Hitler's acquiescence, and Mussolini, in reply, instructed him to seek a Four-Power Conference.

12.15 p.m. Henderson arrived at the Chancellery to express Chamberlain's willingness to come to Berlin. Escorted through the milling officers and aides up to the Führer's suite, he noticed a change in the atmosphere. 'It is going better – stick to it,' whispered one German confidant.[98] Henderson read Chamberlain's proposal. The Führer replied he must consult Mussolini before giving an answer. Then the interview was interrupted: Attolico once more. Henderson was left to 'argue desultorily' with Ribbentrop, while in the next room the sweating Italian told Hitler of Mussolini's proposal. Hitler was being begged for a meeting by both Italian and British leaders. He returned to Henderson, who noticed no difference in Hitler's attitude – indeed, those listening on the other side of the doors feared talks were going badly because of the noise of Hitler's shouting.[99]

At 1 p.m. two signals from Lord Perth had arrived at the Foreign Office. Halifax was told Hitler had agreed to a 24 hour postponement; the Duce would advise Hitler to accept proposals for a Berlin conference.[100]

2.35 p.m. Back at the British Embassy, Henderson contacted London. 'Issue is still in the balance. I need not urge importance of appealing to House of Commons not to aggravate the situation by attacks on Herr Hitler and National Socialism.... I see a glimmer of hope.'[101] A few minutes later, Chamberlain left Downing Street for the House of Commons. As his official car covered the half mile to Parliament Square, he could see the crowds around the Cenotaph, waiting for news of war.

2.50 p.m. Chamberlain began his speech to the anxious Members and Cabinet Ministers were astonished to hear of his new appeal.

3.15 p.m. Henderson telephoned from Berlin. Cadogan hurriedly scribbled a note for Halifax: 'Sir Nevile Henderson told me ... that the Ministry for Foreign Affairs had just informed him that Herr Hitler invites the Prime Minister to meet him at Munich tomorrow morning. He has also invited Signor Mussolini, who will arrive at 10 a.m. and M. Daladier....'[102] Thirty minutes later the note was in Chamberlain's hands and being read to the House. Peace had been kept; appeasement had been successful; Munich had been arranged.

Mussolini selected Munich as the rendezvous – Hitler had offered him Munich or Frankfurt. Here, in the seedy cafés and beer cellars, Hitler had made a subversive start to his shady career. And here he now intended to dictate terms, though in such a way that he might seem to be conceding more than he demanded. He travelled to meet Mussolini early on Thursday morning, 29 September, and the two Dictators met near the old German-Austrian border at Rosenheim. They continued the journey together in the Führer's special train, Mussolini listening as Hitler held forth. The conference presented an ideal opportunity for striking at the 'democracies'.[103] 'The time will come when we shall have to fight side by side against France and England.'[104] But the time had not yet come: Munich would give him all he wanted, for the moment, without war.

At 12.45 p.m. that Thursday the conference began at the Brown

House. Thirteen hours later it was still continuing. Chamberlain, already tired from the exertions of the previous day, the early rising that morning, the excitement of the pressing crowds at the airport, and the long flight to Germany, described the afternoon and evening as 'one prolonged nightmare'.[105] As rehearsed in the train from Rosenheim, Mussolini produced proposals drafted by Hitler, but described as 'a basis for discussion' as if they were his own creation. The British delegates considered the presentation 'a reasonable restatement of much that had been discussed in the Anglo-French and the Anglo-German conversations'. In other words, the same basic demands made by Hitler at Godesberg were put forward again. He preferred to let Mussolini do most of the talking for him and so gave an impression of calmness and cooperation – this was as important as the demands themselves: his short opening sentences, said Chamberlain afterwards 'were so moderate and reasonable, that I felt instant relief'.[106]

Discussion was mainly concerned with details. Wilson described it as 'to-ing and fro-ing'. He also commented: 'The German proposals for evacuation and occupation surprised us by their moderation and by the degree of latitude which they left to the International Commission.' Everyone agreed in principle that Sudetenland should be ceded; the discussion was therefore restricted to methods. And this issue was settled by midnight. Inefficient organization – the conference had been arranged so quickly – meant that not until just before 2 a.m. next morning were the Agreement and Supplementaries ready for signing. According to Kirkpatrick: 'The final blow came at the moment of signature when it was discovered that the pompous inkstand contained no ink.' This was rectified and 'Hitler scratched his signature as if he was being asked to sign away his birthright'.[107] Proceedings were concluded by 'brief expressions of satisfaction'.[108] A better description would have been self-satisfaction.

The Czechs had been hovering nearby, understandably anxious for news. The day before, when Chamberlain was preparing for Munich, Newton had sent a message from Benes; he had heard there was to be a conference – he had not been informed by London – and begged the Prime Minister 'to do nothing at Munich which would put Czechoslovakia in a worse situation.... I beg ... that nothing may be done at Munich without Czechoslovakia being heard. It is a most terrible thing for her if negotiations take place without her being given an opportunity to state her case.'[109] Chamberlain did try to have the Czechs admitted, 'but it was represented that the matter was too urgent to permit of the delay that this course would involve'.[110] While the talks were continuing throughout the Thursday afternoon, arrangements had been made for the Czech Ambassador at Berlin, M. Mastny, to be available with other officials at Chamberlain's hotel. When the agreement had been signed and the expressions of satisfaction concluded, 'then arose the question what to do about the Czechs?' Daladier declined a suggestion that he take the Agreement to Prague. He and the Prime Minister would together see the Czech representative, which they did in the Prime Minister's room about 2.15. 'Mastny was given a prepared copy, and a map; and he was also given a broad hint that – having regard to the seriousness of the alternative – the best course was for his Government to accept what was clearly a considerable improvement upon the German Memorandum.'[111] Dr Hubert Masarik wrote, for the Czech Foreign Ministry, a bitter account of this tragic meeting. 'The atmosphere was oppressive; sentence was about to be passed.... The French, obviously nervous, seemed anxious to preserve French prestige before the court.... Mr Chamberlain was yawning continuously, without making any effort to conceal his yawns. M. Léger added hurriedly and with superficial casualness that no answer was required from us, that they regarded the plan as accepted, that our Government had that very day, at the latest by 3 p.m. to send its representative to Berlin to the sitting of the Commission.... Then they finished with us and we could go.'[112] The Czechs rushed off to Prague.

Chamberlain later gave the British Cabinet his version: 'I did my best for Czechoslovakia in the absence of a Czech Government representative, and I think that the arrangement secured could, taken as a whole, be regarded as satisfactory.' He pointed out the main differences between the Munich Agreement and the Godesberg Memorandum, as he saw them. First, 'Godesberg was in fact an ultimatum with a time limit of six days. The Munich Agreement reverts, although not in express terms, to the Anglo-French plan.' Secondly, 'under the Munich Agreement, evacuation and occupation would be carried out in five clearly defined stages between 1 October and 10 October instead of one operation on 1 October.' Thirdly, 'the line to be taken by German troops was to be fixed by an International Commission on which both Germany and Czechoslovakia would be represented. Fourthly, all plebiscite areas would be defined by Hitler. Fifthly, the plebiscite areas would be occupied at once by an international force. Sixthly, there would be better voting procedures.... Lastly, although the Czech Government must leave "existing installations" untouched in the evacuated areas, the people could take foodstuffs, goods, cattle and raw materials, all of which would have had to be left behind under the Godesberg Memorandum.'[113]

But for Chamberlain, far more resulted from the conference than agreement over Czechoslovakia. Equally important, or even more so, was the scrap of paper he and Hitler had agreed to sign while they were waiting for the Munich documents to be drawn up.

'I asked Hitler, about one in the morning, while we were waiting for the draftsmen, whether he would care to see me for another talk,' he later wrote to his sister. 'He jumped at the idea and asked me to come to his private flat, in a tenement house where the other floors are occupied by ordinary citizens. I had a very friendly and pleasant talk.'[114] Hitler thanked Chamberlain 'for his great efforts to bring about a peaceful solution', according to Schmidt's notes, and added that even if the Czechs 'were mad enough' to reject the terms and he had to take forcible action, 'he would always try to spare the civilian population and to confine himself to military objectives. He hated the thought of little babies being killed by gas bombs.'[115] Chamberlain had had more in mind than a general conversation, and this time he had not even told his immediate entourage of his intended initiative. He pulled out a prepared document and asked Hitler if he would put his signature to it. As Schmidt read the document aloud, Hitler kept saying '*Ja, ja, ja ...*' and when he heard it all he said: 'Yes, I will certainly sign it.'

'We, the German Führer and Chancellor, and the British Prime Minister,' it declared, 'have had a further meeting today.... We regard the Agreement signed last night, and the Anglo-German Naval Agreement, as symbolic of the desire of our two peoples never to go to war with one another again....'[116] Mussolini, when he heard that Hitler had signed, commented: 'You do not refuse a glass of lemonade to a thirsty man.' Chamberlain returned to the Regina Palace Hotel, pleasantly sleepy and satisfied. Daladier, on the other hand, had looked like 'a completely beaten and broken man'. He feared the Paris crowd might stone him for deserting the Czechs. Hitler and Mussolini by contrast swaggered amidst their admirers – Hitler's nervous tic seemed to have disappeared.[117]

Only slightly refreshed by a little sleep, Chamberlain returned home to his hero's welcome. Stepping from the aircraft he waved the piece of paper at Halifax, who was waiting, and cried 'I've got it. I've got it.' He wrote later: 'Even the description of the papers give no idea of the scene in the streets as I drove from Heston to the Palace. They were lined from one end to the other with people of every class, shouting themselves hoarse, leaping on the running board, banging on the windows, and thrusting their hands into the car to be shaken.'[118]

'All this will be over in three months,' he said as the car nosed through the cheering crowds. According to Churchill's memoirs, Chamberlain referred to peace and so contradicted his famous Downing Street statement. But according to Halifax, to whom the words were in fact spoken, he was talking simply of his acclaim.[119]

The crowds were largest and noisiest in Downing Street, shouting and screaming for the new beloved Neville Chamberlain. In an effort to disperse the throng, he agreed to appear at an open window for a moment, 'the same window as that from which Dizzy announced peace with honour 60 years ago'.[120] With this thought in mind, the elderly and very tired Prime Minister quoted Disraeli's words, which he had dismissed as unsuitable only two days before. They were as unfortunate this time as after the Berlin Congress in 1878. 'This is the second time in our history that there has come back from Germany to Downing Street peace with honour. I believe it is peace for our time.'

Almost immediately, Chamberlain regretted the statement. And that same night he received a note from Lord Baldwin. 'You have everything in your hands now – for a time – and you can do anything you like. Use that time well, for it will not last.'[121]

4

Consequences

Two matters had to be tidied up on that same Friday, 30 September. Czech acquiescence had to be confirmed and Chamberlain had to report to his Cabinet. Benes could only submit, and Czechoslovakia officially did so at lunchtime, 'under protest to the world'. At 5 p.m. General Jan Sirovy, the new Prime Minister, declared in a broadcast: 'We were abandoned. We stand alone.' The Czech Government had accepted the terms because they now knew they would receive no help if they refused. 'We accepted with bleeding hearts.' Evacuation would start the next day, and a plebiscite would take place later.[1] Five days later Benes resigned, broken by humiliation. Afterwards he fled his country; the nation he came to was Britain.

The Cabinet met at 7.30, after Ministers had pushed their way through the admiring crowds still cramming Downing Street. As soon as the meeting began, Sir John Simon rose to his feet. 'I think the present occasion justifies a departure from the normal procedure.' He wanted to express on behalf of the whole Cabinet, their profound admiration for the unparalleled efforts the Prime Minister had made, and for the success he had achieved. 'I would also like to say how proud we are to be associated with the Prime Minister at this time.' Graciously Chamberlain accepted the praise, then gave his report. 'I think it is a triumph for diplomacy that representatives of the Four Powers concerned should have met and reached a peaceful settlement of this matter.' Czechoslovakia, of course, was not included in this reference. He explained that provision was included in an Annex to the Agreement for help to Czechoslovakia against unprovoked aggression. The guarantee of France and Britain entered into operation at once, while that of Germany and Italy would come into effect after the Hungarian and Polish minorities issue had been settled. 'This question of guarantees had been a difficult one to deal with.' He pointed out the differences between the Munich Agreement and the Godesberg document, and expressed his satisfaction at the treatment dealt out to the Czechs. Discussion was short, in recognition of his exhaustion, but the

63

debate was long enough for Chamberlain to learn he was to lose one of his Ministers. Duff Cooper swiftly injected bitterness into the congratulatory atmosphere. He admitted that he could see more differences between Godesberg and Munich than he had first thought. 'Nevertheless, I think it right that I should say I still feel considerable uneasiness. I am afraid that we might get into the position in which we are drawn into making further concessions to Hitler.' He felt it his duty to resign.

Chamberlain quickly moved to confine dissent. The First Lord should have a private talk with him, he suggested. He was relieved to find rebellion restricted; and especially pleased with the attitude of Halifax, whose opposition seemed temporarily over. Duff Cooper stood alone. The Prime Minister had carried off his *fait accompli*; the Agreement had been signed; the Czechs had agreed; peace had been kept. Perhaps Ministers believed that a stand against Chamberlain would achieve nothing now; perhaps – probably Halifax did – they felt too committed, or too loyal; later Halifax would tell Eden 'he was very unhappy and counting the hours to the time when he should leave office'.[2] Perhaps Ministers hoped to accomplish more by staying. But, in Eden's words, 'The Cabinet, with some doubters, had taken its decision and now events must speak.' Inskip closed the meeting by saying the Chiefs of Staff recommended a standstill of emergency measures.

Chamberlain had achieved a 'diplomatic triumph' at the cost of one Minister. Hitler's diplomatic triumph was greater, and without cost: he had brought the British Prime Minister hurrying on three occasions, and had more than reversed the wrongs of the Versailles Treaty.

Munich was partly the result of allied military weakness. As the crisis unfolded, more deficiencies were revealed in Britain's defences. Gaps in the anti-aircraft system were evident, equipment of all kinds shown to be inadequate; and the British people realized – or thought they did – just how vulnerable they were. RAF Fighter Command had only 29 squadrons of fighters, and the 93 Hurricanes in the Command were useless above 15,000 feet because their guns would jam in the cold. Remembering the outdated Gladiator biplanes on which Britain would have had to rely, Air Chief Marshal Lord Dowding later admitted 'We had so very little.... It was a very good thing [Chamberlain] did act in that way.'[3] Air Marshal of the RAF, Sir John Slessor agreed: 'I find it impossible to convince myself that any British Government could have brought itself to face taking the country into war in our then shocking state of unpreparedness in the air.'[4] The British Army was still not organized for fighting in Europe: strategy, planning and equipment were designed for colonial warfare. Armoured divisions were short and there were still serious manpower deficiencies. The French were likewise unprepared, more so than Gamelin's account had revealed. France had no armoured divisions and only 68 infantry

64

divisions, grossly deficient in training and equipment, faced Germany. And the French Air Force was even weaker than the RAF, as the British Cabinet was soon to discover.

On the other hand, unknown to the Allies, Germany was also unready. Keitel was to tell the Nuremberg Court after the war: 'We were extraordinarily happy that it had not come to a military operation because ... our means of attack against the frontier fortifications of Czechoslovakia were insufficient.'[5]

Both appeasers and anti-appeasers believed the Luftwaffe could destroy London. Experts expected 50 casualties per ton of high explosives: that meant 600,000 killed and 1,200,000 injured in the first raid. The blitz in fact, though, caused 15-20 casualties per ton – terrible, but by no means the massacre expected. And, in Autumn 1938, the German Air Force was concentrated upon Czechoslovakia: it had neither the strength, nor, without taking France and the Low Countries, the range, to launch a full onslaught on both London and Prague. Yet fears of attack had led hundreds to contemplate suicide should war come; relief produced the jubilation after Munich.

Chamberlain has been fiercely criticized for not using adequately the extra, precious time he bought with Munich. But the Cabinet records make clear how anxious he was to increase the defence budget, and how completely economic and financial dictates prevented him. Only by switching the country at once to a wartime footing could more money have been found. Chamberlain believed the people would not stand for that, and his encounters with Trade Union and Labour Party opposition proved him right. The resulting high taxes, restricted freedom, and bureaucratic impertinence would have created political upheaval – which would not have prepared Britain for war. Chamberlain had to balance the militants against the mood of the country – he dared not push too fast. Besides, wartime economy could not be maintained for long: the right moment must be chosen.

Eden and other critics agreed with the assessment, but not the conclusion. They claimed that if the people were told the truth, they would respond. Eden told a meeting at Cardiff on 14 October: 'The gaps in our defences and the public demand for a speeding up of rearmament, arise from the fact that the armament industry in this country and in France is being operated on a peacetime basis.... In the totalitarian states, armaments are being piled up on a basis which we have hitherto only consented to adopt in time of war.'[7]

Germany, a dictatorship, could be viciously taxed, though, again, not indefinitely; even Hitler had to loosen the screw – hence the drop in armament expenditure in the last months before war.

At Munich, France had ingloriously abandoned attempts to influence Eastern European events. Yet in Paris, Daladier too was welcomed with flowers, not the stones he had feared. Only residual entanglements – results of the 1925 Locarno Treaty – threatened to complicate the next few months.

Britain now needed a policy for the future. Appeasement and re-armament would preoccupy the Cabinet. Views would range from the realistic and far-sighted to the cowardly and blind. In Autumn 1938 Chamberlain had a powerful weapon in the overwhelming support of the people. An elected politician, he had conducted Britain's foreign affairs as *they* wanted him to do. Hoare, in his memoirs, stressed this. 'Was it not to his credit that he tried to save the simple people from the catastrophe of war and the devastating effects of an immediate invasion?'[8] But apart from the humanitarian aspects, somewhat sickeningly expressed by Hoare, there were practical ones: Chamberlain believed that if he had 'stood up to the dictators' in 1938, he would have been denied support from the electorate, from the powerful potential ally across the Atlantic, and from the Dominions. Churchill and his few colleagues would have been inadequate compensation; the voices for peace were still shouting down the cries for war.

Chamberlain's belief found justification. Roosevelt cabled just two words: 'Good man.' King George VI sent his 'most heartfelt congratulations', *The Times* declared: 'No conqueror returning from a victory on the battlefield has come home adorned with nobler laurels.' From the Empire came a message from Smuts: 'A great champion has appeared in the lists, God Bless him. The path of the peacemaker was difficult and dangerous, but he gave no thought for himself, or his future.' King Leopold of the Belgians expressed 'the heartiest thanks of one to whom destiny has entrusted the sacred responsibility of many human beings'. The Belgians struck a medal to 'the apostle of peace', Greeks requested a piece of his umbrella, to be made a holy relic, Germans, Dutchmen, Italians, many hundreds wrote to praise him.[9]

Some said Chamberlain should call a sudden general election and use his massive support to strengthen his political position, and firmly silence his critics. Halifax was among those who urged him not to heed this call. On the way to Downing Street from Heston airport, he had said 'there were two things which I wished to leave in [Chamberlain's] mind before we got to London. One was that he would find there people who would urge him very strongly to have an immediate election.... I told him that I thought he ought to resist that counsel, for he was no longer only a party leader: for better, for worse, what he had just done made him a national leader and he must act accordingly.... From that, indeed, followed the second thing I wanted to say – which was that by the time he met the House of Commons on Monday [in three days' time] he ought to have reconstituted his Government, bringing in Labour if they would join, and Churchill and Eden. He seemed surprised, but said he would think it over. Nothing however happened, and I have often wondered whether or how the course of history might have been changed if he had acted in the sense that I suggested.'[11]

The time would come, and Chamberlain knew it, when the public mood would change. He had to be ready for that moment. And Baldwin's sad words remained to haunt him ... 'use the time well, for it won't last'.

5

Reaction and Reprieve

Late on the day of Chamberlain's return, the British, French and Italian Ambassadors met Weizsäcker in Berlin. The group formed the International Commission on the new Czech frontiers. Czech representation was originally planned, but never proceeded with; and only a few weeks later, the British Chargé was to comment: '[the Commission] might as well be dead for all the use it is. All questions arising out of the Munich Agreement have been and will be decided at German Nazi direction.'[1] So much for the 'international supervision' of the transfer.

Never had the Nazis been so confident. 'This fellow Chamberlain shook with fright when I said the word war,' scoffed Hitler. The unity of Greater Germany had been achieved, now diplomats, politicians and soldiers anxiously wondered where Hitler would move next.

But in the first hours after Munich Poland caused most apprehension. On about 20 September the Polish Foreign Minister, Colonel Jósef Beck, had hardened his demands for the Teschen region, taken by Czechoslovakia 19 years before. Frontier incidents were exaggerated, mass demonstrations organized, half-hourly broadcasts made. And, an hour before midnight on 30 September, a Polish note was handed to the Czechs: the Teschen and Freistadt areas must be evacuated, and a reply was demanded by mid-day, 1 October.[2] Newton warned Halifax early on Saturday morning: 'In view of Munich Agreement ... and the guarantee given by Great Britain and France, the President appeals for protection.'[3] But at 1.30 on Saturday afternoon, the British Ambassador at Warsaw, Sir Howard Kennard, reported 'the Czechoslovak Government have accepted Polish demands in their entirety'. Tension eased.[4]

For Chamberlain, this was almost the last straw. Next day he travelled down to Chequers, and wrote: 'I came nearer to a nervous breakdown than I have ever been in my life. I have pulled myself together, for there is a fresh ordeal to go through in the House.'[5] In Czechoslovakia, appalling confusion continued in the areas being ceded to Germany.

Families were only given a few hours in which to tear up their roots; refugees clogged the muddy roads. The administrative problems were immense. Chamberlain told the Cabinet on 3 October, that the Czechs were asking the Government to guarantee a loan of £30 million, to help deal with the immediate refugee problem and to reconstruct the country's economic life. Chamberlain believed it too early to assess how much help Prague needed; Simon agreed: 'I do not think that this is an occasion on which this country need adopt an apologetic attitude.... On the contrary ... a world war has been averted and thereby Czechoslovakia has been saved.' So the Cabinet decided to allow an immediate advance of £10 million – more examination was required before the remainder could be offered.[6]

One chair gaped empty at this meeting; and in the afternoon Duff Cooper gave his official resignation speech in the Commons, at the opening of the three-day debate on the Munich Agreement. 'I besought my [Cabinet] colleagues not to see this problem in terms of Czechoslovakia ... but rather to say to themselves, "a moment may come when, owing to the invasion of Czechoslovakia, a European war will begin, and when that moment comes we must take part in that war, we cannot keep out of it, and there is no doubt upon which side we shall fight". ... The Prime Minister has believed in addressing Herr Hitler through the language of sweet reasonableness. I have believed that he was more open to the language of the mailed fist.' This was Chamberlain's 'ordeal'. Now he rose to reply. Nicolson wrote in his diary: 'He is obviously tired and irritable and the speech does not go down well.'[7] He stressed the importance of the Anglo-German declaration signed after the Munich Agreement. 'I believe there are many who will feel with me that such a declaration ... is something more than a pious expression of opinion.... I believe that there is sincerity and good will on both sides in this declaration.' The significance of the joint statement therefore went far beyond the actual wording. 'After everything that has been said about the German Chancellor today and in the past ... I do feel that the House ought to recognize the difficulty for a man in that position to take back such emphatic declarations as he had already made, and to recognize that consenting to discuss with representatives of other Powers those things which he had declared he had already decided for once and for all, was a real and substantial contribution on his part.'

The applause was loud, but not tumultuous. As Sir Sidney Herbert said in the speech which followed, everyone felt relief that there would be no war, but nevertheless a grave humiliation had been suffered. Ill, leaning heavily on his stick, Sir Sidney continued: 'I was led to suppose that the locusts had stopped nibbling about two years ago, but I can hear their little jowls creaking yet under the Front Bench.' Eden then condemned the Munich Agreement in an attack which, after a slow start, finished on a rousing level. 'Surely the House will be agreed that foreign affairs cannot indefinitely be continued on the basis of "stand and deliver!" Successive surrenders bring only successive humiliations, and they, in their turn, more humiliating demands.'

But the Prime Minister's position was not in danger. Early that morning the National Labour Executive had pledged him support; many agreed with Henderson's comment on Duff Cooper: 'I am glad that he has gone – he is a frightful fellow.'[8] Hoare sneered that Duff Cooper had been yachting in the Baltic in August, when the crisis was reaching a climax, and had therefore been absent from Cabinet discussions, 'but he had unreservedly agreed on his return to the demand for self-determination'.[9] A favourable account of Duff Cooper's speech written by the Lobby Correspondent of *The Times* remained unpublished. Even one of Churchill's greatest orations, delivered when the debate was nearing an end on 5 October, could not seriously harm Chamberlain. 'All is over,' Churchill growled. 'Silent, mournful, abandoned, broken, Czechoslovakia recedes into the darkness.' Chamberlain, impassive, listened as Churchill went quietly, reasonably on. 'I do not begrudge our loyal, brave people ... the natural, spontaneous outburst of joy and relief when they learned that the hard ordeal would no longer be required of them at the moment.... But they should know the truth. They should know that there has been gross neglect and deficiency in our defences. They should know that we have sustained a great defeat without a war, the consequences of which will travel far with us.... They should know that we have passed an awful milestone in our history ... the terrible words have for the time being been pronounced against the Western democracies – "Thou art weighed in the balance and found wanting." And do not suppose that this is the end. This is only the beginning of the reckoning.'

Chamberlain had to wind up the debate the following day; and he faltered under the pressure. He admitted his 'peace for our time' was perhaps unwise. 'I hope Honourable Members will not be disposed to read into words used in a moment of some emotion after a long and exhausting day, after I had driven through miles of excited, enthusiastic, cheering people – I hope they will not read into these words more than they were intended to convey.' The confession shocked Members on the Government Benches and the Opposition jeered as he continued: 'I realize that diplomacy cannot be effective unless the consciousness exists, not here alone, but elsewhere, that behind the diplomacy is the strength to give effect to it.'

Chamberlain made clear no immediate General Election would be held, and support or opposition to him would therefore have to be declared then and there. As Nicolson realized, the Conservatives were placed in a difficult position. 'It is difficult to say: "This is the greatest diplomatic achievement in history, therefore we must redouble our armaments in order never again to be exposed to such humiliation." '[10]

The Commons voted on Thursday, 6 October; and the policy of His Majesty's Government, 'by which war was averted in the recent crisis', was approved by 366 to 144. About 35 dissident Conservatives stayed in their seats as a sign of abstention, among them Anthony Eden, Winston Churchill, Duff Cooper, Leo Amery, Lord Cranborne, Lord Wolmer, Roger Keyes, Sidney Herbert, Harold Macmillan, Richard Law, Robert Boothby, Duncan Sandys, Anthony Crossley, Brendan Bracken and Paul Emrys-Evans. 'It is not our numbers that matter, but our reputation,' claimed Nicolson, also in the group. 'It was clear that the Government were rattled.'[11] Chamberlain was indeed disturbed; and he had decided on a step he avoided mentioning to his Cabinet. On Wednesday, the day of Churchill's attack, he had sent a secret message to Hitler, who was to speak at the *Sportpalast* that evening; he asked if in the speech 'he could give the Prime Minister some support in forming public opinion in Britain'.[12] Hitler apparently obliged: in his address he attacked Chamberlain's critics, mentioning Eden and Cooper. But the divided weakness of his opposition – different factions were headed by Churchill and Eden – was perhaps a more substantial help to him. Churchill was even considered a politically dangerous associate. On one occasion Lord Maugham, the Lord Chancellor, said agitators like Duff Cooper and Churchill should be 'shot or hanged'.[13]

While Chamberlain had been manoeuvring for support at home, international diplomacy had grown confused. On 3 October, a councellor at the German Embassy in Moscow reported to Berlin that the Soviet Union felt snubbed at not being asked to Munich. He thought Russian foreign policy would grow 'more positive' towards Germany. Bonnet had told Phipps the day before that Litvinov was 'highly incensed at recent events'. 'If our two countries had stood firm,' he had declared, 'they would, with Russia's help, have made Hitler climb down.' Bonnet, reported Sir Eric, had 'smiled when he referred to the probable extent of Soviet help had war broken out, and also at Russia's extreme valour from a safe and respectable distance from the scene of hostilities.'[14]

With British defences urgently in need of improvement, on 6 October the Committee for Imperial Defence – the CID – discussed means. Hore-Belisha stressed that production and defence must be coordinated; he pleaded for a Supply Ministry, but this idea was shelved again – it would dislocate 'peacetime' economy and create trade-union opposition. The CID would not go beyond asking the Service departments for reports on the defects the crisis had disclosed, with suggestions for improvements.[15]

Even Henderson was increasingly apprehensive. The same day he wrote sadly to Halifax. 'To me personally all this affair has been intensely disagreeable and painful. I want to wash the taste out of my mouth, and I will rejoice from the bottom of my heart if you'll remove me to some other sphere. I never want to work with Germans again.... For some days last week I believed war to be inevitable. I hated the very thought of British men, women and children being killed for the sake of Czechs or Sudeten, or to free Germany of the monstrous incubus of Hitler, Himmler, Ribbentrop & Co.'[16] Already suffering from illness, stress and overwork, he would soon return home and hand over for a while to the First Secretary, Sir George Ogilvie-Forbes.

Extremists in Germany were considering new targets. They supported the Poles in their opportunist grab for Czechoslovak land, but far less the Hungarians. Slovakia, which Budapest wanted, also featured in German plans. Her semi-independent status, awarded by Prague soon after Munich, suited Berlin. 'An independent Slovakia would be weak constitutionally,' wrote Ernst Woermann, Head of the Political Department at the Foreign Office, 'and would therefore best further the German need for penetration and settlement in the East.'[17] On 8 October, Hitler violently attacked Britain in a speech at Saarbrücken. Following inquiries by Halifax about treatment of non-Nazi Sudeten Germans, Hitler, already angry at being dubbed a gangster by some MPs, lashed out at British interference. 'It would be a good thing if people in Great Britain would gradually drop certain airs which they have inherited from the Versailles period,' he shouted. 'We cannot tolerate any longer the tutelage of Governesses.' Hitler credited Chamberlain's Cabinet, indirectly, with wishing for peace – as asked – but claimed these men were likely to be ousted. 'They govern in countries whose domestic organization makes it possible that at any time they may lose their position to make way for others who are not anxious for peace.... It only needs that in England, instead of Mr Chamberlain, Mr Duff Cooper or Mr Eden or Mr Churchill should come to power, and then we know quite well that it would be the aim of these men immediately to begin a new World War.... I have therefore decided ... to continue the construction of our fortifications in the West with increased energy.'[18] And while publicly announcing these measures for the West, Hitler secretly prepared for renewed offensive in the East. Keitel, asked how many extra troops would be needed to take Bohemia and Moravia, and how much time preparations would take,[19] could reply on 11 October: 'It would be possible to commence operations without reinforcements, in view of the present signs of weakness in Czech resistance.'[20]

The French viewed the Czech situation with increasing concern. Phipps reported on 12 October: 'It is considered certain ... that the political and economic influence of Germany in Central and Eastern Europe will be increased, and that of France diminished, if not extinguished.... There are undercurrents of defeatism which feel that

72

France's future as a Great Power is dangerously compromised.... At the moment of such uncertainty and depression French opinion is leaning heavily on Great Britain for leadership and guidance.'[21] Henderson wrote the same day from Berlin that 'a period of stocktaking' had begun; he detailed a number of lessons to be learnt from the recent crisis. One was the growth of the Rome-Berlin alliance, the other was the strength of German air power – 'according to my information the Germans have a first-line strength which is at least double ours. In design and performance they are far ahead of us.... The conclusion to be reached is that the Germans, if they do not intend to commit an act of aggression on us, propose to use their air force as a big stick to enforce a *Pax Germanica*.'[22]

By coincidence, the next day Britain introduced new anti-aircraft measures. German newspapers promptly attacked Britain's 'provocative' rearmament policy, while Göring presided over a conference on accelerated German arms production.

Chamberlain still had to balance rearmament with conciliation. 'While hoping for the best,' as Halifax put it, 'it was also necessary to prepare for the worst.' But preparations for war might undermine the attempt to keep the peace. If he invited Eden into the Cabinet, as Halifax still proposed, the 'conciliatory part' of his policy might suffer.[23] So typically he played safe and made Lord Stanhope, his close friend, First Lord in place of Duff Cooper, and the Cabinet's overall outlook remained unchanged.

On 17 October, Hungary announced 'precautions' at the frontier with Czechoslovakia, and it seemed increasingly likely that the Munich Powers would be called in. Newton reported from Prague on a recent interview between the Czech Foreign Minister and Hitler, who declared: 'If the dispute is referred to the Four Munich Powers, Germany and Italy would insist on something very different, and if Britain and France had any other terms in mind they would only end by advising the Czech Government to accept those laid down by the Powers of the Berlin-Rome Axis.'[24] Weizsäcker had said much the same to Henderson. Germany seemed aiming at a Munich-type conference, to push her terms through. The next day Hitler revealed his thoughts to François-Poncet, who was leaving Berlin to take charge of the French Embassy at Rome. His face pale and marked with fatigue, he launched another attack on the British, who he claimed had destroyed 'the spirit of Munich'; he had been insulted in the House of Commons; Britain was 'feverishly' rearming.

The Cabinet hardly touched on Czechoslovakia when they met on 19 October. Instead, unaware of Hitler's latest attack, they spent most of the morning discussing rearmament. They studied Inskip's 'Most Secret' memorandum on the 6 October CID meeting, which explained that Service departments would report on military deficiencies. Inskip hoped to be able to submit proposals soon, but believed more equipment could only be produced by 1 August 'by somewhat drastic use of compulsory powers'. But he still ruled out a Supply Ministry.[25] With Duff Cooper gone, Hore-Belisha was the Minister most likely to rebel, and the Supply Ministry question was a likely cause. Certainly after his call, in Cardiff on 21 October, for 'drastic changes' in the armament programme, the press were quick to speculate on a possible Cabinet split. Chamberlain made a note to call Hore-Belisha to see him.[26]

Meanwhile Hitler had been taking positive action to increase Germany's military readiness. Following Keitel's 11 October memorandum, he told his Generals 'It must be possible to smash at any time the remainder of Czechoslovakia.'[27] During the weekend German newspapers again criticized British rearmament. Hardly consistent. as Ogilvie-Forbes reported, they also dismissed British efforts as puny. *Der Angriff* stressed Germany's superior position: the nation in peace was geared for war. So while the German papers applauded Hitler's energetic arms production, Chamberlain was berating Hore-Belisha for his modest plea. 'I assured him that I did not wish to make things difficult,' wrote the War Secretary in his diary. 'But I felt I must make my conclusions clear. I asked him, if he could not see his way to setting up a Ministry of Supply, if he would tell the House that he was exhausting all other means.'[28]

Britain and Germany both stepped up their search for strength through diplomacy. On 24 October Ribbentrop gave the Polish Ambassador, Jósef Lipski, an excellent lunch in Berchtesgaden. 'It is time to arrive at a general settlement of all possible points of friction between Germany and Poland,' he enthused. If the Danzig question could be settled, and if Poland joined the Anti-Comintern Pact against Russia, the Polish-German Treaty could be extended and Poland's frontiers guaranteed. Lipski promised to report to Beck.[29]

For her part, Britain considered a new approach to Italy. On 26 October, the Cabinet debated whether the Anglo-Italian agreement, originally initiated on 16 April, should be brought into force.[30] The agreement had been designed to preserve the *status quo* and persuade Italy to withdraw her troops from Spain. Only about half the troops had left, but Halifax felt he had an opportunity to edge Mussolini away from Berlin. Certainly Perth thought that if the agreement did not come into force, Anglo-Italian relations would reach 'the parting of the ways'.[31] Halifax, it was decided, should contact Mussolini secretly.

The Cabinet next turned back to armament. The Service department reports were ready now, and Inskip presented them.[32] Two major questions seemed to be raised: Did 'recent events call for any revision of the scope of the authorized programmes of the three services'? Was there 'any ground for immediately altering our central supply organi-

74

zation' with a Supply Ministry? Certainly the situation revealed was disquieting. Chamberlain, though, stressed the need for a strong financial base: 'Our financial resources will be one of our great assets in any long war, and I think that any big war will necessarily be a long war.' A committee, chaired by Inskip, should be set up. Chamberlain moved next to the Supply Ministry question, repeating that Trade Unions and employers would claim that the possibilities of voluntary cooperation were not exhausted yet; and he carried the cabinet with him, in spite of Hore-Belisha's preference 'on merits' for 'an immediate decision in favour of taking compulsory powers'; so that topic was shelved.[33]

Discussions over the Anglo-Italian Agreement proceeded well and when Ribbentrop visited Rome on 28 October, he failed in his attempt to strengthen German-Italian relations. Ribbentrop, described by Ciano as 'vain, frivolous and loquacious', wanted Mussolini to sign the draft defensive military alliance between Germany, Italy and Japan. Mussolini hesitated; Ribbentrop applied pressure: 'The Führer is convinced that we must inevitably count on war with the Western Democracies in the course of a few years, perhaps three or four.'[34] But Mussolini still stalled; and the next Monday, Chamberlain could tell his Cabinet that he intended to make a statement to Parliament, saying the agreement would be put into effect on Tuesday, 1 November.[35]

On Monday Chamberlain proposed Sir John Anderson be made Minister responsible for air raid precautions and national voluntary service. Entitled Lord Privy Seal, he would in fact be Minister for Civil Defence.[36] Inskip presented a memorandum on the Supply Ministry Proposal.[37] He was still against it, and proposed labour should be supplied through the Employment Exchange system; but to give some relief to Service Ministers, he suggested a Parliamentary Secretary be appointed to his own office to deal with defence supply questions. Hore-Belisha was sure this did not go far enough: 'The right solution is the appointment of a Minister of Supply with compulsory powers. Failing this, I think the right course is to appoint a Minister who would have full responsibility for supply work.' But he was still in the minority; nor was Sir Thomas's suggestion received favourably. The Cabinet decided 'the setting-up of a Ministry of Supply with compulsory powers was undesirable', and one 'without compulsory powers was also undesirable'.

Chamberlain then indicated a statement he intended to make the following day when Parliament reassembled. 'Our foreign policy is one of appeasement.... We must aim at establishing relations with the Dictator powers, which will lead to a settlement in Europe and to a sense of stability.... A good deal of false emphasis has been placed on rearmament, as though the one result of the Munich Agreement has been that it was necessary for us to add to our rearmament programme. Acceleration of existing programmes was one thing, but increases in the scope of our programme which would lead to a new arms race was a different proposition.' Chamberlain hoped it might be possible to 'take active steps and to follow up the Munich Agreement by other measures, aimed at securing better relations. The putting into effect of the Anglo-Italian Agreement will be one step in this direction.' He therefore still intended to proceed cautiously: 'I propose to make a reassuring statement tomorrow.'[38]

MPs reassembled in London; they heard the 'reassuring statement' but if they were reassured at all, it soon faded. 'We are constantly giving, and they are constantly taking,' Eden told the Commons on 2 November. Next day Herbert Morrison moved a Vote of Censure condemning the Government for the lack of preparations 'to protect the civil population when the country was brought to the brink of war'. Anderson was thrown into the struggle, but the task of defending the Government fell mainly upon Chamberlain's chief critic in the Cabinet, Hore-Belisha, who now had to support the Government's policy. His speech appeared both a defence of measures so far taken, and a plea that more should be done in the future. He warned that a defence programme was a developing and not an instantaneous phenomenon. Time was needed. 'It must be borne in mind that practically the whole of the armament industry in this country was closed down after the war.' But in his closing sentences he swung back to attack complacency and delay. 'Nothing, of course, could atone, or will atone until our programme is complete.... I have dealt frankly with the present state of our deficiencies and it is not a state which will endure....'[39] The Opposition motion of Censure was defeated. But Hore-Belisha was even more suspected by Chamberlain, while he himself considered his criticisms amply proved by information given to the Cabinet at its next meeting, 7 November. Two 'Most Secret' documents were presented for consideration: both revealed frightening deficiencies in the country's fighting forces.

First discussed was the report of the Cabinet Committee appointed on 26 October, containing proposals from the Service Departments and the Home Office.[40] The Admiralty, which 'during the crisis ... had been impressed with the shortage of vessels for escort and convoy work', proposed the building of 20 escort vessels, 10 to be laid down at once, and 10 more before May 1940. In the delicate balancing of rearmament with conciliation, it was Halifax's turn to hesitate: 'I do not feel very strongly about the proposal.... I think that steps should be taken in the near future to prevent the Munich wax setting too hard before we take some further action towards implementing our policy of appeasement.' And it was Chamberlain's turn to incline towards armament and 'though not altogether happy about the proposal', recommend its approval. Inskip proposed that production of guns for the Army should be stepped up, and that new capacity should be created for the purpose so that anti-aircraft defence could be given absolute priority 'without still further postponement of the provision of field guns'. The Home Secretary felt this increase was inevitable, doubted in fact whether it would be adequate; and so a further review of Home Defence was agreed.

Discussion turned next to improvements in the RAF.[41] Sir Kingsley Wood pointed out: 'It is Germany's strength in the air, and the relative weakness in this sphere of the other Powers, which is the main factor causing unrest and anxiety in the world today.... If our air strength could be increased, it would give strength to the Prime Minister in his further efforts for peace.' Not only that: 'If we had had to engage in war in September ... we could only have continued an effective fight in the air for a very short period.' To remedy this, Wood suggested first, considerable increases in reserve strength plus the supply of up-to-date equipment, then, more fighters, and then – perhaps mainly – 'if our real aim is to prevent war, it is necessary that we should have sufficient bomber force to ensure that any country wishing to attack us will realize that the game is not worth the candle.' In terms of cost-effectiveness, he felt heavy bombers were preferable to medium ones. Wood's emphasis on bombers had two important drawbacks: it might restrict production of fighters needed to defend Britain, and, as clearly an offensive measure, might arouse Hitler's wrath. And it was based on two prevalent beliefs: that the bomber would always get through, and that it would then cause crippling damage. Both these later proved false.

A serious obstacle faced these plans. Where was the money coming from? Simon now issued a stern warning. Two and a half years before the country had embarked upon a five-year rearmament programme; the cost had been put at £1,500 million, of which £400 million were to be borrowed and £1,100 million found from taxation. 'It is certain that the cost of the programmes as now presented will be over £2,000 million, and it might well be £2,100 million for the quinquennium.' So far, £631 million had been spent under the five-year plans; if therefore the cost of the remainder of the previous programme, plus the new projects, came to £2,000 million, 'we should have to find about £1,400 million over the next three years. We could probably find £675 million from taxation on the existing basis, leaving £725 million to be met either from borrowing and/or from an increase in taxation.... The real question is whether this task is within our powers.' It was of 'vital importance that we should not get into a position whereby we undertook a very large programme, and announced our intention of carrying it through, and then found that for financial reasons we were unable to do so'. He pointed out that the cost of the new fighter programme amounted to £45 million, and the cost of the bomber programme, £175 million.

Eventually the Cabinet made a number of important decisions. The Admiralty proposals were approved, and agreement was confirmed for the Army's anti-aircraft gun increases. But the RAF received the greatest boost. Approval in principle was given to the full programme of fighters, totalling 3,700, proposed by Wood. Consideration of very heavy bombers was delayed though sufficient orders would be placed to avoid substantial personnel dismissals, and to maintain an adequate production flow.[42]

Apart from the brief objection raised by Halifax, finance had been the only major hindrance to the extended rearmament plans. Yet Chamberlain was still trying to balance these plans with a peace offensive, including through visits to Paris and Rome. About flying over to Paris, he had written on 6 November: 'I felt it to be the right thing for many reasons – to give the French people an opportunity of pouring out their pent-up feelings of gratitude and affection, to strengthen Daladier and encourage him to *do* something at last to put his country's defences in order, and to pull his people into greater unity, to show France, and Europe too, that if we were anxious to make friends with Germany and Italy, we were not on that account going to forget our old Allies.' Talks in Paris would perhaps make possible the ambitious idea of a visit to Rome. 'I feel that Rome at the moment is the end of the Axis on which it is easiest to make an impression.... An hour or two *tête-à-tête* with "Musso" might be extraordinarily valuable in making plans for talks with Germany.... In the past, I have often felt a sense of helpless exasperation at the way things have been allowed to drift in foreign affairs, but now I am in a position to keep them on the move, and while I am PM I don't mean to go to sleep.'[43] All the ingredients of Chamberlain's attitude are in this letter: conceit, desire to mix conciliation with rearmament, determination that his hands alone should grasp the tiller.

Hitler was meanwhile concentrating on attacking Britain's 'warmongers'. He continued to scoff at 'that man with the umbrella' – 'Thank God we have no umbrella politicians in this country,' he barked.[44] On 6 November, he had made a number of ill-tempered jabs at Churchill and Arthur Greenwood. Churchill replied in a letter to *The Times*, while Ogilvie-Forbes sent a message to Halifax: 'I asked Herr Dietrich, Head of the Reich Press ... why Herr Hitler at Weimar, having openly attacked Messrs Churchill and Greenwood, did not vouchsafe one word of tribute to Mr Chamberlain. All that Herr Dietrich could reply was that Herr Hitler, who spoke *extempore*, must have forgotten.'[45] The Führer continued to speak *extempore* and to issue threats as to Germany's reaction. More, the terrible events of the next few days formed a damning indication of the type of leader and régime with which the British Prime Minister had to deal. On 7 November, a 17-year-old boy pulled a revolver from under his coat and fired five shots into Ernst vom Rath, of the Germany Embassy, in Paris. The boy, Herschel Grunspan, had sought revenge: he was a German Jew. But vom Rath's death was to bring a nightmare for Jews in Germany.

A month earlier, on 6 October, the Polish Government had issued a decree invalidating all Polish passports unless marked with a special frank obtainable only in Poland; Polish Jews outside the country had until the end of the month to acquire the necessary stamp. But the Berlin Foreign Ministry believed Poland aimed to be rid of the Polish Jews resident in Germany, and the Nazis retaliated on 28 October; some 17,000 Polish Jews were arrested, herded into box-cars and man-handled to the Polish frontier. They were then pushed across the border. Among those 17,000 unhappy Jews caught between one hostile nation and another, was Herschel Grunspan's father.[46] Herschel had intended to assassinate Welzeck, the German Ambassador at Paris; vom Rath had approached to see what the boy had wanted – tragically, he was a Jewish sympathizer being shadowed by the Gestapo for his anti-Nazi opinions. The murder of a diplomat was exactly the kind of incident needed by Joseph Goebbels, head of the Nazi propaganda machine. 'It is clear that the German people will draw its own con-clusions from this new deed,' screeched the *Völkischer Beobachter* on 8 November. Anti-Jewish riots were already erupting, and by early next day the Nazi-organized mobs were smashing and looting Jewish property.

British Ministers were attending a Cabinet meeting as this holocaust began. A heated argument was taking place, not on the international situation in general nor the Jews in particular, but on the question of a new armoured vehicle training range. Hore-Belisha wanted per-mission for the War Office to buy 6,000 acres at Linney Head, Pem-brokeshire. Simon complained: 'I have a personal knowledge of this piece of coast, which is one of the most beautiful and unspoilt places in these Islands ... this piece of country would be ruined.' Hore-Belisha retorted: 'The people of this country must realize that the needs of defence must be supreme,' and 'unless an area is discovered in the near future, the units cannot be properly trained in 1939.' A Sub-Committee was appointed to deal with the problem.[47]

But the plight of the wretched German Jews would soon be forced upon the Cabinet's attention. Dr Weizmann, President of the World Zionist Organization, telephoned Halifax 'in considerable distress' that afternoon, 9 November. German Jews believed the only means of saving the situation would be 'for some prominent non-Jewish English-man to go over to Berlin immediately'. Halifax cabled Ogilvie-Forbes in Berlin at 6.15 p.m. to ask his advice on the suggestion, adding '*prima facie* it seems to be fraught with difficulties'.[48] Goebbels was meantime intensifying the anti-Jewish barbarities. Late that evening instructions were issued for more 'spontaneous demonstrations' and an hour after midnight a message was sent to all HQ units of the State Police and SS: 'As many Jews, especially rich ones, are to be arrested as can be accommodated in the existing prisons.'[49] Destruction and deaths multiplied during Thursday, 10 November. That night, Halifax received a reply from Ogilvie-Forbes. 'I can see no advantage and indeed every objection to the proposal.... The treatment of German Jews is fiercely and jealously regarded as a purely internal matter.... Visit of prominent Englishman, far from being a deterrent, would have exactly the opposite effect.'[50] Next day Göring presided over a conference to discuss preliminary reports on the riots, and satisfaction was expressed over the scale of pogroms: over 119 synagogues had been set on fire, another 75 completely destroyed; 20,000 Jews had been arrested; 36 Jewish deaths reported, but the number was confidently expected to be several times higher. British action was confined to a protest made by Halifax over this passage in *Der Angriff*: 'The Jewish murder-urchin Grunspan also assumed the post of a world improver and avenger. Thereby he took the same line as is pursued by Messrs Churchill, Eden, Duff Cooper and their associates, indefatigably and in the most varied fashion in association with the International of Jews and Freemasons.' This indefensible attack was 'not in harmony with the spirit of previous Anglo-German discussions'. Ogilvie-Forbes attempted to deliver the protest on 12 November; but Ribbentrop was in Munich, and Weizsäcker in Paris. Under-Secretary Woermann would be available – would he be a suitable person to hand the protest to? Halifax took nearly 36 hours to consider this. Meanwhile, on 12 November, Göring held another conference. Damage valued at 25 million marks had been caused to Jewish property, and the Jewish insurance claims would damage the German economy; Göring therefore decided: 'The Jew shall get the refund from the insurance company but the refund will be confiscated.... The swine won't commit another murder. Incidentally, I would like to say that I wouldn't like to be a Jew in Germany.'

Ogilvie-Forbes cabled Halifax the following day: 'I can find no words strong enough in condemnation.' But 'I feel that inevitable public condemnation and censure should be tempered by consideration that it will be visited on the unfortunate Jews'.[51] Halifax received this message at breakfast-time on Monday, 14 November; he immediately instructed Ogilvie-Forbes to deliver the delayed protest over the *Angriff* smear – he was to see Woermann 'if he could not conveniently see anyone else'.[52] Also on the Monday, America made a more vigorous protest over the Nazi treatment of Jews. Hugh Wilson, their Ambassador, was recalled 'for consultation'; he never returned to his post.

And according to the German Ambassador at Washington, Hans Dieckhoff, later also recalled, 'a hurricane' was raging in the United States as a result of the pogroms.

Anti-Jewish riots subsided but ill-treatment continued. Halifax instructed Ogilvie-Forbes on Tuesday to make representations, as a member of the International Commission, over alleged expulsions of Jews from the Sudeten area. 'While realizing uselessness of general protest to Government against treatment of Jews,' he said, 'I am anxious to do everything we can where good grounds for intervention exist.'[53] The latest horrors were discussed at the Cabinet meeting starting at 10 a.m. next day, 16 November. Halifax was 'much impressed by the powerful repercussions all over the world of the action recently taken in Germany against the Jews'. The US Ambassador, he reported, believed 'one very important result of the action taken by Germany has been to produce a strong anti-British atmosphere in the United States'. Halifax felt 'public opinion in the United States is now about as critical as it could well be, but that the position could be restored if this country could give a lead, which would force America in turn to take some positive action.... For example, we might undertake that we would make some locality in the Empire available for Jewish settlement.' 'It is important not to exaggerate the possibilities of settlement in the Colonial Empire,' warned the Colonial Secretary; he doubted whether it would be possible to increase settlement in Kenya in the near future, and Jewish settlements met with unanimous opposition in North Rhodesia. But something might be possible in Tanganyika, and the position was much more hopeful in British Guiana.

'Any approach to Germany is, for the time being, out of the question,' announced Chamberlain – but he now hinted at the possibility of a trip to Rome. In the meantime, 'I assume that we will press on with the acceleration of our defence measures ... with a view to encourage the moderate opinions and discourage the extremists in Germany.'[54]

The Cabinet also heard that the final boundary between Germany and Czechoslovakia had now been agreed; according to Chamberlain: 'The result might be described as a compromise with which Czechoslovakia has conceded everything and gained nothing. A further 30,000 Czechs and 6,000 Germans have passed under German rule.... The result is to be deplored, yet there is nothing that we can do.'[55]

Later in the day, Perth cabled from Rome: 'Count Ciano and I signed the declaration bringing Anglo-Italian Agreement of 16 April into effect at 5.00 p.m. this afternoon [16 November].'[56] The same day Perth also wrote to say Mussolini had agreed to Chamberlain's visit and suggested the second week in January.[57] Churchill wrote next day: 'Everyone must recognize that the Prime Minister is pursuing a policy of most decided character and of capital importance.... He has his own strong view about what to do, and about what is going to happen.... He believes that he can make a good settlement for Europe and for the British Empire by coming to terms with Hitler and Sr. Mussolini.... By this time next year we shall know whether the Prime Minister's view of Herr Hitler and the German Nazi Party is right or wrong. By this time next year we shall know whether the policy of appeasement has appeased, or whether it has only stimulated a more ferocious appetite.'[58] And Chamberlain's relations with Hitler were now deteriorating faster than ever before, despite his conciliatory efforts, despite his 'relationship of confidence ... between myself and the Führer'. Ogilvie-Forbes cabled on 18 November to explain the 'exceptionally violent' attacks on Britain in the German press over the previous three weeks. Hitler had recently given a private interview to a select party of German journalists, and told them 'friendship with Britain was not a practical proposition as the Prime Minister had replied to the Munich declaration with rearmament'.[59]

'There is a general feeling in the air that the Chamberlain Government is shaking to its fall,' wrote Harold Nicolson on 23 November. 'The poor old man has gone to France in a gale.'[60] And as the Paris discussions were taking place next day, members of the Eden group met in London to hear the views of Austin Hopkinson, who had just refused the post of Government Whip. 'His account of our unpreparedness is appalling,' noted Nicolson. If Britain had gone to war in September, Hopkinson claimed, the RAF would have been wiped out in three weeks. He had seen Sir Kingsley Wood, and claimed the Air Secretary had admitted 'quite frankly' that Britain could do little without a Ministry of Supply, but to appoint such a Minister would arouse the anger of Germany. Nicolson commented: 'That is a dreadful confession. We all sit there very glum, Anthony Eden, Duff Cooper, Amery, Wolmer and the rest.'[61] These kinds of rumours and half-truths were running loose throughout Parliament and Whitehall. Churchill accused Chamberlain of not considering British rearmament sufficiently seriously; Hopkinson claimed the Prime Minister was blaming Inskip for the deficiencies; and, at the same time, members of the Opposition were attacking Chamberlain's Government for being too active in strengthening the country's forces. This varied criticism was the consequence of Chamberlain's delicate balance between diplomacy and defence. And far from admitting to Britain's military deficiencies, in Paris Chamberlain was throwing doubts on figures claimed for France's future aircraft production. Daladier alleged his country would produce 400 aircraft a month by the end of the following spring, and would accumulate a total of 4,000 aircraft by the end of 1939. Chamberlain was sceptical; he was 'very impressed' by the claim, but France was only producing 80 machines a month at that moment.

Daladier insisted his forecast was accurate, but emphasized in return the need for Britain to give more land forces in the event of a German attack. 'It is not enough to send two divisions after three weeks.' Chamberlain stressed his Government's first duty was to make Britain as safe as possible: the development of aviation had seriously altered the position in Europe: 'London is now the most vulnerable capital in the world. Within 24 hours of warfare London might be in ruins, and most of the important industrial centres in Great Britain as well.' This meant a heavy emphasis on anti-aircraft production. 'As a result, the strength of any force which would come to the assistance of France must be limited by incomplete equipment.' Daladier commented: 'It is better to defend London by having bombers which might go and bomb German towns,' and Chamberlain replied hastily: 'Britain is, in fact, increasing her bombing force in the same measure as her fighting force.'

As expected, the question of the guarantee for Czechoslovakia occupied a good deal of the Anglo-French debate. Chamberlain insisted Germany and Italy should be among the guarantors; then 'the situation of Czechoslovakia would be one of almost complete safety'. But the French feared this arrangement might lead to restricting conditions. France had already guaranteed Czechoslovakia individually against unprovoked aggression. 'I fear it would have a very adverse effect upon France's position if she were now to say that her new guarantee was subordinated to certain conditions.' Practicalities had to be considered, Halifax maintained. 'There is perhaps some danger in establishing a position where a future Czechoslovak Government might look to France and Great Britain for support in pursuing a policy not entirely in conformity with German wishes. That would constitute a certain element of provocation to Germany; and France and Great Britain would be powerless to intervene.' Chamberlain believed: 'From the Czechoslovak point of view it would certainly be better to have a guarantee which would bring in Germany and Italy willingly rather than a sham guarantee which could not work if it were really wanted.' While the haggling continued, the Führer was issuing new military plans. Ribbentrop's diplomatic approach to Poland failed; Beck refused to transfer Danzig; now Hitler sent another directive to his military commanders. 'Preparations are ... to be made to enable the Free State of Danzig to be occupied by German troops by surprise.... The plans of the branches of the armed forces are to be submitted by 10 January 1939.'[62]

Chamberlain pronounced the Anglo-French talks most satisfactory. He had enjoyed the cheering Parisians, though disliked the bullet-proof car. 'No point of difficulty arose,' he said, 'except in regard to the proposed guarantee to Czechoslovakia.' The French had finally agreed the Czechs should be consulted. Halifax had discussed with the French their attitudes to Russia. 'It is clear that they are rather anxious to disentangle themselves from the Russian connection.' The Prime Minister commented: 'I am quite clear that Germany will not acquiesce in any arrangement which allowed Russia to be associated with Czechoslovakia. Germany would, no doubt, make this attitude quite clear to the Czechs, who would have no choice in the matter.' In Halifax's view, 'the dangers which the guarantee is intended to guard against are largely hypothetical. At the same time, it is desirable that we should avoid, if possible, a position in which we might find ourselves asked to take action with France and Russia against Germany and Italy, on behalf of a State which we were unable effectively to defend.' In only a few months Britain would manoeuvre herself into just such a position.

Chamberlain confirmed that he and Halifax would be going to Italy, probably in January. 'As the prospects of appeasement are not very bright in Berlin,' he told Ministers, 'it might be useful that we should visit Rome.'[63] While the Cabinet had been in session, a memorandum was being prepared by the British Military Attaché in Berlin: the German army had gained invaluable experience during the Austrian and Sudetenland operations, 'especially so as regards the handling of motorized and mechanized formations, and the practical working of mobilization.... Germany's strategical position has been greatly strengthened by the intensive work on defences carried out during the year, especially on the western frontiers, and by the acquisition of Austria and Sudetenland.... As far as can be foreseen the German army ... should reach its approximate final maximum peace strength with the intake of the recruit class in the autumn of 1939 ... [and] will be passing through its last period of real difficulty, during which war would take it at a very considerable disadvantage, in the winter 1939-1940.'[64]

As November ended, there came the first sign of a threat to this cherished Rome visit. Ciano made a speech in the Italian Chamber on 30 November, and emphasized the importance of the Anglo-Italian Agreement, but applause was mixed with cries of 'Tunis ... Tunis,' in provocative references to rival Italian and French claims to North African colonies. Halifax cabled to Perth: 'Today's press is full of allegations that ... this demonstration was deliberately planned.'[65] With French support for the visit already weak, the incident could make it impossible. And on Friday Perth confirmed that the shouts resulted from Fascist instructions.[66] But for the moment the matter was allowed to rest.

Bedecked with medals, looking more like a General than a Foreign Minister, Ribbentrop arrived in Paris on 5 December. With arrogance and forced joviality, he graciously agreed to put his name to a Franco-German Declaration: 'The French Government and the German Government fully share the conviction that peaceful and good neighbourly relations between France and Germany constitute one of the essential elements for the consolidation of the situation in Europe and the maintenance of general peace....'[67] He failed to cause a breach between France and Britain, although he later tried to create difficulties by alleging he had been assured France, unlike Britain, was no longer interested in Central and Eastern Europe. Phipps reported Ribbentrop 'rather disappointed with the results of his Paris visit. On the spiritual plane Herr von Ribbentrop seemed to have expected to be greeted with more enthusiasm by the population....[68] The German head of the Protocol Department, and the German Ambassador, made light of Italian shouts for Tunis and Corsica, and indicated that shouting was perhaps the strongest point of Italians: the former went so far as to say that no reliance could be placed on Italy, and that she was really more of an anxiety as a friend than as an enemy.'[69] The Cabinet discussed the Italian incident on 7 December. Ciano had said the outbursts had been entirely spontaneous, but refused to dissociate himself from them. 'We have thus not obtained any very definite result,' said Chamberlain, 'but at least we have been able to say publicly that we've made representations.'

Ministers were told that the Foreign Policy Committee feared Italy and Germany might announce their own guarantee to Czechoslovakia, hence avoiding the international group proposed by Britain. Chamberlain said this 'would put us in an awkward position, since we are unwilling to see the guarantor Powers divided into two *blocs*'. The FPC believed the Czechs should be told Britain 'might have to reconsider her position' if Prague agreed to this dual arrangement.[70] Next afternoon, 8 December, Halifax sent a long despatch to Newton on this question, and this brief revealed how limited any British pledge would be. 'HMG are not prepared to consider a guarantee which might oblige them, alone or with France, to come to the assistance of Czechoslovakia in circumstances in which effective help could not be given. This would be the case if either Germany or Italy were the aggressor and the other declined to fulfil the guarantee.... If Czechoslovakia thought herself able to count securely upon French and British help, she might be tempted to adopt an attitude towards Germany which would only create the trouble we all wish to avoid.' Halifax told Newton that if a choice had to be made between Germany and Russia as guarantors, Britain would prefer the former. 'A Russian guarantee would be ineffective in the probable event of Poland and Roumania refusing passage to Soviet troops.'[71] The same day, Newton drew attention to the 'disintegrating tendencies arising from the discord between the Czechs and Slovaks.... It may be asked whether ... this country has so far lost her independence that a new situation has arisen which alters the whole basis on which HMG made their statement.'[72] This prophetic suggestion arrived in London at about the same time as an ominous warning of German aims, sent by Ogilvie-Forbes. Hitler, according to rumours, was about to embark upon a new programme, 'namely, expansion beyond the boundaries of the old Territories inhabited by the Germans.... I learn from an official source ... that the tiger is in his lair and waiting to see which way to spring.'[73]

Chamberlain became increasingly depressed and despairing as 1938 neared its end; worried by opposition at home, and by the attitude of some of his Ministers – notably Hore-Belisha. 'Worse than that are the continued venomous attacks by the German Press and the failure of Hitler to make the slightest gesture of friendliness. At the same time "Musso" takes the opportunity of writing offensive articles.'[74] The Rome visit seemed in jeopardy. Cadogan wrote to Perth on 12 December: 'The Prime Minister ... is beginning to feel considerable difficulty about his projected visit to Rome.' He said Chamberlain had always suspected the idea would be criticized by some people in Britain; now, however, their attacks had been multiplied by the anti-French outbursts. More disquietening news arrived on 13 December: Germany intended to boost her submarine force and to undertake other naval improvements. Under the terms of the 1935 and 1937 Anglo-German Naval Agreements, she had the right to build up to 100 per cent of Britain's tonnage, but her submarine strength had so far been only 45 per cent; now she planned to make good the difference, and also to provide greater armaments for two cruisers, *K* and *L*, already under construction.

Chamberlain's depression deepened that night: he told the Foreign Press Association at a London dinner that he was 'forced by circumstances to walk continually through dark and perilous ways'. And Stanhope, the First Lord, was uneasy over the German programme. 'Public opinion here might take the view that Germany is now definitely rearming against us, and that there is no hope of any real appeasement between the two countries.... If Germany built submarines to the extent proposed, there might have to be a considerable increase in our destroyer strength.' The German Government would be notified that discussions must be held, under the terms of the Anglo-German Agreements.[75]

The Japanese Ambassador at London, Shigemitsu, noted in a secret despatch on 16 December: 'There is mistrust of Chamberlain's policies in Britain, and the atmosphere of opposition is consequently a strong one.' He believed a growing body of opinion was convinced Germany must be attacked as soon as Britain was strong enough.[76] This communication was intercepted *en route* to Tokyo by German intelligence agents. Only a few hours later Keitel issued his 'Supplement to Directive of 21 October: TOP SECRET: With reference to the liquidation of the rump Czech State, the Führer has given the following orders. The operation is to be prepared on the assumption that no resistance worth mentioning is to be expected. To the outside world it must clearly appear that it is merely a peaceful action. . . .'[77]

Early the following week two political attacks were launched on Chamberlain's Government. On Monday, he had to defend his policy on a Vote of Confidence; and to admit he was still awaiting some sign from Germany. This was immediately seized as an indication of wavering: next day's *Manchester Guardian* headline declared 'THE AWAKENING'. On Monday night, banner headlines in the London *Evening Standard* stated: 'JUNIOR MINISTERS IN REVOLT'. Ironically, Hore-Belisha, chief opposer to Chamberlain in the Cabinet, was not the instigator, but the main target of the 'revolt'. He was criticized for not doing more to strengthen the Army, despite his desire and attempts to do so. He saw the Prime Minister, and learned that Rob Hudson, Secretary of Department of Overseas Trade and one of the Junior Ministers named in the rebellion, had made complaints against various Cabinet Ministers, including Inskip and himself. The War Secretary said he was ready 'at any time to answer for my record'. Chamberlain, according to Hore-Belisha's diary, replied 'that I had no need to do that, that I had done extremely well at the War Office, and that he considered me the best Secretary of State for War since Haldane'.[78] The brief disturbance subsided; but to Chamberlain the incident revealed the rising feeling against appeasement, and to Hore-Belisha, it offered a foretaste of events to come.

The disturbance was not discussed at the 21 December Cabinet meeting; instead, Chamberlain began by showing his renewed determination to visit Mussolini. Halifax thought it important 'to improve our relationship with Sr. Mussolini', but 'we should make [him] no concession . . . unless he will help us to obtain the detente which is the object of our policy'.

Ministers heard from Sir John Anderson on protection from bomb attacks. 'The hard core of the problem is to provide protection for the ordinary citizen in, or close to, his own house. . . . For houses without basements – primarily the two-storeyed house not very solidly constructed – we have . . . evolved a special type of steel shelter which is in sections and can be easily put together.' This was the famous 'Anderson Shelter'. The whole programme would cover about 20 million people, and cost about £20 million.[79]

The Cabinet left for their last Christmas of peace. As 1938 closed, long despatches arrived in Whitehall with dismal prospects for the New Year. On 29 December, Mason-MacFarlane sent a report from Berlin: 'Information regarding the commencement of military preparations in February for action in an easterly direction is too good to warrant our taking it anything but seriously.' German reservists had been told to stand by, transport had been requisitioned, and the Colonel had heard of stoppages of leave.[80] Even more ominous was the rumour brought by Ivone Kirkpatrick, back in London to take up a new appointment at the Foreign Office. Kirkpatrick had been informed by a retired German State Secretary that Hitler had ordered preparations for an air attack on London. 'The plan, allocation of squadrons, selection of airfields, assembly of material, selection of targets, etc., is to be completed and submitted in three weeks from now.' The German had picked up a bookseller's catalogue from his desk and promised to send it to Kirkpatrick's London Club as a signal that the operation was to take place. Kirkpatrick had immediately set the story down on paper for Halifax, and a decision was later taken to bring an anti-aircraft regiment from Lichfield and park the guns in Wellington Barracks, where they could be seen from the German Embassy across the park.[81]

In Paris, prospects were also being assessed as dangerous. On 29 December, Phipps described serious French misgivings over Chamberlain's Rome visit. And next day he signalled: 'I have the impression that the French General Staff are quite convinced that war is coming in Europe, and before very long.'[82]

6

Ides of March

'It has been a bad year,' wrote Harold Nicolson. 'A foul year. Next year will be worse.'[1] Would Hitler now try to take Danzig, or Memel, or both, back into the Fatherland? Was he eyeing the remainder of Czechoslovakia? Or did he intend to seek colonies further East? And if so, did he intend to use peaceful economic penetration, or mobile mechanized divisions? The questions nagged Chamberlain as he tried to relax at Chequers. Britain's domestic situation lent no strength or support. His opponents were still active; unemployment was deplorably high; he had failed to gain the Trade Unions' confidence, essential if the people were to accept the strain of re-armament. Chamberlain could bemoan his invidious inheritance as Prime Minister; if only rearmament had been pushed before he took office, if the 1935 election had been fought on the defence issue, as he had urged, the country would now be better prepared. Had he not initiated the first serious expansion of the Air Force, in 1934? But Baldwin had restricted his efforts and now the hour had passed. It took so long to build destroyers, aircraft, tanks, and so much money to pay for the new production lines. He could only continue to seek more time, knowing that sooner or later the country would have to make sacrifices; until then as much as possible must be done without damaging the already weak economy. As he himself had said in May 1938: 'Wars are not won only now with arms and men, they are won with the reserves of resources and credit.'[2]

And also with the help of allies. So, as 1939 opened, both Germany and Britain intensified their search for support. Chamberlain could at least take some encouragement from news across the Atlantic. On 4 January, Roosevelt's message to Congress called for defence against aggression, though it emphasized 'methods short of war'.

'Anxiety, arising out of uncertainty, breeds rumour and gossip of all description,' cabled Ogilvie-Forbes from Berlin. 'There is only one direction in which Hitler with comparative ease could possess himself of many of the raw materials lacking to Germany, and that is in the

East.... Consequently, the agricultural and mineral resources of the Ukraine and even Roumanian territory are the subject of much talk. It is in that direction that Germany appears most likely to break out.'[3]

On Thursday 5 January, as this report reached Whitehall, Hitler was entertaining Beck at Berchtesgaden. The visit caused added unease in London, which vague reports to the Foreign Office did nothing to alleviate. Ogilvie-Forbes cabled on 7 January: 'Hitler asked M. Beck for an explanation of his attitude towards Soviet Russia.'[4] And two days later: 'Press Attaché has learnt questions of Danzig and Ukraine were discussed.'[5] In Warsaw, Kennard saw Beck on 11 January but found him 'extremely evasive'.[6] Ogilvie-Forbes cabled the same day that Beck had agreed to a corridor across the Danzig Corridor, and that Ribbentrop would visit Warsaw at the end of the month to sign an agreement.[7] But 48 hours later he was informed by the Polish Ambassador at Berlin that the Corridor had not been discussed, and Hitler had 'scoffed at the report of intended German aggression in the Ukraine'.[8] The Foreign Office had to make its assessments in 'a thick fog'.[9]

Hitler had indeed brought up the 'Corridor' question. 'Danzig is German, will always remain German, and will sooner or later become part of Germany' – but he assured Beck 'no *fait accompli* would be engineered', and a settlement could be reached. Hitler said he also wanted a German highway and railroad across the Corridor. Beck was not persuaded and told Ribbentrop he 'saw no possibility whatever of agreement'.[10] For the moment Hitler remained unprovoked: Czechoslovakia had finally to be dealt with first. The Poles, still, stubbornly refused to disclose the nature of the discussion to London or Paris, then or later.

Chamberlain and Halifax left on their heralded mission to Mussolini, leaving Simon in charge in London. They journeyed via Paris, for informal talks with Daladier and Bonnet. Forty-five minutes were sufficient to show that Franco-Italian relations were indeed fragile, and that the French Government would make no concessions.[11]

The British Party reached Genoa on Wednesday, 11 January; Chamberlain had to step on to the platform to inspect the glittering guard of honour, accompanied by clapping, shouting, and noisily-played national anthems. Halifax wrote: 'The final edition of the National Anthem, however, so far as we were concerned, was cut short by the train starting off while we were still standing at attention on the platform, forcing us to make a rather rapid and unceremonious re-entry.'[12] From Genoa the train proceeded without further stops or mishaps. 'Rome station,' wrote Halifax, was 'much carpeted and beflagged', and the pageant continued as the party was driven through cheering crowds to the Villa Madama. One western newspaperman, hearing that Chamberlain was 'much affected' by the reception, asked incredulously: 'Can it be he doesn't know it's *arranged*?'[13] Formalities over, the British were taken to the Palazzo Venezia for the first talks with the Duce. 'The feeling of the stage play came over me strongly,' wrote Halifax. 'As I walked with Chamberlain to be received by Mussolini along a not very wide passage between lines of black-shirted young men, all standing rigidly to attention, with drawn daggers held out at shoulder height, I had the uncomfortable feeling that if I stumbled I must infallibly impale my throat upon a dagger point.... Chamberlain being shorter would fare better and fall beneath the dagger line.'[14]

Talks began, the noise of the crowd causing difficulty, till Mussolini tinkled a tiny bell and, when an attendant appeared, put his fingers to his lips. In a few seconds the cheering had been switched off. And so the visit continued: much pomp, much lavish entertainment, many professions of peace. Halifax departed for Geneva early on the 14th and managed to slip away without fuss. But Chamberlain was given the full treatment. 'The scene at the departure,' said Lord Perth, 'was very similar to that on the arrival: the same crowds, the same troops, the same officials at the station.'[15]

'I may say at once,' wrote Chamberlain of his visit, 'that I consider I have achieved all I expected to get and more, and that I am satisfied that the journey has definitely strengthened the chances of peace.... To give first my impressions of Mussolini, I found him straight-forward and considerate in his behaviour to us, and moreover he has a sense of humour which is quite attractive.'[16] Ciano's impressions were very different. 'How far apart we are from these people!' he wrote in his diary. 'It is another world.' Mussolini had said: 'These, after all, are the tired sons of a long line of rich men, and they will lose their Empire.' Ciano's diary continued: 'The British do not want to fight. They try to draw back slowly as possible, but they do not fight.' Of the conversations: 'Nothing was accomplished. I have telephoned Ribbentrop that the visit was a "big lemonade".'.... And of the final departure: 'Chamberlain's eyes were filled with tears when the train started moving and his countrymen began singing "For he's a jolly good fellow". "What is that little song?" the Duce asked.'[17]

Chamberlain reported on his 'highly successful' journey when the Cabinet met on 18 January – for the first session of 1939. 'I was very favourably impressed with Sr. Mussolini's demeanour and attitude throughout the visit,' he said. 'The Duce appeared quite straight-forward and sincere in everything he said, and never at any time during the visit did he make any statement which was in the least embarrassing to his visitors.... It is difficult to explain how heartfelt, spontaneous and universal was the feeling of welcome.... I am convinced that Signor Mussolini and Herr Hitler cannot be very sympathetic to each other, and that although they have some interests in common their interests are not identical.... Accordingly I, on several occasions, gave Mussolini a chance to express his real feelings of Herr Hitler. He never took the opportunity offered to him, but remained throughout absolutely loyal to Herr Hitler. At the time I was somewhat disappointed at this attitude, but on reflection I think that it reflects credit on Signor Mussolini's character.'[18] Halifax wrote later, though, that he had 'left at the end of two days with a general impression that the visit had probably done a little good'.[19]

The meeting continued with the Chancellor's statement on the financial situation. Up to about a year before there had been a massive flow of capital funds towards London, he said, but 'since last April anxieties on the part of foreigners as to the fate of this country in the war, which they regarded as impending, have led to a great efflux of these funds, chiefly to America, which was regarded as a safe repository.... It appears only too evident that the view continues to be persistently held abroad that war is coming, and that this country may not be ready for it.... I am afraid we must say that the recent conditions have been painfully reminiscent of those which obtained in the country immediately prior to the financial crisis of September 1931.[20]

On 9 January Hore-Belisha had asked every member of the Army Council to give a frank statement of the position, and to specify the difficulties hampering the progress of rearmament. These reports were now ready, and next day, Hore-Belisha revealed their disturbing contents to Sir Horace Wilson over lunch. He was critical of variations in policy, which affected the whole military machine, and of indecision on the scale of war provision, which was holding back increases in factory construction. Every item in the Army's programme, he told Sir Horace, had to be subjected to meticulous examination before sanction was given; every project had to be 100 per cent right 'and full value was squeezed out of every halfpenny'. He then saw Chamberlain. 'I had a long talk with Neville,' he wrote in his diary, 'and told him about the Army Councillors' reports. I repeated what I had said to Wilson. Feel a bit depressed.'[21] While Hore-Belisha was trying to speed approval for rather modest manpower increases in the British Army, in Germany a new military decree was published. With one stroke it became the 'moral duty' of every German, on reaching 18, to qualify for proficiency in '*Wehrsportabzeichen*' – 'military sport'. Thousands of Germans were brought under direct influence of the notorious *Sturmabteilung*, the SA.[22]

Early on Saturday, 21 January, Ogilvie-Forbes informed Halifax that the Czech Foreign Minister, Chvalkovsky, would arrive in Berlin during the day. The Czech Ambassador had told him 'the visit should be of a routine nature'.[23] As far as Hitler was concerned, the visit was indeed routine: he treated Chvalkovsky as he normally did represen-

92

tatives of nations he intended to eliminate. Unless the Czechs behaved, they would be 'annihilated', and as evidence of good behaviour, the country must quit the League of Nations, slash the size of her Army – which 'did not count anyway' – and accept German direction of foreign policy.[24] Yet Dr Masarik, Chvalkovsky's deputy, told the British Chargé, Troutbeck, the following Tuesday, that 'the German Government had shown an entirely correct and courteous attitude'. Troutbeck, though, did not find Masarik 'in buoyant spirits. Indeed, rather the contrary.'[25] This cable failed to reach London until 28 January, a week after the interview, so the meeting of the British FPC on 23 January was not primarily concerned with threats to Czechoslovakia. The session, the first since 6 December, discussed rumours of German action against Holland. Halifax and Vansittart believed Britain should try to enlist United States support: it would be of 'very great value if President Roosevelt could be persuaded to make some announcement on the subject before the speech which Herr Hitler was to deliver on 30 January.' Chamberlain wondered 'whether we should let the United States know that in the event of a German invasion of Holland we should intervene'. Halifax thought so; and added: 'there was a growing feeling in certain quarters in France that Britain is proposing to make her effort on the sea and in the air, leaving the French to fight on the land.' He clearly disagreed with this impression, but Chamberlain immediately pointed out that 'whatever might eventually transpire, it must be clear that at the outset there can be, in fact, no possibility of Britain landing a large army on the Continent'.

Chamberlain suggested the Chiefs of Staff Sub-Committee should be invited to make a report for the Cabinet meeting in two days' time on the major issue, 'namely whether the integrity of the territory of Holland is so vital to the interests and safety of this country that we should be bound to intervene in the event of German aggression against Holland'. At a later date, he added, they should be invited to make a second report, 'namely, if the answer to the first issue is in the affirmative, what military action could this country take?' Halifax asked whether the Prime Minister might make some reference to the subject in the speech he was to make on Saturday, 28 January. Chamberlain said he might 'use some expression which could not be construed as involving us in any new commitment'.[26]

The old pattern was continuing: reluctance to enter into commitments and even greater reluctance to declare them, yet also, recognition that these commitments could not be entirely avoided. Diplomatic decisions were still being taken, before military means were considered to carry them out; not vice-versa.

Halifax assessed the international situation at the long Cabinet session on 25 January. 'The atmosphere is much like that which surrounds a child, in which everything is possible and nothing is impossible.'

Repeating a message just sent to Roosevelt, he described Hitler's anger following Munich, directed against 'the Prime Minister in particular and Great Britain in general'. Exasperation, he explained, had been fanned by the worsening German economic situation in the last quarter of 1938; Hitler had seemed likely to 'explode' in some direction in 1939, to distract attention from his own failures, to provide an excuse for suppressing the German 'moderates', and perhaps mainly to conquer areas which could supply raw materials. But until the end of 1938 Hitler had seemed to be looking East. 'Unfortunately, towards the end of the year, and during the present month, we began to receive reports that the minds of the rulers of Germany were moving in a different, and for us a more sinister, direction.' Shortly before Christmas Hitler had apparently declared: 'These English, arrogant apes that they are, think that they can rule the world forever with 15 battleships. They won't however. Our Air Force, and the German and Italian U-boats will take care of that.' The same report had claimed Hitler was planning another crisis, in which Italy and Japan would also take part, in January or February. Hitler had declared: 'Then you will see how Chamberlain and Daladier will again fly to Berchtesgaden, to the accompaniment of a laughable howl from their Left Press.'

Halifax detailed other reports: that Germany was pressing to convert the anti-Comintern Pact into a full military alliance; that the inner circle of the Nazi Party was convinced there would be war, at the earliest in March, at the latest in April; that a surprise air attack on London was being studied. 'A further report has come in during the last ten days from a very high German source which has always proved reliable in the past. According to this report, about January 12 not only Dr Schacht [President of the Reichsbank], but also the Finance Minister, Count von Krosigk, sent a memorandum to Herr Hitler describing the internal situation as desperate and saying that there were only two possible remedies: first, a drastic cutting down of public expenditure; second, a large increase in taxation.... To all these criticisms Herr Hitler had in substance replied: "Very well. All this means that the vital decision must come at once and it is coming at once."' The German General Staff had apparently been instructed to furnish plans, by 15 February, for an attack on the East, and for a combined attack on Holland and Switzerland, which would involve simultaneous actions against England and France. Halifax thought: 'Herr Hitler seems to be relying on the advice of Ribbentrop more than that of anybody else and Ribbentrop is alleged to be dominated by his hatred of England. At the end of the Munich Conference, for instance, he is reliably reported to have said: "Gentlemen, the obituary notice of England is on the table."' Confirmation of these pessimistic rumours might well be found in the dismissal of Dr Schacht, on 20 January. But Chamberlain was a 'long way from accepting all this information.

Some allowance must be made for the rather disturbing atmosphere in which those who received these secret reports necessarily worked. Again, while many of the forecasts received from these sources had proved correct in the past, this was not always the case.... I also think it is somewhat curious that the Führer should now be described as intensely irritated as the result of Munich.'

The Chiefs of Staff presented their report on Britain's reaction should Germany invade Holland. And they believed such an invasion should be held by Britain as a *casus belli*. If this invasion took place, said Chamberlain, Britain would have to intervene, 'but I doubt whether it is advisable that we should say so at once. I am influenced by the fact that if we made an immediate statement we should enter into a binding commitment which, in certain circumstances, might prove embarrassing.' He thought it best to await a second Chief of Staff report, dealing with military action Britain could take.

Inskip said the Chiefs of Naval and of Air Staff had advised him that, 'if the Government decided to act on the assumption that the information referred to in the Foreign Secretary's statement could not be ignored, then we should at once start taking certain precautionary measures'. But Wood, the Air Secretary, warned: 'The moment we start to take certain precautionary steps, it is inevitable a larger number of persons will be informed, and there will almost certainly be some leakage.... There is little advantage to be gained by making an immediate statement as to our interest in the integrity of Holland.... There is always the possibility that such a statement might be used by Herr Hitler to suggest to the German people that we were threatening them.' Stanhope, the First Lord, also hesitated: 'It is desirable that we should know what action the Dutch themselves will propose to take in the event of an invasion, before definitely deciding upon our own action. I would not be at all surprised if a good deal of the information which has reached the Foreign Office through various sources has not been deliberately planted by Germany with some ulterior motive.'

The Cabinet was clearly uncertain how much determination to show the world, but eventually agreed that, 'while there was little scope for acceleration of the Defence Programme over the next two or three months, it was important to take all practicable steps to put the Defence Services into a state of readiness to meet ... a possible emergency in the near future'. But 'for the time being no public statement should be made as to our attitude in the event of a German invasion of Holland'.

In Warsaw, on January 25, Ribbentrop met Beck, who was still unwilling to agree over Danzig. This added to the German conviction that stronger action should be taken over Poland, and Beck for his part became anxious to secure support.

Still believing Holland, and not Czechoslovakia or Poland, to be

Hitler's next target, the FPC met again next day. They now had the second Chiefs of Staff report to consider. The three Service Ministers, the three Service Chiefs, and Major-General Ismay, the Secretary of the Committee of Imperial Defence, were all there. Britain, the report held, might 'be confronted with a position more serious than the Empire has ever faced before. . . . The ultimate outcome of the conflict might well depend upon the intervention of other Powers, in particular of the United States of America.' However, 'failure to intervene would have such moral and other repercussions as would seriously undermine our position in the eyes of the Dominions and the world in general. We might thus be deprived of support in a subsequent struggle between Germany and the British Empire. . . . Therefore we have, as we see it, no choice but to regard a German invasion of Holland as a direct challenge to our security.'

Halifax 'warmly assented' to these conclusions. But Newall, Chief of Air Staff pointed out 'we could do little or nothing to prevent Holland from being overrun and that the restoration of her territory would depend on the later course of the war'. Even though the Chiefs of Staff had concluded an invasion of Holland would constitute a direct challenge, a precise answer to the question of whether Britain ought to intervene had been avoided.

As at the last Cabinet meeting, there was considerable confusion over what steps to take. Chamberlain said the Dutch might not resist the Germans, which might make Britain's position difficult. Wood and Stanhope agreed such a situation was possible, but Halifax declared that the Foreign Office thought it unlikely. Chamberlain, however, still tried to avoid a firm declaration. 'No useful purpose will be served by the Committee attempting to reach a decision on improbable hypothetical assumptions.' Malcolm MacDonald, though, had to admit that 'if an invasion of Holland evoked no response from this country, the Dominions would conclude that our sun had set'. Finally, the FPC did take the drastic step of endorsing the Chiefs of Staff's conclusion. 'We have no choice but to regard a German invasion of Holland as a direct challenge to our security . . . consequently, if Germany should invade Holland, we must go to war with Germany, assuming always that Holland resists invasion.'[27]

On the same day, the CID discussed Britain's military preparations, and once again fears were voiced by Hore-Belisha. In his diary he noted 'If we were involved in war, it would be a struggle for our very existence, and not a war in which we could limit our liability. . . . The impact of the next war, I said, would be so overwhelming that if a Ministry of Supply were not already in being at the outset, there was a danger that the war would be lost before the organization could be set up.'[28] Hore-Belisha was supported by Halifax, whose anxieties about the international situation were still further increased by telegrams received in the next three days. First came a message from Ogilvie-Forbes: Hitler was 'relying on our lack of preparedness for a major war this year' and intended to break out westwards in March, in order to 'turn the Maginot Line through the Low Countries'.[29] With this message came an assessment from Mason-MacFarlane in Berlin, who also believed Hitler would move West, not East. The German army was 'definitely preparing for possible action on a large scale'.[30] The Colonel's next telegram explained: 'It is logical to suppose that Hitler may contemplate forcing a major war this year, as he most probably considers that his military position *vis-à-vis* France and England is now better than it will be for the next two or three years.'[31] This was immediately followed by discouraging news from Washington. The Secretary of State, Cordell Hull, had sent for Mallet that morning and said, 'in his most oracular style', that 'at present moment reasons of internal politics made it necessary for the President to proceed with great caution ... he hinted that the President would not be sending you any specific message or making any definite suggestions.' Clearly the President would also make no public statement.[32]

So America would not help; threats to Holland were increasing; an invasion of Holland would draw Britain into war, though her forces were still deficient – this grew daily more evident. Chamberlain's fears that any bellicose statement would provoke rather than deter Hitler, multiplied.

Among the signals to the Foreign Office on Saturday, 28 January, were two which, though comparatively unimportant then, had far-reaching implications. The first was from Kennard in Warsaw. Beck had told him the night before that he could not come to London at the beginning of March, as he had hoped, but would probably come towards the end. 'I have the impression he is anxious to make this visit.'[33] The second came from Berlin: the Soviet Embassy had told Ogilvie-Forbes that the Germans were to send a small trade mission to Moscow.[34] Later in the day, Halifax mentioned this to Maisky, the Soviet Ambassador at London, who avoided confirming or denying it but also said 'he anticipated some new crisis before very long, but did not anticipate that this would arise over the Ukraine.'[35]

That evening, Halifax instructed the Paris and Brussels Ambassadors to tell the respective Governments what the FPC had concluded and discover their views. He himself saw the Belgian Ambassador at London, who hinted 'the Belgians would wish to keep out of it, unless obliged to take part by being themselves made the object of attack'.[36] But, during the busy Saturday, news had reached the Foreign Office which conflicted with the assessment that Holland was probably Hitler's next victim. M. de Margerie, of the French Embassy, had said: 'Transports full of German troops had crossed Czechoslovakia in the direction of Austria,' and 'further trainloads of troops, amounting to a division, were likely to be sent.'[37] But no more news was forthcoming.

Meanwhile, news of the French position over Holland arrived at lunch-time on Sunday. 'M. Daladier is inclined to think that German attack on Holland should be considered a *casus belli*,' cabled Phipps, 'whether or not Holland decides to defend herself.' The French leader also inquired anxiously whether Britain 'would not soon introduce compulsory national service. I replied that this seemed to be impossible.'[38]

No clear picture of the situation was emerging from the mass of telegrams from Paris, Rome, Prague, Berlin, Moscow, the Hague, Warsaw, Durazzo, Belgrade, Bucharest, Budapest, Danzig, Bratislava and Washington. Hitler's next objective was Holland, Switzerland, Poland, the Ukraine, Czechoslovakia – nobody knew. So, Sir William Seeds' short telegram from Moscow attracted no special attention. 'Member of my staff learns in strict confidence from an entirely reliable informant recently in Memel and in touch with German official circles there that "*Anschluss*" is expected to take place about 15 March.'[39] The date was exactly correct; the target only slightly wrong.

Listeners in Paris and London anxiously awaited the Führer's broadcast on 30 January, marking his sixth anniversary as Chancellor. But they learnt nothing. Halifax gave his verdict to the Cabinet two days later: the speech 'did not alter the situation very much'. At the Cabinet meeting Holland was still the main topic, and after lengthy discussions formal approval was given to the FPC's recommendation that Britain should consider 'as a direct challenge' German invasion of Holland – or Switzerland, on the grounds that actions against this small country 'would be clear evidence of an attempt ... to dominate Europe by force'. Ministers agreed 'this was a big step forward ... almost tantamount to an Alliance', but one which must be taken.[40] So, for the first time, the Chamberlain Cabinet had agreed to commit Britain to defending a country which could not, in fact, be saved if Germany invaded, though this inability had prevented their helping Czechoslovakia before Munich. It could be argued that invasion of Holland would challenge Britain's security, but not of Switzerland. Chamberlain had felt that Germany had a legitimate grievance over Sudetenland, and could not have over Switzerland. This assessment indicated a new attitude: before Munich he could believe Hitler's aims were limited. Now he could not; appeasement was outdated. Thus, the Cabinet meeting of Wednesday, 1 February 1939, marked the real turning point. Future events, including the actual alliance which would commit Britain to war, merely followed the sequence already begun.

For the Prime Minister the transition had been coming gradually for some weeks – 1 February stamped the official seal on his change of heart and mind. The charade of conciliation might continue, but with no conviction. Britain's rearmament might continue to move slowly, but only for economic reasons. Chamberlain still tried to avoid enraging Hitler with an accelerated arms programme, but only to gain time. No evidence in the Cabinet discussions or FPC debates shows Chamberlain opposed to rearmament measures for any reasons but these – and a fear that people would not tolerate the restrictions and sacrifices which further preparations for war must mean. This fear prevented his agreeing to conscription or a Ministry of Supply. He wanted to wait as long as possible before introducing these final, drastic measures; but he knew they would come.

The next morning's meeting clearly revealed the Cabinet's changed attitude. Although final decisions from this session were deferred for more detailed study, the Ministers now accepted in principle a fundamental change in Britain's military deployment. In the past, Britain's forces had been equipped and deployed for general purposes – assumed to mean a colonial war. Now, they were to include elements specifically equipped for war on the European Continent. Hore-Belisha had prepared a Memorandum: the General Staff, he said, wished to point out that 'present arrangements would not permit the Army to meet satisfactorily or safely the responsibilities it might be called upon to discharge' in accordance with its approved *role*', and to ask for modifications in the programme which would cost an estimated £81 million. The Mobile Division should be organized into two smaller divisions, and these plus four Regular Army and four Territorial Army divisions, should be re-equipped on a continental scale. 'When I first put forward proposals for the role of the Army a year ago,' he said, 'I was governed by the hope that we should not have to send land forces to the Continent. . . . I stress that the General Staff are greatly perturbed lest the present state of affairs might result in our soldiers having to run undue and unnecessary risks if they are sent overseas equipped as at present. . . . If my proposals are approved, the British Army will have divisions specially allotted for European service, and Colonial divisions for minor campaigns elsewhere.'

'This is rather a new conception,' said Chamberlain. 'The Secretary of State for War had described his proposals as modest. Far larger proposals could, of course, have been submitted. It is clear that an unanswerable case could be made out for increased armaments in every arm, if the financial aspect of the proposal is ignored. But finance cannot be ignored, since our financial strength is one of our strongest weapons in any war which is not over in a short time.' Simon strongly supported this. 'In the year 1937-38, the Army Estimates . . . stood at £82 million. The proposals which are now under discussion are therefore broadly equivalent to the whole cost of the Army in 1938-39. Next year the Army Estimate will stand at about £160 million, and the total for the three Defence Services will be over £500 million.' But where was the money to come from? 'There are limitations to

99

what we can borrow.' In the budget for the financial year 1938-39, he had provided for the largest sum ever acquired out of taxation by Britain for defence. This would amount to £270 million. 'Since then there has been a depression in trade, and considerable falling off in the productivity of certain taxes. It is unlikely, therefore, that revenue will provide £270 million in the current year as anticipated, and there will be a substantial Budget deficit.... In the ensuing year there will be a vast gap to bridge between the sum available for defence from the Budget and a defence expenditure of over £500 million.... Further, it is now becoming clear that the maintenance of the defence forces now being equipped will cost an annual figure far in excess of any figure which we have ever raised out of revenue to meet defence services. It will be substantially in excess of £300 million a year.'

Simon added: 'I do not dispute that the proposals can properly be represented as both urgent and necessary. But have they any better claims to be so described than, for example, proposals in regard to further financial assistance to agriculture and shipping, an extended shelter policy, or proposals submitted by the Foreign Office to find money to help states in the East or the Far East, or the increased Air Defence programme, which I understand is shortly to be submitted.' He concluded with another grim warning. 'During last autumn I was faced with serious difficulties in maintaining the level of the pound. Once a loss of confidence shows itself on a wide scale, there will be no means of arresting it. We might be faced with a financial crisis as grave as that of 1931, but with the foreign situation far more serious.'

Chamberlain had already told Ministers that he proposed to make a Cabinet change: Sir Thomas Inskip, Minister for Coordination of Defence, was to become Secretary for the Dominions. His successor was to be Admiral of the Fleet Lord Chatfield; and Chamberlain now told the Cabinet it was important the new Minister should have a chance of considering the proposals. But Halifax was against delay; a reply had just arrived from the French to a British request for wider Staff talks: 'I think there are strong indications in the reply that French opinion is sensitive in regard to the size of the Field Force to be sent by this country to France.... While I realize the full force of what the Chancellor of the Exchequer has said, I wonder whether the present wholly abnormal conditions are such as to make it unjustifiable that we should borrow for current defence expenditure for a period.' Oliver Stanley thought, 'From one point of view we are already at war and have been for some time.... It is clear that some of the conditions under which we are now living cannot last much longer – perhaps not for another year – and the present is probably the crucial year.'

Chamberlain proposed the discussion be adjourned for further examination by Simon, Hore-Belisha and Chatfield. Hore-Belisha was disappointed: 'I had rather hoped that we might be able to agree without further delay to certain proposals in my memorandum.' The Cabinet agreed the War Office should start discussions with the Treasury over the extra equipment needed.[41]

On Sunday evening a telegram arrived from Lord Perth. 'I am not happy at what is happening here. I learn from a most confidential source that a good deal of secret calling up among the younger officers is going on.'[42] Chamberlain took firm action to warn Italy against hostilities with France. 'Any threat to the vital interests of France,' he told the Commons on 7 February, 'from whatever quarter it came, would evoke the immediate cooperation of Great Britain.' 'Really, Chamberlain is an astonishing and perplexing old boy,' Harold Nicolson wrote to his wife. 'This afternoon, as you will have heard, he startled the House and the world by proclaiming something like an offensive and defensive alliance between us and France.... And the old boy gets up and does it as if it was the simplest thing on earth. ... the House was absolutely astounded. It could not have been more definite. It was superb. I felt more happy than for months.... But this is a complete negation of his "appeasement" policy and of his Rome visit. He has in fact swung suddenly round. What does it mean? I think it can only mean that he realizes that appeasement has failed.'[43] That same day Chamberlain wrote to Lord Tweedsmuir – John Buchan. 'I am afraid there are still such volcanic elements at work that we can hardly expect tranquillity for some little time to come.' Yet, rather than being depressed, Chamberlain even felt a 'greater brightness'.[44]

Next day an attempt was made to obtain a German view of the Czechoslovak guarantee. Negotiations had been desultory and abortive; now, French and British *notes verbales* were delivered in Berlin. Each stated the 'time has now come to regularize the guarantee,' and requested 'the views of the German Government as to the best way of giving effect to the understanding reached at Munich'.[45] Paris and London would have to wait 20 days for a reply. International affairs continued dangerously unsettled, and the Cabinet discussed the situation again that same Wednesday morning. Halifax had heard from the French Government, reaffirming that they would consider an invasion of Holland a *casus belli*. The French had said: 'The gravity of the situation ... demands on the part of all the interested party nations the immediate and unreserved adoption of every measure liable to increase the human and material forces already at their disposal. The French Government, for their part, are ready for this community of efforts and sacrifices ... recourse to conscription appears an essential part of the effective participation of Great Britain.' Halifax told the Cabinet: 'I propose to ignore the suggestion in regard to conscription. M. Corbin [the French Ambassador] has informed me that he regretted its inclusion in the French reply.... No further information has been received which would confirm the earlier rumours as to possible

German intentions to attack in the West. Indeed, the relative quietness of the atmosphere is regarded by some people as an ominous symptom.'

Nothing had so far resulted from Hore-Belisha's meetings with Simon over proposals to modify the deployment plans for the Army. But now the Chancellor asked for approval to increase borrowing powers for the defence programme, indicating that he was giving way to Hore-Belisha's insistence. The Cabinet agreed to the preparation of a Defence Loans Bill, which would increase borrowing powers to the extent of a further £400 million.[46]

Events seemed to be steadily working towards a climax. Chamberlain wrote on Sunday, 12 February: 'We are getting near to a critical point, when the whole future direction of European politics will be decided.'[47]

A furtive visitor slipped into the Reich Chancellery in Berlin on Sunday. Dr Vojtech Tuka, once a respected Slovak professor, then sentenced to 15 years in jail for seeking Slovak autonomy, had come to plead with the Führer to make Slovakia independent. 'I lay the destiny of my people in your hands, my Führer.' Emerging from the audience, he commented: 'This is the greatest day of my life.'[48]

Next day, 13 February, the tall, thin, sad-faced figure of Sir Nevile Henderson was again seen in the British Embassy, Berlin, after four months recuperation from serious illness and exhaustion. 'Physically I was still unfit,' he admitted later, 'but morally I was somewhat recovered from the pessimism and disgust which I had felt.' He believed the rumours of German aggression against Holland, Switzerland and even against London, had been circulated largely by the Nazis, and were premature.[49] He immediately began to see his old contacts; in only five days he believed he had sufficient material to send his first assessment. And in it he made the most unfortunate misjudgement of his whole colourful career.

Fears of a German attack on Holland were subsiding. The decrease in tension was reported to the Cabinet on Wednesday, 15 February, when Halifax described a meeting with the Dutch Foreign Minister the previous day. 'Dr Patijin did not attach great importance to the rumour of a possible German invasion of Holland.... I did not say very much to Dr Patijin as to our position, except to point out that we are almost as nearly interested as the Dutch themselves in the maintenance of the integrity of Holland.' Signs of military activity in Germany were reported by Mason-MacFarlane, he continued, but 'there is nothing, however, which definitely portends military activity on a large scale or even partial mobilization'. Likewise, a report by the War Office Intelligence Section, dated 8 February, claimed there were no German military measures pointing to action in the West, East or South.[50]

This report was infinitely more mistaken than Henderson's first detailed assessment, which reached the Foreign Office at breakfast-time on Sunday, 19 February.[51] Sir Nevile had seen Göring on the previous morning and had had a 'long and as usual frank talk. My definite impression since my return here is that Herr Hitler does not contemplate any adventures at the moment, and that all stories and rumours to the contrary are completely without foundation.' Subsequent events apparently showed this bold statement to be ludicrously incorrect. Yet, Sir Nevile did qualify his assertion in a rarely quoted passage, soon to be proved almost totally accurate: 'That Memel will eventually and possibly sooner rather than later, revert to Germany is a foregone conclusion and a settlement as regards Danzig is equally so. Czechoslovakia may also be squeezed, but in these respects I doubt whether Herr Hitler wishes to force the pace unless his own hand is forced. I believe in fact that he would now like in his heart to return to the fold of comparative respectability.' He admitted: 'These may sound strange opinions in the light of all rumours current during the last few months.'[52]

Perhaps Chamberlain had seen the telegram when he wrote that Sunday: 'With a thrush singing in the garden, the sun shining and the rooks beginning to discuss among themselves the prospects of the coming nesting season, I feel as though spring were getting near.... All the information I get seems to point in the direction of peace.'[53] As usual, Halifax doubted, and rebuked Sir Nevile in a telegram the following day. Prospects of improvements in Anglo-German relations were faint, he said 'unless and until your German friends can really show more than smooth words as evidence of friendly hearts'.[54] But Sir Nevile was not to be subdued. On 22 February he sent a further despatch, with more details of the 'loose ends' of his talk with Göring the previous weekend. Göring had been 'very anxious' to know all about a decoration Sir Nevile had received from the King. 'I spoke in glowing terms of it and referred to mantles, chains and banners etc. Göring clapped me on the shoulder and said "Such orders are never given to foreigners, are they?" I told him very, very seldom, which made him look regretful. He has always in mind a visit to London one day and the decoration part might be decisive. It is a point to bear in mind if ever the day came....' As regards matters of more immediate business, 'My instinctive feeling is that this year will be the decisive one, as to whether Hitler comes down on the side of peaceful development and closer cooperation with the West or decides in favour of further adventures eastward.... If we handle him right, my belief is that he will become gradually more pacific. But if we treat him as a pariah or mad dog we shall turn him finally and irrevocably into one.'[55]

The momentum of British Army improvements, which had been set in motion by the threat to Holland, now resulted on 22 February in approval for Hore-Belisha's proposals to reorganize the Mobile Division into two smaller divisions, and equip these and four Regular divisions for Europe. The first echelon of the regular army was to be sent to Europe within 21 days of the outbreak of war, and the second within 60. The four Territorial divisions would also be fully equipped for a Continental conflict. Chamberlain had come to this conclusion 'with some reluctance', but saw no alternative.

Halifax said he was worried over the lack of a definite reply from France on the question of staff talks. 'I hope the French are not occupying time in working out a number of suggestions that would prove inconvenient to us, such as, for example, conscription.'[56]

At the end of February, Henderson was still sending optimistic cables from Berlin: one, on the disturbing reports of German troop movements, claimed, in concurrence with Mason-MacFarlane, 'The German Army is passing through a phase of its evolution in which very much that would normally be abnormal is in point of fact normal.'[57] A second gave another long description of the current situation. 'During the last few weeks a period of calm has ensued.... Although it is suggested in some quarters that this calm may only be a prelude to another storm, I am not inclined to take that pessimistic view at present. Both from the economic and political points of view, the moment is more one for stocktaking than planning new adventures.'[58] This did not reach the Foreign Office until 2 March, by when Henderson had had his first doubts. His first indication of imminent trouble came at the annual banquet, on 1 March that year, which Hitler gave to the diplomatic corps. 'He carefully avoided looking me in the face as he was speaking to me: he kept his eyes fixed over my right shoulder and confined his remarks to general subjects, while stressing the point that it was not Britain's business to interfere with Germany in Central Europe.... I had heard it before, but though he said nothing new or startling, his attitude left me with a feeling of vague uneasiness.'[59]

But the Cabinet seemed to have forgotten its fears of attack in the West. At the 2 March meeting, Holland and Switzerland were not mentioned, for the first time for many weeks. Halifax was unwell and Chamberlain took his place. The French had finally agreed to Staff talks, but Gamelin wanted them conducted at Chief of Staff level. The CID felt this level too high and a signal had accordingly been sent to Paris. The question of a Supply Ministry was again discussed. This time the topic was brought up by the new Minister, Lord Chatfield, who, with Lord Winterton, had prepared a paper against the idea.[60] 'A Ministry of Supply should not be set up in peacetime,' he urged, although 'all preparations should be made at once for the setting up of a Ministry of Supply in time of war', and the decision on when it should actually be brought into operation deferred until the onset of emergency; 'compulsory powers for the Ministry of Supply over labour are not practicable.' Hore-Belisha said if the Ministry were inevitable in an emergency, it should be established now, 'when it can be without dislocation'. The existing supply branches should be left in their present offices, but placed under the control of a single Minister. This, he maintained, could be done without compulsory powers. But most of the Cabinet felt public opinion would be in opposition and the main recommendations of the paper were approved.[61]

Now, in the first days of March, the first ripples of the impending crisis appeared, hardly discernible in the general ebb and flow of international manoeuvring. A letter from the British Consul at Bratislava, to Troutbeck in Prague, reached the Foreign Office on 3 March. 'Last week certain rumours reached me from fairly well informed sources which are rather disquieting.... The financial position of the [Slovak] Government seems to be growing rapidly worse. The Czechs are withholding their financial support and it looks as if in a few months a disastrous situation may arise.' Germanophile extremists might undertake 'some kind of violent action'.[62]

Three days later, Halifax received Hitler's reply to the British and French Notes delivered to him on 8 February, on the question of a German guarantee for Czechoslovakia. It dwelt at length with 'wild tendencies' of some sections inside Czechoslovakia. 'The German Government ... considers it to be necessary first to await clarification of the internal development of Czechoslovakia and the improvement of that country's relations with the surrounding States which may result therefrom, before the time for any further statement of its attitude can be said to have arrived.'[63]

As this message arrived, Newton was cabling from Prague: 'Relations between Czechs and Slovaks seem to be heading for a crisis.'[64] The Czech President, Hacha, had dismissed the Ruthenian Government, whose separatist intrigues had seemed dangerous. Ashton-Gwatkin, Chief Clerk at the Foreign Office and newly returned from meeting Ribbentrop, Funk and Göring in Berlin, had an optimistic report to offer. While he 'did not rule out the possibility of further pressure ... on Czechoslovakia', he felt in general that 'the atmosphere had been very friendly. He had gained the impression that no new adventures of a large type were contemplated.'[65]

Hore-Belisha now introduced his Army Estimates in the House of Commons, and embodied in his speech was the new principle that Britain should have a Continental Army, capable of taking the field against a first-class European power. This speech was welcomed by the Conservatives; the Labour opposition made no protest. Some murmurings came from the press; according to the *Evening Standard*, a 'willingness to send this heavy complement of land power across the water can only prescribe our strategy and shatter our finances', and the *Daily Sketch* commented: 'Our help to France would best be rendered in the air, not by the Army.... To undertake this military burden is unnecessary and unwise.' But the *Observer* made the most accurate point; many of Hore-Belisha's statements were couched in the future tense and 'would not be realized if "the day" were to supervene say, tomorrow.' But a start had been made. Duff Cooper said the speech was 'probably the most satisfactory statement with regard to the Army that had ever been made in the House'. Churchill praised the 'carefully considered statement ... which will be looked upon as one of the definite pronouncements on behalf of the War Office on military policy'.[66] Abroad, the news of Britain's revised military deployment plans was greeted by elation in Paris, anger in Berlin and scepticism in Moscow. Maisky declared he was quite convinced Britain could not stand against German aggression, even with French help, without Soviet support.[67]

Also on 9 March, Henderson was enjoying his last day of optimism. He wrote another long, hopeful, unfortunate despatch for the Foreign Office. 'The German people as a whole are longing for peace. Hitler himself fought in the World War and his dislike of bloodshed, or anyway of dead Germans, is intense. His personal tastes are artistic and he has the artist's desire to satisfy them.... On every reasonable ground Hitler should be sincere when he says that he is looking forward to a long period of peace.... I can find no justification for the theory that he is mad or even verging on madness; I am of the opinion that he is not thinking today in terms of war.' Much depended on whether Britain could count on Hitler's word, if he gave it. 'Personally, I would not go further than to say that, as an individual he would be as likely to keep it as any other foreign statesman.' He did, however, finish with a note nearer to truth. 'I would sum up Germany's immediate objectives, i.e. within the next year or so, as follows: Memel, Danzig and colonies, and the complete subordination of Czechoslovakia politically and economically to Germany. We may dislike the latter, but geographically speaking it is inevitable.'[68]

Sir Nevile would not have to eat his words alone: on 10 March Sir Samuel Hoare told his constituents that the Five Years' Peace Plan was a realistic hope, and that it would lead to a 'Golden Age', though – he admitted – only *if* the statesmen of Europe could work together.[69] And Chamberlain, leaving for a long weekend's fishing, gave an extremely hopeful assessment to Lobby Correspondents: a disarmament conference might meet before the end of the year, he said. Confident or not himself, he intended at least to make the British people so. Halifax, though, disagreed with Chamberlain's briefing to the newspapermen, and on 10 March wrote to tell him so. 'I tried to see you today, but found that, very wisely, you had managed to get away ... as we can't talk, you won't mind my putting my difficulty quite frankly.' He feared the publicity given to the hopes of early progress in disarmament, 'which, however desirable, I cannot regard as probable', would not 'do good' in Germany, and he also feared the

French might be disturbed. 'You know that I never wish to be tiresome or take departmental views! And, of course, I realize all the time how immense is the personal burden on you, and how personal is the contribution that nobody but you can make. But none the less I think that when you are going to make such a general review about Foreign Affairs it might be helpful and well if you felt able to let me know in advance.'[70] 'Your rebuke is most delicately conveyed and was fully merited,' replied Chamberlain from Chequers on 11 March. 'I was horrified at the result of my talks to the press.... I promise faithfully not to do it again, but to consult you beforehand.'[71]

At the very moment that Hoare spoke to his constituents; that Henderson's despatch was being prepared for transmission; that Chamberlain was receiving Halifax's letter of admonishment, Czechoslovakia was collapsing. And although Sir Nevile still sent his report to London where it was received on 16 March, he hurriedly added a sad sentence: 'P.S. The above despatch was written before the present crisis in Czechoslovakia became acute, and is consequently to that extent academical for the moment.'[72]

Talks between the Czechs and Slovaks broke down on Wednesday 8 March and that night Hacha dismissed the core of the Slovak Government, including the Premier, Tiso. Czech troops prepared to move in and martial law was declared on 10 March. At 8.36 p.m. Henderson cabled from Berlin to report rumours of plans to send in German troops. He added: 'If Hitler seeks adventure the most obvious form which it would be likely to take would be some coup in Czechoslovakia.' Sir Orme Sargent added a minute to this telegram when it arrived at the Foreign Office: 'I cannot refrain from contrasting this very accurate forecast with the one he gave in his telegram as recently as 18 February.'[73] Hitler, initially caught by surprise at the speed of events in Czechoslovakia, reacted rapidly. On Saturday, 11 March, he instructed Keitel to draft an ultimatum on Bohemia and Moravia, which he intended to take. Orders were sent to Nazi agents in Czech and Slovak territory. When Karol Sidor, named by Hacha the new Premier of Slovakia, held his first Cabinet meeting on the Saturday evening, the session was abruptly interrupted by Hitler's henchmen, who ordered Cabinet Ministers to proclaim Slovakia's independence immediately. Sidor, to gain time, insisted on another Cabinet meeting. To avoid Nazi intimidation he decided to hold it in his own apartment – or, this being still deemed too dangerous, local newspaper offices. But Tiso escaped from captivity, and announced he had been invited to see the Führer.

'I doubt whether Herr Hitler has taken any decision yet,' Henderson telephoned from Berlin that day. But the next, the Consul at Munich told him: 'I understand state of emergency has been declared for Munich garrison. There have been troop movements during the weekend in direction of Austria.'[74] Yet after hearing this, Sir Nevile sent another hopeful cable to London: 'Up to the present I have no evidence that the German Government intend to exploit the present unrest in Czechoslovakia.' He believed that Hitler, 'a master of turning circumstances to suit his purpose' was waiting to see how events developed.[75] Early on Monday, the anniversary of the Great War – and of Hitler's *Anschluss* – Tiso set off by train for Vienna on his way to Berlin. In Berlin, Henderson 'adjured Weizsäcker to see that nothing was done to violate the Munich Agreement', or upset Oliver Stanley's proposed visit to Berlin. 'I found Weizsäcker completely noncommittal,' he wrote, 'and all that he could assure me was that whatever was done would be done in a "decent" manner. He repeated that phrase more than once.'[76] By now even Sir Nevile was 'filled with the gloomiest forebodings'. Soon afterwards he advised the Czech Ambassador, Mastny, to propose an immediate visit to Berlin of his Foreign Minister who was known to favour co-operation with the Germans[77] – but he made no mention of this proposal to Halifax.[78]

Tiso reached Vienna and was rushed to an aircraft for Berlin. In London, Foreign Office officials were drafting a Memorandum 'On the Position of HMG in connexion with possible Developments of the Slovak Crisis'. 'If German intervention takes place there will clearly be considerable pressure on HMG to take some action.... It is clearly undesirable to make any protest which we are are not prepared to implement or to make statements which would only irritate Hitler without affecting his plans.... If the internal situation in Germany has convinced him that some action is essential in Czechoslovakia, there is nothing we can do to stop him short of war.' It might be held that Britain was bound by her undertaking in the annex to the Munich Agreement to stand by the offer of an international guarantee. 'We could not, however, take any effective action unless the French Government also decided to take action.' Ogilvie-Forbes claimed that by Monday, 13 March, Hitler had changed his mind to present an ultimatum to the Czechs and had decided instead to march. The Czechs for their part made one last desperate and dangerous attempt to preserve their nation's independence: Hacha asked for an interview with Hitler. Tiso, meanwhile, arrived in Berlin and at the same time, Henderson telephoned London to say that the Slovak extremists had also been invited to Berlin. Hitler, by Monday evening, was almost ready to move. Already Hungarian support had been bought by the promise of Ruthenia. 'Heartfelt thanks!' gushed Miklos Horthy, Hungarian Regent.[79]

Now Hitler needed only a suitable stooge. At 7.40 p.m. Tiso was taken into the Führer's room at the Chancellery. Conditions inside Czechoslovakia had become intolerable, Hitler ranted. 'The old Benes spirit has come to life again.' The Slovaks had let him down – he had

108

protected Slovakia after Munich, and had thought the country wanted to be independent. Did she or did she not want her freedom? Give the answer now, Tiso was told. 'It was a question not of days but of hours.' Hungary had wanted Slovakia after Munich, Hitler continued, and he alone had prevented it. But for how much longer? And, brilliantly cued, Ribbentrop handed Hitler a report announcing Hungarian troop movements on the Slovak frontier.[80] Tiso telephoned Bratislava to request an emergency meeting of the Slovak Cabinet, and was hastily sent back home from Berlin. Despite an attempt by some Slovak deputies to discuss the subject at least, independence was announced, as planned, on the morning of 14 March. Also followed, as arranged by Hitler and Tiso, an appeal for German protection.

In Prague, Hacha and Chvalkovsky had been anxiously awaiting a reply to their request for an interview with Hitler. On the afternoon of the 14th Hitler graciously consented to see them, and they left by train – immediately after receiving a Hungarian ultimatum.

In London urgent discussion began at the Foreign Office between Corbin and Cadogan: 'There was probably nothing effective they could do to prevent the execution of a German plan,' said Sir Alexander 'if Hitler had determined to carry it out.' Corbin said that he supposed that the British Government were under some obligation in view of their promise of a guarantee. To this Sir Alexander replied that 'it might be held that they were morally under some obligation in view of their promise of a guarantee; it could equally be maintained, however, that they had been released from it by the fact that they had tried to negotiate an international guarantee of Czechoslovakia, but had failed through no fault of their own. . . . They had always made it plain that they would not contemplate an individual British guarantee of Czechoslovakia.'[81] Chamberlain stood in the House of Commons during the afternoon of Tuesday, 14 March, to answer angry questions over Germany's activity and Britain's inactivity. What were the effects of Germany's interference in Czechoslovakia on Britain's guarantee to that country? The guarantee, he retorted, referred only to unprovoked aggression. 'No such aggression has taken place.' That evening Henderson was urgently instructed. 'Please take earliest opportunity of conveying following message to the German Government. . . . His Majesty's Government have no desire to interfere unnecessarily in matters with which other Governments may be more directly concerned than this country. They are, however, as the German Government will surely appreciate, deeply concerned . . . they would deplore any action in Central Europe which would cause a setback to the growth of . . . general confidence.'[82] Vague and useless, the message was in any case not delivered till next morning, when all was over.

'Nothing but the direct and immediate threat of war would have stopped Hitler at that stage,' wrote Henderson afterwards.[83] Chamberlain too thought Britain could do nothing except watch Czechoslovakia crack and crumble into a confusion of minorities. The Cabinet desperately thought of reasons why Britain need not honour her guarantee: first it had yet to be agreed upon by all four Powers involved; second there had not *yet* been unprovoked aggression. A third, and even more shameful, reason was to be put forward by the Cabinet when it next met. All were attempts to hide the real one: Britain's military power was totally inadequate.

The frail, aged, trembling Hacha arrived at Berlin's Anhalt Station on Tuesday night, 14 March. His weak heart prevented him flying. As he walked slowly towards the SS guard of honour on the station platform, he leant heavily on his daughter's arm. Ribbentrop strode forward, his smooth face beaming, one arm outstretched to welcome Hacha, the other tenderly cradling an abundant bouquet of flowers for his daughter. The Czech party was taken to luxurious rooms at the Adlon Hotel, where Mlle Hacha found another present, a large box of chocolates from Adolf Hitler.

Hacha knew that advanced units of the German Army had already crossed the border of his country. The takeover had begun; Hitler merely wanted the appearance of approval from the Czech leader. Yet he did not condescend to see Hacha and Chvalkovsky until after 1 o'clock in the morning. They were then confronted by Hitler, Ribbentrop, Weizsäcker, Göring, Keitel and, nearby for Hacha's benefit, Hitler's doctor, Theodor Morell. Old man Hacha begged for the life of his country. He debased himself – 'he was convinced that the destiny of the Czechs lay in the Führer's hands' – he grovelled and he pleaded; he 'felt that it was precisely the Führer who would understand his holding the view that Czechoslovakia had the right to live a national life'. All the while Hitler listened; then rapped out his reply: 'I have given the order for the invasion by the German troops and for the incorporation of Czechoslovakia into the German Reich.' Hacha and Chvalkovsky sat as if carved from stone. 'Only their eyes showed they were alive,' wrote Schmidt.

Hitler's voice continued flat and metallic. 'Tomorrow morning at 6 o'clock the German Army will enter from all sides. The German Air Force will occupy the Czech airfields.' Two methods could be used: either brute force, or peaceful entry. 'I am doing all this not from hatred but in order to protect Germany ... the hours are passing; at 6 the troops will march.' Saying he was almost ashamed to admit it, Hitler added: 'For every Czech battalion there is a German division.' The abject, shaken Czech Ministers were led into an ante-room and Ribbentrop and Göring took over where Hitler had left off. Half of Prague would lie in ruins within two hours, the Czechs were told. Documents were pushed in front of them, pens thrust in their hands for them to sign the surrender. 'I should be sorry if I had to bomb beautiful Prague,' threatened Göring. Hundreds of bombers would leave at dawn if the papers were not signed. Hacha suddenly slumped, his face white under the harsh lights. 'Hacha has fainted,' cried Göring in horror. The Nazis almost panicked; if the Czech President died on them, reported Schmidt, they feared 'the whole world will say tomorrow that he was murdered.'

Morell ran into the room. He opened his bag, pulled out a syringe, and doped Hacha back to life – sufficiently at least to sign his country's death certificate. Hitler ran into his inner office, threw his arms around his women secretaries. 'Kiss me!' he invited: 'Children! This is the greatest day of my life! I shall go down into history as the greatest German!' The time was 4 o'clock: two hours later German columns wound their way into Moravia and Bohemia, and Hungarian units moved into Ruthenia. The date was 15 March – the Ides of March.[84]

7

Crossing the Stream

News of the invasion reached the Foreign Office at 7.25 a.m., when Newton telephoned from Prague. The *Wehrmacht* forced forward against minimum resistance. The proclamation announcing the transfer of the country into a German protectorate was declared from the windows of the historic Hradshin Palace. The first comment from Henderson on these dramatic events, came at 9.50 a.m. 'HMG will doubtless consider advisability of postponing the visit of the President of the Board of Trade to Germany.'[1] Sir Nevile wrote in his memoirs: 'There was some question of my sitting up on the night of 14 March.... But I could do nothing more, and preferred to go unhappily to bed.' His first glance at the morning newspapers was sufficient to confirm his worst fears. 'It was the final shipwreck of my mission to Berlin. Hitler had crossed the Rubicon.'[2]

'Do you wonder that I regard Berlin as a soul-scarifying job?' he wrote to Halifax. 'Hitler has gone straight off the deep end again.' Then: 'What distresses me more than anything else is the handle which it will give to the critics of Munich.'[3] British Ministers hurriedly assembled to discuss policy; and the Minutes of the meeting seemed to indicate that those critics of Munich would be justified, that appeasement was by no means finished, and the change at the beginning of February merely temporary. And yet the attitude displayed was a legacy of appeasement, not appeasement itself; Chamberlain's excuses for not assisting the Czechs may have been shameful, but he believed he could do nothing else.

The meeting opened with Halifax's report; the French Government, he said, 'took much the same view of the matter as we do, and held that there is no possibility of effectively opposing what is taking place, or of influencing the position.' Phipps had seen Bonnet and Beranger, who both felt that 'the less we interfered in this crisis the better. They had both remarked that this renewed rift between the Czechs and the Slovaks showed that we nearly went to war last autumn on behalf of a State which was not "viable".' Almost immediately, Chamberlain put forward his reason for British non-intervention, based on these remarks. 'I think the fundamental fact is that the State whose frontiers we undertook to guarantee against unprovoked aggression has now completely broken up.' He conveniently ignored the fact that German aggression, direct or indirect, was partly responsible. Halifax put forward another suggestion. 'We ... regarded the terms of our guarantee as morally binding before the guarantee had technically come into force, because we intended our action to be a means of steadying the position during what was thought to be a purely transitional situation. We had, however, never intended permanently to assume responsibility for a monopoly of obligation in this matter.'

But this excuse clashed with Chamberlain's who therefore declared: 'If it is agreed that the argument which I have suggested is valid, it will perhaps be undesirable to supplement it with the argument put forward by the Foreign Secretary. I also think that it would be wise to take an early opportunity of saying that, in the circumstances which have arisen, our guarantee has come to an end.' Then, sensing no doubt the obvious criticism of his excuse for non-action, Chamberlain added: 'It might be true that the disruption of Czechoslovakia has been largely engineered by Germany, but our guarantee was not a guarantee against the exercise of moral pressure.' The German actions had all been taken under the guise of agreement with the Czech Government, and the Germans could, therefore, plead innocence.

The Cabinet agreed Stanley's visit should be postponed, though he warned: 'The German Government's reaction is likely to be to break off the existing trade talks.' Halifax wondered whether Henderson should be recalled: 'On the whole I am against this step, since, although it is easy to recall an Ambassador, it is not so easy to find reasons to justify his return.... The same argument, however, does not apply if we recall our Ambassador to report, in which case he could return to Berlin after a week or so. While I do not feel strongly on the matter, I think there is something to be said for adopting this course. I am reluctant to allow public opinion in America or in South-Eastern Europe to think that we are inert.' But the general view of the Cabinet was that 'the step suggested was premature. The postponement of the visit of the British Minister to Berlin will be a signal mark of our disapproval.'

The Prime Minister's statement to the House was discussed. The Opposition was pressing for a debate, in which Chamberlain would have to make a full speech. Chamberlain proposed to start by 'expressing HMG's regret', and to end with an announcement of the cancellation of Stanley's visit. Halifax evidently wanted something stronger. 'It is significant that this is the first occasion on which Germany has applied her shock tactics to the domination of non-Germans. I think it is important to find language which will imply that Germany is now being led on to a dangerous path.' Chamberlain and Halifax would prepare a draft.

Of the loan to Czechoslovakia, Simon disclosed that £3 million had so far been drawn; he had sent a message that further payment should be suspended.[4]

Chamberlain defended his Government's policy in the Commons debate that afternoon. 'The position has altered since the Slovak Diet declared the independence of Slovakia. The effect of this declaration put an end by internal disruption to the State whose frontiers we had proposed to guarantee, and HMG cannot accordingly hold themselves bound by this obligation.' Chamberlain added: 'It is natural that I should bitterly regret what has now occurred, but do not let us on that account be deflected from our course. Let us remember that the desire of all the peoples of the world still remains concentrated on the hopes of peace.'

But despite the apparent unity at the morning Cabinet meeting, some Ministers were uneasy. Hoare, an ardent supporter of appeasement, 'felt that my part in the Government was finished, and that I had better retire from public life'.[5] Halifax seemed to want to take a vigorous line, but to feel that such an attitude would be useless. He told the German Ambassador that afternoon: 'I can well understand Herr Hitler's taste for bloodless victories, but one of these days he will find himself up against something that will not be bloodless.' But he told the French Ambassador later he wanted to avoid either of the two countries taking a position which might lead to conflict.[6]

Within hours, though, Chamberlain was to display – publicly now – his radical change of attitude. He took this drastic step for three reasons: first, he had simply had more time to think; and second – adeptly – he now realized that public opinion had changed. *The Times* and the *Daily Mail*, both strong supporters of appeasement, both now hardened their attitudes. More startling was the reaction to Simon's speech in the Commons, when he tried to explain away Germany's invasion. Members erupted 'in a pitch of anger rarely seen'. By contrast Duff Cooper labelled Hitler 'thrice-perjured traitor and breaker of oaths', and was massively applauded.

The third reason was a sudden alarm over Roumania, on Thursday, 16 March. The Roumanian Ambassador, V. F. Tilea, asked for an urgent interview at the Foreign Office, and told Sir Orme Sargent that his Government, from secret sources, had good reason to believe the Germans would reduce Hungary to vassalage within the next few months, and would then proceed to disintegrate Roumania as they had Czechoslovakia.[7] In the turmoil of Foreign Office activity, Tilea's warning attracted minimum notice; concentration was still fixed on Prague – the first German mechanized units had squealed through the cobbled streets of the Czech capital at 9.30 a.m., and during the day

Hitler strutted into Hradschin Castle to announce the Protectorate of Bohemia and Moravia.

Meanwhile Henderson, like Chamberlain, had had time to think: in a telephone call to Halifax on 16 March, he strongly condemned Hitler's action as 'entirely contrary to right of self-determination and utterly immoral. It constitutes a wrong which will soon call for redress.'[8] Opinion in Britain and especially in Parliamentary circles was strengthening so fast that Chamberlain's position would be untenable unless he acted soon. 'The feeling in the lobbies is that Chamberlain will either have to go or completely reverse his policy,' wrote Nicolson next day.[9] And, contrary to the Cabinet decision of 15 March, Chamberlain and Halifax now decided temporarily to recall Henderson, who, on 18 March, 'left Berlin feeling that I might well never return'.[10]

Also on 17 March, Tilea came again to the Foreign Office, and this time saw Halifax. During the last few days, he said, the Roumanian Government had received a 'request' from the Germans to grant them a monopoly of Roumanian exports, and 'to adopt certain measures of restriction of Roumanian industrial production in German interests'. Tilea added: 'If these conditions were accepted, Germany would guarantee the Roumanian frontiers.' It seemed to his Government 'something very much like an ultimatum'. He stressed an invasion might follow in a matter of days; pointing out that 'Germany had more troops in Czechoslovakia than were needed in that country'.[11]

A terrifying account of Hitler's warlike preparations was now given by a correspondent newly returned from Berlin. Rumours reaching the Foreign Office indicated that Mussolini might emulate Hitler and make exorbitant claims in North Africa, or occupy Albania; other reports said Hitler might launch a surprise attack on the British Fleet; a note arrived from Phipps in Paris, the typing full of mistakes because he had done it himself. 'Hitler's personal wish ... is to make war on Great Britain before June or July....'[12] Together with these other alarms, Tilea's warning now had dramatic effect. Chamberlain had urgent talks with Halifax; they studied the draft text of the speech which Chamberlain was to make in the evening in Birmingham, mainly on domestic affairs and social security – and they began to make alterations.

Soon afterwards Halifax told Joseph Kennedy that 'the speech that the Prime Minister was making ... would be generally regarded as an indication of how deeply British opinion was moved and what might be the reactions from this emotion in the fields of policy'. He added that a great many people were re-examining past attitudes.[13] Next, he telegraphed Henderson a last task before leaving Berlin. 'Please inform German Government that HMG desire to make it plain to them that they cannot but regard the events of the past few days as a complete repudiation of the Munich Agreement.... HMG must also take this occasion to protest against the changes in Czechoslovakia by German military action, which are in their view devoid of any basis of legality.'[14] As this telegram was despatched, the Prime Minister was delivering his speech in Birmingham's ornate Town Hall. Chamberlain, man of peace, small and insignificant in the huge chamber, issued a solemn public warning to Hitler.

'Public opinion in the world has received a sharper shock than has ever yet been administered to it, even by the present régime in Germany.... I am sure that it must be far-reaching in its results upon the future.... It has been suggested that this occupation of Czechoslovakia was the direct consequence of the visit which I paid to Germany last autumn ... really, I have no need to defend my visits to Germany last autumn, for what was the alternative? Nothing that we could have done, nothing that France could have done, or Russia could have done, could possibly have saved Czechoslovakia.' Another reason for Munich, he added, had been the belief that by 'mutual goodwill and understanding of what were the limits of the desires of others, it should be possible to resolve all differences by discussion'. But now had come the 'disappointment, the indignation, that those hopes have been so wantonly shattered.... What has become of this declaration of "No further territorial ambition"? What has become of the assurance "We don't want Czechs in the Reich"? What regard has been paid here to that principle of self-determination on which Herr Hitler argued so vehemently with me?' The invasion marked a new turn in German policy. 'The events which have taken place this week in complete disregard of the principles laid down by the German Government itself seem to fall into a different category, and they must cause us all to be asking ourselves: "Is this the end of an old adventure, or is it the beginning of a new?" "Is this the last attack upon a small State, or is it to be followed by others? Is this, in fact, a step in the direction of an attempt to dominate the world by force?"' And he warned: 'No greater mistake could be made than to suppose that, because it believes war to be a senseless and cruel thing, this nation has so lost its fibre that it will not take part to the utmost of its power in resisting such a challenge if it ever were made.' The small figure sat down; Birmingham Town Hall echoed with acclaim; appeasement had been publicly ended.

Meanwhile, Halifax worked late at the Foreign Office over Tilea's warning: he was anxious to sound out other countries who might be affected, and at 10 p.m. cables were sent to the British Ambassadors at Warsaw, Ankara, Athens and Belgrade, with instructions to report the opinions of the respective Governments.[15] Similar instructions were despatched to Phipps, and Seeds was asked to discover whether the Soviet Government would actively help Roumania if requested.[16] But at lunchtime next day, an urgent message arrived from Bucharest:

the British Ambassador, Hoare, asked Halifax to cancel the telegrams. The Foreign Secretary had to wait another three hours to learn why and meanwhile disturbing news reached him from Riga. Arms were apparently being brought into Memel from Germany, and German troops were being moved by sea to East Prussia.[17]

Hoare telephoned from Bucharest at 3.40 p.m. 'It appeared to be so utterly improbable that the Minister for Foreign Affairs would not have informed me that an *immediate* threatening situation had developed here that I called on him as soon as your telegram had been deciphered.... He told me that there was not a word of truth in it.'[18]

A special Cabinet meeting had been called for 5 p.m. The Prime Minister, celebrating his 70th birthday, opened with regrets for having asked his colleagues to meet at the weekend, 'but it seems we are entering upon another rather troubled period.' Halifax reported: 'Although it seems that Roumania is not faced with the immediately threatening situation which was thought to exist, I think that it will be an advantage if the Cabinet took this opportunity of considering what our position would be if a situation such as was envisaged were to arise in the future.' Gone were the times when Britain's position would remain undecided, in the hope that entanglements would thereby be avoided. It made no difference that the threat to Roumania was non-existent; and the subsequent Cabinet discussions, stemming from the false ultimatum report, were to have consequences which led Britain to war.

'Looking at the matter on political grounds,' said Halifax, 'my view is that, if Germany committed an act of naked aggression on Roumania, it would be very difficult for this country not to take all the action in her power to rally resistance ... and to take part in that resistance herself.' Lord Chatfield gave the military view. The Chiefs of Staff believed Britain alone could not stop an invasion of Roumania without the support of Poland and Russia.

Chamberlain gave the reasoning behind his speech the night before. 'Last Wednesday, the German action in Czechoslovakia had only just been taken, and the information available was so imperfect, that neither I nor any of you had had time to give the matter proper consideration, or to decide how far the situation had changed. It was unfortunate that, owing to the Opposition's demands, it was necessary to have a debate in the House of Commons immediately on the heel of these events.' Since then, he had 'come definitely to the conclusion that Herr Hitler's attitude makes it impossible to continue to negotiate on the old basis with the Nazi régime.... No reliance can be placed on any of the assurances given by the Nazi leaders.' The Cabinet expressed full agreement.

'The real point,' said Stanley, 'is not whether we can prevent Roumania from being overrun, but whether, if we went to war with

Germany, we could defeat her. If this happened, the fact that Roumania might be temporarily overrun would not affect the final issue.' A danger existed of speaking in terms of military attacks on this or that country, warned Hore-Belisha. 'We are now faced with a new technique, which brought about collapse from inside.' He was 'in favour of reconsidering our policy and contracting frank and open alliances with countries such as Poland and Russia. I also think it will be necessary to take steps vastly to increase our military strength.' The Prime Minister declared: 'I think Poland is very likely the key to the situation.' The Cabinet agreed. And the decision had been taken which would lead Britain direct to conflict. At this crucial meeting, Chamberlain wanted to move even faster than his colleagues, to raise the issue of compulsory conscription, or the establishment of a Supply Ministry – but the Cabinet decided to defer further consideration of these points.[19]

The next step must be to approach Poland. But that evening Phipps cabled from Paris that the Secretary-General of the Foreign Ministry, Léger, 'strongly suspected that M. Beck had betrayed Roumania or was in the process of doing so'. Léger had declared: 'M. Beck was entirely cynical and false.' His theory must have caused considerable embarrassment in London – he wondered 'whether HMG knew what was the real object of M. Beck's journey to London. He [Léger] knew from a source very secret, but absolutely sure and highly authoritative, that the plan of the Polish Foreign Minister was to ask HMG to make an alliance with Poland, so that there would be a triple Anglo-Franco-Polish alliance under which Great Britain should undertake to come to Poland's help if attacked.... [Beck] knew that HMG could not undertake a definite commitment of the sort.... He would then return to Poland and report his request and its rejection ... and that now it was clear Poland must lean on Germany.'[20]

'It would be wrong,' the German Ambassador at London cabled to Berlin, 'to cherish any illusions that a fundamental change has not taken place in Britain's attitude towards Germany.'[21] The Bulgarian Ambassador reported back that 'energetic diplomatic activity' by the British was imminent in the Balkans; this report was intercepted by German intelligence.[22] Russia's reaction to latest events was revealed to Halifax in a message from Seeds on Sunday morning. 'The Soviet Government proposed that delegates appointed by Britain, the Soviet Union, France, Poland and Roumania should meet to discuss possibilities of common action.'[23] Maisky followed this up with Halifax on Sunday afternoon: he urged Britain to answer Litvinov's call for a conference, but Halifax in his reply said Britain was against the idea for two reasons; first, 'we could hardly in present circumstances manage to send a responsible Minister to take part in the conference,' and second, 'to hold such a conference as M. Litvinov suggested without any certainty that it would be successful was dangerous'.[24] Instead, Britain preferred a less drastic step. Chamberlain told the Cabinet next morning, Monday, 20 March, that at a meeting the previous day, Halifax, Simon, Stanley and himself, had concluded that an announcement by France, Russia, Poland and Britain should be made as soon as possible. The Cabinet agreed to this draft declaration: 'We, the undersigned, hereby declare that inasmuch as peace and security in Europe are matters of common interest and concern, and since European peace and security may be affected by any action which constitutes a threat to the political independence of any European state, we have pledged ourselves immediately to consult together if it appears that any such action is taken.' This declaration, with its reference to 'any European state', widened the area of commitment from the Cabinet conclusion, which had specified 'South-East Europe'. Now Chamberlain claimed: 'The precise form which the *casus belli* might take is perhaps not very material. The real issue is that if Germany showed signs that she intended to proceed with her search for world domination, we must take steps to stop her by attacking her on two fronts. We should attack Germany, not in order to save a particular victim, but in order to pull down the bully.' His statement, in its no-nonsense determination, was worthy of Churchill. Only for a brief moment did Munich seem to echo in the Cabinet Room: the Prime Minister considered 'writing to Mussolini, expressing my unease at Herr Hitler's attitude', but he added immediately that the letter must not convey 'the impression that the Democracies were alarmed at the position, and wanted the Duce to get them out of a difficulty'. This had been precisely the motive for the Munich appeal to Mussolini. The Cabinet agreed to Chamberlain's proposal.[25]

The letter was sent later on Monday. Meanwhile Mussolini's distress was even more acute that that in London or Paris. The Duce had always believed Munich his personal triumph; now, as Ciano noted, the Czechoslovakia of Munich had been shattered. The day before Chamberlain sent his letter, Mussolini had agreed with Ciano that the alliance with Germany must be broken – if it were continued, 'the very stones would cry out'.[26] With Mussolini in this state of mind, action by Chamberlain might well have persuaded him to move away from Hitler, though Mussolini rather believed that even if Italy and all other nations worked together, Germany would still be victorious. But the shadow of appeasement still lingered, and the message did have the effect Chamberlain feared it might. 'Mussolini will answer after striking at Albania,' wrote Ciano. 'This letter strengthens his decision to act, because in it he finds another proof of the inertia of the Democracies.' And the Führer had also decided to write to the Duce; when this message arrived it would drench the weak Italian leader in praise.

Hitler was about to demonstrate his strength once more, this time over Memel. Lithuania's Foreign Minister, Juozas Urbays, was in Berlin on his way back from Rome, and at noon on Monday was summarily informed by Ribbentrop that the question of a Memelland cession could be postponed no longer. Urbays was told to telephone President Smetona of Lithuania 'at once', or 'the Führer will act with lightning speed'; frightened, he hurriedly flew back to Kovno to convey the message in person.[27]

Even if Memel could not be helped, a British initiative to deter further aggression seemed all the more imperative. 'It seems to HMG to be desirable to proceed without delay to the organization of mutual support,' cabled Halifax to the Ambassadors at Paris, Moscow and Warsaw just before Monday midnight. He revealed the declaration agreed by the Cabinet, and instructed the Ambassadors to sound out the respective Governments. 'HMG would be prepared to sign Declaration immediately the three other Governments indicate their readiness.'[28] Events of the last few days had made Beck's visit 'even more opportune than before', Halifax told the Polish Ambassador, Count Raczynski, next morning, 21 March. He told the Ambassador 'that I would put the question to him quite bluntly ... if Roumania was threatened by Germany, would Poland come in?' The Pole replied 'there was a 99 per cent chance'. When the Count was told of Britain's proposal for a joint declaration, he 'warmly applauded the idea'.[29]

As Halifax was seeing Raczynski in London, von Ribbentrop had 'invited' Ambassador Lipski to see him at the German Foreign Ministry, and for the first time displayed a hostile attitude. The Führer was becoming 'increasingly amazed at Poland's behaviour.... Poland must realize that she could not take a middle course between Russia and Germany.' She must have a 'reasonable relationship' with Germany, which must include a joint 'anti-Soviet policy'. Beck should visit Berlin for talks with Hitler, soon, 'lest the Chancellor should come to the conclusion that Poland was rejecting all his offers'.[30] And as this meeting took place, Urbays arrived back at Kovno, to be told that Hitler demanded Lithuanian representatives before him in Berlin – the following day. These delegates should have authority to sign over Memelland. The Lithuanian Cabinet hurriedly assembled; five hours later they agreed to despatch representatives. Hitler, on hearing the news, decided to make a triumphant sea voyage to Memel on the pocket battleship *Deutschland*; plans were made for the warship to leave early next day. A week had passed since his victorious entry into Prague.

There were serious difficulties in the way of the joint declaration by Britain, France, Russia and Poland, despite Raczynski's enthusiasm. 'It is clear that our invitation faces Polish Government and particularly

M. Beck with the necessity for a crucial decision,' cabled Kennard.[31] Acceptance would almost certainly entail an immediate German reaction, and Poland disliked the idea of strengthening ties with Russia, especially after Ribbentrop's threats to Lipski. The possibility increased of the British Cabinet having to choose between Poland and Russia – but, Halifax pointed out: 'It would be unfortunate if we were now so to act as to give the Soviet Government the idea we were pushing her to one side.' With these considerations in mind, the Cabinet met on 22 March. Halifax reported that the general French reaction was favourable. As far as Russia was concerned, 'M. Litvinov seems to be somewhat perturbed that we have not been more enthusiastic over his proposals for a conference'. He added: 'It is probably true that an *Anschluss* of Memel with Germany is to be expected,' and that the reports in the morning newspapers were based upon fact. 'There is, of course, more justification for this course than for certain recent events.' The takeover could be explained away under the list of Versailles grievances.

Chamberlain told the Cabinet that he had had talks with Chatfield and the Service Ministers on defence preparations. 'From the point of view of a sudden air attack without warning, the position is very disturbing, and we are totally devoid of ground defences against such an air attack.' Some way had to be found of bringing stations into action sooner. Conscription would be one answer, to enable stations to be continually manned; but he stressed: 'Unless there is a very marked change in their opinion, the Labour Party will continue to oppose conscription strongly.' Hore-Belisha would have to wait longer for conscription – but Chamberlain was wavering.[32]

On Wednesday the Lithuanian delegation arrived in Berlin, to be confronted by Ribbentrop. Hitler had already sailed for Memelland. But the Nazi Foreign Minister was to find the Lithuanians more stubborn than expected, and by the time night fell the talks were still continuing. In London, Anglo-French discussions began. Attending, apart from Chamberlain and Halifax, were Cadogan, and Phipps who had just flown from Paris; on the French side were only Bonnet and Corbin. Bonnet suggested Britain and France should ask Poland this question: supposing Germany attacked Roumania and Britain and France rendered assistance, what would Poland do? 'If the question were to be put in this form, it would be difficult for Poland to give a negative answer.' It would be an advantage if Soviet help could be obtained, but 'the important thing, however, was not to give Poland a pretext for running out on account of Russia.' Halifax stressed that Russia should not feel ignored.

Chamberlain then apologized for raising a 'rather delicate point'. In Paris in November 1938, Daladier had told him French aircraft production would reach 400 machines a month by the end of spring,

1939. 'Present information seems to confirm the doubts I expressed.' Bonnet admitted 'he had his doubts about the figures given by M. Daladier'; the previous month 100 aircraft had been produced. Chamberlain displayed great satisfaction at the British record. 'Our own difficulties have been successfully overcome, and our production is now nearly 600 aircraft a month.'[33] Could Britain help France build up her output?

Discussions ended at 6.45 p.m. with a firm assurance from France that she would join Britain in the declaration, and shortly a cable arrived from Warsaw with the Polish answer. 'M. Beck said today that he is instructing the Polish Ambassador to propose that HMG and the Polish Government should immediately enter into a secret agreement of consultation.' By keeping the agreement secret, Beck believed, the Poles would not be compelled openly to insist on the exclusion of the Soviets.[34] But now the situation suddenly became still more complicated. As Halifax was considering this Polish suggestion, Litvinov told Seeds: 'We are in agreement with the British proposal and accept the text of the declaration.' But he then insisted on informing the Press the following day. Seeds, unable to dissuade him, hurried off to cable London.[35]

Meanwhile Hitler, seasick on the tossing warship, waited anxiously for news from Berlin. During the evening he had twice sent to Ribbentrop for information on the talks with the Lithuanian delegation. At 1.30 a.m. on Thursday, 23 March, the good news was radioed to the *Deutschland*: Memel belonged to the Reich. This latest news reached London early on Thursday morning. Chamberlain, like Léger, believed the seizure did not call for Anglo-French action; it did not affect the European balance; occupation of the port did not materially increase Germany's strength or her capacity to wage war against France or Britain. And Memel was a residual problem of Versailles. Roumania was a different matter, because she possessed vital war materials which would boost Germany's military potential. The takeover of Memel might even be an advantage to Britain and France – the Poles might now be more willing to cooperate.[36] Chamberlain made a statement on Memel in the Commons on Thursday: Britain would not intervene, but Germany would meet determined opposition if she went further. Bonnet, in resumed talks with Halifax during the afternoon, again raised the question of conscription; once more he met British hesitation. In fact, earlier in the day Chamberlain and Chatfield had seen representatives of the TUC, to discuss this, and possible methods of accelerating rearmament. The response had been 'most unsympathetic'.[37]

Thursday was therefore Hitler's day of triumph. Final signatures were put to the German 'Treaty of Protection' with the Czechs; and the Führer strutted ashore at Memel, his latest conquest. 'You have returned to a mighty new Germany,' he declared. Back in Berlin, Poland became a major preoccupation for Hitler – as she still was for the British Government. On Friday, 24 March, Halifax received the Polish Ambassador with Poland's proposal for a secret agreement. He had also to bear in mind the contents of a report received during the day from Seeds: Stalin was vigorous in his condemnation of the 'so-called Democracies', and especially of the British. His criticisms were more violent than those he made of the Fascists, 'for whose tactics he seems to nourish a certain admiration.... Those innocents at home who believe that Soviet Russia is only waiting an invitation to join the Western democracies should be advised to ponder M. Stalin's advice to his Party: "To be cautious and not allow Soviet Russia to be drawn into conflicts by warmongers who are accustomed to have others pull chestnuts out of the fire." '38

And in Poland, fears were multiplying. The German treaties with Memel and the Czechs were followed by a trade agreement with Roumania on 24 March. 'Signature in rapid succession by Germany of one-sided treaties ... has made Polish public opinion indignant, alarmed, and at the same time defiant,' reported Kennard. According to the Military Attaché, about 10,000 Polish reservists had been called up.39 On Sunday, 26 March, Lipski was scheduled to return to Berlin, after consultations following the heated interview with Ribbentrop. Lipski would bring with him a reply to Germany's demands for Danzig. Hitler reacted almost nervously to the possibility of a Polish refusal: he left Berlin on Saturday night, 25 March, leaving negotiations to Ribbentrop. Before his departure, he conferred with General von Brauchitsch, C-in-C of the German Army, who wrote: 'The Führer does not wish to solve the Danzig question by the use of force. He would not like to drive Poland into the arms of Great Britain by doing so.'40 Hitler was prepared to wait, but not for too long. So Lipski was received by Ribbentrop; as expected, Poland refused Germany's demands, and Ribbentrop reacted with routine bluster – Polish mobilization measures 'reminded him of certain risky steps taken by another State'.

It seemed a race between Hitler's reaction to Poland's defiance and the conclusion of a protection arrangement by Warsaw; yet Poland still feared that Russian inclusion in any declaration would bring dangers both from the Soviet Union, whom Poland suspected, and from Germany. Nor did Chamberlain believe the Soviets valuable allies. 'I must confess to the most profound distrust of Russia,' he wrote that Sunday. 'I have no belief whatever in her ability to maintain an effective offensive, even if she wanted to. And I distrust her motives.' And later: 'I can't believe that she has the same aims and objectives as we have, or any sympathy with democracy as such. She is afraid of Germany and Japan, and would be delighted to see other people fight them.'41 Chamberlain displayed his attitude at an FPC meeting on 27 March. In view of Poland's reluctance to be linked with Russia in a Four-Power declaration, he proposed a public declaration, plus a secret-bilateral understanding. Britain, France and Russia should join in the first, Britain and Poland in the second. Existing Franco-Polish obligations would be merged into this framework. Efforts to build a front against Germany would be frustrated if Russia were too closely involved. 'In these circumstances ... we must abandon the policy of the Four-Power Declaration and concentrate on the country likely to be the next victim of aggression – Roumania.' Roumania had to be protected both for her oil and because 'control of that country by Germany would go far to neutralize an effective naval blockade' by Britain. Roumania, moreover, shielded Poland's flank. 'Poland is vital to the scheme, because the weak point of Germany is her present inability to conduct war on two fronts.' Chamberlain added: 'It will be observed that this plan leaves Soviet Russia out of the picture.... We should have to explain to her that the objections to her open inclusion come not from ourselves but from other quarters.' Chamberlain emphasized the necessity for urgent and immediate action, but 'did not think it expedient to summon an emergency meeting of the Cabinet ... this might cause undue publicity.' Halifax prepared to take the necessary steps.[42]

Lipski had been summoned to the German Foreign Ministry for a further meeting during the day. He was given no opportunity to talk; Ribbentrop harangued him over Polish outrages against the German minority in Poland – an ominous tactic.[43] At the War Office in London, Britain and France attempted talks on closer military cooperation. The French were horrified by details of the size and condition of the troops Britain hoped to use in France, and the British equally perturbed at French reluctance to disclose plans.

Just before midnight on the 27th, Halifax cabled to the Ambassadors at Warsaw and Bucharest: 'It will not be possible to proceed without modification to the proposed Four-Power Declaration.... In any scheme, the inclusion of Poland is vital as the one strong Power bordering on Germany in the East, and the inclusion of Roumania is also of the first importance, since Roumania may be the State primarily menaced by Germany's plans for Eastern expansion.' Although the Cabinet had not been consulted, Halifax claimed the Government had decided on a new idea. Poland and Roumania were to be asked if they were prepared actively to resist if their independence were threatened by Germany; if so, Britain and France would be prepared to come to the help of the threatened State. The assurance to Poland would be dependent upon Poland agreeing to help Roumania, and vice-versa. The Ambassadors were instructed to be ready to discover the views of the Polish and Roumanian Governments.[44]

A Nazi press campaign against the Poles opened next day. German women and children were being molested in the Polish streets, claimed *Die Zeitung*, Göring's newspaper; German houses and shops had been smeared with tar, German farmsteads attacked at night.[45] Ciano noted in his diary that the campaign was a disagreeable reminder of the previous press attacks on Austria and Czechoslovakia. Beck summoned the German Ambassador and gave a strong warning against aggressive attempts to change the Danzig *status quo*. A veiled warning to Hitler came also from Chamberlain, who told the Commons that contacts with European countries went a good deal further than mere consultations. Meanwhile, work hurriedly continued both to complete the work on Britain's new commitment in East Europe and to further improve Britain's ground forces. Both were fully discussed at the Cabinet meeting on 29 March, but even now, Ministers were not informed of the initiative considered in their name; Chamberlain and Halifax merely described the differences encountered with the joint declaration proposal, and hinted that Russia might have to be left out. Germany must be faced with war on two fronts simultaneously, so Poland was 'the key to the situation'. Halifax would, however, 'take what steps are possible to keep in with Russia'.

'I wish at this point to deal with a matter of great urgency and importance, which is not on the agenda,' said Chamberlain. 'Although we are not actually at war, the state of affairs in which we now live could not be described as peacetime in the ordinary sense of the word.' But compulsory conscription could have a 'disastrous effect' on relations with the Labour Party and the Trade Union movement; organized, open opposition would mean decreases in industrial output, and a deplorable psychological effect. So for the moment he still ruled this out; instead, he had asked the War Secretary if he could find any alternatives, and if he could design a scheme which would secure a large increase in the territorial force. Hore-Belisha said the peace strength of the territorial Field Divisions amounted to 130,000 men: he now proposed to raise these divisions to war strength, 170,000 men, and then to double the Field Army to 340,000. Every Territorial Army (TA) unit would be over-recruited, to form in due course two duplicate units.[46] For maximum effect abroad, Chamberlain himself would announce these measures to the Commons. And when he did so, his critics immediately condemned them as grossly insufficient: Eden's group combined with Churchill's in tabling a resolution demanding immediate conscription and a National Government. Thirty-six signed the resolution; a few days later, 180 Tory loyalists countered with a resolution pledging full support for Chamberlain. Both were eclipsed by events.

Meanwhile, recruits poured into the TA headquarters throughout Britain; drill halls were crammed; severe shortages arose of instructors, equipment, and uniforms. But training began at weekends, in the evenings, and even in lunch-hours. Time was short.

Britain would have declared war almost immediately, if Mason-MacFarlane had had his way. Ogilvie-Forbes reported: 'The Military Attaché here is in a very warlike mood, and is anxious that we should declare war on Germany within the next three weeks!' He believed: 'If we delay I believe that from the military point of view we shall be taking an unwarrantable risk, and an indefinitely greater one than war in the immediate future ought to represent if we play our cards properly and swiftly.'[47]

Fears of a German attack upon Poland suddenly increased late on Wednesday night and early on Thursday, 29-30 March. British Ministers hastily assembled at 11 a.m. for a special meeting. Halifax apologized for summoning them at such short notice: 'My reason for doing so is that information received yesterday appeared to disclose a possible German intention to execute a *coup de main* against Poland.' The US Ambassador, Mr Kennedy, had received a message from his colleague in Warsaw, which reported Hitler's plan to act against Poland while Britain and France were still discussing action they should take. This information had been reinforced by a report brought to London by the Berlin Correspondent of the *News Chronicle* – contacts in Germany had told him Poland was the next item on Germany's programme. Halifax continued: 'This thesis was supported by a good deal of detailed information, including the statement of a local industrialist that he had been given orders to accumulate rations opposite Bromberg by 28 March.' The journalist had also brought Mason-MacFarlane's despatch. Halifax feared Hitler might make some immediate move. 'We should make a clear declaration of our intention to support Poland, if Poland is attacked by Germany.'

Halifax admitted this drastic idea had a number of drawbacks. 'First, we should be giving Colonel Beck what he wanted without obtaining any reciprocal undertaking from him. Second, there is some risk of upsetting the prospects of direct agreement between Germany and Poland. Third, such a declaration would be very provocative to Germany. Fourth, it has the appearance of leaving Roumania out of the picture.' And he added: 'The draft statement is a rather heroic action to take, on the meagre information available to us.' A draft should therefore be made ready for use at a moment's notice. And Chamberlain declared: 'The action now proposed is a serious step, and is the actual crossing of the stream.'

'We would be exposed to great humiliation,' said Halifax, 'and would suffer a serious set-back, if Germany took any action against Poland before we are prepared.' To speed matters, Chatfield suggested it might be better to issue a more general statement at an earlier date, 'which would give more timely warning.' Ministers agreed the Prime Minister should make this preliminary announcement to Parliament next day.

First, telegrams would have to be sent to Warsaw and Paris; Chamberlain now revealed that the Opposition leaders had already given their general consent. The Cabinet approved a draft statement, with this critical paragraph: 'I wish to say on behalf of HMG in the United Kingdom, that, in the event of resort by the German Government to any action which the Polish Government feels obliged to regard as a threat to their independence and accordingly to resist, His Majesty's Government will at once lend the Polish Government all support in their power.'[48]

Replies from Warsaw and Paris arrived that evening. 'M. Beck agreed without hesitation,' said Kennard, who then hinted that he himself disagreed with the move; 'Your Lordship doubtless possesses much information not available to me,' but while Poland was unlikely deliberately to provoke Germany, the 'possibility of some impulsive action cannot altogether be excluded'. Britain would then be involved in war, even though Germany might not have made the first move. 'I venture to suggest insertion of word "unprovoked".... I might add for what it is worth that both the German Ambassador and M. Beck have assured me today that German Government have not made any demands in the nature of an ultimatum, and that there is no indication that they intend to take more menacing action in the immediate future.'[49] Phipps's message was short: 'French Government agree. They do not apprehend any imminent *coup* against Poland.'[50]

Coup or not, Chamberlain intended to go ahead. But on 31 March came a last minute delay. On the afternoon of 30 March, Arthur Greenwood, acting Labour leader, and Sir Archibald Sinclair, Liberal leader, both warned of trouble 'in certain quarters' if Russia were to be excluded; Chamberlain replied 'the present arrangement is only intended to cover the interim period, and that the position in regard to Russia would no doubt be cleared up during Colonel Beck's visit.' Pressed to include in his statement that Russia had been consulted, he answered that Halifax intended to see Maisky next morning.[51] He had to agree to delay the statement until the Friday afternoon, to give Halifax more time. Chamberlain also told Cabinet Ministers the draft statement had been modified to read: 'As the House is aware, certain consultations are now proceeding with other Governments. In order to make perfectly clear the position of HMG in the meantime before those consultations are concluded, I now have to inform the House that during that period, in the event of any action which clearly threatened Polish independence, and which the Polish Government accordingly considered it vital to resist with their national forces, HMG would feel themselves bound at once to lend the Polish Government all support in their power.' He pointed out that two conditions were embodied in the new draft. First, the action must clearly threaten Polish independence, and in the new version 'it would, of course, be for us to determine what action threatened Polish independence, and this left us some freedom of manoeuvre'. Second, the Poles must themselves resist with their national forces. 'This will prevent us becoming embroiled as the result of a mere frontier incident.' Halifax had been unable to see Maisky that morning, but would try to do so before 3.00 p.m. Chamberlain commented that the Labour Party seemed to feel the Government 'were prejudiced against Russia and were neglecting a possible source of help.'[52]

'Chamberlain comes into the House looking gaunt and ill,' wrote Harold Nicolson in his diary. 'The skin above his high cheekbones is parchment yellow. He drops wearily into his place.' A few moments later, he rose to make his announcement. He read his statement very slowly, his grey head bent down as if he were having difficulty in seeing the words; and the cheers and shouts from MPs contrasted with his quiet voice. He had not had such an enthusiastic reception from the House since he announced his invitation to Munich.

Britain's continuing at peace now depended on Hitler's not attacking Poland, and despite the final changes in the statement, also on Poland – until recently an active scavenger for scraps dropped by Hitler, and an unreliable ally. Chamberlain, after years of caution, had run to the other extreme; he had jumped into committing Britain following false reports of a German invasion, and without a pledge of support from Russia. Halifax finally saw Maisky on Saturday morning, and later admitted: 'I was not surprised that M. Maisky took the opportunity of saying that, as he had not been consulted yesterday, it was obviously impossible for him to say at a moment's notice what the position of his Government would be.'[53] Soviet trust in Britain, already low, plummeted to new depths.

But, at last, Britain was committed. And united. 'This was no time for recriminations about the past,' wrote Churchill. 'The guarantee to Poland was supported by the leaders of all parties and groups in the House. "God helping, we can do no other," was what I said.... But no one who understood the situation could doubt that it meant in all human probability a major war, in which we should be involved.'[54] Britain now blocked Hitler's path. 'I'll cook them a stew they'll choke on,' raged the Führer when he heard the news.

8

Eastern Entanglements

On 28 March, Franco's forces took Madrid; and on 1 April, hostilities in Spain officially ended. And now came signs of a new area of conflict. 'There are fresh rumours of Italian pressure on Albania,' wrote Sir Andrew Ryan from Durazzo on the first day of the month.

In Poland the atmosphere was calm. In Britain, urgent measures to improve the nation's forces continued. A few days before, Sir Hugh Dowding, C-in-C RAF Fighter Command and under threat of retirement since July 1938, had at last been informed by the Air Ministry that 'no change of command was likely during 1939'.[1] Dowding was to be there for the Battle of Britain, and was recognized as the architect of the RAF's victory.

Also on 1 April, a cable from Perth in Rome brought Mussolini's reply to Chamberlain's letter of 20 March. The Duce refused to try to influence Hitler. 'I do not consider that I can take the initiative before Italy's rights have been recognized.'[2] And during the evening, Hitler made his first public pronouncement on Britain's initiative over Poland: 'He who declares himself ready to pull chestnuts out of the fire for these powers must realize he burns his fingers.... When they say in other countries that they will arm and will keep arming still more, I can tell those statesmen only this. "Me, you will never tire!"'[3] The same night, Seeds sent a depressing cable from Moscow. 'I have just seen M. Litvinov, who made it quite clear HMG's action is misunderstood and not at all appreciated.'[4]

To add to this gloomy international picture, a split appeared once again between Churchill and Chamberlain, over the question of cooperation with Russia. 'Having begun to create a Grand Alliance against aggression, we cannot afford to fail,' Churchill told the Commons on 3 April. 'The worst folly ... would be to chill and drive away any natural cooperation which Soviet Russia in her own deep interests feels it is necessary to afford.' Lloyd George agreed. 'If we are going in without the help of Russia, we are walking into a trap. It is the only country whose arms can get there.' And a fresh alarm arose during this Monday evening. Ogilvie-Forbes telephoned: 'Informant who is in contact with the War Ministry has stated that the first sign of German intentions ... will be a lightning attack on the British Fleet. ... There will be neither an ultimatum nor a declaration of war.... I feel that as we are dealing with a maniac who is violently aroused against Great Britain, you should be aware of this contingency.'[5] The 'maniac' was indeed making preparations for conflict: 'Case White', the directive for dealing with Poland, was being drawn up. 'The present attitude of Poland requires ... the initiation of military preparations, to remove, if necessary, any threat from this direction forever.... A surprise attack is to be aimed at and prepared.... Preparations must be made in such a way that the operation can be carried out at any time from 1 September 1939.'

A succession of telegrams on Tuesday, 4 April, revealed a steadily increasing likelihood that Italy would invade Albania. But Britain's main concern was for Poland. An Anglo-French staff appreciation on 4 April urged 'all the resources of diplomacy should be directed to securing the benevolent neutrality or active assistance of other powers, particularly the USA.' The paper recognized that in the first phase of war only economic measures – that is, a blockade – could be used against the Germans. This meant Britain would be unable to prevent Poland being overrun, unless Soviet forces intervened.[6]

Also on 4 April, Beck arrived in London, and his visit, originally planned to discuss general topics, now assumed extreme importance. His first public function was luncheon at the Savoy; Churchill asked: 'Will you get back all right in your special train through Germany?' 'I think I shall have time for that,' replied the Colonel.[7]

Beck was distrusted by many British diplomats and politicians. Secretive, aloof, suspicious, he was only too ready to take – and give – offence. Intensely self-reliant, he could be unscrupulous and unprincipled, and bore traces of his time as one of Pilsudski's conspirators against both Russian and German domination. He was a marked contrast to his political rival, the sociable and popular Benes.

Talks began at once. Beck welcomed the British proposal for a declaration, but repeated 'it would be dangerous to bring Russia into any discussions'. On Danzig, he said his country would not accept a *fait accompli*, though 'she would not close the door to reasonable and free negotiations'. He made no mention of the recent Ribbentrop demands for the return of Danzig, presented exactly a fortnight before. Halifax said it was vital for Britain to know whether, if she were attacked by Germany, Poland 'would be with us'. This would clearly be so, replied Beck. Halifax turned to the question of Russia: what value did Beck place upon the Soviet military forces and upon the Soviet transport system? Not very much, Beck answered. 'One of the difficulties about Soviet Russia in this country,' commented Halifax, 'is that some members of the Labour Party believe that, if Great Britain and the Soviet Union could join hands, the world would be safe for ever more.'[8]

Later talks were attended by Chamberlain. Beck reaffirmed for him that the agreement with Britain would be reciprocal, but despite pressure, refused to shift his position over Soviet participation. If Britain wanted to negotiate with Russia, 'Poland would keep clear and not join in, leaving the matter to the judgement of HMG, though continuing to be sceptical about it.' Chamberlain asked whether any discussions on Danzig were at present taking place; Beck replied: 'No negotiations are in progress, but conversations about Danzig have been going on for some time.' He implied they were of no great importance. Had Germany ever asked for an *autobahn* across the Corridor (she had, on 21 March)? Beck replied: 'Nothing that has happened has passed beyond the stage of conversations. No written demands have been presented to the Polish Government.' Beck added, 'privately and confidentially', that possibly Ribbentrop was 'the inventor of some of these ideas, but I doubt whether they have received the approval of his chief.' Chamberlain was 'much obliged to M. Beck for putting his views so frankly.'[9]

Beck had a busy day: he next met Eden for 45 minutes before attending a Foreign Office dinner. Eden reported his conversation to Halifax: 'M. Beck expressed the belief that the results of his visit and of the agreement reached in London would be to deter Germany from taking any further step against Poland. Germany would be angry and would bluster, but there was nothing she could do.'[10]

Halifax summed up the situation for the Cabinet next morning, 5 April. A reciprocal Anglo-Polish guarantee seemed obtainable, but Beck was apparently reluctant to extend this to cover Roumania. 'I was surprised at the vigour and persistence of Colonel Beck's reactions to the Russian problem.' 'You will appreciate,' said Chamberlain, 'that while the conversations with Colonel Beck have been by no means unsatisfactory, they have not turned out quite as we expected. . . . We are thus offered by Poland not even a Three-Power Pact, but a Two-Power Pact, and every attempt which we made to suggest that other Powers should be brought into the arrangement have been quietly but firmly resisted. . . .' But, Chamberlain confessed, 'I have very considerable distrust of Russia. I have no confidence that we will obtain active and constant support from her. . . .' Poland, he reminded his Cabinet, was the key to the situation. 'Our next step should be to convert our temporary arrangement with Poland into a permanent arrangement.' Albania was also discussed, and clearly Britain would not intervene. Halifax pointed out that Italy's special position with regard to Albania had been recognized by the Conference of Ambassadors after the war.

Hore-Belisha sought to increase the size of the Regular Army; substantial deficiencies had long existed which could only be remedied by an increase in manpower. 'I require, in the current year, an intake of 100,000 men for the Regular Army,' he said. 'The Field Force cannot be mobilized without an addition to its strength. Garrisons abroad are below war establishment.' Despite the crisis situation, Simon was opposed to this; he had agreed the previous week to doubling Territorial Army strength, and added: 'I feel it is impossible for me ... to accept this further very large commitment. The total liability involved is more than we could possibly bear.' And Hore-Belisha had to agree to reconsider his estimates.[11]

Litvinov's *amour-propre* had been wounded, Seeds cabled on 6 April.[12] On the same day, Halifax saw Maisky to explain the general lines of the Anglo-Polish talks, and to show him Chamberlain's statement to the Commons, declaring that a permanent Anglo-Polish agreement was now being considered. He reported later: 'After a process of cross-questioning that seemed likely to be interminable, M. Maisky took his leave, giving me as he left a warning against the possible unreliability of Polish policy.... The Ambassador's general attitude was friendly, but his ingenuity in the formulation and examination of hypothetical problems is unrivalled.'[13]

Also on 6 April, Italian warships appeared off Durazzo. Before nightfall they had slipped mysteriously away again. Meanwhile, the Italians presented a document to the King of Albania, which, if he signed, would mean the handover of his country. He referred the matter to his Ministers, and, according to a despatch from Sir Andrew Ryan, 'was very bitter with the Italians for catching him bending under the preoccupation of his wife's confinement.'[14] Early in the morning of Good Friday, 7 April, the Italian Fleet returned. This time the warships opened fire; Italian forces streamed ashore; the King fled.

The Albanian takeover, planned originally by Ciano as a move to lessen German influence, merely increased it: Mussolini, isolated by world opinion after his conquest, had to lean even more on the Führer. But now, he was in a position to push north into Yugoslavia, or south via the Greek island of Corfu; and Britain had close relations with Greece. The Duce tried to soothe the British; the Italian Chargé in London called to see Halifax that Friday morning, and handed over a message: the Duce gave 'formal assurances that the solution of the Italo-Albanian question will take place in such a form as not to provoke a crisis in Anglo-Italian relations, or the international situation in general'.[15] Phipps reported France's attitude the same day: Bonnet thought 'the most optimistic explanation would be that the Italians were tired of constant German successes and wanted a fairly easy victory of their own'. He remarked that France was not bound in any way to defend Albania, and seemed still anxious to improve Franco-Italian relations.[16] That evening Halifax instructed Perth to tell

Ciano that Britain felt 'deep concern at the course events seem to be taking', and, under the Anglo-Italian agreement, felt entitled to the 'frankest and fullest explanation'. Four courses seemed immediately open, he later told the Cabinet, 'enquiry, protest, threats, or action'. The first seemed clearly right. Apart from the telegram to Perth, cables had been sent to Belgrade, Athens, Ankara and Paris. 'It is clear Yugoslavia does not intend to take any action; the Government in Greece is watching the position very closely; if the present situation develops further, Greece will be on our side.' The Turkish attitude was similar, but no firm information had yet arrived concerning the French position. 'If, in the course of a few days, the Italian Government comes to some arrangement which leaves unimpaired the sovereignty, and frontiers, of Albania, it might be contended that such an arrangement is within the letter, at any rate, of the Anglo-Italian Agreement.' But later he added: 'It looks as though the invasion of Albania has been deliberately timed to take place during the Easter Recess [of Parliament], and as a riposte to the Anglo-Polish Agreement. Again it looks like a demonstration by the Dictators against the Western Powers.' He continued: 'No doubt public opinion in certain countries, such as America, will be likely to take the view that, while we use brave words, our action is less heroic.'

'We should not go to war over Albania,' was his verdict, 'but should endeavour to secure further time, which we should use to improve our position.' Early steps should be taken to reach agreements with both Greece and Turkey, but the Ambassador should not be withdrawn from Rome.

'The situation is still somewhat obscure in regard to a number of important factors,' stated a Communiqué issued after the meeting, 'and it has therefore been arranged that the Ministers concerned should remain in or near London for the present. No further meeting has, however, yet been fixed.'[17] Churchill pressed for more vigorous protest and for more positive protection for threatened Greece. 'I am hoping Parliament will be recalled at the latest on Tuesday,' he wrote to Chamberlain on Sunday, 9 April. 'I hope the statements which you will be able to make will enable the same united front to be presented as in the case of the Polish Agreement.... It is imperative for us to recover the initiative in diplomacy.... What is now at stake is nothing less than the whole of the Balkan peninsula.' He also urged Britain should send warships to occupy Corfu.[18]

Sunday brought fresh reports of a possible Italian landing there. The British Ambassador at Athens, Waterlow, had been summoned by the Greek Prime Minister at midnight on Saturday, and afterwards reported: 'Greek Military Attaché at Rome has learnt from reliable source that Italians intend to attack Corfu between 10 April and 12 April. Same source foretold date of invasion of Albania.'[19] Following a similar warning from the Greek Ambassador, Halifax decided firmer British action was required; he immediately telephoned Chamberlain, then drafted a telegram to Mussolini: 'HMG have no intention of occupying Corfu, but a situation of the gravest nature would arise if it were occupied by the Italian Government. Any Italian act of aggression by the Italian Government upon Greek territory would be regarded by HMG as a threat to vital British interests and treated as such.'

The warning was clear enough. But while the telegram was still being prepared, the Italian Chargé called to see Halifax again, with fervent assurances that Italy 'intended to base her relations with Greece on a cordial and solid friendship'.[20] So Halifax and Chamberlain agreed to scrap the telegram. But in Paris, an even more disturbing theory was causing anxiety. Daladier, according to a telephone message from Phipps on Sunday night, believed the Albania *coup* was merely a prelude 'to a big Italo-German offensive, from the North Sea to Egypt'. Daladier told the British Ambassador, in strictest confidence, that extensive military precautions were being taken, and the National Defence Committee was still in session.[21]

Next morning, 10 April, the Cabinet discussed improving relations with the Mediterranean countries, especially Greece, Yugoslavia and Turkey. Halifax was against denouncing the Anglo-Italian Agreement – 'we derive far more benefit from it than Italy'. Discussion was aimless and unsatisfactory. At the close of debate Chamberlain suggested the FPC should meet later in the day to consider what steps could be taken.[22] Tension ebbed during the day; war scares subsided; in Rome, Perth refused to believe that an attack on Corfu was intended. The FPC, meeting at 4 p.m., refused to agree to precipitate British action. While Greece was the more immediate issue, the Committee believed it necessary also to take Roumania's position into account; in turn, the attitude of Turkey was important with regard to both Greece and Roumania, and the decision was taken to make a formal approach to Ankara over the possibility of a joint declaration.[23] The Committee believed British policy should be restricted to strictly diplomatic moves, yet Chamberlain was nevertheless getting into the same situation over the Balkans as he had over Poland; in both cases as a result of an invasion scare.

Meantime, as the threat to Greece began to diminish, fears for Poland persisted. 'German troop movements were reported as taking place towards Poland,' cabled Phipps after a meeting with Bonnet. And unknown to the Western diplomats, Hitler, on 11 April, added details to his 'Case White' directive of 3 April: he still hoped to achieve Warsaw's diplomatic isolation in the 'not too distant future', and the date for the completion of all military preparations was confirmed as 1 September.

Chamberlain had still to contend with domestic political problems:

suspicions over his policy had been revived by his apparently meek line over Albania. 'There is a theory that the appeasers – Simon, Hoare and Horace Wilson – have regained their influence,' wrote Nicolson on 11 April.[24] Yet although intervention had been ruled out – and not even Churchill had believed this should be attempted – Chamberlain was still firmly against undue emphasis upon appeasement, and was at this moment considering the establishment of a Supply Ministry. He wrote to Hore-Belisha on 11 April that he had reached the conclusion 'that the matter ought to be considered afresh'. He had asked Chatfield and Morrison to prepare a report for the Cabinet.[25]

Meanwhile, the French were pressing to guarantee both Greece and Roumania. On 12 April, Halifax was handed the text of a declaration, to be made in Paris next day, which embodied this protection offer, but he was opposed to including Roumania, which would complicate negotiations. 'Turkey is the key to Balkan solidarity, achievement of which seems to us of the highest importance.'[26]

France's attitude was perhaps 'the most difficult point', Halifax told the Cabinet next morning. A reply had been received from the Turkish Government: they were apparently not prepared to commit themselves to a public statement of the kind Britain wanted without the consent of the Turkish Chamber, and without some guarantee of their own security. This reply had arrived before a second British telegram had reached Ankara, proposing the British and Turkish Governments should come to the help of each other. 'I think this telegram will set their doubts to rest,' said Halifax. Meanwhile, the Prime Minister's statement to the Commons that afternoon would only refer in a general way to Turkey: Chamberlain proposed to say 'we should be fully justified in denouncing the (Anglo-Italian) Agreement, but that we did not propose to do so.' The Cabinet approved, and also authorized him to say: 'If aggression took place against Greece or Roumania and these countries resisted, we would come to their aid.'[27]

During this session, a message arrived at the Foreign Office from Phipps: Paris was still insisting upon a formal declaration which would include Roumania. 'M. Daladier addresses strongest appeal to you and the PM,' he said. According to Daladier, Roumania was 'the key to the whole situation'.[28] Only a few minutes later a telephone call from the Ambassador at Bucharest reported Hungarian claims of Roumanian mobilization; if Roumania was not controlled, the Hungarian Government would be 'obliged to have recourse to military measures'.[29] So Halifax told Phipps: 'In the interests of solidarity, we do not feel that we can fail to respond to M. Daladier's appeal.'[30] So Roumania was again included in the British scheme of agreements, and her area of commitment in East and South-east Europe was widened still further. Chamberlain told the Commons: 'His Majesty's Government ... have come to the conclusion that, in the event of any action being taken which clearly threatened the independence of Greece or Roumania, and which the Greek or Roumanian Governments respectively considered vital to resist with their national forces, HMG would feel themselves bound at once to lend ... all the support in their power.' Churchill immediately launched a harsh attack on the country's military unpreparedness. 'We have committed ourselves in every direction, rightly in my opinion, having regard to all that has happened.... How can we bear to continue to lead our comfortable, easy lives here at home, unwilling to pronounce even the word "compulsion", unwilling to take even the necessary measures by which the armies which we have promised can alone be recruited and equipped?' And he added: 'How can we continue – let me say with particular frankness and sincerity – with less than the full force of the nation incorporated in the governing instrument?'[31]

Faint signs of cooperation appeared from Moscow. Maisky called to see Halifax on 14 April. In view of British interest, he said, 'in the fate of Greece or Roumania, the Soviet Government are prepared to take part in giving assistance to Roumania'. Halifax asked Seeds to approach Litvinov, to see if Russia might make a declaration over Roumania and perhaps Poland.[32]

When Ogilvie-Forbes telephoned that the 'German Government are contemplating securing the return of Danzig to the Reich by Herr Hitler's birthday, 20 April,'[33] Russian help seemed suddenly even more urgent. Halifax sent another cable to Seeds. Litvinov must be asked if Russia could make a declaration that 'in the event of any act of aggression against any European neighbour of the Soviet Union, which was resisted by the country concerned, the assistance of the Soviet Government would be available'.[34] With this sweeping British request, the long, frustrating and fated Anglo-Soviet negotiations began.

A conference took place at the War Office throughout Saturday, 15 April. The subject was mobilization, and the Chief of the Imperial General Staff (CIGS) warned: 'There is no means of keeping anti-aircraft defences in a state of continuous readiness without some regular nucleus, which could not in the near future be provided except from reservists.' The answer, according to Hore-Belisha, was some kind of compulsory service, and that evening he urged Chamberlain once again to introduce one.[35]

A new appeal for peace came from across the Atlantic that night. Roosevelt sent a long and eloquent telegram to Hitler and Mussolini, seeking assurances that they would not attack nations or groups of nations, which he listed, and which ranged from Finland and Estonia, through Liechtenstein, Luxemburg and Poland, down to Roumania, the Arabias, Egypt and Iran. Britain's reaction came in a written statement handed to the Press, signed by Chamberlain and Halifax.

The President's initiative had come as a surprise, said the statement, but had been received 'with cordial approval', and HMG entirely endorsed the President's estimate of the situation and the means he had put forward to remedy it.[36] Göring was in Rome when Roosevelt's appeal arrived; 'Roosevelt is suffering from an incipient mental disease,' he commented, and thought the appeal not worth answering. Mussolini, trying to match his guest's invective, dubbed the telegram a 'result of infantile paralysis'.[37]

On 15 April, Seeds saw Litvinov, who gave Halifax's proposal a 'friendly hearing', and promised to consult his Government.[38] But next day, Göring and Mussolini in Rome decided that it would be advisable if Germany also extended feelers towards Moscow.[39] Late on Monday, 17 April, Litvinov handed Seeds the official Soviet reply. Moscow proposed an agreement by Britain, France and Russia, under which they would 'render mutually forthwith all manner of assistance, including that of a military nature, in case of aggression in Europe against any one of the contracting Powers'. Assistance would also be given to 'Eastern European States situated between the Baltic and Black Seas and bordering on the USSR'.[40] But in Berlin, on the same day, the Soviet Ambassador, Merekalov, was received by Weizsäcker for the first time since he had presented his credentials almost a year before. 'There exists for Russia no reason why she should not live with Germany on a normal footing,' he declared, 'and from normal, relations might become better and better.'[41]

During this Monday, the Germans took action on Roosevelt's appeal: a circular telegram was sent to all the states, except for Britain, France, Poland and Russia. Ambassadors were to ask two questions: did the respective countries feel themselves threatened by Germany? Had the respective Governments authorized Roosevelt to make his proposal? Ribbentrop explained: 'We are in no doubt that both questions will be answered in the negative. Nevertheless, for special reasons, we should like to have immediate authentic confirmation.' Hitler intended to use the appeal for his own propaganda purposes.

In Paris, Bonnet was in a pessimistic mood. 'Minister for Foreign Affairs lunched here today,' cabled Phipps, and 'feels that the present state of tension cannot last much longer and that the question of peace or war may well be decided within the next two or three weeks.'[42] Monday, 17 April, was also a black day for Hore-Belisha – and the Cabinet came close to a crisis. 'I had come to the end of my tether and I was going to resign,' he wrote.[43] This resulted from Chamberlain's negative reaction to the suggested partial mobilization, and from his failure to have conscription introduced. He arranged to see Chamberlain the following morning; but meanwhile, he talked with Halifax, who, according to Hore-Belisha, commented that 'he had good reason to believe that conscription was the only course that would have any effect on Germany'. France was restive at Britain's delay in introducing conscription. Hore-Belisha said Britain was entering 'into so many pacts and military commitments all over Europe, and that full preparations must be made to fulfil them.' So, strengthened by Halifax's apparent agreement, he saw Chamberlain, but any expectations of a change of mind were soon shattered. 'It was not a pleasant interview,' he wrote. 'He said I was adding to his difficulties and ... that I had a bee in my bonnet about conscription; that the War Office wanted it and that I had therefore a biased view.' Hore-Belisha had warned 'my task was impossible if he rejected some form of compulsory military service'. Later in the day, he saw Simon, a strong Chamberlain supporter. But Sir John, who had resigned as Home Secretary in 1916 in opposition to this very question of conscription, had now changed his mind. 'He was bound to admit that the case I had presented was unanswerable, and that he was in agreement.' With Halifax and Simon – second and third in the Cabinet hierarchy – supporting him, Hore-Belisha's confidence increased. He called a meeting of the Army Council and revealed Chamberlain's views. 'They unanimously agreed there was no alternative to what we had submitted.' Chamberlain had been making his own inquiries, and now realized the dangers of a deep Cabinet split; he weighed the implications of this against Trade Union and Labour Party opposition. Next morning, he asked Hore-Belisha to see him again. 'I went across to No. 10 at 10.45.... His manner had completely changed from yesterday.' Chamberlain promised to give him an opening to present his views at the Cabinet meeting, scheduled to start in about five minutes' time.[44]

The Cabinet met at 11.00 a.m., and the Prime Minister kept his word. But first Halifax revealed the Soviet reply to the British suggestion of a Russian declaration. Moscow now proposed a comprehensive European plan of mutual assistance, and 'it will be necessary to exercise considerable caution'. The plan was held over for the FPC. Halifax then had to deal with a complicated point of protocol – incongruous at the least, among so many crucial items. 'The question has arisen as to whether the Chargé in Berlin should subscribe to the birthday present to Herr Hitler, which has been organized by a certain member of the Diplomatic Corps in Berlin.' Chamberlain had decided no donation be made, provided the French Ambassador and the American Chargé likewise declined. But should the King send a birthday greeting? 'I think that one very important consideration,' said Halifax, 'is the probable effect on Herr Hitler of the discontinuance of the normal birthday message, which he might well regard as a deliberate affront.... I think that the right course will be to send a message not in the customary form, which contains wishes for the recipient's health and welfare, but as follows: "Please accept Herr Reichschancellor my congratulations on your 50th birthday.' Halifax thought

138

it best if Henderson did not return to Berlin until after Hitler's birthday celebrations.

Now Hore-Belisha repeated the views of the Army Council that partial mobilization measures should be adopted immediately. 'Virtually all other nations in Europe have taken substantial mobilization steps.' Anti-aircraft defences were inadequately manned, he warned – and the Prime Minister agreed. 'The process of manning the [search] lights and guns would take twelve hours,' said Chamberlain. 'In the meantime we would be virtually without defence against air attacks.' This, explained Hore-Belisha, was caused by the present reliance on volunteers. 'Unless an emergency is declared, it would be an intolerable burden on Territorial officers and men to be called upon to serve wholetime for an indefinite period.' Regulars were the only answer, and, because of the manpower shortage, this would mean conscription. Chamberlain warned of the opposition to any Governmental proposals, and revealed that he intended to delay a short while longer – 'any rash or sudden decision without proper preparation will be likely to cause so violent a reaction that the rearmament programme would be interfered with.' Chamberlain wanted more time to think. Ministers were obliged to agree.

Chatfield now proposed a Supply Ministry. This would help organize equipment for the Territorial Army, and could be expanded into a large organization serving the three Services. At last, the Cabinet agreed to these proposals. Chatfield was asked to work out details and to report back with a draft Bill.[45] Progress was swift: in the House next day, 20 April, Chamberlain announced the creation of the Ministry to a chorus of 'loud and prolonged cheers'. Then he added that Leslie Burgin, Transport Minister, would be appointed, and the cheers subsided. Members had hoped he would take the opportunity of broadening the basis of his Cabinet. Nicolson recorded: 'There is a very widespread belief that he is running a dual policy – one the overt policy of rearming, and the other ... appeasement.'[46]

But unsuspected by Chamberlain's critics, he had, under pressure, now agreed to conscription, a far more radical step. Later that night, Wilson told Hore-Belisha, who made no attempt to hide his satisfaction, 'that it had been decided to introduce conscription and that it was to be kept secret'.[47]

Still no reliable information on Hitler's plans was forthcoming. In the uneasy pause, rumours ran rife through Europe. Attolico reported to Rome on the 20th that German action against Poland was 'imminent'. 'That would be war,' wrote a worried Ciano in his diary.[48] Meanwhile, Britain's diplomatic representation in Berlin and Rome was changing. Lord Perth was leaving Rome – and in Berlin, Ogilvie-Forbes was warned by Weizsäcker that unless an Ambassador returned soon, 'the German Government would adopt the attitude that it did not care whether there was a British Ambassador here or not.'[49] This message reached Halifax on 22 April, and next day, by coincidence, Henderson returned. Almost immediately despatches from Berlin received his highly individual stamp.

On the afternoon of Sir Nevile's arrival, Ogilvie-Forbes sent a cable which cast doubt on Beck's statements in London. According to a member of Hitler's personal staff, German proposals had been made to Beck over Danzig. 'Herr Hitler assumed that Colonel Beck informed you of them when he was in London.'[50] Halifax jotted on the telegram: 'Is it not the case that Beck gave us to understand that there had been no definite proposals, and that the matter had not reached the stage of negotiation? If so, he has been less than frank and I should be disposed to say something to him.' With doubts raised of Beck's credibility, talks now opened in London with Gafencu, the Foreign Minister of Roumania, also sought by Britain as an ally. Asked by Chamberlain whether he believed 'Germany had, for the time being, decided not to make a further push in the direction of Roumania', Gafencu replied, 'The next push will be towards Poland, and towards Danzig in particular.'[51]

The same day, 24 April, the Prime Minister circulated a paper containing his conclusions on conscription, reached since the last Cabinet meeting.[52] His proposals had one important restriction. 'Unless and until war breaks out, Compulsory Military Training will be confined to purposes of Home Defence.' Chamberlain proposed a Military Training Bill, involving between 200,000 and 250,000 men. 'Personally, I have long been in favour in principle of a scheme for compulsory military service,' he claimed, 'but until recently I regarded the introduction of such a scheme as impracticable because of the opposition which it would arouse in Trade Union circles.' The scheme now envisaged would overcome principal objections, and he intended to announce the proposals before Friday. 'It would be desirable for H.M. Ambassador in Berlin to communicate the decision to the German Government, before it is publicly announced, and this is one of the reasons why I thought it desirable to expedite the Ambassador's return.' In this way, German reaction to British conscription might be tempered. The proposals were discussed at a second Cabinet meeting,[53] and instructions sent to Henderson, and to Sir Noel Charles, Chargé at Rome. They were to announce that the Prime Minister would be making a statement in the Commons next day: the new Bill, 'due very largely to a change in public opinion,' was a consequence of Britain's new liabilities in Europe, but, the Ambassadors were to say, the object was 'not to wage war but to prevent it'.[54]

Sir Nevile had to move quickly to tell the Germans before Chamberlain's statement was made, though in fact they had already guessed. He later wrote: 'By this time the intention of HMG was an open secret', and for this reason he thought it unnecessary to tell Ribbentrop, contacting instead Weizsäcker, who said 'he was aware of the object of the visit', and agreed to see Sir Nevile at noon. Because he had not seen Ribbentrop, Press stories immediately appeared that he had been 'rudely rebuffed'.[55]

Meanwhile, Britain had been discussing with the French a reply to Russia's proposals of 18 April, for a tripartite Agreement. The FPC had considered Britain's reply on 19 April, armed with a memorandum by Cadogan, which ran: 'This Russian proposal is extremely inconvenient. We have to balance the advantage of a paper commitment by Russia to join in a war on one side, against the disadvantage of associating ourselves openly with Russia.' Russia's military usefulness outside her own frontier was limited (an opinion fully endorsed by the Chiefs of Staff). The implication was clear: Poland was more valuable than Russia. This view was expressed by the FPC, though Hoare pointed out that 'Poland would be able to offer little military resistance to German invasion, and would soon come to the end of her munitions. We should be in no position to supply her, and Russia was the only possible source for munitions for Poland and the other countries of Eastern Europe.' Chamberlain pushed this to one side: the Committee, he said, was considering 'the Soviets' present proposal for a definite military alliance between England, France and Russia. It can not be pretended that such an alliance is necessary in order that the smaller countries of Eastern Europe should be furnished with munitions.' The Committee therefore decided the Soviet proposals should be rejected. French agreement would be needed, and Halifax told the Cabinet on the 26th that an outline of Britain's proposed reply had been sent to Paris five days before, for comments. The main point, he said, was that the Soviet proposals 'took too little account of practical difficulties.... In particular, Poland would object to a tripartite Agreement providing for Soviet assistance to Poland whether or not the latter wanted it. There is also the point that Poland would object to a tripartite Agreement of mutual assistance between the three Great Powers, since certain forms of Soviet assistance could only be afforded through Poland.... The time is not ripe for so comprehensive a proposal, and we propose to ask the Soviet Government to give further consideration to our plan, which aims at giving early protection where it is most needed, and does not ask the Soviet Government to do more than to come in when we would be already involved.' Paris had agreed to the British views on 24 April, two days before, he said, but the French had also gone further than the Prime Minister had intended. 'The French Government proposed a tripartite Agreement between Britain, France and Russia, providing, first, that if Great Britain and France were at war with Germany in consequence of fulfilling their obligations to Eastern European countries, Russia would assist them;

secondly, that if, as a result of giving this assistance, Russia was at war with Germany, Great Britain and France would assist her.' Although Britain had originally wished to open discussions with the Soviet Union on the grounds that she might be prepared to help Poland, Halifax now disagreed with the French scheme because it involved 'some degree of Soviet assistance to Poland'. His change of attitude had resulted from Poland's obvious unwillingness to be associated with the Soviet Government. He now told the Cabinet: 'The French Government's proposal is open to the objection which they themselves have urged. In other respects also the French proposals seem to be somewhat confused.' On 25 April the FPC had decided he should reply to Paris and criticize the scheme on these grounds.

'The value of Russia as a potential ally,' declared Halifax, 'is by no means as high as seems to be believed by prominent members of the Labour Party.... We should, of course, endeavour to order our policy so that, if war broke out, Russia would be either neutral or would come in on our side. At the same time, it is essential to bear in mind the effects of our relations with Russia on Poland, Roumania and other countries, not excluding Germany.... We should not act in such a way as to forgo the chance of Russian help in war; we should not jeopardize the cause of peace.' The difficulty lay in achieving all these aims at the same time.[56]

As planned, Chamberlain gave notice in the Commons that afternoon of a conscription Bill. The announcement was now expected, and Parliament was packed – more so, according to Nicolson, than it had been at the time of Munich. The previous day, Chamberlain had seen Trade Union leaders in a vain attempt to gain their support – an angry Bevin had condemned the Government for violating its pledge, and he threatened that the TUC would have to reconsider the promise to cooperate in the voluntary national service scheme already started. The proposed Bill would lead to full-blooded conscription, Bevin added, and would divide the country. Hoare, who had attended this meeting as Home Secretary, wrote: 'Until I listened to Bevin's attack, I had never realized the extent of the personal bitterness felt by the Labour leaders against the Prime Minister.'[57]

Chamberlain expected a hostile reception in the Commons; and received it. 'Is the Prime Minister aware,' asked Attlee, 'that this decision will break the pledge solemnly given to this country and re-affirmed only four weeks ago, that compulsory service would not be introduced in peacetime, that it will increase the already widespread distrust of the Prime Minister, that so far from strengthening this country, it will be sowing divisions in the ranks of this country, and will gravely imperil the national effort, and that this departure from the voluntary principle will meet with strenuous opposition?' Chamberlain was indeed very well aware: he had forecast these points would

142

be used against him. Nicolson observed: 'He puts on his obstinate face which would be irritating were it not that one sees signs of extreme exhaustion and profound mental suffering.'[58] The Opposition clamoured for, and received, an Emergency Debate for the following day.

Ambassadors, Commonwealth and Dominions' representatives, Military Attachés, Members of Parliament – all crowded the galleries and benches of the House for this debate. For the first time in peace, Britain was to compel citizens to join the armed forces. Chamberlain admitted the departure from former promises and traditional policy, but the voluntary system no longer sufficed. Britain's acceptance of what was the universal rule on the Continent would be convincing evidence of her wholehearted cooperation in resisting domination. He pleaded for a united front, to oppose aggression and give Britain the means of doing so. But he had seen Trade Union leaders again in the morning, and they had reaffirmed their disagreement; now Attlee again ranged the Labour Party against the proposals. An Opposition motion claimed the voluntary principle provided sufficient manpower for defence. 'This country provides the greatest fleet in the world,' said Attlee. 'It has a rapidly growing Air Force. It has to provide munitions for them ... for its allies, and it cannot, in addition to that, provide a Continental Army.'

The House was tense and excited by the time Hore-Belisha wound up the debate. 'Let those whose slogan is "Stand up to the Dictators" give us the trained men with whom we can stand up.... What infringement is it of our freedom to take steps to secure it?' And all would serve alike, rich and poor, skilled and unskilled, professional and lay. 'This is as democratic a proposal as has ever been made to this House.... Far from dividing the nation, it should do much to bring the younger generation together and unite it by a common experience.' MPs crowded through the division lobbies to vote; the motion was carried by a large majority – 380 votes to 143. The verdict was decisive, and revolutionary. If conscription was a further mark against Chamberlain, it also brought triumph for Hore-Belisha, to whom, Churchill wrote, belonged the credit of forcing this belated awakening. 'He certainly took his political life in his hands.... I saw something of him in this ordeal, and he was never sure that each day in office would not be his last.'[59]

As expected, Hitler's reaction was extreme. On 28 April, the day after the Commons debate, he scrapped the Anglo-German naval agreement – a step which Henderson had warned back in 1937 would 'inevitably lead in the end once more to war with Britain'.[60] In a two-hour speech to the Reichstag, he also renounced the 1934 Non-Aggression Pact between Germany and Poland, and he heaped ridicule on Roosevelt for his appeal for peace. But, as one or two observers carefully noted, he made no condemnation of Russia. His main attack was launched not on Britain, nor even Poland, but on America. He had asked all the nations mentioned in the President's letter if they felt threatened, and 'the reply was in all cases negative'. Nevertheless, he added amid laughter: 'I here solemnly declare that all the assertions which have been circulated in any way concerning an intended German attack or invasion on or in American territory are rank frauds and gross untruths.' But in the list of countries there was one omission – Poland.

At the end of April it was more than ever apparent that *Kriegper-manenz* – undeclared but existing war – was being intensified. In Cabinet discussions, preparations for conflict, including debates on accumulation of supplies and reserves, use of manpower, completion of plans, evacuation, civil defence organization, rationing, emergency regulations, mobilization, or strategy, now had first priority. And the search for allies continued. So, on 28 April, Halifax told Kennard the latest position in the Russian negotiations: Britain still wanted to persuade the Soviet Government to make a public declaration, and Soviet proposals for a more comprehensive agreement were still being rejected; the British idea took account of the 'susceptibilities of Poland and Roumania. Neither country is mentioned by name; the Soviet declaration ... would, in form, be unilateral, and the assistance of the Soviet Government would only be made available if required.' Sir Howard was asked to obtain Beck's comments on the scheme.[61] Next day, Halifax saw Maisky, newly returned from Moscow, and told him Britain regretted not having replied to the Soviet Union, but would do so after having consulted the French. Phipps told Halifax the French would send their opinions on 2 May.

Meanwhile, war scares increased. On the morning of 2 May, Henderson talked with Ribbentrop, who 'spoke very bitterly on the subject of Poland.... I was struck by the similarity of his language to that employed by him last year in regard to Czechoslovakia. He himself drew open comparison between the Polish and Czech cases.'[62] He cabled another warning late in the day. 'A diplomatic colleague informed me this evening ... that all preparations were being made for an invasion of Poland through Lithuania or Latvia within the next 14 days.'[63]

Halifax revealed his anxiety when the Cabinet met next morning, 3 May, and he was especially concerned over Danzig. 'Colonel Beck is believed to be somewhat pro-German.... On the other hand, public opinion in Poland is now aroused, and there is all the makings of trouble.' He was also anxious about possible implications of the Anglo-Polish guarantee. 'It will be dangerous to allow the issue of peace and war to be dependent solely on the judgement of the Polish Government.... We hold the view that the mere fact that we have given the guarantee gives us the right to be kept informed as to any situation which arises.' Lack of Polish cooperation was causing disquiet at the Foreign Office, and with good reason. Yet because of Poland, negotiations with Russia were being delayed. 'Time must not be lost,' commented Churchill on 4 May. 'Ten or 12 days have already passed since the Russian offer was made. The British people ... have a right, in conjunction with the French republic, to call upon Poland not to place obstacles in the way of a common cause.... Not only must the full cooperation of Russia be accepted, but the three Baltic States, Lithuania, Latvia, and Estonia, must also be brought into association.'[64]

Halifax was already aware of Churchill's views, but both he and Chamberlain thought it far easier to make vigorous declarations when one was out of office. He told the Cabinet on 3 May that the previous day he had seen Churchill, who had been 'entirely in favour of the tripartite Pact proposed by Russia'. Halifax said: 'A tripartite Pact on the lines proposed would make war inevitable. On the other hand, I think that it is only fair to assume that if we rejected Russia's proposal, Russia will sulk. There is also always the bare possibility that a refusal of Russia's offer might even throw her into Germany's arms.' This latter point had also occurred to Hore-Belisha. 'Although the idea might seem fantastic at the moment, the natural orientation suggests an arrangement between Germany and Russia.' And Malcolm Mac-Donald agreed. 'We do not wish to give offence to Russia – it would be a serious matter if Russia were neutral and supplying Germany with food and raw materials. Would it not be possible to keep negotiations continuing for some further period, in the hope of finding a compromise?' Chamberlain approved of this suggestion, and said no decision was called for at the present time. 'We are at present awaiting a formal reply from the French Government.... When that has been received, we should send a reply to the Russian Government, setting out our counter-proposals. I assume that the Russian Government will not thereupon break off negotiations, but will send a further communication.' In other words, there was no emergency.[65]

But any hopes of Russia becoming, in time, more flexible, suddenly received a serious setback. On 3 May, Seeds had seen Litvinov, who had shown no sign of anything unusual disturbing him. Yet on 4 May the Ambassador opened his Moscow newspaper to find an announcement that 'M. Molotov, President of Council of Peoples' Commissars, has been appointed Commissar for Foreign Affairs.' An inconspicuous four-line notice on the back page stated: 'The Presidium of the Supreme Council of the USSR has released M. Litvinov at his own request from his duties as Commissar for Foreign Affairs.' This shuffle of Soviet Ministers would mean a new twist in Moscow's foreign policy. 'My impression,' cabled Seeds, 'is that ... we are faced with a more truly

Bolshevik – as opposed to diplomatic or cosmopolitan – *modus operandi*.... Reactions to what we say or do not say will be more violent, and the great men in the Kremlin will be more apt to plunge off into the deep if disappointed or indignant.'[66] Litvinov had been an advocate of collective security, an attitude which Stalin opposed but which he had allowed until, according to Maisky, Britain rejected Moscow's proposals for a conference after the Nazi occupation of Czechoslovakia in March.[67] And Litvinov, as the German Ambassador stressed, was a Jew. German hopes had now been increased that Anglo-Soviet negotiations would be further complicated by Molotov's take-over, and Berlin's chances of an accommodation with Russia would improve. 'I am filled with the gloomiest forebodings for the future,' wrote Henderson to Halifax, 'and am far more apprehensive of war than ever I was last September.'[68] On 5 May, Halifax received a startling signal from Rome. 'My French colleague,' cabled the new British Ambassador, Sir Percy Loraine, 'propounds the astonishing theory that Stalin has sacked [Litvinov] in order to make an arrangement with Germany, which would of course enable the latter to attack Poland and retake the Corridor with relative impunity.' He added that he found François-Poncet's theory 'difficult to swallow'. But on the same day Georgi Astakhov, Soviet Chargé at Berlin, was conferring with Dr Julius Schnurre, expert of East European affairs, at the German Foreign Office. Russia and Germany were carefully sounding one another out.[69]

Beck made an important policy statement on this day; Halifax had hoped he would be 'firm and unprovocative' and not close 'any door to free and reasonable negotiation'. But instead, Beck displayed a vigorous opposition to German intimidations. 'It is clear that negotiations in which one State formulates demands, and the other is to be obliged to accept these demands unaltered, are not negotiations in the spirit of the Declaration of 1934, and are incompatible with the vital interests and dignity of Poland.'[70] Hitler did not respond publicly to this stubbornness, but continued his secret planning instead – there would be no further negotiations between Germany and Poland.

Saturday saw manoeuvrings for allies by Britain, Germany and Italy. In the morning, Halifax told Maisky Britain was at last about to submit a reply to Moscow; instructions were sent to Seeds that evening. He was to inquire whether Molotov believed his appointment had changed the Soviet outlook; if he believed a change had come about, he should suspend action and inform London. If not, then he was to hand over the British reply, criticizing the Soviet proposals for taking 'too little account of practical difficulties', which would delay negotiations. Britain's suggestion was a Soviet statement on the lines agreed by the Cabinet and now approved, with some reservations, by the French.[71] Seeds presented this British proposal on 8 May. Soviet policy had not changed since Litvinov's departure, Sir William was assured, and the Note was therefore presented. Seeds found his position complicated by the fact that Bonnet had given a slightly different proposal to the Soviet Ambassador at Paris. Molotov said the British laid great stress on Poland's reluctance to be associated publicly with the Soviet Union, and claimed 'his own information was that the Polish Government had now changed their attitude in this respect'. Careful consideration would however be given to the British proposals. According to Sir William's report: 'He repeated that Soviet policy had not changed, but added cryptic remark that it was liable to be altered if the other States changed theirs. I should add that he commented unfavourably on our delay in answering.'[72]

'The tone of the interview did not seem too promising,' Halifax told the Cabinet two days later. 'I have no information bearing on the likelihood of some secret agreement being concluded between Herr Hitler and M. Stalin. I find it difficult to attach much credence to these reports, which might be spread by persons who desired to drive us into making a pact with Russia.' One or two Cabinet members were disturbed over the situation. 'I am more and more impressed,' said Hoare, 'by the serious consequences which would ensue from a breakdown of the negotiations.' He suggested Halifax might invite Molotov to meet him at Geneva, where Halifax was going for a League of Nations meeting. Halifax agreed it was important to avoid a breakdown, but reminded the Cabinet of the importance of maintaining good relations with Spain, for example. But Chamberlain and Halifax were to think further about this idea of a meeting with Molotov.[73]

In Berlin, Henderson was worried that Germany did not believe Britain would go to war over Poland, and proposed an ingenious scheme. He had received a telegram from Halifax, instructing him to give a quiet warning to a number of leading Germans, including Keitel, that Britain was not bluffing. He suggested this message be sent to him again, only transmitted 'as if by error' in a cypher the Germans could easily decode. The scheme was put into practice, and the warning duly noted by German intelligence.[74] But with no apparent results; nor was the effort needed: that day, Hitler was making further plans, based on the assumption there would eventually be hostilities with Britain and France.[75]

While word was awaited from Moscow, Foreign Office officials were wearily approaching the conclusion of the first stage of another series of negotiations – for an Anglo-Turkish Declaration. Britain and Turkey were to lend each other all the support in their power, if an act of aggression should lead to war in the Mediterranean. The second stage – permanent agreement – was to follow. Britain had yet another commitment.

Germany was also negotiating. On 13 May, Ciano received the text of the Italian-German 'Steel Pact', which had appeared to be a modest document when Ribbentrop had shown it to him earlier. Now Ciano exclaimed: 'I've never seen a pact like this – it's dynamite.' Hitler's document was one-sided, aggressive, and permanent. Mussolini, trying to moderate the terms, could only cut the duration from eternity to a decade.[76]

Late on Sunday, 14 May, Seeds was handed the Soviet reply to the Anglo-French proposals of 8 May. Once again the Soviets had answered in only minimum time; once again, discussions went back rather than forward. The British appeal 'did not contain principle of reciprocity' and placed Russia 'in a position of inequality', because no obligation by Britain and France to guarantee the Soviet Union was included. Also, the north-western frontier of the USSR, Finland, Estonia and Latvia – would remain unguaranteed. The Soviet Government insisted on 'an effective pact of mutual assistance against aggression', and on guaranteeing states in central and eastern Europe, plus Latvia, Estonia and Finland. Halifax had asked Seeds to ask if Molotov could visit Geneva, but the Soviet Minister was 'unlikely to be going himself' to the League of Nations Council; so there were no prospects of a personal discussion.[77]

The FPC discussed Britain's next move. The Soviet Union should be induced to approve a simple agreement covering Poland and Roumania with a tempting offer of military staff talks. Maisky, at a lunch with Vansittart, had hinted such a solution might be acceptable.[78] This idea was put to the Cabinet next morning. 'There are two particular objections,' said Halifax, 'the Russian proposal ignores the attitude of the four Baltic States .... Finland, indeed, is unwilling to be guaranteed by *any* other country.' Second, 'if we went beyond the scope of our previous proposals, namely Poland and Roumania, it will be necessary for us to consult the Governments of those countries, and this would involve considerable delay....'[79] Sir Robert, in a personal capacity, asked Maisky's advice: it was important to avoid delay, he said; Britain objected to the inclusion of the Baltic States, but was prepared to hold Staff conversations. If the arrangements were initially limited to Poland and Roumania, possible expansion could be discussed later. Maisky promised to submit the ideas to Moscow immediately.

Delay could be even more disastrous than the British imagined; on the same day, the Soviet Chargé in Berlin had again seen Schnurre. 'Astakhov,' reported the German, 'stated that there were no conflicts in foreign policy between Germany and the Soviet Union ... he commented on the Anglo-Soviet negotiations to the effect that, as they stood at the moment, the result desired by Britain would hardly materialise'.[80] And hints of Soviet-German contact had reached the British Embassy. The day after the Schnurre-Astakhov meeting, Henderson reported: 'I have little doubt that the Germans are doing all they can to secure the definite neutrality of Soviet Russia.'[81] The following day, 19 May, Chamberlain complained in the Commons of 'a sort of veil, a sort of wall, between the two Governments [Britain and Russia]'. But opposition to the British delays was embarrassingly loud: Russia had made 'a fair offer', declared Churchill, Soviet proposals were 'more simple, more direct, more effective', than those of Chamberlain's Cabinet. Ministers should 'get some brutal truths into their heads. Without an effective Eastern front, there can be no satisfactory defence in the West, and without Russia, there can be no effective Eastern front.' Lloyd George agreed: 'For months we have been staring this powerful gift horse in the mouth.... Why did we not make up our mind, and make it up without loss of time, that we should come to the same terms with Russia as we did with France?' Eden urged Halifax to go to Moscow, without success, and even offered to go himself.[82]

In Moscow, Seeds heard the BBC report of the debate, and feared the Russians would use these arguments to reinforce their own. He was therefore relieved to receive Halifax's cable giving him something to say. 'We now know the difficulties that have to be overcome in order to secure cooperation which both our Governments desire,' and a British answer would be sent 'without delay' after the Cabinet and other Governments had been consulted.[83]

Count Friedrich Werner von der Schulenburg, the German Ambassador, walked into the gloomy Soviet Foreign Ministry that same day. Molotov, in a 'most friendly' mood, declared Soviet-German economic negotiations could be resumed, but added that the necessary 'political basis' should first be laid down. Schulenburg asked what was meant, and Molotov gave a tantalizing reply: it was, he said, something both Governments would have to think about.

Meanwhile, Henderson had long since decided the Poles were to blame for the Danzig flash-point: the port should be handed to the Reich. 'If Scotland were separated from England by an Irish Corridor,' he had written on 26 April, 'we would want at least what Hitler demands.' Now, on 20 May, his next plea reached the Foreign Office. 'Although the arguments in support of the Polish case may be extremely strong,' he wrote, 'it is impossible to close one's eyes to the natural effect which the present Polish attitude must have on a mentality such as that of Herr Hitler.... From the point of view of prestige in his own country, to say nothing of the economic pressure from within, he must, by hook or crook, obtain before September some settlement of the Danzig and Corridor question.'[84] During that Saturday night, a crowd of demonstrators milled round a Polish customs station at Kalthof, in the Danzig area. Shots were fired; a German was killed, and tension immediately intensified. Only a few hours before, such a possibility had been discussed in Paris by Halifax, Daladier and Bonnet, Halifax stressed that Beck would regard a German seizure of Danzig or entry into the Corridor, as a threat to her independence. If this were so, 'Great Britain would be with Poland'.[85]

Germany required at least three years of peace, claimed Ribbentrop to Ciano, who had just arrived in Berlin to sign the Steel Pact on 22 May. At a sumptuous dinner given by Attolico that evening, Ciano invested Ribbentrop with the glittering Collar of the Annunziata, and so made him a cousin of the King of Italy. Ciano noticed tears in Göring's eyes – he wanted a Collar too. Before leaving for this dinner, Weizsäcker had despatched a cable to Schulenburg; commenting on Molotov's search for a 'political basis' for agreement, he said: 'We must now sit tight and wait to see if the Russians will speak more openly.'[86] Rumours of German-Russian talks were increasing, and were immediately denied in Moscow. 'Soviet Chargé at Berlin had reported that Germans were busy spreading rumours of that kind,' Seeds was blandly told that night.[87]

The Steel Pact was duly formalized, Ribbentrop proudly wearing his Collar. But as usual, most Berliners were plainly unimpressed by Nazi pomp. When Ciano went to lay a wreath at the War Memorial next day, reported Sir Nevile, 'the only person who was really spontaneously cheered by the Berliners was a solitary sanitary inspector who rode his bicycle along the *Unter den Linden* two minutes before Count Ciano was scheduled to pass'.[88]

Ciano left for home and Hitler next turned to his apprehensive Generals. In his Chancellery study he barked: 'Further success can no longer be won without bloodshed.... We cannot expect a repetition of the Czechoslovakia affair. There will be war. Our task is to isolate Poland.... There is no question of sparing Poland, and we are left with the decision: *To attack Poland at the first suitable opportunity.*' The italics were in the German original.[89]

'While the French were insistent that negotiations with Russia should not be allowed to break down,' Halifax, returned from Paris and the League of Nations, told the Cabinet on 24 May, 'they were a good deal less interested in the form that the agreement with Russia should take.... M. Daladier seemed almost disinterested about the actual wording....' Subsequent talks with Maisky at Geneva had been frank and fruitful. Maisky had made it clear his country insisted on a triple relationship as a 'fundamental condition'. If this were accepted, 'the Russians would not prove difficult on other matters'.

Halifax had had an important change of mind. Before, he had been prepared to dally with the Russians; now, he had realized the urgency. A breakdown would have a 'definitely unfavourable' effect and also: 'the idea of some *rapprochement* between Germany and Russia is not one which can be altogether disregarded....' And Chamberlain was also changing his mind. 'As my colleagues will be aware from the attitude which I have hitherto adopted, I view anything in the nature of an alliance with Russia with considerable misgiving. I have some distrust of Russia's reliability and some doubt of her capacity to help us.' But, like Halifax, he thought Britain should go ahead. The Cabinet agreed he should state in the Commons that afternoon, that no great difficulties need be anticipated with Russia. But the search for conciliation with Germany should continue; this, he said, would be 'the positive side of our policy'.[90] Important new instructions were sent to Seeds: 'HMG ... are now disposed to agree that effective cooperation between Soviet, French and British Governments against aggression in Europe might be based on a system of guarantees, in conformity with the principles of the League of Nations.'[91]

But next day, 25 May, Ribbentrop told Weizsäcker and Friedrich Gaus, director of the Foreign Office Legal Department, that the Führer intended 'to establish more tolerable relations between Germany and the Soviet Union'. Plans were being drawn up.[92] So, on this Thursday, draft instructions were being prepared for two Ambassadors in Moscow. First to arrive were the British proposals, but the French and British Ambassadors were to see Molotov together, and approval was needed from Paris. Yet Britain still retained the lead: briefly, Hitler hesitated. Weizsäcker told Schulenburg on 26 May to 'maintain an attitude of complete reserve'; the Führer had seen Chamberlain's optimistic statement to the Commons and been told the Anglo-Soviet negotiations might be too advanced to be broken. His offer might suffer a humiliating rebuff.

Meanwhile, leaks of an intended German initiative had reached London: on the 26th the French Ambassador showed Kirkpatrick an accurate report of the German moves from the French Ambassador at Berlin.[93] Seeds was instructed to present the new proposals 'as soon as possible'.[94] The British and French Ambassadors did so the following afternoon. Details of the proposals had already reached Molotov from Paris and from Maisky. Bolstered by the knowledge that Germany was also likely to bid for his attentions, he was well prepared. He received the two diplomats at the Kremlin, instead of at the Foreign Ministry, and to add to the majestic effect, sat behind a huge desk on a raised dais, while they sat in small chairs at his feet.

Molotov's personal reaction was, he declared, negative. 'The impression produced on his mind was that Great Britain and France wanted to continue conversations *ad infinitum* but were not interested in obtaining concrete results.' Seeds was shocked and dismayed; both he and Halifax genuinely believed that the main Soviet requirements had now been met. Molotov's criticism was certainly not true now. He asked Molotov to explain. 'The introduction of references to the League of Nations,' said Molotov, 'was a clear indication that Britain was prepared to make effective cooperation dependent on the interminable delays of League of Nations' procedure.' The Soviet Government, on the other hand, wanted an immediate guarantee of effective mutual assistance. Sir William insisted 'over and over again' that the reference was to 'the spirit' and 'the principles' of the League, but Molotov maintained this meant reference to the League's 'procedure'. 'He seemed to be either blindly acting on instructions or else capable of misunderstanding.' Molotov claimed: 'Britain and France were deliberately making no serious contributions towards concrete action ... his views remained unchanged, but they were, of course, only personal; he would report to his Government.'[95]

As news of this depressing interview reached London during the evening of 27 May, Weizsäcker was writing to Schulenburg at Moscow. An Anglo-Russian agreement would 'not be easy to prevent,' he said, and a German offer might provoke 'a peal of Tartar laughter.... Thus we now want to wait and see how deeply Moscow and Paris-London mutually engage themselves.' But he did not post this letter for another three days; and when it was finally despatched, it contained an important postscript.[96]

On 29 May, Halifax made an urgent attempt to clear up Russian misunderstandings. 'There is not the slightest ground for the assumption that HMG wish to adopt League procedure,' he cabled to Seeds. Britain was prepared to embark immediately on conversations of a concrete arrangement. Molotov's 'attitude is doubly disappointing in that I had understood that all the Soviet Government wanted was complete reciprocity and a guarantee of immediate effective support. This HMG are ready to give and their proposals have no other aim.'[97] Sir William immediately set off to see Molotov again, but reported back that he doubted the success of his long and tedious interview. 'My impression ... is that it is my fate to deal with a man totally ignorant of foreign affairs, and to whom the idea of negotiation – as distinct from imposing the will of his party leader – is utterly alien. He has also a rather foolish cunning of the type of the peasant.'[98]

Britain's temporary advantage in the race was soon to end. Early in the morning, Astakhov told Weizsäcker that Molotov had 'no intention of barring the door against further Russo-German discussions'. Weizsäcker then sent Schulenburg the letter he had written on 27 May, to which he had added a few more lines. 'With the approval of the Führer, an approach is nonetheless now to be made to the Russians.' A second message, stamped 'Most Urgent', stated: 'Contrary to the tactics hitherto planned we have now, after all, decided to make a certain degree of contact with the Soviet Union.'[99] Exactly one month was to pass before Germany's next formal move; but by then the ground would be even better prepared.

On 31 May, Molotov gave, to the USSR Supreme Council, his first public speech as Foreign Minister. He criticized the Democracies for hesitating, and he questioned whether they seriously wished to reach

152

agreement. A successful conclusion could only be reached if all the states of Central and Eastern Europe, including those bordering on the Soviet Union in the north, were given a guarantee. He did not criticize Germany – as Schulenburg immediately reported.[100] Hitler's enthusiasm for agreement with Russia grew; and at the same time the Führer tried to insure himself against a possible Anglo-Russian guarantee of Latvia and Estonia by hurriedly drawing up a non-aggression pact with Denmark on 31 May. 'Hitler will risk war if he does not have to fight Russia,' the French Ambassador at Berlin warned Bonnet on 1 June. 'On the other hand, if he knows he has to fight her too, he will draw back rather than expose his country.'[101]

London and Paris could only wait for the reply from Moscow, and this came next day. Molotov had modified the proposals into a new draft plan; but the modifications raised new problems without solving the old. Objections to the draft were discussed at an FPC meeting on 5 June, and Halifax pointed out: 'While we are called upon to guarantee all Russia's western neighbours, Russia would not guarantee all the countries neighbouring upon us.' Some way had to be found out of the deadlock. Halifax cabled Sir William to return,[102] and asked William Strang, Head of the Foreign Office East European Department, then visiting Warsaw, to be ready to accompany him.[103]

Next day, 7 June, Hitler's non-aggression pact with Denmark was followed by similar agreements with Latvia and Estonia. In London, the Estonian Minister, saying 'he was sorry to have to do this,' immediately presented an *aide-memoire*. If press reports were true, and Russia, Britain and France agreed to assist Estonia whether she liked it or not, 'the Estonian Government would be compelled to consider such proposals as an unfriendly act directed against the neutrality of Estonia'.[104] Negotiations with Russia were further complicated. During the day, Seeds was ushered to bed with a temperature, and could not travel to London as planned.

Halifax and Chamberlain decided to send Strang to Moscow. Halifax explained the so-called Strang Mission to Maisky on 8 June. 'I had at one time thought of suggesting to the Prime Minister that I should go myself, but it was really impossible to get away.'[105] Whether the outcome would have been different if Halifax had found time is an unanswerable question; it was probably already too late. He had in any case already been rebuffed over Geneva.

'German Embassy has, I understand, been very active recently,' cabled Seeds on 11 June. 'The German Ambassador leaves tonight for Berlin. It would seem that commercial negotiations are in progress.'[106] Next day, Strang left London for Moscow, and on 14 June, Halifax revealed to the Cabinet the written instructions he had with him, which tried to make the British position as flexible as possible. 'The draft treaty should be short and simple in its terms. It is better the agreement should be quickly reached than that time should be spent in trying to cover every contingency.'[107] However plausible Halifax considered the British attitude the central point was that the Soviet Union must be convinced that Britain's offer was better than Hitler's would be. Probably in the early days of the negotiations, Russia hardly considered an agreement between her and the arch-enemy Germany; yet in those first weeks Britain had deliberately delayed progress. Then had come the signs that an understanding with Hitler was not, after all, out of the question. The Anglo-French draft might have been successful if it had arrived earlier. But by then contact had been opened with Berlin; and Hitler could offer far more. Strang had indeed a daunting mission.

Eastern Approaches

Not only the Soviets believed Britain too weak to stand up to Hitler's armies. At a dinner on 14 June, the day Strang arrived in Moscow, Churchill was appalled to hear from Walter Lippmann that the US Ambassador, Joseph Kennedy, considered Britain would be defeated. 'It may be true,' he declared, waving familiar cigar in one hand, clutching familiar whisky tumbler in the other. 'It may well be true that this country will at the outset of this coming and, to my mind almost inevitable, war, be exposed to dire perils and fierce ordeals. It may be true that steel and fire may rain down upon us day and night scattering death and destruction far and wide. It may be true that our sea-communications will be imperilled and our food supplies placed in jeopardy. Yet these trials and disasters, I ask you to believe me, Mr Lippmann, will but serve to steel the resolution of the British people and to enhance our will for victory.' Sadly he went on: 'No, the Ambassador should not have spoken so, Mr Lippmann; he should not have said that dreadful word. Yet supposing, as I do not for one moment suppose, that Mr Kennedy was correct in his tragic utterance, then I for one would willingly lay down my life in combat rather than, in fear of defeat, surrender to the menaces of these most sinister men. It will then be for you, for the Americans, to preserve and to maintain the great heritage of the English-speaking peoples. It will be for you to think imperially, which means to think always of something higher and more vast than one's own national interests....'[1]

In Moscow that evening a plan of action was discussed by Strang, Seeds and his French colleague, Naggiar. The three met Molotov next morning. 'He undertook to study the material which we had supplied to him,' reported Sir William, 'and we expect to have another meeting with him shortly.'[2] Just before the meeting Seeds had cabled: 'I understand that the German Military Attaché and Commercial Counsellor have now also gone to Berlin.'[3] There, Schnurre warned a special conference that a breakdown of economic negotiations with the Soviet Union would be a severe political as well as economic setback.

Also on 15 June, the Führer was handed the top secret plan drawn up by Brauchitsch for operations against Poland. The order of deployment for the German forces would be put into operation on 20 August. 'All preparations must be concluded by that date.'⁴ While the German *Wehrmacht* worked out details of the offensive, British war preparations were being intensified. Naval reservists were organized on 15 June, against surprise attack; and the same day, General Sir James Marshall-Cornwall, Director-General of Air and Coast Defence, expressed optimism at the rate of anti-aircraft defence progress. In a few months, he claimed, London would be the safest place in the world.⁵

But a new fear arose: 'German exercise ... is due to begin on 20 June,' Phipps cabled from Paris on 16 June. 'It is thought that this may mark the first stage of an operation designed to cover eventual military action against Poland.'⁶ On 17 June Goebbels ferociously criticized Poland in Danzig itself. For some weeks German arms and personnel had been smuggled there to train local inhabitants; the Poles were taking counter-measures, which increased apprehension among Western diplomats.

Meanwhile, the scene was being set for the retreat of the British and French from Moscow. On Saturday, 17 June, Molotov met Seeds, Strang and Naggiar, and gave them a devastating reply to the latest Anglo-French suggestions. As Cadogan had feared, the Soviets seized on the alleged imbalance between the Western desire for a guarantee for Holland and Switzerland, and their reluctance to guarantee Estonia, Latvia and Finland. 'If His Majesty's Government and the French Government treated the Soviet Government as being naïve or foolish,' Molotov declared, 'he himself could afford to smile, but he could not guarantee that everyone would take so calm a view.'⁷ Yet, despite Molotov's latest reply, both the FPC and the Cabinet were still optimistic. Strang's instructions had contained a possible solution to the difficulty of states which did not want a guarantee. 'It should be agreed that the three Powers should consult together if one of them considered that its security was menaced by a threat to the independence or neutrality of any other European Power. If the other two Powers agreed that such a menace existed, and if the contracting Power in question was involved in hostilities in consequence, the other two Powers would go to its assistance.'⁸ The formal guarantee to the Baltic States, which Russia wanted but they did not, might thus be avoided. Consequently, Halifax sent further instructions to Seeds. As far as the Baltic States were concerned, he said, Molotov 'appears to overlook completely the fact that our draft treaty was intended to provide precisely for this assistance'. And in answer to the Soviet criticism that the proposals were unequal, he pointed out that the neighbouring countries whose integrity was important for Russia were Poland, Roumania and the Baltic States; for Britain and France they were Belgium, Holland and Switzerland. The West should receive the same treatment for the latter as Russia did for the former. If these matters could be settled, he would be prepared to agree to staff conversations starting immediately the agreement had been signed, and also to the omission of references to the Covenant of the League of Nations. The FPC was convinced that only these 'misunderstandings' obstructed a satisfactory outcome to the talks.[9] And Halifax told the Cabinet on 21 June: 'Provided Russia is really keen on reaching an agreement, I think there are no outstanding points which are likely to give rise to difficulty.'[10]

The Anglo-French team saw Molotov again that afternoon, and carefully repeated their main points as Halifax described them. But Molotov insisted the names of the countries concerned should be given in the Treaty, and that 'the guarantees which the Soviet Government would receive ... should be precisely stated and not left vague'. He said 'the proposal we had made did not represent any progress. He would however submit it to the Soviet Government'.[11] And back came the reply the same evening, short and sour. 'In view of the facts that these proposals constitute a repetition of previous proposals made by England and France, which, as already stated, have met with serious objections on the part of the Soviet Government, the latter have come to the conclusion that these proposals must be rejected as unacceptable.'[12] 'You are doubtless as bewildered as I am by the attitude of M. Molotov,' cabled Halifax to Seeds late the next night. 'The position as I see it is that we have declared ourselves ready to give him the substance of everything he requires.'[13]

While Halifax had been puzzling during the day over the next move, Hitler had been approving a 'preliminary timetable for "Case White"'.[14] Planning was on an immense and meticulous scale, with total military and civil mobilization. Problems involved were discussed at a top-level meeting of the Reich Defence Council next day, 23 June, with Göring in the chair. Seven million men would be drafted; concentration camp inmates would be used for labour supply; coordination details were to be fully drawn.[15]

On the same Friday, the Belgian Government informed Britain that they could not agree to basic military staff conversations between the two countries. No joint plans were to be prepared. British and French forces would have to operate with minimum information on the preparations in this vital section of the Front.

Halifax had another frustrating interview with Maisky on Friday: the Soviet Ambassador was, as usual, cooperative, but powerless. He was asked 'point-blank' whether his Government wanted a treaty at all. Halifax added: 'Throughout the negotiations the Soviet Government has not budged an inch and we have made all the advances and concessions.' He added that 'saying "No" to everything was not my idea of

157

negotiation and that it had a striking resemblance to Nazi methods of dealing with international questions'.[16] The FPC met in a pessimistic mood on 26 June, and concluded that to avoid a possible breakdown of negotiations, they must if need be accept the listing of States to be covered by the guarantee.[17]

But German feelers were to be extended again towards Russia. On 27 June, Schulenburg reported to Berlin that the Russians seemed anxious talks should not stop after the commercial bargaining had finished. 'They are afraid that as soon as we have gained this advantage we might let the negotiations peter out.[18]

Acting on the FPC's conclusion, Halifax told Seeds: 'In the last resort we should agree ... to a published list of States.' But Holland and Switzerland should be included on the list and the pre-liminary wording should read 'the following States which the con-tracting country concerned felt obliged to assist in maintaining its inde-pendence or neutrality....' A third condition laid down that the changes would have to result in a final settlement. There was to be no insistence that the non-guaranteed States should be on a 'consultative' basis. This, he hoped, would stop criticisms that the Anglo-French draft gave unequal treatment to Russia with regard to the Baltic States.[19] No more concessions could possibly be made. 'If we fail to reach agreement on the basis now proposed,' he told the Cabinet next morning 'there will be no possibility of reaching an agreement except on the basis of a simple tripartite pact.'[20]

But as the Cabinet in London approved this 'last effort', Schulenburg was enjoying a long interview with Molotov. 'My impression,' he reported, 'is that the Soviet Government is greatly interested in learn-ing our political views ...'[21] He asked for further instructions from Berlin.

'BRITISH AND FRENCH GOVERNMENTS DO NOT WANT A TREATY ON THE BASIS OF EQUALITY FOR THE USSR,' declared *Pravda* on 29 June. An article by Zhdanov, member of the Politburo and President of the Soviet Parliament's Foreign Affairs Committee, accused Britain and France of insincerity, even of manoeuvring for a settlement with Germany. One purpose of this article, suggested a hopeful Schulenburg, was 'to lay the blame on Britain and France for the possible breakdown of the negotiations'.[22]

On that day Henderson was 'thinking aloud' in a letter to Halifax. 'I do not believe that Hitler himself has yet decided what line to follow this autumn. He is simply waiting on events and testing nerves.'[23] He had recently attended a 'lively' party, and talked to Dr Funk, Economics Minister and President of the Reichsbank. 'I remarked ... "Heaven knows what Hitler's plans are." Funk's answer was "Hitler does not know himself". *In vino veritas*, for Funk at the time was not very sober.' While Hitler kept his policy close-hidden, Halifax made every attempt to make Britain's clear. It had two aims, he said in an important speech at Chatham House. 'One is our determination to resist force. The other is our recognition of the world's desire to get on with the constructive work of building peace.' But 'the threat of military force is holding the world to ransom, and our immediate task is ... to resist aggression. I would emphasize that tonight with all the strength at my command so that nobody may misunderstand it.' But the speech stood slim chance of success; Chamberlain and his Cabinet were too tainted with appeasement. To the Russians the speech meant Britain might yet conclude an agreement with Germany; to the Führer, despite his contingency plans for economic war against Britain, it meant Britain might not oppose him by force. And next day Halifax received another depressing cable from Henderson: 'The anti-British campaign both in the German press and in speeches by National Socialist leaders, particularly Dr Goebbels, has been intensified during the past few weeks.'

And also on 30 June, the name first appeared in Foreign Office documents of another prominent figure in Britain's attempt to make her position known. Mr Dahlerus, 'a very important industrialist', and a 'personal friend of Field-Marshal Göring', was in London and might be able to help. He was to see Göring again on 5 July ... and had asked the Field-Marshal to arrange an interview for him with Hitler at Berchtesgaden.' Dahlerus asked to be briefed on British policy to pass it on to the Germans.[24]

During 30 June new instructions were sent to Schulenburg: he was to delay resumption of economic discussions for the moment.[25] Perhaps Hitler believed progress would be easier after the Democracies had failed; or perhaps that the British and French had appeared too eager.

Seeds, Strang and Naggiar saw Molotov next day, 1 July, to hand over the 'final' Anglo-French concessions. At first the talks seemed hopeful: Sir William suggested the list of States might be contained in an unpublished annex to the Treaty, and Molotov said 'he thought that the Soviet Government would be willing to agree to this'. But then Molotov introduced a new problem: the question of 'indirect aggression'. He cited the example of Hacha, who had been intimidated into surrendering Czechoslovakia the previous March. 'We told him that this was a new point,' reported Seeds. 'There was nothing about such indirect aggression in the Soviet draft of 2 June; and indeed our new draft gave the Soviet Government everything they had asked for in their own draft. He replied that the question of indirect aggression had been discussed during conversations, and that the Soviet Government were as much entitled as [we] were to raise new points during discussions.' The delegates went away to consult their Governments; Molotov took their draft for consideration.[26] The reply came 48 hours later, on 4 July. The Russians agreed to a secret list of names – but not to including Holland and Switzerland. And they insisted on the words 'indirect aggression' being inserted.[27] Seeds, tired, bitter and frustrated, reacted strongly. Molotov replied that Switzerland and Holland marked a new extension of Soviet liabilities and that the Soviet Government had anyway made a concession by agreeing to a secret rather than published list of the countries.[28] The FPC hurriedly assembled that evening. In view of the urgency, they decided two alternatives should be submitted to the Soviets: 'The first alternative is that the Soviet Government should drop their definition of "indirect aggression" and that we should abandon our insistence on the inclusion of Switzerland and Holland in the secret protocol ... the second alternative is to fall back on a tripartite pact.' As far as the omission of Holland and Switzerland was concerned, 'the wheel has come full circle from the early days ... when Russia pressed for full reciprocity....' But 'it can well be argued that it is of first importance to make some arrangements in Eastern Europe, which would ensure Russian support for Poland, and that any failure to achieve this will act as an encouragement to Herr Hitler.'

The 5 July Cabinet meeting also discussed rumours of an imminent *coup* at Danzig. Chamberlain disclosed that on 1 July the French had asked him to join in a formal statement, but he had decided against it, believing the rumours were German-inspired and that 'the issue of such a statement might be playing the German game'. But a message was sent to Mussolini via Loraine, warning that any attempt to transfer Danzig to the Reich 'would undoubtedly lead immediately to a European war'.[29] And another leader in the West was also issuing a warning: the Soviet Ambassador in Washington, departing for a leave in Russia, carried with him a message from Roosevelt to Stalin. 'If his [Stalin's] government joined up with Hitler, it was as certain as the night followed the day that as soon as Hitler had conquered France he would turn on Russia.'[30]

But while Britain joined in the chorus of warnings, money had still to be found for essential military improvements. The Cabinet's second session on 5 July was one of the most significant of this period. Discussion revealed why Britain's rearmament programme was not advancing faster; indeed, experts held that existing projects were crippling the economy.

A memorandum on the financial situation had been prepared by Simon. So secret was this document that, together with a second paper on the German financial situation, it had to be handed back at the end of the meeting. The first section, headed 'War Chest', explained there were four possible sources from which Britain might pay for imported goods in wartime: exports, gold stocks, foreign securities owned by British subjects, and loans from abroad. The first of these, exports, could not be counted any considerable source of strength. On the second, Simon commented 'the sterling balance held in London by countries of the sterling *bloc*, is estimated to be falling by some £80 million per annum.... If this continues, it will soon become a serious economic activity even in peacetime. But the greatest anxiety is that it may gravely affect our staying power in war.' He continued: 'Our gold stock, together with such assets as we may be able to sell or mortgage in wartime to countries overseas, constitutes our sole war chest.' The third item, available foreign securities, totalled only about £200 million. As far as loans from America were concerned, 'the position under the Johnson Act is that we cannot borrow in the US today, either privately or from the Government'. Simon told Ministers: 'The broad upshot ... is that we should realize that we are steadily reducing our War Chest. It is impossible to say when war might break out. If it should break out some years hence, it is important that those who are responsible for policy should realize that our financial strength is then likely to be much weaker than it is today.'

The paper also dealt with 'Money for Defence'. The Cabinet review of February 1938 had allotted roughly £1,000 million for defence in 1939, 1940 and 1941. This had grown to about £1,100 million by September 1938 and subsequently a total of £2,100 million: £750 million in 1939, £700 million in 1940, and £650 million in 1941. The memorandum stated: 'On the basis of existing taxation ... the balance of expenditure to be found somehow may be guessed as follows: 1939, £500 million or a little less, 1940, £360 million, and 1941, £330 million or a little less.' Britain would therefore have to find, from new or additional sources, almost £1,200 million over the coming three years in order to meet only the existing defence programme. One obvious remedy was to increase taxation, but increases had already been substantial. 'In the course of time,' continued the paper, 'and it may be a short time, it is likely to be necessary to contemplate a variety of controls, especially prohibition of new issues, control of advances by banks, control of advances by Building Societies, control of companies' dividends and of the investment of their reserves, and possibly also the control of prices.' These measures were being studied. And Simon believed this section of the memorandum 'probably too favourably stated'. In conclusion: 'Further expenditure on armaments in this country cannot be undertaken without counting the cost in gold.... Indeed, as there is a prospect of the continuance of the present armed peace, if not of the outbreak of war, finality of expenditure (unless for overmastering reasons) should now be declared.'

Sir Richard Hopkins, Second Secretary to the Treasury, was allowed into the Cabinet meeting to be questioned. The Air Secretary asked: 'Is Britain unable to fight a long war?' Sir Richard replied: 'The situation undoubtedly grows more difficult with every month that passes.' On money for defence, he pointed out that 'from the point of view of our internal economy, it is impossible to proceed on the existing basis'. Lord De La Warr, President of the Board of Trade, gave an opinion which others, including Churchill, had long held. 'At the present time we are being subjected to a war strain in times of peace and are trying to maintain the position by peace methods.'

Germany had the advantage of being a dictatorship, stated a second report considered by the Cabinet, but this could be of dwindling value. 'The present régime in Germany started in a period of great depression with quite a small national debt, and was in a position to use inflationary methods on a very large scale, while merely taking up the slack in employment.' But the memorandum continued: 'The country is now fully employed and as much of their borrowing has been and remains inflationary, they may be approaching the end of these resources, and the advantage in this one respect may lie in the future on our side.'[31]

If the Treasury's assessment of Britain's situation was accurate, allies to share the burden of war, or neutralize Germany's advantages, were needed more than ever; next day, 6 July, Halifax sent the new instructions to Seeds. Before doing so, he asked Maisky to see him, and explained that if any further difficulties emerged, it might be better to fall back on a purely tripartite agreement. Maisky claimed 'the fuss made by the Baltic States', including a recent protest by Finland against being included in any Anglo-Soviet agreement, 'was about 75 per cent for purposes of show'.[32] In Moscow, Sir William sought another interview with Molotov.

Meanwhile in Berlin, Ribbentrop boasted to Attolico that a Russo-German treaty would soon be signed; if the Poles misbehaved over Danzig, they would be attacked; if France intervened, she would be crushed; if Britain stirred, her Empire would be destroyed; as for America, one speech by Hitler had put her to flight. 'I listened in wondering silence,' reported Attolico to Rome.[33] Informed of this frightening conversation, Mussolini saw Loraine on 7 July to receive Chamberlain's warning, and he made a statement which sounded awesome and harsh. 'Tell Chamberlain that if England is ready to fight a war in defence of Poland, Italy will take up arms with her ally, Germany.' Outwardly bold, Mussolini was inwardly very afraid, and his next words could have been a plea: 'the Danzig question is not worth a world war.' This interview was conducted in secret for fear of German reaction. 'Count Ciano is most anxious that the fact of my having seen Signor Mussolini should not be divulged,' wrote Sir Percy in his report. 'He says it would cause a fearful to do.'[34]

On Saturday, 8 July, Seeds presented the latest 'limits of concession' to Molotov, who still insisted Holland and Switzerland be excluded 'unless the Soviet Government obtained some compensation'. On indirect aggression, Molotov proposed a modified definition; this would read 'covering the use by a European Power of the territory of one of the undermentioned States for purposes of aggression either against that State or against one of the three contracting countries'. Seeds, Strang and Naggiar agreed to recommend it to their Governments. These two points could therefore be cleared out of the way if, at the next meeting, Sir William agreed Holland and Switzerland could be left off the secret list, and his instructions enabled him to do so providing the 'indirect aggression' issue was settled. But a third point pushed itself forward. Molotov now demanded this Agreement must depend on the conclusion of a separate Military Agreement. This requirement, made much earlier, had since been put to one side.

Sir William rushed his report off to London, where it was received on 9 July. Halifax replied that Sir William should not give way on the question of a Military Agreement. As for Molotov's definition of indirect aggression, he confessed he was puzzled at the meaning of the formula. 'At first sight his formula seems narrower than ours and fact that he prefers his is somewhat suspicious.'[35] But on the previous evening, at another meeting in Moscow, Molotov had abandoned the definition of indirect aggression which he had proposed on the Saturday. The expression now 'covered action accepted by any of the listed States under threat of force by another power, or without such threat involving the use of territories and forces of the State in question for purposes of aggression against that State, or against one of the contracting parties and consequently involving the loss of, by that State, its independence or violation of its neutrality'. He also emphasized that 'without a military agreement the political agreement would be a mere empty declaration'.[36] As for Holland and Switzerland, the Soviet Government agreed to include them on the list if separate pacts of mutual assistance had been signed by Turkey and Poland with the Soviet Union, and the Governments of Holland and Switzerland established diplomatic relations with Russia.

Molotov's new definition of indirect aggression was considered by the FPC on 11 July. They decided it gave the Soviet Government 'a wide range of intervention in the internal affairs of other countries', and was unacceptable. They would accept that a military agreement must be concluded before the final signing of the political treaty, provided this definition could be altered.

Seeds was not granted an interview with Molotov until 17 July, when the Anglo-French team argued without progress with the Soviet Minister over 'indirect aggression'. They told him their Governments had agreed to omit Holland and Switzerland, but would like a clause allowing consultation 'in the event of aggression or threat of aggression by a European Power against a European State not named in the foregoing list'. Molotov said this would be considered, but emphasized that his country demanded simultaneous political and military agreements. 'In

163

Soviet conception there would not be two agreements but a single Politico-Military Agreement.... On this point there should be no mis-understandings.' Unless Britain and France agreed, there could be no point in continuing, and he claimed this had been the Soviet scheme since talks started. Seeds reported to Halifax: 'In the circumstances we did not think that any useful purpose would be served by arguing about this.... I said frankly that my reports on our latest conversations had produced a painful impression in London, where it was felt that we were making fruitless concessions.'[37] Halifax was now convinced that the lack of Soviet cooperation meant the finish of negotiations.

The Russians made another tentative approach to the Germans during the day. The Soviet Trade representative in Berlin, Barbarin, told Schnurre that Moscow would like to extend economic relations with his country. A detailed memorandum explained how this could be done. Barbarin also disclosed that he could sign a trade treaty – such a treaty, Schnurre observed, 'will not fail to have its effect at least in Poland and Britain'.[38]

Halifax told the Cabinet next day, 19 July, that the Anglo-Soviet talks might collapse, but if they did 'this will not cause me very great anxiety, since I feel that, whatever formal agreement is signed, the Soviet Government will probably take such action as best suits them if war breaks out'. He added: 'It seems that discussions of some kind are proceeding between the German Government and the Soviet Government. It is impossible to assess their real value, but it seems likely that these discussions relate to industrial matters.' Chamberlain could not bring himself 'to believe that a real alliance between Russia and Germany is possible'.[39] Five days were to pass before the next Anglo-French meeting with Molotov. But Strang, described by the American Ambassador as having 'run aground',[40] sent a depressing report to London. 'Molotov does not become any easier to deal with as the weeks pass.... On the whole the negotiations have been humiliating experience.' And, prophetically, he added: 'The negotiations of the military part of the agreement will be a very difficult matter.... Poland, for instance, would have to agree to Soviet passage through their territory.'[41]

On Saturday, 24 July, a short cable arrived from Seeds. 'Following statement issued ... in the Soviet press this morning: "During the last few days negotiations with regard to trade and credit have been renewed between Germany and the USSR...." '[42] And during the day Schulenburg received important instructions from Weizsäcker. German-Soviet trade negotiations in Berlin would be acted on 'in a markedly forthcoming manner.... As far as the purely political aspect of our conversations with the Russians is concerned, we regard the period of waiting stipulated to you in our telegram [of 30 June] as having expired.'[43]

'If faced by the alternative of a limited treaty or complete break-down,' Halifax asked Sir William, 'do you think that M. Molotov would become more amenable to argument, or would he cheerfully accept the prospect of an immediate breakdown?' He was considering summoning Strang home if a deadlock could not be avoided, 'so as to be able to say that the discussions had not broken down but had only been suspended'.[44] Sir William felt an attempt should still be made to obtain a satisfactory definition of indirect aggression: he and his French colleague had drafted an alternative formula. He requested approval in time for a meeting with Molotov next day.[45] But Halifax wired: 'I cannot give you definite decision in time.... In no circum-stances should you commit HMG without further instructions.'[46] Seeds therefore went unarmed into the discussions. But Molotov had apparently lost interest in talk of a definition. 'He did not think ... that these questions would raise insuperable difficulties and he was con-vinced that the three Governments could find a formula which would satisfy them.' He was now primarily concerned with the military agree-ment. Sir William had to insist that the British Government, as he had said at the last meeting, wanted agreement on the outstanding political points before military talks began. Molotov attempted to brush this aside; repeating that no insuperable difficulties remained and 'it was essential that there should be no further delay about opening military conversations'. Accusing the British and French of wasting time, he insisted the military discussions should begin 'immediately'.[47] 'While disappointed at M. Molotov's attitude as regards definition of indirect aggression,' reported Sir William, 'I do cherish hopes that his repeated assertions that there would be no real difficulty over this question represents his intention to do his best for us.... I am not optimistic as to the success of military conversations ... but to begin with them now would give a healthy shock to the Axis Powers.'[48]

On the 25th the 'Big Four' – Chamberlain, Halifax, Simon and Hoare, met and decided, without consulting the full Cabinet, to make this important concession. Seeds was instructed to agree to immediate military conversations at Moscow.[49] Halifax told the Cabinet next day. Military conversations would have 'a good effect on world opinion', he explained. But some Ministers felt uneasy: Britain might put herself in a weak position if confidential information were given to the Soviet Government before a pact had been concluded. After con-siderable general discussion, a solution was found: '... our represen-tative should be instructed to proceed very slowly with the conversations until a political pact had been concluded.'[50]

But, unknown to the Cabinet, German-Soviet negotiations had advanced another stage. The previous night, Schnurre had dined Astakhov at an expensive Berlin restaurant. The Russian declared that a Soviet-German political *rapprochement* was in the vital interests of the two countries and asked: 'Why has Germany been so hostile?' 'German Policy in the East has now taken an entirely different course,' replied Schnurre.[51]

During the afternoon of 27 July, Molotov was informed by Seeds and Naggiar that military discussions could start. News of the agreement to start military talks reached the German Foreign Office on 28 July.[52] The same day came the first indication of Britain's leisurely approach to these talks. A telegram from Halifax to the French leaders announced that the British team would be led by Admiral the Hon. Sir R. A. R. Plunkett-Ernle-Erle-Drax, and the question of whether they should go by sea or air was under consideration. Had the French any preference in the matter?[53] The French replied next day that train transport would be preferred, but this would mean travelling through Germany, 'unnecessarily provocative' as Henderson pointed out. General Doumenc, head of the French team, 'did not appear attracted' to the idea of flying. The problem received full attention at the FPC meeting on Tuesday, 1 August. Chatfield said the only civil aircraft available were two old 'Hannibals' and these would have to land in Germany, according to air regulations. Another regulation prohibited the flight of Service officers over Germany. The only suitable service aircraft were Sunderland flying boats, but it would take six or eight of them to carry the party and they were 'urgently required for Fleet exercises' – although they could reach Russia via Denmark, flying outside territorial waters. Wellington bombers were available but 'would mean travelling in great discomfort'. In the end a passenger ship was chartered which would sail from London on Saturday, 5 August – and which would not reach Russia till the 11th. Chamberlain did not think 'that a difference of two days in the date of arrival ... will be very important'.[54] They were indeed.

On 29 July, a German courier had been rushed to Moscow by Weizsäcker, with a secret despatch for Schulenburg. 'It would be important for us to know whether the remarks made to Astakhov... have met with any response in Moscow. If you see an opportunity of arranging a further conversation with Molotov, please sound him out on the same lines.' Schulenburg should state that Germany would safeguard Soviet interests in Poland and in the Baltic area.[55] Weizsäcker anxiously awaited a reply.

Also on the 29th, Henderson attempted to talk with Hitler, but the Führer was making himself suspiciously difficult to contact. Convinced the Danzig situation was about to explode, mainly because of the Polish attitude, Sir Nevile set off to see Hitler, who was attending a Wagner Festival at Bayreuth. 'I had car trouble on the way down and when I arrived there I found that Hitler was away inspecting the Siegfried Line, accompanied by Ribbentrop – an ominous combination. ... He got back on the last afternoon of my visit, but I only saw him at a distance in the opera house.... But if he had wanted to speak to me Hitler could have done so, for he must have been informed that I was there.'[56]

Chamberlain was now convinced a breakdown of talks with Russia was highly probable, and the only chance of peace, he wrote on 30 July, rested in convincing Germany that 'the chances of winning a war without getting thoroughly exhausted in the process are too remote to make it worth while.... But the corollary ... must be that she has a chance of getting fair and reasonable consideration and treatment from us and others if she will give up the idea that she can force it from us.'[57]

On the last day of July, Weizsäcker cabled Schulenburg. His impatience had got the better of him. 'Please report by telegram the date and time of your next interview with Molotov as soon as it is fixed. We are anxious for an early interview.'[58] That same afternoon, Chamberlain announced to the Commons that a military mission was being sent to Moscow. And R. A. Butler, winding up the debate for the Government, committed an indiscretion which further complicated the talks. 'We have proceeded with the utmost vigour to discuss with Russia our outstanding difficulties and the main question has been whether we should encroach on the independence of the Baltic States.'[59]

The last month of peace opened with the largest German air exercises the country had ever seen. Mason-MacFarlane's staff in Berlin noted that officers and men were recalled from the reserve for short periods of training, and remained there long after. 'We noticed the absence of many individuals we knew, the shortage of petrol at garages, the restricted supplies of certain goods in the shops, and the curiously worded Press announcements.'[60] Henderson still believed that if war came the Poles would be almost as much to blame as Hitler. In a letter to Halifax on 1 August, he admitted his views were sometimes unorthodox – this was one reason why many of his letters were addressed privately to the Foreign Secretary. 'My views in an official form might be embarrassing to you.... I live on the other side of the Rhine, British internal politics are not my affair and if I may well see too much of the other man's view, in England one may well see too little.... I regard it as essential that the Poles, in their own ultimate interests, should be persuaded to be reasonable.' They should hand over Danzig.[61]

Halifax told the Cabinet next morning, 2 August. 'I have observed a certain tendency ... for it to be stated that we are committed to fight for Danzig. The true position is that Danzig, of itself, should not be regarded as providing a *casus belli*. If, however, a threat to Polish independence arose from Danzig, then this country would clearly become involved.' To Halifax's legalistic mind, the difference might be important; to others, notably Churchill, no difference existed. While having 'no wish to be more Polish than the Poles,' Churchill was anxious that the Government should not put pressure on the Polish Government to take action which, in their view, would be destructive to their State'.[62]

Seeds saw Molotov that afternoon, and the outcome was a virtual suspension of political discussions. 'Mr Butler had grossly misrepresented the Soviet attitude as regards Baltic States. . . .' Sir William attempted unsuccessfully to steer discussion back to the definition of indirect aggression. Molotov was a changed man. Unless Britain attempted a fresh approach, reported Seeds, political conversations would lapse.[63]

In London the Cabinet was about to disperse for summer holidays. 'I hope all my colleagues will have a really good holiday. In saying this I am also thinking of the Civil Service, which has worked under exceptional pressure for a very long time. . . . It is of the utmost importance that Civil Servants should also have a good holiday, so that they could return with renewed energy.'[64] But with Parliament about to go into recess, there were those who feared Chamberlain and Halifax would be free to produce a second Munich. In the Commons Churchill and Greenwood tried in vain to have the date of Parliamentary reassembly brought forward from 3 October to 21 August. Chamberlain declared that a vote for an earlier return would be a vote of no confidence in his leadership, and Churchill failed to raise sufficient support. Henderson was relieved: 'The proceedings in Parliament do not help the temperature in Europe to fall and to my mind that is what is above all needed at this moment.'[65]

Chamberlain left first for Chequers then for the wilderness and isolation of Northern Scotland. He intended to stay until 21 August, when he planned to return to London for a day or so. 'My movements thereafter depend on the state of affairs,' he had told the Cabinet. On 4 August, the 25th anniversary of the outbreak of the Great War, Parliament closed. But 20 days of holiday were all that the Cabinet would be allowed.

10

Account Presented

'I learn from an excellent source,' wrote the British Consul at Danzig, Shepherd, to the Foreign Office on 2 August, 'that German Ambassador ... is making his next steps dependent on an outcome of the Moscow discussions.'[1] And next day, German hopes soared, while those of Britain and France slumped. 'I think we may take it that M. Molotov will not volunteer any new proposals in the near future,' cabled Seeds, 'so unless we make a fresh approach to him, there will be a pause in the political conversations.... A pause in the conversations at the present stage would do no harm, since it would give time for the squall about Mr Butler's speech to blow over, and for the military missions to arrive and start their work.'[2]

Schulenburg had arranged to see Molotov, and Ribbentrop sent him an urgent cable. 'Yesterday I had a lengthy conversation with Astakhov ... in response to his desire for more concrete conversations on topical questions, I declared myself ready....'[3] An hour later, Weizsäcker also contacted Schulenburg, and told him that in the interests of speed, German-Soviet talks would be continued in Berlin while he negotiated in Moscow.[4] And in line with this, Schnurre saw Astakhov and made it clear the Germans wanted 'to make use of the *next few days* for continuing the conversations, in order to establish a basis as quickly as possible.' Schulenburg met Molotov during the evening, and reported later that he had 'abandoned his habitual reserve and he appeared unusually open'. Back in Berlin, the situation seemed highly satisfactory.

Well-informed as usual, the French Ambassador at Berlin reported on 3 August that the Nazi leaders had entered 'a new phase'. Attolico seemed also to sense the new attitude: Henderson found him unusually uncommunicative and hostile.[5] From Shepherd at Danzig came fresh reports of military activity. 'Evidence of the continued importation of military equipment is seen in the large proportion of rifles carried by detachments of auxiliary police.'[6]

Next day, 4 August, the day the British Parliament went into recess, saw a new surge of tension. The predominantly German Danzig Senate decided that Polish customs inspectors should not be allowed to carry out their duties. The Polish Government reacted quickly to this challenge, requesting 'immediate confirmation the Polish customs inspectors will be allowed to carry out their duties'. A reply must arrive by the following evening.[7] To Hitler, their 'ultimatum' was another clear sign that the Poles would not be intimidated, that sterner action was required.

The Anglo-French military missions sailed on their slow boat to Russia, and a cable from Halifax to Seeds indicated the political talks were to be kept firmly in abeyance. 'I shall not be replying in any detail to urgent points dealt with in your telegram for some days.'[8] Yet under the previous Cabinet decision the military talks were to proceed as slowly as possible, so that these political discussions could first arrive at some conclusions.

On Saturday it appeared the Polish ultimatum to the Danzig Senate had been successful. The Senate President informed the League of Nations' High Commissioner, Dr Karl Burckhardt, that orders concerning the Polish Customs inspectors had been given 'by a subordinate without my knowledge', and telephoned the Polish representative to say the regulations would not be put into effect, for the moment. Reporting this to London, Shepherd said the Polish Representative, although believing the matter would be settled, had still sent his family away to safety and had advised the High Commissioner to do the same.[9] Next day, Sunday, the Nazi Gauleiter of Danzig, Albert Forster saw the High Commissioner to express his 'irritation' at the Polish ultimatum, and, said Burckhardt, was 'inclined towards forcible measures'. Ominously, Shepherd reported, 'Herr Forster leaves by air for Bavaria tomorrow morning'.[10]

In Bavaria, Hitler's anger had been increased by information from the German Ambassador at Warsaw. 'Hardly any doubt' existed that Poland would fight over Danzig.[11] Ciano's diary entry for 6 August reads: 'We must find some way out. By following the Germans we shall go to war and enter it under the conditions least favourable for the Axis, and especially for Italy.' And on 7 August Mussolini proposed that Ciano and Ribbentrop should meet immediately.

Forster arrived at Berchtesgaden on the Monday, where the Führer told him he had reached the limits of his patience with the Poles; Hitler was working himself into an intense emotional state, witnessed by the Hungarian Foreign Minister, Count Czaky, on 8 August. A letter from the Hungarian Premier on 24 July had stressed that on moral grounds Hungary could not take armed action against Poland. The Führer was 'shocked' at the message; he stormed that if Germany were defeated in war, Hungary 'would be automatically smashed'. Poland did not present any problems anyway, nor did any other country: 'No power in the world could penetrate Germany's western fortifications. Nobody all my life has been able to frighten me, and that goes for Britain. Nor will I succumb to the oft-predicted nervous breakdown.'

'There is undoubtedly a feeling here that a serious crisis is inevitable before the end of the month,' cabled Kennard from Warsaw. 'Reports are reaching here regarding increased German military activity.'[12] Weizsäcker handed a note to the Polish Chargé: 'The German Government are compelled to call attention to the fact that repetition of such demands having the nature of an ultimatum and addressed to the free city of Danzig, as well of threats and reprisals, would lead to an aggravation of Polish-German relations, for consequences of which responsibility would fall exclusively on Polish Government.' As Beck pointed out to Kennard: 'It was the first time the Reich had directly intervened in the dispute between Poland and the Danzig Senate.'[13]

During the evening of 29 August, while London was plunged into a trial 'blackout', the *City of Exeter* slowly edged into Leningrad; on board were the British and French military missions, in full dress uniform. Next morning they were welcomed by a deputation of Soviet officers and left the docks in a fleet of cars, to spend the day sight-seeing. In Warsaw, Beck answered Germany's Note. Sarcastic, and belligerent, this reply was unlike any other the Führer had received from a threatened country. 'The Polish Government ... can see no judicial basis capable of justifying intervention of Germany ... and will consider any future intervention by German Government to detriment of their rights and interests as an act of aggression.'[14] German newspaper headlines screamed invectives and threats: 'POLAND? LOOK OUT!' 'WARSAW THREATENS BOMBARDMENT OF DANZIG.' Henderson to Lord Halifax: 'It's just like last year, everything is ready for *all* eventualities.'[15]

A young SS agent, Alfred Helmut Naujocks, was now given top secret instructions by his chief, Heydrich. He was to travel to the Polish border and prepare plans for a fake attack on the German radio station at Gleiwitz. In the attack, he was to leave 'evidence' that the violators of peace had been Poles.[16] In Danzig, Forster presented Burckhardt with an invitation to visit Hitler at Berchtesgaden. Göring was seeing a party of businessmen, most of them British but including the Swede, Dahlerus. Dahlerus later told the Foreign Office Göring believed a four-power conference of the Munich nations 'a good idea' and would mention the suggestion to Hitler. Dahlerus had also been told he could talk to Göring at any time, 'and convey him views which were difficult to convey in any other way'.[17]

On Friday, 11 August, Salzburg airport saw the separate arrivals of Ciano and Burckhardt. Ciano had a conference with Ribbentrop at his castle at Fuschl; Burckhardt met Hitler at Berchtesgaden. Both came away appalled and frightened at the pitch of frenzy now reached by the Nazis.

Mussolini's plea for a conference was dismissed. 'The decision to fight is implacable,' wrote Ciano in his diary. '[Ribbentrop] rejects any solution which might ... avoid the struggle. I am certain that even if the Germans were given more than they ask they would attack just the same, because they are possessed by the demon of destruction.... I am becoming aware of how little we are worth in their opinion.' Germany, said Ribbentrop, was bound to destroy the Poles for their recent attitude, but he claimed the conflict would not become general – even if France and Britain did intervene 'they are faced with the physical impossibility of injuring Germany or the Axis'. Lunch at Ribbentrop's castle was eaten in cold silence, except for a brief discussion on the difference between woodcock and snipe. After a further six hours of talks, which Ciano described as 'pretty dramatic', an official communiqué stressed 'the perfect identity of views' existing between the two Governments.[18] Ciano then went on to Berchtesgaden.

Burckhardt's encounter with the Führer had been even more terrifying, and he later sent Halifax a dramatic account of the two and a half hour ordeal:—

HITLER: The State Secretary has sent for the Polish Ambassador and told him the hour has struck.... That is my answer to ultimatums and lost war of nerves. (Fortissimo) If the slightest incident happens now I shall crush the Poles without warning in such a way that no trace of them can be found afterwards.... Listen to that.

BURCKHARDT: I am listening. I know that that will mean a general war.

HITLER (agitated and almost appealingly): So be it. If I have to wage war, I would rather do it today than tomorrow.... Italy (and here an impression of slight uncertainty) will fight with us whatever happens (hesitation), Japan also. Thanks to my fortifications I will hold the west with 74 Divisions, the rest will be hurled against the Poles, who will be liquidated in three weeks.... The Russians have no offensive strength and will not pull chestnuts out of the fire for others. A country which kills off its officers [Stalin had recently purged his army] does not intend to fight a war....'

Hitler advised Burckhardt to send his children to Switzerland; and added 'I have been glad to see you. You come from a world which is strange to me. But you have worked for a peaceful solution. I have great sympathy for another man, Lord Halifax. They have said much ill of him to me since, but my first sentiments prevail. I thought he was a man who saw things on a big scale and desired a peaceful solution.' Part of Burckhardt's account was not communicated to the French, including the possibilities of a visit to Hitler by an Englishman; this idea, according to Shepherd at Danzig, had been hinted at by Hitler at his meeting with Forster, and Shepherd had asked Burckhardt if he would try to discover more. In his talks with the High Commissioner, Hitler agreed to the idea of an Englishman – one who could speak German – coming to see him, and suggested General Ironside, who had recently visited Poland. Burckhardt agreed to pass the idea to London. And part of the conversation was not communicated either to France or to Britain; this, described in Burckhardt's memoirs, included a startling revelation of Hitler's plan. The Führer apparently stated that he would conclude an agreement with the Soviet Union, defeat the West, and then turn back against Russia.[19]

Meanwhile, the Anglo-French military missions had at least arrived at Moscow. And when officers sat down for the start of discussions, a ludicrous difficulty immediately arose. Marshall Voroshilov produced a document which gave him power to sign an agreement; General Doumenc had power to discuss but not to sign – and Admiral Drax had no written credentials at all. 'Please send by airmail,' cabled Seeds to London.[20] As these preliminaries took place in Moscow, Astakhov in Berlin informed Schnurre that 'he had received instructions from Molotov to state that the Soviets were interested in a discussion of the individual groups of questions',[21] and the Führer told Ciano at Berchtesgaden 'the Russians have agreed to a German political negotiator being sent to Moscow'. Ciano mentioned Mussolini's proposed conference, and Hitler did not reject it completely, but pointed out: 'Russia could no longer be excluded from future meetings.' The Italian Minister tried to discover Hitler's contemplated date for the attack on Poland; the Führer declared: 'I am determined to use the opportunity of the next political provocation ... to attack Poland within 48 hours and to solve the problem in that way.' At a second shorter meeting next day, Hitler stressed that because of the bad weather in the autumn, 'it is of decisive importance, firstly, that within the shortest possible time Poland should make her intentions plain, and secondly that no further acts of provocation of any sort should be tolerated by Germany.'[22] Ciano, disillusioned and frightened, confided to his diary: 'I return to Rome completely disgusted with the Germans, with their leader, with their way of doing things. They have betrayed us and have lied to us. Now they are dragging us into an adventure which we have not wanted.'[23]

In Moscow, the military missions were still holding initial talks; but Seeds had doubts about the instructions issued to the British team, that 'until such time as the political agreement is concluded, the delegation should ... go very slowly with the conversations, watching the progress of the political negotiations, and keeping in very close touch with HM Ambassador.'[24] Sir William warned Halifax that 'M. Molotov on his side will ... evade coming to any agreement with us on these political points, until he has reason to believe that the military talks have at least made very considerable progress.'[25] And now the Russians forced the pace, catching the Anglo-French military missions off-balance; they were never able to recover themselves. In order to give effective help in a war against Germany, declared Voroshilov on Monday, 14 August, Russian forces would have to be allowed 'to move against East Prussia through Polish territory and in particular through Vilno Gap ... (and) to use Roumanian territory.' But would the Poles and the Roumanians allow these operations? 'Without an unequivocal answer, continuance of military conversations would be useless.' Seeds cabled the latest development to London, and added: 'I beg to stress the need for extreme urgency.'[26]

While the military talks in Moscow had reached stalemate almost as soon as they had begun, Ribbentrop had instructed Schulenburg to give Molotov a long declaration of German policy, which mentioned the possibility of a visit to Moscow by Ribbentrop himself. Halifax, a few days before, had told Maisky he himself was too busy to go to Russia; Ribbentrop was apparently certain he could find the time. 'In my view, only through such direct discussions can change be brought about, and it should not be impossible thereby to lay the foundations for a final settlement of German-Russian relations.'[27] Also on this eventful Monday, Hitler called a conference of his Commanders-in-Chief – his *Schweinhunde* as he liked to describe them. 'The great drama is now approaching its climax,' he declared. He thought it unlikely Britain would join the conflict, and hinted at agreement with the Soviet Union. Nevertheless to avoid Anglo-French intervention 'it would be necessary to crush Poland within a week or two'.[28] During the evening, Henderson reported a discussion he had had with Attolico. Clearly very worried, he had told Henderson that 'unless something was done and done before Hitler has occasion to make his next public speech either at Tannenberg on 27 August, or at Nuremberg, we would drift inevitably into war'.[29] Later that night Kennard added his quota of gloom. 'There has been a marked increase in German military activities; the Polish Government has decided to reinforce their troops on the frontier.'[30]

German military preparations reached a new level next day, 15 August, when instructions were issued to call-up 25,000 men for the Western Front. The party rally at Nuremberg, scheduled for early September and proclaimed by Hitler on 1 April as the 'rally for peace', was suddenly cancelled. In Britain, large scale exercises of the 19 squadrons of coastal command began on 15 August and would last until 21 August.[31] The same day, Churchill was touring the French fortifications, escorted by General Georges. 'The French Front cannot be surprised,' he reported to Hore-Belisha. 'It cannot be broken at any point except by an effort which would be enormously costly in life.'

174

But 'the flanks of this Front however rest upon two small neutral states. The attitude of Belgium is thought to be profoundly unsatisfactory. At present there are no military relations of any kind between the French and the Belgians.'[32]

Back in London, the idea of delaying the progress of military talks with Russia was abandoned. In Paris, Bonnet saw the Polish Ambassador and urged 'with every argument at his command' that Warsaw should give immediate consent to Russian assistance.[33] But in Berlin the British and French Ambassadors called on Weizsäcker and were scornfully told that not only would Russian help to the Poles be negligible, but in the end Russia would even join in sharing in the spoils.[34] And also that evening, Molotov replied to Ribbentrop; Russia 'warmly welcomed German intentions of improving relations with the Soviet Union', although Molotov added that Ribbentrop's visit would require adequate preparation and should not be hurried. He hinted that a non-aggression pact between the two countries might follow.[35] Ribbentrop hurried to Hitler at Berchtesgaden.

Wednesday, 16 August, saw frantic activity at the Foreign Office in Whitehall, in an attempt to break the Russian deadlock. Halifax and Strang, now back in London for further briefings, discussed the Russian demand for consent to move into Poland and Roumania. Strang told the French Ambassador the Polish and Roumanian Governments should be approached, and 'the situation put frankly to them'. In fact the French had already decided to sound out the Polish General Staff, using the French Military Attaché at Warsaw.

New instructions were being rushed to Schulenburg. He was told to tell Molotov that 'Germany is prepared to conclude a non-aggression pact with the Soviet Union.... Further, Germany is ready to guarantee the Baltic States jointly with the Soviet Union.' Ribbentrop stressed the urgency of an agreement, 'in view of the present situation and of the possibility of the occurrence any day of serious events'. He added : 'For these reasons I am prepared to come by aeroplane to Moscow at any time after Friday, 18 August ... if the occasion arises to sign the appropriate treaties.'[36]

The same day, Admiral Drax cabled London from Moscow : 'Hopes of military agreement ... seem to depend primarily on a favourable reply regarding Poland and Roumania.'[37] Yet if the latest assessment by Henderson was accurate, Polish cooperation was doubtful. 'If there is to be a truce (and it is the last hope) the ill treatment of the German minority in Poland must be stopped.... Of all Germans, believe it or not, Hitler is the most moderate so far as Danzig and the Corridor are concerned.... Warsaw ... is one thing. Outside in the country the Poles are an utterly uncivilized lot.... We could not say Boo to Benes last year till we were on the abyss of war. And we can't say Boo to Beck this year.'[38]

On Thursday morning, 17 August, Berchtesgaden, London and Paris anxiously awaited news from Moscow and from Poland. In Warsaw, Beck urgently discussed with Polish military chiefs the French query about Russian help. Hitler, impatiently waiting for a report from Schulenburg, issued final instructions for 'Operation Himmler' – the fake attack on the German radio station at Gleiwitz, where anti-German slogans would be shouted into the radio microphone and bodies would be left. These, concentration camp victims, were code-named 'canned goods'.[39] At noon, the Führer sent to Schulenburg, demanding information. None came for another eight hours, when an exasperated Schulenburg replied that he was to see Molotov that evening. A single sentence was cabled to London by Seeds. 'Due insistence that no use continuing until reply from Governments is received, conference has adjourned until Monday.'[40] Everything still depended on the Poles.

Schulenburg saw Molotov at 8 p.m., and the Russians had decided to dally. 'Until very recently,' Molotov said, 'the Soviet Government have proceeded on the assumption that the German Government are seeking occasion for clashes with the Soviet Union.' They therefore insisted that negotiations should be by 'serious and practical steps', rather than by one drastic action such as Ribbentrop proposed. First, trade and credit agreements should be concluded; and, although Ribbentrop's proposed visit was highly gratifying, and contrasted sharply with the despatch of a British official of 'second class rank' to Moscow, it would take a while to prepare.[41]

Just before midnight on 17 August, Halifax sent further instructions to Seeds. 'Now that the military conversations are in progress, it is desirable that the discussions on outstanding political points should be continued.'[42] He was woefully misguided: military talks had shuddered to a stop. The clearest warning so far of the need for drastic action reached Halifax next morning in a message from Lindsay, Ambassador at Washington, revealing the interview between Schulenburg and Molotov on 15 August. The conclusion of a non-aggression pact between Germany and Russia was not only possible, but imminent.[43] On Friday morning Hitler was impressed by the need for a vigorous initiative, when Schulenburg's report revealed the Germans would have to force the pace.

Rumours of early action increased during this Friday. Loraine reported from Rome: 'Senior official of Ministry of Foreign Affairs, who accompanied Count Ciano to Salzburg and Berchtesgaden is convinced that Hitler has definitely decided, unless it is surrendered, to take Danzig, then march on Warsaw. He also said that Herr Hitler's language and behaviour showed clear signs of mental abnormality.'[44] A letter reached London from Henderson. 'I don't usually take tickets in the "dates" lottery, but I did venture to write to the S of S early in

July to the effect that I foresaw the big crisis round about 27 August. I am afraid that I may not be far out.'⁴⁵ In another message Sir Nevile suggested 'a letter, if possible accompanied by a German translation, from the Prime Minister to Hitler'.⁴⁶

In Warsaw, the French Ambassador saw Beck; the interview was 'not satisfactory'. 'If Poland agreed to passage of Russian troops,' said Beck, 'this would lead to an imminent declaration of war on the part of Germany, as Herr Hitler would consider such a step was a further critical development in the policy of encirclement, and given his anti-Bolshevik complex he would see red and not hesitate to precipitate the war.' This information was sent to London by Kennard, who added : 'I will try to do my best to convince Colonel Beck further, and even try, if all else fails, to get him to agree to concession of tacit acceptance.'⁴⁷ During the Friday evening yet another 'most urgent' telegram was sent by Ribbentrop to Schulenburg. 'We too, under normal circumstances, would naturally be ready to pursue a realignment of German-Russian relations through diplomatic channels, and to carry it out in the customary way.' Ribbentrop continued : 'But the present unusual situation makes it necessary, in the opinion of the Führer, to employ a different method which would lead to quick results.' He proposed to make 'an imminent departure for Moscow', and Schulenburg was to prepare the way. 'Please emphasize that German foreign policy has today reached an historic turning point.'⁴⁸

Saturday, 19 August, was a glorious day on the wide Scottish moors. The grouse-shooting season had been open one week; the birds were plentiful, the air was fresh and sweet. Chamberlain was enjoying his rest, despite the despatches from the different world in London. And now came a letter from Halifax : German hostilities could be expected to start in about six days' time. 'If the appreciation is in fact a true one, it is also a black one, and there is no time to lose.... There are indications that Herr Hitler still believes we do not mean to fight or that, alternatively, he can crush Poland before we come in.... I would suggest that we should find a means of conveying to him a clear message.... It is for consideration whether this should best be done through the agency of someone like Ironside, who might speak verbally to Hitler, or by means of a letter to Herr Hitler from yourself.' Halifax enclosed a draft communication for Chamberlain to study.⁴⁹

Britain's peace-loving Prime Minister packed away his guns and hurried south to face the prospect of imminent war. The Cabinet was also soon scurrying to London. Meanwhile, early on 19 August, Kennard had been received by Beck. 'I fear that my conversation with M. Beck was, if anything, more unsatisfactory than that of the French Ambassador,' he cabled.⁵⁰

Tension in Berlin and at Berchtesgaden was as unbearable as in Whitehall. Schnurre reported the discussions with the Russians on the trade agreement had ended the previous evening with 'complete agreement', but the signature which was to have taken place that day, 19 August, had been delayed. The Russians had telephoned to say they were awaiting instructions from Moscow.[51]

Then, at 7.10 that evening, the teleprinter at the German Foreign Ministry began to chatter out a message from Moscow. 'The Soviet Government agree to the Reich Foreign Minister coming to Moscow one week after the announcement of the signature of the economic agreement.' Schulenburg added: 'Molotov handed me the draft of a non-aggression pact.' Molotov said Ribbentrop could arrive on 26 or 27 August if the trade treaty were signed and made public on 20 August. 'Molotov did not give reasons for his sudden change of mind. I assume that Stalin intervened.'[52]

Top priority telegrams and telephone messages continue to pass between Moscow, Warsaw, Paris, Berlin, London and Rome during the Saturday night and Sunday. At 2 o'clock on Sunday afternoon the commercial treaty between Germany and Russia was signed in Berlin; final preparations for the 'incidents' on the Polish frontier had been made; German troops moved off in closed trucks to assembly points in the Gleiwitz, Pitschen and Hochlinden areas.[53] In Rome, Loraine reported the Italians anxious to avoid war, and Halifax sent him a warning for the Duce that Britain would fight. But Mussolini was now resigned to the fact that the fate of his country was linked to Hitler. 'The Duce made an about face,' wrote Ciano in his diary. 'He wants to support Germany at any cost in the conflict which is now close at hand.... I try to debate the matter but it is useless now.'[54]

Once the pact was signed with Russia, Hitler could act, and on Sunday he sent a personal telegram to Stalin. 'I accept the draft of the non-aggression pact that your Foreign Minister, M. Molotov, handed over, but consider it urgently necessary to clarify the questions connected with it as soon as possible.' Hitler, who had so often and so recently vilified Stalin, now pleaded for his assistance. 'The tension between Germany and Poland has become intolerable.... I therefore again propose that you receive my Foreign Minister on Tuesday, 22 August, but at the latest on Wednesday, 23 August.'[55]

During the day a cryptic message had arrived at the Foreign Office from Berlin suggesting that Göring should come to London and see the Prime Minister. Halifax discussed the suggestion with Chamberlain, and it was decided to agree. Arrangements were started for Göring to come over secretly on Wednesday, 23 August. 'The idea was that he would land at some disused aerodrome, be picked up in a car and taken direct to Chequers.' But no answer was to come until 24 August, when a message arrived that Hitler did not think the idea immediately useful. 'Nothing further therefore happened,' wrote Halifax, 'and except that it was obviously wrong to neglect any chance however unpromising, I think we all felt it resembled stage melodrama rather than even the feverish diplomacy that immediately precedes the catastrophe of war.'[56]

Hitler was almost collapsing under the strain and tension as he waited for a reply from Stalin, and he paced the room during the night of 20/21 August, unable to sleep. His doctors were nearby. At 3 o'clock on Monday morning came an almost intolerable message that Schulenburg had still to receive the telegram containing Hitler's message for Stalin. Ribbentrop, under equal strain, sent another cable. 'Please do your utmost to ensure that the journey materializes.'[57] Four German Divisions were now poised ready on the Polish frontier. In France, precautionary military measures were being taken; all men on leave were recalled and units in training camps were sent back to their barracks ready for deployment.[58]

'I am to see Molotov at 3 p.m. today,' cabled Schulenburg just after noon on the 21st.[59] Meanwhile the French were making a last effort at the Moscow military talks: if Warsaw would not give consent to Russian troops moving into Poland, then this consent would be given 'in principle' on Poland's behalf. M. Corbin, French Ambassador at London, called at the Foreign Office to say the French Ambassador in Moscow, and General Doumenc, head of the French military mission, were going to inform the Russians that the Soviet request had received an affirmative answer. The slim excuse for this initiative was to be that, in refusing the Russian request, Beck had insisted his negative reply should not be communicated to the Soviets. Corbin asked for Britain's cooperation. Strang told Cadogan, after this conversation, that 'the French Government have gone ahead without consulting us and now ask for our support. It may well be that their judgement of the Polish attitude is the right one.'[60] But it came too late. Voroshilov had suggested a long adjournment to allow the members of the Soviet mission to atend 'autumn training exercises'. The military missions had held their last meeting; now, at last, written credentials for Admiral Drax arrived from London.[61]

By 10.30 p.m. Stalin's reply was in the Führer's hands at Berchtesgaden. 'The Soviet Government have instructed me that they agree to Herr von Ribbentrop's arrival in Moscow on 23 August.'[62] Shortly after 11 p.m., light music on the German radio was interrupted for an announcement: 'The Reich Government and Soviet Government have agreed to conclude a pact of non-aggression.' Within moments the news, transmitted first by press agencies, had reached London. One journalist telephoned Hore-Belisha, now back in London and still studying the flood of reports of German troop concentrations. 'A complete bombshell,' he scribbled in his diary. 'Ribbentrop is to go to Moscow immediately to bring negotiations to conclusion. Germany has two million men under arms.'[63] An urgent meeting of the Cabinet was called for the next day, 22 August, and, early in the morning, a cable arrived from Shepherd at Danzig, written before the announcement of the German-Soviet pact. 'Atmosphere in Danzig is tense. High Commissioner feels that whereas at the time of his interview, Herr Hitler was hesitant, something has since occurred to tip the scales.'[64]

Goebbels' newspaper, *Der Angriff*, declared: 'The world stands before a towering fact; two peoples have placed themselves on the basis of a foreign policy which during a long and traditional friendship produced a foundation of a common understanding.' Yet this newspaper had been among the most hostile to the Bolsheviks. The French Minister of Marine recalled all men from leave, ordered booms to be placed in position, sent ships to war stations. Reports of German troop movements continued to jam the wires. Corbin told the British Foreign Office that Paris proposed to treat the report with 'calm and reserve'. Guidance given by the Foreign Office to newspaper queries also said the reports should be treated with 'calm and reserve', adding: 'It does not modify the attitude or policy of HMG.'[65] Slightly less calm were instructions sent to Seeds, who was instructed to tell Molotov that a German-Soviet agreement would 'seem to render negative the results already achieved during the negotiations between the three powers, and to constitute an act of bad faith on the part of the Soviet Government. It would indeed be incredible that the Soviet Government should have been carrying on, let alone concluding, such negotiations without a single word to HM Government or the French Government.'[66] Sir Nevile struggled to find some consolation. 'If pact does not materialize within the next few days, and von Ribbentrop is faced with negotiations like ourselves and no simple guarantee signature, the effect in Germany and on public opinion might be correspondingly depressing.'[67] Later in the day he had doubts of even this advantage. Claiming not to be surprised by the announcement: 'I have always felt that our policy with Poland would only end by driving Germany and Russia together,' he commented: 'I imagine everything must be cut and dried and that Ribbentrop will merely sign on the dotted line and come back with drums and trumpets, greater prestige and kudos. I hate the thought of that. It is too much to hope that Moscow will play with Germany as they have with us.'[68]

With pendants fluttering, German staff cars accelerated up the winding mountain road to the Berghof. The German military chiefs were assembling for a conference called by the Führer. The weather was peaceful and warm, and the views across the peaks were magnificent, as the officers crunched across the gravel into Hitler's mountain retreat and took their seats in a half circle. Hitler stood behind his massive desk to address his Chief Commanders. Excited, exultant, extolling his own greatness, he announced action would now be taken against Poland. A treaty with Russia would be concluded in 48 hours' time, and with political preparations completed, the way was open for the soldiers. A 'propagandist reason' would be given for starting the war – 'never mind whether it is plausible or not'. The date for opening hostilities would probably be Saturday, 26 August. A number of those present at this highly emotional meeting scribbled surreptitious notes, and one General passed his to a staff officer, who in turn handed them to a journalist in Berlin. The notes finally arrived in the hands of Sir George Ogilvie-Forbes at the British Embassy. By 26 August the Foreign Office therefore had a reasonably accurate account of the meeting, and of the Führer's frenzied attitude. Hitler was quoted: 'I experienced those poor worms Daladier and Chamberlain in Munich. They will be too cowardly to attack. After Stalin's death – he is a very sick man – we will break the Soviet Union. Then there will begin the dawn of the German rule of the earth.... I have but one worry, namely that Chamberlain or some other such pig of a fellow will come at the last moment with proposals or with ratting. He will fly down the stairs, even if I shall personally have to trample on his belly in the eyes of the photographers. No, it is too late for this. The attack upon, and the destruction of, Poland begins Saturday early.... For you, gentlemen, fame and honour are beginning as they have not since centuries. Be hard, be without mercy, act more quickly and brutally than the others. The citizens of western Europe must tremble with horror. That is the most humane way of conducting a war. For it scares the other off.' The secret informant had added that the speech was enthusiastically received. 'Göring jumped on a table, thanked bloodthirstily and made bloodthirsty promises. He danced like a wild man. The few that had misgivings remained quiet.' During his interrogation at Nuremburg, Göring refuted this description. 'I dispute the fact that I stood on the table, I want you to know that the speech was made in the great hall of Hitler's private house. I do not have the habit of jumping on tables in private houses. That would have been an attitude completely inconsistent with that of a German officer.'[69]

Meanwhile, a top level meeting had also begun in London, in a vastly different atmosphere. Cabinet Ministers had assembled for their first meeting since their summer holidays. Ministers were tense; the Town Clerk of Westminster had just made a terrifying announcement. 'Parents and Guardians residing in Westminster are asked to bring their infants up to two years of age to one of the below-mentioned centres during the week commencing Thursday, 24 August ... to be fitted with gas helmets.'

'I am sorry to have to recall the Cabinet in circumstances which can only be described as grave,' apologized Chamberlain. Halifax gave an account of the military discussions with Russia, and added that Sir William had been instructed to ask Molotov 'how we stood'. Chatfield admitted: 'In the course of the Staff conversations we have given the

Soviet Government certain secret information as regards our plans on the Western Front, but only in general terms. The French have given a good deal more.' 'The effect of the pact on Poland has been to confirm suspicions of Russia,' said Halifax. 'It will certainly not make Poland more inclined to accept Russian assistance.' He added: 'I think that if it is true that the German-Soviet pact has been concluded, this is perhaps not of very great importance in itself. Nevertheless, the moral effect ... will be very great.'

Later in the discussions Halifax said there was a good deal of information, from a number of sources, that Germany proposed to attack Poland, and the dates 25 August to 28 August had been mentioned. 'If these are Germany's intentions they are probably based on the assumption that if they attack Poland they would win a speedy victory, and that other Powers will not interfere.' Chamberlain then revealed the suggestion of a message from him to Hitler, possibly using Ironside as emissary. The Cabinet felt, however, that if a letter was to be sent it would have to make suggestions on how the German-Polish dispute could be settled, and any emissary would have to deal with very delicate negotiations. Ironside would not be suitable. The Prime Minister commented: 'It is unthinkable that we should not carry out these obligations, and I think an announcement should be made ... that, whatever ... the arrangement between Germany and Russia, it made no difference to our obligations to Poland, and to our determination to support Poland.' He also said Parliament should be recalled on 24 August, and both Houses should be asked to push the Emergency Powers Bill through during the day, and after these steps, 'there is no reason why the proposal to send a personal letter to Hitler should not be carried out.... I feel that the letter should be passed through ordinary diplomatic channels.' Halifax interrupted to say a telegram had just been received from Shepherd at Danzig, stressing that the letter should be sent to Hitler next day. Ministers agreed that Chamberlain and Halifax should draft it.

The Cabinet also decided to set up a Committee on increasing defence preparations. Meanwhile, Ministers agreed to a number of precautions: the First Lord was to call up 5,000 further reservists, the War Secretary to call out key parties of all coast defences and anti-aircraft units, with discretion to call out the remainder without reference to the Cabinet. All squadrons of the Auxiliary Air Force were to be brought into operation, including the balloon squadrons, and Anderson was asked to take action on Civil Defence measures, including the blackout. Evacuation measures were to be prepared. 'It will shortly be essential,' warned Simon, 'to take steps with regard to the loss of gold which has been very heavy in the last few days, amounting on one day to £30 million. The amount of gold remaining ... must now be regarded as the minimum required for our War Chest.'[70] The

Cabinet issued a categorical statement that Britain would stand by Poland, and in Paris a National Defence Council meeting reached the same decision. 'France has no choice ...'

As Ribbentrop arrived by air at Königsberg on the first stage of his flight to Russia, Molotov, in Moscow confirmed to Seeds that a non-aggression pact was about to be signed, and the British Ambassador reacted with a brave display of anger. He was delighted, 'after months of patience and self-control, to accuse the Soviet Foreign Minister of "bad faith", a charge which an accuser cannot usually make and survive'.[71] As Sir William was releasing steam, in Rome Loraine was told by Ciano that Mussolini had studied very carefully Chamberlain's request that the Duce use his influence. When Ribbentrop returned from Russia, the message would be conveyed to him; meanwhile, Britain should urge the Poles to re-establish direct contact with Germany. Sir Percy commented to Halifax: 'In difficult circumstances, Sr. Mussolini's response is handsome.'[72]

Halifax, on this busy night of 22 August, telephoned Henderson to warn him that a letter for Hitler would soon be sent; this communication read: 'Apparently the announcement of a German-Soviet agreement is taken in some quarters in Berlin to indicate that intervention by Great Britain on behalf of Poland is no longer a contingency that need be reckoned with. No greater mistake could be made.... It has been alleged that, if His Majesty's Government had made their position more clear in 1914, the great catastrophe could have been avoided.... HMG are resolved that on this occasion there should be no such tragic misunderstanding.'[73] Sir Nevile hurriedly arranged to fly to Berchtesgaden next morning, 23 August. He arrived at Salzburg at noon. Also at noon, two large Condor transport aircraft swept down on to the concrete at Moscow airport with Ribbentrop and the German delegation on board. They hurried to the Embassy in Moscow for a hasty meal.

Henderson drove to Hitler's retreat at Berchtesgaden, and was received by Hitler just after 1 p.m. Hitler was excitable and uncompromising, his language violent; he condemned the British support for the Czechs and Poles. Sir Nevile repeated that Britain intended to honour her obligations to Poland, while Hitler repeated that the Poles were persecuting German nationals. It was agreed the Führer would send or hand Sir Nevile the reply to Chamberlain's letter in two hours' time, and Henderson returned to Salzburg to wait. Seven days later Sir Nevile heard a report, which he believed, that Hitler had had a nervous breakdown after this Wednesday lunchtime visit. Weizsäcker, in his memoirs, gave a different version. 'Hardly had the door shut on the Ambassador,' he wrote, 'than Hitler slapped himself on the thigh, laughed, and said "Chamberlain won't survive that conversation; his Cabinet will fall this evening".'[74]

Halifax had been trying to push Mussolini into action. He dismissed the Duce's excuse that a communication could not be sent to Berlin until Ribbentrop had returned. 'I sincerely hope,' he cabled to Loraine, 'that if Sr. Mussolini is contemplating any representation in Berlin, he may think that now is the time for it, when Herr Hitler has the Prime Minister's message before him.'[75] Before this cable reached Rome, Loraine had seen Ciano again at the latter's request. 'In the Duce's opinion ... if peace was to be saved there was not a moment to be lost.' Only if Poland were freely to recognize the right of German Danzig to return to the Reich would the present deadlock stand a chance of being broken.[76]

Late in the afternoon, Henderson was summoned from Salzburg to receive Hitler's reply. He found the Führer calm – 'he never raised his voice once'. Conversation produced little new, except that Hitler stressed his determination to attack Poland if 'another German were ill-treated'. Sir Nevile reported: 'I took the line at the end that war seemed to be quite inevitable, if Hitler persisted in direct action against Poland.' And he wrote in his memoirs: 'My last remark to him was that I could only deduce from his language that my mission to Germany had failed, and that I bitterly regretted it.'[77]

In Moscow, talks had begun three hours before, and progress had been smooth. The atmosphere became warm as the documents were prepared for signature, and drinks and compliments flowed freely. And while congratulations oozed across the Kremlin banqueting hall, in Warsaw Beck had at last adopted a more flexible attitude over co-operation with Russia. He agreed that General Doumenc could tell the Russians: 'We have learnt for certain that in the event of common action against German aggression, collaboration, and the technical conditions to be settled subsequently between Poland and the USSR are not excluded.'[78] But German and Soviet officials were already allotting parts of Poland to Stalin and Hitler. And even before the documents were signed in Moscow, the French decided to take extensive military measures to face an immediate war.

Hitler was now also prepared. After receiving a confident cable from Ribbentrop, he decided the definite date and time for the onslaught on Poland: 4.30 a.m., Saturday 26 August – in under 60 hours' time. In the early hours of 24 August, the pact of non-aggression between Germany and the USSR was signed.

'Who could have imagined,' wrote General Ismay, 'that two gangsters, who had been heaping the vilest abuse on each other for many years, would kiss and make friends overnight?.... It seemed certain we should find ourselves at war in a matter of days.'[79] Churchill had just returned from Paris, 'in high fettle', and reported the French to be unperturbed. But in London the atmosphere of impending conflict weighed heavy. Late that night Nicolson travelled through the streets of the city. 'As I drive back to the Temple, I pass a motor cyclist in a steel helmet. A sinister sight. It is very hot and still.'[80] Diplomatic activity died down for a while on the morning of 24 August. Ribbentrop, the 'second Bismarck', returned to his hero's welcome; he had been in Moscow less than 24 hours. In London, Paris, Warsaw – and Rome – it was a moment for collecting thoughts and wondering what next could be done. 'Consider remaining in Moscow most undesirable,' cabled Drax. 'Unless contrary instructions received, Franco-British missions leave 2200 hours tonight.'[81] Henderson continued to blame the Poles: 'However exaggerated German Press reports ... there is no doubt there is much ground for German complaints.' He wrote again a few hours later: 'My conversation with that man yesterday confirmed me in the view that it is practically hopeless to deal with him.... I have held from the beginning that the Poles were utterly foolish and unwise. But there it is, and perhaps Providence regards war as necessary to teach us not to do it again.'[82]

The Cabinet met at 12.45, but only for a few minutes. The latest events were explained, and Simon referred to the announcement which had been made 45 minutes before that the bank rate was being put up to 4 per cent. Hore-Belisha wanted to call out the whole of the Regular Army Reserve and the Territorial Field Army, but Chamberlain wished to wait a few hours longer.[83] And the Cabinet refused to abandon all hopes that peace could be prolonged a few more days. At 1.33 p.m. came news that negotiations between the Germans and Poles might yet come about: Kennard cabled to say that Beck had at last instructed his Ambassador to see Weizsäcker. A few minutes later Halifax contacted Rome with another message for Mussolini. The Duce was asked if he could obtain some assurance from Hitler that if the Polish Government agreed to return Danzig, the Führer would agree to an international guarantee to the independence of Poland. If such an assurance could be given, 'there might be a possible basis for an approach to the Polish Government.'[84] Nor was the military mission allowed to flee from Moscow. In answer to the cable received from Drax two hours before, Halifax telephoned the Embassy at Moscow, instructing him to try to see Molotov at once and discover whether, despite the pact with Germany, a chance still remained of an Anglo-French agreement with Russia 'on the basis hitherto contemplated'. Only if Molotov gave a definite No could the team depart.[85]

Parliament fully approved Chamberlain's decision to stand by the Poles. The Emergency Powers (Defence) Bill, which authorized the Government to make regulations by Order of Council, was passed by both the Commons and Lords. Speeches by Chamberlain and Halifax were vigorously applauded. But from Poland came disturbing news. Kennard reported that the 'Polish Government have felt it necessary to take serious military measures involving mobilization of practically two-thirds of the Polish Army'.[86] And in Danzig that evening Forster was appointed *Staatsoberhaupt* – Head of State – by the Senate. SS units were put on stand-by alert near the Polish border; Berliners heard the sound of German bombers roaring over the city; anti-aircraft guns were being hoisted to the roofs of buildings in the capital. Early on Friday morning, 25 August, Halifax learnt the Poles were still delaying direct contact with the Germans, and Kennard reported that the proposed interview between the Polish Ambassador and the German State Secretary would not come about for some time. 'M. Beck said that Herr Weizsäcker was in Berchtesgaden and would probably not return until the end of the week.'[87]

Less than a day remained before German troops were scheduled to march. Yet Hitler, tired, strained, his face almost yellow, had doubts. Only a few hours before, he had expected Chamberlain's Cabinet to collapse; he had pestered his press bureau for news of political crises in London and Paris – and instead had been given reports of strong speeches by Chamberlain and Halifax, the passing of the Emergency Powers Bill, and warlike declarations from Paris. During the morning of the 25th, Hitler drafted a letter to Mussolini: 'In case of intolerable events in Poland, I shall act immediately ... no one can say what the next hour may bring.... I can assure you Duce, that in a similar situation I would have complete understanding for Italy, and that in any such case you can be sure of my attitude.'[88]

Hitler's doubts steadily increased during the morning, over whether Mussolini would stand by him, and over the British and French attitudes. He decided to test Chamberlain and his Cabinet. At 12.45 Henderson added a short PS to a report he was drafting for Halifax. 'Have just got a message that Hitler wishes to see me at 1.30 p.m.'[89] The Ambassador drove to the Chancellery; the city was tense, with Berliners quiet on the pavements. And as Sir Nevile went to see Hitler, Halifax sent a short cable to Drax: 'Military mission should leave as soon as possible.'[90] The Admiral thankfully prepared to depart.

Sir Nevile was handed by Hitler a communication for Chamberlain: once the Polish problem had been solved he would offer Britain a 'large and comprehensive' settlement, which would guarantee the British Empire and would include German help 'regardless of where such assistance should be necessary'. But Hitler insisted that the Polish 'provocation' had become intolerable, that Chamberlain's present attitude would only mean 'blood and incalculable war'. He told Sir Nevile: 'This is my last attempt.' He suggested the Ambassador fly to England to put the case; Sir Nevile repeated that the offer would not be considered unless it meant a negotiated settlement of the Polish question, but this Hitler refused to guarantee, on the grounds that Polish provocation might any time render German intervention necessary. After 60 minutes, during which Hitler spoke 'with calm and apparent sincerity' and Ribbentrop stayed silent – much to Sir Nevile's relieved surprise – the Ambassador agreed to fly back to London. Soon afterwards he met Lipski, and urged him to ask Warsaw for instructions to see Ribbentrop. The Polish Ambassador agreed, but Sir Nevile feared the Polish Government would be too suspicious, too afraid of seeming to weaken.[91]

At 3 p.m., half an hour after Sir Nevile had left Hitler, provisional orders were sent to German field units for the start of the offensive against Poland next morning. At 3.30 p.m. Halifax belatedly sent a cable to Paris, saying the time had come for the British and French military staffs to agree to joint plans for putting the Polish guarantee into practice.[92] Ten minutes before this despatch left Whitehall, Mussolini had received Hitler's letter; he began to draft a reply – which was to confirm Hitler's worst fears. Loraine had accurately assessed the Duce's unwillingness to fight, and had suggested to Halifax that he should be tempted to break his alliance with Germany. 'Do you think it is possible or desirable to convey in any manner to Sr. Mussolini that, in the event of our being at war with Germany, and in his event of finding himself in difficulties owing to his failure to act with Germany, we should be ready for our part to afford him our collaboration and support?'[93] Even without this offer, Mussolini intended to risk Hitler's wrath. And even before Mussolini's reply reached Berlin, Hitler's confidence received a further jolt. Not only had the British Cabinet managed to survive but now had the audacity to decide that the Anglo-Polish agreement should be formalized into a full treaty; at 5.30 p.m. the Polish Ambassador signed in London the document which transferred Britain's guarantee into a binding mutual assistance pact. Attached was a secret protocol: the European power whose aggression would bring about military assistances was specified to be Germany, hence later removing British obligations to declare war against Russia when she marched into the tottering Poland.[94]

The Führer sat brooding, the report of the signing of the Anglo-Polish treaty in front of him. He believed this formalization could have been a deliberate rejection of his offer to Chamberlain, not knowing that Sir Nevile had cabled this message rather than used the telephone, and hence the text of the communication had only just reached the Foreign Office. Sir Nevile had telephoned Weizsäcker to say he would be flying to London the next day. 'I said that I doubted if I would get back before the day after tomorrow.... He begged me "to return as soon as possible, as the situation was very strained".'[95] Hitler needed to know for sure if his offer had been turned down – and to speed Sir Nevile on his mission, a German aircraft was put at his disposal.[96]

Hitler's depression deepened. And at 6.30 p.m. Attolico brought Mussolini's reply: 'I must emphasize to you that I cannot assume the initiative of warlike operations, given the actual conditions of military preparations which have been repeatedly and in timely fashion, pointed out to you, Führer, and to von Ribbentrop. Our intervention could however be immediate if Germany were to give us at once the munitions and raw materials to sustain the shock which the French and British would probably inflict upon us. In our previous meetings, war was envisaged after 1942, and on this date I should have been ready.' So Hitler may have gained Russia, but he had temporarily lost the support of Italy; Britain, Poland and France were joined against him; German forces were planned to move in only nine hours' time. In the space of a few moments, Hitler had made his decision, and, as Attolico left Hitler's room, Keitel was told to enter. He rushed out. 'The order to advance must be delayed,' he shouted to his adjutants. Orders flashed from Berlin to German field units; some columns were already moving forward – one of them could only be stopped in the early hours of the following morning by a German staff officer landing in a light aircraft in front of the advancing men, a few yards from the Polish border. Hitler then sent a curt reply to Mussolini's plea for aid: he asked to be informed 'what implements of war and raw materials you require and within what time'.[97]

Dahlerus telephoned the Foreign Office early Saturday morning, 26 August, and was seen by an official at the Carlton Hotel. He had just had a long telephone conversation with Göring, who had talked 'of an even graver situation owing to the signature of the Anglo-Polish Pact yesterday.' Later in the morning Dahlerus met Halifax, and afterwards flew off to Germany with a note from him to Göring. '...We are not at present fully clear as to the implications of [your] message on which the Ambassador may be able to help us. But while we must have time to frame our considered reply after consultation with him, we shall endeavour to preserve the same spirit as the Führer has shown, namely, a desire to find a satisfactory solution.'[98] While Dahlerus was flying to Berlin, Henderson was approaching London. He had left Ogilvie-Forbes in charge of the noisy, crowded Embassy, crammed with belongings left by British subjects who had fled the German capital – it looked like a furniture depository, said Sir George.

Mussolini had received Hitler's note at 9.30 p.m. the previous night, and on Saturday morning the Duce drew up details of military requirements – 'enough to kill a bull', wrote Ciano. The list was sent during the day, with a letter attached for Hitler: 'It is my duty to tell you that unless I am certain of receiving these supplies, sacrifices I should call on the Italian people to make ... could well be in vain and could compromise your cause along with my own.' The Führer wrote an immediate reply, which Ribbentrop telephoned to the German Ambassador in Rome.[99] At 3.22 p.m., 14 minutes after this telephone call by Ribbentrop, Halder made an important entry in his diary. '(1) Attack starts 1 September. (2) Führer will let us know at once if we are not to strike.'[100]

Hitler's forces were tight-geared to action; he either had to pull them back and stand them down, or throw them forward, and despite the exceptionally dry weather, Hitler knew only a few days remained before the autumn rains would bog down his mechanized units and reduce visibility for his Stuka dive-bombers. All hopes of securing a rapid Polish collapse, and hence of presenting Britain and France with a *fait accompli*, would be stuck in the Polish mud. A timetable had therefore to be maintained. At the same time, Hitler typically kept his options open: his military chiefs were told to be ready for further orders 'if postponement is necessary'. It might still be possible to gain his objectives through political pressure on London, Warsaw and Paris, or by causing a breach between the nations opposing him; and, in the meanwhile, as much support as possible had to be prised from the weak Italian leader. When Attolico had delivered Mussolini's list of military requirements to Hitler, he had insisted on his own initiative that the material 'must be in Italy *before* the beginning of hostilities'; Hitler, in his reply, said this deadline was clearly impossible; but: 'Duce, I understand your position, and would only ask you to try to achieve the pinning down of Anglo-French forces by active propaganda and suitable military demonstrations, such as you have already proposed to me.'[101]

The British Cabinet met at 6.30 p.m., with Henderson also present. Halifax thought it undesirable to send an answer to Hitler that afternoon, 'since this might create the impression we could be rushed,' and Sir Neville had said to Ribbentrop that he hoped to return to Berlin sometime the next afternoon. Neither Halifax nor the rest of the Cabinet were deceived by Hitler's message, which showed 'the not unfamiliar techniques.... It is clearly one purpose of the letter to divide us if possible from the French and the Poles, and to try to make us realize that, in the new situation created by the Russo-German pact, Poland's friends could do nothing to help her and should therefore make no attempt to do so.' Two conflicting wishes were expressed in the letter, Halifax believed. 'The first is his keen desire to settle the Polish question. The second is his desire to avoid a quarrel with the British Empire.... The ultimate question is, of course, whether he wants a settlement with Poland on his own terms more than he wants to avoid war with Great Britain. I feel no confidence as to the answer. ... In the course of the day, fairly precise information from sources alleged to be reliable, has reached us to the effect that Germany intends to march into Poland tonight, or, according to later reports, tomorrow morning.... I myself think, however, that for the German Government to arrange for our Ambassador in Berlin to fly to this country with a special message in a German aeroplane is not consistent with such an intention.... It might well be that the object in causing these reports to be circulated is to influence the substance of our reply.' A 'neutral person' had told him the Anglo-Polish treaty had had a great effect in Berlin and this same person (obviously Dahlerus) had asked him to send a message to Göring; a suitable one had been despatched. In answer to questions, Henderson said 'no reasonable person' could now have any doubt that Britain would honour her obligations to Poland. 'I think however, that we must not rule out altogether the possibility that Herr Hitler might still hope that he could detach us from the Poles, and get us to dishonour our obligations.' As regards the Russo-German alliance, Sir Nevile commented: 'It seems likely that there is some big *quid pro quo* which does not form part of the published agreement.' He added: 'I have thought all along Herr Hitler intended to start a war of nerves and to see how much he could get without fighting. At the same time, if we get into a position in which neither side can give way, war will result.' In reply to another question, he said the general position was quite different from the previous year when Hitler had 'entertained a great hatred for Benes and refused to meet him. He is quite well disposed towards Colonel Beck and M. Lipski.' Ministers discussed a draft reply to Hitler, and agreed it should be 'stiffened up'.

Lord Chatfield presented a report by the Chiefs of Staff dealing with the preparation of a declaration of war, an issue which was soon to cause acute difficulties for Chamberlain and his Cabinet. 'The main points which emerge from this report,' he said, 'are that if an ultimatum is not to be issued until all essential war preparations have been completed, the earliest date for the ultimatum will be Thursday, 31 August. This assumes that action is to be taken which enables evacuation to start by Monday, the 28th.'[102]

While British Ministers were holding their meeting, Hitler had received another letter from Mussolini. 'I leave you to imagine,' simpered the Duce, 'my state of mind in finding myself compelled by forces beyond my control not to afford you real solidarity at the moment of action.'[103] Hitler could only salvage the remains. 'I respect the reasons and motives which led you to take this decision,' he wrote late that night. He asked Mussolini 'to support my struggle psychologically with your Press or by other means' and added: 'This winter, at latest in the spring, I shall attack in the West with forces which will be at least equal to those of France and Britain.' He would be grateful if Mussolini could help by sending Italian labourers for German agriculture and industry.[104] Exhausted, Hitler went to bed. But he was soon called again by the arrival of the unorthodox Dahlerus bringing Halifax's message. 'Mr Hitler was calm and composed, but evidently speaking under the strain and the importance of the situation,' wrote Dahlerus to Halifax in a hastily scribbled and misspelt note the next day. 'He asked me point blank if I was satisfied that there was no desire in Great Britain towards war I unhesitatingly replied that there was no such desire in Great Britain.... [Hitler] finished off by saying that he wanted me to convey to Mr Chamblin a message that it went entirely against his nature to have to fight the Germanic race and that he himself by nature desired to devote his time to build up the German empire and guide the people in establishing an efficient industry and erecting publich buildings this must be approved that I am not planning for war.' Hitler asked Dahlerus to return immediately to London, and retired again.[105] At Chartwell, Kent, Churchill had also just gone to his bed, his pistol nearby to defend himself against possible German parachutists. 'In those hours I knew that if war came – and who could doubt its coming – a major burden would fall upon me.'[106]

Scarlet and gold, a huge German flag flapped in Danzig market-place on Sunday, 27 August, and loudspeakers, newly erected in the streets, were ready for a mass proclamation. The weather remained hot and sultry. In Berlin, food rationing was announced; all naval, military and air attachés were refused permission to leave the city. In London, work had almost been completed on the British War Book: this Top Secret file, which Ismay had started to revise 13 years before, contained the instructions and procedures for the administration of the country when it embarked on war. But in the British capital some optimism remained, and indeed had grown stronger during the last few hours. Hitler had not taken the final step, and the longer he delayed the better the chances of a peaceful settlement. 'It is curious to recall and analyse the general mood during those dark days since 22 August,' wrote Harold Nicolson. 'The House when it met on 24 August was in the depth of gloom. People scarcely spoke to each other above a whisper, as if some close relation was dying upstairs. Then, when nothing happened on Saturday and Sunday, and when Hitler consented to enter into an argument, hope revived.'[107]

If this hope was to be justified, much depended upon the energetic amateur emissary. Sunday was Dahlerus's day. Arriving at Croydon at 2.30 p.m., he was rushed through back streets to Whitehall, to see Chamberlain, Halifax, Wilson and Cadogan, and present the scribbled note prepared on the aircraft. Dahlerus was adamant that Hitler wanted peace, but Halifax pointed out that Britain could not start discussions while German troops might at any time invade Poland. Direct discussions between Germany and Poland were essential, and for these to take place confidence had to be re-established. Dahlerus agreed to fly back to Germany yet again, 'to prepare the way for the main communication' which Henderson would bring. Dahlerus was given rough guidance, which read: '(1) Solemn assurance of desire for good understanding between G and Gt B. Not a single member of the

Govt who thinks different. (2) Gt B bound to honour obligations to Poland. (3) Therefore German-Polish differences must be settled peacefully. If this can be done it would lead to better relations all round, which are quite impossible without it.'[108] Dahlerus's mission offered one slim means of gaining more time; Italy might provide another. As the Swede had been hurried from Croydon through the south London suburbs on his way to Whitehall, Loraine had been speaking to Ciano in Rome. During the talk Ciano had decided to telephone Halifax, and the two spoke over the crackling line a few minutes before Dahlerus arrived at Downing Street. Ciano believed talks would allow more time for a settlement to be reached and 'Mussolini was quite willing to cooperate'.[109]

Soon after 3 p.m. Chamberlain and Halifax entered the Cabinet Room.[110] Halifax opened the meeting by informing Ministers of his conversation with Ciano, and Chamberlain commented: 'I am strongly in agreement with Count Ciano's view that it is desirable that we should work to gain time. I am also impressed by the fact that if time is given, world opinion gathers force, and that after active negotiations with a view to maintaining peace have continued for a long time, it is harder for any Government to take action which will result in war breaking out.' 'The position in Berlin at the present time is somewhat confused,' said Halifax. 'It appears that the firm attitude we have adopted has had a considerable effect.' Ministers therefore decided to delay the reply to Hitler until the next morning, and agreed to a Press communiqué that Hitler's communication was being carefully studied.

Halifax reported on the actions of a 'neutral person, Mr D' and read the message he had brought to London that afternoon. The draft reply to Hitler was discussed again and Ministers generally felt the words needed tightening still more, to avoid any impression that Britain might change her attitude.

Late on Sunday afternoon, the Duce replied to the Führer's letter: Italy would tie down as many Anglo-French forces as possible; he would send Italian workers as requested; he would keep secret the fact that Italy was not joining the struggle immediately – 'the world would not know before the outbreak of hostilities what the attitude of Italy is.'[111] Mussolini was both a weak partner for Hitler and a frail proponent of peace for the allies. And Hitler himself, despite his decision the previous day that the attack on Poland should be prepared for 1 September, still wavered; by Sunday afternoon he seemed to favour less than full scale conflict. At a conference at the Chancellery at 5.20 p.m., Hitler revealed his changed attitude; according to notes made by Colonel Oster: 'Minimum demands – return of Danzig, settling of Corridor question. Maximum demands – "depending on military situation".' The Führer, nearing complete exhaustion, retired to his room with his SS bodyguard. By late evening rumours of compromise had increased so much that Ribbentrop had to counter them; he telephoned the German Ambassador at Rome at 10 p.m., with orders to deny firmly all report of a *detente*. 'The armies are on the march,' he said.[112] Forty-six minutes later an urgent cable reached the Foreign Office from Kennard at Warsaw. 'M. Beck has just informed me that in view of the nature of Herr Hitler's language regarding Poland in his conversation with Sir N. Henderson, the Polish Government have decided on full mobilization, which is to take place at once.'[113] Sir Howard was told to plead with Beck to delay this drastic step.

Dahlerus reached Berlin again late on Sunday evening and gave the British message to Göring. But in his exuberance – and perhaps because he was not given clear enough instructions – he extended his brief: Britain rejected the idea of Germany pledging herself to defend the British Empire; discussion on the Colonies could not be held while Germany stayed mobilized; Polish boundaries must be guaranteed by the five great powers; Britain proposed that immediate negotiations with Poland should start on the Corridor issue. As for Hitler's statement that 'Germany wanted a pact or alliance with Britain', Dahlerus reported to Göring that 'England is willing in principal to come to an agreement with Germany,' an answer which offered Hitler a possible means of splitting the Allies. So, although Göring considered the reply not very favourable, Hitler was eager to display generosity, and at 1 a.m., Göring telephoned Dahlerus at his hotel that Hitler would 'accept the English standpoint' – providing Henderson's official version tallied with that given by Dahlerus. Sir George Ogilvie-Forbes telephoned to London: 'Dahlerus states that atmosphere is favourable for negotiations.'[114]

Dahlerus's comments formed a main item of discussion at the Cabinet meeting at noon on Monday, 28 August. Halifax said that apart from Sir George's message, he had also been given some notes by Sir Harold Wernher, whom Dahlerus had telephoned. 'The latter stressed to Sir Harold that the Government's reply should be neither cold nor "governessy".' But despite Dahlerus's advice and optimism, the Cabinet refused to accept Hitler's bait. 'Final draft reply expressed in much stiffer terms,' wrote Hore-Belisha. Chamberlain said that in view of the further mobilization measures announced by the Poles, it would be best if Parliament met on Tuesday, 29 August.[115]

'It is more than possible,' cabled Halifax to Loraine at 1.30 p.m. 'that despite the friendly nature of the communication Sir Nevile Henderson will be taking back to Berlin this evening, Herr Hitler may take tomorrow the irrevocable step of invading Poland.' The Ambassador was told to warn Ciano of Britain's fears, in case Mussolini could see his way 'to take immediately any action which might avert the possibility'.[116] Thirty minutes later Halifax cabled Kennard, instructing him immediately to obtain Beck's permission for Britain, in the reply to be taken by Sir Nevile, to say 'that Poland is ready to enter at once into direct discussion with Germany'. Late in the afternoon the authorization was rushed to London.

'The sun beats very hot and all the autumn mist melts, and the spider webs also upon the yews,' wrote Harold Nicolson. 'It looks as if war will burst upon us tomorrow.'[117]

The Last Days of Peace

At 4 o'clock on Monday afternoon, 28 August, the War Office staff practised an air raid warning, girls giggling, shirt-sleeved men embarrassed as they ran self-consciously down the corridors. In Berlin, troop convoys were moving east through the sunny streets. An odd assortment of vehicles had had to be commandeered because all military transports were already in full use elsewhere. And girls giggled as they pointed to troops crammed into furniture removal vans and grocery delivery trucks, while the soldiers looked the other way, embarrassed.

Henderson reached the German capital at 9 p.m. Three hours before, the text of the reply he was to give to Hitler had been telephoned to the Embassy to await his arrival; it read: 'Everything ... turns upon the nature of the settlement and the method by which it is to be reached ... the next step must be the initiation of direct discussions between the German and Polish Governments on a basis which would include the principles stated above, namely, the safeguarding of Poland's essential interests and the securing of a settlement by an international guarantee.' Britain had already received a definite assurance from the Poles that they were prepared to enter discussions, the message continued; failure to reach a just settlement 'might well plunge the whole world into war. Such an outcome would be a calamity without parallel in history.'[1] 'Could any reply have been more precise or straightforward?' asked Sir Nevile afterwards. 'It made it easy for Hitler to avoid the calamity of war, if he had really wished to do so.'[2]

The Ambassador had barely begun a hurried meal at his Embassy when a message arrived to say Hitler wished to see him at 10 p.m., in only a few minutes' time. Sir Nevile suggested a short delay. 'At 10.30, fortified by half a bottle of champagne, I drove down the Wilhelmstrasse to the main entrance of the Reich Chancellery. A good many people were waiting outside the Embassy and a considerable crowd outside the Chancellery. No hostility as far as I could see, absolute silence, possibly uneasiness.' He was received by a guard of honour in full state, 'as if I had been presenting my letters of credence'. Nor was he kept waiting; Ribbentrop – courteous for once – ushered him along the corridors to an equally unexpected reception from the Führer. 'The Chancellor looked well, was absolutely calm and normal. No fireworks or tirades of any kind.' Sir Nevile told Hitler that the British people sincerely wanted an understanding with Germany, and no one more so than the Prime Minister. Ribbentrop remarked that Mr Chamberlain had once said to him that it was his dearest wish. 'Today the whole British public was behind the Prime Minister.... There was absolutely no truth in the idea sometimes held in Germany that the British Cabinet was disunited or that the country was not unanimous. It was now or never and it rested with Herr Hitler. ... Herr Hitler must choose between England and Poland.' Hitler continued to argue, although 'in moderate terms', that Poland could never be reasonable. Ribbentrop asked whether Sir Nevile could guarantee that Chamberlain would carry the country with him in a policy of friendship with Germany. 'I said there was no possible doubt whatever that he could and would, provided Germany cooperated.'

This was the opening for which Hitler had been waiting; according to Sir Nevile's official account: 'Herr Hitler asked whether England would be willing to accept an alliance with Germany. I said, speaking personally, I did not exclude such a possibility provided the developments justified it.' The Führer could hardly have hoped for a better answer. The interview closed down soon afterwards with Hitler saying he would give Chamberlain a reply when he had carefully studied the British message.[3] He held an immediate Cabinet Meeting at the Chancellery: his manipulations seemed to be working; he had manoeuvred Britain into obtaining Polish agreement for direct negotiations – and, after the experiences of Austria and Czechoslovakia, such 'negotiations' would surely mean a German victory. And Hitler had apparently secured British acceptance of the idea of an alliance with Germany, a step which would surely force a gap between the allies. So, at 1.30 a.m. on Tuesday, 29 August, Dahlerus received a telephone call from one of Göring's adjutants, that the British reply was 'highly satisfactory and there was every hope that the threat of war was past.' Early next morning Dahlerus twice rang the Foreign Office in Whitehall: he had been told that the German Cabinet were agreed on 'certain broad principles' and 'both the Field Marshal and Herr Hitler considered that there was now a definite possibility of a satisfactory settlement.'[4]

Hitler was still using the same tactics with Chamberlain as he had done at Munich. If appeasement had still been Chamberlain's prime policy, the tactics would probably have worked. But now these methods were outdated, and the implications of the situation into which he was trying to push Britain were clearly understood at the Foreign Office;

thus Ivone Kirkpatrick attached a revealing Minute to Sir Nevile's report of his interview. 'It is inevitable that we should be in danger of being manoeuvred by Hitler into a very dangerous position. Hitler now has two courses open to him. Either to ignore our offer and go to war, in which case the issue is plain. The second course is to reduce his demands on Poland to an acceptable level. In that case he will have fulfilled his promise to recover Danzig bloodlessly and obtain other advantages as well.... The next stage will be the understanding with England. Herr Hitler will naturally endeavour to drive a wedge between us and France ... [the world] will, of course, despise and blame us if we allow Hitler to play his old game of securing concrete concessions in return for purely illusory promises.' Later in the day another Minute, by Sir Orme Sargent, was attached to this document. 'I am afraid there is a third course open to Hitler ... to use the proposal for direct negotiations between Germany and Poland in such a way that he will be able, under threat of breaking off these negotiations, to exact settlement.' Halifax added on 30 August that while he agreed with Kirkpatrick and Sir Orme, a peaceful solution should still be sought.

Sir Robert Vansittart commented that while Henderson had conducted his interview with Hitler satisfactorily, he had made one mistake – his answer to Hitler's question concerning an alliance. 'This, I think, is very dangerous indeed. It is the third German reference that I have seen to such a possibility. It is not of course practical politics.' He pointed out the diplomatic dangers – 'the merest suggestion of it would ruin us in the United States' – and Halifax agreed. 'We might put Sir Nevile Henderson in possession of our views,' he wrote, 'so that he may fully realize how boggy the ground is.'[5] Nor were the Poles apparently going to oblige Hitler's request for direct negotiation: the Warsaw leaders were to show a marked reluctance to send an emissary to Berlin. Meanwhile, Hitler and his henchmen continued to hope, and even to expect, that Britain and Poland would undertake what was asked of them. 'There will be peace!' crooned Göring to Dahlerus when the two men met at 10.50 that Tuesday morning. Pumping the Swede's hand and slapping his back, he declared that peace was definitely secure, and Dahlerus rushed happily to the British Embassy.

London, Berlin, Rome, Paris – each waited to see what the other would do. The mood in the House of Commons was generally more optimistic than that in the Cabinet; Henderson's journeys were seen as a hopeful sign, and many MPs believed the anti-gas doors being fitted and the sandbags being heaped around the windows would no longer be necessary. Meanwhile, Ciano assured Loraine later in the afternoon that Mussolini was continuing to press for discussions: the Duce had sent an urgent personal telegram to Hitler only a few minutes before, said Ciano, in which he had declared the British reply 'offered the basis of an honourable and peaceful settlement, and at the moment when he [Hitler] was about to take a decision fraught with gravest consequences, his [Mussolini's] counsel to Herr Hitler, as a true friend, was not to reject it but to agree to open discussions.' The message was very warm, clear and emphatic.[6] In Warsaw, by contrast, there seemed no grounds for optimism; outwardly the atmosphere remained calm as usual, yet accumulating reports dashed all hopes of peace. Traffic through Danzig had been stopped; Russian troop movements were being carried out in the East; German troops had entered Slovakia; British and French determination to fight seemed to be wavering. At 5.10 p.m., Kennard phoned London: 'Vice-Minister for Foreign Affairs has just informed my French colleague and me that the Polish Government have, in view of gravity of the situation, decided on general mobilization.' Kennard added that he had made an immediate protest.[7]

The German reply would be delivered to Henderson that evening, reported Dahlerus. No difficulties need be expected over the contents, he added, but warned, the British Government should tell the Poles 'to behave properly', giving perhaps the first indication that progress was soon to be abruptly reversed.[8] Just five minutes after Dahlerus had telephoned London, Henderson returned to the Chancellery to see Hitler. The Führer had meanwhile decided that the period of patience must be finished; the bait had been offered, Britain had apparently accepted it, and had agreed to direct discussions between Poland and Germany – and had seemed tempted by the possibility of an alliance with Germany. Now pressure should be increased; time was short – Poland was fast mobilizing, the Indian summer would soon be gone, his troops could not remain at peak readiness for very much longer. The British had been wooed, and now the Poles had to be won.

Sir Nevile was totally unprepared for the reception he now received. 'Interview this evening was of a stormy character,' he telephoned afterwards. 'Herr Hitler was far less reasonable than yesterday. Press announcements this evening said five more Germans had been killed in Poland and news of Polish mobilization had obviously excited him.' As usual, Sir Nevile was ready to blame the Poles. Hitler's reply listed Polish misdeeds – 'barbaric actions of maltreatment which cry to heaven' – which Germany could no longer tolerate. His demands, he added, 'are in conformity with the revision of the Versailles Treaty with regard to this territory.... While the British Government may still believe that these grave differences can be resolved by way of direct negotiations, the German Government unfortunately can no longer share this view.' Nevertheless, the British proposal would be accepted and direct discussions started – if a Polish emissary with full powers arrived in Berlin on Wednesday, 30 August. Poland had there-

198

fore only until the following day in which to send a negotiator scurrying to Berlin.[9] Hitler obviously intended to use the tactics he had employed with the Czechs. 'I pointed out to His Excellency that this ... sounded very much like an ultimatum. This was strenuously and heatedly denied by Hitler himself, supported by Ribbentrop.' The deadline merely emphasized the urgency of the situation, when Germans were being massacred in Poland. 'His Excellency asserted that I did not care how many Germans had been slaughtered in Poland.' At this, Sir Nevile lost his temper. Diplomatic composure thrown to one side, he launched an attack on the Führer, which, in volume at least, was worthy of one of his own tirades. 'I proceeded to outshout Herr Hitler. I told him that I would not listen to such language from him or anybody. Such a statement was intolerable and an example of all his exaggerations. I added a good deal more, shouting at the top of my voice.' Listeners in the corridors of the Chancellery stood white-faced and horrified.

The Henderson-Hitler interview was closed, wrote Sir Nevile in his memoirs, 'by a brief and, in my opinion, quite honest – since it represented his feelings at the moment – harangue on Hitler's part in regard to the genuineness of his constant endeavour to win British friendship, of his respect for the British Empire, and of his liking for Englishmen generally.' Nevertheless, 'I left the Reich Chancellery that evening filled with the gloomiest forebodings.'[10] The Ambassador sent the first short summary of Hitler's reply at 9.15 p.m. At 10 p.m. Göring summoned Dahlerus to his home, and subjected him to a violent, hysterical outburst against the Poles and against the British. The meeting between Hitler and Henderson had been 'most unsatisfactory', he spluttered, then switched tactics: the Führer was drafting a 'magnanimous' offer to Poland, and Dahlerus should fly to London and emphasize that Hitler still sought peace.

Beck summoned the British and French Ambassadors at Warsaw and 'begged' for the gist of Hitler's reply to be sent as soon as possible; Kennard telephoned this request to London – but Beck was to be disappointed. Although Sir Nevile's initial report had requested the information should be sent on to Warsaw, this action was delayed, and for many hours the only information Beck received was a sketchy account given by Sir Nevile to Lipski. Halifax's first impression of Hitler's reply, based on the summary sent at 9.15, was intensely pessimistic. But he told Kennard: 'Summary of German reply just received. It does not appear to close every door.'[11] Halifax's opinion of the German reply underwent a sharp change when the full account arrived half an hour after midnight. Halifax and Chamberlain were discussing a draft communication to Hitler when this text reached the Foreign Office; Halifax hurried back to his room and, at 2 a.m. another message was despatched to Kennard: 'Summary is misleading. Full text which is not so unpromising is being considered and reply will be sent to you as soon as possible.'[12] This reply, and the official version of Hitler's statement, were sent in the early hours of the morning – but were not to be communicated to the Polish Government until midnight that night, though under the terms of Hitler's demands, a Polish delegate had to be in Berlin by that day. The Poles were therefore kept deliberately uninformed to avoid precipitate action. Meanwhile, Halifax told Sir Nevile at 2 a.m. on the 30th: 'It is of course unreasonable to expect that we can produce a Polish representative in Berlin today, and German Government must not expect this.' German intelligence agents intercepted this telephone message, as they did most others during those critical hours.[13]

Halifax and Chamberlain received advice from Berlin, Warsaw, and Dahlerus. Henderson telephoned: 'While I still recommend that the Polish Government should swallow this eleventh hour effort to establish direct contact with Herr Hitler ... one can only conclude from the German reply [that Hitler] is determined to achieve his ends by so-called peaceful, fair, means if he can, but by force if he cannot.'[14] Kennard, now in possession of Hitler's reply but with instructions to keep it from the Poles, gave his opinion: 'I feel sure that it would be impossible to induce the Polish Government to send Colonel Beck, or any other representative, immediately to Berlin ... they would certainly sooner fight and perish rather than submit to such humiliation.' Yet such was the British determination not to give way that the Poles were not even asked if they would in fact 'submit'.

Thirty minutes after Sir Howard's telephone call, Dahlerus arrived at 10 Downing Street, and was immediately seen by Chamberlain, Halifax, Wilson and Cadogan. He handed over Göring's message of the previous night, but found the British Ministers 'highly mistrustful' and 'inclined to assume that nothing would now prevent Hitler from declaring war on Poland'. The emissary had barely left Downing Street, with the promise that he would keep in close touch, when Ministers assembled for the Cabinet meeting. Halifax reported the events of the previous night: 'Although the full text is open to several interpretations, nevertheless I think that the line we should take in regard to it is fairly clear. It might be that Herr Hitler is playing for time, or that he is hoping to manoeuvre us into breaking off negotiations.... The terms of Herr Hitler's reply are somewhat bombastic, but I think that stripped of its verbiage, it reveals a man who is trying to extricate himself from a difficult position.' Ministers were told of the latest arrival of 'Mr D'. 'The main point which Mr D made was the remarkable effect of our reply in Berlin.... Göring had been thrown into a state of almost hysterical anger by stories of Germans being shot. But for our reply, war would have broken out yesterday morning.... I think the general line which our reply should take, should be to pin

Herr Hitler down to the points in his reply in which he met our point of view, and on other points to endeavour to safeguard the position of ourselves and our allies.' He believed a reply should be sent as soon as possible. He gave no indication of wishing to soften Britain's attitude, despite the danger of war; nor did Chamberlain. 'The most unsatisfactory thing in Herr Hitler's reply,' believed the Prime Minister, 'is the demand that the Polish emissary should go to Berlin today. This is definitely part of the old technique. It is essential that we should make it quite clear that we are not going to yield on this point.' Ministers agreed the Polish Government was entitled to insist the talks should be held on neutral ground.[15]

By late afternoon the British reply had almost been completed by Halifax, Wilson and Cadogan, and at 5.15 the Foreign Office contacted the Embassy in Berlin to describe the next steps. This conversation was also recorded by the German *Forschungsamt*, or Research Office. Henderson was told he should not 'get so worked up', and, according to the *Forschungsamt* account, that 'the Prime Minister had personally looked into the matter and thought that the telegram which Henderson was now going to get would help him out... [he] had declared that he fully understood the situation, for he had after all been over there himself....' The account continued: 'In London, the unidentified Foreign Office voice went on, people were quite unperturbed, as Henderson was aware. The Voice thought that they were on the right track now. They (the Germans) really could not expect to succeed again by summoning people to them, handing over documents to them, and having them sign on the dotted line. All that was over now....'[16] Fifteen minutes after Sir Nevile had been told not to get excited, Phipps telephoned Halifax with the French reaction. 'M. Daladier tells me ... he considers it very bad indeed, and that it indicates Herr Hitler's intention to dismember Poland.' Sir Eric had suggested Daladier might go to London for talks, but the French leader had felt unable to leave Paris at the moment.[17]

No word had reached Hitler during the day of a possible Polish surrender; instead, reports of Polish mobilization had been increasing. The Führer, despite the skill of his intelligence agents, was unaware that the Polish leaders had not yet even received the official text of his demands, and he believed the Poles to be defiantly refusing to come to Berlin. Hopes for a peaceful acquisition of his aims seemed to have gone, and his army must move; he confirmed the date for his offensive. Halder noted in his diary: 'Make all preparations so that attack can begin at 4.30 a.m. on 1 September. Should negotiations in London require postponement, then September 2.'

At 7 p.m. Kennard was told that when further instructions arrived, he could hand the full text of Hitler's reply over to the Poles, together with the latest British answer. They were to be told that, 'in view of the fact that the Polish Government have authorized HMG to say that they are prepared to enter into direct discussions with the German Government, HMG hope that, provided method and general arrangement for discussion can be satisfactorily agreed, Polish Government would be prepared to do so without delay.' Henderson was sent the British reply at 7.40, also with instructions not to hand it over without further orders; the British Government, said this reply, 'fully understand that the German Government cannot sacrifice Germany's vital interests, but the Polish Government are in the same position. HMG believe that the vital interests of the two countries are not incompatible.' Detailed differences could be solved at a conference, but: 'the method of contact and arrangements for discussions must obviously be agreed with all urgency between the German and Polish Governments, but in HMG's view it would be impracticable to establish contact so early as today.'[18]

At 9.15, Sir Nevile was told he could present this reply, and he arranged an interview for midnight. The Foreign Office was informed at 12.10 a.m. that he had left for this meeting, and only then was Kennard instructed to pass the British communication, together with the first full account of the German reply, to the Polish Government. The time selected by Sir Nevile for his appointment with Ribbentrop could hardly have been less provocative: midnight marked the end of the deadline for a Polish representative to arrive for talks in Berlin. Ribbentrop believed Sir Nevile's visit, originally fixed for 11.30, had been postponed deliberately, but according to Sir Nevile in his memoirs, he had needed longer for the telegram from London to be deciphered.[19]

Ribbentrop's attitude, hostile from the start, increased in violence as Sir Nevile read the British note. 'He kept jumping to his feet in a state of great excitement, folding his arms across his chest, and asking if I had anything more to say. I kept replying that I had, and, if my own attitude was no less unfriendly than his, I cannot but say in all sincerity that I had every justification for it.' At one point, according to the interpreter, Dr Schmidt, both men leapt from their seats and glared at each other so angrily that Schmidt thought they were coming to blows. The provocation came from the Poles, roared Ribbentrop. Nonsense, shouted Sir Nevile. 'I have reason to believe that the German press accounts are greatly exaggerated.' Ribbentrop retorted that Britain's advice to Poles to avoid provocative action had had 'cursed little effect'. 'I am surprised to hear such language from a Minister for Foreign Affairs,' replied Sir Nevile, and said he would report his comments and remarks to the British Government. Ribbentrop hastily added he was merely voicing his own thoughts and it was for Herr Hitler to decide. He produced a document listing 16 German points of view, which, according to Sir Nevile, he 'gabbled through to me as fast as he could, in a tone of the utmost scorn and annoyance'. The Ambassador, only able to get the gist of six or seven of the points, asked to read the document. Ribbentrop refused, flinging it on the table and saying it was out of date since no Polish emissary had arrived on time. 'I observed,' said Sir Nevile in his report to London, 'that to treat matter in this way meant that request for Polish representative to arrive in Berlin on 30 August constituted in fact an ultimatum, in spite of what he and Herr Hitler had assured me yesterday.' The allegation was denied by Ribbentrop, who still refused to hand over the document. Nor would he agree to Sir Nevile's suggestion that the Polish Ambassador should be asked to call. 'In the most violent terms Herr von Ribbentrop said that he would never ask the Ambassador to visit him. He hinted that if Polish Ambassador asked him for an interview it might be different.' Sir Nevile continued: 'We parted on that note; but I must tell you that von Ribbentrop's whole demeanour during an unpleasant interview was aping Herr Hitler at his worst.'[20]

'I returned to HM Embassy that night convinced that the last hope of peace had vanished,' Sir Nevile wrote in his memoirs.[21] He was justified in his fears; although the German 'sixteen points' were more liberal than previous demands, they were also irrelevant. Hitler had decided on the military *fait accompli*, and, at midnight, as Sir Nevile had arrived to see von Ribbentrop, the German radio had announced the formation of a War Cabinet, a 'Ministerial Council for the Defence of the Reich'. Chosen to preside over this group was Sir Nevile's confidant, Hermann Göring. But despite his conviction that no hope remained, Sir Nevile immediately asked the Polish Ambassador to see him at 1.30 a.m., and told Lipski 'in very strongest terms', that he should telephone Beck and request permission to seek an interview with Ribbentrop. Sir Nevile doubted much would come from the move. After seeing Lipski, the weary British Ambassador saw Attolico, who 'vehemently urged immediate action by Polish Government',[22] and then Weizsäcker, and finally Ulrich von Hassell, former German Ambassador in Rome, a confirmed anti-Nazi, and closely watched by the SS. As a result, at 9.15 in the morning of 31 August, he telephoned Halifax: 'Have just been informed on best possible authority, that if nothing happens in next two or three hours, i.e. possibly by mid-day, German Government will declare war.' This telephone conversation, like so many others made by the British Ambassador, was heard clearly by the vigilant German intelligence agents.[23]

Kennard in Warsaw had also been active throughout the night. After midnight he had contacted Beck to inform him of Britain's reply to Hitler, and, as instructed by Halifax, to ask Poland to open discussions with Germany as soon as possible. But at 5.35 a.m. he reported a further delay was inevitable: the Polish Government would have to be consulted, Beck had said, although he promised a considered reply by noon.[24] In Berlin, Sir Nevile was still trying to press Lipski into action, and at 8 a.m. committed another indiscretion by warning Lipski over the telephone that unless Poland made concessions by noon, the country would probably be attacked.[25]

Dahlerus had been with Göring for most of the night; he had been assured that the German proposals were 'extremely liberal' and had been 'formulated in order to show how extremely anxious the Führer is to reach an agreement with Great Britain'. When he heard from Ogilvie-Forbes of Ribbentrop's behaviour with Sir Nevile, he admonished Göring – 'this was no way to treat the Ambassador of an Empire like Great Britain' – and obtained from him a typed list of the sixteen points, which he took to the British Embassy. Then Dahlerus and Sir George hurried to show Hitler's demands to Lipski – who scolded Sir George for having brought a complete stranger at such an important moment. Lipski, having read the sixteen points, declared: 'The German plan was a breach of Polish sovereignty, a trap, and acceptance was quite out of the question.'[26]

Dahlerus and Sir George returned to the British Embassy, where Sir Nevile not only allowed the Swede to use the telephone in his room to send a report which he, as Ambassador, should have communicated to London, but then allowed Dahlerus to commit even worse breaches of security than he himself could manage. Sir Horace Wilson took the call at the Foreign Office, and immediately afterwards wrote a shocked Minute on the undiplomatic conversation. 'He said that "we" ... had been to see Lipski ... at this point I heard a German voice apparently repeating D's words and therefore interrupted to tell D that he had better give his information to Henderson; he, however, went on. He said they had given Lipski the terms ... Lipski had replied that the terms were out of the question. (I again interrupted to tell D not to get ahead of the clock and that, in any case, if there is anything to say Henderson should say it in the ordinary way, but again I failed to stop him.) His next remark was that the Poles did not intend to give way and it was "obvious to us" that the Poles were obstructing the possibilities of a negotiation. I again told D to shut up, but as he did not do so I put down the receiver.' After reporting the conversation to Chamberlain and Halifax, a telegram was sent to Sir Nevile: 'You really must be careful of use of telephone. D's conversation at mid-day from Embassy was most indiscreet and has certainly been heard by Germans.'[27]

The Italians had been trying to cool the situation. Attolico, as a result of Sir Nevile's information, had warned Rome that unless 'something comes up, there will be war in a few hours'. Ciano therefore telephoned Halifax to suggest the Poles give up their rights to Danzig, but Halifax hedged: 'The immediate difficulty is to make the first contact between the Poles and the Germans,' and he urged that the Germans should be persuaded to ask the Polish Ambassador to call.[28] Thirty minutes later Attolico saw Weizsäcker, and said the Duce needed time to press his peace plan: if the German Government asked to see Lipski, this might be obtained.

But, at last, the Polish Ambassador himself contacted the German Foreign Ministry at 1 p.m. to ask for an interview. This was not to be granted for another five and a half hours. Meanwhile, a few minutes earlier, Ciano had telephoned Halifax again with Mussolini's last attempt at peace: he proposed that a conference should be called for 5 September, aimed at revising the clauses of the Versailles Treaty 'which are the cause of the present grave troubles in the life of Europe'. Halifax discussed the proposal with Chamberlain, then asked Corbin for the French reaction; according to a subsequent Minute by Halifax: 'M. Bonnet had spoken on the telephone with M. Coulondre in Berlin: the latter did not believe that the question was one of such urgency. M. Bonnet would like to consult M. Daladier.' By then, Hitler had completed final details for the offensive. Halder had noted in his diary at 11.30 a.m.: 'General Stuelpnagel reports on fixing of time of attack for 04.45. Intervention of West said to be unavoidable; in spite of this Führer has decided to attack.' At noon the SS personnel received the codewords – 'Canned Goods' – for the attack on the radio station at Gleiwitz. And also at twelve, Hitler, Supreme Commander of the Armed Forces, issued his first 'War Directive'. 'Since the situation on Germany's eastern frontier has become intolerable and all political possibilities of peaceful settlement have been exhausted, I have decided upon a solution by force.' The time of the attack was inserted in red pencil.[29]

The telephone shrilled in Naujocks' drab hotel room at Gleiwitz. 'Call back,' said a high pitched voice. He called a Berlin number and the same tinny voice told him: 'Grandmama dead.' Naujocks was to carry out the fake attack on the radio station that night at 8 o'clock. He hurried to collect his men – his assistant Oppeln Müller collected the corpses ready for laying out at the transmitter.[30]

Meanwhile, Henderson, Ogilvie-Forbes and Dahlerus were having a tea-party with Göring. Dahlerus had proposed this strange gathering, after having treated the Field-Marshal to an exceptional meal at the Hotel Esplanade. Now, at the tea-table, he suggested a novel idea for last minute talks: he urged that Göring should meet a Polish representative somewhere in Holland. Henderson, wrote Dahlerus later, promised to submit the proposal to the Foreign Office, but no mention of the suggestion was made in any of his subsequent telegrams and reports. Instead, he wrote that the conversation led nowhere. 'I augured the worst from the fact that he [Göring] was in a position at such a moment to give me so much of his time.' The gathering was still in session when Lipski finally obtained an interview with Ribbentrop just before 7 p.m.[31] Lipski curtly informed Ribbentrop that he had no power to discuss or negotiate. Instead, he read an official declaration by his Government. 'Last night the Polish Government were informed by the British Government of an exchange of views with the Reich Government as to the possibility of direct negotiations between the Polish and German Governments. The Polish Government are favourably considering the British Government's suggestion, and will make them a formal reply on the subject during the next few hours.'[32] Lipski made a dignified withdrawal, returned to his Embassy – and found himself unable to communicate with Warsaw because all lines had been slashed.

Up to 54 German Divisions were now poised on the Polish frontier, according to a despatch from the Military Attaché in Warsaw. And, as this signal was on its way to Whitehall, 'incidents' were being perpetrated against Germany. Naujocks and his picked team were approaching the transmitting station at Gleiwitz on the German side of the border. Just before 8 p.m. the disguised Germans burst into the station engine house and raced up the stairs to the broadcasting studio, pushed the startled staff into a cellar and fired shots at the ceiling 'to make a bit of a shindy and frighten people'. Naujocks pulled out a document written in Polish, and soon afterwards surprised listeners in Germany heard a 'Polish' voice speaking through a babble of shouts and crackling pistol shots. Four minutes later Naujocks and his men withdrew; as they sprinted through the gates they stumbled over the bodies of the concentration camp inmates, dressed in Polish uniforms. Similar charades were enacted at the Hochlinden Customs House and at other points just inside Germany. 'Evidence' had been prepared for the German invasion of Poland.[33] Nearly one and a half million German troops were in their final positions; ammunition had been distributed; tanks and armoured vehicles clanked and squealed into line and waited in the darkness; aircraft stood ready on the tarmac at bases throughout Germany, bombs slung heavy under their wings.

Yet in Berlin, the atmosphere seemed normal. Traces of war preparation were limited to anti-aircraft gun emplacements; few sandbags had been filled, no Berliners had been evacuated. In Britain, 3 million mothers and children were to move the following day from areas believed to be most threatened; barrage balloons were ready for hoisting above London. The War Book had been completed, and plans for the composition and style of the War Cabinet had been handed to Chamberlain for his consideration by Bridges and Ismay, the civilian and military Cabinet secretaries. In Paris, the Ministerial Council was having a late night emergency meeting. Despite Daladier's afternoon insistence that he would rather resign than accept Mussolini's invitation to a conference, the Council now 'quite realized that it would now be impossible to decline the Italian proposal off-hand.'

As the long day dragged to a close, the Foreign Office received one welcome item. Loraine telephoned an hour before midnight. 'Italy will not fight against either England or France.... This communication was made to me by Count Ciano at 21.15 under seal of secrecy ... and moved by the deepest emotion.' Ciano recorded that when he gave the British Ambassador this information, Sir Percy wept and clung on to his hand.[34] Henderson made his last telephone call of the day. 'War may be justified on ground that Nazi régime is an immoral one which one must fight sooner or later.' But, 'I submit that on German offer it would be completely unjustifiable.... I can only suggest that Polish Government be urged in unmistakable language that they should announce tomorrow, in the light of German proposals which have now been made public, their intention to send a plenipotentiary to Berlin.'[35]

For a few hours, diplomatic activity died down; duty staff at the Foreign Office relaxed; teleprinter machines and telephones stood silent – until just before dawn next day, Friday, 1 September. Guns suddenly erupted and tracer fire flickered across the dawn streaked sky, and German tanks rumbled forward over outlying Polish positions. At 5.40, one hour after the invasion began, German radio listeners were told the news and heard Hitler's proclamation to his army. 'Polish State has refused peaceful settlement of relations which I desired and has appealed to arms. Germans in Poland are persecuted with bloody terror and driven from their homes. A series of violations of frontier, intolerable to a Great Power, prove that Poland is no longer willing to respect the frontier of the Reich. In order to put an end to this lunacy, I have no other choice than to meet force with force from now on.'[36] Newspapers were rushed on to the Berlin streets, and the special edition of the *Volkischer Beobachter* declared: 'Polish insurgents cross the German frontier,' and described the Gleiwitz incident as 'clearly the signal for a general attack on German territory by Polish guerrillas'.[37]

News of the offensive had reached the War Office in London at 5.20 a.m. At 8.30 a.m. a message came over the appalling telephone line from the British Embassy at Warsaw. 'Ministry of Foreign Affairs learns that Cracow, Katowice and other cities were bombed at 6 a.m. General Staff confirm bombardment early this morning.... Frontier crossed by small German detachments.' The message faded. 'Please inform....'[38]

Hitler's military planners aimed to make full use of Poland's geographical vulnerability. Polish forces would be overwhelmed by a double attack, with both German thrusts converging on Warsaw; the enemy would then be trapped and crushed with no time to retreat behind the line of the rivers San, Narew and Vistula. Fifty-four German Divisions were initially put into the field; this included all the German armoured, light, motorized and mountain units, and about two-thirds of the first line infantry. In support were about 1,600 aircraft. From the start the Poles were resigned to heavy losses and much

207

abandoned territory. But they believed they could retreat into defensive position and keep the Germans occupied, while the British and French attacked on the Western Front. The Polish Ambassador told Halifax the invasion was 'a plain case as provided for by the Treaty'.

'War has broken out because the Poles attacked the radio station at Gleiwitz,' declared Göring to Dahlerus at 8 a.m. Dahlerus rushed to the British Embassy and telephoned London. 'The Poles are sabotaging everything.'[39] Henderson sent similar messages. 'I understand that the Poles blew up the Dirschaw bridge during the night and that fighting took place with the Danzigers. On receipt of this news Herr Hitler gave orders for the Poles to be driven back from the border.... Herr Hitler may ask to see me after the Reichstag meeting.'[40]

The Führer had received two blows to his pride. The Italians had delivered the first, early in the morning, when Mussolini had instructed Attolico 'to entreat Hitler to send a telegram relieving him from the obligations of the alliance'. Hitler obliged in a starchy telephone call to the German Embassy at Rome. 'I am convinced that we can carry out the task imposed upon us with the military forces of Germany. I do not therefore expect to need Italy's military support.' But Hitler warned Mussolini that he had not entirely escaped – 'I also thank you, Duce, for everying which you will do in the future for the common causes of Fascism and National Socialism.'[41] The second damage to Hitler's self esteem came as he drove to address the Reichstag at the Kroll Opera House soon after 10 a.m. Instead of the hysterical demonstations, the tossed flowers, the frantic cheering, which had marked the start of the First World War, the thin crowds of Berliners were apathetic and silent. And Hitler's speech was almost defensive in tone. 'Seems like a swansong,' whispered one listener.[42] Henderson later reported that Hitler had interviewed a number of Generals immediately after his speech, and had 'confessed his policy had broken down and that guns alone could now speak. Herr Hitler broke down and left the room without completing his speech.'[43] But he soon recovered his nerve and noise. Göring took Dahlerus to see him, and although the Swede believed Hitler was 'upset inside', a violent attack was launched against the British for refusing to come to terms. Hitler was still not fully convinced Britain and France would intervene – Henderson reported: 'On the night of 31 August – 1 September, Herr Hitler had quarrelled with Herr von Ribbentrop on the subject of Britain's resolve to fight.'[44]

In London, the Commons had been summoned to meet at 6 p.m. Meanwhile, at 11.30 a.m. the Cabinet gathered. Chamberlain immediately declared Britain's determination to fight. 'The events against which we have fought so long and so earnestly have come upon us. But our consciences are clear, and there can be no possible question now where our duty lies.' Halifax said the Polish Ambassador had called to see him earlier. 'He expressed the opinion that circumstances have arisen which call for the implementation of our guarantee. I replied that providing the facts were as stated, I did not suppose that we would differ from his conclusions.' Halifax had then telephoned the German Chargé to ask whether he had any information or message to convey to him; the German had rung 15 minutes later to say reports that Warsaw and other cities were being bombed were untrue – the Poles were shooting and the Germans shooting back.

Ministers agreed that reports of the bombing of Warsaw were probably premature: 'It was pointed out that there was at present no very definite information as to what hostile action had taken place in Poland, and that it was desirable not to take any irrevocable action until we had some greater assurances.' Consideration would have to be given to the terms of a communication to Hitler, said Chamberlain; this would warn the Führer that unless hostilities ceased, Britain would fulfil her obligations, but, the Cabinet would have to decide whether this communication should contain a time limit – whether it should be an ultimatum. Chatfield said he had discussed this matter very briefly with his Service colleagues, the Lord Privy Seal, and the Chiefs of Staff; the evacuation process had just started, and from that point of view, a further delay was obviously desirable before an ultimatum was sent. But the Chiefs of Staff believed the enemy must not be allowed to steal an advance by attacking first – for the same reason, when an ultimatum was sent, the time period should be as short as possible. The Foreign Office, continued Chatfield, thought the period should be not less than six hours – in 1914 the time allowed had been four hours.

Discussion of the draft continued. Then Halifax interrupted with a message from the French. 'They wish to declare war before we do. The reason given for this is said to be public opinion in France, since the French Government are not anxious to appear to be dragged into war by us.' Ministers insisted war should be declared by France and Britain simultaneously. They also approved the idea of an interim reply being taken to Berlin by 'Mr D'. This reply ... 'should be stiff, and should stress the fact that the only way in which the World War could be stopped would be if the German troops left Polish territory. ... No hope should be held out that we could act as mediators between Germany and Poland.'

Discussion reverted to the communication to be given to Hitler by Henderson. 'It is possible', warned Chamberlain, 'the Germans might take aggressive action on the receipt of this telegram. Although it is unlikely that they should start an air attack on this country, they might start an attack on our merchant shipping and ships of war.' The communication should therefore not be in the form of an ultimatum, at this stage, and Britain would act in consultation with the French.

A meeting of the Defence Preparedness Committee had been hurriedly summoned that morning, said Chatfield, and had authorized departments to put the 'Precautionary Stage' into force. Decisions included the completion of mobilization. Ministers agreed the Advanced Air Striking Force and British Field Force should be sent to the Continent at once. Simon believed the Bank Holiday planned for the outbreak of war should be on Monday, 4 September.[45]

There was some confusion between the allies over last possibilities of negotiation. François-Poncet told Ciano that France now welcomed Mussolini's idea of a conference, provided it did not try to deal with the problems of countries not represented.[46] But Loraine told him that 'the action of the German Government has now rendered it impossible'.[47]

The ubiquitous Dahlerus telephoned from Berlin at 12.20 and told Cadogan 'that he supposed I had heard the news that fighting had begun.' Cadogan had clearly had enough of the well-meaning Swede. Dahlerus had insisted he should fly to London with Ogilvie-Forbes. 'I said I could not see what purpose could be achieved by that.... Any idea of mediation while German troops are invading Poland is quite out of the question.'[48]

Gradually, steadily, government departments were being organized for war. Shepherd cabled from Danzig: 'High Commissioner left 9.15 hours this morning at the request of local authorities who gave him one hour's notice. I hope to leave with Consular Staff for Riga via Königsberg this afternoon.' Henderson had asked the American Chargé 'to be good enough to take charge of British interests in the event of war'. All ciphers and confidential documents at the British Embassy at Berlin were being burnt, and the staff left their homes and camped in the hotel next door to the Embassy. At Downing Street, Chamberlain planned the composition of his War Cabinet, and, during the afternoon at last invited Churchill to re-enter the Cabinet. 'He told me that he saw no hope of averting a war with Germany,' wrote Churchill, whose actual position in the Government was so far unspecified.

Henderson was warned at 4.45 p.m. to be ready for the text of a communication to be handed immediately to the German Government. Halifax added: 'For your information: If the German reply is unsatisfactory the next stage will be either an ultimatum with time limit or an immediate declaration of war.' An hour later the text arrived: 'By their action the German Government had created conditions ... which called for the implementation by the Governments of the United Kingdom and France of the undertaking to Poland to come to her assistance.' The text continued: 'I am accordingly to inform Your Excellency that unless the German Government are prepared to give HMG satisfactory assurances that the German Government has suspended all aggressive action against Poland, and are prepared

210

promptly to withdraw their forces from Polish territory, HMG will without hesitation fulfil their obligations to Poland.'[49] Sir Nevile requested an interview with Ribbentrop for 7.15 p.m., but the Germans already knew the contents of the message – the communication had been sent *en clair* and had immediately been noted by the intelligence system. The Note was to be presented by both the British and French Ambassadors: France now seemed determined to open hostilities within a short time, yet still refused to abandon completely the hopes of a conference. Twice during the afternoon Bonnet told his Ambassador at Warsaw to ask if Poland would agree to the Italian proposal. 'We are in the midst of war,' snapped Beck in an impatient reply that evening. 'It is no longer a question of a conference but of common action.'[50]

Lights at the House of Commons had been lowered and Members stumbled through the dim lobby. Chamberlain arrived, welcomed by a loud cheer. With him was Arthur Greenwood, Acting Leader of the Labour Opposition. Up in the distinguished strangers' gallery the seats were crowded, and the Polish and Russian Ambassadors found themselves sitting next to one another. Chamberlain immediately rose to speak. The time had arrived, he said, when action rather than words was required. With some emotion, he reminded the House how he had prayed that it would never fall upon him to ask the country to accept the 'awful arbitrament of war', but 'I fear that I may not be able to avoid that responsibility.... Responsibility for this terrible catastrophe lies on the shoulders of one man, the German Chancellor, who has not hesitated to plunge the world into misery in order to serve his own senseless ambition.' Cheers broke out from all benches, then Members listened as Chamberlain told them the British and French Ambassadors had been instructed 'to hand to the German Government the following document ...'. Chamberlain rummaged through his papers to produce the message Sir Nevile was to deliver, and which he began to read, very slowly.

Sir Nevile saw Ribbentrop at 9.30, but the German Foreign Minister refused to see the French Ambassador at the same time: Coulondre would be received at 10 p.m. Ribbentrop was 'courteous and polite'. After reading the message, he claimed Poland had provoked Germany, who was therefore blameless; nevertheless he would pass the British communication to the Führer. Sir Nevile was 'inclined to believe that Hitler's answer will be an attempt to avoid war with Great Britain and France, but not likely to be one which we can accept'.[51] Berlin was darkened in fear of an air attack, but no Polish bombers came. The British War Cabinet was later told that the Polish air units had not received orders in time, and many airfields had been overrun before precautions could be taken.[52] And so Berliners packed into cafés, restaurants and beerhalls and were apprehensive but safe. Many Londoners also feared the terrible devastation and death which experts had prophesied. They, like Berliners, were calm, reluctant to fight, but determined to do so. Mussolini still sought his second Munich; the Duce had no straws left to clutch – except one: the attitude displayed by France the previous day. So, early on 2 September, he telegraphed Berlin that he still had a chance of bringing the Powers together, that a mere halt of the German army might be sufficient. His message contained a renewed appeal for a conference, which, said Mussolini, 'is now supported particularly by France'; this information was handed to Weizsäcker by Attolico at about 10 a.m., von Ribbentrop was 'unwell'.[53] The French, after briefly cooperating the evening before, were now proving a serious embarrassment. Phipps reported to London that according to Daladier, if conflict became inevitable 'it would be constitutionally necessary to summon Parliament in order to declare war,' and there would be many other matters to discuss, because the French Parliament would be meeting after a long interval. A joint Anglo-French declaration of war, or even a firm ultimatum to Germany, might therefore be delayed; Chamberlain would be under attack in Parliament for apparently hesitating to fight; Hitler would believe he could continue to act without interference; the Poles would believe they had been deserted. Halifax therefore told Sir Eric: 'For your information: Delays in Paris and attitude of the French Government are causing some misgiving here. We should be grateful for anything you can do to infuse courage and determination into M. Bonnet.'[54]

Ribbentrop, rapidly recovering his health, saw Attolico at 12.30 p.m. Mussolini's message had come too late, he said, because the British and French Ambassadors had already delivered an 'ultimatum' the previous evening. Attolico pleaded the contrary, and as Ribbentrop remained unmoved, offered to ask the British and French Ambassadors whether their communications had been intended as an ultimatum or not. Schmidt wrote later: 'I can still see Attolico, no longer in his first youth, running out of Ribbentrop's room and down the steps to consult Henderson and Coulondre.'[55] At 1.00 a.m., 2 September, he arrived back again, 'as breathless as he had left'. Ribbentrop still refused to allow the weary Ambassador any encouragement; the Germans would draft an answer to Mussolini's appeal 'in a day or two', and, when Attolico pressed for an earlier answer, finally agreed to reply by noon the next day, Sunday, 3 September.

Parliament met at 2.45 p.m. The session was unemotional and business-like and dealt with the practical preparations for war. The Conscription Bill was passed with only slight discussion. Chamberlain warned: 'It is impossible to wait for more than a very limited time before resolving the present situation, and HMG do not intend to do so.... It is, however, highly desirable that the action of HMG and that of the French Government should be simultaneous and identical.'

The French Parliament had been called for 3 p.m., and Chamberlain promised he would make a further statement to the House. But already rumours were circulating that Mussolini proposed another conference, and the French were inclined to listen – and suspicion returned that Chamberlain might still succumb to another Munich. His opponents thought the absence of a firm declaration would be clear evidence that the Government was attempting to shuffle from their responsibilities. Immediately following the afternoon Parliamentary session, the Cabinet met to discuss this urgent question of a British ultimatum to Germany. Halifax explained provisional conclusions reached by Chamberlain and himself. 'First, that the communication which Sir Nevile Henderson had made to the German Government was a final warning rather than an ultimatum. Secondly, if the German Government asked for further time, for consideration of their reply to our communication, we should be prepared to allow them until 12 noon tomorrow ... subject to their agreeing to an armistice. Thirdly, the primary condition for any conference should be that German troops should first withdraw from Polish soil.'

Chamberlain's opponents could not have wished for a stronger attitude; unfortunately, the Prime Minister was soon to find himself unable to reveal it. Halifax told the Cabinet: 'We might be prepared to consider an extension of the time limit from 12 noon tomorrow to 12 midnight, if this would facilitate consideration of a conference.' While the Chiefs of Staff were opposed to further delay, the French Government did not want the ultimatum to expire for another 48 hours. The Air Secretary and the First Lord strongly disagreed with this disturbing suggestion; Hore-Belisha was 'strongly opposed to further delay which I think might result in breaking the present unity in the country. Public opinion here is strongly against our yielding an inch. If the Germans are prepared to consider a standstill, it shows that they are weakening and that we should show the greatest possible strength.' He therefore favoured giving Germany until midnight of that night to accept the proposal to withdraw her troops; 'otherwise we should regard ourselves at war'. Chatfield agreed; Hore-Belisha also thought Hitler and Mussolini were most likely working in collusion. Chamberlain read a despairing message from Lipski, who had been instructed to request the immediate fulfilment of British obligations to Poland and sought an urgent reply. He had also handed over a grim telegram from Warsaw. 'Battle today over the whole of the front has increased in intensity and has acquired a very serious character. Our troops are opposing strong resistance. The whole of German air force is engaged against Poland. Villages and factories bombarded. The engagement of German aircraft by allied forces of greatest urgency.'

'I think there is general agreement in the Cabinet on two main points at issue,' said Chamberlain. 'First, that there should be no negotiation with Germany unless she is first prepared to give an undertaking to withdraw her troops from Poland and Danzig. Secondly, it is undesirable to allow Germany longer than until midnight tonight to make up her mind on these points. A communication in these senses clearly constitutes an ultimatum. At the same time it is evident that the precise terms of the communication to be made to Germany, and the statement to be made in Parliament this afternoon, will have to be settled in consultation with the French.'[56] These conclusions therefore had one flaw. The terms of the ultimatum had to be settled with the French. And Bonnet told Cadogan on the telephone immediately after the Cabinet meeting that 'if they [the British] insisted on a midnight ultimatum, they would incur a grave responsibility vis-à-vis France, because French evacuation ... will take two more days to complete'. The French Cabinet would reach their decision 'by 9 o'clock'.[57] The French therefore clashed with the British conclusions; and Parliament would expect a firm statement from the Prime Minister when it assembled at 6 p.m.

Halifax made another urgent attempt to establish Anglo-French cooperation: Phipps was told at 6 p.m. that if Bonnet still proved obstinate he must try and persuade Daladier. MPs were meanwhile milling in the Commons Lobby, impatient, tense and anxious. Chamberlain hurriedly summoned a meeting of his Ministers at his room in the House, and explained the position: the Cabinet had agreed on an ultimatum expiring at midnight, yet also believed that action against Germany must be coordinated with the French, and the French were refusing to cooperate.[58] Meanwhile, the French Cabinet was hopelessly divided, and Gamelin and the French General Staff were reluctant to agree to an immediate ultimatum. France must have at least two days more in which to carry out general mobilization and defensive precautions. Britain was in a far easier position – she would not be immediately threatened, and France would have to stand alone on the Western Front until British forces arrived – and how long would this take, and how large would the forces be?

Chamberlain could wait no longer before addressing Parliament. He could neither announce the conclusion agreed upon in the afternoon Cabinet meeting, nor, in view of the need to maintain Anglo-French loyalties, reveal the reason for delay. He later described these 'final long-drawn-out agonies' as 'nearly unendurable as could be'.[59] Members filed into the Chamber at 7.30 p.m. 'We wait there exactly like a court awaiting the verdict of the jury,' wrote Harold Nicolson. At 7.44 Neville Chamberlain walked to the Government Front Bench and immediately began his speech. 'His voice betrayed some emotion as if he were sickening for a cold,' noticed Nicolson. 'He is a strange man. We expected one of his dramatic speeches. But none came.'[60] Instead, he confined himself to giving a chronological review of recent

214

events and he informed the House that no reply had come from Berlin in answer to the Note delivered by Henderson the previous night. 'I should be horrified,' Chamberlain continued, 'if the House thought for one moment that the statement that I have made to them betrayed the slightest weakening, either of this Government or of the French Government.' The French Cabinet were in session and a communication would be received from Paris 'in the next few hours'. In an attempt to reassure the House he added: 'I anticipate that there is only one answer I shall be able to give the House tomorrow ... and I trust the House will believe me if I speak in complete good faith.' The Commons gasped with astonishment: no decision had apparently been reached. Greenwood, acting Labour leader, leapt to his feet to cries of 'Speak for England Arthur'. 'I am gravely disturbed. An act of aggression took place 38 hours ago. The moment that act of aggression took place one of the most important treaties of modern times automatically came into operation.... I wonder how long we are prepared to vacillate at a time when Britain and all that Britain stands for, and human civilization, are in peril.' Unwittingly ironic, he added: 'We must march with the French.'

Shocked MPs dispersed to discuss the deplorable speech. And some Ministers gathered in Simon's room at the House. 'We pressed that the Cabinet should meet at once and deputized Simon to see PM,' wrote Hore-Belisha. Meanwhile, Halifax, just about to go out to dinner with his wife, was asked to see Chamberlain, who told him how badly the statement had gone in the Commons. 'I had never known Chamberlain so disturbed,' he wrote. Cadogan was also summoned, and the three men were discussing the situation when the fourth of the 'Inner Cabinet', Simon, arrived with a message from the anxious Ministers. Chamberlain agreed to meet them at his room in the House. He told them of the continued French delay, and that he wanted to retrieve immediately the impression he had made in the House. The Ministers urged a statement should be made, irrespective of the French, and while Chamberlain returned to Downing Street, remained in Simon's room to draft a letter to him setting out their points.

At 9.50 p.m. Chamberlain telephoned Daladier personally to plead for French action: an angry scene had taken place in the Commons, he said, and his Cabinet colleagues were very disturbed because they had wanted to fix a midnight deadline for an ultimatum. As a compromise, Chamberlain proposed an announcement be made that the Ambassadors had been instructed to present the ultimatum at 8 a.m. the next morning, to expire at mid-day. Unless British bombers were ready to act at once, replied Daladier, France would prefer to delay the expected attacks upon her armies. The two leaders agreed to resume the conversation in about 15 minutes. When, soon after 10 p.m.

Simon and Anderson walked from Parliament to Downing Street, they found Chamberlain and Halifax had now decided Britain must act, without France if necessary. Half an hour later Halifax telephoned Bonnet in Paris, and proposed Britain should be free to act by sending separate instructions, provided the French would give an assurance they would follow suit within 24 hours. Bonnet tried vainly to persuade Halifax that Britain should wait.[61]

Ministers assembled for an emergency late-night Cabinet session. Chamberlain explained what had happened so far, and told the Cabinet he would like to make a statement at noon the following day. 'I therefore suggest that Sir Nevile Henderson should be instructed to see Herr von Ribbentrop at 9 a.m. tomorrow, and to say that unless a reply is received by 12 noon a state of war will exist between England and Germany as from that hour.... It is just possible that when the French Government become aware of our decision, they might bring forward their times a little, but I doubt whether they will.' Simon pointed out that if the ultimatum expired at noon, there would be insufficient time before the Prime Minister made his statement; he suggested the ultimatum should finish at 11 a.m. The Cabinet agreed.[62] With true drama, the meeting ended with a violent clap of thunder, and lightning flashed outside in Downing Street.

Even while the Cabinet had been sitting, Halifax had sent a precautionary message to Henderson, followed by another at 12.25: 'You should ask for an appointment with Minister for Foreign Affairs at 9 a.m. Sunday morning.' The instructions sent, Halifax relaxed 'and seemed relieved'. He called for a glass of beer, brought by a Resident Clerk in pyjamas.[63] The French had finally made their decision, and Bonnet had cabled Coulondre at midnight to instruct him that a new *démarche* would be forwarded to him in the morning, to be presented 'at noon'. Yet even now Bonnet refused to abandon his fading hopes of peace. 'During the night,' wrote Ciano in his diary on 3 September, 'I was awakened by the Ministry because Bonnet had asked ... if we could not at least obtain a symbolic withdrawal of German forces from Poland.... I throw the proposal in the waste paper basket without informing the Duce. But this shows that France is moving toward the great test without enthusiasm and full of uncertainty.'[64]

The text of Britain's ultimatum to Germany was telephoned to Berlin early on Sunday morning, 3 September, and Sir Nevile was instructed to tell Ribbentrop that Britain had still to receive assurances, sought on 1 September, that the Germans would suspend all aggressive action against Poland. 'Although this communication was made more than 24 hours ago, no reply has been received, but German attacks on Poland have been continued and intensified. I have accordingly the honour to inform you that unless not later than 11 a.m., British Summer Time, today, 3 September, satisfactory assurances

216

to the above effect have been given by the German Government and have reached HM Government in London, a state of war will exist between the two countries as from that hour.' Sir Nevile was told by Halifax that if the assurance referred to were received, 'you should inform me by any means at your disposal before 11 a.m. today, 3 September. If no such assurance is received here by 11 a.m., we shall inform the German representative that a state of war exists as from that hour, and you shall at that time act in accordance with the war instruction.'[65]

An hour before the time appointed for delivery of this document, Dahlerus sprang into action again. Hearing from Ogilvie-Forbes that the British ultimatum was to be delivered at 9.00, he went in a panic to Göring and begged him to ensure the German reply was 'reasonable'. Dahlerus claimed Göring then agreed to, and secured Hitler's permission for, a plan for him to fly to London that morning, 'to negotiate'. If the claim were true, the suggestion came far too late.

Meanwhile, the presentation of the ultimatum had run into humiliating difficulties. Henderson was informed Ribbentrop would not be available at such an early hour, especially on a Sunday. Instead, he had to arrange to see Dr Schmidt, merely an interpreter. And this hardworked official overslept on the crucial morning of 3 September, and rushing down the Wilhelmstrasse saw to his horror Henderson already mounting the Foreign Ministry steps. He had barely time to sprint into a side door, run up the stairs and regain his breath, before Sir Nevile was announced, precisely at 9 a.m. 'He came in looking very serious, shook hands, but declined my invitation to be seated, remaining solemnly standing in the centre of the room.' Sir Nevile performed his duty. Schmidt rushed the British document to the Chancellery to inform Hitler and Ribbentrop – now available. 'When I entered the room, Hitler was sitting at his desk and Ribbentrop stood by the window. Both looked up expectantly as I came in. I stopped at some distance from Hitler's desk, and then slowly translated the British ultimatum.... Hitler sat immobile, gazing before him ... after an interval which seemed an age, he turned to Ribbentrop, who had remained standing by the window. "What now?" asked Hitler with a savage look, as though implying that his Foreign Minister had misled him.' Schmidt left the room and met Göring outside, who said: 'If we lose this war, then God have mercy on us!' Goebbels stood in a corner, downcast and self-absorbed. 'Everywhere in the room I saw looks of grave concern.'[66]

At 10.15, 45 minutes before the ultimatum expired, Dahlerus again telephoned the Foreign Office. 'If there could be give and take on both sides the conference could be arranged,' he lectured, adding he was satisfied the Germans were 'most anxious to try to satisfy the British Government ... and to give assurances not to violate the independence of Poland'. Overlooking the detail that this independence had already been mutilated, Dahlerus continued: 'Never in world history has an army withdrawn before negotiation.' Thirty minutes later, he telephoned yet again. 'As a last resort,' wrote Cadogan, 'he suggested that Field-Marshal Göring should fly over to London to discuss matters. The Secretary of State sent a reply to the effect that our position had been known to the German Government for some time, and we could not now delay our procedure.'[67] The telephone clicked silent; at long last the public-spirited Dahlerus had finished 'trying his damnedest' to patch up the quarrels between the great powers.

Fifteen minutes later, just after 11 a.m., Henderson received a summons to see Ribbentrop. Already the ultimatum had expired; and in London at 11.15 Halifax handed the German Chargé a formal note stating that since no German assurances had been received, 'I have the honour to inform you that a state of war exists between the two countries.' Before Henderson set out to see Ribbentrop, the Embassy staff had been informed Britain was at war. A few minutes before 11.30, Sir Nevile was handed the German Government's reply: 'The German Government and the German people refuse to receive, accept, let alone to fulfil demands in the nature of ultimata made by the British Government.'[68] The document detailed the German grievances against Poland. 'My only comment on reading this completely false representation,' wrote Sir Nevile, 'was "it will be left to history to judge where the blame really lies".'[69] Ribbentrop replied that nobody had striven harder for peace and good relations with England than Herr Hitler; history, he claimed, had 'already proved the facts'.

While Sir Nevile was talking, for the last time, to Ribbentrop, Chamberlain was broadcasting to the British people. 'I am speaking to you from the Cabinet Room at 10 Downing Street....' Britain was at war. 'You can imagine what a bitter blow it is to me that all my long struggle to win peace has failed.' He had scarcely finished when, in Churchill's words, 'a strange, prolonged, wailing noise, afterwards to become familiar, broke upon the ears.' The air raid warning – but so soon? Churchill went to the flat roof of his house and saw all around him the roofs and spires of London, clear in the cool September light, and above them were already rising thirty to forty fat cylindrical barrage balloons. He went to the air-raid shelter, 'armed with a bottle of brandy and other appropriate medical comforts'.[70] The crowd scattered from the railings in Parliament Square; in the House of Commons, Members crammed into the improvised shelters; the Chiefs of Staff, who were just emerging from the underground War Room where they had been having a top-level meeting, now disappeared below again. Air Chief Marshal Dowding was in his office at Headquarters, Fighter Command, and immediately went to the Filter and

Operations Room, to discover within a few moments that the alarm had been caused by a French aircraft bound for Croydon, bringing some French officers to London on official business.[71]

At noon, loudspeakers in the Berlin streets suddenly crackled out the news of war. Berliners listened in stunned silence as they stood on the sunlit pavements; faces expressed depression, shock and no elation. At six minutes past noon, Chamberlain rose to address the Commons; it was the first Sunday meeting of Parliament for nearly 120 years. His face looked old and very tired. He formally revealed latest developments, and told the House that the French Ambassador in Berlin was at that moment making a similar *démarche*, accompanied by a definite time limit. 'This is a sad day for all of us, and to none is it sadder than to me. Everything that I have worked for, everything that I have fought for, everything that I have believed in during my public life, has crashed into ruins. There is only one thing left for me to do. That is to devote what strength and powers I have to forwarding the victory of the cause for which we have to sacrifice so much. I cannot tell what part I may be allowed to play myself; I trust I may live to see the day when Hitlerism has been destroyed and a liberated Europe has been re-established.' Churchill, sitting in his place and listening to the speeches, felt a 'very strong sense of calm' coming over him. 'I felt a serenity of mind and was conscious of a kind of uplifted detachment from human and personal affairs. The glory of Old England, peaceloving and ill-prepared as she was, but instant and fearless at the call of honour, thrilled my being.' The sirens continued through the debate, but were only calling the equally unaccustomed 'All Clear'. The National Service (Armed Forces) Bill was passed through all its stages before lunch.[72]

Meanwhile, at 12.30 the French ultimatum had been delivered after a farcical refusal by Weizsäcker to accept it. Coulondre had arrived punctually at noon, only to find Ribbentrop was welcoming the new Soviet Ambassador at the Chancellery. Weizsäcker said he himself had insufficient authority to act; Coulondre still tried to pass over the ultimatum document. Weizsäcker refused to cooperate and told the diplomat to 'be good enough to be patient'. Thirty minutes later he passed over the document to Ribbentrop, and in reply to Ribbentrop's statement that France would be the aggressor, echoed the words of his British colleague: 'History will be the judge of that.' The French ultimatum was scheduled to expire at 5 p.m. – twelve hours earlier than originally intended. Hitler's shock at Britain's determination to stand against him poured out in an angry, virulent proclamation issued during the afternoon. 'Great Britain has for centuries pursued the aim of rendering the peoples of Europe defenceless against British policy of world conquest.' He also issued his War Directive No. 2. 'Offensive naval action should start against England.' Restricted air attacks on English naval forces would also be launched, but the opening of hostilities in the West 'will be left to the enemy'.

In London, Chamberlain offered Churchill the post of First Lord of the Admiralty. 'I naturally preferred a definite task to that exulted brooding over the work done by others which may well be the lot of a Minister, however influential, who has no department.'[73] No time was specified for the appointment to take effect, but Churchill was anxious to be at work. 'I therefore sent word to the Admiralty that I would take charge forthwith and arrive at six o'clock.' 'WINSTON IS BACK' signalled the Admiralty to all Royal Naval vessels. Chamberlain saw another of his previous critics during the afternoon. Anthony Eden had received a hint from Churchill the previous evening that he would be offered 'one of the major offices of State', but he was offered only the post of Secretary of State for the Dominions, which would not have a Cabinet seat. Reluctantly, Eden accepted; he wrote in his memoirs that he disliked this 'somewhat anomalous position in the Cabinet. If it had not been for the emergency of war, nothing would have induced me to return.'[74]

Berlin was quiet, the streets almost empty. A single *Schupo* paced the pavement before the British Embassy. In London, the War Room was silent, waiting. In the Filter and Operations Room, nerve centre of Fighter Command, the huge mapped table showed no aircraft plots; then a spindly 'daddy longlegs' whirred from the window, settled on the map in the area of Dover, and walked daintily down the coastline of the English Channel. Dowding broke the silence. 'A Coastal Command sweep I presume.'[75] At 5 p.m., Ministers once more assembled at Downing Street. But now there were fewer than before; the decision-making centre of the Government was to be streamlined to meet the needs of stress and acute urgency. Its title had a sinister ring – the British War Cabinet.

12

War

Chamberlain believed he might soon quit the Premiership. 'One thing comforts me,' he wrote on 10 September. 'While war was still averted, I felt I was indispensible, for no one else could carry out my policy. Today the position has changed. Half a dozen people could take my place while war is in progress, and I do not see I have any particular part to play until it comes to discussing peace terms – and that may be a long way off.'[1] Eight months to the day after he wrote these words, Chamberlain was to leave 10 Downing Street. During those weeks of tension, followed by acute anti-climax, Chamberlain the pursuer of peace, was to command Britain in conflict, his character and methods unchanged; the Cabinet Minutes reveal his manner at the war meetings was as secretive, quiet, obstinate, self-centered and often infuriating, as it had been during the peacetime sessions.

The Cabinet itself was radically altered; it took over not only from the peacetime version, but also superseded the Committee of Imperial Defence and the single secretariat which had served both these groups under Sir Edward Bridges. On 31 August, the latter had handed Chamberlain guidance papers on the possible composition of a War Cabinet; next day, Chamberlain announced at the 11.30 a.m. Cabinet meeting: 'I have no doubt that the right course is to set up a War Cabinet at once on the model ... established in the last war.' He asked his colleagues to be prepared to resign collectively.[2] The World War One model, set up as late as 1916 under Lloyd George, had consisted of merely five members, of whom only the Chancellor of the Exchequer had firm departmental responsibilities. Newspaper opinion, especially *The Times*, also supported this idea of 'five men with nothing to do but run the war'. So Chamberlain sought a group which would be flexible, manageable, without factional or Ministerial pressures, able to reach decisions rapidly and smoothly. 'My sole purpose was to find a Cabinet that would work, which means that personalities must be taken into account.'[3]

Reluctantly, he was forced to abandon hopes of persuading a Labour member to join; the Liberals also declined. And Chamberlain refused to consider his sharpest Tory critics: at a War Cabinet meeting on 4 October he rejected, 'with an irritated snort', the idea of inviting Leo Amery and Duff Cooper.[4] Ministers Chamberlain readmitted after previous disagreements found it difficult to work with former opponents. And, as 'personalities must be taken into account', nine members in all gathered for the initial session of the War Cabinet. If Churchill, through the force of his personality, was to be a member as First Lord, the other two Service Ministers must be included: Hore-Belisha and Wood. These three, Halifax as Foreign Secretary, and Simon as Chancellor, made five members responsible for important departments of State, so Chamberlain's hope for a high proportion of ministers without portfolio had therefore been abandoned. With three Service Ministers, Chatfield must also be included as Minister for Co-ordination of Defence, though the Committee of Imperial Defence (CID), which he had supervised, had ceased to exist. Other members were Sir Samuel Hoare, now Lord Privy Seal, and Lord Hankey, Minister without Portfolio.

Nine members still represented a drastic reduction from the peace-time twenty-two. Chamberlain's War Cabinet had also what appeared an important advantage over Lloyd George's. In the First War the two Chiefs of Staff had advised the Prime Minister independently, which led to confusion and rivalry; but since 1924 the Chiefs of Staff Sub-Committee had advised the Cabinet on overall defence policy. During peacetime, this Sub-Committee acted as a subsidiary of the Committee of Imperial Defence, and reported to the Cabinet via that. Now it could report direct to the War Cabinet, and it was hoped – in vain as it turned out – this would speed the decision-making process.

Meanwhile, policy-making was concentrated upon the War Cabinet and the Chiefs of Staff Committee. The former met at least once each day, usually at 11.30 a.m., and apart from the nine members, other ministers, officials and experts were called in for specific discussions; these included Sir John Anderson, for Home Affairs; Anthony Eden, for the Dominions; Sir Horace Wilson, Permanent Secretary to the Treasury; W. S. Morrison, Chancellor of the Duchy of Lancaster, and various departmental heads. The three Chiefs of Staff attended regularly for military business.

The Chiefs of Staff Sub-Committee met each day at 10.00 a.m., in time for conclusions to be passed on to the War Cabinet later. Comprising this committee were General Sir Edmund Ironside, Chief of the Imperial General Staff, Air Chief Marshal Sir Cyril Newall, and Admiral of the Fleet Sir Dudley Pound. Their secretary was the previous secretary of the CID, Major-General Hastings Ismay, who was also Deputy-Secretary under Sir Edward Bridges at the War Cabinet. The official terms of reference of the Chiefs of Staff Committee were 'to hear reports and consider the situation, to decide day-to-day problems concerning operations', and to deal with specific matters referred to them by the War Cabinet. Before long this committee became, in effect, a battle headquarters, an executive body, which sent instructions to field commanders. Further down the scale were two more inter-Service bodies, the Joint Planning and the Joint Intelligence Sub-Committees.

A French 'Law for the Organization of the Nation in War-time', passed on 11 July 1938, empowered the President – Daladier – to govern by decree from the day hostilities started. Daladier also controlled foreign affairs (Bonnet went to the Ministry of Justice) and his chief technical adviser was General Gamelin, Chief of Staff for National Defence. Coordination links between Paris and London had been worked out in the summer of 1939. A memorandum by Chatfield and the Service Ministers, 'Supreme Command in War', was adopted by the CID on 6 July, and formed the basis of the subsequent structure. All Allied Powers should be represented on a single Supreme War Council, which should meet preferably in England. Both Powers should be represented by their Prime Ministers and one other Minister, and both should send permanent military representatives. The Council would have no executive authority, but would enable the respective Governments to make decisions. A French and British secretariat was established, and branches of the new organization began to function on both sides of the Channel.[5] With this Supreme Command structure went a Higher Command system for the forces in France. In 1918, Foch had been appointed Allied C-in-C, and Haig had been instructed to obey 'loyally' the French C-in-C, or appeal to the British Government if he thought an order imperilled the British Army. This scheme was adopted again in 1939. But Bomber Command, the advanced air-striking force in France, would receive its operations directly from its own C-in-C, Bomber Command, back in England.[6]

Broad strategic policy for the conduct of the war had been laid down at Anglo-French Staff talks in early Spring, 1939; and, in general, conclusions reached at these discussions were to be followed remarkably closely. 'We should be faced by enemies who would be more fully prepared than ourselves for war on a national scale,' stated the conclusions, 'would have superiority in air and land forces, but would be inferior at sea and in general economic strength. In these circumstances, we must be prepared to face a major offensive directed against either France or Great Britain or against both. To defeat such an offensive we should have to concentrate all our initial efforts, and during this time our major strategy would be defensive.'[7]

Much needed to be done to bring Britain's forces to war efficiency. The recent changes to the Army took time to be introduced and for administrative problems to be solved. The abrupt switch from readiness to police and garrison a global Empire, to readiness to fight in the fields of Europe, had imposed an immense strain on the army structure, on the War Office, and on the new Ministry of Supply. Hardly a unit was to go to France completely equipped. On the outbreak of war, only two of the nineteen Regular and Territorial Divisions which were to go to the Continent were approaching readiness; and because of the call-up of industrial workers, factory production was dislocated, retarding armament production. The decision to send all Regular units abroad meant units left in Britain were semi-trained and deficient. The flower of the British Army went across the Channel, though this offering was proportionately small.

Nor was the RAF anywhere near adequate strength. Scheme M, the production programme under way at the outbreak of war, would have produced a powerful air force – but not before March 1942. As it was, first-line aircraft for fighting over Britain and France only totalled 1,460, of which 608 were fighters and 536 bombers. 'There was still so much to be done,' said Dowding, 'and I was being asked to give up too much for despatch overseas.' As C-in-C Fighter Command, Dowding had the equivalent of 34 squadrons to defend Britain; staff talks before the war had agreed there should ideally be 53.[8] The first-line combat strength of the Luftwaffe amounted to 1,180 long-distance bombers and 366 dive bombers.[9] Until the end of 1936 the construction of capital warships and cruisers was limited by treaty, and the Royal Navy, even after 1936, was hampered by an assumption that its primary operational role would be in the Far East. Yet the Navy was relatively far stronger than the other two services. The main shortage was of destroyers and cruisers, especially for convoy escort duties: the Royal Navy had 184 destroyers, but none designed specifically for escorting, and Churchill was constantly to remind the War Cabinet of gross deficiencies in this essential naval role.

After the first five weeks of war the British had landed in France two corps, each of two divisions, and four fighter and eight reconnaissance squadrons. Allied strategy on the Western Front had been much discussed since the Cabinet had decided, in February 1939, to extend the scope of Anglo-French military conversations. From the start, problems caused by Belgium neutrality loomed large, and on 2 May had formed the subject of a joint Anglo-French staff paper. If the Germans invaded the Low Countries, the allies were to move into Belgium to take up defensive positions. But permission would first be needed from Brussels. Yet the Belgians consistently refused to join in staff talks, even after the outbreak of the Polish campaign. So detailed plans were difficult to elaborate, and were based on hazy and dangerous assumptions.

The shock of war soon passed, to be followed by anti-climax. Restrictions became resented. With no fighting on the Western Front, and no air raids, the reasons for restrictions were not apparent. The condition of war caused friction, without any fire of enthusiasm. Only a few days after war had begun, Chamberlain wrote: 'One can see how this war twilight is trying people's nerves.'[10]

The 'war twilight', the 'Bore War', the 'Phoney War', the 'Sitzkrieg' these were all tragic misnomers to the bombed, battered, abandoned Poles. The French and the few British troops were 'sitting still and sheltering behind steel and concrete while a quixotically valiant ally was being exterminated'.[11] The Franco-Polish Military Convention of 19 May 1939, had laid down that the French would 'progressively launch offensive operations against limited objectives towards the third day after General Mobilization Day'. And the French plan had specified that 'as soon as the principal German effort develops against Poland ... France will launch an offensive action against Germany with the bulk of her forces – "*les gros de ses forces*".' This would start on the fifteenth day after mobilization. Gamelin claimed '*les gros*' – the main bodies – was vastly different from '*le gros*' – the bulk; an assault on the Siegfried Line had definitely not been promised; and, by 23 August, Gamelin had told his Government that a serious offensive could not possibly be launched 'in less than about two years'. Anyway help depended on signature of the political agreement, then in the course of preparation but not yet signed.[12]

Britain's attitude was equally devious. Staff discussions during the summer led to the conclusion that Poland's retaining up to thirty-five German Divisions in the East, would increase the time available for the preparation of Allied forces in the West. But the overall conclusion was that Britain and France could do little to help the unfortunate Poles, whose fate 'will depend upon the ultimate outcome of the war', which, 'in turn, will depend upon the ability to bring about the eventual defeat of Germany, and not on our ability to relieve pressure on the Poles at the outset'. So Chamberlain and his Cabinet – and his War Cabinet – believed Poland could only be saved after she had first been destroyed. Nevertheless, the March guarantee had centred on the clear assurance that Poland could count on Britain's 'immediate and full support'. The Poles soon made clear they had expected far more than they were given; and the War Cabinet Minutes of Ministers' twisting and wriggling to avoid answering desperate Polish appeals make painful reading. And Churchill twisted and wriggled as much as any other. If Belgian neutrality, and insufficient troops, restricted a land offensive against Germany, there still remained possibilities of bomber raids. But on 2 September the British and French Governments announced their intention to confine bombardment to strict military objectives in the immediate area of the Western Front, and these limited. This course was adopted partly for humanitarian reasons, but more from fear of retaliation. Besides, vital resources must be conserved. The RAF had to be content with dropping propaganda leaflets and undertaking limited attacks on military targets; only the Navy, as Churchill never failed to mention, was truly active. The Poles were left to face the German invasion alone; Britain's 'immediate and full support' amounted to a meagre list of hardware items, some of them hastily stopped *en route* when it appeared the Poles might be defeated.

When the War Cabinet began its daily, sometimes twice daily, meetings, discussions were bitty, jumping from one topic to another without lengthy debate: War Cabinet members seemed unsure of themselves and still confused. But, gradually, the rhythm of proceedings became apparent as procedures became routine – and, before long, the routine became dull to those tied to it. A number of subjects constantly recurred: the need to find allies and deter potential foes; to improve collaboration with France; and, again before long, to find something to do in this period of half-war; and above all to build up forces before twilight darkened into terrible night.

Death of an Ally

War Cabinet members assembling for their first meeting at 5 p.m. Sunday, 3 September, six hours after war had been declared, had to choose someone to command Britain's forces in France. Incredibly, this crucial appointment had so far not been discussed at Cabinet meetings, and yet the British Field Force was about to start leaving for the Continent. Many British officers took Ironside's selection for granted. On the outbreak of the First War General Sir John French, Inspector-General of the Forces, had been made C-in-C of the British Expeditionary Force and this had led to the subsequent belief that Inspector-General meant in effect C-in-C designate – and Ironside had been appointed Inspector-General of the Overseas Forces when the office was revived earlier in 1939. If, unexpectedly, Ironside was not chosen, another likely candidate seemed to be Lieutenant-General Sir John Dill, who held the Aldershot command and was considered Britain's leading strategist.[1]

But Hore-Belisha wanted neither, and proposed instead General Viscount Gort, V.C., then Chief of the Imperial General Staff. Younger, junior, Gort was an unexpected choice. His bravery in the First War was legendary, but many senior officers believed him better suited to be a Corps or Army commander. Hore-Belisha met Chamberlain before the first War Cabinet meeting and was told it was up to him to propose the man he considered most suitable, though he might confer with Wood and Churchill. Both concurred with Hore-Belisha's choice, although Wood hesitated over his plan to make Ironside Chief of the Imperial General Staff. Gort's appointment was agreed at the Cabinet meeting and, despite opposition from Wood, so too was Ironside's. Churchill swung round the doubters with an energetic speech in support of Hore-Belisha: already he was stamping his domineering personality on the discussions. General Sir Walter Kirke was appointed C-in-C, Home Forces.[2]

The War Cabinet now considered the first operation plans of the conflict: action against the German Fleet; action by the French; action by the RAF over Germany. A bomber force would attack the German Fleet which was reported to have sailed from Wilhelmshaven during the afternoon. Ministers were worried over possible French violation of the agreement to be cautious in selecting bombing targets. 'It would be desirable to take steps to restrain the French from taking precipitate action in this matter.' The RAF would drop leaflets during the night in the Hamburg, Bremen and Ruhr areas. This 'might well have its maximum effect in the first few hours of war. The risk to pilots is not regarded as great.'[3]

Hore-Belisha had an audience with the King at 7.30 p.m. – in view of the exceptional circumstances he was told he need not change into morning clothes – and the senior officer appointments were confirmed. But Ironside's appointment was unpopular at the War Office, he wrote, despite his own belief that 'he had that dynamic strength which was essential in the present crisis'. And the appointment of Gort – an officer junior to Dill – also caused resentment; it seemed and indeed was, typical of Hore-Belisha's policy of favouring younger men. Older, more senior, officers had already been passed over since Hore-Belisha became War Secretary, and for many months had felt bitter. War brought them opportunity to act upon their grievances, since civilian interference was easier to attack than in peacetime, and before many weeks Hore-Belisha was to feel the result.[4]

Meanwhile, at 9 p.m. on the first night of war, the liner *Athenia* steamed 200 miles west of the Hebrides, outward bound from Britain. German submarines were known to be in the area, but fears of attack were slight. U-boats had been ordered not to attack passenger liners, only to sink merchant vessels after they had been stopped and searched; only troopships, escorted vessels, and vessels taking action which might help the enemy could be sunk without warning. The *Athenia* fitted none of the categories. But U-30 hovering in the area, saw the lights of the target, and within minutes the liner slipped beneath the black water; 112 lives were lost, including 28 American. First reports reached the Admiralty during the night and fears that Germany intended unrestricted submarine warfare immediately increased. 'Let me have a statement of the German U-boat forces, actual and prospective, for the next few months,' wrote Churchill in his first Admiralty minute of the war, to the Director of Naval Intelligence.[5] Almost immediately he was told the enemy had 60 U-boats and at least 40 more would be ready by 1940. Churchill told the War Cabinet next day that routing of merchant ships was now in force, and the convoy system was to be introduced without delay.[6]

Meanwhile, since all U-boats were maintaining radio silence, the German Naval High Command could not make an immediate check on the reports of the sinking. First reports – which reached Berlin from London – were disbelieved; nevertheless, during 4 September all U-boats were signalled: 'By order of the Führer, on no account are operations to be carried out against passenger steamers, even when under escort.' Weizsäcker summoned the US Chargé to deny that a German submarine had been to blame; and within a few days the German Propaganda Ministry was to seize the opportunity to allege that Churchill had personally ordered a bomb to be placed on board the *Athenia* to prejudice German-United States relations.

The Chiefs of Staff Committee held their 4 September meeting before the Cabinet assembled. Discussing Roumania, they concluded there would be more advantage in her remaining neutral than her joining in the struggle against Germany. If Hitler attacked Roumania, nothing could stop him. Neutrality would 'avoid ... the possibility of giving Germany a cheap success.'[7] They also discussed Norway, and Narvik was mentioned – a name which was soon to become tragically familiar. Hitler needed Narvik to transport ore supplies and, in consequence, he needed a neutral Norway and was unlikely to commence hostilities; if he did, a seaborne invasion would be exposed to Britain's superior naval forces.

The Cabinet, as well, discussed diplomatic rather than military matters for most of its morning meeting. Discussion covered the reactions of a wide range of countries. Turkey headed the list: the Turks were increasing their demands for financial help, and Halifax warned that until these demands were met, the Turks were unlikely to sign the French-Anglo-Turkish Agreement. The French were unlikely to help 'although it is to their interests as much as to our own that we should keep Turkey within our orbit'. He pointed out that in two or three months' time Polish resistance might be broken, and a long period of stalemate would follow on the Western Front. Britain and France could only strike at Germany through Turkey and Roumania. On Italy, he said: 'There is good reason to believe that Mussolini is as anxious to avoid becoming involved in war against us as he is to keep out of a war with Germany.' But an ultimatum to make him declare Italian neutrality would 'throw him into the arms of Germany'. The position in South Africa was confused: a telegram from the High Commissioner reported that the Union Cabinet had split over neutrality; their Parliament would probably be dissolved and new elections held. Eire had declared her neutrality, as expected, and no help could be expected from that direction.

Only towards the end of the meeting were military topics mentioned. Newall said he had been pressed by the French to employ the Air Striking Force in collaboration with the French Army. 'I am opposed to any such action at a time when the French Army is not undertaking active operations.' Despite the decision that Poland could not be helped until Germany had been defeated in the overall struggle, Churchill now stated: 'The main German effort is concentrated against Poland

and every means possible should be employed to relieve pressure. This could be done by operations against the Siegfried Line, which was at present thinly held.' The Cabinet approved this new attitude: 'It was generally agreed ... that the Chiefs of Staff should make immediate contact with General Gamelin, with a view to concerting the action of the British and French forces.' Ironside and Newall later flew to France to discover Gamelin's plans – such as they were. Unfortunately, this determination to help Poland was soon to fade. The Polish situation was discussed last. 'The concentration of as many as 32 German divisions in Slovakia has come as a surprise,' reported Ironside. But the country between Slovakia and Poland was extremely difficult for military operations. However, if the Germans broke through, the Poles would have to face an attack in enormous strength from the South. Yet Ironside was optimistic that Poland would be able to survive for at least a few weeks.[8]

Henderson had just left the British Embassy for the sad journey home. Berlin was quiet – and Berliners were surprised that bombers had not appeared the previous night. The Ambassador and his staff left the capital in two well-appointed Pullman railway cars. Diplomatic niceties were being observed. The staff of the French Embassy, headed by Coulondre, had already left. In France chaos spread along the frontier from tiny Luxembourg south through Strasbourg to Basle. Civilians crammed the road as they fled back from the battle-zone; troops and reinforcements pushed forward for the Maginot Line garrisons. Over 250,000 *Strasbourgeois* left their city in forty-eight hours. Women and children flocked from towns and villages, some taking no more than they could carry in their arms. Farms were left empty, animals left untended, with cows bellowing in agony from their swollen udders. French motorized infantry divisions were still *en route*; many of the infantry units in front of the Maginot defences were at peacetime strength; ammunition columns had still to arrive; the air force concentration was incomplete. Advance parties of the British Field Force stepped on to French soil during the day. Also on 4 September the RAF made its first raid on Germany, acting on the Cabinet's decision the previous afternoon. Twenty-nine bombers took off to attack naval units at Brunsbüttel and Wilhelmshaven – seven aircraft were reported lost, and damage to the enemy was reported slight.

The day had an unfortunate ending for Henderson. All had gone well until nightfall when his train reached a small station, Rheine, near the German-Dutch frontier. 'We were suddenly held up there pending further orders.' Some problem had apparently arisen over German officials' journey from Paris and the French mission in front was not being allowed to escape until Hitler's diplomats had reached neutral territory. 'We were similarly detained, until the steamship with the staff of the Germany Embassy from London should arrive in Dutch territorial waters.' Sir Nevile had to remain at Rheine; he ended his first full day of war playing bridge in his Pullman railway car.[9]

The battle for the Danzig corridor had ended. Stukas had shattered Polish communication links – carefully avoiding damage to roads so that the approaching German tanks would not be hindered. Whole divisions of these tanks had pushed their way through the Polish lines, screeching forward thirty or forty miles in a single thrust. Motorized columns had raced across the flat countryside, dragging heavy guns, carrying thousands of grey helmeted troops. That night the Polish sky-line glowed red and vivid yellow. *Blitzkrieg* had begun. 'The crushing of Poland by Germany in a few weeks is most improbable,' Ironside had declared at the Cabinet meeting only a few hours before.

'You will understand how hateful I find my personal position,' wrote Chamberlain to the Archbishop of Canterbury when he had heard of the first RAF deaths early next morning, Tuesday, 5 September. 'I simply can't bear to think of these gallant fellows who lost their lives last night in the RAF attack and of their families who have first been called upon to pay the price. Indeed, I must put such thoughts out of my mind if I am not to be unnerved altogether.... But it was just the realization of these tragedies that has pressed upon me all the time I have been here. I did so hope we were going to escape them, but I sincerely believe that with the madman it was impossible.'[10]

Polish defences at Czeestochowa had been broken by three or four German motorized divisions, Hore-Belisha told the War Cabinet on 5 September. 'This threat must be taken seriously since it might result in Germany capturing Poland's main industrial area.... It might also mean that the Polish army will have to withdraw to the line of the Vistula.'[11] Henderson had remained stranded. While waiting at Rheine, he and his staff learnt from German newspapers that the RAF had raided Wilhelmshaven, and that the first leaflets had been dropped, some of them not far from where they sat in their siding. Then, at about two in the afternoon, the train clanked forward again, over the frontier and into neutral territory.[12]

The War Cabinet met again at 3 p.m., to receive a full report from Ironside and Newall on their discussions with Gamelin in Paris. After his armies had completed their concentration, Gamelin intended to open a limited offensive, between the Rhine and the Moselle, to relieve pressure on the Poles. The first phase would involve an advance to the Siegfried Line. Then, from 17 September onwards, Gamelin proposed the French would 'lean against it' to test its strength. A breakthrough might be achieved, but Gamelin's aims were strictly limited. The War Cabinet took note of this plan and agreed that RAF bombers might exploit any successes.[13]

At 10 p.m. Churchill presided over a lengthy conference at the

Admiralty, on the security of the Navy's Home Fleet, which must have as safe a base as possible. As Churchill wrote: 'In a war with Germany Scapa Flow is the true strategic point from which the British Navy can control the exits from the North Sea and enforce blockade.' Scapa Flow was vulnerable to submarine and air attack. 'I was surprised ... that more precautions had not been taken in both cases to prepare the defences against modern forms of attack.' Anti-submarine booms were inadequate, and the narrow and tortuous approaches on the east of the Flow were an especial source of anxiety. The submarines of the last war could not cope with the currents in these passages but now submarines were considerably more powerful. As for air defences – they hardly existed.[14] Following Admiralty discussion, the Chiefs of Staff completed a memorandum on the air defence of Scapa Flow, on 6 September, recommending, among other improvements, two flights of balloons, and two extra fighter squadrons based in the area.[15] As if to emphasize Britain's vulnerability, the first German air raid on Britain took place the same day. German bombers struck at points along the east coast, although little damage resulted.[16]

Meanwhile, depressing news came from Poland. At the War Cabinet meeting on 6 September Ironside changed his assessment: the situation was 'deteriorating very rapidly. Information is very meagre, but the Polish Army still appeared to be intact.' War Cabinet members were still unaware that by now the Polish Air Force had been virtually eliminated, most of the 500 first-line aircraft destroyed by German bombs before they could even take off. The same day, Cracow, Poland's second city, was occupied by German troops. The War Cabinet agreed that the need for a Turkish treaty 'is becoming still more urgent by reason of the growing deterioration of the situation in Poland'. But Turkey was proving difficult. They demanded a gold loan of £15 million, still too much although France had agreed to help. But the Cabinet resolved to agree, if a lesser sum could not be negotiated.

Leslie Burgin, Minister of Supply, had discussed British Field Force equipment allocations at a War Office meeting. During 6 September he examined the supply problems involved in sending the Field Force to France and, at a special War Cabinet meeting that evening, revealed some startling findings. Britain could not send as many troops as estimated. 'The present plan is to despatch overseas 32 Divisions in the first year of war,' he reminded the War Cabinet. But 'the capacity already developed will admit of only sixteen....' Factory programmes would have to be expanded immediately, especially for production of cordite and explosives. It was urged that the size of the Army, on which planning was to be based, should be laid down at an early date. Sixty Divisions was the figure proposed – the rest would be Dominion and foreign units.

Hore-Belisha felt 'the assumption should be the war will be of long duration, say at least five years, and that our effort should be an extreme one'. There was personnel for thirty-two Divisions and supply must accelerate to match. He believed there should be sixty Divisions for France and planning for Britain's Land Forces should be based on that. 'It is essential to take steps to accelerate the production of guns and tanks. While the supply and use of ammunition can be rationed, it is impossible to ration guns.' The War Cabinet agreed a Land Forces Committee should be set up to examine the problem, comprising Sir Samuel Hoare (as Chairman) with the three Service Ministers, plus Leslie Burgin.

'The position in Poland is, for the moment, a little easier,' Ironside told the Cabinet on Thursday morning. 'This is probably due in part at least to the Germans having to reorganize and refuel their armoured fighting vehicles, after their first rapid advance. A big battle is in progress some 40 miles north of Warsaw.' The French appeared to be considering a Balkan operation, Halifax reported. This had been planned before the war on the assumption that Italy would have joined the conflict; Ministers feared French action might in fact bring them in. The British representatives at the Supreme War Council would have to tell the French this.

'The strength of the Home Fleet is more than sufficient to deal with the German Fleet,' claimed Churchill.[17] In fact, during that day, 7 September, Hitler instructed Admiral Raeder to slacken German naval actions. France was displaying 'political and military restraint', and the British were proving 'hesitant'. U-boats in the Atlantic should therefore spare all passenger vessels without exception and the pocket battleships *Deutschland* and *Graf Spee*, respectively in the North and South Atlantic, should be signalled to withdraw to 'waiting stations' for the time being. Hitler also held a conference with Field-Marshal Brauchitsch.

'Operation in the West not yet clear,' wrote Halder in his report of this meeting between the Führer and the Commander-in-Chief. 'Some indications that there is no real intention of waging a war.... French Cabinet lack heroic calibre. Also first signs of sobering reflection from Britain.' But despite, or because of, the lack of apparent activity on the Western Front, Halder began to work out full-scale plans for the transfer of German troops to the area. By nightfall on 7 September, German units were within thirty miles of Warsaw, and an offensive from eastern Slovakia towards Lvov had begun. And Sir Nevile Henderson returned home. 'Shortly after 8 p.m. we reached Victoria Station. It had taken us three days and eight hours to get from Berlin to London. My mission to Berlin had terminated and the failure was complete.'[18] Back in Berlin, citizens were being told that the German troops had almost conquered Warsaw in the victorious 'counter-attack'.

On Friday, 8 September the War Cabinet heard depressing information from Simon on the country's financial state. 'There are two pressing dangers in the financial sphere, first the exhaustion of our exchange resources, second, inflation.' The sum total of resources, including the requisition of private holdings, was not more than £700 million. 'There is no real chance of any addition to this figure on capital account, for example by borrowing abroad. The door is doubly barred on borrowing in the United States by the Johnson Act against war debt defaulters and by the Neutrality Legislation.' Neutral countries were anxious to be rid of their sterling. 'We hold more gold than in 1914 and in some respects, for example stocks of oil, are far better equipped. Our holdings of useful foreign securities are much less. Our total resources are vastly inferior. At the beginning of the last war our balance of payments was so favourable that we were able to invest abroad at the rate of £200 million a year. When we entered this war we had not only abandoned the practice of lending abroad, but were already to some extent drawing on our past investments.' As far as the second danger, inflation, was concerned, he proposed 'to introduce and carry through a supplementary budget this month if possible, in which severe additions to existing rates of taxation will be imposed'.[19]

Despite criticisms, the restricted bombing policy would be continued; according to the Cabinet Minutes: 'there was strong feeling in some quarters that it was not right that, while Poland was being severely bombed by Germany, our operations should be confined to the dropping of propaganda. On the other hand, there was good reason to believe that the German authorities feared the effect of our propaganda and the fact that our aircraft were able to fly with impunity all over the north-west of Germany would have a depressing effect on the morale of the German people.' Leaflet dropping was a 'valuable operation which should be repeated from time to time as and when opportunity offered'. 'On the French front it seems that the French Armies have everywhere reached the Franco-German frontier,' reported Ironside, 'and perhaps have crossed it in a few places.' When Chamberlain asked if the French were fully prepared against a possible turning movement through Holland and Belgium, Ironside assured him that plans had been made. The most important Polish engagement was thirty-four kilometres north of Warsaw, Ironside continued. 'On the rest of the front the Germans appeared to be reorganizing. The Polish Army is fighting well and has not been broken.' But Hore-Belisha revealed that an urgent appeal for help had just come from Poland. An emissary had flown to London with a message from General Carton de Wiart, head of the British Military Mission at Warsaw, and the Polish military situation was described as extremely serious. Britain and France would have to find some means of delivering military supplies; particularly aeroplanes, machine guns and ammunition. But the Cabinet had by now reverted to their original attitude: 'Without in the least minimizing the effort which Poland was making, there was only one way in which we could give her substantial help, namely by waging war on Germany until Poland was rehabilitated.'[20]

Meanwhile, the Russians had come to the conclusion that if they failed to move soon they might be too late for the Polish spoils, and Soviet forces on the border began to mobilize. Friday afternoon, 8 September, saw the German 4th Panzer Division reach the outskirts of Warsaw. To the south, Riechenau's 10th Army took Kielce, and the 14th Army under List arrived at Sandomierz, at the junction of the Vistula and San rivers. In Berlin, Admiral Canaris protested against the brutality of SS personnel to the Poles. Also in Berlin, radio programmes were suddenly interrupted at 7.16 p.m. to announce, prematurely, that German troops had taken Warsaw. Most Berliners greeted the announcement with little apparent emotion, but the Nazi leaders were pleased to hear from the Spanish Ambassador that Bonnet, 'in view of the great unpopularity of the war in France, is endeavouring to bring about an understanding as soon as the operations in Poland are concluded'.[21] The French 4th Army was in fact preparing a minor offensive, aimed at securing positions to attack enemy defences around Saarbrucken. Troops began to move forward during the night of 8/9 September and by morning had advanced nine kilometres.[22]

Soon after midnight, Ribbentrop wrote an urgent top secret message to Schulenburg in Moscow: as operations in Poland were 'progressing even beyond our expectations', Germany would like to know 'the military intentions of the Soviet Government'. Molotov officially congratulated the Germans 'on the entry into Warsaw' in a message the following morning, but Ribbentrop had to wait for information.[23] Despite Nazi claims, Ironside told the Cabinet on 9 September there was little change in the situation in Poland. Chamberlain said he had just received a telegram from Daladier, urging the British Government to do all they could to reinforce the Polish Air Force: Newall announced that 40 modern French fighters were being sent via Marseilles and a further 40 or 50 were being sent to Syria for forwarding to Poland when the opportunity came. The Chiefs of Staff had received an oral report that morning from a Captain Davies, of the Polish Military Mission, who had just returned from Poland: he emphasized the importance of immediate material assistance. Churchill said the Admiralty could let the War Office have 15 million rounds of .303 ammunition for Poland, but no other offers were made. Yet the Cabinet agreed that 'Germany will now endeavour to convince the Poles that we are about to desert them and that they had better surrender'. A statement should be issued to the Press, 'stating in solemn form that HMG were mobilizing the entire resources of the country with a view to the successful prosecution of the war, and that to this end they were making all their plans on the assumption that the duration of the war would be at least three years.'[24]

The statement, surely one of the most hypocritical since the birth of appeasement, could have done nothing to ease the minds of the struggling Poles; no Minister seemed to consider what would happen to Britain's ally during those three terrible years. Where now was Churchill's loud voice to demand that Britain should honour her moral commitments? Apart from his offer of second-hand bullets, he now remained silent with the rest. He had joined the appeasers.

Poland's Military Attaché in Paris persisted in asking awkward questions during this Saturday. What was happening to the general attack in the West? When would allied bombers begin to strike? No answers came. And to warn off the British and French, Göring threatened that if the allies bombed Germany, terrible revenge would follow. Within a week seventy German Divisions, now in Poland, would be released for service 'elsewhere', he added.[25] But Hitler, in his War Directive No 3, issued on 9 September, ordered his forces to treat the British and French gently for the moment. 'Even after the half-hearted opening of hostilities by England, at sea and in the air, my personal approval must be obtained: (a) for any crossing of the German land frontier in the West, (b) for all flights beyond the western frontier of Germany, unless they are necessary to meet heavy enemy air attacks, (c) for air attacks against England.'[26] The reason for caution lay precisely in the 'half-hearted' British and French actions – the allies might yet agree to negotiate a peace.

The German in the street was beginning to wonder whether this was a general war at all. Why had the formal declaration of hostilities by France and Britain not been translated into action? Why had only leaflets been dropped? Tension eased as life in Berlin returned nearly to normal; cheerful Berliners crowded to the theatres, operas, cinemas. The German newspapers reported two hundred football matches played throughout Germany on Sunday, 10 September.[27]

The Sunday Cabinet meeting in London was short and attended by only three Ministers, following a decision that the Sabbath sessions should only be attended on a rota basis. Lieutenant-General Sir Ronald Adam, Deputy Chief of the Imperial General Staff, reported the Poles intended to withdraw to a line covering the Galician oil fields and would attempt to keep open communications to Poland from the south-west. As for the Western Front, the French were continuing their methodical advance through 'No Man's Land' between the Maginot and Siegfried Lines. No German troops had so far been transferred from the Polish front to the West.[28] For Churchill this Sunday was no day of rest. While the Cabinet was meeting, he had been drafting a long letter to Chamberlain. 'I hope you will not mind my sending you a few points privately,' he wrote, and proceeded to give his views on bombing, Army equipment, naval programmes, army-air relations.

236

Despite the devastation being suffered by the Poles from the German bombers, Churchill wrote: 'I am still inclined to think that we should not take the initiative on bombing, except in the immediate zone in which the French armies are operating, where we must of course help. It is to our interest that the war should be conducted in accordance with the more humane conceptions of war.' This was to gain time, as appeasement had been. 'Every day that passes gives more shelter to the population of London and the big cities.'[29] Churchill also dropped a note to Burgin, on reconditioning heavy artillery which he, Churchill, had ordered to be stored when he was at the War Office in 1919.[30] Burgin was at a meeting of the Air Council, called to discuss the aircraft building programme. A scheme to raise the output of aircraft frames from 2,000 to 3,000 a month within 18 months was considered, but found impracticable. Instead, an increase of 550 was agreed, comprising an extra 300 in Britain and 250 from Canada and Australia.[31]

The Poles had still to receive a reply to their request for urgent help. The Germans, who needed no military assistance for their Polish Campaign, heard the Soviets' intentions towards the Polish victim. Russia would move against the enemy 'within the next few days'. Molotov decided that the excuse for Russian intervention must be 'that Poland was falling apart and that it was necessary for the Soviet Union, in consequence, to come to the aid of the Ukrainians and White Russians "threatened" by Germany'. He told the astonished Schulenburg: 'This argument is necessary to make the intervention plausible to the masses and at the same time avoid giving the Soviet Union the appearance of an aggressor.'[32]

Next day, Monday, 11 September, more detachments of British troops landed secretly in France; the limited French offensive in front of the Siegfried Line halted. Further attacks in Lorraine would, Gamelin believed, involve profitless losses, and the Divisions facing the Sarre were ordered to consolidate. 'The French have established a line of infantry along the whole front of the Siegfried,' Ironside told the Cabinet meeting, adding – which destroyed the effect – 'There are now no Germans in front of that line.' This inactivity on the Western Front was to continue while Poland's desperate and hopeless struggle came closer to its finish. 'The Poles are putting up a good fight,' said the CIGS, 'and are defending Warsaw vigorously. Their main army is still intact. Eight divisions have been caught in the Posen salient, but it is hoped some might break through. A line of defence is being taken up on the Vistula. Polish difficulties are increased by the very dry weather, which has made the Vistula fordable at all points.'[33] The Poles were still pleading for help, for pressure on the Western Front – or an allied bombing offensive. The latter was firmly ruled out by the Chiefs of Staff report on Monday. A large part of Poland had been rapidly overrun, said the report, but 'this was always expected.... Nothing that we can do in the air in the western theatre would have any effect on relieving pressure on Poland.' Despite the devastation, the Chiefs of Staff believed the Germans had avoided all-out aerial warfare. 'Accepted principle had so far not been violated.... Both Hitler and Göring have publicly affirmed their intention ... to restrict the operations of the German Air Force. And we have no definite or reliable proof that in fact they have not done so in Poland though possibly on a somewhat elastic interpretation.' The Chiefs of Staff thought it would therefore be unwise not to display extreme caution over RAF bombing; moreover a wider bombing policy would cut down the support Britain could give the French offensive. The longer the delay in introducing an expanded bombing policy, the better Britain could prepare for it.[34]

With German victory imminent in Poland, reports reached London that Hitler might soon make a peace offer. When the War Cabinet met again at 6 p.m. for a second meeting on the Monday, Halifax said that Count Czaky, the Hungarian Foreign Minister, had recently been in Berlin, and 'had been struck ... by the evident desire of the German Government for the war to be brought to a rapid conclusion, and he anticipated that Herr Hitler might make some peace offer after the fall of Warsaw.' He added: 'Information has also reached us from another source that very valuable results might be secured if HMG were to make a direct appeal to the German Army.' While in Berlin, Czaky had seen Ribbentrop and been offered a slice of Poland, but had declined. 'He suspected that Herr von Ribbentrop's offer was a prelude to a demand being made by Germany for the grant by the Hungarian Government of transit facilities.'

Chamberlain announced that he and Chatfield would be flying to France the following day for discussions with the French leaders. They would try to obtain the latest information, in order to be able to make a statement to the Commons. He anticipated three main topics would be considered: the attitude of the allies towards Italy; General Weygand's plans for the Balkans, and the possibilities of a German peace offer.[35] In Berlin, one evening paper's headline outdid all previous fantastic propaganda: 'Poles Bombard Warsaw.' Another report claimed two British Secret-service agents had organized the slaughter of Germans at Bromberg.[36] Also in Berlin Canaris complained again to Keitel of barbarities inflicted on the Poles by SS *Einsatzgruppen* – Task Forces – which followed the German troops. 'The world will one day hold the Wehrmacht responsible,' he warned.[37] Hitler himself was still unsure what should be done with Poland as a whole. A discussion on board his special train at Ilnau next day, 19 September, showed the Führer to be undecided between complete partition of the country with Russia, and creation of a small, nominally independent Polish State. Paradoxically, Ironside's report to the Cabinet at 11.30 contained one scrap of favourable news on the campaign. 'Rain has begun in Poland. This will not only slow up the German operations.... A good fall of rain ... will effectively prevent an attack ... on the Western Front before the winter.'

French concentration on the Western Front must now be almost completed, the CIGS continued. 'An unsatisfactory feature of the position is the lack of contact between the French and the British on the one hand and the Belgians on the other.... In the event of a German invasion through Belgium, British and French forces will require to move rapidly in support of the Belgian Army. For this purpose conversations with the Belgians, and reconnaissance by French and British officers, is most desirable.' But the Belgians were refusing to cooperate. 'The Belgian attitude is indefensible,' declared Churchill. 'I hope they will be left in no doubt as to the effect it will produce on British minds. ... The Belgians owe everything to us, and retention of their Colonial Empire will depend entirely on our victory.' Halifax was asked to examine the possibility of pressing the Belgium Government to consent to military talks.

Reports from the Ambassador at Moscow, said Halifax, indicated that 'the Soviet mobilization is of a precautionary nature, but there is a possibility that later the Soviets might desire to secure a portion of Polish territory'. Five days later this assessment was proved correct.[38]

'There is a remarkable identity of two views between our two Governments,' said Chamberlain on 13 September, reporting on his Paris talks. 'Even more so than I had expected.' He told the meeting agreement had been reached on all matters discussed. As far as a possible French action in the Balkans was concerned, Daladier had agreed 'it would be unfortunate if any steps were taken which gave Italy the impression that we were forming a Balkan *bloc* against her,' and had confirmed that military objectives should be carefully considered. Gamelin had said he was 'perfectly satisfied with the present arrangements for Franco-British liaison'. The military situation was 'developing in the way anticipated by the French General Staff'. The War Cabinet expressed 'great satisfaction'.

Meanwhile in Rome, Lorraine believed Mussolini 'would hold the scales between war and peace as long as he could and dared'. But as Halifax commented, he was 'now slightly less optimistic than before as to the outcome'.

Ironside reported that the Poles were 'fighting better'. But during the day the Polish situation deteriorated rapidly. By the evening Warsaw had been completely surrounded, and the west of the country completely conquered. German troops were in transit from the Eastern to the Western Fronts. By next day, Thursday, 14 September, about eighteen Divisions had left Poland. Ironside thought Germany's next move might be an attack on Roumania. This would be very difficult without passing through Hungary; if Germany were to make the attempt, it would remove all possibility of an attack by them in the West, at any rate until the spring. The further the Germans became involved in the East, the more difficult it would be for them to withdraw their mechanized formations. The Chiefs of Staff had been considering whether, from a military point of view, it would be better for the Balkan Entente to be neutral so long as Italy were so, or whether Turkey, Greece and Roumania should fight with the allies, even if this involved hostilities with Italy. They plumped for the former, and Halifax agreed, while having to report disquieting news from Ankara: the Turkish Council of Ministers had expressed 'extreme dissatisfaction' at the British delay in meeting Turkish requirements. The British Ambassador expected to see the Turkish Foreign Minister again, and proposed to offer to increase the gold loan to £15 million. Ministers agreed the Turkish Government 'were probably trying to drive a still harder bargain'.[39]

Russia was becoming increasingly anxious that her forces should enter Poland before the total collapse. Schulenburg was summoned to the Kremlin on 14 September and was asked when Warsaw would fall; in order to justify Soviet intervention, said Molotov, the Russians must be able to blame the Germans for destruction of Poland, and would therefore send forces into the country as soon as possible after the Polish capital was taken.[40] Schulenburg wired for instructions. That same evening Churchill left to inspect the defences at Scapa Flow. 'I spent most of the next two days inspecting the harbour and the entrances, with booms and nets. I was assured that they were as good as in the last war, and that important additions and improvements were being made or were on the way.[41] Complacency was soon to be abruptly and tragically shattered.

Churchill's absence from the Cabinet meetings failed to prevent his continued bombardment of the Prime Minister with letters, statements, points of view. 'First Lord to Prime Minister. As I shall be away till Monday, I give you my present thoughts on the main situation.' In this minute, dated 15 September, he declared: 'It seems to me most unlikely that the Germans will attempt an offensive in the West at this late season.... Surely his obvious plan should be to press on through Poland, Hungary and Roumania to the Black Sea.' Nonetheless, preparations to oppose Hitler in the West should be increased. Above all, the Belgians should cooperate. 'I hope you will consider carefully what I write to you. I do so only in my desire to aid you in your responsibilities and discharge my own.'[42] Chamberlain's irritation at Churchill's condescending attitude was revealed in his reply next day. 'All your letters are carefully read and considered by me, and if I have not replied to them it is only because I am seeing you every day and, moreover, because as far as I have been

240

able to observe, your views and mine have very closely coincided.'[43]

'The military situation in Poland has greatly deteriorated since the last meeting of the War Cabinet,' reported the CIGS on Friday, 15 September. And Ministers believed even the limited amount of aid given to Britain's ally should perhaps be further restricted. The War Cabinet agreed: 'The Chiefs of Staff Committee should consider, in consultation with the Foreign Office, what action should be taken with regard to the various consignments of war stores which are already on their way to Poland or were about to be despatched to Poland.' The Belgians were still refusing to cooperate in joint discussions on the defence of the Western Front. 'Disastrous results will accrue to Belgium,' warned the CIGS, 'if, through refusing to permit the establishment of military contacts now, she were to be invaded by Germany.' The War Cabinet agreed Lord Halifax should consider sending a special emissary to Belgium armed with a memorandum prepared by the Chiefs of Staff. Further consideration should be given to the idea of an appeal from George VI to the Belgian King.[44]

That evening, Ribbentrop replied to Schulenburg's telegram sent the previous day. Warsaw, he claimed, would fall 'in the next few days' and Germany would 'welcome the Soviet military operation now'. But Russia's idea of justifying intervention by blaming Germany was 'out of the question ... contrary to the true German intentions'. It would 'make two states appear as enemies before the whole world'.[45] Meanwhile, Polish units were being squeezed towards the Roumanian border and, as the CIGS told the Saturday Cabinet meeting: 'The Poles are endeavouring to hold the line in the south-east corner of Poland.... It seems doubtful whether many Polish Divisions will be able to retire behind this line. It will probably take the Germans at least a week before the position is cleared up.'[46]

At 6 p.m. Schulenburg had another interview with Molotov, who 'declared that military intervention by the Soviet Union was imminent – perhaps even tomorrow'. Soviet justification would be that Poland had disintegrated as a state and 'third powers might try to profit by the chaos'. Schulenburg objected the only possible third power would be Germany; Berlin should not 'stumble over this piece of straw' replied Molotov, and should understand Russia's difficulty.[47] Eight hours later, at 2 o'clock on the Sunday morning, the Ambassador was summoned suddenly to see Stalin. He reported to Berlin at 5.20 a.m. 'Stalin ... declared that the Red Army would cross the Soviet border at 6 o'clock.... Soviet aircraft would begin today to bomb the district east of Lvov.'[48] On schedule, 20 Divisions of the Workers' and Peasants' Red Army began to roll on to Polish soil; first vague reports reached London soon afterwards and the Deputy CIGS opened the noon Cabinet meeting by announcing 'the most serious news, received early this morning, concerning the Russian invasion of the eastern frontier of Poland'. No news had come from the British Military Mission at Warsaw, he continued, but a telegram had arrived from Seeds in Moscow: the Soviet Government had stated 'there was no proper Government in Poland with whom they could get in touch, and that without abandoning their neutral attitude, they felt compelled to protect the interests of White Russians and Ukrainian minorities'.

The British Ministers agreed the invasion would be especially serious if the Russian troops overran south-east Poland and severed Polish communications with Roumania; but less so if the invasion was limited to the north-east, north of the Pinsk Marshes, the area mainly inhabited by White Russians. In any event the Russian advance was expected to be slow, and it could complicate German actions in south-east Poland. The invasion might have followed some kind of Russo-German arrangement, in which case 'it was disturbing to think that some similar secret agreement might have been made between the two countries in regard to Roumania'. The Cabinet had to face the difficult question of Britain's reaction to the Russian invasion. Under the terms of the Anglo-Polish Agreement, should Britain now declare war? Fortunately, Halifax had discussed this very problem the day before with the French Ambassador, and told him 'the provisions of the Anglo-Polish Agreement would not come into operation as a result of Soviet aggression ... since the Agreement provided for action ... only if Poland suffered aggression from a European Power, and there was a further understanding between the two Governments that the European Power in question was Germany.' Corbin had agreed.

Poland was prostrate; all her forces surrounded; the campaign was finished, except for the brave, stubborn, decimated units determined to die. Churchill was still in Scotland, enjoying the peace of Loch Ewe. He motored to Inverness, stopping on the way to picnic by a sparkling stream in the pleasant sunshine. Gloomy thoughts intruded. 'What of the supreme, measureless ordeal in which we were again irrevocably plunged? Poland in its agony; France but a pale reflection of her former warlike ardour; the Russian Colossus no longer an ally, not even neutral, possibly to become a foe. Italy no friend. Japan no ally. Would America ever come in again? The British Empire remained intact and gloriously united, but ill-prepared, unready. We still had command of the sea. We were woefully outmatched in numbers in this new mortal weapon of the air. Somehow the light faded out of the landscape.'[49] The words could well have been written by Chamberlain. Churchill caught the overnight train to London. Reaching Euston he was surprised to see the First Sea Lord waiting for him on the platform. Admiral Pound reported tragic news: 'The *Courageous* was sunk yesterday evening in the Bristol Channel.' Over 500 of her crew had perished. Churchill's reaction showed his difference from Chamberlain. 'We can't expect to carry on a war like this without that sort of thing happening.' He added in his memoirs: 'And so to bath and the toil of another day.'[50]

During Sunday night the Russian forces had pushed into Poland on a broad front; now, on Monday, Vilna was occupied – and at Brest-Litovsk, scene of the Russo-German peace-making in 1918, the Soviet troops met their German allies.

In Britain, the Chiefs of Staff completed a report on 'The Possible Future Course of the War'. Germany, it said, had three alternatives. She could merely consolidate her position in Poland and adopt a defensive attitude towards the West, although this was considered unlikely, since a long war was against German interests. Secondly, Germany might launch an offensive in the West, either through an unrestricted bombing campaign against Britain, or through a land offensive, probably turning the Maginot Line by an advance through Holland and Belgium. If the Germans invaded the Low Countries, 'we understand the French idea is that, provided the Belgians are still holding out on the Meuse, the French and British Armies should occupy the line Givet-Namur, the British ... on the left.' The report commented: 'We consider it would be unsound to adopt this plan unless plans are concerted with the Belgians for the occupation of this line in sufficient time before the German advance.... Unless the present Belgian attitude alters and plans can be prepared for early occupation of the Givet-Namur line, we are strongly of the opinion that the German advance should be met in prepared positions on the French frontier.' This advice was to be ignored, with drastic consequences.

Germany's third course of action, said the Chiefs of Staff, would be to continue on the defensive in the West, while extending political and military control in south-eastern Europe. Then, Roumania would probably be Germany's next victim. Turkey might be expected to resist and should be encouraged to do so, as the first step in building up a Balkan Front against Hitler. The report was referred to the War Cabinet, and from there to the Supreme War Council.

Meanwhile, Ministers were told on Monday, 18 September, that the problem of cooperation with Belgium was no nearer solution. Halifax had decided against sending a special emissary; instead, Sir Robert Clive, Ambassador at Brussels, would be brought back for consultations.

This Monday was a day of jubilation in senior circles of the German Army. The first objective had been gained with success beyond all expectations. Generals were in no mood to heed a warning from the German Chargé in Washington, Hans Thomsen. 'The sympathies of the overwhelming majority of the American people are with our enemies, and America is convinced of Germany's war guilt.'[51] Hitler had set up his headquarters in a special train near Gogolin and each morning had driven to the front line to inspect the troops. Now, on the evening of the eighteenth, he moved to the luxurious Casino Hotel at the Baltic resort of Zoppot, ready to make his triumphal entry into Danzig next day. Only one item marred his complete success: Warsaw continued to hold out.

Reporting this refusal to surrender, the CIGS told the Cabinet on 19 September that 'little opposition was being offered to the Russians. The Vilna salient has been cut off and large numbers of Poles are streaming into Lithuania....'

With an urgent decision needed on dispositioning the British Field Force, the Cabinet asked Hore-Belisha to cross to France for talks with Daladier and Gamelin. But talks with the Belgians were no nearer; Halifax reported that 'while the Belgian Government appreciated the necessity for Staff Conversations, they did not realize the need for urgency'. The Cabinet agreed that the Ambassador should return to London for instructions.

Chamberlain reported 'a most gloomy view of the situation,' from the American Ambassador, Kennedy, who 'did not believe Congress would agree to modifying the neutrality legislation, although the President took the opposite view. The Ambassador thought the action of the USSR would throw public opinion in the United States into the arms of isolationists.'

The Cabinet considered a memorandum from the Minister of Information on criticism of the Government in the newspapers.[52] The press was dissatisfied because 'we are not ourselves as yet taking part in warlike operations of the first importance'. Churchill was considering a plan to rectify this. He drew the Cabinet's attention 'to the large imports of iron ore which Germany imported from Sweden and which are vital for the German munitions industry. In the summer the imports can reach Germany by way of the Gulf of Bothnia. In winter the Gulf is closed by ice, and the trade goes from Narvik along the whole length of the Norwegian coast, from north to south.... The ships protected themselves against interference from the British Navy by keeping within the three mile limit.' If this passage were not stopped through pressure by Britain on the Norwegian Government, 'I will be compelled to propose the remedy which was adopted in the last war, namely, the laying of mines inside Norwegian territorial waters, which drove the ore-carrying vessels outside the three-mile limit'.[53] For the moment Churchill pursued the matter no further at Governmental level; the War Cabinet merely took note of his statement. But the Narvik issue was to become increasingly dominant, pushed on all possible occasions by the persistent First Lord. Later in the day he asked Admiral Pound for details of the 1918 case and studies of the steps necessary to put the scheme, which he described as of 'the highest importance in crippling the enemy's war industry',[54] into operation.

244

For the moment the Cabinet was preoccupied with the Western Front and with the need for Belgian collaboration, as German troops could now be moved 'en masse' from Poland. By the evening of the nineteenth the first corps of the British Field Force had landed in France; despatch of the next troops was pushed to maximum speed. That night Hitler gave his victorious address in the ornate Guildhall, Danzig, his first public speech since his Reichstag address on 1 September, which had started the Polish campaign. 'I have no war aims against Britain and France,' he declared, and if London and Paris continued to fight then they were the warmongers. To many Germans, talk of an offensive on the Western Front was outdated. It had not been launched before; and now Poland was defeated, why should the British and French want to continue the fight? Spirits rose; within the next month peace would probably come.

At the Cabinet meeting next morning, 20 September, Halifax undertook to draft a suitable statement in reply to Hitler's speech. And he also said that Corbin, the French Ambassador, had told him the previous day, that his Government had delivered a protest to Moscow over the Russian invasion of Poland. Somewhat relieved, he pointed out that Britain's opportunity to join with the French over the protest had therefore gone.

Meanwhile, Hore-Belisha had flown to France that morning. Soon after his arrival he saw Lord Gort, C-in-C of the BEF, and discussed a number of subjects which needed to be taken up with the French, among them the basic question of which area should be occupied by British forces. During the afternoon, Hore-Belisha saw Daladier, who remarked that 'operations in Poland had shown the importance of fighting on prepared positions'. Gamelin feared a sweep through the Low Countries but, without previous conversations with the Belgians, French forces could not cooperate with Belgian defence of the Albert Canal-Meuse line. He was determined to avoid an encounter battle in the centre of Belgium. Hore-Belisha said Gort wanted the BEF deployed in a sector south of Lille and north of Valenciennes. Gamelin saw no difficulty in this, but emphasized his need for more British fighter aircraft in France and for the largest possible land effort.[55]

Next day, while Hore-Belisha was recounting to a 'thoroughly satisfied' Gort his conversations with Daladier and Gamelin, Gamelin was himself told by French Intelligence that within a week the Germans would be able to attack in the West.[56] Up to 47 German divisions had now been concentrated in the West and in the East the better troops had been replaced by inferior units. French forward units should pull back to the best defensive positions, he was advised. Yet when the Supreme War Council met next day, 22 September, the French changed their minds over where the British troops should be deployed; it would now be between Lys and the Scheldt. Reporting to the

Cabinet later, Chamberlain said: 'The French urged that British troops should advance to the frontier as soon as possible in order to counteract German propaganda to the effect that the British intended to let the French troops bear the brunt of the fighting.' They had also asked for six more British fighter squadrons – about eighty aircraft – as well as more anti-aircraft batteries: Gamelin was expecting an attack within the next few weeks and was anxious for an increase of fighter strength in Lorraine. Newall told the Cabinet he had previously agreed to sending three extra fighter squadrons, and did not feel justified in further reducing the number of squadrons available for Home Defence. The Air Secretary agreed, and so did Churchill.[57]

Despite Gamelin's fears of an imminent offensive, a growing number of military experts believed it too late in the year for a German attack. Churchill put this view to the War Cabinet next morning, Saturday, 23 September. 'I very much doubt whether a land offensive in the West will be mounted this winter.... The Eastern Front has more or less closed down owing to the Russian action and I suggest that Germany's most likely move will be an attack on our air force and aircraft industry in the near future.' Chamberlain, on the other hand, thought 'there is a considerable danger of a "peace offensive"'. But Lord Hankey, Minister without Portfolio, still believed 'the possibility of an offensive in the West this autumn should not be underrated. The French regard such an offensive as probable.'

The day before, the Chiefs of Staff had decided restrictions on British bombing might soon have to be relaxed. Presenting their report to the Cabinet, Newall said reliance could not be placed on demolition work stopping a German advance into the Low Countries, but if air attacks were then made on the German units, there would be killing of Belgian and Dutch civilians. The Chiefs of Staff therefore sought authority for these operations now, to avoid delay in seeking it later.[58] But Ministers expressed reluctance to sanction such a course and concluded it would be better to concentrate on persuading the Belgians to start staff talks.

The Turks were again causing difficulties over the proposed Treaty – the Turkish Foreign Minister was on his way to Moscow. Halifax pointed out that an assurance of Turkish cooperation was now less necessary than before; the Russian occupation of south-east Poland had made an immediate invasion of Roumania much less likely. However, diplomatic success or failure could be influential at this time.[59]

Almost overnight the urgency seemed to disappear from Cabinet discussions, as the feeling grew that the Western Front would remain quiet. Germany would be stopped not by the Maginot Line, but by the autumn and winter weather. Yet Chamberlain had a new fear – could the British stand the irksome restrictions and strain of waiting? 'Without the strong centripetal forces of mortal danger,' he wrote on

23 September, 'all the injustices, inconveniences, hardships and uncertainties of war-time are resented more and more, because they are felt to be unnecessary.... Last week 17 per cent of my correspondence was on the theme of "stop the war". If I were in Hitler's shoes I think I should let the present menacing lull go on for several weeks and then put out a very reasonable offer.'[60] Poland, the ally, and the reason for going to war, was dead; the British and French might now be defeated by a different weapon – an offer of peace.

14

War Twilight

Now the real 'Phoney War' began. Troops became increasingly bored; housewives and civilians increasingly annoyed by restrictions, rising prices, low wages, unemployment. By February 1940, food prices would have risen by one-seventh, and even before rationing was officially introduced, shops had had to start unofficially.[1] Sniping, carping newspaper attacks on the Administration began to increase, and Chamberlain condemned the press for commercialism and disloyalty. Yet Chamberlain himself was unable to inspire confidence or enthusiasm: at his most recent weekly statement, on 20 September, about a dozen MPs slumbered in the benches. 'The Prime Minister has no gift for inspiring anybody,' wrote Nicolson, 'and he might have been the Secretary of a firm of undertakers reading the minutes of the last meeting.'[2] Yet less than a month before, the House had been excited, apprehensive, alert for any war news. Nicolson summed up the situation. 'The effect of the blackout, the evacuation and the general dislocation has been bad for morale. The whole stage was set for an intensive and early attack by Germany, which would have aroused our stubbornness. The Government had not foreseen a situation in which boredom and bewilderment would be the main elements. They concentrated upon coping with panic and they have been faced with anticlimax.... The result is general disillusion and grumbling, from which soil defeatism may grow.'[3]

But the Cabinet were also bewildered. Not only was the domestic atmosphere difficult, but in the international arena no clear, obvious policy seemed to offer itself. Cabinet meetings and Anglo-French discussions degenerated to jumbles of half-formed, half-pursued ideas. Thus there was no definite policy for meeting a German invasion on the Western Front; and misunderstandings and hazy misconceptions form one of the few constant themes in the Cabinet minutes for this period. Time bought by the Poles, and extended by deteriorating weather, had to be used to find a strategy in the West. One major drawback was the complete absence of Belgian cooperation. Halifax saw the Belgian Ambassador who, he told the Cabinet on 24 September, 'while appreciating our point of view, made it quite clear that it would be out of the question for the Belgian Government to agree to our suggestion. They are satisfied that Germany did not intend to violate their neutrality, but fear that the news of Staff conversations, which would be sure to reach German ears, would precipitate an attack.' This blind stubbornness was to persist till too late.

Yet this same Sunday, 24 September, Gamelin told the British Chiefs of Staff it was likely that 'when Germany wishes to make her military effort against the Western Powers, she will invade Luxembourg, Belgium and all or part of Holland.... The moment at which she will make this effort cannot be accurately determined, since it is dependent upon the action which Germany is now able to complete in the East ... but this moment may be close.' What action the allies took against invasion of the Low Countries would depend on when the Belgians asked for help.... 'If this call is not made in time, the Anglo-French troops will absorb the Belgian troops, and possibly the Dutch troops if they retired in that direction, on the French frontier.' If it *were* made in time, the Anglo-French forces would enter Belgium to support Belgian resistance.[4] Ironside, like Churchill, did not think the Germans would attack soon. He told the Cabinet next morning, 25 September: 'There is every indication the Germans are concentrating on defence on the Western Front.'[5]

Churchill completed a long memorandum that Monday, setting out his thoughts on the situation. Hitler seemed to have three options in the West: first, a major attack, probably through Belgium, second, an intense air attack on Britain, third, 'what the Prime Minister calls "the peace offensive"'. Churchill wrote: 'Personally, I shall believe that (1) is imminent only when at least 30 divisions have been concentrated opposite Belgium and Holland. As to (2), it seems a very likely thing for that man to do.... As for (3): if he has not tried (2), it would seem our duty and policy to agree to nothing that will help him out of his troubles, and to leave him to stew in his own juice during the winter, while speeding forward our armaments and weaving our alliances.... The general outlook, therefore, seems far more favourable than it did in the autumn of 1914.... But there always remains (2). That is the pinch.'[6]

Members listened with now customary apathy as Chamberlain made a statement to the Commons on 26 September – his clothing matched the mood: 'He is dressed in deep mourning relieved only by a white handkerchief and a large gold watch-chain.'[7] Then they began to stir in anticipation; Churchill was about to give his first full Parliamentary speech since entering Chamberlain's Government. His subject was the general naval situation, and he believed he had 'a good tale to tell' – though many believed the old master had lost the power to tell it. In answering routine Commons questions since taking office he had stumbled over words, and had seemed to have lost his sensitive touch. 'It is true that Churchill had been at the Admiralty only a few days,' wrote the Tory MP Beverley Baxter, 'but then we did not look upon him as an ordinary man who would take time to play himself in. Therefore there was some shaking of heads. The old bandit, who had been the terror of the mountain passes, was cornered at last, and the fire in him was burning low.'[8]

The 'old bandit' lumbered to his feet. His head thrust forward, he peered at the audience. Slowly and cautiously, as if exploring the way, he began to speak. 'It is a strange experience to me,' he said with deep solemnity, 'to sit at the Admiralty again, after a quarter of a century, and to find myself moving over the same course against the same enemy and in the same months of the year.' He paused; the House waited for some typically eloquent and even far-fetched phrase to sum up the incredibility of the coincidence. Instead, with relished understatement, he caught the House unawares. 'It was,' he said, 'the sort of thing one would hardly expect to happen.' A roar of delighted laughter swept through the Commons, a huge grin spread across Churchill's ample cheeks, and he was back where he belonged. 'In the first week our losses by U-boat sinkings amounted to 65,000 tons. In the second week they were 46,000 tons; and in the third week they were 21,000 tons. In the last six days we have lost only 9,000 tons.' This remarkable progress had been achieved through setting in motion the convoy system, arming merchant ships, and counter-attacking U-boats.

The First Lord may have been temporarily satisfied; the War Secretary was decidedly not. Hore-Belisha believed the Maginot Line must be extended; that British positions must be strengthened and more troops sent. 'I feel that the great thing is to get a very strong defence on the whole line before the spring,' he wrote to Gort the same day. 'What I would like to be sure of is that the French are going to do exactly the same. If they are not, we would consider giving them help.'[9] Also the same day, Hitler's 'peace offensive' began. The German press and radio made a call to end the war: nothing was left to fight about. At the least, the campaign might persuade the German people that the British and French, and not Hitler, were responsible for the continuation of conflict and all the unpleasant domestic restrictions that went with it – during the day new German limitations were announced on clothing, shoe repairs and soap.

Next day, Wednesday, 27 September, Warsaw finally surrendered. Dishevelled, bleeding Polish troops and militiamen emerged from the rubble; German troops swarmed over the carcase of the proud dead city. Ribbentrop hurried to Moscow to improve the German-Soviet arrangements for the partitioning of Poland. News of Warsaw's fate had still to reach London when the Cabinet met at 11.30, but information had already arrived about Ribbentrop's flight to Moscow – and Sarajoglu, the Turkish Foreign Minister would be there at the same time; in view of the delicate Anglo-Turkish negotiations, said Halifax, 'this is somewhat disturbing.'

Units of the BEF II Corps were starting to land in France, reported Hore-Belisha, and another rumour of ominous German activity had arisen. 'The Belgian Military Attaché in Paris has informed the French that he has had news of a large German concentration near Aachen, and that he believes it is only a question of hours before Belgium will be invaded.' Hore-Belisha added that the General Staff did not attach much credence to this report, but 'it indicates a state of mind in the Belgian Staff which might be of use....' The War Cabinet discussed Anglo-French plans in the event of invasion; and this discussion was to be of critical importance in the muddle over vital strategic plans. Hore-Belisha pointed out that both he and Lord Hankey had 'made it quite clear' to Daladier and Gamelin that in no circumstances would the British Government agree to the BEF leaving their prepared positions to advance into Belgium unless it were safe to do so.[10]

While the British War Cabinet was considering this question, Hitler was holding a military conference; and his Service chiefs were instructed to prepare plans for 'an attack in the West as soon as possible, since the Franco-British army is not yet prepared.'[11] Gamelin had apparently been correct, and he repeated his assessment in a memorandum to the British Chiefs of Staff later in the day. 'Offensive action against France on the frontier between the two countries is not so very improbable.... Certain information even leads to the belief that it is imminent.' Hitler, he claimed, could soon have a strength of 130 Divisions. The allies had 65 or 70.[12]

At 6 p.m. on the 28th the treaty of mutual assistance between Britain, France and Turkey, was finally initialled in Ankara – although, as feared by Halifax, the Germans and Russians were later to attempt to hinder the formal conclusion. Meanwhile in Moscow, German-Russian talks on Polish partition had also gone smoothly. At five in the morning of Friday, 29 September, the 'German-Soviet Boundary and Friendship Treaty' was signed. Stalin smirked 'with obvious satisfaction', and a joint communiqué expressed the view that 'after the definite settlement of the problems arising from the collapse of the Polish State ... it would serve the true interests of all people to put an end to the state of war existing between Germany on the one side, and England and France on the other.' One part of the treaty was published, the other kept secret; the latter added Lithuania to the Soviet 'sphere of influence', Lublin and Eastern Warsaw to the German.[13]

Stalin's attention turned to Finland and the Baltic. Meanwhile, on this same day, Churchill again took up the subject of Scandinavia in a memorandum to the War Cabinet. 'It must be understood that an adequate supply of Swedish iron ore is vital to Germany, and the interception or prevention of these Narvik supplies during the winter months i.e. from October to the end of April, will greatly reduce her power of resistance. For the first three weeks of the war no iron ore ships left Narvik owing to the reluctance of crews to sail and other causes outside our control.' But this 'satisfactory state of affairs' might not however continue. Churchill did not deal with possibilities of stopping the ore supply after it had left the Norwegian outlet port of Narvik, instead, he considered means of persuading the supplier, Sweden, to cooperate. But during the afternoon of the twenty-eighth, Halifax had seen M. Boheman, Secretary-General of the Swedish Foreign Ministry, who adopted 'a very stiff and unhelpful attitude'. It seemed as if Churchill's fear of a resumption of iron ore supplies might soon be realized.[14]

Halifax told the Cabinet of the reports of German-Soviet agreement: the two countries would apparently make an effort to bring a rapid end to the war through a 'peace offensive' and 'if this failed, they would consult together regarding the necessary measures to be taken'. The same Cabinet meeting heard Ironside change his mind over the likelihood of a German offensive in the West. 'On the whole,' he said, 'General Gamelin's forecast of the time which might elapse before the Germans could stage an offensive in the West agreed with my own.' The first possible date was 16 October, but the danger would not be over until 10 November. 'I am inclined to think that the collection of the Divisions from Poland might take some time, and I think we still have three weeks before an attack can be launched.'[15]

In Berlin, Halder jotted down a reminder to explain to Hitler that the 'technique of Polish campaign no recipe for the West. No good against a well-knit Army.'[16] But the allied armies were by no means 'well-knit'. Allied plans were confused, and now the misunderstandings were to be increased; in an attempt to 'clarify' policy, Gamelin sent two Instructions, dated 29 September and 30 September, to Lord Gort. These laid down that if the Belgian cry for help was received in sufficient time, the allies would advance to support the Belgians on their line of resistance along the River Meuse – Albert Canal – Antwerp. If the call did not arrive in time, the allies would stay where they were. But the British War Cabinet had stated categorically on 27 September that British units should not risk advancing into Belgium if they might be caught exposed. So far the Belgians showed no signs of cooperating. Meanwhile, the War Cabinet continued in ignorance of Gamelin's schemes as fresh reports arrived, at the end of September, of increased German activity on the Western Front.

Not only were adequate plans for an advance into Belgium lacking. If the allies stayed and fought where they were, inadequate defensive positions in France would cause British units serious difficulties. On

2 October, General Sir Alan Brooke, Commander of BEF II Corps, visited the I Corps area at the frontier near Lille, and afterwards wrote a shocked account. The positions were deplorable, consisting of nothing but a shallow tank-ditch and a number of very scattered and ill-concealed pill-boxes, most of them unfinished. Units of I Corps, commanded by Dill, were being subjected to extreme risks, and the front which the French had allocated to the Corps extended for twenty-five miles, with a large gap between the British left and the nearest French troops. Little could be done to stop a German advance across the Belgium plains. 'It surely would not take them long to cross the intervening ground,' commented Brooke, 'and thus take advantage of the unpreparedness of the French and ourselves.... We are facing this war in a half-hearted way. The forward area is still crammed with civilians that ought to be evacuated, and no real serious efforts seem to be made to organize civilian labour to prepare defences that are essential.' Gort, he believed, was cheerfully unconcerned by the defects. 'Both the War Office and GHQ appear to be thinking of the war in six months' time. Our immediate danger in the event of an attack does not appear to be fully realized.'[17]

Brooke's criticisms of Gort, then and later, were not fully justified. He was seriously concerned, despite his cheerful appearance. On 2 October, he revealed to Hore-Belisha fears of inadequate cooperation and inadequate BEF resources. Simon had suggested the country could not afford the number of Divisions now proposed. 'I had hoped those wearying arguments were over for good,' Gort commented. 'The French will certainly expect us to pull more and more weight on land as the war proceeds.... It is indeed cheering news to hear you are pressing hard to get us more aircraft for our use, as we must aim at effecting paralysis in their rear areas. They will undoubtedly give us a rotten time until we have more AA guns and fighters.'[18]

Yet, despite the defects of the frontier defences, the French and to a lesser extent the British were obsessed with the idea of the defensive strategy. Experts believed the Poles had been defeated not because the German offensive had been good, but because their defence had been bad.

Deficient plans for a move into Belgium; defective positions along the French frontier; undue emphasis upon the defensive and a failure to appreciate the implications of Germany's victory in Poland. And added to these potential seeds for disaster was another misunderstanding. Chamberlain told the War Cabinet on 2 October that Daladier had written, not only repeating a French request for AA guns and fighter aircraft, but also asking that new British fighter and bomber squadrons should be sent at an early date to occupy bases in France. Yet Newall immediately pointed out that Gamelin had 'definitely agreed' the second contingent of the Air Striking Force should remain in England.

To sort this out, the Cabinet appointed a special committee to re-examine the situation on the Western Front, especially as regards Anglo-French cooperation. The committee, consisting of the Minister for Coordination of Defence, the three Service Ministers, and the Minister without Portfolio, were asked to report as soon as possible.

Churchill at least had dramatic news for the meeting. Since war began the Admiralty had been anxiously trying to trace the huge German pocket-battleships, the *Deutschland, Graf Spee* and *Admiral Scheer*. These were the most valuable naval prizes: sink one of these, and Britain would have accomplished a tremendous prestige victory. Besides, lurking along the sea-lanes, they seriously threatened British shipping. British warships had searched the high seas; intelligence reports had been studied at the Admiralty. On 30 September, the British liner *Clement* was sunk off Pernambuco; and now an excited Churchill told the Cabinet: 'According to the survivors, the ship had been stopped by a sea-plane, and then sunk by gunfire by the *Admiral Scheer*.[19] Churchill wrote in his memoirs: 'The news electrified the Admiralty. It was the signal for which we had been waiting.' A number of hunting groups were immediately formed, comprising all available aircraft carriers and supported by battleships, battle-cruisers and cruisers. Nine hunting groups were to operate during the next few weeks; and the search for the *Scheer*, later identified as her sister ship *Graf Spee*, was to be one of the most dramatic naval operations of the war.[20]

Meanwhile, chaotic misconceptions over the most crucial operation of the war continued. That Monday evening, 2 October, the committee appointed to consider the Western Front situation first met. Members decided Newall and Ironside should 'go over and have a frank exchange of views with General Gamelin'. Chatfield, the chairman, told the Cabinet next morning that the Chiefs of Staff had 'expressed their anxiety at what seemed to be frequent changes in General Gamelin's idea of the German plan'. The first idea, after the collapse of Poland, had been that the Germans would advance through the Low Countries; this had been succeeded by the hypothesis that the Germans would overrun the French right flank through Switzerland. 'Now it appears that a direct attack on the Maginot Line is considered likely.... The Chiefs of Staff feel that they are not in sufficient close touch with the French headquarters.'[21]

They were even less in touch than they realized. In a memorandum dated 18 September, they had made clear to Gamelin their opposition to an allied advance to the Givet-Namur Line (or Meuse-Antwerp Line) unless the Belgians offered full cooperation before the German invasion. This advance deep into Belgium, called Plan D by Gamelin, was subsequently discussed by the Supreme War Council, and Gamelin's comments invited. He had merely referred to a French Delegation report, which stated: 'If the call is made in time, the Anglo-French troops will enter Belgium, but not to engage in an encounter battle. Among the recognized lines of defence (in Belgium) are the line of the Scheldt and the line Meuse-Namur-Antwerp.' An alternative had therefore been introduced to Plan D: the shorter advance to the Scheldt. The Chiefs of Staff, in their report to the War Cabinet on 4 October, paid close attention to this Scheldt line, but made no mention of Plan D. The Cabinet therefore assumed that it had been dropped. 'I was present,' wrote Churchill, 'and was not aware that any significant issue was still pending. During October, there being no effective arrangements with the Belgians, it was assumed that the advance was limited to the Scheldt.' But the assumption was incorrect; unknown to the Chiefs of Staff, not only was Plan D still being contemplated by Gamelin, but he was soon to negotiate secretly with the Belgians for its implementation.[22]

While this confusion continued in the West, the subject of Scandinavia pushed itself steadily forward. Oliver Stanley told the War Cabinet on 5 October that the Norwegian Trade Delegation visiting London had received instructions to return home; the question of the iron ore reaching Germany via Norwegian ports – especially Narvik – was unsolved. Ministers considered Churchill's 29 September suggestion that Sweden be persuaded to restrict its export of vital ore to the Germans.[23] Stanley agreed that firm action was required. So far, only non-military means of persuasion were being considered, and the Cabinet concluded: 'No action on our part will be necessary unless supplies from Narvik to Germany start to move once more. In that event the Royal Navy will take drastic action.'[24] And Norway was also preoccupying Admiral Erich Raeder, Chief of the German Naval Staff. Two days before, on 3 October, he submitted a proposal to Hitler 'with the aim of improving our strategic and operational position'. The proposal was 'Gaining of Bases in Norway'.[25]

Meanwhile, for some days talk of peace had hung in the air. German newspapers had alternated between peace hints and nonsensical propaganda stories – on 3 October *12-Uhr Blatt* proclaimed: 'England's Responsibility – For Outrageously Provoking Warsaw to Defend Itself.' On 5 October the Cabinet had discussed the possibility of Hitler offering peace, and had considered a telegram from General Smuts. 'Any German peace offer now,' Smuts had written, 'will not be sincere but will simply be meant as a peace offensive to weaken us. It will be dangerous for two reasons: (1) the idea of peace is infectious ... (2) Germany has just won first round in a spectacular way.' The Cabinet agreed. Hitler returned to Berlin from reviewing his triumphant troops in the smoking, stinking, Warsaw wasteland, and at noon next day, 6 October, made his expected proposal in an address to the Reichstag. Towards the end of one of the longest speeches he ever made, Hitler declared: 'Germany has no further claims against France.... At no time and in no place have I ever acted contrary to British interests. ... I believe even today that there can only be real peace in Europe, and throughout the world, if Germany and England come to an understanding.' He proposed a conference, adding: 'Let those who consider war to be the better solution reject my outstretched hand.' 'I am coming more and more to the view,' said Halifax next day when the Cabinet discussed the speech, 'that my chief war aim is the elimination of Herr Hitler. It is not, however, politic to say so.' Ministers agreed Britain's reply should point out the obscurities and contradictions in Hitler's words, and draw attention to Poland, Czechoslovakia and the disarmament issue. Chamberlain would deliver this reply in the Commons, probably on 11 October, and broadcast afterwards. Halifax would prepare a draft, and also ask the French not to reply before Britain.

Sir Cyril Newall reported on the 'frank exchange of views' he and Ironside had had with Gamelin the previous day. And the British Chiefs of Staff were apparently still unaware that Gamelin still contemplated Plan D. Instead, the talks had mainly concentrated on the French appeal for more aircraft; the Cabinet now authorized Newall to despatch, at his discretion, two fighter squadrons to France if the situation demanded.[26] On Friday, Hitler had repeated that 'Germany will in no circumstances impair the inviolability of Belgium and Holland'; now, on Saturday, new instructions were issued to the Army Group leaders – 'to make all preparations for immediate invasion of Dutch and Belgian territory, if the political situation so demands.'[27]

The first reply to the Führer's peace proposal came during the day. Halifax had not had time to ask the French not to answer first: Daladier declared France would not lay down her arms until guarantees for a 'real peace and general security' were obtained. Some high-ranking German officers genuinely hoped the peace offer would be accepted, on the grounds that if Germany continued the war, she would be defeated. So strong were doubts among military chiefs that, during this Saturday, Brauchitsch and Halder were pressed into presenting to Hitler a report of Army deficiencies. General Jodl warned Halder: 'A very severe crisis is in the making.'[28] But one German officer was about to bring off an astounding success for his Fatherland. On Sunday, 8 October, in bright, crisp weather, Lieutenant Günther Prien directed his submarine, U-47, from Kiel harbour, and through the cold water of the Kiel Canal to the sea; his course was north-north-west; his destination the Orkney Islands and Scapa Flow.

Britain's II Corps was now going into the line, reported the Deputy CIGS at the Sunday War Cabinet meeting. But 'the Field Force is experiencing some difficulty in taking over a portion of the Franco-Belgian frontier which is not adequately marked, and across which there is a great deal of traffic.'[29] Yet the possibility of imminent action, and the crucial importance of the Western Front, were stressed again in a report completed this Sunday by the Chiefs of Staff. The Russo-German Agreement meant that Germany's flank and rear were to some extent protected; 'In consequence the West is more than ever the decisive front and is likely to be the scene of any immediate German offensive.'[30] 'Should it become evident in the near future,' declared Hitler in his War Directive No 6 issued next day, 'that England, and under her influence France also, are not disposed to bring the war to an end, I have decided, without further loss of time, to go over to the offensive.... An offensive will be planned on the northern flank of the Western front, through Luxembourg, Belgium, and Holland. This offensive must be launched at the earliest possible moment and in greatest possible strength.'[31]

Britain's reply to Hitler had still to be made, but Chamberlain commented on Hitler's offer in a letter dated 8 October. 'I was, I confess, anxious when I read Hitler's clever speech, and especially when the first American reaction was reported that he had made a very attractive series of proposals.... I was clear in my own mind that it offered no real advance in mind or spirit towards a reasonable peace.'[32] And he underlined his opinion at the Cabinet meeting on Monday, 9 October, the day of Hitler's War Directive. Three main points had to be borne in mind: first, the reply should be 'stiff'. Second, 'Herr Hitler's speech said in effect that there was to be no further discussion about Poland, as her future is the concern of Germany and Russia exclusively. Our reply should draw attention to this, and make quite clear that it is an impossible basis for starting peace negotiations.' Thirdly, 'in regard to the more general proposals in Herr Hitler's speech, the answer should be that it would be no use discussing them, since it is impossible to believe anything that Herr Hitler says. This should be illustrated by reference to his past words and deeds.'[33]

Ministers agreed with Chamberlain, and decided the statement should still be made in two days' time, on 11 October. Meanwhile Hitler, while waiting, was continuing his preparations for the offensive. On 10 October he summoned his Generals to a conference, and read them a long and impressive memorandum, in which he showed a skilful grasp of both military history and tactics. The struggle might be hard, he warned his wavering Generals, and time was on the enemy's side. Germany must therefore strike first, and hardest. The positional warfare of 1914-1918 must be avoided at all costs; instead, the armoured divisions must force the crucial breakthrough, 'to maintain the flow of the army's advance, to prevent fronts from becoming stable by massed drives through identified weakly held positions.' Luxembourg, Belgium and Holland constituted 'the only possible area of attack', and he added: 'The start cannot take place too early. It is to take place in all circumstances (if at all possible) this autumn.'[34] German staff officers immediately set to work drawing up details of the offensive.[35] Hitler's Generals may have needed prodding; not so his Admirals. On the day of the army conference, Raeder had a long discussion with Hitler, and, acting on his 3 October approach, urged that close consideration be given to operations to secure bases in Norway. Hitler told Raeder to leave his papers for further study.

Britain's reply was still not ready, said Chamberlain at the War Cabinet meeting on 10 October. Modifications were still being made to the draft, and as Dominion Governments should be consulted, Ministers agreed the statement should be postponed twenty-four hours, to 12 October. On the 12th it seemed a further delay might be necessary, following objections to the wording from Smuts. 'I cannot for a second time postpone making the statement,' complained Chamberlain. 'I am very averse to any further alterations of the draft.'[36] He therefore gave the British reply in a Commons speech during the afternoon, rejecting Hitler's proposals as 'vague and uncertain'. He added: 'They contain no suggestions for righting the wrongs done to Czechoslovakia and Poland.' No reliance, said Chamberlain, could be put on the promises 'of the present German Government' – hence making an appeal to the German people to put their house in order. If the German Government wanted peace, 'acts, not words alone, must be forthcoming'. Chamberlain demanded convincing proof from Hitler that he really sought peace. The statement was received by the Commons with moderate applause. Hitler's reaction was to issue a German statement, that Britain had been offered peace and had chosen war. Fears of a German bombing offensive immediately increased. The Chiefs of Staff, on the other hand, pressed again for a revision of the restricted Allied bombing policy. In a report completed on the 12th, they pointed out that when they had previously raised the subject of air operations in the event of a German invasion of the Low Countries, a decision had been deferred in the hope that staff talks might be arranged with the Belgians. 'This hope had proved false, and a German attack now seems to be impending.' It would be vital to put bombing plans into operation 'without a moment's delay', and so they asked for authority to take such a decision without referring back to the Cabinet, should this situation develop.[37] Next morning, Friday the thirteenth, the War Cabinet reluctantly consented. Chamberlain was soon to see the Belgian Ambassador, and undertook to leave 'no illusions as to what action we should take in the event of a German invasion of Belgium. We should attack the enemy wherever we might find him' – even if this resulted in civilian deaths.

Churchill told the Cabinet there appeared to have been an increase in U-boat activity. 'An early attack on our shipping, ports and East coast convoys must now be anticipated.'[38] One U-boat was indeed to be tragically active. As Churchill spoke, Lieutenant Prien's U-47 was nearing the Scottish coast. For past days, the German submarine had been stealthily cutting her way through the North Sea; now, at 7 p.m. this Friday the thirteenth, Prien was ready to surface. The dripping black conning tower sliced through the swell, and Prien scanned the sea around him; no ships were in sight. The submarine throbbed closer inshore; carefully and slowly, Prien edged her around Holm Sound, then through the dangerously narrow – and therefore un-defended – passage of Kirk Sound. The whole wide bay of Scapa Flow lay in front of U-47, and, her massive bows now vulnerable and help-less, a Royal Navy battleship lay berthed beneath the shadow of the land. Torpedoes whispered through the water; twenty seconds later the black shadow of the battleship burst into vivid yellows and reds, and the noise of the explosion echoed around the islands of Orkney and Hoy. More explosions followed, and HMS *Royal Oak* slid to the bottom of Scapa Flow with the bodies of 786 men. Prien slipped back through the gap.

For Churchill the disaster would mean a personal attack from his critics. Scapa Flow was ultimately his responsibility, even though he had been First Lord only one and a half months. But Churchill emerged unscathed, despite the appalling gap revealed in Britain's naval defences. 'Winston has been through a rough sea over the Scapa incident,' wrote Sir Samuel Hoare. 'Being for the moment the war hero, he has come through it fairly well. I shudder to think what would have happened if there had been another First Lord and he had been in Opposition.'[39] For Chamberlain, the tragedy reinforced his personal revulsion of war. 'How I hate and loathe this war. I was never meant to be a War Minister, and the thought of all those homes wrecked with the *Royal Oak* makes me want to hand over my responsibilities.'[40]

Cabinet Ministers heard the formal report of the sinking when they met next day. 'It is believed she was attacked by a submarine,' said Churchill, his voice tired, 'which, by some unknown means, had pene-trated the defences.... The first sign of attack was an explosion for-ward, which at first was thought to have been the result of some internal cause. About twenty minutes later, there were other explosions, and the ship sank. Admiral Blagrove ... and about 800 officers and men are believed to have been drowned.' A search was still being made for the submarine, 'which is thought might have been unable to make its way out of the Flow'. He concluded: 'The loss of the ship, though an extremely regrettable disaster, does not materially affect the general naval position.'

The Cabinet had other matters to worry them that Saturday. Hore-Belisha reported an increase in German activity on the Western Front – thirteen bridges had now been built across the Saar. Ironside once again warned that a German attack appeared imminent. 'It might even start as early as tomorrow.' Ministers felt that 'Herr Hitler is confronted with the dilemma in the West that, if he were not to take the offensive, he runs the risk of severe loss of morale, while if he were to attack the Maginot Line, he would be taking a gamble which might lead to his destruction.'[41] General Brooke failed to share the Cabinet's optimism. 'It is hard to realize we are at war,' he wrote in his diary next day, and he gave his opinion of the French – 'the whole country dressed in their Sunday best and apparently oblivious that they may be sitting on a volcano.'[42]

At the Sunday Cabinet meeting, the Deputy CIGS gave the latest reports. German troops were drifting steadily towards the Moselle; and might therefore attack towards Metz. 'The new dispositions all seem to indicate that the original German plan of an invasion through Belgium has been abandoned.'[43] But late that Sunday night the most serious scare so far caused near panic in France. The French High Command expected an immediate attack – through Belgium. Messages and signals flashed from headquarters to headquarters, unit to unit; and the British Corps Commanders were told Gamelin had decided the Anglo-French forces would now advance into Belgium, to meet the German invasion – despite the continued lack of Belgian cooperation. Troops would move forward within a few hours. The very action which the British War Cabinet and Chiefs of Staff had warned should be avoided, was now threatened. To Brooke and Dill, such an advance seemed madness. Their half-formed, unarmoured units would meet the German Panzers and aircraft in open country. Full equipment had still to be supplied; no reconnaissance had been carried out. To Brooke, the only sensible decision would have been to stay in the defensive positions on the Franco-Belgian frontier; and this, although Brooke never knew it, was the plan which the Chiefs of Staff had said should be followed – the plan which the Cabinet had been led to assume would be adopted in the absence of Belgian cooperation.

Rumours of impending German invasion of Belgium fortunately faded next day. Meanwhile, at the morning Cabinet meeting Hore-Belisha underlined the difficulties Britain would face if she tried to challenge too strongly French direction of the war in France. He referred to a telegram from the Ambassador at Paris, reporting 'unfair comparisons' between the size of the BEF, now 158,000 men, and the total of the French Army, 3,500,000 men. The French naturally insisted they should have the more powerful voice in strategical planning. Hore-Belisha told Ministers he intended to make a broadcast on 21 October, in which he would point out that the BEF was only an advance guard. Ministers thought the fact should be emphasized that the British force already despatched was larger than that originally promised.[44]

Confusion over strategic plans increased still further. No new directives reached Corps level after the 15 October scare, and as far as Dill and Brooke were concerned, the plan was still to advance into Belgium if the Germans attacked. 'Spent the morning planning for our advance into Belgium,' wrote Brooke on 17 October, 'in the event of the Germans violating her neutrality. In the afternoon attended two and a half hours GHQ conference.... Before the conference Dill and I got hold of Gort and tried to make him realize the serious aspects of the contemplated move, the danger of leaving our present prepared position for one totally unprepared, and the exposure of our left flank if Falgalde's 16th Corps does not come up on the left.'[45]

Minor alarms and excursions continued on the wet and depressing Western Front. The Germans had attacked east of the Luxembourg border, reported Hore-Belisha to the War Cabinet on the seventeenth. 'The attack appears to have the limited objective of gaining some high ground, probably as a preliminary to later attacks on a larger scale.'[46] 'The Germans have again advanced on to French soil at some points,' stated Hore-Belisha on the 22nd, 'although only to seize minor tactical features'. But the weather deteriorated rapidly. At this 22 October meeting, Ministers heard a report from the Military Attaché at Brussels, describing the Belgian roads as waterlogged and mostly impassable for tanks. The Deputy CIGS commented on his recent visit to the BEF; among his main points was the 'very wet state of the British front, which made an attack on it quite impracticable at the moment.'[47] Next day Hore-Belisha reported Gamelin now gave the impression 'that he was thinking more in terms of a German offensive in the Spring'. Churchill asked if the General Staff now believed no major German attack was impending. 'It is not possible to be absolutely definite,' replied Ironside, 'but a major operation in the present state of the weather, so late in the season, is not one which I myself would be prepared to undertake.'

Cabinet discussion turned for a moment to another potential war area. Britain's Ambassador at Helsinki had sent a telegram recommending that 'in the event of Soviet aggression against Finland, we should either formally or informally declare a state of belligerence between the USSR and ourselves'. Reporting this telegram to the War Cabinet on 23 October, Halifax commented: 'It appears also that Mr Snow anticipates that the Government of the USSR might be preparing to establish themselves on the north coast of Norway. I suggest it would be useful if the Chiefs of Staff Committee could take into consideration the advantages and disadvantages of our declaring war against the USSR.' And the Cabinet agreed.[48]

The French, especially Gamelin, were still not satisfied with Britain's contribution to the defence of France, much to the Cabinet's annoyance. By next spring, Germany would have 160 Divisions, of which between 120 and 130 would be available for the Western Front. Gamelin intended to find more French troops to meet the threat, and hoped to be able to raise ten new Divisions; he calculated the British Army would be able to provide 650,000 men. 'He doubts whether this would be sufficient,' said Hore-Belisha at the 24 October Cabinet meeting, 'and therefore asks that we should examine the possibility of speeding up our programme.' Ministers immediately expressed their irritation: 'It was clear from these repeated appeals from General Gamelin that he was not aware of the very great war effort which was being made by this country.... The additional Divisions which were now being raised by both the Germans and French would be poorly equipped. By contrast our plans contemplated that all the British Divisions would be fully equipped and armed.' Hore-Belisha would draft a suitable reply.[49]

In France, Brooke and Dill continued to warn Gort of the consequences of the plan to advance into Belgium. The two Corps Commanders were unaware of the difficulties the British Commander-in-Chief was himself experiencing. Brooke wrote in his diary on the 27th: 'He refuses to face the difficulties we may be up against and makes light of them all.' And on this same Friday, Hitler informed his Generals that 'Operation Yellow' would now start on 12 November, just over two weeks away. 'Brauchitsch tired and dejected,' noted Halder.[50] But Gort wrote to Hore-Belisha next day: 'Everything here is fast becoming quite waterlogged and unfit for any attack. For an army which depends for success on tanks and low-flying, I can imagine no worse combination than Flanders mud and low cloud.'[51] Rain continued to saturate the soldiers and save them from attack. At home, the bad weather merely added to the depression, and in London the streets took on their wartime winter appearance. With the disappearance of Indian summer, the drabness of conflict cloaked the city; men and women buttoned themselves in last year's coats against chill Thames draughts; shop-windows suffered an increasing scarcity of goods. In Berlin, the citizens – or at least women – were asked to make an even greater sacrifice. Himmler issued a decree on 28 October: 'It will now be the great task, even outside the marriage bond, for German women and girls of good blood, not in frivolity but in deep moral earnestness, to become mothers of the children of soldiers going off to war.' It seemed as if the Nazis were planning for a long conflict, spreading into the next generation. But good living had not entirely disappeared from Europe, as Brooke found while visiting French messes. 'A wasted day as far as work was concerned,' he wrote on 31 October. 'Champagne-lunch consisting of oysters, lobsters, chicken, pâté-de-foie-gras, pheasant, cheese and fruit, coffee, liqueurs....' He commented: 'I could not help wondering, whether the French are still a firm enough nation to again take their part in seeing this war through.'[52] Twilight War had become a routine: in France the troops were lethargic, and Gort complained he would be glad when there came 'some real soldiering to do'. At home the civilian boredom increased, and more MPs fell asleep each week as Chamberlain gave his report to the Commons: Halifax wished 'the PM would give up these weekly statements, it is as if one were in East Africa and received the *Times Weekly* at regular intervals'; and Harold Nicolson felt ashamed when Dominion representatives crowded into the Gallery to hear the proceedings. 'They had come expecting to find the Mother of Parliaments armed like Britannia. They merely saw an old lady dozing over her knitting, while her husband read the evening paper aloud.'[53]

Sudden war scares still came to stimulate the atmosphere. Hore-Belisha told the War Cabinet on 31 October, for example, that 'rumours of an impending German attack on Great Britain, either by a sea-borne expedition or by large air forces, are now being received from sources as widely diverse as The Hague and Peking'. But he added: 'There seems little doubt that these rumours are being deliberately spread by Germany.'[54] Hore-Belisha described these rumours and the Cabinet's reaction to them in a letter to Gort. 'On Friday night last (27 October), at Winston Churchill's request, a committee of Service Ministers was assembled, with military advisers.' The reason for the meeting was a report from the French Military Attaché in Yugoslavia that 'an enormous invasion was being planned on this country by sea, land and air, and would take place at any moment.... We tried to riddle the arguments, but nevertheless we were instructed to prepare plans for meeting the invasion and even for bringing back Divisions, if necessary, from France.' The rumours dwindled before such drastic steps could be taken.[55]

The end of October saw changes to the Government's decision-making machinery. It had become increasingly clear that the War Cabinet suffered from a number of defects, due partly to personalities, but mainly to Cabinet structure. The first of these defects was the presence of two natural leaders, Churchill and Chamberlain: the First Lord, not content with Departmental responsibilities, nor with the slow tempo of the war, had continued to bombard the Prime Minister with Minutes, letters and memoranda, some of which Chamberlain considered unnecessary. Churchill found it difficult to be a subordinate member of the Cabinet, and this was reflected in the poor and over-defensive performances he had given at question time in the Commons. More fundamental was a weakness in the existing War Cabinet system. In time of peace, the Chiefs of Staff Committee had reported to the Cabinet via the Committee of Imperial Defence, but now, with the CID gone, they reported direct to the War Cabinet; and, as a result, the Cabinet found themselves involved in formulating military policy too early and in too much detail. Insufficient ground-work was done before the Cabinet stage, and too much Cabinet time taken up in dealing with this necessary preparatory study. Vice-versa, the Chiefs of Staff were being asked to consider problems which strictly speaking should have fallen outside their brief. And another consequence was the tendency to direct military operations from the War Cabinet room. Churchill had suggested one improvement in a Minute to the Prime Minister on 21 September. 'I wonder if you would consider having an occasional meeting of the War Cabinet Ministers to talk among themselves without either secretaries or military experts. I am not satisfied that the large issues are being effectively discussed in our formal sessions.'[56]

Chamberlain decided to re-introduce an intermediary body to concentrate on defence and link War Cabinet to Chiefs of Staff Committee. On 31 October, he announced his proposal for a standing committee, to consider long-term strategic projects. The group would be called the 'Ministerial Committee on Military Coordination', and would comprise Chatfield and the three Service Ministers; it would 'keep under constant review, on behalf of the War Cabinet, the main factors in the strategical situation and the progress of operations, and to make recommendations from time to time to the War Cabinet as to the general conduct of the war.'[57] A fifth member, Leslie Burgin, was later added. But the innovation failed to improve the decision-making process. Instead, experience soon showed that discussions which had taken place at Chiefs of Staff level were often repeated at the Military Coordination Committee stage, and then again at the War Cabinet meetings. The business of explanation, disputation and formulation of conclusions was repeated three times.[58] The correct balance had still to be found between speed, which required a streamlined structure, and the delegation of more detailed discussion to a subordinate body.

Meanwhile, as November began, Hitler's preparations for attack continued. On the second of the month he left for two days' inspection of the Western Front; a few days before, tentative German inquiries had been made to the Dutch Government, asking if positions could be taken up inside their frontier – and, when reports of this ominous request reached Brussels, alarm inevitably increased; on 2 November, Hore-Belisha therefore informed the War Cabinet of a report that the Belgians had asked the French what their attitude would be to a request for staff talks. The news of this move by Brussels was highly welcome, but hopes of cooperation were soon to be disappointed once again. Hitler had difficulties with his commanders as he visited the German positions. 'None of the higher headquarters,' wrote Halder on 3 November, 'thinks the offensive ... has any prospect of success.'[59] But the Führer refused to be deterred. 'I have led the German people to a great height, even if the world does hate us now,' he told his Generals on that day. 'I risk the loss of this achievement. I have to choose between victory or destruction. I choose victory.... My decision is unchangeable. I shall attack France and England at the favourable and earliest moment.' But his Generals continued to express their anxiety; and German civilians began increasingly to chafe – war, particularly twilight war, was irksome.

Meanwhile in London, Sir Samuel Hoare was saying: 'People in general are willing to accept controls if they are convinced that they are justified, but at the moment they are not satisfied with the Government's policy.... They do not, for example, understand the need for the commandeering of buildings; they question the need for rationing coal while miners are still unemployed; and there have also been criticisms of a number of economic controls, on the ground that the people administering them are not altogether impartial owing to their business affiliations.' Ministers believed 'one cause of the discontent in Press circles, and of the attacks on the Government, is the absence of real war news'. Chamberlain attacked the unpatriotic newspaper industry, which only sought profits and stimulated a 'mass-produced and artificial indignation'. The War Cabinet agreed that a survey should be made of controls and restrictions, and the Prime Minister was invited to consider the best method of approaching newspaper proprietors.[60] Hitler was still trying to whip up his Generals' enthusiasm. On Sunday, 5 November German units were scheduled to begin the move forward to jump-off points opposite Holland, Belgium and Luxembourg; and on the same day, Brauchitsch drove to the Chancellery to urge Hitler to abandon the plans for the offensive. Pushed into action by dissatisfied and anxious senior officers, he claimed the weather was unsuitable. Hitler answered that the enemy had to suffer exactly the same conditions. But the morale of the German troops was low, protested Brauchitsch. And at this, Hitler shrieked and stormed at the Commander-in-Chief until he fled in fear. German units moved to their positions as planned; the date for the offensive was still 12 November, one week away.[61]

'The disposal of the Divisions opposite the Dutch frontier is consistent with the possibility of a German attack on Holland,' Hore-Belisha reported to the Cabinet the following day. The total number of German Divisions on the Western Front remained at 133, he added. Churchill had just made a rapid visit to France, and reported his impressions: Daladier had seemed 'to be labouring under a sense of imminent crisis ... Unless the Germans take the offensive either in France or against this country in the near future, the opportunity for doing so, with any hope of success, will not present itself again until next Spring.' And if the Germans remained inactive until then, 'it would be tantamount to a great victory in the field for the Allies'.[62]

Hitler had already drafted proclamations to be made to the Dutch and Belgians justifying his invasion – his pretext would be French violations of the Belgian border. On 7 November the King of the

Belgians and the Queen of the Netherlands issued a joint appeal for peace, probably as a result of a message which had reached their Governments from Berlin. Soon after the disastrous Brauchitsch-Hitler interview, when it appeared Hitler would never be dissuaded, one officer had decided to take dangerous and drastic action. Colonel Hans Oster sent a message to the Belgian and Dutch Legations in Berlin warning them to expect an attack on the morning of 12 November.[63]

A reply to the Dutch and Belgian appeal was to be discussed by the British War Cabinet on 12 November. But by then, Hitler's plans had altered again. Weather conditions over the Western Front had continued to deteriorate. Low cloud restricted aircraft movement; mud, churned by tanks, bogged vehicles and slowed marching men; ditches overran with stormwater; atmospheric static crackled wireless communications. Forecasts predicted worse to come. And on 7 November a short signal was sent to Field Commanders from Keitel in Berlin. 'The Führer and Supreme Commander of the Armed Forces, after hearing reports on the meteorological and railway transport situation, has ordered: A-Day is postponed by three days. The next decision will be made at 6 p.m. on 9 November.'[64] This postponement of the attack was to be followed, at varying intervals, by fourteen more.

One of the firmest dates in Hitler's crowded diary was his speech at the annual reunion of fighters of the 1923 Munich *Putsch*. The ceremony was held in the Munich *Bürgerbrau*, and the Führer drove there on Wednesday, 8 November, gave his address and then left – unusually early. Twelve minutes later a massive explosion ripped open the hall; and the eye of the damage was the spot where Hitler had stood such a short time before. The 'attempted assassination' was probably organized by the Gestapo, in an effort to increase Hitler's popularity and to stir up resentment against those lukewarm over the war, including some Generals. Two British Secret Service agents, who were involved in shady dealings with alleged German conspirators, were kidnapped and charged with attempted murder. A trial was never held.

The German attack was postponed again on 9 November, and set for 19 November. But Holland and Belgium 'appear to be thoroughly alarmed' Hore-Belisha told the Cabinet. 'The CIGS and the Chief of the Air Staff are discussing the situation with General Gamelin at this moment.' This was at a conference in Vincennes, with an impressive list of participants. Gamelin warned of a move by the Germans in the near future, probably a '*Blitzkrieg* against Holland'. General Georges, immediate superior to Gort, then proceeded to explain how this offensive would be dealt with – and all the fears of officers such as Brooke and Dill were fully realized. The Anglo-French force would advance into Belgium, declared Georges, either to the farther line of Namur-

Wavre-Antwerp, as under Plan D, or to the nearer line of the Scheldt. Yet the decision of the British Chiefs of Staff and the War Cabinet still stood: the forward movement should not be attempted unless adequate forward defensive positions were prepared and full Belgian cooperation obtained. But no British objections were raised at the Vincennes meeting. General Ironside remained silent, and he explained his reasons for doing so when the Cabinet met for another session that night. When asked if he thought the plan to advance into Belgium should be adopted, he replied that under the structure for the Higher Command in France, the British Commander – Lord Gort – was subordinate to the French commander, Gamelin, and his deputy, General Georges, and, while Lord Gort had the right of protest to the British Cabinet, he had not done so. Until he did, the War Cabinet should not intervene: Gort apparently accepted the proposed advance, so, therefore, should the Cabinet. Besides, the Belgians were believed to be working hard at constructing defences between Namur and Wavre. But despite this reassuring information and Ironside's devious explanation, the War Cabinet nevertheless showed concern by asking Halifax to send a telegram to the Ambassador at Brussels, asking him to press again for staff talks.[65]

Four days later, on 13 November, Gamelin received what he claimed were satisfactory assurances that the Belgian military authorities would fulfil necessary conditions for him to advance the allied armies deep into Belgium. These included Belgian mobilization and the construction of adequate defences for the Anglo-French forces to occupy when they reached the forward lines. So, on Tuesday, 14 November, General Gamelin expounded his plan of campaign at a meeting at General Georges' headquarters. Following his secret negotiations with the Belgians, the Allied commander now proposed his 'personal and secret Instruction No. 8': an advance into Belgium which would not halt at the Scheldt, but which would move 'if circumstances permitted' to the line from Namur to Antwerp. The British would hold the sector along the line of the River Dyle, covering Brussels, extending from Wavre to Louvain.

Chamberlain had been absent from the War Cabinet meetings since 9 November, suffering from his first attack of gout for two years. He returned for the Cabinet meeting on the fourteenth, and heard a report from the Military Coordination Committee that the Chiefs of Staff were again urging they should have discretion over bombing policy, in the event of a German invasion of Belgium. This proposal included provision for bombing military targets in the Ruhr. But the Cabinet still agreed 'it was not possible to authorize in advance of the event any specific policy'.[66] Meanwhile, the French were continuing to grumble, 'in a most friendly way', at the scale of British military efforts on the Western Front. Reynaud, the French President of the Council, had pointed to a considerable disproportion between the British and French mobilization figures. 'Whereas one in every eight of the French population was at present mobilized, the corresponding proportion in Britain was only one in every forty. France was languishing owing to the absorption of manpower in the armed forces.' Hore-Belisha told the Cabinet that Reynaud feared hostile propaganda could be made of the difference, and Reynaud believed his country could find equipment for more British troops. But Churchill was concerned over the equipment for the existing programme; he drew attention to recent forecasts from the Supply Ministry, which showed Britain would only have sufficient equipment for 15 Divisions by the end of the first year of war. 'This reduction from the original forecast of 20 Divisions is most disquieting.... I cannot believe that we could do no better than this.' 'A deficiency in any one item delays the final completion of the Divisions,' retorted Hore-Belisha. He added however that he was visiting France at the end of the week, and he proposed he should discuss possible supplies of equipment from the ally.[67]

Many thousands of miles away in the waters of the Mozambique Channel, the German pocket-battleship *Graf Spee* re-emerged from obscurity. The giant warship attacked and sank a small British tanker before disappearing again. But Royal Navy warships had been on the alert since the liner *Clement* had been sunk by the *Spee* on 30 September. The search was now intensified. The Captain of the *Spee*, Hans Langsdorf, feinted towards the Indian Ocean, then doubled back and headed for the South Atlantic. The decision was fateful. Churchill was now to spend many hours in the naval War Room, enthralled in an adventure which suited him perfectly – small brave British warships hunting the wide oceans to harry the massive German vessel. But on Thursday, 16 November, Churchill turned his thoughts in an opposite direction – to Russia, and to the subject of possible Soviet advances in the Baltic. 'No doubt it appears reasonable to the Soviet Union to take advantage of the present situation to regain some of the territory which Russia lost as a result of the last war, at the beginning of which she was the ally of France and Britain.... This applies not only to Baltic territories, but also to Finland. It is in our interests that the USSR should increase their strength on the Baltic, thereby limiting the risk of German domination in that area. For this reason it would be a mistake for us to stiffen the Finns against making concessions to the USSR.'[68] Churchill would soon have chance to prove if he believed his words.

Meanwhile, Gamelin's crucial Plan D was discussed at a meeting of the Supreme War Council in Paris on 17 November. Gamelin put forward a vigorous case, and Chamberlain conceded that as much territory in Belgium should be saved as possible. Daladier felt the defence of the forward Antwerp-Namur line was as essential as the defence of France herself. So the Council endorsed the strategy, with all the implications involved in an advance deep into largely unreconnoitred, largely unprepared country. The Supreme War Council also discussed air policy, and Chamberlain put forward the view of the British Air Staff that in the event of a German invasion of Belgium, waves of bombers should strike at the Ruhr, prepared to accept heavy losses. Daladier doubted the wisdom of risking such losses, feared retaliation, and did not believe bombing targets in Germany would stop the German armies in Belgium. The Council therefore agreed that allied air action should still be confined to military targets in the immediate battlefield area, unless the Germans bombed allied aircraft factories. In the political field, the 17 November Council meeting recorded a solemn agreement that neither of the two allies would make a separate peace or armistice with Germany.

But despite the ease with which Gamelin had managed to have his Plan D accepted, many still doubted the judgement behind it. Why go so far? Why not stop at the Scheldt, only a day's march away? But it was more tempting for Gamelin and the political leaders to adopt the more ambitious advance: by moving the sixty miles to the River Dyle, the Belgium capital and the port of Antwerp could be saved, communications with Western Holland would be kept open, and the line of defence on the Dyle would, it was believed, be shorter and therefore allow more men to be retained as reserves. Military and political advantages therefore seemed to make the risk worthwhile. But the risk was nevertheless considerable. To reach the Dyle meant the troops would have to race across strange country, perhaps under air attack, and, because the appeal for help from the Belgians might be late, the timetable had to be rigidly planned for maximum speed – and this did not allow for unforeseen delay *en route*. The original objection raised by the British Chiefs of Staff in their 18 September report remained valid: 'We consider it would be unsound to adopt this plan unless plans are concerted with the Belgians for the occupation of this line in sufficient time before the German advance.' General Brooke believed: 'If we can get there in time to organize ourselves properly, it is without doubt the right strategy.' All would be well – if the army could push forward fast enough through the panic-stricken refugees who would be clogging the roads; if the Belgian units could hold back the Germans long enough; if the defensive positions along the Dyle were adequately prepared. To Generals Brooke and Dill, to the French General Billotte, commander of the Army Group One, to many of their colleagues, the obstacles were too large. But Gort did not voice his objections, and the War Cabinet remained ignorant of the depth of unease. 'Of these differences we knew nothing,' claimed Churchill afterwards.[69]

During the afternoon of 17 November, Hore-Belisha left foggy

Hendon airfield for a visit to the Western Front, a visit soon to have serious repercussions on his career. He spent the next day, Saturday, travelling almost the whole length of the British sector, accompanied by Gort, Dill and Brooke. 'A great deal of digging is in progress along the front, but I was surprised to see only two new pill-boxes being constructed.... I mentioned this to Gort.... A bigger conception will have to be taken of the defences.'[70] Back in London this Saturday, Ironside was reporting to the Cabinet on the latest situation. 'Information tends to show that the troops for an invasion of the Low Countries are still concentrated ready on the German frontier.... There is a limit to the length of time for which troops can be kept closed up for the attack, without relief. If the Germans, therefore, do not stage their attack very shortly, they will probably have to release the tension and carry out reliefs.'[71]

A new threat to Britain had emerged: British shipping was in danger from newly sown magnetic mines. These devices, which exploded without contact, by magnetic influence, had been used by Britain on a small scale at the end of the First World War; now the Germans appeared to be dropping them in large quantities around the British East coast, especially at harbour entrances. Sweeping was difficult owing to the depth at which these mines could be placed. Naval experts desperately thought of ways to render them inactive; Churchill thought of means for retaliation. On 19 November, he completed several papers, and among them was a scheme for striking at Germany's artery, the Rhine. 'As a measure of retaliation it may become necessary to feed large numbers of floating mines into the Rhine. This can easily be done at any point between Strasbourg and the Lauter, where the left bank is French territory.' This would create havoc and widespread damage among the river traffic, especially the heavy barges, and shatter the boat bridges which had recently been thrown across the Rhine for troop movements. Churchill went into the idea in great detail, and asked his experts to consider the proposal.[72] Another of Churchill's proposals was for a 'Northern Barrage', a gigantic mine-field from Scotland almost to the coast of Norway, aimed at hindering U-boat and German surface raiders. If the Barrage were extended far enough, and entered Norwegian territorial waters, it would also serve to sever Germany's iron ore trade routes.

Hore-Belisha's visit had made him anxious over the state of the BEF defences, and he mentioned his disquiet at an Army Council session on 20 November. 'I discussed various questions of policy and dealt at length with the question of pill-boxes. I emphasized that far more concrete pill-boxes were essential.' Next morning, he reported on his visit to the War Cabinet apparently uncontentiously.[73] But the so-called 'Pill-Box Controversy' was arising. Writing to Gort on 22 November, Hore-Belisha commented: 'I am seeing the engineers tomorrow. I really think the pill-boxes should spring up everywhere.' Dominion representatives had recently visited France with Eden and they too, he claimed, had commented on the absence of these necessary defences.[74] During the afternoon, he made a statement to the Commons on the BEF. 'This is a fortress war. The House can see in its mind's eye the busy work of our soldiers, digging and building. Under their hands blockhouses and pill-boxes take shape, and with digging machines and with squelching spades they throw up breastworks or carve out entrenchments....' But was all this being done fast enough? Eden was among those who had serious doubts. Hore-Belisha had asked him to see him. 'I could only report what I had stated before,' wrote Eden. 'Considerably to my surprise, the Secretary of State then put the blame on Gort, who, he said, "has everything he asked for".' Hore-Belisha revealed his opinions of the C-in-C. 'He told me that he had made the appointment to poularize the army and help recruiting – "a Viscount and a VC". I showed my incredulity.'[75] With this attitude, complications would inevitably arise.

The same day, the Cabinet meeting heard a report by the Chiefs of Staff on a subject which would soon take over as their main preoccupation – possible British intervention in Norway.[76] The Chiefs of Staff had previously been asked to study the military implications of giving an assurance of support to the Scandinavian countries, in the event of aggression by Russia or Germany. An initial report by the Chiefs of Staff, considered and approved by the War Cabinet on 1 November, had concluded Britain was at present in no position to undertake additional burdens: if Russia attacked Finland, Britain should not declare war on her, but the despatch of a small expedition to Norway, in the event of aggression, might be a practical proposition. Now, in their latest report, the Chiefs of Staff hesitated to give continued approval for even this limited commitment. After reconsidering the problem, they believed that 'once British troops had landed in Norway, it might be difficult to limit their commitment'. While they still believed a small expedition would be practicable, they did not consider it desirable. This conclusion, the report added, might affect the assurances Britain had already given to Norway. 'It was for consideration whether a further communication should be made to the Norwegian Government, explaining that the extent of our support must be limited to naval action.' For the moment, the War Cabinet came to no decision: Halifax told Ministers he would like longer to study the implications.[77]

The pill-box issue re-emerged on Friday, 24 November. 'I saw the Prime Minister in the morning,' wrote Hore-Belisha, 'and he mentioned to me the recent visit of the Dominions' ministers to GHQ. He said it was the opinion of some of them that a great increase of concrete pill-boxes was required.' The War Secretary had already taken steps to increase the BEF defences: a Territorial Army officer and a civil engineer had been sent to France to organize a civilian task force. Immediately, a number of officers at GHQ complained of Hore-Belisha's meddling. Talk of 'civilian interference' became louder – especially among those officers who already disliked the War Secretary's 'flashy' attitude. Five days after Hore-Belisha had discussed the shortages of pill-boxes with the Prime Minister, Ironside left for a visit to the BEF. Unknown to the War Cabinet, and even to Hore-Belisha, a telegram preceded him, addressed to Gort's Military Assistant, and stating that the CIGS was coming 'to inspect defences in BEF area on War Cabinet instructions'. The cable was to form excellent ammunition for those who wished to drive a gap between Gort and the War Secretary.[78]

First, Churchill and the Admiralty came under attack, for their responsibility in letting German pocket battleships slip away unharmed after an encounter in the North Atlantic. Churchill reported to the Cabinet on 24 November that an armed cruiser, SS *Rawalpindi*, was believed to have been sunk after a clash with the *Deutschland* between the Faroes and Iceland. Warships had been sent rushing to the area. Next day, Churchill reported that survivors from the *Rawalpindi* claimed there had been two warships of the *Deutschland* class. 'It is possible that the *Scharnhorst* and *Gneisenau* are also out, though the Admiralty thought this improbable.' Not until much later was it confirmed that these had in fact been the *Scharnhorst* and *Gneisenau*, and that they had slipped through the Royal Navy cruiser line off the Norwegian coast. 'Public impressions are unfavourable to the Admiralty,' wrote Churchill.[79] Especially galling was the belief, later proved correct, that the pocket battleships had made use of Norwegian territorial waters in order to escape. Churchill declared at the 25 November Cabinet meeting: 'I think it would be intolerable if the British Navy had to stand aside while the *Deutschland*, after having sunk the *Rawalpindi*, crept down the Norwegian coast inside Norwegian territorial waters.'[80] The episode reinforced his conviction that something must be done to take away the advantages Germany gained from Norway's neutrality. Two days later, Churchill addressed a long Minute to Admiral Pound, on the subject of the iron ore supply. 'Pray examine and advise upon a proposal to establish a minefield, blocking Norwegian waters at some lonely spot on the coast as far north as convenient. If the Norwegians will do this themselves, well and good. Otherwise a plan must be made for us to do it.' This idea, Churchill stated, was preferable to two other suggestions made verbally to him by the Naval staff: the violation of Norwegian neutrality by landing a force, or by stationing a ship at Narvik.[81] And on 30 November, he raised this suggestion of a minefield in Norwegian waters at a Cabinet meeting. Ministers began by discussing his proposals for a Northern Barrage, and Churchill explained this would extend from the Orkneys to the fringe of Norwegian territorial water; preparations would take about six months, and the total cost would be about £3 million. A similar scheme had been put into operation in 1918, and the Norwegians had agreed to extend the barrier into their waters as a result of 'influence exerted by the Allied military success and by Germany's internal weakness.... We have not yet arrived at a similar stage, and it would be imprudent to count on being able to persuade Norway to close the eastern end of our projected Barrage.' The War Cabinet agreed preparations should be started.

Then Churchill moved on to the linked, but far more controversial question of a specific operation to mine Norwegian waters. 'It seems certain that ... we shall have trouble with the Norwegian Government over the trade in Swedish iron-ore between Narvik and German ports.' The iron-ore vessels hugged the coastline in winter, continued Churchill; in the last war this had been prevented by the use of mines, which had driven the vessels out into the open sea. 'The time is coming when we shall have to consider taking similar measures. A few small minefields, each of perhaps three or four miles square, would be enough for the purpose.' Halifax warned: 'We should meet with a flat refusal from the Norwegians.' A decision, he thought, would have to await three investigations being carried out: the military problems involved, the economic implications, and the moral and legal aspects. 'They might show that we should be well advised to proceed cautiously.' Ministers nevertheless agreed these preliminary investigations should begin.[82]

Rumours of possible Soviet aggression against Finland had been increasing for some time. Four days before, on 26 November, a telegram had arrived from Seeds in Moscow: 'The Soviet Government, as a result of a serious incident on the Soviet-Finnish frontier, has addressed a Note to the Finnish Government demanding that the Finnish troops on the Karelian Isthmus should be withdrawn.' Halifax had told the Cabinet next morning: 'It is alleged that the presence of Finnish troops at their present strength so near Leningrad represented not only a danger, but a hostile act.' But the Foreign Secretary had pointed out that the Soviet Note had not taken the form of an ultimatum, and token withdrawals by Finnish and Soviet troops could be possible.[83] During the afternoon of the twenty-sixth Halifax had seen Maisky, the Soviet Ambassador, who had described the Finnish attitude as unreasonable and alleged that the Finns 'have shelled Russian territory'.[84]

'According to an unconfirmed report,' Hore-Belisha had told the War Cabinet on Wednesday, 29 November, 'the USSR has concentrated 350,000 men, a large number of aircraft, and 750 tanks along the Soviet-Finnish border. The Finns have 400,000 men under arms, and are in possession of a strong line.... They are

273

plucky people, and it looks as though they intend to fight.'[85]

And on 30 November, while Ministers were discussing Churchill's scheme for laying mines in Norwegian waters, a message was brought into the Cabinet Room: 'The War Cabinet were informed that confirmation had been received that the Soviet forces had crossed the Finnish border north-east of Lake Ladoga, and that firing had taken place across the Karelian Peninsula. There was also a report, not as yet confirmed, that Helsinki had been bombed.' The Russo-Finnish War had begun.[86]

Ivan Maisky had made an illuminating diary entry for 27 November, the day he had seen Halifax. The Britisher, he wrote, 'is energetically marking time, and trying to throw out his chest like a champion. It seems as though he is bursting to go into the attack: but in reality he desperately doesn't want to fight, and is only waiting for the first suitable occasion to throw off this unusual disguise, put on a dressing gown and sit down by the fire to read the evening paper.... Oh no! there's no smell of a warlike spirit in Britain today.'[87] Clearly, Maisky had no fears of British intervention to help Finland.

'I will have to make a statement on the Finland situation in the Commons,' said Chamberlain at the 30 November Cabinet meeting. Halifax thought the statement should 'show our strong disapproval of Russia's action, but at the same time should not lose sight of the fact that there is no effective action which we can take in the matter.' 'I think we ought not to be deterred,' said Churchill, 'in expressing disapproval by consideration of the possible effects on the Russians, who are impervious to words.'[88]

For the first few hours the Russian invasion seemed cautious and exploratory. Both sides manoeuvred for position. The main Russian offensive was launched initially upon the Finnish frontier position in the Karelian Isthmus, the 'Mannerheim Line' so-named after the Finnish C-in-C. From the start, the outnumbered Finnish units fought well, despite equipment shortages; included in the Finnish armoury was a home-made hand grenade, soon nicknamed the 'Molotov Cocktail'. Hitler was far from pleased with Soviet aggression against Finland, a country which had close ties with Germany, and whose independence had been won from the Soviet Union largely through the intervention of German troops in 1918, but he had officially to condone the unprovoked attack – while despairing over the reduction of Soviet economic aid to Germany which was likely to result. The Soviet assault had radical implications for both Germany and Britain. It focused attention on the Scandinavian and Baltic regions, while the Western Front became overshadowed. If British troops were to be sent to help the Finns, they could only arrive via Norway or Sweden; and if transit were allowed by these two countries, Germany believed her supply of Swedish iron ore would be threatened, and she risked being outflanked in the north. Temptations for Germany and Britain to act first were consequently increased.

Finland appealed to the League of Nations on 2 December, which could only cause embarrassment to the Western Allies in view of their inability to take effective action. The same day, the Russian invasion was fully discussed at the Cabinet meeting, and it emerged that the Soviet actions might hold advantages for the allies. 'Russian expansion in the Baltic will have no direct adverse effect on the allies,' maintained Hore-Belisha, 'and might indeed sow dissension between Russia and Germany.' On the other hand, 'the offensive might be a prelude to further Russian expansionist schemes, especially in South-East Europe.... The Chiefs of Staff have consistently advised against being drawn into war with Russia, but if Russian aggression occurred in South-East Europe, we might be forced to declare war on her whether we liked it or not.' Indignation was likely to be expressed in Britain against the Soviet action, and 'it might be difficult politically to avoid a more open condemnation of her action in Finland, in view of its similarity to German aggression in Poland'.[89]

Hore-Belisha was taken from his study of the implications of Soviet aggression by the re-emergence of the 'Pill-Box Controversy'. During the day Ironside came to see him to report on his recent visit to the BEF, and, according to Hore-Belisha's diary, 'with great emphasis told me that the officers were most upset at the criticism made about lack of defences and that everyone was talking about it. I told him I was amazed that the matter had been so widely spread. He said that Gort greatly resents it.... Instead of Ironside explaining the misunderstanding, it is clear that he has not put the matter right. He said Gort was threatening to resign.' The War Secretary tried to reassure the British C-in-C. 'The speed of the achievement is quite remarkable,' he wrote to Gort on the Second.[90] No reply came, and the misunderstanding, if misunderstanding it was, would soon be important. So too, would another event of that Saturday. The *Graf Spee* reappeared to sink a ship on the Cape-Freetown route; three thousand miles away across the Atlantic off the River Plate, Commodore Sir Henry Harwood heard of this, and believed the battleship could be heading towards his patrol area to attack the rich shipping lane. If so, she would arrive about 13 December; Harwood immediately signalled his forces to concentrate by 12 December.

The first request came from Finland for British help. Halifax told the Cabinet on 4 December that the Finnish Ambassador had called to see him the previous afternoon: Finland desperately needed at least thirty fighters. Halifax pointed out that the Soviet Union might attempt to edge round and seize the northern ports of Norway, and therefore, 'from the practical point of view, I consider it would be in our interest to try to give the Finns this measure of help. While it is to our advantage that Russia should be causing embarrassment to Germany, we must, at the same time, realize that the Russian invasion of Finland might, in time, prove very embarrassing to ourselves.' Sir Kingsley Wood objected strongly. 'The air defence of this country is becoming an increasing burden which makes it almost impossible to meet outside demands of this nature.' But Chamberlain agreed with Halifax: Wood should give further study to the request and report as soon as possible.[91] This he did by the next meeting: 'From the purely military point of view, there is no case for supplying Finland with fighters, since we have insufficient for our own needs.' But the Air Staff appreciated the wider aspects and proposed 20 Gladiators should be supplied. 'The War Cabinet must realize, however, that in making this offer we are running a certain risk ourselves.'[92]

At successive War Cabinet meetings the War Secretary continued to report 'no change on the Western Front'. Air activity against Britain continued to be small-scale; Churchill was confident the convoy system was working efficiently. Nevertheless, Britain was beginning to suffer from the war, as the Cabinet heard on 6 December. Sir John Gilmour, Minister of Shipping, reported: 'There is urgent need for removal of every avoidable cause of delay to shipping, and for every economy in our internal consumption.' The same meeting decided sugar should be rationed as from 8 January, and meat from not later than 5 February, 1940.

The Western Front remained quiet; the Russian advance in Finland was slower than expected. But Norway was again actively discussed, in London and in Berlin. Hitler was being urged to make an offensive in Norway, and the name of Major Vidkun Abraham Quisling, C.B.E., was to feature large in German plans. This ex-Norwegian Defence Minister and founder of the Norwegian Fascist Party had established contact with the Nazi Alfred Rosenberg. Immediately after the Russian attack on Finland, Admiral Raeder had begun to receive reports from his Naval Attaché at Oslo of imminent allied landings in Norway, and he mentioned these to Hitler on 8 December, advising him: 'It is important to occupy Norway.'

Next day, 9 December, the day when the first British soldier died on the Western Front, the Cabinet discussed procedure for peace settlement with Germany. Ministers agreed there should be an understanding with the French Government 'by which we and they bind ourselves not to make a separate peace'. This declaration 'might lose some of its effect if announced during the present period of inactivity,' and New Year's Day was therefore selected as a possible time for the statement to be issued.[93]

Churchill, impatient with the inactivity, began to increase pressure for a Norwegian operation. He told Ministers on 11 December that he had arranged with the American Ambassador 'to ascertain privately President Roosevelt's reactions to the suggestion we should mine Norwegian territorial waters.... the President's reactions are more favourable than I had hoped.' He also declared : 'I think it would be to our advantage if the trend of events in Scandinavia brought it about that Norway and Sweden were forced into war with Russia.... We would then be able to gain a foothold in Scandinavia with the object of helping them, but without having to go to the extent of ourselves declaring war on Russia. Such a situation would open prospects in the naval war which might prove most fruitful.' The Cabinet invited Halifax to study the implications of this.[94] On the same day, 11 December, Quisling met Raeder in Berlin. A British invasion of Norway was being planned, he claimed; and the German naval chief, enthusiastic already, was warned by Quisling of the dangers to Germany which would result from a British occupation. Raeder saw Hitler the following day; and told him Quisling 'made a reliable impression on me'. Also on 12 December, Hitler issued another directive, once more postponing the attack in the West. A further decision would not be made until 27 December, and the earliest day for the offensive would be 1 January.

Early in the morning of the 13th, Commodore Harwood's hunch proved correct. On board the cruiser *Ajax*, 400 miles off Montevideo, smoke was sighted in the east. The time was 6.15 a.m. The German pocket battleship *Graf Spee*, still believed by Harwood to be the *Scheer*, was approaching. Harwood immediately dispersed his small force in order to attack and harry the huge German warship from different directions. Langsdorf, Captain of the *Spee*, over-confident of the power of his 11-inch guns, advanced direct at the *Exeter*; salvoes from all three British vessels began to batter the *Spee*. The *Exeter* was crippled, her bridge destroyed but the small 6-inch cruisers continued their bombardment. Langsdorf put down smoke and made for the neutral sanctuary of the River Plate, but the battered *Ajax* and *Achilles* clung like determined terriers. By 7.25 a.m. the two after turrets of the *Ajax* had been shattered and Harwood had to ease the pressure. Yet the German warship was still engaged at intervals throughout the day and evening, until, shortly after midnight, she limped into the port of Montevideo. The British force lurked outside territorial waters; for the moment Langsdorf was safe, but sooner or later he would have to leave the River Plate, and the *Exeter*'s sister ship, the *Cumberland*, was steaming up at full speed. During the day Churchill had been in the Admiralty War Room, excited as a schoolboy, enthralled by the prospects of this tremendous prestige victory. Next morning, 14 December, while the German public read newspaper claims of great naval success for the Fatherland, he reported to the War Cabinet. The *Spee* was entitled to remain in a neutral port until necessary repairs could be completed to make her seaworthy, but not for action. 'The ship must be very short of ammunition, and the Naval Attaché (at Montevideo) has been warned to watch the position very closely. If the ship does not leave neutral territorial waters as soon as she is fit for sea, it is the duty of the neutral to intern the crew.'[95]

The same day, Hitler had decided preparations should be made to take war into Norway. He had seen Quisling and was suitably impressed; and in the evening he ordered Keitel to draft a plan, in consultation with the Norwegian traitor. Two alternative schemes were to be submitted, one for a *coup* engineered from within by Quisling, with only minor military assistance from Germany; the other a joint naval, land and air operation in case the political scheme should fail.[96] 'The abuse of Norwegian territorial waters,' Churchill told the Cabinet next morning, 'has now come to a head with the sinking of one Greek and two British ships inside the three-mile limit. I consider that this action on the part of the enemy makes it necessary that we should, in our own interests, claim and make use of a similar latitude without delay.' Churchill repeated his two proposals – the Barrage and the mining of Norwegian waters. He now added a third, 'which can be justified as a *quid pro quo* for the German action in sinking ships inside Norwegian territorial waters.' This scheme was to send four or five destroyers into the lonelier parts of those waters, to arrest all ships carrying ore to Germany. The ships would not be sunk, but would be taken as prizes. 'I am ready to accept the fact that such action would undoubtedly provoke a violent protest from the Norwegians, but consider that such protests can be satisfactorily disposed of by reference to diplomatic channels.' Halifax was plainly alarmed by the suggestion; he claimed the proposal was 'new to me and I would be glad of the opportunity to examine it'. Churchill was asked to circulate a memorandum.

It took the First Lord only twenty-four hours to produce this memorandum. It appeared on Saturday, 16 December, written in Churchill's usual stirring style. 'The final tribunal is our own conscience,' he declared. 'We are fighting to re-establish the reign of law and to protect the liberties of small countries. Our defeat would mean an age of barbaric violence. The letter of the law must not in supreme emergency obstruct those who are charged with its protection and enforcement.' Churchill maintained the effective stoppage of the ore supplies to Germany ranked as a major offensive. 'No other measure is open to us for many months to come which gives so good a chance of abridging the waste and destruction of conflict, or of perhaps preventing the vast slaughters which will attend the grappling of the main armies.... Humanity, rather than legality, must be our guide.'[97] Yet at the meeting, he concurred with Halifax's suggestion that a decision should await further reports. He agreed, he said, because 'after further consideration, the Naval Staff has come to the conclusion that it would be wiser to adopt the alternative plan, which is to lay a mine-field in Norwegian territorial waters, so as to force the traffic out on to the high seas.' The Deputy Chief of Staff had explained there were only four points in Norwegian waters at which ships had to show them-selves: everywhere else they were in waters in which they could not be easily obstructed by British warships.

Churchill also told the War Cabinet that the *Graf Spee* had been ordered by the Uruguayan Government to leave Montevideo at 2 a.m. GMT on 17 December – the next morning.[98] In Berlin, Goebbels instructed the German press to give plentiful space to a fake despatch from Montevideo, claiming the *Spee* had only suffered 'superficial damage'. British reports were 'pure lies'.

Chamberlain, touring the positions in France, whispered to General Montgomery: 'I don't think the Germans have any intention of attacking us, do you?'[99] At that time, he was correct. Temporarily the tide seemed against the Führer. On 16 December, Ciano delivered a two-hour anti-Communist and anti-Hitler speech, hailed in Italy as a denunciation of the Steel Pact and 'the funeral march of the Axis'.[100] And next day came the tragic and inglorious end of the *Graf Spee*. At a conference presided over by Hitler, Langsdorf had been instructed by cable to 'attempt by all means to extend the time in neutral waters ... fight your way through to Buenos Aires if possible....' Efforts to extend the time limit failed, and during the afternoon of the seven-teenth more than 700 men were transferred from the *Spee* to a German merchant ship in Montevideo harbour. Shortly afterwards the battle-ship weighed anchor; at 6.15 p.m. she steamed slowly towards the sea, awaited by British cruisers. But at 8.54 p.m. the *Ajax*'s aircraft reported: '*Graf Spee* has blown herself up.' And that night, to Hitler's rage, Langsdorf shot himself.

Nor was the situation favourable to Russia. Hore-Belisha told the Cabinet on 18 December that the Finns had achieved a considerable success north of Lake Ladoga and had severely damaged three Russian Divisions. Hoare thought this might be the decisive moment, and suggested the three Service Ministers should meet to consider further offers of help. The War Cabinet agreed.[101] The Supreme War Council, meeting in Paris the following day and attended by Chamberlain fresh from the Maginot Line, also concluded that all possible material aid should be given to the Finns. Daladier advocated breaking rela-tions with Russia, but Chamberlain preferred a more cautious line.

Returning to London on 20 December, Chamberlain told the Cabinet that in the British sector, 'the defences already constructed appeared to me extremely formidable,' but 'much work remained to be done'.[102] He saw Hore-Belisha for a few minutes after the meeting, and told him the row over the pill-boxes was still being discussed at GHQ. 'The feeling was strong,' wrote Hore-Belisha in his diary. 'They were resentful at what they regarded as my criticism of them. He had the impression, with all the gossip going about – it was just like an officers' club – that there were people who were out to make trouble, and he advised me to be careful. He added that he had appointed me Secretary of State for War, and he did not want me to be tripped up by this kind of thing.'[103]

The same day, a long meeting of the Military Coordination Committee considered four important papers on Scandinavia. The first, from the Minister of Economic Warfare, considered economic arguments for stopping iron ore exports from Sweden to Germany. 'It would be likely to cause by next spring such a substantial curtailment of German steel production as to have an extremely serious repercussion on German industrial output.... From the purely economic standpoint, in fact, her position would, in that event, be so serious as to appear to justify the risk of considerable handicaps to ourselves ... to bring it about.' A paper from Churchill stressed that every effort should be made to cut off Germany's ore supplies by the end of 1940. 'We have a right and, indeed, are bound in duty, to abrogate for a space some of the conventions of the very laws we seek to consolidate and reaffirm. Small nations must not tie our hands when we are fighting for their rights and freedom.' Commenting on this paper, the Foreign Office agreed Britain could not be expected to fight the war on the basis of allowing Germany to break all the rules while Britain kept them. Halifax would 'certainly not desire to take unnecessary objection to any course of action which could be shown to be vital to the prosecution or abbreviation of the war.' The Chiefs of Staff had prepared an appreciation of the military factors involved. Three main possibilities existed, they said: stationing a naval force in Norwegian territorial waters; laying a minefield; sabotaging railways carrying the ore – or the mines themselves. The first would probably bring a clash between the Royal Navy and the Norwegians, the second and third would also violate Norwegian neutrality. Legally, such a violation could only be justified if a prior violation by Germany had taken place – which it had. The possible German reaction had to be considered; according to the Chiefs of Staff, the Germans would be unlikely to invade southern Sweden, but an invasion of southern Norway was more feasible. 'There is little prospect that the Norwegians, whose whole army amounts to little more than one scattered Division, could offer much resistance.' The Chiefs of Staff therefore decided that the first proposal, stationing a naval force, would be technically most effective. The third idea, sabotage inside Norway, would react against Britain because it would also stop the supply of ore to Britain, while sabotage of other stretches of railway, which would not affect Britain to the same extent, would require a strong military force. If a naval force were sent to Narvik, Russia might also intervene. 'In these circumstances considerable additional commitments might have to be accepted.'[104]

These documents were put before the War Cabinet two days later, on 22 December. Very wide issues were involved: forces might have to be withdrawn from France, priorities might have to be completely re-arranged, and, as Chamberlain said, the eventual decision could mean one of the turning points of the war. Arguments were to continue in the Cabinet for almost three months. Meanwhile, on 22 December, more information was deemed necessary. The Chiefs of Staff were to consider the question of indirect assistance to Finland, and assistance to Sweden and Norway if Germany should react as a result. They were also to give further consideration to 'all the military implications of a policy aimed at stopping the export of Swedish iron ore to Germany'.[105]

Christmas intruded itself into this atmosphere of uncertainty and indecision. Cabinet members snatched a few hours of relaxation. Chamberlain went to Chequers depressed, suffering from twinges of gout and the beginnings of another, far more serious disease. 'I find war more hateful than ever, and I groan in spirit over every loss and every home blasted.'[106] Churchill had a typically contrasting attitude. 'The transition from peace to war has been accomplished,' he wrote to Pound on Christmas Day. In the German press Churchill had been dubbed *Lügenlord* – Lying Lord – or was simply referred to by his initials, letters which, as in Britain, were stamped on toilet cisterns. Germans, like the British, struggled to make Christmas festive, and the Nazi Government eased rationing restrictions for a few days: an extra quarter-pound of butter and 100 grammes of meat were allowed, plus four eggs in Christmas week instead of one. But the sleet-showered Berlin streets were as sad as London's. The Führer left for the Western Front – where, it was announced on 27 December, the offensive was again postponed, for 'at least a fortnight'.

On Boxing Day, the British War Cabinet considered the Chiefs of Staff report on Finland, Sweden and Norway. It recommended that Finnish demands for war material made so far should be met. These covered aircraft ammunition and rifles to buckles, mess tins, boot-leather, and 2,000 tons of peas. The report also said the question of sending volunteers to Finland should be examined. But the Chiefs of Staff hesitated over aid to Norway and Sweden if these countries were invaded by Germany. 'The most likely action by Germany against Norway and Sweden would be the seizure of Norwegian and Swedish shipping in the Baltic, and attacks on this shipping in the North Sea and the Atlantic, and seaborne land attacks on southern Norway and Sweden. It is possible that she may by air attack on the cities of south Scandinavia attempt to compel them to submit to her demands ... Britain would not be able to do much about this. Virtually the only measure recommended was an early declaration that an air attack on Scandinavian cities would be regarded 'in the same light as an air attack on Great Britain, and would invite a similar reaction on our part.'[107] The War Cabinet agreed to the aid to Finland, and also to inform the Swedish and Norwegian Governments, at once, that Britain and France were prepared to give such help as they could in the event of a German hostile reaction. The opinions of the Scandinavian Governments should be sought on warships in Norwegian waters stopping coastal traffic to Germany. The War Office was to proceed with preliminary plans for despatching a force to Narvik. The first tentative steps had been taken.[108]

1939 ended with no signs of a close to the Twilight War. In France, autumn rains had been followed by exceptional falls of snow and widespread ice. Frozen rivers prevented water transport, roads were impassable, soldiers huddled under waterproof capes or trudged through the slush and mud. Instead of death and destruction, allied bombers had dropped badly-written propaganda sheets. Only at sea had the war been pursued full-scale. The Admiralty now believed the U-boats could be handled: by the end of 1939, out of 5,756 ships which had sailed in convoys, only four had been sunk by submarines. Germany had only 33 U-boats left for active duty.[109] Hitler issued his New Year proclamation. 'United within the country, economically prepared and militarily armed to the highest degree, we enter this most decisive year in German history.... May the year 1940 bring the decision.' The day before, a small group of conspirators had decided on an ambitious scheme to throw the Führer from power: a number of Divisions would stop in Berlin while in transit from west to east; the SS would be dissolved; Beck would take over Supreme Command of the army; a doctor would declare Hitler incapable of office. The scheme stood no chance of success. Hitler's opponents could do nothing but get drunk – Berlin's Kurfürstendamm saw more drunkenness on 31 December 1939, than most people could ever remember.

15

A Question of Ore

Britain's Cabinet were unaware of Hitler's plans for imminent action on the Western Front. Rumours persisted but Ministers turned their attention elsewhere – to highly dangerous, illegal and strength-consuming operations in the terrible conditions of Scandinavia. Military plans for Scandinavia were discussed in two important reports completed on 31 December 1939. According to the Chiefs of Staff, widescale British military intervention should take place in Northern Scandinavia, Southern Norway and Southern Sweden. These reports were considered by the Cabinet on 2 and 3 January, together with a memorandum by Churchill.

The main Chiefs of Staff report gave the first comprehensive estimate of what operations in Scandinavia would entail; it was based on two essential assumptions: that interruption of the export of Swedish ore to Germany would be decisive, and that Swedish and Norwegian cooperation would be forthcoming. If these two conditions were met, 'our military aim will be to gain control over as great a volume of Swedish iron ore as we can and to retain that control for a sufficiently long time, to bring Germany to the point of surrender'. Naval actions alone would be insufficient. 'Once the Germans were established (in Southern Norway) it would require a major operation to dislodge them. Hence, it will be necessary to forestall them.... The role of any forces landed in Norway would be to delay, by guerilla tactics, a German land advance to capture the bases concerned, and to defeat any attempts at airborne attack.' To obtain a complete stoppage of the ore supply to Germany an expedition would have to be despatched to northern fields. And to obtain Scandinavian cooperation 'we may be called upon to send a force to support the Swedes and Norwegians against German attacks. This would involve the employment of a substantial Allied Land Force.' Such a force could be maintained from a base at Trondheim.

The Chiefs of Staff emphasized that operations in Northern Scandinavia, Southern Norway and Southern Sweden would have to be complementary and 'it is vital to the success of the project that we should be prepared to carry out all three concurrently'. The report concluded: 'It must be realized that to embark on an offensive in Scandinavia in the Spring of 1940 represents a fundamental change in our policy. Up to date that policy has been to remain on the defensive on land and in the air, while our armaments are increased. The plan under review, however, would enable us to initiate, in March, offensive operations which might well prove decisive. The opportunity is a great one and we see no prospect of an equal chance afforded us elsewhere.'[1]

Supplementary to this drastic document was a second report considering the relation of this major operation with Churchill's proposed partial stoppage through naval action. The Chiefs of Staff still believed the major operation 'might well bring German industry to a standstill, and would in any case have a profound effect on the duration of the war'. If this were the case, priority should be given to it. Since it could not be started until March, the smaller scheme might perhaps be attempted meanwhile, but they believed that such an interim measure might be unsound.[2]

'With many of the larger arguments of the Chiefs of Staff report I am in full accord,' wrote a disgruntled Churchill in a memorandum on 31 December. 'But I fear that its effect will lead to a purely negative conclusion.' He pointed out that according to the Chiefs of Staff, the 'minor operation of stopping the ore from Narvik and at Oxelosund must not be tried because it would jeopardize the larger plan. The larger plan must not be attempted unless Sweden and Norway cooperate.' But, he asked, 'is there any prospect of Sweden and Norway actively cooperating with us of their own free will to ... (a) ruin the trade of their ironfield and the shipping which carries it; (b) involve them in a war with Germany; (c) expose the whole southern part of both countries to German invasion and occupation? ... Thus, the minor operation is knocked out for the sake of the bigger, and the bigger is only declared practicable on conditions which will not occur.'[3]

The War Cabinet had therefore to decide, on 2 and 3 January, whether the economic prize of a large-scale operation was worth the risk, and whether Scandinavian cooperation could be expected. And as Newall declared, if the Chiefs of Staff recommendations were accepted, 'Scandinavia would have to be regarded, for the time being, as the decisive theatre of war. Subject to being secure at home and in France, all else would have to be relegated to second place.' On the supplementary report, Newall said operations against the Narvik traffic would be unsound for two reasons. 'We might antagonize the Norwegians, and possibly the Swedes, and thus make it most unlikely that they would cooperate with us in the larger project. Secondly, we might give the Germans a pretext for immediate demands on Norway and/or Sweden.' Chamberlain pointed out that the value of the larger operation depended on the assumption that severing the ore supply to Germany was of crucial importance to the duration of the war. He asked the Minister of Economic Warfare if he were satisfied that this was correct. Sir Frederick Leith-Ross thought a complete stoppage of Swedish iron ore would probably bring war to an end in about a year.

The Chiefs of Staff had therefore a powerful argument against the Narvik operation. But Hore-Belisha opposed them. Stoppage of the Narvik trade was, he maintained, 'a perfectly legitimate operation in retaliation for the sinking of British ships in Norwegian waters, and would be unlikely to antagonize Norway, or to provoke Germany into invading her'. Churchill agreed: 'The sequence of events would probably be as follows: Norway would make a protest at our action. A German reaction might then follow, possibly in the form of an invasion of Norway. The effect of this would be vexatious, but would in no way be decisive.... On the other hand, it would open the way to our next action, which would be the occupation of the Northern ore field. The Norwegians would undoubtedly resist a German invasion, which would be a violation incomparably greater than the violation of territorial waters of which we should be guilty.' He therefore reached a convenient conclusion: 'Thus, by interrupting the trade from Narvik we should be paving the way to the major operation.' Chamberlain was sympathetic. He too was 'very anxious' to stop the trade from Narvik, but also feared a German invasion of Southern Norway which might result. If the Chiefs of Staff could remove his fears on this point, he said, 'I would be prepared to support the proposal to take immediate steps to stop the Narvik traffic.' The Chiefs of Staff were therefore to undertake further studies.[4]

In the Cabinet discussion on Wednesday, 3 January, Chamberlain came out in stronger support of the Narvik idea; he agreed with Churchill it was in Germany's interest to keep war out of Scandinavia, and did not regard a German invasion of south Norway as likely. But the Cabinet also agreed that as Norwegian cooperation was essential for operations on a large scale in Scandinavia, soundings should be taken of the possible Norwegian reaction to a stoppage of the ore traffic. Should forces be made ready for occupying Stavanger, Bergen and Trondheim 'should this prove necessary'? Hore-Belisha was against the idea; he feared that in the long run too many troops would be swallowed up. Churchill thought troops should at least be ready for despatch to Stavanger and Bergen in the event of a German invasion. 'There is no reason why this small diversion should develop into a large commitment, unless we wished it to.'

French approval would be needed; and Halifax would tell Paris that Britain proposed to inform the Norwegian Government that:

'Having regard to the violation by German naval forces of Norwegian territorial waters, we were taking appropriate dispositions to prevent the shipment of goods down the Norwegian coast to Germany and for this purpose it would be necessary for His Majesty's Naval Force at times to enter and operate in Norwegian territorial waters.' This would only be sent if the French agreed; America was also to be informed.[5] The War Secretary was asked to prepare an assessment of forces needed to occupy Stavanger, Bergen and Trondheim. But he never completed this report. Instead, in another 48 hours he had resigned; within a week he had left the Government, unwillingly, amid cries from Press and politicians for an inquiry into the reasons for his departure.

Hore-Belisha attended the session next morning, 4 January, completely unaware that anything was amiss. During the meeting he was handed a note from the War Office: a telephone message had come from No. 10 that the Prime Minister wished to see him at 2.45. He arrived five minutes early, to find Chamberlain enjoying a cigar. 'He started by saying that what he had to say to me might be disappointing to me. He spoke of the very high opinion he had of my work and then said there was prejudice against me. Because of it he thought it was in my interest to leave the War Office now.' Hore-Belisha asked: 'Can you give me some details of the prejudice you refer to?' 'No, but it exists,' replied Chamberlain, refusing to enter into details. He offered Hore-Belisha the post of President of the Board of Trade.

'You were prepared for this interview,' said Hore-Belisha, 'I was not. I am completely taken aback and would like time to think.' Chamberlain seemed surprised there should be any need to hesitate – 'you surely do not want to go out into the wilderness.' He was against the idea of delay, he said, because the news might leak out – although he assured Hore-Belisha that the two of them were the only people who knew. It was finally agreed Hore-Belisha would give Chamberlain his answer next morning at 10 o'clock. Later in the day he received a short but pleasant communication from Chamberlain which began: 'My dear Leslie – I feel so much distress myself at the thought of the trial through which you are passing.' Hore-Belisha had found time during the afternoon to hint to Lord Beaverbrook that 'it is by no means certain that I shall be staying on at the War Office'. Beaverbrook came round to dine with him and urged that Churchill be told of the news. But he had left for France during the day in order to explain to the French High Command his scheme for laying mines in the Rhine, 'Operation Royal Marine', and another scheme for an automatic trench cutting machine, 'Cultivator'. A telephone message was sent asking him to call Hore-Belisha's number; when he eventually rang both Beaverbrook and Hore-Belisha were astonished to discover he knew the news already. Chamberlain had told him before he had left for Paris. He urged Hore-Belisha to accept the Board of Trade, but without success.

Late that night Hore-Belisha wrote a long letter to Chamberlain, declining the Board of Trade. 'It was only on 20 December last, when the controversy about the defence in France was at its height, that you assured me of your complete support and of your desire that I should remain at the War Office to see the job through.' He claimed that if he went to the Board of Trade he would have no confidence that the same reversal might not happen again; much still needed to be done at the War Office: 'If the Maginot Line policy is the correct one ... how dangerous is it to leave the Line incomplete!' Hore-Belisha added that he realized his views had been 'resented as an interference by a civilian Minister in military matters', and that this had led to the 'pressure to which you feel bound to yield'. He demanded to know more about this pressure when he saw Chamberlain at ten next morning. Chamberlain admitted it stemmed from prejudice in the Command in France, which also existed at the War Office; and he said that although this feeling had been known for some time, it was only now he had come to the conclusion 'that it would be in your best interests to change from the War Office'.

Returning to the War Office, Hore-Belisha drafted his letter of resignation, which he showed to Chamberlain after the War Cabinet meeting. 'This is very nice,' the Prime Minister commented, then asked if Hore-Belisha would mind adding a sentence to say no difference of policy existed between them; Hore-Belisha agreed. He spent the rest of the day at the War Office, attending a routine Press Conference in the late afternoon, and working until 10 p.m. By then a Press announcement had been made; next morning the newspapers, which also revealed that Oliver Stanley would succeed Hore-Belisha, Sir Andrew Duncan go to the Board of Trade, and Sir John Reith to the Ministry of Information, exploded with front-page stories on the Great Belisha Scandal. Churchill had strongly urged that Eden should be War Secretary, and Eden himself would have liked the appointment. But at least by not being chosen by Chamberlain, he was to be spared the unfortunate repercussions of the Norwegian campaign which Stanley was to suffer.

'Of course,' wrote Chamberlain on Sunday, 'the enemies of the Government will do their best to exploit the incident by representing it as a victory for brass hats who don't like the democratization of the Army. This is grossly unfair to them, and I may say that none of the Generals have ever taken the initiative in complaining to me or asked directly or indirectly that he should be moved.' The Prime Minister added: 'The friction is due to personal incompatibility and not policy or administration.' The difficulties in December had been smoothed out but, Chamberlain believed, they would be likely to break out again. Hore-Belisha had done more for the Army than anyone since Haldane but, 'unfortunately, he has the defects of his qualities – partly from his impatience and eagerness, partly from a self-centredness which makes him careless of other people's feelings'. So Hore-Belisha, who had hung on to his Cabinet seat despite differences with Chamberlain towards the end of the appeasement period, had to go because of 'personal incompatibility'. And Chamberlain made it clear that this clash of personalities arose between Hore-Belisha and Gort. 'Nothing could be worse than perpetual friction between the Secretary of State and the Commander-in-Chief in the Field.' Of the two men Gort must stay and Hore-Belisha had to depart, despite the fact that Gort himself, as Chamberlain stressed, had never hinted such a drastic step should be taken. In fact the basic troubles lay deeper: Hore-Belisha had 'interfered' and had been doing so since he became War Secretary; many of the older officers had been affronted and passed over; it had been they, rather than Gort, who had exerted the pressure – war had given them the opportunity and they took advantage of Chamberlain's belief that his colleague was more dispensable than the officers in the field.[6] Hore-Belisha was by no means blameless. If, as he had stated to Eden, he had chosen Lord Gort 'to popularize the Army and help recruiting', then his list of priorities at that time – the first days of war – was sadly out of order. 'Though Hore-Belisha had some good qualities as a War Minister,' wrote Eden, 'and showed courage in enforcing National Service, attention to detail, however important, was not one of them. It was a weakness of his that being publicity conscious he was too eager about appearances and too indifferent about what lay behind them.'[7]

Demands for an early recall of Parliament were refused by Chamberlain and Hore-Belisha would not make his resignation speech until 16 January. Meanwhile, on Saturday, 6 January, Scandinavia again monopolized Cabinet discussion. Halifax reported a conversation with the French Ambassador: 'M. Corbin informed me that the French Government were in complete agreement with the general lines of the Note which we propose to address to the Norwegian Government.... They think, however, that it would be preferable to base our argument in support of the action we propose to take on general grounds, rather than to justify it as a specific reprisal.' Halifax agreed and had redrafted this paragraph: 'By these hostile acts German naval forces have turned Norwegian waters into a theatre of war, and have in practice deprived them of the enjoyment of neutrality.'[8] The Norwegian Ambassador, Herr Colban, was asked to the Foreign Office after the Cabinet meeting. 'I gave him the *aide-memoire*,' Halifax later reported, 'he remained silent for a time and then, speaking with some emotion and evidently choosing his words with care, he said that this communication had come as a complete surprise to him and that, being without detailed information on the subject, he could not say whether the facts of the German action were as stated.' But even if the British allegations were true, 'his first personal reaction was that there was no logical ground for maintaining that three unfortunate occurrences had deprived Norwegian waters of their neutral character. ... In consequence he found it necessary at once to enter a strong and formal protest against the idea of any foreign naval forces operating in Norwegian waters.' He had also warned that the Germans 'would not remain passive' if British warships stopped and searched vessels. 'Norway might be involved in the war as a result.'

Immediately after this interview, Halifax had seen Herr Prytz, the Swedish Ambassador and had shown him the same document. 'Speaking unofficially,' Prytz had commented, 'he could say that he had expected His Majesty's Government to take this step, and had so informed the Swedish Government.' He had added: 'He did not think it would produce much reaction in Sweden, since Swedish interests were not directly involved except in the case of shipments of iron ore.' But next day, 7 January, a telegram had been received from the British Chargé at Stockholm, Mr Pollock. He had been summoned late the previous evening by the Secretary-General of the Swedish Foreign Office, whom he had found 'clearly angry'. The consequence of this step would probably be the German occupation of Denmark and possibly the end of the independent existence of all the Scandinavian countries and the Swede had added: 'I should have thought that the British Government had the fate of a sufficient number of small states on their conscience as it was.'[9]

On Wednesday, 10 January, Hitler gave definite orders for the attack on the West to begin on 17 January, 'fifteen minutes before sunrise'. The Luftwaffe would start the softening-up process three days before by attacking enemy airfields in France – not in Belgium and Holland. The weather in the West had recently been more settled, although still very cold; the Führer hoped it would remain clear long enough for the massive attack to gain momentum. But only a few hours later came the dramatic incident of the captured plans: a German aircraft, flying from Münster to Cologne, became lost in clouds over Belgium and was forced to land. One of the two passengers was Major Helmut Reinberger, who carried plans of the attack in the West in his briefcase, including orders for the 22nd Airborne Divisions for an air attack across the Meuse. He hurriedly attempted to burn the documents, but was stopped from completing the destruction by the arrival of Belgian soldiers. He tried again at the nearby military quarters and later told the German Embassy at Brussels that too little remained to reveal any information. This message was passed to Berlin. But enough remained undestroyed for the Belgians to learn the fate in store for them. And yet even now, they still refused to cooperate in

289

making joint preparations with the Allies. When the news of the mishap to the documents reached Berlin, panic struck the military planners, despite Reinberger's insistence that the evidence had been burnt. 'If the enemy is in possession of the files,' wrote Jodl, 'the situation is catastrophic.' But in London and Paris the scare died down when no invasion took place; it was assumed the documents had been faked. Halifax was to say at the War Cabinet meeting on 2 February: 'The whole incident of the alleged capture of these documents is, in my opinion, extremely suspicious and I doubt very much whether the documents are genuine.'[10]

Despite recurring alarms on the Western Front, the Cabinet continued preoccupied with Scandinavia. On 10 January, as Reinberger made his forced landing in Belgium, Halifax reported to Ministers a conversation between Mr Charles Hambro of the Ministry of Economic Warfare and the Swedish Ambassador.[11] The discussion confirmed the intense reaction to the British proposal by the Swedish Government. Three courses were open, Halifax told the Cabinet: to do nothing; to continue as planned; or, as a compromise solution, 'to use the threat of naval intervention as a lever to press the Scandinavian countries to concede what we want'. Halifax favoured the third suggestion, which received support from other Ministers. Churchill thought it had much to commend it, but stressed the need for urgent action: 'Every week the prize is melting. Time will be consumed in the proposed negotiations and, if we failed, we should be back again just where we started.' Lord Chatfield believed the idea should be tried and he suggested that in return for Swedish cooperation, Britain should point out an Allied force might possibly be deployed to protect the northern ore fields against a Russian invasion. M. Wallenberg, head of the Swedish Trade Delegation, was scheduled to arrive in London for talks next day. The War Cabinet therefore agreed to defer a decision until discussions had been held with him.[12]

The Swedes were frightened of a harsh German reaction, Wallenberg told Halifax, and in a roundabout way, if Britain carried out her plan the Finns might suffer. This idea, apparently overlooked by the War Cabinet, immediately captured Halifax's interest and sympathy. The Swedes, said Wallenberg, had given and were giving a great deal of material help to Finland, in some cases up to 20 or 30 per cent of all Swedish equipment. 'From the point of view both of Sweden herself and of Finland, it is vital that Sweden's rearmament should not be interrupted. At the present time, Germany is replacing the arms which Sweden is supplying to Finland.' Wallenberg continued: 'If the rearmament of Sweden by Germany is made impossible by outside action, Sweden's ability to help Finland might be gravely affected, if not destroyed, and public opinion in Sweden will feel that Sweden had been stabbed in the back in their struggle against Russia.' This argument placed the Cabinet in an extremely awkward position. The enemy, Germany, was helping to arm a friend, Finland, against Britain's other potential enemy and Germany's supposed ally, the Soviet Union. And in putting forward this argument Wallenberg had unwittingly beaten Britain at her own blackmail game. 'My conversation with M. Wallenberg,' Halifax told the Cabinet next day, 12 January, 'has definitely weighed the balance of my judgement against the Narvik project.' Moreover, the Scandinavian reaction clearly indicated that the larger project for a complete stoppage of the ore supply would be seriously endangered. The War Cabinet therefore decided no action should be taken for the time being. Conversely it was also very plain that if Scandinavian cooperation was completely lacking for the Narvik operation, hopes for consent to the larger project were also unlikely to be fulfilled, and the Cabinet therefore invited the Chiefs of Staff to consider the possibility of capturing the Galivare orefields 'in the face of Norwegian and Swedish opposition'. Lord Chatfield had also pursued the idea for support for Finland and the Cabinet considered his memorandum on the methods by which assistance could be given short of direct military intervention.[13] The despatch of even a small number of volunteers to Finland would have a good moral effect.[14]

On 13 January Göring saw the Military Attaché from Brussels, who had been rushed back to Berlin to discuss the question of the captured German plans; and although they concluded that the documents had indeed been destroyed, orders were sent out to halt the attack in the West, scheduled to begin in four days' time. The risk from the captured plans was too great, and the weather had deteriorated as well. No more dates would be set for the start of the offensive for another four months. 'Operation Yellow' was placed on the shelf; instead, before many days had passed another plan, 'Weser Exercise', would be taken out and spread on the operations table: it dealt with a German advance into Norway and Denmark.

Yet because of the captured plans Brussels was in a state of panic; allied troops were alerted; alarming reports continued to reach London.[15] The Belgian Government was convinced of an imminent German attack, and Chatfield told Ministers on 14 January: 'the Belgians now looked to us and the French for support.' He had spoken on the telephone to Chamberlain – who was spending the day at Chequers – and a telegram was to be sent to the British Ambassador at Brussels, stressing the importance of starting staff conversations as soon as possible. Churchill reported that Sir Roger Keyes, MP and Admiral of the Fleet, had just had an interview with King Leopold in Brussels and had telephoned a message. The King had asked whether the British Government would agree to a number of conditions before Belgium consented to collaborate. The first specified there should be 'no opening of negotiations for peace without participation by Belgium'; the second, that guarantees should be given for the complete restoration of Belgian political and territorial status, and that of her colonies; the third, that help should be given for economic and financial restoration of the country. Keyes believed that if these conditions were met, the King could be persuaded to invite French and British troops into Belgium immediately. Chamberlain had told Churchill over the telephone that he 'strongly disliked the suggestion that the Belgians should, at this late hour, attach conditions to receiving help from us'. Apparently the Belgians feared the French would retain part of the country at the end of the war.

The Cabinet agreed Sir Roger should tell the King that no reply could be given yet. The French would be consulted; the CIGS would enquire from Gamelin how much notice the allied armies would need before starting their forward move through Belgium; and the Cabinet would assemble again later in the afternoon.[16] Meanwhile, alarm escalated among the Germans. During the day the German Ambassador at Brussels sent a 'most urgent' despatch to Berlin, warning that the Belgians were ordering 'Phase D' in their mobilization procedure, which, he pointed out, meant only one step from going to war.

Cadogan called at the French Embassy in London and told Corbin of the Belgian King's message. Corbin immediately contacted Paris, then confirmed his Government's agreement. Ironside was unable to speak to Gamelin, but had been told by Gort that Allied troops were standing at a four hour notice to move. The forward motorized troops could reach the Namur-Antwerp line in about six hours. So, when the War Cabinet met again at 6.30, with Chamberlain now in the Chair, it was agreed the stiff conditions laid down by King Leopold should be accepted. A message was sent to Keyes.[17] The Cabinet assumed his message from the King – that allied troops would be able to enter Belgium 'immediately' if the conditions were met – meant exactly what he had said: once the conditions had been agreed the invitation would be issued and the Anglo-French forces would start to move. At last it appeared the doubts and confusion over Belgian cooperation had been finished for good.

But next day, 15 January, this expectation proved false. By 'immediately' the King meant 'immediately the Germans invaded'. The Cabinet was told at 3 p.m. that the King had expressed great reluctance to hold staff conversations, and had said all details of Belgian military preparations – which the Allies urgently required in order to work out their plans for advance into Belgium – would be placed in sealed envelopes and given to the British and French Military Attachés in Brussels, with instructions not to open them until hostilities had started.[18] Plans for collaboration were therefore no further forward, and the ebbing of alarms in Brussels meant less hope the Belgians would be frightened into agreement. At the War Cabinet meeting, Stanley complained: 'It will take between 24 to 48 hours for the troops to get back into positions occupied before the emergency move.' Units had been put to considerable hardship. Churchill growled his irritation and wrote to a colleague afterwards to explain remarks he had made. 'My disquiet was due mainly to the awful difficulties which our machinery of war-conduct presents to positive action. I see such immense walls of prevention, all built and building, that I wonder whether any plan will have a chance of climbing over them.' His scheme for the Narvik operation had run into opposition from all quarters, he continued, despondent: 'I have two or three projects moving forward, but all, I fear, will succumb before the tremendous array of negative arguments and forces. Pardon me, therefore, if I showed distress.'[19] Nor was Churchill's mood lightened by a decision he made during the day to abandon plans for 'Catherine' – his idea for forcing a passage into the Baltic with specially built warships.[20] Ironside saw Churchill from a slightly different angle: 'the difference between Chamberlain and Churchill during this little crisis is most marked', he wrote next day. 'Churchill, fully seized with the military value of going to Belgium, is enthusiastic and full of energy. Chamberlain negative and angry at Belgium making conditions.'[21]

The Cabinet decided on the seventeenth against the idea of a mission to Norway and Sweden, to explain British views of the Narvik ore traffic,[22] but Halifax saw the respective Ambassadors in London and, on the nineteenth, told his colleagues the Swedish Ambassador had 'expressed himself personally in complete agreement with the argument put to him, and would telegraph for permission to pay a visit to Stockholm in order to put his view before his Government.... The Norwegian Ambassador did not react too badly to the suggestion that the Norwegian Government should themselves lay a minefield in their territorial waters. But I do not delude myself into believing that the Norwegian Government are likely to accept this suggestion.' The French, it appeared, were 'much concerned that we have done nothing to stop the Narvik traffic'.[23]

Ministers had before them that day two Chiefs of Staff reports on Norway and Sweden. The first, on preparations for operations in Northern and Southern Sweden, assuming *with* Swedish consent, had been requested on 10 January. Since then, hopes of cooperation had faded quickly; so on 12 January the second study had been prepared, considering capture of the Northern ore fields in the face of Scandinavian opposition. Very great difficulties would apparently have to be faced. First, Narvik would have to be captured; 'the real difficulties however would only begin when the force commenced its advance from Narvik. To reach Galivare, the expedition would have to undertake a 150-mile advance over some of the most difficult country in Europe.' Establish-

293

ing lines of communication would be almost impossible. 'If German troops and aircraft reinforced the Scandinavian forces opposing us, as they well might in the circumstances, we have no hesitation in saying that we should be courting complete failure.'[24] The report reinforced Churchill's belief in limited action against the ore supply route in Norwegian territorial waters. Nevertheless, the Cabinet approved the reports in principle and ordered further preparations.[25]

In fact there was little time. Just before Christmas a special German agent had been sent to Norway to prepare, with Quisling, for German seizure of Norwegian bases; initial plans were titled 'Study North'. Now, on 27 January, Hitler ordered Keitel to issue a top-secret directive: Further work on 'Study North', retitled 'Weser Exercise', would be continued under the Führer's 'personal and immediate supervision'. Keitel was placed in charge of all preparations.[26] 'Come then: let us to the task,' exhorted Churchill in a speech at Manchester on the twenty-seventh, 'to the battle, to the toil – each to our post, each to our station. Fill the armies, rule the air, pour out the munitions, strangle the U-boats, sweep the mines, plough the land.... There is not a week, nor a day, nor an hour to lose.'

While both British and German attention turned increasingly to Scandinavia, the Western Front remained quiet. Defences continued to be improved along the Franco-Belgian border; on the Franco-German border French loudspeakers blared out recordings of Hitler's old speeches, in which the Führer had denounced Bolshevism and Stalin before the German-Soviet Pact, and German soldiers tried to shoot the loudspeakers into silence. Sales of pocket editions of 'Mein Kampf', especially printed for troops at the front, reached 5,950,000. General Alan Brooke continued pessimistic: he wrote on 30 January: 'Instead of attacking this spring, we are far more likely to be hanging on by our eyelids in trying to check the German attacks.[27] Yet Gamelin, now convinced the Germans would not even attempt an attack in the West in 1940, had come up with a scheme, to London's astonishment, for active Allied operations in Finland, against the Russian Red Army. At the Cabinet meeting of 29 January, Halifax was so surprised he had to admit he was 'uncertain as to the meaning'. The Chiefs of Staff were perturbed enough to go to Paris to find out. Chamberlain told the Cabinet: 'Events seem to be leading the Allies towards open hostilities with Russia,' and yet: 'It might well be that Allied assistance to Finland might well be the only way of getting a footing in Scandinavia.'[28]

On 31 January, Gamelin outlined his plan for the Chiefs of Staff, and additional details were provided by Admiral Darlan and General Vuilemin. The British military chiefs disagreed with a number of points in the plan and, returning on 2 February, told the War Cabinet 'it appeared to us that certain features of the French project lacked precision'. The main features of the project included landing at the Arctic port of Petsamo (now in Russian hands – it would be taken in a joint operation with the Finnish forces) and despatching to Finland through neutral countries between 30,000 to 40,000 Allied volunteers. The Chiefs of Staff insisted Narvik was a far better choice of entry point: to land at Petsamo a base would still be needed in Norway, whose neutrality would still be infringed. Another difference had emerged over the expected reaction from Norway and Sweden; according to the French, 'Norwegian and Swedish opinion is not yet ripe for direct intervention through their countries. Allied intervention in Finland would, however, stiffen and encourage them, and might ultimately secure their cooperation.' But 'the British Foreign Office predicts precisely the opposite effect. It is thought the more successful our action in aid of the Finns, the more will Norway and Sweden retire into their shell of neutrality.'[29] General Ironside commented: 'General Gamelin is now no longer convinced that the Germans will attack in the West this year and believes that if we could force the Germans to undertake operations in Scandinavia, these would involve a large diversion of German effort.'

The Cabinet thought the French plan 'not ... well thought out'. Everything depended on the sending of a large force into Finland through Norway and Sweden yet, 'if this were possible it would be unnecessary to go to Petsamo at all'. Besides, occupation of Northern Finland might have a local success, but would have no effect on the outcome of the Russian invasion; because the project was by no means certain of stimulating Scandinavian countries into action, 'we should accept all the disadvantages of war with Russia, without ... securing a valuable prize, such as we should get if we occupied Galivare'. Hoare suggested: 'We should make Norway and Sweden face the realities of the situation and urge on them that Finland, if unaided, is almost certain to collapse in May. We should tell Norway and Sweden that we are ready to intervene effectively to save her, provided that we have [their] cooperation.... If these countries then refused ... the onus of Finland's betrayal would rest upon them.' The Cabinet finally agreed 'it was of the utmost importance to prevent Finland being overrun by Russia in the Spring and that this could only be done by considerable forces of trained men entering Finland from, or via, Norway and Sweden.'[30] But at the 3 February Cabinet meeting the Prime Minister read a report by the Military Attaché at Stockholm which gave a clear warning of the dangers in a Scandinavian involvement. The Attaché had been told by his Roumanian colleague, who had recently served at Berlin, that 'Germany's Number One war-aim is the overthrow of the British Empire, and they hope to achieve this by actually defeating Great Britain whilst remaining upon the defensive against France. Scandinavia is to be used as the stalking horse.'[31]

Yet intervention in Scandinavia was still viewed with enthusiasm. The 2 February report still stood: 'The stakes are high, but the prize of success is great. We therefore consider that, if an opportunity to occupy the Galivare ore fields should be presented, or could be created, we should seize it with both hands.'[32]

So, armed with this plea for intervention in Sweden, Chamberlain travelled to Paris for the Supreme War Council meeting on 5 February. Also armed with the British view that the French proposal for the Petsamo project was unrealistic and ill-prepared, he put forward a new scheme: an operation to help the Finns, but also to secure Galivare. This expedition 'ostensibly and nominally designed for the assistance of Finland, would kill two birds with one stone'. Daladier agreed with the idea and the War Council decided the force would be provided from Allied units, disguised as 'volunteers' after the example of the Italian 'non-intervention' in Spain. This would be mainly British and the French agreed in principle the BEF might have to be reduced; the 44th and 42nd Divisions should not therefore proceed to France as planned. Norwegian and Swedish cooperation was still essential; so as soon as the expedition was ready the Finns should appeal publicly for help – to Norway and Sweden, who could then hardly refuse to allow the Allied force through their territory. Daladier, not quite so certain on this, insisted that if neutral opposition prevented the seizure of the Swedish ore field, the French proposal for an operation through Petsamo should be reconsidered.[33]

The ambitious Scandinavian undertaking had a number of serious drawbacks, some already stressed by the Chiefs of Staff. Norwegian and Swedish cooperation was by no means certain, despite Chamberlain's optimism. The danger of Soviet hostility was apparently minimized. Administrative difficulties were considerable, both in deploying the Allied force in Finland and in the operations in Sweden and Norway. The terrain would make communication links vulnerable, and supply transportation slow and difficult. The principal base port would be Trondheim, yet from this centre only a single line railway ran east and this, in addition to moving supplies, might have to carry imports to Sweden should Germany blockade the Baltic ports; and Trondheim, Newall warned, was within range of 1,300 German heavy bombers. Above all, resources perhaps urgently needed elsewhere would be dispersed. Because of activity dwindling in the West, and no fresh reports of German troop movements, an almost desperate belief had grown that Allied operations should be started somewhere else. 'The Finnish wild-goose chase,' thought Brooke, would 'provide better chances than ever for our losing the war'. Planning went ahead at the War Office, though the Finns asked on 10 February for an urgent supply of weapons, especially fighter aircraft and heavy anti-aircraft artillery, rather than men.[34]

Nor, despite the possibility of a large new commitment, could the Cabinet hope to mobilize faster than at present. Indeed, at the end of the first week in February, Lord Stamp, Simon's adviser, told Ministers that even the existing programme should be scaled down or spread over a longer period. Unless economies were made, the country would be in serious financial difficulties. 'If the view of the memorandum is accepted,' wrote Churchill, 'we must now definitely curtail our war objective in men and material, and the impression will be spread in all quarters, including French quarters, that we are definitely recoiling from the task we set ourselves.' Yet the day Churchill wrote these comments, the Cabinet approved the idea of the Scandinavian operation – which would involve over 100,000 men. Churchill for one refused to be deterred by Stamp's warning; in his memorandum, written as if it were one of his celebrated war speeches, he declared: 'We aim only at 55 Divisions by the twenty-fourth month. Now it is argued that even this is too much for us. So far from accepting any diminution of objective, we ought to hurl ourselves into the task with a new surge of impulse and face all the sacrifices, hardships and exertions which this entails.'[35] And despite the warning from Stamp and the increasing problem of finding sufficient equipment, on 13 February the War Cabinet decided 55 Divisions should remain the objective.

Suddenly the whole issue of Norwegian neutrality was brought into sharp focus. *Altmark*, an auxiliary vessel for the pocket-battleship *Graf Spee*, had been known to be sailing homewards from South America. On board were believed to be nearly 300 British merchant seamen, captured by German warships. For nearly two months the *Altmark* had been hiding in the South Atlantic; now she had been sighted steaming for Germany and she was sailing in Norwegian territorial waters. On Thursday, 15 February, the official War Diary of the German Naval Staff stated: 'Supply ship *Altmark* proceeding southwards through Norwegian territorial waters. Ship has been located by the enemy. According to our radio monitoring, the British Admiralty warns Naval Commands, particularly the cruiser *Glasgow* and the submarines *Seal, Triad* and *Orzil*, that according to a report from Tromso, a large German tanker of some 10,000 tons, painted black, passed off Tromso at 12.15 hours on 12 February.'[36] A British aircraft confirmed the identification and location of the *Altmark* – according to Churchill's memoirs, this confirmation was made as early as 14 February, but at the Cabinet meeting on Saturday, 17 February, he reported she had been identified the previous afternoon. In a minute to Admiral Pound, on 16 February, Churchill ordered cruisers and destroyers to sweep northward to the coast of Norway, 'not hesitating to arrest *Altmark* in territorial waters should she be found. This ship is violating neutrality in carrying British prisoners of war to Germany.

... The *Altmark* must be regarded as an invaluable trophy.' The orders were passed to a destroyer flotilla in the area, under the command of Captain Philip Vian, of *HMS Cossack*. The subsequent events were described in Churchill's report to the Cabinet the following morning. A destroyer from the flotilla, *HMS Intrepid*, had located the *Altmark*, which had fled to find refuge in the Josing Fiord. 'This fiord being a cul-de-sac the *Intrepid* took station off the entrance with two Norwegian torpedo boats between her and the *Altmark*.' At 4 p.m. Captain Vian had reported he was in Josing Fiord with the *Altmark*, and had demanded the release of the British prisoners; the two Norwegian torpedo boats were still standing by. After receiving this report Churchill immediately consulted Halifax, who 'gave his concurrence within five minutes' and the following signal was sent: 'Unless Norwegian torpedo boats undertake to convoy *Altmark* to Bergen with a joint Anglo-Norwegian guard on board and a joint escort, you should board *Altmark*, liberate the prisoners, and take possession of the ship pending further instructions. If Norwegian torpedo boat interferes, you should warn her to stand off. If she fires upon you, you should not reply unless attack is serious, in which case you should defend yourself, using no more force than is necessary and ceasing fire when she desists. Suggest to Norwegian destroyer [sic] that honour is served by submitting to superior force.'

This signal crossed with a despatch from *HMS Cossack*, which said the Norwegian torpedo boat, *Kjell*, had told Vian that *Altmark* had been examined in Bergen on 15 February, 'whence she had been authorized to proceed South through Territorial Waters. The captain of the *Kjell* had further said that *Altmark* was unarmed and that nothing was known of the prisoners.' The *Cossack* had withdrawn to await further instructions, and the Admiralty had signalled that the German vessel be boarded; if no prisoners were found the Captain and officers were to be brought off for questioning in order to discover where the prisoners were; if prisoners were found, the ship should be taken as a prize. But before this signal could reach Vian, he had acted on the previous instructions. *Altmark* had been boarded and between 300 and 400 prisoners had been released. *HMS Cossack* was now on her way home. Halifax told the Cabinet: 'It is likely that the Norwegian Minister will come to see me this afternoon. If the Ambassador makes a protest I will take the line that it is we and not the Norwegians who have strong grounds for complaint.' The War Cabinet agreed 'the case should prove a powerful lever for obtaining Norwegian assent to the laying of a minefield in Norwegian territorial waters'.[37] For Hitler, the *Altmark* incident had exactly the opposite effect. The Führer was now convinced the Norwegians would not seriously oppose a British display of force in their own territorial waters. As the German Naval War Diary stated on 16 February: 'Our

298

previous assumption of the complete safety of the Norwegian territorial waters cannot be supported any longer.'[38] So, while Britain would try to make use of the incident to secure greater Norwegian cooperation, Hitler would speed up his plans to forestall allied action in Scandinavia.[39]

Meanwhile, regardless of the lack of progress to gain Scandinavian consent for the operation to help Finland, preparations continued on the assumption that it would be forthcoming. On 18 February the War Cabinet considered a Chiefs of Staff/Foreign Office report on the time factor involved with this project. From the military point of view 'the earliest date on which we can land a force in Norway is 20 March. To enable this to be done store ships would have to sail on 12 March, and personnel ships on 15 March. . . . On the other hand, in order to make sure of getting established at Galivare and Lulea before the earliest known date on which the latter would be ice-free, we must commence landing in Norway on 3 April at the latest. The force intended for Stavanger, Bergen and Trondheim, known as Force Stratford, could start earlier, by 28 February. Sir Orme Sargent gave the diplomatic assessment. As soon as possible Field-Marshal Mannerheim, the Finnish C-in-C, should be informed of the project; on 5 March the Finns should issue their appeal; between 5 and 12 March negotiations with Norway and Sweden should take place, allowing for the departure of the first ships on 12 March.[40]

Yet the Swedes had already made their position plain; and, as expected, the Norwegian Ambassador communicated on 17 February his Government's condemnation of the 'gross violation of Norwegian territorial waters'. Britain replied with a protest of her own on the same day. '. . . So far as the facts were at present known to HMG it appeared to them that the Norwegian Government had failed in their duties as neutrals.' Churchill urged Britain should take more advantage of the situation. 'It has been very painful to watch during the last two months the endless procession of German ore ships down the Norwegian territorial waters, carrying to Germany the materials out of which will be made the shells to kill our young men in 1941.' Britain had already been accused, even justly, according to Churchill, of 'the most flagrant breach of neutrality of a technical character which could be imagined. . . . The plunge has been taken . . . why then should we stop here? . . . Strike while the iron is hot.' On 18 February the War Cabinet concluded that a decision on Churchill's renewed proposal for Norwegian waters to be mined should be deferred for further consideration, but Churchill raised the matter again next day, stressing his anxiety to begin preparations. And this time the Cabinet agreed the opportunity created by the *Altmark* affair should not be ignored, and he was therefore authorized to undertake the preliminary work for laying mines.[41] Late the same day instructions were sent to the British Embassy at Helsinki that Mannerheim should now be informed of the Anglo-French plan.[42]

But the same day, General Jodl, Chief of the German Operation Staff, noted in his diary that Hitler had 'pressed energetically for the completion of "Weser Exercise"'. Jodl had been ordered: 'Equip ships. Put units in readiness.'[43] Two days later General Niklaus von Falkenhorst, who had taken part in the German campaign in Finland in 1918, was appointed commander of the planned German expedition to occupy Norway.

Meanwhile, the French wanted use made of the *Altmark* opportunity which even Churchill would not have countenanced. Halifax told the War Cabinet on 22 February, that he had just received an important communication from Paris which proposed that Britain should seize Stavanger, Bergen and Trondheim, on the strength of the incident. Churchill strongly disagreed. 'Even the firing of a few shots between the British and Norwegian forces would be a most unfortunate affair.' Laying mines carried with it no such risk. Lord Halifax drew attention to an important telegram from Helsinki, in which it appeared that the Finnish President was appealing for British and French help – and an appeal from the Finns was to have been the signal to send in allied forces. The message came in a telegram from the British Ambassador, Mr Snow, giving an account of his farewell audience with President Kallio. Present had been the Finnish Foreign Minister, who had confirmed the Swedish refusal to allow troops to cross Sweden *en masse*, and who told Snow that 'the Finnish Government had informed the Swedish Government in consequence that they now had no alternative but to appeal to the Allies for help.... The Finnish President said that he wished to request that HMG and the French Government would at once inform the Soviet Government that if the latter would not respond to the Finnish Government's known desire to bring hostilities to an end, it would have an unfavourable effect on the future course of relations between the Allied Governments and the Soviet Union.' The President had added that this step offered the only chance of immediate help to Finland; munitions and men would take longer. 'The message might be the Finnish Government's supreme appeal to the United Kingdom and France.' Full discussion would have to wait while Halifax studied the telegram. But without Swedish support 'the prospects of an Anglo-French military operation in aid of Finland, in the form originally contemplated, must now be considered as extremely dubious.' The Cabinet agreed that 'the language which it is suggested the British and French Governments should hold to Russia amounted almost to a declaration of war'.[44]

Ironically, this same day, unofficial talks were taking place between R. A. Butler and Maisky on the possibility of Britain helping Finland

and Russia to start negotiations. Maisky had been told that Russia wanted peace as soon as possible and Britain should be invited to take part in the arrangement of talks. The invitation was turned down, wrote Maisky, because 'the Chamberlain Government did not wish to commit itself in any way and preferred to keep its hands free to be able, if necessary, to attack Russia'.[45]

Mine-laying was discussed again next day, 23 February, and Halifax was hesitating. 'We could not make much of a case for our proposed action on purely legal grounds,' he told the Cabinet, 'since we have not sufficient proof of Germany's transgressions in Norwegian waters.' However, 'we could make a broad case, on grounds of rough justice, for taking the gloves off and dealing with Norway in a rather high-handed manner'. But a number of drawbacks had to be taken into account: the effect on neutral public opinion, the possibility of German reaction and the probability that the Swedes would no longer feel bound by their 'gentleman's agreement' to reduce the export of iron-ore through the Baltic ports. Churchill agreed 'no one could make an accurate balance beforehand of all the possible consequences. It might be more a question of following an instinct,' but therefore pleaded for immediate action. 'Such action would be more than a naval foray. It might well prove to be one of the main fulcra on which the whole course of the war would turn.' 'Although my instincts are in favour of taking action,' said Chamberlain, 'I cannot take the proposed step lightheartedly. We entered the war on moral grounds and we must be careful not to undermine our position.' The Cabinet agreed that more discussions should be held, including consultations with the Dominions and with the Parliamentary Opposition.[46]

But discussions over Norwegian territorial waters, over Finland, over the Swedish ore-fields, took for granted a continued stagnation of the Western Front. Stanley reminded the Cabinet on 22 February: 'Our present plans for assistance to Finland are ... delaying very considerably the stage at which the BEF could play any considerable part on the Western Front.... It might even be necessary for a time to suspend entirely the flow of equipment and ammunition to the BEF.'[47] 'All indications show that the War Office now look upon this front as one of stalemate,' wrote Brooke in his diary on 25 February. 'They may well have a rude awakening.' A few days before, Brooke had spoken to the War Secretary in France, and had warned him how dangerous was any idea of taking equipment from the BEF for use in other theatres, and he had added that war in the West was a certainty some time in 1940. He despaired over the lack of equipment – especially tanks.[48]

Uncertainty even existed over which French officer the British Commander of the BEF, Lord Gort, should answer to. 'It has recently come to light,' declared a Chiefs of Staff report on 23 February, 'that there is some misunderstanding as to whether the BEF in France is under the command of General Georges (Commander of *"Front Nord Est"*) or directly under the command of General Gamelin (C-in-C, *Forces Terrestres*).' The War Office had always understood the BEF had been placed under General Georges by General Gamelin; Gort had held the same opinion, the report continued. 'One or two matters have recently occurred which throw doubt upon the situation.' Ironside asked Gamelin for clarification on 17 February; Gamelin, in a reply the next day, said: 'I have always considered the BE Corps in France as being directly under my orders.... It has never been in my mind to put the BE Corps under the orders of a Commander of an Army Group. It was merely understood, in order to simplify matters, that General Gort could in all matters of routine service deal directly with General Georges.' The reply therefore revealed a different situation from that understood by Gort and the War Office; the CIGS asked Gamelin to make this decision formal. 'You will appreciate,' he wrote, 'that I am most anxious that there should be no ambiguity as to the Commander from whom the C-in-C, BEF, receives his orders.'

By 27 February, the situation was even more unsatisfactory. 'It is clear,' Stanley told the Cabinet, 'that we were mistaken in thinking that General Gamelin had delegated his command of the BEF to General Georges. General Gamelin clearly wished to treat Lord Gort as the equal of General Georges. This situation is most unfortunate.' Relations between Gort and Georges had been 'most happy', and Gort wanted to avoid any change. 'The position is, indeed, worse than unfortunate and might become extremely dangerous. The CIGS and Lord Gort both agree that there is a serious risk if the BEF is in an indeterminate position with regard to the Command of the French armies on either side of it, more particularly when our Army is comparatively small.' Stanley and Ironside believed the best step would be for Gamelin to be 'induced to revert to the arrangement which has hitherto existed'. Chamberlain thought 'the root of the trouble' lay in a recent deterioration in the relationship between Gamelin and Georges.[49]

And while the British Chiefs of Staff were trying to find out who commanded the army in France, Hitler had changed his mind over the plan his forces would use in 'Case Yellow' – the offensive in the West. Previously the strategy had been for the main German assault to be launched through Belgium and northern France, aimed at the Channel ports in order to separate the French and British armies and to secure air and naval bases, from which he could threaten Britain. Anticipating that the German right flank, striking through Belgium, would be the main enemy drive, Gamelin had formulated his Plan D to advance into Belgium and block this thrust. Now, however, the original 'Case Yellow' scheme had been abandoned by the Führer.

General von Manstein, Chief of Staff of Rundstedt's Army Group A, had conceived the idea of a sharp thrust in the centre. A massive German armoured force would shatter the French defensive lines, cross the Meuse just north of Sedan and then race to the Channel at Abbéville. Meanwhile, a feint by the German right wing towards Belgium would bring the BEF and part of the French Army rushing forward – as under Gamelin's Plan D. The attack in the centre would be unexpected, especially as the terrain, hilly and wooded, was considered unsuitable for tank movement. Once the French line had been pierced in the centre and the German thrust had wheeled north, the main Anglo-French force would be trapped up against the German right flank. Rundstedt campaigned for this plan and the scheme was outlined to Hitler at a dinner on 17 February. By 24 February the Führer had enthusiastically approved this strategy and his army commanders were instructed accordingly. Halder, the German Chief of Staff, believed the idea crazy until he thought it advisable to alter his opinion.

The War Cabinet had decided the Finnish President's appeal, made to Snow, was not after all the signal for Anglo-French intervention. Besides, to respond to this request would have entailed a strong statement to Russia – and the Cabinet was anxious to avoid a full declaration of war. But on 29 February, came another 'appeal scare'. Corbin told Halifax the Finnish Ambassador at Paris had called to tell Daladier his Prime Minister would like aid accelerated. Daladier 'had reached the conclusion that we should take the Finnish Prime Minister's message ... as a kind of appeal, if not the actual appeal which figured in our plan.' The Cabinet agreed Halifax should cable Snow, instructing him to ask if this was the appeal, and if so, whether the Finns wanted Britain and France to approach the Swedish and Norwegian Governments.

At this meeting, Churchill's mines scheme failed again. Chamberlain had now consulted the Opposition leaders: Sinclair was in favour of action, but Attlee and Greenwood believed Britain should not take steps which might injure a third party, and 'the laying of a minefield in Norwegian waters would expose that country to attacks by Germany'. Dominions representatives thought the advantages insufficient to balance the risks. Chamberlain concluded: 'In principle, I am in favour. I am however not at all convinced that the measure proposed would be opportune at the present moment.' Norway and Sweden might not allow troops through to Finland; America might react badly – 'many people in that country are looking out for a stick to beat us with'.

Churchill's reaction to this was surprisingly generous: 'It would not be right to press the Prime Minister unduly in this matter.... There could be no question of embarking on positive action of the first order of importance against the better judgement of the Prime Minister on whose shoulders fall the principal burden of the conduct of the war.' But he warned of the general danger of remaining inactive. 'It is dangerous to give Germany an opportunity of quietly preparing and perfecting plans for large-scale operations.'[50]

Churchill was more correct than he could ever have known. On this same day, Hitler approved Falkenhurst's plans; next day, Friday, 1 March, the Führer issued the formal directive for operations against Norway and Denmark.[51]

'The situation at Helsinki seems somewhat confused,' Halifax told Ministers on 1 March. The Finnish military position had suddenly deteriorated, according to reports reaching London – and these reports were so frequent, contradictory and vague that he did not think it worthwhile to read them out. But despite the confusion, Halifax now believed the Swedes should be asked for permission to send the Allied intervention force across their territory. The Finnish Ambassador, Gripenberg, had called at the Foreign Office early in the morning, and seemed to think the force would not be able to arrive until the end of April, 'which in their view was too late', and had expressed his Government's disappointment over the size of the contingent which would be despatched. Halifax had corrected Gripenberg over the date the force would arrive, but agreed that Swedish consent was still not obtained.

Yet if the British delayed action it might come too late. 'M. Gripenberg also informed me that the Finnish Government have to decide today whether they will negotiate with the Soviet Union.... The time has now come when we should address our appeal.' Daladier 'felt he could not maintain his position if effective steps were not taken to help Finland'. So pressure was being applied by Finland and France. But what if the Norwegians and Swedes refused consent? Four courses would be open, said Halifax: an ultimatum to Norway and Sweden; a strong request for passage backed up by the arrival of the force off Narvik; a request for transit permission of unarmed volunteers; the despatch of material to the Finns, rather than men. Churchill favoured the second course. 'We should arrive off Narvik and demand passage.' Newall pointed out that if military pressure were to be applied, the expedition would have to be reorganized, and 'if we had to encounter even relatively mild opposition from the Swedes, it would be impossible for our forces to reach Finland in time to render effective help'. The Cabinet agreed telegrams should be sent to the British Ambassadors at Stockholm and Oslo, instructing them to ask for 'active cooperation essential for the success of the scheme'.[52]

Gripenberg called Halifax again later in the day. 'He told me the Finnish military situation was serious,' Halifax told the second Cabinet meeting at 6 p.m. 'The Finnish Government have to make up their minds whether to enter into negotiations with the Russians. They have to decide in the course of the next twenty-four hours and their decision will be largely governed by the amount of immediate assistance which can be furnished by the French and British.' Gripenberg had then made a sensational request for help: immediate despatch of 100 bombers and crews; 50,000 troops by the end of March, with more later, to fight anywhere in Finland and under the orders of the Finnish General Staff; pressure on Norway and Sweden to agree to passage; confirmation that if this agreement were not forthcoming Britain would not change her mind over helping Finland – in other words, if consent were not obtained the expedition should force its way through. Mannerheim had apparently asked the French to provide 50,000 allied volunteers and 30 bombers – with British crews.

The Chiefs of Staff had only had a short time to study the requests, said Pound. But the enormity of the list was obvious. 'It is ... clearly impossible for us to comply with the Finnish demands.'

A message from Paris was brought into the Cabinet Room. Halifax told the Ministers: 'M. Daladier has told the Finnish Ambassador that the French Government are prepared to accede to the Finnish request on all points. The French troops are ready and are awaiting British transports.' Ministers angrily criticized the premature French action. 'It was generally agreed that this was a most disquietening message and that the French action was a bad example of lack of cooperation. The French were apparently prepared to bluff, knowing that they could throw on us the whole blame for the failure to redeem their promises, as we had undertaken the direction of the enterprise.' Ministers were also puzzled why the military situation in Finland had deteriorated so rapidly. 'It was doubtful whether Field-Marshal Mannerheim was really at the end of his tether. It was agreed the most encouraging message possible should be sent to the Finns.'[53] Unknown to the Cabinet the Finns had already, on 23 February, made tentative peace approaches to the Russians.[54] The Finns were undoubtedly in a serious military position; the Soviet offensive had succeeded in piercing the Mannerheim Defence Line and ammunition was running low. British and French aid was intended as a counter in the forthcoming talks as much as an attempt to restore the military situation.

M. Mallet, Ambassador at Stockholm, reported the Swedish view in another telegram received on 2 March. The Foreign Minister had made it clear his Government would not consent to the passage of foreign troops across Sweden. 'He seemed faintly surprised that we should even imagine that there was any hope of their returning an affirmative reply.'

Early on Monday, 4 March, the British Ambassador at Helsinki spoke to the Finnish Prime Minister and tried to make the limits of

British help clear. 'During the interview the Finnish Foreign Minister, who was also present, had been querulous, not to say, defeatist, in attitude. He had laid stress upon the immediate despatch by us to Finland of 100 bombers.' Reporting these cables to the War Cabinet later on Monday, Halifax said: 'the Finnish Government might be trying to get the best of both worlds; on the one hand gaining time in their negotiations with the USSR and on the other hand awaiting the reactions of the Swedish and Norwegian Governments.' Mr Mallet, in his interview on Sunday with Bohemann, had been told that during the previous week the Finns had been on the point of 'agreeing to a not unreasonable Russian offer', but they had changed their minds at the last moment. And on Sunday afternoon, Cadogan had had an interview with Gripenberg, who claimed: 'The sincerity of our desire to help Finland will be judged by the material we now send her.' Cabinet Ministers were beginning to suspect the Finns were playing a devious game, and decided a decision on the despatch of additional aircraft to Finland should be deferred and no further approach made to Norway and Sweden until the Finns had made it clear whether they intended to make a public appeal for help.[55]

Suspicions were increased next day, Tuesday, 5 March. 'The War Office has made an appreciation of the situation in Finland,' said the War Secretary, 'which led to the conclusion that things were by no means desperate'.[56] But by Wednesday, 6 March, Halifax was beginning to waver; this policy 'might have a result different from that we anticipate; the Finns might decide to give in on the ground that they did not know the extent on which they could rely on us for the supply of material'. Chamberlain refused to be moved. 'I consider that such an attitude would be wholly unjustified.' But Halifax wondered whether Britain could perhaps send 50 bombers and bring them back to this country if Britain were attacked. Newall was doubtful – 'I do not believe that in the circumstances we should be likely to get back more than ten out of the 50 bombers.' To add to the difficulties Sir Stafford Cripps, who had just completed a visit to Russia, cabled his belief 'that the Government of the USSR are anxious to improve their relations with us and not to become too closely tied to Germany'.[57]

Churchill injected a different topic into this long and involved talk of Finland. At the meeting on the sixth he urged that preparations be made for his scheme for floating mines down the Rhine. 'The object is not to create a sudden surprise on a large scale, but permanently to arrest traffic on the Rhine,' and although the RAF could not start to drop mines until mid-April, the Royal Navy could release them from the French bank of the river almost immediately. Mines would be introduced into a tributary of the Rhine on a level with Karlsruhe, and these would reach Mainz in approximately 34 hours, travelling at three feet below the surface. It would be very difficult for the Germans to contrive effective counter-measures without themselves disrupting traffic. Halifax saw no objections to the scheme, provided neutral barges were given adequate warning; the War and Air Secretaries believed the operation should be used as a form of retaliation. So the idea was approved and the Chiefs of Staff asked to consider the question of notice to neutrals. Naval preparations should then begin, and Halifax would seek French agreement.[58]

After this interlude the Cabinet turned again to Finland for the next meeting, 7 March. And by now attitudes had changed. Peace prospects had increased – and if Britain did not offer more aid before agreement was reached, other nations would condemn her for betraying the Finns. Halifax described an interview between Cadogan and Corbin, who told him the Finns had started negotiations with Russia, though had so far rejected the terms offered. Ministers agreed the situation had altered since they had decided against sending aid until the Finns made the public appeal. Plans for large-scale intervention were clearly blocked by the Swedes; but Simon came closest to the truth when he declared: 'The offer of 50 bombers would make a very big difference in the presentation of our case to the world.' Chamberlain now suggested this offer should be made, although when Halifax raised the idea on 5 March, he had avoided giving him support. Newall objected: 'To weaken our bomber force in this country might invite attack on us by the Germans,' and Sir Kingsley Wood asked for time to consult his technical advisers. Chamberlain, Halifax and Newall were asked to draft a telegram to Helsinki asking for a definite answer, within a specified period, on whether the Finns intended to appeal, and conveying the promise of 50 more bombers. Contrary to the previous decision, the offer did not depend on the appeal.[59] But Gripenberg called on Halifax again before this telegram could be sent. The Finns expected 'to receive shortly from the Soviet Government the minimum terms on which the Russians were prepared to make peace.... They are not hopeful of being able to accept these terms, but they do not wish to make their appeal until they have had time to see whether acceptable terms emerged from the ensuing discussions.' Halifax emphasized that the Finns' attitude during their negotiations might well be largely influenced by the British attitude over aid. But the Cabinet could not decide whether an end to the Russo-Finnish War would be for or against British interests, and agreed on a neutral communiqué.

The Chiefs of Staff had completed their report on the 'Royal Marine Operation'. It held out 'promise of important results and should be carried out as soon as possible'. One possible drawback had been ingeniously overcome: under the Hague Convention, nations were forbidden to lay unanchored, automatic contact mines unless they would become harmless after one hour; but, said the report, 'it would appear from the preamble to this Convention, which reads as follows – "inspired by the principle of the freedom of the seas as the common highway of all nations" – that the Convention could not be held to apply to rivers and waterways in the enemy's country.' If this interpretation was considered correct, no notice was required before the mines were laid; if however the War Cabinet decided that from humanitarian considerations some notice should be given, the Chiefs of Staff recommended 24 hours. The report suggested operations should start on 12 March, laying at first 300 mines a night, and later settling to 1,000 a week. The Fifth Sea Lord had been to France the previous day and seen Gamelin, who was 'in favour of the operation in principle', and was to hold a meeting of the French Chiefs of Staff on Sunday, 10 March. The French Cabinet would consider the scheme on Monday.[60]

Later on Friday, 8 March, a Finnish delegation left for talks with the Russians. Talks began during the weekend. And at last the Finns admitted that their plea for assistance had been made to bargain with the Russians. Halifax reported to the Cabinet on 11 March, that the Finnish Ambassador had 'asked the Prime Minister for a statement in the House to strengthen Finnish hands in the negotiations with Russia, and had pleaded for the immediate despatch of bombers.'

Ministers discussed the possibility of sending a force to help Finland even if the Norwegians and Swedes continued to refuse consent. The Chiefs of Staff believed there should be simultaneous landings at Narvik and Trondheim; Churchill outlined a possible scenario: 'I envisage that the Admiral will immediately go ashore and inform the authorities that he intended to land a force for the assistance of the Finns. Meanwhile, parties from the ships will be making their way ashore, and agents of ours would be doing their best to influence the local population in favour of allowing our forces to pass through without opposition. It would be a matter of persuasion and cajolery. ... 'I don't think that the Norwegians could vigorously oppose our landing by force of arms. Once ashore we should have secured a valuable prize, not only in the possession of about a million and a half tons of iron ore, but also in our occupation of the harbour.[61] Churchill still considered the Finland operation a pretext to secure the ore fields.

The Cabinet learned on 12 March, that the commanders had been chosen for the intervention force: Admiral Sir Edward Evans would run the naval operation, and Major-General P. J. Mackesy the military. The Chiefs of Staff made clear that landings at Trondheim must be undertaken at the same time as those at Narvik; and also recommended that the naval commanders should be authorized to use 'sufficient force to enable them to achieve their object'. Halifax pointed out that this latter recommendation was new. 'It has been generally agreed,' he said, 'that our force should not allow itself to be deterred from landing by a show of resistance, but now ... the warships might open fire to silence forts'. Casualties could be vastly increased. 'I think it would be a profound mistake to use force to this extent.'

The War Cabinet agreed on a further meeting to discuss the commanders' instructions; this session had to settle orders to cover the force's intervention expedition to Finland, but also secure control in Norway and Sweden. Evans and Mackesy were told the campaign was to render assistance to Finland, while ensuring that the North Swedish ore fields were denied to Germany and Russia for the longest possible period. Instructions seemed to concern the latter rather than Finnish intervention: the first task would be to establish a force at Narvik; the second, to secure the railway link into Sweden; the third, to concentrate the force in Sweden so that the ore fields could be controlled. Firepower would only be used 'as an ultimate measure for self-defence should their forces be in jeopardy'. No communication would be made to the Government of Norway until the transports had actually arrived off Narvik.[62]

But while this meeting was taking place, peace talks in Moscow were coming to a successful conclusion. The Finns accepted the Russian terms; hostilities in Finland's wastelands and forests slowed to a halt. Britain had lost her excuse for intervening in Norway and Sweden.

Norway

'The conclusion of peace,' wrote Jodl on 12 March, 'deprives England, but us too, of any political basis for occupying Norway.'[1] Hitler's justification had been the British intention to intervene in Scandinavia; both Britain and Germany would now have to seek another pretext, but military plans were shelved, for the moment, in Berlin and London; the British force was partially dispersed, and the two Divisions held back were now allowed to proceed to France.

Churchill was especially disappointed; and lack of progress over his 'Royal Marine Operation' made his depression worse. On 11 March he had reported 'hopeful signs' that the French would join the project. But within hours French opposition began to grow, and on the afternoon of 11 March he flew to Paris to talk the ally into cooperating. 'General Gamelin strongly supported the immediate execution of this operation as planned,' he reported, 'but said that the Council had asked for more time.' He had dined with Daladier in an attempt to discover the reason for delay, and had been told that everyone in the Council had supported immediate action, except the Air Minister, who warned that the 300 aircraft at Villacoublay might be a target for reprisals. He wanted three weeks to move them; far too long, retorted the First Lord. Daladier promised to look into the matter.[2]

Worse news arrived next morning, 13 March. 'I have now heard,' Churchill told the Cabinet, 'that the French wish the proposed Royal Marine Operation to be postponed for two months.' Reasons were being sent; meanwhile, the First Lord declared 'The issue is of sufficient importance to justify its discussion at an early meeting of the Supreme War Council.' Halifax also wanted a meeting soon. 'Events of the last few days have shown some absence of harmony of view over Finland,' and another problem was what Allied strength the French High Command believed necessary for the Western Front: this information would indicate how many troops were available 'for employment in other theatres'.

While Britain and Germany prepared plans for Scandinavia, an emissary from the American President had been flitting around European capitals in an attempt to find some basis for a peace settlement. Sumner Welles had arrived in Berlin on 1 March, and had long depressing talks with German leaders before leaving for Rome on 3 March. He reached London via Paris, on 12 March, with plentiful evidence that hopes were forlorn. Chamberlain reported on initial conversations with Welles at the War Cabinet meeting on 13 March; he had said any peace proposals which America might put forward would have to be based on two requirements: a necessary sense of security for the Allies, and, for the Germans, the non-elimination of Hitler. Chamberlain said '...Mr Welles is aiming at the impossible. The more he helps to make it possible for Herr Hitler to retire from the nominal headship of Germany, and while securing peace, to be able to claim that he had come out of the war without loss of prestige, the more unacceptable to the Allies would be the proposed solution.' He had told the American that 'the Allies had gone into the war to convince Germany and the world that force did not pay, but a solution on the lines suggested would enable Herr Hitler to claim that it did.'[3]

'Führer has not yet decided how to justify the "Weser Exercise"' recorded Jodl on 14 March. That day, Churchill showed he had more initiative, imagination, or gall, than Hitler: he admitted that the Finland plan had been a 'cover' to secure control in Scandinavia, and he suggested justification was still obtainable. He presented a memorandum to the War Cabinet on the effect of the Russo-Finnish Treaty,[4] apologizing for doing so at such short notice, but maintaining the matter was of greatest urgency, 'since a decision has to be taken almost immediately whether the whole Scandinavian expedition should be dispersed, or whether we should allow the troop movements which are already in progress to continue'. He pointed out that the 'concessions extorted from Finland, which allow free access to Russia through Finland into Norway and Sweden, are in effect an act of aggression against us, and raise an altogether new situation'. Britain had an excuse for intervening which Hitler, ally of Russia, could not use. 'It is for consideration whether we should now give Norway and Sweden means of reinforcing their neutrality.' (That is, violate this neutrality.) 'We might go on with our plans to secure possession of Narvik for this purpose.' Churchill then made an admission new even in the tight privacy of the Cabinet Room. 'Our real objective is, of course, to secure possession of the Galivare ore fields.... Up till now we have had assistance to Finland as "cover" ... but we have now lost this justification ... the only chance seems to be to take the line that our national interests are directly threatened.'

'If our principal object is to secure possession of the Galivare ore fields,' maintained the Prime Minister, 'the despatch of the expedition to Narvik would serve no useful purpose.' Norway and Sweden had feared they might be involved in hostilities while the Russo-Finnish war had been taking place, and, 'a better way of achieving our object seems to be to make capital out of the feeling of relief in the Scandinavian countries'. Halifax was against an expedition to Narvik: like Chamberlain, he believed it would not succeed, and Simon pointed out another embarrassing drawback. 'It would be difficult to take the step proposed ... the House of Commons has just been assured that our intervention in Scandinavia would only take place as a result of an appeal by the Finns.' Churchill warned: 'I fear we shall never get another opportunity of gaining a foothold in Scandinavia.' But the Cabinet decided that as soon as Halifax was satisfied hostilities would not break out again in Finland, 'steps should be taken to disperse the forces prepared for the Scandinavian expedition'.[5]

'Our radio reconnaissance intercepts two very important items,' stated the official diary of the German Naval Staff on Friday, 15 March. '(1) The British submarine deployment in the North Sea off the Skagerrak and the German Bight is being dispersed.... From this information we can conclude that in consequence of the unexpected Finnish peace, the planned operation has been *postponed*. (2) Our decoding service has also succeeded in partially decoding an order issued by the Admiralty at 13.47 hours on 14 March to the C-in-C, Home Fleet... preparations for troop embarkations on a major scale have been put in hand and are complete.... There is *nothing* in the signals which indicates a complete *cancellation* of the Norway operation.'[6]

France was as anxious as Churchill to go into Scandinavia, and equally devious. Corbin had a long conversation with Halifax during the evening of the fifteenth, reported to the War Cabinet next morning. He had been instructed to suggest again that the Allies take control of Scandinavian waters, and, if necessary, occupy certain Norwegian ports. The French doubted 'whether the behaviour of Norway and Sweden during the Finnish war was, in fact, as neutral as the Allies had a right to expect, since in practice these States had adopted an attitude which favoured German policy, and they had, moreover, clearly accepted German recommendations'.[7]

Later during this Saturday, Hitler at a military conference in Berlin, fixed D-Day for operations against Norway and Denmark provisionally for 9 April. Raeder warned that although the danger of a British landing in Norway was no longer acute, the object 'has been and still is to cut off Germany's imports from Narvik'. Rumours of British intervention would justify Hitler's own invasion; and because these rumours were probably true, Hitler had to ensure his forces arrived first.

Meanwhile, Halifax grew rapidly enthusiastic for the 'Royal Marine Operation'. 'Making full allowance for the ill-effects we have suffered by the Finnish collapse,' he said on 19 March, '... we have now to ... see what positive action we can take.... The "Royal Marine Operation" seems much the most promising idea.... The French reasons for not carrying it out are unconvincing.'[8] The need for some action to break the Twilight War was emphasized later that day, when Chamberlain made a speech in the Commons, attempting to refute the charge that the allies had deserted Finland. Britain did all she could, he claimed; German threats had terrified the Scandinavian countries into withholding the help which might have saved Finland, while Britain had been concerned to respect the neutrality of Norway and Sweden. A force larger than that requested by Mannerheim had been prepared, but the Finns had not made the formal appeal for it to be sent. Despite Chamberlain's detailed account, some MPs still suspected unnecessary delays, and made a strong call for greater vigour in the conduct of the war. No division was taken and Chamberlain's Government emerged unscathed. Daladier was less lucky. Criticism had been mounting, especially over the lack of activity, and the close of the Russo-Finnish war proved fatal. On 20 March the Daladier Cabinet resigned; next day Paul Reynaud became the new President of the French Council although Daladier remained at the War Office and Defence Ministry.

In the absence of activity elsewhere, attention turned back to the West. The War Cabinet, on 21 March, considered action in the event of a German invasion of Holland and Belgium, and came to the radical conclusion that Belgian wishes should not be taken into account. If an invasion took place the allied forces should 'immediately move into Belgium, without waiting for an invitation....'[9]

Steadily, pressure increased for an end to the Twilight War. The pressure had toppled Daladier, and Reynaud was determined not to suffer the same fate. On Wednesday, 27 March, the War Cabinet discussed a long communication from Reynaud. The allies should not be too legalistic in their concept of neutrality, he declared, and resolute steps should be taken to control navigation in Norwegian waters, including occupation of vantage points on land. Efforts should also be made to cut off German supplies from the Caucasian oilfields. Above all, time was working against the allies. 'I find little of value in the French Note,' commented Chamberlain, 'which, while proposing certain ostentatious actions, gives no details and decides no arguments for carrying them out.'

The latest Chiefs of Staff report on 'Certain Aspects of the Present Position',[10] had a bearing on this discussion. The allies should not be 'stampeded into undertaking unprofitable military projects ... merely for the sake of doing something.'

Chamberlain agreed, but was anxious lest the Government appeared inactive. 'The appetite of the public for spectacular operations remains,' he said, 'and this psychological factor cannot be ignored.... It is of the utmost importance that we should make the best use, for propaganda purposes, of our exploits.' The 'Royal Marine Operation' seemed an ideal undertaking. 'It is difficult to understand why the French hesitate to agree to its execution. I feel that the psychological effect would be tremendous. It would give us the initiative and encourage our own people and the neutrals.' Churchill could also take some slight encouragement from Chamberlain's comments on his scheme to sever the Narvik ore trade. 'I feel that the laying of the minefield is an operation which could be carried out at any time ... and it is only a question of choosing the right moment.' The Supreme War Council would meet in two days' time; the French representatives would be pressed to agree.[11]

Churchill, who had already written to Reynaud to enlist his support, had good hopes that 'Royal Marine Operation' would be accepted by the Council on 28 March. Initially his hopes were justified: Reynaud said the French War Committee had previously rejected the proposal through fear of German reprisal, but he now thought sanction might be given if the scheme were linked with another, and he urged that the Norwegian Leads should be mined without delay. Both Churchill's favourite projects had therefore been agreed, and a provisional time-table was arranged.[12] The War Cabinet endorsed the Council's decisions the following day; and Chamberlain, Churchill and Lord Halifax were well-pleased. At last, positive action was to be taken. Churchill wrote later: 'After all this vain boggling, hesitation, changes of policy, arguments between good and worthy people unending, we had at last reached the simple point on which action had been demanded seven months before.'[13]

But on 31 March came news that the French War Committee had refused to endorse the Supreme War Council's decision on the 'Royal Marine Operation'. Corbin asked for an interview; Chamberlain, Churchill and Halifax met at Downing Street. Chamberlain was still determined to push the French into action. Paul Reynaud was known to be anxious to have the mines laid in the Norwegian Leads, and it was decided to insist that if this action was to be carried out, so should the Rhine operation. When Corbin arrived at the Foreign Office, he was told: 'Britain had agreed to the plan for action in Norwegian territorial waters and the "Royal Marine Operation", as one whole. If we were to carry out the former plan only, we should be accused of violating the neutrality of a small nation. We could, however, overcome this criticism if, at the same time, we took vigorous and effective action against Germany herself.' He was asked to put this point of view to his Government. Corbin had been 'in a gloomy and apologetic mood'. Objection to 'Royal Marine' had come from Daladier, who claimed the Germans might retaliate against French munition and aircraft factories. He wanted three months' delay. Apart from any other objection, this could easily result in a disastrous leak of information.[14]

Meanwhile, also on 1 April, Chamberlain altered his Cabinet. Hoare, Lord Privy Seal, and Wood, Air Secretary, changed places, to the intense annoyance of Churchill, who had wanted Eden at the Air Ministry. The changes promised to be interim and uneasy: only a few weeks before Wood had told Eden 'Hoare's stock has never been so low',[15] while Hoare wrote in his memoirs 'it was clear to both the House of Commons and the Cabinet that he [Kingsley Wood] was a tired man and needed a change'.[16] Only six weeks later Chamberlain was to write a letter describing the intense dislike he believed Hoare felt for him; Eden, not knowing of this, commented 'Neville had his particular friends and would stick to them as long as he could, and longer than the country wished. He had only accepted Winston and me because he could not avoid it.'[17] With such feelings in the Cabinet, creating a harmonious body would have defied any powers.

While the Cabinet waited for the French to change their minds over the 'Royal Marine Operation', and the Norwegian mining was delayed as a result, Hitler was taking further positive steps towards renewed action. After a long conference on 2 April, attended by Göring, Raeder and Falkenhorst, plans for the Norwegian campaign were confirmed, and a formal directive issued.[18]

A revealing report from the Foreign Office reached the War Cabinet on the third. '... When the project of the "Royal Marine Operation" was first broached, M. Daladier had regarded it as a dangerous toy, but not one to be taken seriously. Later, when we pressed this proposal, he became irritated, fearing serious German reprisals on the French aircraft industries. Political reasons probably also entered into the picture, but M. Daladier is a sick man, and must not be judged too harshly.' It was therefore suggested that the Ambassador at Paris should find out from Reynaud whether he objected to Chamberlain's writing to Daladier. If he had, or if Daladier's reply proved unfavourable, Norwegian waters should be mined anyway. Whatever the French decision, Churchill hoped the mines would be laid in the Leads on 5 April as arranged. 'It must be realized that it is very difficult to hold the operation in suspense.'

Norway would be warned on the fifth, the mines laid on the eighth. Later he had to settle for less. Meanwhile a report had been received, said Churchill, that the Germans had blown up a Rhine bridge on 31 March, and another report stated a net was being positioned across the Rhine. 'This suggests that news of the proposed [Royal Marine] operation has leaked.'

Oliver Stanley, War Secretary, also had disturbing news. A 'somewhat garbled' report had arrived that the Germans had been collecting a strong force at Rostock, to take action in Scandinavia. Halifax added that a telegram from Stockholm tended to confirm this: it looked as though the Germans were preparing a counter-strike against a British attack on Narvik or other Norwegian ports.[19] Meanwhile, a small group of German merchant ships was heading through the North Sea, loaded with military supplies and carrying a number of troops. Their destination was Narvik. These vessels formed the initial section of Germany's task force for the takeover of Norway.[20]

The same day, 3 April, Chamberlain made another Cabinet change. The post of Minister for Coordination of Defence, held by Lord Chatfield, had become superfluous when the CID had been abolished at the outbreak of war. In spite of the CID wartime equivalent, the Military Coordination Committee (MCC), the appointment was unnecessary, and Chatfield had been asked to resign. His departure was announced on 3 April to the shock of the rest of the Cabinet.[21] Churchill, as senior Service Minister, would preside over the Military Coordination Committee.

Late in the evening of 3 April, Halifax received an optimistic telephone call from Campbell in Paris: he believed Reynaud would agree to Chamberlain's personal letter to Daladier. But next morning, he telephoned Halifax again to say Reynaud, after all, disliked the idea, 'since he thought that this would only strengthen M. Daladier's position'. Chamberlain, Churchill and Halifax met again at Downing Street, and as a result Churchill set off for Paris. He dined with Reynaud in the evening, and, he wrote later, 'we seemed in pretty good agreement'. Daladier had been invited, but ominously had pleaded a previous engagement. Arrangements were made for a meeting the following morning.

While Churchill talked with Reynaud, Chamberlain addressed the Central Council of the National Union of Conservative and Unionist Associations – and in a long and unusually optimistic speech, he uttered a statement for which he would soon be ridiculed. 'After seven months of war, I feel ten times as confident of victory as I did at the beginning. I feel that during the seven months our relative position towards the enemy has become a great deal stronger than it was.' When the conflict started, he continued, German preparations had been far ahead of those in Britain, and Hitler could have been expected to make use of this advantage. 'Is it not a very extraordinary thing that no such attempt was made?' And Chamberlain added: 'One thing is certain: he missed the bus.' Churchill commented: 'This proved an ill-judged utterance.' Chamberlain may have wished to convince his audience that the dreary, boring, taxing Twilight War was not in vain. And he was not alone in unfortunate declarations; Ironside was quoted in a newspaper next morning: 'Our army has, at last, turned the corner.... We are ready for anything they may start.'[22]

On the day of Chamberlain's speech, the German Naval Staff diary stated: 'A race is beginning for Scandinavia between ourselves and Britain.' German warships were being prepared at Wilhelmshaven; and the Danish Naval Attaché at Berlin, Captain Kjölsen, rushed to Copenhagen with an accurate and highly alarming report of imminent action against his country.

The Cabinet was told of Churchill's mission to Paris when they met on 5 April. Halifax said Churchill was seeing Daladier at that moment, and if talks failed, would tell him that Britain agreed to mining the Norwegian Leads as planned. Churchill now telephoned a report on his talks with Daladier. He had apparently undergone a complete about-face, and 'been convinced by the French arguments that a serious risk would be run if the ["Royal Marine"] operation took place now.... It would be a very great mistake to try to force the French.' However, the French *were* prepared to put a definite date in writing for the initiation of the operation. The Norwegian mining plan was sanctioned. Halifax was authorized to warn Norway and Sweden.

'Our aircraft have sighted some 50 or 60 ships,' reported Newall, 'presumably mine-sweepers and anti-submarine craft, in the Heligoland Bight, steaming northward.'[23] That evening, a film show was held at the German Legation, Oslo; guests included many distinguished Norwegian politicians and Ministers. The film depicted Germany's successful Polish campaign, with plentiful scenes of death and destruction, and with a warning caption: 'For this they could thank their English and French friends.' Guests departed in gloom and considerable fear.

The delivery of Notes to Norway and Sweden produced an electric effect. The Swedish Foreign Minister declared: 'This [the mine-laying] brings our countries very close to war.'[24]

Bustling activity was reported on wharves and roads near Kiel, Hamburg and Lübeck; early on Sunday morning, 7 April, five powerful German naval groups put to sea, their departures so timed that they would arrive simultaneously. Destinations were Narvik, Trondheim, Bergen, Egersund, Kristiansund, and Oslo. Waiting at Narvik, Trondheim and Stavanger were German merchantmen with troops concealed in their holds.

No British War Cabinet meeting was held that day, a Sunday, and Ministers had to wait until Monday to hear latest developments. 'The minefield in the Vest Fiord was laid between 4.30 and 5.30 this morning,' reported Churchill. At 5.30 in the morning, said Halifax, the British and French Ambassadors had presented a Note to the Norwegian Foreign Office. Extremely disturbing reports were reaching the Admiralty, Churchill told Ministers. The previous evening a German Fleet had been located moving towards the Naze across the mouth of the Skagerrak. 'It has been hard to believe that this force could possibly be intending to go to Narvik, although a report from Copenhagen on 6 April indicated that it is Hitler's intention to seize that port. It was thought that the German ships would probably turn into the Skagerrak.' But at 8.30 a.m., *HMS Glowworm*, who had been delayed and who was now in a position about 150 miles south-west of the entrance to the Vest Fiord leading to Narvik, had reported she was engaged with an enemy destroyer to the southward. The enemy had appeared to be concentrating with another destroyer, and *HMS Glowworm* had withdrawn to the north to lure them towards the other British warships. 'Shortly afterwards she reported seeing another destroyer ahead of her. And at about 9.45 a.m. she became silent. Since then nothing has been heard from her.... From this, it appears that the German force is undoubtedly making towards Narvik. It is calculated that if they were to be unopposed, they could reach there about 10 p.m., but they will no doubt be engaged by His Majesty's ships ... and an action might take place very shortly.'[25]

Churchill was exhilarated; at last there was conflict. Ismay, who attended both this and the Military Coordination Committee meeting later in the day (the first at which Churchill was chairman) was fascinated by the effect of events on him. 'Winston is back from France full of blood.... He was like a boy this morning describing what he had done to meet the Germans. His physique must be marvellous, but I cannot think he would make a good Prime Minister. He has not got the stability necessary for guiding the others.'[26] The Home Fleet, under Sir Charles Forbes, and the Second Cruiser Squadron, had cleared Scapa Flow the evening before and were now steaming for Norway. The First Cruiser Squadron, which had been embarking troops at Rosyth for Bergen and Stavanger under the original plans for British landings in Norway en route to Finland, now sailed without the soldiers. The escort for the troopships previously intended for Narvik and Trondheim was ordered to move into Scapa, ready for sailing to Norway. The intervention force for Scandinavia had been scrapped, yet this force, 'R4', would have been ideal for subsequent operations. Although it could never have reached Norway in time to prevent the German landings, it would have been able to attack before they had fully consolidated their positions. But the Royal Navy was chosen to deal with the German threat: the patchy reports reaching London on 7 April and early 8 April had still to indicate a full-scale German invasion of Norway was taking place, and fleet actions were envisaged instead.[27]

By the time the War Cabinet met next day, 8 April, for a special early meeting at 8.30 a.m., an almost complete picture of the German operation had emerged. But by then it was too late. Newall revealed the situation to horrified Ministers. Oslo fiord: four large German warships had reached as far as Tönsberg; Stavanger: one enemy war-

318

ship approaching; Bergen: five enemy warships had been reported approaching at 3.25 a.m., and, at 6 a.m. the British Consul had telephoned to say the quay was occupied by Germans; Trondheim: two enemy warships were in the port, according to an unconfirmed report from Oslo; Narvik: no sign yet of the enemy.

Churchill gave the most up-to-date scraps of information. *HMS Renown* had had a short engagement off Vest Fiord with enemy warships in the early morning and was in pursuit of these to the north, but her wireless had been shot away and the weather was 'very heavy'; British destroyers were covering the mouth of the Vest Fiord to stop enemy transports entering Narvik. *Gneisenau* and *Scharnhorst*, the German pocket battleships, were reported to have moved into the North Sea. A strong Royal Navy force was concentrating off Bergen. The Admiralty had received no further news of *HMS Glowworm* – and only after the war would the fate of this gallant destroyer be fully revealed to the British. She had sunk after gallantly ramming the powerful cruiser *Hipper*. Her captain was posthumously awarded the VC.

Scharnhorst and *Gneisenau* had indeed entered the North Sea. But unknown to Churchill, these had been the two warships engaged by *Renown*. They had been sighted at early dawn on the ninth, about 50 miles off Vest Fiord and believed to be heading for Narvik. *Renown* opened fire at 18,000 yards and smashed *Gneisenau*'s main gun-control equipment. Both German warships slipped away northwards with *Renown* in pursuit, but the British vessel was damaged, and the Germans escaped amidst snow-squalls and smoke-screens. The main British Fleet had arrived off Bergen at dawn, and, ten minutes before the War Cabinet met, a signal was sent to Forbes: 'Prepare plans for attacking German warships and transports in Bergen and for controlling the approaches to the port, on the supposition that defences are still in hands of Norwegians. Similar plans as regards Trondheim should also be prepared, if you have sufficient forces for both.'

As the War Cabinet meeting continued, more messages reached Downing Street. Air attacks were taking place near Oslo; German aircraft were over Stavanger; German troops had landed at Egersund. But Ministers were unaware of the situation in Denmark: German forces had appeared off the Danish coast at dawn and an ultimatum had been presented at 5.20 a.m. to Copenhagen and Oslo. The Norwegians announced their determination to resist, but the defenceless Danes had to submit.

Also unknown to British Ministers was the true situation at Narvik. *Scharnhorst* and *Gneisenau* had not been on their way to the port – they had been returning having landed troops. Other German vessels had also slipped past the British under cover of night and appalling weather. The garrison commander at Narvik had surrendered; the naval commander, despite brave resistance, had been overwhelmed and his men had suffered heavy casualties. Narvik was now in German hands. 'I suggest that our first immediate action should be to go ahead with our plan for seizing Narvik,' said Ironside at the meeting. 'Our information is that the Germans are not in occupation there. One battalion could sail at mid-day today, and could be at Narvik in three days' time.' The Germans must not establish themselves at Trondheim and Bergen. 'If the Norwegians are driven out of Oslo, they would retire on Bergen and Trondheim. The German forces there cannot be very strong, probably not more than 2,000 men, and these have probably accomplished little more than taking the docks. Now is the critical moment.' Churchill, who had already ordered Forbes to prepare plans to attack Bergen and Trondheim, agreed. 'No large forces will be required in the initial stages.' Ministers discussed whether Oslo and Stavanger should also be attacked to destroy their airfields, but the Cabinet agreed more information was needed. But 'everything possible should be done to push preparations for sending expeditions to retake Bergen and Trondheim and to occupy Narvik.'

'Present events might well be the prelude to the opening of a German offensive on land,' warned Churchill. 'We should press the Belgians to come into the open before it is too late.' Cabinet discussion was interrupted by the arrival of the text of a German radio announcement; this declared: 'The German High Command of the German Army announces that, in order to counteract the actions against Denmark and Norway and to prevent a possible hostile attack against these countries, the German Army has taken these two countries under its protection.'[28] Out in the howling winds and heavy seas off the Norwegian coast, four cruisers and seven destroyers had been detached from the main British battle fleet and were heading for Bergen, 80 miles away. Back in the Admiralty, the attack on Trondheim, urged at the War Cabinet meeting, had been postponed until the whereabouts of the German battle-cruisers was established, in order to prevent the main fleet becoming too dispersed.

The War Cabinet met again at noon after a brief Chiefs of Staff conference. Newall now reported that according to a broadcast from Oslo, a 'small German force' had landed at Narvik, and the Chiefs of Staff had agreed British destroyers in the Vest Fiord should probe German strength. Churchill, with his normal resilience, declared: 'As regards the general situation in Scandinavia, I feel that we are in a far better position than we have been up to date. Our hands are now free, and we can apply our overwhelming sea power on the Norwegian coast.' Reynaud and Daladier would be flying to London, said Halifax, for an emergency meeting of the Supreme War Council during the afternoon; the Prime Minister would then make a statement in the Commons.

Churchill told Ministers of orders to British warships to force their way into Narvik and Bergen; Trondheim would be left until later.[29] But when he returned to the Admiralty after the Cabinet meeting, Churchill was told by Pound that opposition at Bergen might be stiff. There were two heavy German cruisers in the harbour, instead of one, and Norwegian shore batteries were now assumed to be in German hands. After a brief discussion, it was agreed that the attack on Bergen should be cancelled.

The Germans had indeed taken the batteries, but had still to restore them to fighting trim. Not two, but three cruisers were in Bergen harbour, plus troops' transports – yet the Germans were fully occupied in getting troops and equipment ashore. A British attack would have stood good chance of success, and Forbes was himself prepared to take the risk, but had been overruled by Churchill, who admitted later: 'Looking back on this affair, I consider that the Admiralty kept too close a control upon the C-in-C ...'[30] This over-direction from Whitehall was to continue throughout the campaign.

Reynaud and Daladier arrived in the afternoon after a meeting of the French War Committee, and the British and French leaders found they agreed largely on the conduct of the Norwegian campaign: troops should not be despatched until the naval situation had been cleared up. Because of this delay, German opposition on land would be stiffer, and forces should be concentrated against one target rather than dispersed. Daladier and Reynaud urged Narvik should be the first objective; the *Chasseurs Alpins*, previously detailed for the Finland intervention operation, would be made available.

The Supreme War Council also discussed the Western Front, and fears similar to Churchill's were expressed. The French leaders proposed the Allied armies should move into Belgium immediately, provided Belgian cooperation was forthcoming. The French High Command was to contact Brussels to seek this permission. If the Allied armies did move forward, the French would agree to the 'Royal Marine' being put into immediate effect.

Gradually, the Norwegian objectives had altered in emphasis during the day. At the Cabinet meeting Ironside had stressed the importance of the southern ports of Bergen and Trondheim, although agreeing the immediate target should be the port of Narvik in the north. The Chiefs of Staff had endorsed this view. Then Trondheim had been dropped and, later, Bergen. The Supreme War Council had emphasized Narvik, anxious still to gain control over the orefields. Yet also throughout the day, evidence had accumulated that German opposition at Narvik was likely to be considerable. By the time the Military Coordination Committee met in the evening, intelligence reports indicated the Germans might have up to 4,000 men there, in addition to six destroyers. The Committee, with Churchill as chairman, re-emphasized that in view of this, British forces should be concentrated on Narvik. Ironside warned that the success of the Narvik action would depend on the most careful planning – which would take time; and Ismay commented, 'amphibious operations are a very specialized form of warfare'. Churchill agreed, and said these operations must 'fit together like a jewelled bracelet'. Closest possible co-ordination was needed between naval and army forces.

When darkness fell on Tuesday, 9 April, the Germans were in possession of Copenhagen, Oslo, Stavanger, Bergen, Trondheim and Narvik. The Danes had capitulated; the Norwegians were still determined to resist, and the King and Government had eluded the Germans and appealed to the allies for help. The Germans had won the initiative. The British were still only sketchily informed as to the overall situation. No attempt had been made to organize a command unit which would coordinate the Norwegian operations and the nature of the operational area meant local strategic questions had to be considered and decided on back in London. This meant, in effect, that 'the distinction between the higher direction of the war and local strategy became blurred in practice'.[31] More strain was thrown upon the Chiefs of Staff, the MCC, and, ultimately, the War Cabinet. The MCC played its part, yet Churchill complained that it lacked incisiveness, and no proper system existed for deciding between the conflicting claims of the Royal Navy, Army, and RAF. Service Ministers also lacked confidence in each other; Eden wrote in his diary: 'He [Churchill] is indignant with Sam [Hoare] whom he suspects of being eager to score off him, Winston, and whom he regards as unsuited to inspire the Air Force at a time like this. "A snake" and some other stronger epithets.'[32]

During the night of 9 April, air attacks were made upon German warships at Bergen, and despite the firm reports of strong German opposition at Narvik, plans went ahead for the probing operation by Royal Navy destroyers, though Captain Warburton-Lee, commanding these five destroyers, knew the odds were against him. The Admiralty, evidently profiting from the Bergen affair, intended to leave the decision to him.

The First Lord reported this 'First Battle of Narvik' to the War Cabinet on Wednesday morning, 10 April, but few details were available of the damage caused by (and inflicted on) the British flotilla. Warburton-Lee was the campaign's second posthumous VC. Reports were also given of the Supreme War Council's decision the previous day, and of the conclusions reached by the MCC, both of which stressed Narvik should be taken. Chamberlain believed the latest information reinforced this choice. 'Narvik, which for another month will be isolated, offers the only possible objective for an allied assault.' Halifax had seen the Norwegian Ambassador, who 'emphasized the importance, from the psychological point of view, of our getting a foothold somewhere in Norway.'

The kind of question now being asked, said Anderson, both by the British public and by neutrals, was how the Germans could have managed to execute such an operation in the face of the Royal Navy. Chamberlain proposed this should be discussed the following day, and the First Lord should prepare a full statement. Ministers discussed possible reasons which could be given for the German success. 'It should be made clear that the blame attached not to us, but to the neutrals, and we should take every opportunity of bringing this point home.'

The Belgian Foreign Minister was 'emphatically opposed' to the allied troops moving forward into his country, reported Halifax, but the Belgians might consider the idea more favourably, 'if they could be assured that the Allied forces would take up a more advanced position, and thus prevent the war being fought in the heart of Belgium'.[33]

Plans were being prepared for the Narvik operation, and following a suggestion by Churchill the idea considered was of establishing an advanced base on Norwegian soil, from which an attack could be launched on Narvik itself. The MCC also adopted the suggestion; this base might also be used as the first step to the Galivare ore fields. The base site selected by the Chiefs of Staff was Harstad, about 15 miles in a straight line from Narvik, but about 60 miles by road and ferry, and the army commander was to be Major-General P. J. Mackesy, who was to have been in charge of the army element in the Finnish force. But the naval commander would be Admiral of the Fleet Lord Cork, despite his unusually high grade of authority for such a small command. Cork had worked closely with Churchill at the Admiralty, and would receive orders direct from there rather than from the C-in-C Home Fleet, and he attended the meeting of the MCC that Wednesday.

General Mackesy was up at Scapa Flow and therefore unable to attend the meeting. But he received instructions very early next day, Thursday, 11 April. These orders stated the aim was to throw the Germans from the Narvik area. 'Your initial task will be to establish your force at Harstad, ensure the cooperation of Norwegian forces that may be there, and obtain the information necessary to enable you to plan your further operations. It is not intended that you should land in the face of opposition.... The decision whether to land or not will be taken by the senior naval officer in consultation with you.' A letter from the CIGS, enclosed with these instructions, seemed to underline that although the taking of Narvik was the main aim, the first step would be to establish a base at Harstad and make preparations. 'You will have sufficient troops to allow you to make a preliminary preparation and reconnaissance.' Then General Ironside seemed to add a contradiction: 'You may have a chance of taking advantage of the Naval action, and you should do so if you can. Boldness is required.'

The War Cabinet was informed of this operation, code-named 'Rupert', at the Thursday morning meeting. But amid all the discussion and activity over Scandinavia, moves were also being made for strategic plans regarding the Western Front, and these plans carried extremely dangerous implications. Halifax told the Thursday meeting that he had sent another message to the French leaders, via Campbell, concerning the attitude of the Belgians. He had asked Reynaud if he could discover Gamelin's views on the suggestion that Belgium might issue an invitation for the allies – if the allies, in return, promised to take up more advanced positions. Gamelin had replied: 'We can promise to do everything in our power to give satisfaction to the Belgian *desideratum.*' Reynaud was seeking Daladier's consent.[34]

General Mackesy and Lord Cork met, for the first time.[35] While final preparations for the force were being made during the afternoon of 11 April, Churchill as First Lord, had to explain to the Commons why the Royal Navy had failed to stop the Germans.

He walked slowly to his seat through the crowded Commons, and sat on the Government Front Bench while other business was completed. 'He is not looking well,' wrote Harold Nicolson, 'and sits there hunched as usual with his papers in his hand. When he rises to speak it is obvious that he is very tired.' 'I had to face a disturbed and indignant House,' wrote Churchill. 'I followed the method I have always found most effective on such occasions, of giving a calm, unhurried, factual narrative of events in their sequence, laying full emphasis upon ugly truths.' 'He starts off by giving an imitation of himself making a speech,' Nicolson continued, 'and he indulges in vague oratory, coupled with tired jibes.' Churchill told Members of the difficulties encountered over Norwegian neutrality. 'It is not the slightest use blaming the Allies for not being able to give substantial help and protection to neutral countries if we are held at arm's length until these neutrals are actually attacked.' And with obvious reference to Belgium, he continued: 'I trust this fact will be meditated upon by other countries who may tomorrow, or a week hence, or a month hence, find themselves the victims.' He then explained the difficulties which the Royal Navy had had to face – the storms, mists, night, uncertainties; command of the sea only meant command of a small area of the wide expanse. He described Warburton-Lee's heroic exploits. 'The House listened with growing acceptance of the account,' he wrote afterwards; Nicolson's diary reads: 'He hesitates, gets his notes in the wrong order ... keeps on saying "Sweden" when he means "Denmark", and in one way and another makes a lamentable performance.... He gives no real explanation of how the Germans managed to slip through.' Churchill warned that other 'reckless'

German operations might soon follow. 'These costly operations may be only the prelude to far larger events which impend on land. We have probably arrived now at the first main clinch of the war.' In his own verdict of his speech, Churchill believed that 'after an hour and a half the House seemed to be very much less estranged'; Nicolson's read: 'It is a feeble, tired speech and it leaves the House in a mood of grave anxiety.'[36]

As General Mackesy sailed for Norway, frantic endeavours were being made to assemble all other available troops. 'They lacked aircraft, anti-aircraft guns, anti-tank guns, tanks, transport and training,' wrote Churchill. 'Thus began this ramshackle campaign.'[37] Yet only an hour and a half before the first troops had left Scapa Flow, he had urged an expedition should also be made to Namsos, in harsh country to the north of Trondheim, despite the previous insistence on concentration upon Narvik. Chamberlain agreed with this new suggestion. 'The Swedes are emphasizing the vital importance of recapturing Trondheim, which is the key to communications into Norway and Sweden, and it looks as if Namsos might be a useful jumping-off place.'

Halifax told the War Cabinet Daladier had now agreed with the proposal for Belgium. The British Ambassador would inform the Belgium Government.[38] But in Paris, at a metting of the French War Cabinet, a leadership crisis was reaching dangerous proportions. Relations between Gamelin and Reynaud had deteriorated: the latter's insistence on the Norwegian campaign and the General's insistence that he wanted little to do with it, led to a clash at the 12 April meeting which offered little hope of firm direction of France's war effort. Gamelin, not for the first time, offered to resign, but was persuaded from doing so by Daladier.[39]

The War Cabinet met again at 4.30 p.m., to discuss in more detail the revised plans for intervention in Belgium. Ministers had received a paper by Churchill, covering a Chiefs of Staff report on an actual or impending German invasion of Holland or Belgium.[40] It was agreed that if Germany invaded Holland, and Belgium refused to go to her aid, the allies should march in whether invited or not; this should not be revealed to the Belgians, but be 'hinted at'. On another point the Chiefs of Staff now had their way – the Cabinet laid down that 'the allied air forces, in the event of a German invasion of Holland or Belgium, without further reference to their Governments, should immediately attack military objectives in Germany.' The 'Royal Marine Operation' would be carried out at the same time.[41]

The Military Coordination Committee had agreed on 11 April that an operation against Trondheim should be studied in detail, but no preparations should begin until the needs of the Narvik expedition could be fully assessed. Now, however, on 12 April, a small naval detachment would be landed at Namsos, and Major-General A. Carton de Wiart, was warned to be ready for overseas service. The new plan received full attention at the War Cabinet meeting next day, 13 April. 'The important point,' stressed Halifax, 'is to secure Trondheim and the railways leading from the port across the peninsula.' Chamberlain agreed, despite a warning from Ironside that so large-scale an operation would mean troop reductions in France. Halifax thought: 'Early action against Trondheim is imperative from the political point of view, while it seems that, if necessary, the operation at Narvik can wait.' Churchill was horrified. 'I am very apprehensive of any proposals which might tend to weaken our intentions to seize Narvik.... Trondheim is, on the other hand, a much more speculative affair.... There is a grave danger that we shall find ourselves committed to a number of ineffectual operations along the Norwegian coast, none of which will succeed.' Narvik, Churchill's long-sought objective, must remain first priority. But Halifax insisted that 'unless we can give the Norwegians and Swedes some assurances of the help which we intend to send them, there is a serious risk that they will collapse.' Narvik was too far to the north. Oliver Stanley agreed. 'It is important that we should correct the impression that our intention to seize Narvik is inspired by the selfish motive that it is the entrance to the ore fields.' Churchill was outnumbered, and the War Cabinet agreed to tell the Swedish and Norwegian Governments 'we intend to recapture both Trondheim and Narvik'. Yet Churchill was supported by the Chiefs of Staff, who had pointed out that the 'Rupert' force could not be split between Narvik and Trondheim, since it had been loaded for a single disembarkation: complete chaos would follow attempts to find the correct equipment for two operations among the packed cargoes. And, as Ironside was to point out, the force had no maps of the Trondheim area.

While the War Cabinet had been meeting, the 'Second Battle of Narvik' had been taking place, and the result was to further influence the Trondheim decision. At noon on 12 April the battleship *Warspite* forced her way up to Narvik, escorted by nine destroyers and supported by dive-bombers from the *Furious*, and the task group, commanded by Admiral Whitworth, completely shattered the Germans. No British ships were lost. In the absence of opposition, the Admiral considered sending a shore party into the port. Churchill, already outnumbered in his opposition to diminishing the 'Rupert' force, had now an excellent reason for changing his mind: Narvik had been virtually taken.[42]

On the fourteenth, both the Chiefs of Staff and the First Lord completely changed their minds. The 146th Territorial Brigade would be diverted at sea, and it might be possible to effect a landing at Trondheim itself. But in any event, some seamen and marines were to be landed at Namsos – 'Operation Henry', and some at Aalsund –

'Operation Primrose'. These landings would attract the Germans away from Trondheim itself.

Halifax turned again to the War Cabinet's other preoccupation – Belgium. The previous evening Cadogan had seen the Belgian Ambassador, who had conveyed from the Foreign Minister, M. Spaak, the reply to the allied request that in return for advancing deep into Belgium, an invitation should be issued as soon as possible. 'There can be no question of the Belgium Government giving an affirmative answer to the Allied request,' M. Spaak had declared. 'The Belgium Government has no certain information that the situation had deteriorated, or that the German forces have been reinforced during the last four days.' The Belgians even accused the allies of moving troops closer to the frontier, and were 'extremely surprised' that no prior information had been given. The Belgians, embarrassingly, required an assurance that there was no intention on the part of the Allied Governments to move troops into Belgium without an invitation. Sir Alexander had tried to hedge the issue, and had declared he was not aware of the troop movements, and anyway the British Government had suggested, more than once, that the Belgian Government should enter into closer consultations.

Halifax told the Cabinet that he had written to the Belgian Ambassador, stressing that any troop movements were due 'solely to the German menace', and were not a prelude to moving into Belgium. 'We assumed that if the Belgium Government were attacked by Germany, they would certainly desire that our troops should be as well placed as possible.' But the Ambassador's suspicions remained. Just before the meeting he had telephoned the Foreign Office and declared himself unsatisfied; he wanted answers to two questions. Had the intention of the two Governments been modified? Had Britain in fact no intention of moving troops into Belgium unless in response to a Belgium appeal? The reply might say, suggested Halifax, that the British and French Governments intended 'to do their utmost to protect Belgium and the Netherlands, and they must reserve their liberty to act as rapidly as possible to give support to those countries, both in their interest and in that of the Allies, the moment the time arrived'. Halifax was still trying to avoid a direct answer, but an indignant Churchill exclaimed: 'We are under no obligation to the Belgians,' and Chamberlain agreed. Britain should ask the Belgians some questions in return – for example, was there a possibility of the Belgian Government coming to terms with the German Government? 'I consider that we should adopt a very stiff line,' he added. Finally, Ministers heard some more disappointing news. The French had refused to agree that if Germany invaded Belgium and/or Holland, the Allied air forces should immediately attack military targets in Germany, without further reference to their Governments. Halifax said the refusal was probably due to Daladier. Ministers decided that the Officer Commanding the British Air Force in France should try to reach agreement with the French High Command.[43]

General Carton de Wiart, commander of 'Mauriceforce' which was to strike at Trondheim, received instructions during the day: the objects of the expedition were to boost the Norwegian Government, to rally local forces, and to secure a base for subsequent operations. The Trondheim area must be secured, but his forces were not to attempt an opposed landing.[44] The General would fly to Namsos, secured that afternoon by 'Operation Henry'. Preparations were therefore well in hand for 'Mauriceforce', while an attack at Narvik stood good chance of success, and Lord Cork, sailing there at high speed, received a welcome signal from Admiral Whitworth. 'I am convinced that Narvik can be taken by direct assault now, without fear of meeting serious opposition on landing. I consider that the main landing force need only be small.'[45]

All went awry. First, the MCC, whose members had been under intensive strain for the past six days, threatened to split apart. Oliver Stanley was critical of Churchill's handling of the meetings; Ironside agreed and wrote in his diary: 'One of the fallacies that Winston seems to have got into his head is that we can make improvised decisions to carry on the war by meeting at 5 p.m. each day.... [Oliver Stanley] is going to see the Prime Minister today and tell him that war cannot be run by the Staffs sitting round a table arguing.... We cannot have a man trying to supervise all military arrangements as if he were a company commander running a small operation to cross a bridge.'[46] Churchill derided the meetings as 'a copious flow of polite conversation' leading to 'a tactful report' and compared them unfavourably with prompt Admiralty methods; matters had to be discussed again and again, he complained, and he admitted his inability to act as an adequate Chairman. Next day, 15 April, Churchill asked Chamberlain to take the chair, which he did at all the subsequent meetings during the Norwegian campaign.[47] The MCC was expected to concert the action of the individual Service departments – and these individual plans were in danger of running wild. 'Our Staff work at this time had not been tempered by war experience,' wrote Churchill. 'Neither I, as chairman of the Committee, nor the Admiralty, were made acquainted with the War Office instructions to General Mackesy, and as the Admiralty directions had been given orally to Lord Cork, there was no written text communicated to the War Office.' Cork had been told to operate directly under the Admiralty, and was independent of the C-in-C, Home Fleet, although he virtually depended upon him for necessary naval forces.

This lack of coordinated direction now had woeful effects. Cork, receiving Whitworth's signal, had altered course and had made for

Skjel Fiord near the Narvik approaches, intending an immediate assault; he signalled Mackesy to meet him there, but communications between the two broke down, and Mackesy made for the original rendezvous at Harstad, where Cork finally had to sail back and join him. Instructed by the Admiralty not to attack except in combination with Mackesy, Cork urged him to launch an assault on Narvik. But Mackesy, who had orders not to attempt an opposed attack, established his HQ in a local hotel, deployed his few soldiers, and awaited reinforcements. Deadlock had quickly been reached.

Reports of this state of affairs had just started to reach London when the War Cabinet met at 11 a.m. on the fifteenth, and their assessment was undergoing a radical change as a result. An equally unfortunate situation had developed at Namsos. A full-scale landing might be extremely difficult. 'Namsos is under four feet of snow,' reported Churchill, 'and offers no concealment from the air. Local deployment before reaching sparsely wooded country is impossible.' The Chiefs of Staff agreed 'it would be unwise to attempt the proposed further landing that night', the main force should keep away at sea until the position became clearer.[48] General Carton de Wiart arrived at Namsos during the day, but without a staff.

Back in London discussion continued. Should Trondheim be attacked directly or indirectly – with forces converging from Namsos and Aandalsnes? The Joint Planning Committee advised against the latter, stressing the dangers of German air strikes; but the Chiefs of Staff still considered direct attack feasible. Meanwhile, the main Namsos force landed after all, lacking some equipment and also their commanding Brigadier – his ship had sailed for Narvik, under the original plan. Yet despite this Namsos landing, the Military Coordination Committee decided that day that Trondheim should be directly attacked, though only best quality troops should be used in view of the dangers. A regular infantry brigade would have to be sent from France.

Stalemate continued at Harstad, far to the north. Mackesy insisted his task was preliminary preparation. Any attack would have to be launched in appalling weather conditions, and his troops would be outnumbered ten to one, the Germans well dug in. By the evening of the sixteenth, more news of delay had reached London: the General proposed to take the unoccupied positions on the approach to Narvik and hold on until the snow melted – perhaps at the end of the month. He believed that by then the first demi-brigade of *Chasseurs Alpins* would have arrived; still unaware that this valuable French unit was being diverted to Trondheim. The MCC met to discuss this disturbing news, and Churchill urged the attack should be made under cover of naval guns. A strong telegram should be sent to Cork and Mackesy to this effect. Reporting to the Cabinet soon afterwards, he said the telegram, now sent, had put 'the arguments in favour of an early assault', while 'in no way overruling their judgement'. Churchill added: 'Casualties in General Mackesy's force caused by exposure in the next few weeks might well be as severe as those which would be suffered in an immediate assault.'[49] But Mackesy refused to be moved.

Meanwhile more doubts were cast on plans for a direct attack on Trondheim. The C-in-C Home Fleet, Sir Charles Forbes, at sea in the *Rodney*, believed such an attack would mean very heavy losses. If warships, rather than the slower troopships, were used to convey the troops, losses would be reduced – but insufficient warships were available. So the Chiefs of Staff concentrated instead on the 'enveloping operation' from Namsos and Aandalsnes, which Churchill detailed to the War Cabinet next day, Thursday, 18 April. When the *Chasseurs Alpins* arrived, he said, Wiart 'would have forces at least as strong as, or stronger than, the total of German forces in the area.'[50]

Plans for advance into Belgium had not yet been fixed. The previous day, 17 April, Halifax had revealed information from secret sources that King Leopold and his advisers had decided, if Holland were invaded, not to help her, though he added that the Belgian Government might decide differently. The Cabinet agreed Halifax should consider telling the Belgians that allied troops would enter their country if Holland were invaded.[51] But on the eighteenth Halifax reported that despite previous allied thinking, Reynaud now believed the Allies should not go into Belgium uninvited. Not till next day was even a little light shed on this remarkable situation – neither British nor French knowing how they would respond – when Sir Ronald Campbell was able to report that instructions to the French Ambassador at Brussels 'indicated' determination to go into Belgium regardless.[52]

Also on 19 April, the Chiefs of Staff concluded that direct assault on Trondheim should be abandoned in favour of the enveloping moves. Now direct activities at Trondheim would merely serve as a diversion.[53] The same day Mackesy reconnoitred the Narvik area from the *Aurora*, and returned even more convinced that immediate attack would be disastrous. And when, later during the day an Arctic blizzard began to rage, serious tactical moves grew even less likely. In Berlin, there were similar frustrations. The attempt to govern Norway through Quisling appeared to be failing, and the Narvik garrisons seemed in imminent danger – on the 17th Hitler had made the hysterical (and impossible) demand that the troops should be air-evacuated from the port.

Cork was made sole commander at Narvik, largely due to Churchill, who 'hoped that by relieving General Mackesy from direct major responsibility we should make him feel free to adopt bold tactics'.[54]

Chamberlain, meanwhile, remained optimistic, writing on 20 April: 'The military keep saying that we are engaged in very hazardous

330

Patrick Cosgrave in "Churchill at War -
Alone 1939-40" P.159 states that, by
failing to quote from Military Co-ordination
Committee minute of later on 13.4.90
Parkinson fails to show that Churchill
moved towards support for Trondheim
operation on 13.4.40
[See also paperback Churchill vol.2
P.191-2]

operations, so I suppose we are, but I shall be very disappointed if we haven't practically captured Trondheim before the week is out.'[55] Within hours these hopes were thoroughly crushed.

Cork wrote to thank Churchill on 21 April. 'Inertia' had to be overcome, he said. Yet fears he shared: the snow was deep; assuming there would be no resistance had been a serious error; supplies were deficient. 'What is really our pressing need is fighters.'[56] Both Cork and Mackesy now believed nothing could be done until the weather improved. This now resulted in a change of emphasis back in London; on 20 April Churchill wrote 'the importance and urgency of reaching a decision at Narvik can hardly be overrated', on 21 April Ismay decided: 'At the present moment our main attention is directed to the Trondheim area... the capture of Narvik is not at the present moment so urgent.'[57]

But on 21 April, Ministers heard that the Trondheim situation had deteriorated: British forces at Namsos had been heavily bombed, and communications disrupted. As usual, Churchill was optimistic, yet even he began to sound anxious. 'The position in Norway generally gives rise to some anxiety, but it is not by any means desperate. We have taken a risk with our eyes open, knowing that it was a very hazardous operation to throw lightly equipped forces ashore without proper maintenance facilities.' Preparing a brief for the Supreme War Council, Ismay summed the situation up. Because of the need to act quickly to help the Norwegians, hastily-improvised forces had had to be put ashore, and the points where they had landed were unsuitable for the maintenance of big formations. 'Thus, until we succeed in capturing Trondheim the size of the forces which we can maintain in Norway is strictly limited.'[58]

But the Namsos-Trondheim situation continued to worsen; a slight thaw allowed German forces to land on the flank of the British advance to the north of Trondheim, and the British units were driven back towards Namsos, itself under heavy Luftwaffe attack. Wiart cabled on 21 April that 'his position was becoming untenable and that he might have to evacuate his troops'. But the War Secretary sent a message 'pointing out the importance of keeping his troops in being, and informing him of steps which are being taken to provide air support'.[59] Neither Churchill nor Chamberlain attended the Cabinet meeting on the 22nd, both had left for the Supreme War Council meeting in Paris. But before leaving, Churchill had left a note urging that Cork should bombard Narvik if he felt it necessary, regardless of civilian casualties. The MCC endorsed this: 'It would be impossible to allow the Germans to convert Norwegian towns into forts by keeping the civilians in the towns to prevent us from attacking.'[60]

Churchill later described this important Supreme War Council meeting. 'M. Reynaud, having welcomed us, opened with a statement on the general military position which by its gravity dwarfed our joint Scandinavia excursions.' He claimed Germany could deploy 150 Divisions on the Western Front, while the Allies could muster only 100, 10 of them British; the Germans also had the advantage of aircraft, artillery and ammunition. The French at last agreed to the bombing of German military targets when invasion began, and the allies confirmed that the armies would also advance immediately into Belgium, with or without an invitation. The extent of the advance would however depend on the Belgian attitude: if Belgium joined the allies with her 20 Divisions the move would attempt to reach the Namur-Antwerp line – Plan D – if not, it would go no further than the Scheldt. Chamberlain then described the Norway situation, using Ismay's brief, and the Council agreed that the immediate military objectives should be Trondheim and Narvik, followed by the concentration of an adequate allied force on the Swedish frontier.[61]

Meanwhile in London, the new Vice-CIGS, Sir John Dill, had given a gloomy account of the Namsos position to the War Cabinet. The Luftwaffe was continuing to threaten any possible British success. 'It has always been recognized that a landing operation in the face of superior air forces is extremely hazardous, and indeed hardly practicable. At Narvik the enemy are not able to bring such a heavy scale of air attack to bear, and at Aandalsnes it has been possible to put up some anti-aircraft defences before heavy air attacks developed. At Namsos conditions are at their worst.'[62]

At 7 a.m. on 24 April, four British warships began to bombard Narvik. Prior warnings had been broadcast over the Norwegian radio, and every attempt was made to avoid shelling houses, many of which contained German strongpoints. For three hours the bombardment continued, watched by local Norwegians, and Germans, from safety in the surrounding hills. Meanwhile, the Chiefs of Staff were thinking again about direct attack on Trondheim, previously discarded in view of the air threat, and because envelopment from Namsos and Aandalsnes had promised success.[63] This suggestion revealed the level of desperation now reached. The Military Coordination Committee discussed it later in the day, but the Joint Planners stressed that even if Trondheim were taken, the lack of anti-aircraft defences would mean the British would be at the Luftwaffe's mercy. And more troops would be needed from France, which would take two weeks to arrange. Later during the twenty-fourth, news arrived that the Narvik bombardment had had only limited results. Nobody could think of a way from the Norwegian quagmire; the appointment of Lieutenant-General Massy, Dill's predecessor as Deputy CIGS, as overall commander of Norwegian operations except Narvik, failed to bring any change for the better. Churchill now wrote a worried letter to the Prime Minister. 'Being anxious to sustain you to the best of my ability, I must warn you that you are approaching a head-on smash in Norway.' He pointed out deficiencies in Chamberlain's decision-making structure. 'I am very grateful to you for having at my request taken over the day-to-day management of the Military Coordination [Committee]. I think I ought however to let you know that I shall not be willing to receive that task back from you without the necessary powers. At present no one has the power.' Six Chiefs and Deputy-Chiefs of Staff, three Ministers and General Ismay all had a voice in the Norwegian operations, 'but no one is responsible for the creation and direction of military policy except yourself'. If Chamberlain thought he could carry this burden, then he would be given unswerving loyalty by Churchill. 'If you do not feel you can bear it, with all your other duties, you will have to delegate your powers to a deputy who can concert and direct the general movement of our war action.'[64] Churchill never sent this plea for the creation of a Minister of Defence; before he could despatch the letter, he was invited to dine with Chamberlain, and the First Lord put all his points verbally. But Chamberlain refused to take the hint. Churchill would have to wait just a short while longer; Chamberlain, now increasingly ill, struggled on. The effect on Churchill became noticeable. Next day, 25 April, the Cabinet discussed moves to push forward from Aandalsnes to relieve pressure on the Norwegians guarding the Oslo-Trondheim road – 'Operation Sickleforce'. 'Winston was a bit wild at the Cabinet,' wrote Ironside, 'trying to command the troops in the field and railing at us for not having carried out demolitions on the front held by the Norwegians.'[65] Major-General B. C. T. Paget, commander of 'Sickleforce', arrived at Aandalsnes that night, after vainly appealing in England for more air support. Next day, the Cabinet learnt that most of a batch of Gladiator aircraft, sent to provide more cover, had been destroyed on a frozen lake cleared as a landing strip.

The same day, the Military Coordination Committee decided plans should be prepared for possible withdrawal from Norway, except from Narvik.[66] Reporting this to the Cabinet a few minutes later, Chamberlain said the Committee believed very little could be done in central Norway without Trondheim. 'The diversion of strength that we should have to make to try and maintain forces ashore would be disproportionate to the ends we might achieve. For this reason, the Committee has come to the conclusion that plans should be got ready for evacuating our forces from Aandalsnes and Namsos in case of need.' Chamberlain continued: 'It cannot be denied that to admit failure in Norway would be serious to our prestige, but we might mitigate the effects of our withdrawal if we could present to the world the picture that we had gone into central Norway to gain time for the achievement of our real object, which is the capture of Narvik.'[67] A meeting in the evening decided Gamelin and the French Staff should be invited to London next day, 27 April, for talks with the British Chiefs of Staff; and when Reynaud heard the British were considering withdrawing from central Norway, in direct contradiction of the Supreme War Council's decision of only three days before, he insisted on coming as well.

Meanwhile, Hitler had chaired an all-night military conference in Berlin, and at 3.30 in the morning of 26 April, had made new offensive plans. His military commanders were now told 'Operation Yellow' – invasions of Holland and Belgium – would start between 1 May and 7 May. In London, Chamberlain, who had written on 20 April that he would be disappointed if Trondheim was not 'practically captured' before the week was out, wrote on 27 April: 'This has been one of the worst, if not *the* worst, weeks of the war.'

Reynaud, Gamelin, Daladier and Darlan had long discussions with the British leaders during the morning of the 27th; Chamberlain emphasized the strain on the Royal Navy, the devastating effect of German air superiority, the adverse weather conditions. He mentioned ominous rumours that Italy might be ready to enter the war. Gamelin suggested that as a preliminary to taking Narvik, the Namsos troops should occupy as many points as possible on the coast running north, and this idea was accepted by the Supreme War Council. Churchill, in the Cabinet later in the day, also hesitated to agree to complete withdrawal. 'Further consideration should be given to leaving the troops now in Norway to put up the best fight they could, in conjunction with the Norwegians.' Ironside disagreed: 'I could find no military reason for doing this. It was all politics.'[68]

Only a few hours later depressing and adverse reports had accumulated to show evacuation from central Norway should start almost immediately. Plans were made for the evacuation to take place at Namsos on the night of 1/2 and 2/3 May. On the night of 29 April the King of Norway and members of his Government were taken aboard the cruiser *HMS Glasgow* at Molde, and sailed to Tromso, north of Narvik. With incredible bravery, skill, and a good proportion of luck, Aandalsnes was successfully cleared without loss by dawn on 1 May, in the face of vicious bombing attacks. Admiral J. H. D. Cunningham, who had sailed from Scapa on 29 April, scorned the idea of taking two nights to lift the troops from the Namsos beach, and planned to accomplish this operation during darkness on 2/3 May.

Meanwhile, Chamberlain had considered Churchill's points, and decided changes were indeed necessary in the decision-making process. At the end of April he gave Churchill greater powers of direction, stopping short of Defence Minister: Churchill would continue to chair all MCC meetings when the Prime Minister himself did not preside, and would be responsible 'on behalf of the Committee, for giving guidance and direction to the Chiefs of Staff Committee'. For this

334

purpose he had power to summon the Chiefs of Staff whenever necessary. To help him, Churchill would have a small Central Staff, as distinct from the Admiralty Staff, under a Senior Staff Officer who would be an additional member of the Chiefs of Staff Committee. The officer selected was Ismay, who wrote: 'These arrangements seemed rather odd. How would the Secretary of State for War and the Secretary of State for Air feel about their respective Chiefs of Staff taking orders from the First Lord?' Ismay voiced his misgivings to Chamberlain, who 'left me in no doubt that the decision was final, and instructed me to report to Mr Churchill forthwith'. The General's doubts increased: he feared Churchill would still have responsibility without any real authority, and would merely be able to guide and direct the Chiefs of Staff on lines already specified by the MCC. Churchill seemed to think otherwise. 'To my surprise he gave the impression of being enthusiastic about the new arrangements.'[69]

The changes were announced on 1 May. On the same day, Harold Nicolson jotted in his diary: 'The tapers and tadpoles are putting it around that the whole Norwegian episode is due to Winston. There is a theory going round that Lloyd George may head a Coalition Government. What worries people is that everybody asks, "But whom could you put in Chamberlain's place?"'[70]

As the last troops left Aandalsnes on 1 May, the Chiefs of Staff rejected a proposal by Massy for a base to the south of Narvik. Now, with the Norwegian campaign dwindling, it seemed increasingly likely that a new campaign would begin – on the Western Front. The 1 May Cabinet meeting saw a telegram from the British Chargé at Rome, Sir Noel Charles, who reported: 'According to a reliable informant just returned from Berlin, the Germans had made all preparations for an almost immediate attack on Belgium and Luxembourg.' The dates mentioned were 1 May and 2 May. An equally alarming cable had come from the Ambassador at Ankara, that the Germans were preparing 'a vast number of aircraft for dive-bombing and ground attack, and a large number of submarines. ... With these, the Germans intended to make a great combined attack on the Home Fleet; after this attack they intended to land 25,000 men in England.' 'In view of the exceptionally large number of mine-laying air raids last night,' Churchill told the War Cabinet, 'orders have been issued for the action to be taken in the event of a German attack on Belgium or the Netherlands to be held at 12 hours' notice, instead of 24.'[71]

And on this gentle Spring day, Hitler ordered his army to be ready to strike on 5 May, four days away. From 4 May the assembled armoured units were to be at a 24-hour notice to leap forward. The temperate weather heralded the new season for war in the West.

'The Dutch authorities are certainly more alarmed than they have been for some time past,' Halifax told the Cabinet on 2 May. 'The situation *vis-à-vis* Italy is a shade easier than it has been, and it is unlikely on balance that Italy will make war on us during, say, the next week or fortnight.'[72] Meanwhile Chamberlain had some explaining to do over British failure in Norway, and, although the evacuation from Namsos was not to take place until that night, 2/3 May, he thought it necessary, in view of rumours and criticisms, to make an evening statement in the House concerning the Aandalsnes withdrawal. At the Cabinet meeting the day before, he had said he intended to make a number of important points in this statement: the withdrawal from central Norway was 'strategically imperative', and if the campaign had been continued up to 60,000 troops would have had to be put into the operation; the result would have been an undue strain upon the Navy. He would include some 'favourable factors', including the 'tangible and irrefutable fact that we have succeeded in destroying half the German navy', and the point that the Germans had been induced to send some eight or nine Divisions into Norway. While this rehearsal was taking place, Eden whispered to Anderson that he wondered if 'Hitler's supreme council were also conducted in similar fashion'.[73]

Chamberlain accordingly made his statement on the evening of 2 May. But in spite of his claims, few MPs did not know that Britain had suffered a major defeat, and this belief became a conviction when Namsos was also evacuated, brilliantly and bravely though this was done. Talk grew of Lloyd George replacing Chamberlain; Halifax was believed to be too tired to carry on; Churchill was considered by many to have been discredited. Uncertainty only increased the gloom. Stafford Cripps, mobilizing opinion for a new Government, met Lloyd George on 2 May and found him 'most pessimistic and disturbed and generally disgruntled.... Rather to my surprise [he said] Winston could not be PM, and that it would have to be Halifax.' 'Considering the prominent part I played in these events,' wrote Churchill, 'and the impossibility of explaining the difficulties by which we had been overcome, or the defects of our staff and governmental organization and our method of conducting war, it was a marvel that I survived.'[74]

On Friday, 3 May, the Cabinet heard that vessels had reached Scapa Flow with the troops from Aandalsnes.[75] During the day Cork ordered a direct attack on Narvik for 8 May, but Mackesy stressed the shortage of landing craft and the lack of surprise, and Cork referred the matter to London. The same day, Hitler postponed the attack on the West by 24 hours, to 6 May, largely to give the German Foreign Office more time to think of excuses for invading the Low Countries. Next day the Führer ordered another 24 hour delay. But rumours continued to reach London, strengthened by reports of increased activity.

Chamberlain escaped to Chequers that Saturday. He felt ill, extremely tired, and anxious over his political position; he hoped his opponents would not succeed in ousting him because 'I should then have to leave this lovely place.' Trying to snatch a few hours' relaxation, he walked through the nearby woods, and wrote another long letter that evening, giving his opinions of the Norwegian campaign. 'I am thankful that at least we got our men out.... We could not give them what they wanted most, namely fighter aircraft.' Even if Trondheim had been taken, he believed success would probably have been only temporary. 'The most common cry, and this of course is chronic in the USA, is "why are we always too late? why do we let Hitler take the initiative?".... The answer to these questions is simple enough, but the questioners would rather not believe it. It is "because we are not yet strong enough".' Britain had plenty of manpower, but most of this was untrained and ill-equipped; weapons were in short supply; air power was especially deficient. 'If we could weather this year, I believe we should be able to remove our worst deficiencies.'[76] Next day, 5 May, Hitler again postponed the attack, this time to 8 May. But Jodl noted: 'The Führer has finished justification for "Case Yellow".'

Lord Cork was instructed on 5 May that the most which could be done at the moment was to set up a forward landing strip at Bodo, about 120 miles from Narvik, from which British fighters could operate. General Auchinleck would go to Harstad, with a senior Air Officer, to spur matters forward, Narvik must be taken as soon as possible. On 6 May the Cabinet considered Churchill's proposal to occupy Iceland 'forthwith', as a base for flying boats and for re-fuelling the Northern patrol. Should the Icelandic Government be informed beforehand that this takeover was to come about? The Admiralty favoured a simultaneous occupation and declaration, and Halifax agreed. 'The main argument against preliminary negotiations with the Government is that they would inevitably refuse,' he said. 'This would make the task of subsequently entering by force even more distasteful.'[77]

A telegram arrived from the British Minister at the Vatican, where it had been learnt that a German invasion in the West would begin 'this week ... this offensive might include not only the Maginot Line and the Netherlands and Belgium, but even Switzerland.' This was read to the War Cabinet next morning, 7 May. Ministers 'took note'.[78] Another from the Hague claimed 'An attack on the Low Countries and the Western Front is to be expected at dawn on the 8th, or shortly afterwards.'[79]

But Ministers had other pressing problems to consider, including their own political future. The *Daily Mail* article on 7 May, unsigned but actually written by Stafford Cripps, called for a coalition Government under Halifax. And in the afternoon was the Commons debate on Norway.

The House was filled to capacity; Chamberlain knew he would have a hostile reception, but remained confident. He rose to speak to cries of 'Missed the bus!' then presented the Government's case. He, and the Service Ministers, dealt almost exclusively with Norway: Norwegian cooperation had been lacking, next time it would be better; he gave details of the Governmental reorganization, including Churchill's new position. But the speech did not go down well: his critics thought it too clinical, too unemotional, too stubborn. And Norway was not the only issue, nor indeed the main one; after nine months of Twilight War, MPs were frustrated, irritated by the lack of positive action and the apparent complacency. And, as the debate went on, it became clear that feeling against Chamberlain was increasing; criticisms were met with louder cheers each time. The turning point came after J. C. Wedgwood, Labour Member for Newcastle-under-Lyme, had suggested the Royal Navy had fled to Alexandria in fear of German bombs. A moment later Sir Roger Keyes, Conservative MP, hero of Zeebruge and Admiral of the Fleet, entered the Chamber, in full uniform with six rows of medals pinned on his chest. A note was passed to him, telling him of Wedgwood's preposterous jibe. He immediately went to the Speaker's chair, and began a devastating speech. After condemning Wedgwood for his 'damned insult', he condemned the Naval Staff for their failure to take Trondheim. 'When I saw,' he told a hushed House, 'how badly things were going I never ceased importuning the Admiralty and War Cabinet to let me take all responsibility and lead the attack.' He had been told, he said, that a naval action at Trondheim was easy but unnecessary owing to the success of the military. Members gasped at this apparent evidence of gross bungling; Keyes, distinguished in his tailored uniform, seemed to symbolize the Government's lack of offensive spirit. (The Cabinet records make no mention of his 'importuning', nor was a naval victory at Trondheim ever considered 'easy'.) And yet Sir Roger seemed to support Churchill for Prime Minister. 'One hundred and forty years ago, Nelson said: "I am of the opinion that the boldest men are the safest," and that still holds good today.' He sat down to massive and prolonged applause, and the Opposition probably decided then to insist on a vote: before the debate began there had been no intention of dividing the House. The first day's debate ended with Amery's dramatic quotation of Cromwell's words to the Long Parliament. 'You have sat too long here for any good you have been doing. Depart, I say, and let us have done with you. In the name of God, go!'

Ministers were subdued when they met for the War Cabinet meeting next morning. Halifax said subsequent inquiries had shown the alarming report from the Hague, which he had read to the War Cabinet the previous day, was probably a deliberate German leak, intended as a feint. But a new rumour had arrived from Brussels.

'M. Spaak has been given to understand, by the Belgian Ambassador in Berlin, that the German authorities are drafting a note to be presented, at an appropriate moment, to the Netherlands and Belgium Governments.' Ministers now went again to face the hostile House.[80]

Herbert Morrison declared the Opposition's intention to vote, and the proceedings, technically continuing on an Adjournment Motion, now became a Vote of Censure. Chamberlain accepted the challenge, and in doing so made a serious mistake by showing he regarded the attack as one against him, personally. He called upon 'my friends in the House – and I have friends in the House – to support us in the Lobby tonight'. Chamberlain had now turned the vote into a verdict on himself as Prime Minister. Lloyd George, aged 77, made the last great speech of his career, condemning Chamberlain and his Government – with the exception of Churchill. He concentrated on Chamberlain. 'It is not a question of who are the Prime Minister's friends. It is a far bigger issue. He has appealed for sacrifice. The nation is prepared for every sacrifice so long as it has leadership, so long as the Government show clearly what they are aiming at.... I say solemnly that the Prime Minister should give an example of sacrifice, because there is nothing which can contribute more to victory in this war than that he should sacrifice the seals of office.' This speech by an old and respected War Leader had deadly effect. Churchill had the unpleasant task of winding up the debate for the Government, a chore which he had volunteered to do. 'Exception has been taken because the Prime Minister said he appealed to his friends. He thought he had some friends and I hope he has some friends. He certainly had a good many when things were going well.... I say, let pre-war feuds die; let personal quarrels be forgotten, and let us keep out hatreds for the common enemy.... At no time in the last war were we in greater peril than we are now....'

The House divided at 11 p.m. The voting figures were announced: the Government's majority, nominally 231, was 81. The result was greeted with tumultuous applause; Wedgwood started to sing 'Rule Britannia,' other Members yelled 'Go, Go, Go'; the Prime Minister, white-faced, walked swiftly from the Chamber.[81] Chamberlain now realized the depth of the issue, and realized the tactical mistake he had made. 'The long period of waiting,' he wrote, 'without any real setback to German prestige, and then the sudden and bitter disappointment over the hopes that had been so recklessly and unjustifiably fostered by the Press, just boiled up, with the accumulated mass of grievances, to find expression. The serving members were acutely conscious of various deficiencies.... The Amerys, Duff Coopers, and their lot are consciously, or unconsciously, swayed by a sense of frustration because they can only look on, and finally the personal dislike of

Simon and Hoare had reached a pitch which I find it difficult to understand.'[82] Hoare denied any personal animosity, and perhaps Chamberlain was once again taking criticism too personally: Hoare wrote in his memoirs that he had done his best to defend the Norwegian operation in the debate following the evacuation, but the Government had, he believed, failed through 'the rashness of undertaking a military operation for which we were not prepared, and in failing to resist the outcry for action when waiting was the only wise course.... A Government in war time must be overwhelmingly strong, if it is to withstand failure.'[83]

Chamberlain asked Churchill to come to his room in the Commons immediately after the debate. He 'felt he could not go on', and a National Government would have to be formed. 'Someone must form a Government in which all parties would serve, or we could not get through.' Churchill, hackles raised by the passion displayed at the close of the debate, wanted to fight, and urged Chamberlain to stick until his majority had gone completely. But 'Chamberlain was neither convinced nor comforted, and I left him about midnight with the feeling that he would persist in his resolve to sacrifice himself.'[84] While Chamberlain turned the agonizing question over in his mind, the war had still to be waged. The Cabinet met next morning in the Prime Minister's room at the House of Commons; the atmosphere was strained and unreal.

The War Cabinet considered a Chiefs of Staff report, making recommendations on the assumption that Germany had decided to seek a decision in 1940.[85] Included in the paper was the suggestion that 'plans already prepared for dealing with an invasion of this country should be revised forthwith and requirements met... financial considerations should not be allowed to stand in the way.'

Late in the morning, while German newspaper headlines proclaimed 'Britain Plots to Spread the War', Churchill learnt from Wood that Chamberlain had decided to form a National Government, and was prepared to stand down, if necessary. 'Thus by the afternoon I became aware that I might well be called upon to take the lead,' he wrote. 'The prospect neither excited nor alarmed me. I thought it would be by far the best plan.' At 4.30 p.m. the Prime Minister summoned Halifax and Churchill to Downing Street. Attlee and Greenwood were to join the discussion, and when they arrived, Chamberlain declared he intended to form a National Government, and asked them to find out if the Labour Party would serve under him. Halifax, in his memoirs, said it was at this meeting, before Attlee and Greenwood arrived, that Chamberlain discussed questions of his successor. 'He had made up his mind that he must go, and that either Churchill or I must take his place. He would serve under either.' Halifax declined: if he were Prime Minister, Churchill would be running Defence and hence a smooth, single, leadership would be difficult, and he [Halifax] would have no access to the Commons. 'I should speedily become more or less honorary Prime Minister, living in a kind of twilight just outside the things that really mattered.... Churchill, with suitable expressions of regard and humility, having said he could not but feel the force of my words, the Prime Minister reluctantly and Churchill evidently with much less reluctance finished by accepting my view.'[86] According to Churchill's memoirs, this selection took place not at this meeting, but next morning.

'However things go these next few days,' Halifax wrote to Chamberlain that day, 'I can't help writing this line to tell you, how much I have learnt from you during the last 24 hours. You have given me a lesson in public spirit, and in the will to set self to one side, which I hope I will remember. I thank you for that, and for very much else.'[87]

Dusk came on 9 May with the clear promise of excellent weather for the morrow. Scare reports had continued to arrive, but many were thought to be German plants. A cipher message from the Belgian Military Attaché in Berlin reached the Belgian Army HQ at 9 p.m., but was not decoded until 10.30; this reported the German attack would be launched the following day. In France, General Brooke and his staff gathered in the garden of his billet to watch a group of German aircraft fly over high above at about 10 p.m., drawing fire from nearby anti-aircraft guns. Later that night, forward outposts along the length of the frontier from Holland to Luxembourg heard a steadily increasing murmuring from the German side, 'as of the gathering of a host'.[88] To this muttering was added the rumble of vehicles, the squeal of tank tracks, the clatter of metal upon metal. The sound grew louder, out there in the dark. And, at 5.30 a.m., Friday, 10 May, after a few moments of silence, the noise suddenly burst to shattering pitch, and the German mechanized Divisions lurched forward on to the fragile frontiers of Holland, Belgium and tiny Luxembourg.

Final Payment

First news reached London about 5 a.m. The Service Ministers rushed to read the reports, then Stanley and Hoare discussed the situation with Churchill at the Admiralty. 'It was six o'clock in the morning,' wrote Hoare of this talk, 'after a fierce House of Commons debate and a late sitting. We had had little or no sleep, and the news could not have been worse. Yet there he was, smoking his large cigar and eating fried eggs and bacon, as if he had just returned from an early morning ride.' Just before 6 a.m., the BEF received orders from Gamelin to advance into Belgium up to the River Dyle – Plan D.[1]

Friday morning was crisp and clear, with the promise of warm weather to come. Ministers, quiet yet excited, began to arrive at Downing Street just before 8 a.m. for an emergency Cabinet meeting. Halifax entered with a thick bundle of telegrams; Churchill was flushed, Chamberlain pale and sombre. Ministers heard the latest news. 'Parachute troops have been dropped between Leyden and the Hague and in the Rotterdam area. The Luxembourg frontier has been crossed by German troops. The Germans are said to have dropped bombs on Nancy, and two of our aerodromes in northern France have been bombed, but missed. One bomb is said to have fallen in Brussels.' Churchill had telephoned Corbin, at 6 a.m. 'I asked him to find out from the French Government if the armies would move into Belgium on the information which had been received up to that hour, namely, that the attack was on Holland alone.' But Belgium had also been invaded and had asked for help. 'The whole plan for the advance of the Allied Forces into the Low Countries has been set in motion. The troops are not at the highest state of readiness, but will certainly be on the move quickly.'

An immediate problem was whether, in accordance with the Supreme War Council decision, bombers should now strike at military targets in Germany. Newall explained: bombers could either attack the Ruhr, or hold back to intervene at a critical point in the land battle; and a new stipulation was now also agreed: 'it would be preferable not to begin bombing operations in the Ruhr until we have definite news that the Germans have attacked targets ... which would cause casualties to civilians.' Meanwhile, the RAF would bomb targets west of the Rhine to impede the German advance. 'The coast defences and home forces are being put at immediate readiness,' said the War Secretary. 'This will involve considerable expenditure in the case of the home forces, but I assume that no objection will be raised.' Agreeing the general public should 'look to the state of their gas masks', the Ministers dispersed, to meet again in three hours.[2]

At 10 a.m., Sir Kingsley Wood, Lord Privy Seal and Chamberlain's close friend, called to see Churchill at the Admiralty. Chamberlain had believed he should stay on as Prime Minister, in view of the opening of the offensive, but had been persuaded otherwise – the new crisis had made a National Government all the more imperative. An hour later Churchill saw the Prime Minister again; it was now, he wrote later, that the choice was made between Halifax and him. It was certainly now that Chamberlain revealed the Labour Party had refused to serve under him. Churchill would therefore move to Downing Street after seeing the King. 'The momentous conversation came to an end,' wrote Churchill, 'and we reverted to our ordinary easy and familiar manners of men who had worked for years together, and whose lives in and out of office had been spent in all the friendliness of British politics.... I then went back to the Admiralty, where, as may well be imagined, much awaited me.' Chamberlain would see the King to offer his resignation during the evening, or the next day; Halifax believed Churchill impatient with the delay.

The Cabinet met again at 11.30. No mention was made of the impending Government upheaval; bombing policy was the main topic. Ministers agreed to meet a Belgian request that if Germany bombed civilians, Britain and France would act 'in the same manner as if the British and French civilian populations were bombed'. A stream of reports of German air attacks had arrived: the British Ambassador at the Hague telephoned at 11.40 to say a bomb had just dropped within 600 yards of the British Legation; Brussels had also been attacked, despite a Belgian statement insisting it was an open town and no troops were stationed there. 'In the light of this information,' Ministers agreed, 'we should be justified in starting bombing operations on military targets in the Ruhr this evening.' But nevertheless a final decision would be deferred until late afternoon.

At 11.35, just after the War Cabinet had begun, a telephone call had come through from the Paris Embassy. 'Our Ambassador has just learnt that the French had no information suggesting that there are large-scale movements of German troops against either Belgium, the Netherlands, or Luxembourg. The enemy appeared to be working with small detachments – parachutists etc.' 'According to reports received,' said Ironside, 'it looks as if the Germans are advancing through Luxembourg and the Ardennes to the lines of the Meuse, and at the same time advancing through Belgium to the line of the Albert Canal. ... Zero hour for the advance of our forces into Belgium is 1.00 this afternoon. It is probable that our advance forces are already on the move.' The situation, so far as it could be gathered, seemed satisfactory. There should be no general evacuation yet, but the Whitsun holidays should be cancelled – 'the population should be urged to bend all their energies to increasing war production'.[3]

Ministers walked back to their Departments, passing newspaper placards which announced, inaccurately: 'BRUSSELS BOMBED – PARIS BOMBED – LYONS BOMBED – SWISS RAILWAYS BOMBED'. Across the Channel, the allied forces began to move. Their deployment was exactly suited to Hitler's strategy: with the enemy forces in the North held deep in Belgium, he would smash through at unexpected points further south.

A third Cabinet meeting started at 4.30 p.m. Reports were read of bombing in Holland, Belgium, France and Switzerland. Five incendiary bombs had dropped near Canterbury, yet according to Newall: 'There appears to be no deliberate attack on civilian populations.' 'Up to the present,' said Ironside, 'the advance of our troops is going to plan. As to the enemy's progress, it appears that although parachutists have been dropped at a large number of places in Belgium, there is as yet no rush of armoured Divisions across the frontier.... In fact it is doubtful whether an invasion of Belgium in strength is actually taking place.... It might be that the German advance will take place tonight, but it might also be that they have miscalculated our reaction to their advance on Holland and Belgium, and had not expected us to advance so rapidly. In any case, it appears that we have got a good start, and our leading troops should by now be on the line of the Dyle. It will take some 48 hours for the main bodies to reach that line.' Leashes were still not to be fully slipped on the bomber assaults: no attacks should be made east of the Rhine that night, and the matter would be considered again next day.

The Cabinet reached the last item on the agenda. Chamberlain shuffled his papers together. 'As you are aware,' he said, 'the Labour Party have been asked whether they would consider, in principle, cooperation in the Government, (a) under the present Prime Minister, or (b) under some other Prime Minister. The Labour Party's answer has now been received.... Their answer to the first question is in the negative, and to the second question is as follows: "The Labour Party are prepared to take their share of responsibility as a full partner in a new Government, under a new Prime Minister, which would command the confidence of the Nation.' He looked up. 'I have reached the conclusion that the right course is that I should at once tender my resigna-

344

tion to the King. I propose to do so this evening. I think it will be convenient that the new Prime Minister should be authorized to assume that all members of the War Cabinet placed their resignations at his disposal.'[4]

'I saw the Prime Minister after tea,' wrote King George VI. 'I accepted his resignation, and I told him how grossly unfairly I thought he had been treated, and that I was terribly sorry.' As for Chamberlain's successor, 'I, of course, suggested Halifax'. Chamberlain told him of the Foreign Secretary's objections. 'I was disappointed over this statement, as I thought H. was the obvious man, and that his peerage could be placed in abeyance for the time being. Then I knew there was only one person whom I could send for to form a Government who had the confidence of the country, and that was Winston.'[5] At 6 p.m. Churchill was summoned and asked to form a Government. He told the King that he would send for the Labour and Liberal leaders immediately, that he proposed to form a War Cabinet of five or six Ministers, and that he hoped to let the King have at least five names before midnight. He then returned to the Admiralty. He had already decided on his Service Ministers – Eden at the War Office; A. V. Alexander, a Labour member, as First Lord; and Sir Archibald Sinclair, Liberal leader, as Air Secretary. He telephoned Chamberlain, and invited him to lead the House as Lord President of the Council; Chamberlain accepted. Halifax was asked to stay as Foreign Secretary. At about 7.30 a.m., the Labour leader, Attlee, was invited to submit recommendations – apart from Alexander, Churchill mentioned Bevin, Morrison and Dalton.

Churchill did indeed have a five-man War Cabinet. Apart from himself, Chamberlain, and Halifax, Attlee entered as Lord Privy Seal and Greenwood as Minister without Portfolio. All others, including Service Ministers, remained outside this inner War Cabinet. And Churchill appointed himself Defence Minister, 'without however attempting to define its scope and powers'. Other appointments included Ernest Bevin as Minister of Labour, and Beaverbrook as the newly created Minister of Aircraft Production. Hoare soon left as Ambassador to Spain.

At 9 p.m. on 10 May, while Churchill was working on the composition of the new Government, Chamberlain announced his resignation in a radio broadcast. 'It came quite spontaneously,' he wrote afterwards. 'I had no time for polishing.' After 8 May debate, 'I had no doubt in my mind that some new and drastic action must be taken, if confidence was to be given to the House of Commons, and the war carried on with the energy and vigour essential to victory.... In the afternoon of today it was apparent that the essential unity could be secured under another Prime Minister.... In these circumstances my duty was plain.... The hour has now come when we are to be put to the test, as the innocent people of Holland, Belgium, and France are being tested already. And you, and I, must rally behind our new leader, and with our united strength, and with unshakable courage, fight and work until this wild beast, that has sprung out of his lair upon us, has been finally disarmed and overthrown.' 'It is a magnificent statement,' wrote Harold Nicolson, 'and all the hatred that I have felt for Chamberlain subsides as if a piece of bread were dropped into a glass of champagne.'[6]

Churchill eventually went to bed at 3 a.m., 'conscious of a profound sense of relief'. Chamberlain wrote next day that the real reason for the Government's failure was the country's comparative weakness; people did not appreciate that 'we haven't yet anything like caught up with the German start ... as that fact remains, whatever the Administration, I am afraid they will presently be disappointed again.'[7] 'I had a short conversation with Chamberlain,' wrote Eden, 'who looked ill and was clearly hating it all. He said that he was staying in the new Government with a heavy heart.'[8] Neville Chamberlain, ex-Prime Minister, ex-appeaser, was dying: in six months' time, cancer would kill him.

The new Prime Minister took the chair for his first Governmental meeting at 12.30 next day, Saturday, 11 May. Chamberlain was there but the Minutes do not record him as saying anything. Churchill announced the 'Royal Marine Operation' had started, and the first fluvial mines ought to reach Mannerheim during the afternoon. Ismay was instructed to discuss with the Home Secretary and War Secretary whether the police should be armed, and Ironside warned of likely 'bombing attacks in the near future on towns on the north and north-east coast, possibly launched from Norway'.[9]

Leading infantry units of the BEF reached their positions on the River Dyle during the day, but in London it seemed likely that a German thrust might reach the river before British forces had established themselves. Fears subsided again during the night; everything still seemed to be going to plan, and in London, after the first excitement and apprehension, there was calm again; in Berlin, noted an American correspondent, the people's apathy was remarkable.[10] Sunday, 12 May, saw the allied forces deploying according to Plan D. General Billotte, commanding the First Army Group, would 'coordinate' the operations of the British, Belgian and French forces in the area. But the German build-up further south had continued; the main thrust forward was almost ready to be launched; Hoth's corps and Kliest's group had pushed ahead, and by darkness on the twelfth Rommel's division was up to the Meuse at Dinant and Guderian's corps at Sedan.

Churchill's third meeting was held at the Admiralty at 10.30 p.m. on the twelfth. Optimism still glowed from all the reports; Newall declared that although 76 aircraft had been lost, and 40 damaged, in the last two days of fighting, 'the German losses are believed to be in the neighbourhood of 300.... I am satisfied with the results.' Ministers were told the German advance had slowed considerably, and allied forces might well establish themselves on the Antwerp-Namur line. But the Holland position had deteriorated; the possibility of helping the Dutch was considered, though no decision was reached. Ministers discussed the German success in landing aircraft on open spaces in Holland, such as car-parks and football grounds; the War Secretary – now Anthony Eden – and Sir Archibald Sinclair, the new Air Secretary, together with Anderson, would look into this question to prevent the same success against Britain.[11]

13 May – Whit Monday – was one of the most crucial days of the war, but did not seem so either to the BEF or in London, despite a 5 a.m. telephone call to King George VI from Queen Wilhelmina of Holland, pleading for aircraft. 'I passed this message on to everyone concerned, and went back to bed. It is not often one is rung up at that hour, and especially by a Queen. But these days anything may happen.'

Parliament was summoned to record formally a Vote of Confidence in the new administration; Chamberlain was cheered more than Churchill when he entered the House. In a rousing, short speech the new Prime Minister declared: 'I have nothing to offer but blood, toil, tears and sweat....' Lloyd George made a moving speech of welcome, and Churchill, sitting between Chamberlain and Attlee, mopped his eyes with a large handkerchief. But 'the proof of the pudding,' warned Cripps, 'will be in the experience of eating.' With this formality over, Ministers met at 6.30 p.m. Everything still seemed satisfactory, although the first tinge of doubt was beginning to appear. 'The general situation on the whole front,' reported Ironside, 'shows strong German mechanized forces advancing in a number of directions, but as yet no signs of infantry columns.' Without the infantry, according to the text-books, a large-scale offensive could not take place. 'The French are not yet certain whether the main German effort is directed through Luxembourg against the left of the Maginot Line, or through Maastricht.' The first phase of the movement of the French and British armies would be completed by 7.00 next morning, and the Anglo-French forces would be engaged in consolidating their positions; 'the Belgian Army does not appear to be putting up a strong resistance'.

'The picture which has been placed before the War Cabinet ... shows there are two alternatives,' said Churchill. 'The Germans might either be launching their great land attack with the object of trying to defeat the Franco-British armies, or they might content themselves with making contact along the line which the Allied armies have taken

347

up in Belgium, and with consolidating their position in Holland preparatory to their great attack on this country.' Ironside commented:
'The extent to which the Germans have committed their air and
mechanized resources indicates the land battle is beginning.'

Further thought had been given to defence against enemy parachutists, said Eden. The Cabinet approved a suggestion for 'a corps
of local defence volunteers'. This later became the Home Guard.

'There has been a fresh outburst of Italian animosity,' said Halifax,
'even more bitter than the last. It seems that Sr. Mussolini is either
trying to give the utmost assistance to Germany without going to
war, or is trying to make Italy war-minded before driving her into
war.'[12]

While the Cabinet was in session, the Battle of France was being lost.
Earlier in the day a motor-cycle battalion from Rommel's division
had managed to secure a small bridgehead over the river Meuse at
Houx; late on 13 May, his tanks moved across the river. And at Sedan,
scene of Napoleon III's surrender to Moltke in the Franco-Prussian
War, Guderian's armoured units crossed the Meuse in a large-scale
assault, closely supported by the Luftwaffe, and Panzers began to
pierce through France's central lines. Few hints of this disaster reached
the BEF; the Belgian forces further forward, on the far side of the
Meuse, were complaining of lack of air support, and had begun to fall
back on the main Antwerp-Louvain-Wavre line – but the situation
still seemed hopeful. The Dutch, however, were in a desperate position, and were appealing for help; next morning came the finish, when
the Germans, impatient with the delay, bombed Rotterdam and the
Dutch capitulated.

First reports of the breakthrough in the centre reached London just
before the Tuesday, 14 May Cabinet meeting. Ministers were told the
most serious German thrust was on the Namur-Sedan front, with the
axis of the German advance through Dinant. Ironside added: 'News
received from Lord Gort this morning shows that the position of the
BEF is satisfactory.'[13] Ministers still felt no undue alarm.

But by mid-afternoon the French situation had changed completely. Another Cabinet meeting was called for 7 p.m., at which
Churchill read a telephone message from Reynaud. German tanks
were streaming across the Meuse, over a specially constructed pon-
toon bridge, which remained intact despite desperate attempts to
destroy it by French artillery and armour and costly RAF attacks.
'Germany intends to deliver a mortal blow towards Paris,' Reynaud
had said. 'The German army has broken through our fortified line
south of Sedan.... We cannot resist the combined attacks of heavy
tanks and bomber squadrons.... To stop the German drive whilst
there is still time, it is necessary to cut off the German tanks and the
bombers supporting them. It can only be done by an enormous force

348

of fighters. You were kind enough to send four squadrons, which is more than you promised, but if we are to win this battle, which might be decisive for the whole war, it is necessary to send at once, if possible today, ten more squadrons. Without such support, we cannot be sure of stopping the German advance.... Between Sedan and Paris there are no fortifications left to be compared with the line to be re-established at almost any cost.'[14] Churchill said he had discussed the message with the Chiefs of Staff; yet, despite the urgency of the appeal, no decision was taken at this meeting. The Panzers plunged on. The gap in the French centre stretched to 30, 40, then almost 50 miles wide; and the German Divisions flooded through and on towards Paris. At 7.30 next morning, 15 May, the Prime Minister was awoken to be told Reynaud was ringing from Paris; he heard Reynaud say in English: 'We have been defeated. We are beaten. We have lost the battle.'

Churchill described this 'alarmist message' to the War Cabinet three hours later. 'M. Reynaud said that the Germans had broken through at Sedan, and that the road to Paris is open. He made an urgent appeal for British help.... I refused to accept so gloomy a picture of the situation. I pointed out that it is impossible for us to send any more divisions to France at the present moment; and even if we had been ready to denude this country of troops, it would be quite impossible to get them quickly to the scene of action.' He had telephoned General Georges, who had 'seemed quite calm', and had told Churchill the situation was fairly satisfactory in the north; pressure was considerable in the centre; in the south the position was undoubtedly serious. 'The Germans had broken through on a fairly wide front, but this has now been plugged – "Colmaté".' He had made no direct request for further help. Churchill went on: 'I have also had a telephone call from General Gamelin, who said that although the position was serious between Namur and Sedan, he viewed the situation with calm. He asked for all possible air assistance.' Ironside confirmed the German thrust at Sedan was blocked for the moment – but he had been misinformed: the Germans were pushing forward and were now about 50 miles inside France.

Halifax said he had been told by the American Ambassador that instructions had come from Cordell Hull to urge US citizens to leave Britain. Then Churchill returned to the questions of aircraft and bombing policy: two points had to be decided, he said; first, 'whether we should send any more fighter squadrons to France in response to M. Reynaud's appeal'; secondly, 'whether we should attack military objectives in Germany east of the Rhine'. He continued: 'I suggest that the War Cabinet will have little difficulty in deciding against the despatch of further fighter squadrons in view of the fact that no demand for these has been received from the Military Authorities in France.' Newall corrected him on this – a request had arrived from the C-in-C British Air Force in France, Air Marshal Barratt. But Newall continued: 'I would not, at this moment, advise the despatch of any additional fighter squadrons to France.' The Chiefs of Staff were 'extremely conscious' of the heavy losses being suffered by the RAF in France – 67 aircraft on 14 May alone.

Attending this meeting was Air Chief Marshal Dowding, Air Officer Commanding Fighter Command, who, in view of his concern over more aircraft being despatched to France, had asked to be able to plead his case. According to his own account, he now did so. 'I got to my feet, and taking my graph with me I walked around to the seat occupied by the Prime Minister. I leant forward and laid the graph on the table in front of him, and I said: "If the present rate of wastage continues for another fortnight we shall not have a single Hurricane left in France or in this country." I laid a particular emphasis on "or in this country".'[15] There is no evidence in the Minutes that this dramatic intervention changed Churchill's mind, nor, contrary to Dowding's later account, is there evidence that Churchill's mind needed changing anyway. From the outset he was firmly opposed to the despatch of fighters.

The Cabinet turned to the second question: bombing the Ruhr. Again, high RAF losses had to be considered. 'The experience of the last few days in France,' said Sinclair, 'points to the fact that, at the present rate, it will be extremely difficult for the RAF to maintain its present effort in support of the land battles by daylight bombing operations.... The extent to which the Army can be supported in the immediate battle zone by night bombing is very limited. I therefore think that the right course will be to extend the activities of our long-range night bombers.' Dowding commented: 'It is the soundest action which we can take in the present situation,' adding ominously, 'We should not be deterred by the fear of attacks from Germany since these, in my opinion, are bound to come sooner or later.' But Churchill was also concerned with effects on neutral opinion: American sympathy had recently been veering very much in Britain's favour, he maintained. 'Would the operations ... produce a revulsion of feeling?' But Halifax believed long-range bombing policy fully justified, and the Cabinet eventually agreed; the operations should start that night.[16]

German pressure on Belgium increased. The French First Army, to the BEF's immediate right, was being heavily squeezed on the Wavre-Namur gap, and the Belgian troops on the BEF left were nervous and unsettled. Brooke wrote that evening: 'The BEF is likely to have both flanks turned, and will have a very unpleasant time extricating itself out of its present position.'[17] Churchill wrote a warning letter to Roosevelt during the day: the scene had suddenly darkened; the danger of a Nazi Europe was imminent; it might be too late – unless the United States used her voice and force. He asked the President to declare 'non-belligerency', which he thought might include the loan of 50 or so destroyers and several hundred aircraft.

Over 100 heavy bombers droned across Europe on the night of 15 May to bomb the Ruhr; the Strategic Air Offensive had begun. But damage was later found to have been slight, and by next morning the situation on the Western Front was deteriorating even faster. The French, Churchill told the 11.30 Cabinet meeting, were again urgently asking for additional fighters, and now the urgency of the position had been confirmed by the senior British officers at the Front. Newall had been in contact with Barratt, who reported 'Our fighter pilots are very tired.... They had to deal all yesterday with waves of 50 bombers, every hour, heavily escorted by fighters.' Instead of the RAF counter-attacking with whole squadrons of fighters, as should have been done, flights of three or five aircraft were being sent up against vastly superior numbers. 'Every pilot was carrying out four or five sorties a day,' said Newall. The French appeared to be making little resistance on the ground, and he added that Air Marshal Blunt, with the British Air Component, had told him 'the Germans are now attacking with waves of 100 bombers at a time.'

Churchill stressed the risk of sending fighters – 'at a time when we are most likely to be attacked ourselves in response to the attacks on the Ruhr last night.' But 'it seems essential to do something to bolster up the French', and he favoured withdrawing two fighter squadrons from Scapa and sending six extra squadrons in all to France. 'More than this we cannot do.' Sinclair told the Cabinet that Dowding was still, even now, opposed to sending fighters to France. Because of this, Sinclair was against despatching more than four squadrons. Halifax interrupted the discussions. 'I have just received a message from our Ambassador in Paris.... M. Reynaud ... fears that German armoured fighting vehicles will reach Paris tonight.' He added that Gamelin was sending a fresh appeal for fighters, proposing they should be based on the lower Seine, where they could be rapidly recalled to Britain in an emergency. The Cabinet agreed to despatch four fighter squadrons immediately, and prepare for two more squadrons to be sent at very short notice. Summing up the military position, Ironside commented: 'There is no doubt that the situation is most critical. The Germans have made this large penetration with mechanized forces, but it does not appear that the infantry have followed up behind. All now depends on whether the French will fight with vigour in the counter-attack which General Gamelin proposes to launch.'

Dill, Vice-CIGS, who had just spoken on the telephone with Gort, now revealed even more disturbing information. The line had been extremely bad, but so far as Dill could make out, the BEF was about to be pulled back. 'On the right, the Second Division has been severely attacked, but has not given ground. There has been a certain penetration by the enemy over the Dyle on the right of this Division, which has caused a slight withdrawal on the part of the French and a consequent readjustment of our line. General HQ are not, however, disturbed.... Further south, however, from the direction of Mezières, the Germans have made a penetration with armoured forces ... orders have been issued, either by General Georges or General Billotte, or both, for a withdrawal tonight.' This retirement would result in a new line from Trelon-Marpent, north-east along the Sambre to east of Charleroi, then along the Sanne to Hal, through Brussels to Malines and on to the Antwerp defences. 'I take an extremely grave view of this news,' exclaimed Churchill. 'I consider that a withdrawal from our line on account of the penetration of the French line, by a force of some 120 German armoured vehicles, is quite unjustifiable, and will expose the British Army to far more serious risks than if they remained in their present position and fought.' He clearly believed the French were still exaggerating the threat; further consultations must take place before withdrawal was given, and Churchill would fly to Paris with Dill and Ismay.[18]

By 5.30 p.m. Churchill was confronting Reynaud, Daladier and Gamelin at the Quai d'Orsay; Gamelin gave a five-minute account of the situation – the Germans had broken through north and south of Sedan on a front of 50 or 60 miles, and were now advancing, unopposed, towards Amiens and Arras. They could then strike up for the coast, or head for Paris. Nobody spoke when Gamelin had finished, until Churchill asked: 'Where is the Strategic Reserve?' Gamelin, according to Churchill's account, answered: 'There is none.' After the war Gamelin claimed he had said: 'There is no longer any.' The discrepancy made no difference to the French plight; and outside the room in which Churchill was talking to the desolate French leaders, secret papers were being burnt to prevent their falling into German hands. French armour was inadequate, Churchill was told; much of the best artillery had been lost – and 400 fighter aircraft out of 500.

Churchill no longer had doubts about the seriousness of the French situation. He telephoned London, and at 11 p.m. the Cabinet met again – with Chamberlain temporarily back in the chair. Churchill had 'urged that six more squadrons of fighters should be sent to France in addition to the four already promised ... and that a larger part of our heavy bombers should be employed on the following nights upon the German masses crossing the Meuse.' 'If six more were sent,' warned Sinclair, 'we will be down to 29 squadrons in all of the United Kingdom.' Dowding had said he could only defend Britain with an absolute minimum of 25. Newall gave more frightening details. 'There remains in the United Kingdom, now, only six complete Hurricane squadrons.' But he proposed a solution: move all these Hurricane squadrons to Kent, and send servicing parties over to northern France.

'Three of the six squadrons to be sent to Kent would work in France from dawn until noon...being relieved by the other three for the afternoon.' This was approved; 'Arranging for bombers as you propose,' Churchill was told in Paris.[19]

The Prime Minister received the welcome news soon after 11.30 p.m. He immediately drove to Reynaud's flat. Daladier was sent for. 'I hoped to revive the spirits of our French friends, as much as our limited means allowed,' wrote Churchill. 'Daladier never spoke a word. He rose slowly from his chair and wrung my hand.' The Prime Minister went to bed at the British Embassy at 2 a.m., and slept contentedly, only slightly disturbed by 'cannon fire in petty aeroplane raids'. For the BEF those hours of darkness were the start of 18 days of hell. The withdrawal had begun, initially back to the line of the Scheldt. Troops blew up bridges after them, and the Germans were close behind; and, while Rommel and Guderian cut through from south of Sedan, Reinhardt's and Hoth's two other Panzer corps were thrusting forward further north, racing alongside the retreating French First Army and heading for the base towns from which the Allies had advanced into Belgium, only six days before.

Churchill flew back early next morning, 17 May, in time for the Cabinet meeting at 10 a.m. In his report, he showed he realized the German strategic plan: 'It is now plain why the Allied troops had not been bombed in their advance into Belgium: the Germans wanted to get us into forward positions, in order to effect a breakthrough and turn our flanks.' He claimed the German advance had now slowed, probably to re-form and re-fuel. 'I made it quite clear to the French that, unless they made a supreme effort, we will not feel justified in accepting the grave risk to the safety of this country, which would be entailed by the despatch of more fighters to France.... I feel that the War Cabinet has been faced with the gravest decision that a British Cabinet has ever had to face.'

'The BEF has withdrawn to the line of the canal running through Brussels,' Dill reported. 'Their position is satisfactory, except on the right flank, where German armoured vehicles have penetrated the line. A strong counter-attack is being made.... Our troops are distributed in great depth; the danger spots are the flanks. The Belgian Army on our left flank has not yet been attacked.' Elsewhere the position was deplorable. 'I have just heard from Air Marshal Evil that the situation is very serious,' said Newall. 'The Germans have made a considerable advance during the night and have reached the line Laon-Soissons. ... The position of the (RAF) Advanced Air Striking Force...is precarious. As a result of the rapid German advance, the large number of damaged aircraft, and the partial breakdown of communications, the Advanced Air Striking Force must be considered virtually out of action until it can be reformed.'[20]

'The Führer is terribly nervous,' wrote Halder on the 17th. 'He is worried over his own success.' Intelligence had been gathered by the Luftwaffe – now in virtual control of the skies – that the French were mounting a massive counter-attack from the south, and on the morning of the seventeenth an order was sent to Guderian, almost a third of the way to the Channel, to halt his advance. But Guderian pleaded to be allowed to push forward, and quoted Hitler's own words: 'Once armoured formations are out on the loose, they must be given the green light to the very end of the road.' And so the advance continued: the German columns rumbling over the French countryside, a vast dust cloud hanging in the hot air behind them. Rommel wrote: 'Civilians and French troops, their faces distorted with fear, lay huddled in the ditches.... Always the same picture....'[21]

A special Ministerial sub-committee meeting took place that day, at Churchill's request, and presided over by Chamberlain. The subject discussed was the plight of Britain, should France collapse. The meeting urged that the Government should take far-reaching powers from Parliament to exercise control over labour, business, property, the whole life of the nation. The War Cabinet was to approve these drastic measures, and a Bill resulted and became law on 22 May. Among the topics which Churchill asked the 17 May group to examine were 'the problems which would arise if it were necessary to withdraw the BEF from France, either along its communications or by the Belgium and Channel ports'. Yet Churchill told the Cabinet next day: 'On the whole the military situation in France is better. The French are bringing up troops, and French artillery has had some success in destroying tanks.... The RAF have covered themselves with glory.' Beaverbrook, Minister for Aircraft Production, told Ministers he hoped to salvage three aircraft a week from wrecked machines, and Halifax reported the Russians seemed anxious at the speed of the German advance: 'it might be possible to make some arrangements with them'. The Cabinet asked Stafford Cripps to proceed to Moscow to explore possibilities.[22]

Cambrai and St Quentin fell during the 18th. As the allied units reeled backwards, Brooke listed the features of this nightmare – 'lack of sleep, irregular meals, great physical exertions of continuous travelling in all directions, rumours, counter-rumours, doubts, ambiguous orders and messages, lack of information on danger-points, and the thousand and one factors that are perpetually hammering away at one's power of resistance'.[23] The same day, Reynaud ousted Daladier from the Ministry of National Defence and took over the position himself. He summoned General Weygand to replace Gamelin, and he invited Marshal Pétain to join his Ministry. Weygand, who officially took over command of the French and British armies on 20 May, was seventy-three years old.

354

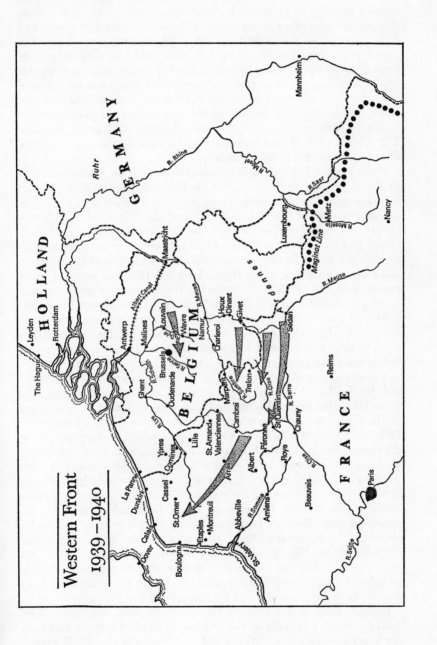

Western Front
1939–1940

The British Chiefs of Staff considered a report on 19 May, titled 'British Strategy in a Certain Eventuality', which examined the situation in the event of a French defeat, a Franco-German agreement, and Italy joining the war against Britain – all soon to come about. The report posed two questions. Could Britain hold out until help came from America? And could Britain ultimately bring sufficient economic pressure to bear on Germany to ensure her defeat? The enemy, said the report, would try one or more of three possible courses: unrestricted air attack on Britain, aimed at a collapse in public morale; starvation through attacks on British shipping and ports; invasion. The Chiefs of Staff concluded, correctly, that in the last resort all depended upon RAF fighter aircraft.

Fresh alarms followed during the afternoon from a telephone call to the War Office by General Sir H. Pownall, Gort's Chief of Staff; Ironside gave Pownall's message to the War Cabinet at 4.30. 'If the gap on the right of the BEF widens, [Gort] has it in mind to withdraw towards Dunkirk, resting his right on the canal running through St Omer, and to fight it out there.' The suggestion was contrary to military theory based on the 1918 experience, which taught the supreme value of an unbroken allied front. 'I replied that this proposal could not be accepted at all,' said Ironside. 'We might at a pinch be able to supply the BEF in a bridgehead resting on the Channel ports for a limited period, but we should certainly never evacuate the force completely.' Churchill agreed: 'the BEF would be closely invested in a bomb-trap, and its total loss would only be a matter of time. Our forces must therefore at all costs move back towards Amiens.'

The decision was confirmed at a Defence Committee (Operations) meeting held at the Admiralty that night, at which a letter was read from Dill, who was in France and had seen General Georges earlier in the day. An unfortunate rumour had reached French ears, wrote Dill. Lord Gort was believed to be 'contemplating taking action independent of ... General Billotte and withdrawing on Boulogne'. Such an action would have a disastrous psychological effect 'at this moment'. Churchill drafted instructions which Ironside immediately flew to Gort.[24] He travelled throughout the night of 19/20 May, along roads crammed with refugees, to reach Gort before he took the disastrous step. Back in London, Cabinet members were feeling increasingly apprehensive. 'Our only hope, it seems to me,' wrote Chamberlain on the nineteenth, 'lies in Roosevelt and the USA. But unfortunately they are so unready themselves that they can do little to help us now.'[25] And Monday, 20 May, was to be perhaps the most disastrous day of the entire war for Britain and free Europe.

Ironside reached Lord Gort's HQ at 6 a.m., and was horrified by what he found, especially by the attitude of General Billotte, C-in-C of the French Armies in the North and coordinator of the Anglo-French forces. 'No plan, no thought of a plan,' wrote Ironside. 'Ready to be slaughtered. Defeated at the head without casualties.... I lost my temper and shook Billotte by the buttons of his tunic. The man is completely beaten.... Gort told me when I got back to his headquarters that they [the French] would never attack.' He telephoned a brief message to Churchill in time for the Cabinet meeting at 11.30 a.m. Reporting this conversation Churchill told Ministers: 'Everything possible will be done to help the Belgian Army, which will have to conform to the British movements.' But according to Eden: 'The War Office feels that there is very little chance of the Belgian Army being able to conform to the movements of the BEF. Their communications are very bad and they are without mechanical transport.' German mechanized units were advancing upon Arras, which was held by the partially trained 23rd Division. And yet the BEF was to withdraw on Arras under the existing War Cabinet plans. Eden claimed: 'The BEF are holding the line of the Scheldt from Oudenard to St Amand. It appears probable that a German attack will be made during the course of this afternoon. The British troops are tired but in very good heart.'

While Eden was speaking, the transcript was handed to him of another, longer, telephone call made by Ironside to the War Office: a start was being made with the withdrawal to the south of three BEF divisions; two had been ordered to attack Arras, and were on the move. 'General Ironside said that Lord Gort's main difficulty will be to extricate himself from his main present position on the Escaut. He [Gort] is in contact with the enemy on this line, and his units on the right are mixed up with General Billotte's army.... Further, the lines of communication of the two armies are crossed. General Ironside has seen General Billotte and has tried hard to make him attack; he rather gathers that an attack on Cambrai is intended, but he expressed no great faith in this attack, or in General Billotte. He has also spoken to General Weygand, who is full of fire.' Ironside would stay in France until the next morning.[26]

As expected, the Germans attacked during the day with renewed vigour. Seven armoured Divisions drove relentlessly west from the Somme; for the first time it became clear the objective was not Paris, as the French had expected when the German offensive began, but the sea and the Channel ports. Following the armoured divisions came six supporting motorized divisions with Guderian's Second Panzer Division spearheading the attack. Amiens fell, and Abbeville. Scattered units of two recently landed British territorial divisions were overrun. So fast was the advance that one British battery was captured with all its guns in the market square at Albert. And by nightfall, Guderian's units were at the coast, ready to strike north at Boulogne, Calais – and Dunkirk. The last line of retreat for the northern armies – nearly one million men – was about to be severed; already the remaining communication links with Paris and the base areas had been slashed.

Also on the twentieth, as a contingency plan and before full news of the disaster had reached London, Admiral Ramsay at Dover had his first conference to decide on action in the event of a BEF withdrawal. The operation was code-named 'Dynamo'.

By the morning of Tuesday, 21 May, the implications of the German success were realized in London, yet the War Cabinet still refused to consider withdrawal to the Channel ports; instead, the trapped BEF and French forces would have to fight their way to the south. Churchill, as usual, reacted bravely and optimistically: he had the audacity to tell the War Cabinet 'The situation is more favourable than certain of the more obvious symptoms indicate. Our forces still enjoy an overwhelming superiority of numbers in this theatre of operations. We must now be ready to fight hard under open war conditions.' Ironside reported on his visit to France. 'Indecision reigned in the French High Command in the north until the arrival of General Weygand and myself. General Billotte was expressing the gloomiest forebodings, but was doing nothing. He had failed to carry out his duties of coordination for the last eight days and appeared to have no plans. I complained on the telephone to General Weygand, who has spoken sharply to General Billotte.... I believe there is nothing wrong with the French troops themselves in Flanders. The BEF are in very good heart and ready for the fight.' One of the main difficulties was the mix-up of British and French communications, and 'all the roads on both lines are filled with hundreds of thousands of refugees.... The first thing to be done, in order to get a grip on the situation south and west of Arras, is to clear the towns of refugees, to block entrances to the towns and to hold them.... The next step will be to deal with the German armoured columns.'[27]

Fortunately for the BEF and for Britain, Ironside's plan was never attempted. Cooped in the towns, the BEF would have been at the mercy of the Luftwaffe; the offensive strength of the BEF and French units was severely limited; ammunition was short; logistic difficulties almost insuperable; communication links were patchy or non-existent. A meeting at Ypres on the twenty-first between Weygand, Gort, Billotte and King Leopold of the Belgians failed to achieve the required coordination. The most Lord Gort could accomplish that day was a small push south of Arras, when elements of two British infantry divisions and the First Army Tank Brigade, cooperating with French mechanized cavalry, gained ground against superior German numbers. But they had to retire again, and by the evening Gort told Brooke that the Germans were believed to be sneaking round behind, and were near Boulogne and Calais. Confusion was increasing; fragile contact between the French, British and Belgians had almost snapped.

The War Cabinet meeting at 10.30 a.m. next day opened without Churchill. 'In view of the very grave news from France,' explained Chamberlain, 'and of the difficulty of knowing exactly what was taking place in that country, the Prime Minister decided to go to France and is now on his way to Paris.' 'The BEF are still holding their position on the Escaut,' Ironside reported. 'Owing to a breakdown in communications, no recent information has been received direct from HQ, and for this reason we have had no news of General Weygand's conference with Lord Gort (at Ypres) yesterday.' It was known, however, that General Billotte had been injured in a car accident on his return from Ypres, and had been replaced – in fact Billotte died as a result of this accident, and General Blanchard took over from him. General Ironside told the War Cabinet: 'The German armoured column which was advancing on Boulogne yesterday has penetrated no further than the river Canche, where it has been heavily attacked by us from the air.... The commanding officer at Calais has reported all well, and the coast road to Dunkirk is open.' Reinforcements were being sent to the Boulogne-Calais area to secure the ports.[28]

Churchill had discussions during the day at the headquarters of the French Supreme Commander in the Château de Vincennes. The elderly Weygand, tough and wizened like a walnut, described the situation and unfolded his plan, which Churchill rushed back to London to reveal to the Cabinet at 7.30 p.m. The BEF and the French First Army would strike south-west, he said, and a new French Army Group would strike north from the Somme towards Amiens to meet them. The operation would start next day, 23 May, and the RAF would give all possible help, night and day, while the battle lasted. Ironside expressed doubts. 'So far as is known, no preparations have been made for these attacks.... I think the attacks will take some time to mount.' And Eden reported a conversation with Lord Munster, Gort's *aide-de-camp*, who had telephoned at 5 p.m. from 'some point on the coast' with a message for Churchill. 'The situation is very grave. All the lines of communication of the BEF are cut. Conversation is impossible either with Paris or London. There is a serious shortage of the essential commodities of war both in respect of food and munitions. Above all, there is no coordination between ourselves and the French on our right.' The message had continued: 'The gap must be closed at all costs on our right. The French should clear our lines of communication. As yet, however, they are not prepared to fight, nor did they show any sign of doing so.'

In the midst of this anxiety, the half-forgotten war in Scandinavia re-emerged. Churchill told the War Cabinet that Reynaud believed if the battle in France were lost, a success at Narvik would be 'of little avail'. On the other hand, if the battle in France was indeterminate, 'a small success at Narvik would be an enheartening contribution'.

359

Churchill agreed; yet on 21 May he himself had first suggested Narvik should perhaps be evacuated once it had been captured, and now, on 22 May, this was clearly recommended by the Chiefs of Staff. Next day the War Cabinet gave authorization for withdrawal plans to be prepared.[29]

Meanwhile, the critical situation to the south of the BEF, and the highly extended nature of the Front, led to Gort's decision to retire from the Scheldt to the frontier defences during the evening of 22 May – just as the War Cabinet was hearing of Weygand's unattainable plan for an advance. The BEF was, after all, to occupy the defence positions on the Belgian border which had been so carefully prepared during the winter months; but now the BEF was far too thin on the ground to hold them, and the enemy was encircling the British units. Back moved the BEF; soldiers, vehicles, fleeing refugees, all crowded into a steadily contracting area. The refugees were increasingly a problem: Brooke wrote: 'The continual sight of agonizing humanity drifting aimlessly like frightened cattle becomes one of the worst daylight nightmares. One's mind, short of sleep, is continually wracked by the devastating problems of an almost hopeless situation, and on top of it one's eyes rest incessantly on terrified and miserable humanity cluttering the lines of communication on which all hope of possible security rest.'[30]

Churchill told the War Cabinet next morning, Thursday, 23 May: 'The situation which has developed round the Channel Ports has become so critical that I have instructed the CIGS to remain at the War Office, in order that he might in person supervise the conduct of these operations.' This 'personal' supervision from London, by the CIGS and even more by Churchill, was rapidly to become a source of bitter controversy. Churchill continued: 'It appears that very much larger German forces have succeeded in getting through the gap than was at first supposed.' Yet he still thought an allied breakthrough should be attempted to the south. 'The whole success of the plan agreed with the French depends on the French forces taking this offensive. At present they show no signs of doing so.' He had therefore sent Reynaud a stiff telegram: 'Strong enemy armoured forces have cut communications of northern armies. Salvation of these armies can only be obtained by immediate execution of Weygand's plan. I demand that French commanders in North and South and Belgian HQ be given the most stringent orders to carry this out and turn defeat into victory. Time vital as supplies are short.'

Clement Attlee, the Lord Privy Seal, made one of his few interventions in the War Cabinet discussions, and the eventual result was to be of utmost importance. 'Are we not in danger of falling between two stools,' he asked, 'neither the plan agreed with General Weygand will be carried out, nor will we use our forces to best advantage in

360

retaining our hold on the Channel Ports?' He suggested the BEF move back to these Channel Ports; the Minutes do not record that any other Minister agreed.[31]

But Churchill opened a second Cabinet meeting at 7 p.m., by admitting: 'I have been giving further consideration to the observations made by the Lord Privy Seal this morning.' He had spoken to Reynaud, and had stressed the BEF's difficult position; at 6 p.m. he had also contacted Weygand, who had spoken to the CIGS as well. The French Commander had told General Ironside that the French had retaken Amiens, Albert and Peronne, and the manoeuvre was continuing under good conditions; Weygand believed the only solution was to continue this operation – 'the rest is disaster'. Both Ironside and Dill agreed with Weygand, 'since, if the BEF were to retire on the Channel ports, it would be unlikely that more than a small part of the force could be got away'. But Eden said a telegram had been sent to Gort, that 'if he found it impossible to continue operations in accordance with General Weygand's plan, he should inform the British Government, so that the French could be informed, and all possible naval and air steps taken to cover the move to the coast'. Churchill closed the meeting with his view. 'I feel ... that we have no choice in the matter but to do our best to conform to General Weygand's plan. Any other course would wreck the chance of General Weygand's plan succeeding.'[32]

But the alternative – withdrawal – had been brought into the open by Attlee, and almost hourly it became increasingly evident that hopes of fighting to freedom were totally unrealistic. Brooke started his diary entry for the day: 'Nothing but a miracle can save the BEF now, and the end cannot be very far off.'[33] The whole of the BEF had been put on half-rations during the night of 22/23 May, and, during the night of 23/24 May, instead of attacking south of Arras, British troops in the town only just avoided encirclement. Two days before, the 20th Guards Brigade had been hastily despatched to Boulogne and the 30th Infantry Brigade and 3rd Royal Tanks to Calais, in a desperate attempt to stop Guderian from sweeping along the coast behind the British, French and Belgian forces. But Churchill told the War Cabinet meeting on Friday, 24 May that Boulogne had been evacuated during the night; one thousand men had managed to escape. Calais was still being held, although the pressure was becoming intolerable – and after Calais only Dunkirk remained. The CIGS warned Ministers: 'It is possible that Dunkirk already contains as many troops as it could hold.' And yet the order to withdraw to Dunkirk had still to be given.

But now came a startling development: the War Cabinet was informed of air reports indicating a definite halt in the movement of the German armoured divisions. 'This might be due to lack of petrol or the need for repairs, as otherwise there is no reason why these forces should not push on.'[34] The information given to the War Cabinet was in fact a few hours premature; at the time of the Cabinet meeting, Hitler was in conference with Rundstedt at the latter's Army Group A headquarters, Charleville; and, due to Runstedt's timidity, to Hitler's fear of a French counter-offensive from the south, and to Göring's plea that his air force be allowed to administer the *coup de grace,* orders were now issued that for the second time Guderian's tanks should halt their advance – yet these armoured units were within 30 miles from Dunkirk. This mistake served as the 'miracle' Brooke had hoped for the evening before.

But while Guderian's tanks were halted, Beck's Army Group to the north-east was not, and on 24 May this German thrust sliced through the Belgian lines above Courtrai and between Courtrai and Menin. The BEF left flank was directly threatened. Gort had to pull back his forward units, and, with some difficulty, was persuaded by his staff officers and by Brooke that the BEF should withdraw to the Ypres-Comines canal. This withdrawal began that evening, despite the absence of orders from London, where the attempt to run the war from long distance continued, and where, incredibly, Churchill and Ironside still apparently believed the BEF should fight through to the south. Churchill told the Cabinet on 25 May: 'At about midnight last night I had a telegram from M. Reynaud, saying that the British Army was no longer conforming to General Weygand's plan and had withdrawn towards the Channel ports. At that time, we had had no information of any such move on Lord Gort's part.' Churchill said that after consulting Ironside he had replied 'we believe that Lord Gort is still persevering in the southward move'. Churchill continued: 'Later, however, a staff officer reported to the War Office confirming the withdrawal of two divisions from the Arras area.' No doubt Gort's action had been forced upon him by his position. 'Nevertheless, he should at once have informed us of the action which he had taken, and the French have grounds for complaint.... But this is no time for recriminations.' Chamberlain agreed: 'I hope that no hasty judgement will be passed on Gort's failure to keep the Government informed. There might be some explanation for his apparent omission.' Ironside provided this. 'It seems certain that Lord Gort's communications have been almost completely severed. Only the line to Dunkirk remains.... I have sent a message ... in the briefest terms possible, asking him to say whether he is (a) advancing on the ports, (b) advancing on Amiens, or (c) fighting it out on his present position.'[35] In other words Ironside, and the War Cabinet, had no idea whatsoever of the situation.

And at the GHQ conference during this Saturday, 25 May, Gort decided the withdrawal, which had been made necessary by the crumbling Belgian defences, should be made a full-scale race back to the coast. The same conclusion was now reached by a meeting of Service Ministers and Chiefs of Staff in Whitehall during the evening. 'Lord Gort should march to the coast, in battle order, under strong rearguards, striking at all forces between himself and the sea.' The meeting agreed a plan should be prepared on these lines, 'and the Navy should prepare all possible means for re-embarkation, not only at the ports but on the beaches.... The RAF should dominate the air above the area involved.' A warning was to be sent to Gort to draw up a scheme 'on the assumption that the march would start on the night of 26/27 May, but informing him not to give effect to this plan without further notice from the War Cabinet'.[36]

Churchill reported this decision to the Cabinet next morning, and told them Reynaud was coming to London during that day. 'It seems from all the evidence available that we might have to face a situation in which the French are going to collapse, and that we must do our best to extricate the BEF from northern France.' As usual he made the best of a calamitous situation; reversing his previous assessment, he now told the Cabinet 'there is a good chance of getting off a considerable proportion of the BEF,' but added: 'We must however be prepared for M. Reynaud ... to say that the French cannot carry on the fight. I will make every endeavour to induce M. Reynaud to carry on, and I will point out that they are at least in honour bound required to provide, as far as lay in their power, for the safe withdrawal of the BEF.' Calais was still holding out, said Ironside, and the First Sea Lord declared: 'The Admiralty are putting in hand all preparations for the despatch of a fleet of ships and small boats to evacuate the BEF.' But Halifax gave the gloomiest assessment of all. 'We have to face the fact that it is not so much now a question of imposing a complete defeat upon Germany, but of safeguarding the independence of our own Empire, and, if possible, that of France.' The evening before, he had had an interview with the Italian Ambassador, who 'clearly made soundings as to the prospects of our agreeing to a conference'. More was soon to be heard of this possible approach to Mussolini.[37]

'The blackest day of all,' wrote Chamberlain. 'Reynaud coming over ... plain from his attitude that he had given up all idea of serious fighting, and if we are to go on, we shall be alone.'[38]

A second Cabinet meeting was called at 2 p.m. for Churchill to report on conversations so far with the French leader. 'I do not think M. Reynaud will object to the BEF being ordered to march to the coast,' he said. Reynaud had warned Churchill that the French had only 50 divisions left with which to face 150 German divisions, and Weygand had sent a message making it clear the enemy, with their superiority of numbers and tanks, could pierce the flimsy French defences. The French commander had said he would obey orders and fight it out as long as he was told to do so, and would be prepared to 'go down fighting for the honour of the Flag', but he did not think France's resistance would last very long against a determined German onslaught. Churchill had told Reynaud the British 'were not prepared to give in on any account. We would rather go down fighting than be enslaved by Germany.' The meeting finished with discussion of a possible approach to Italy; at this stage Ministers did not believe such an initiative would meet with success.[39]

Talks with Reynaud continued during the afternoon, and, at 4.05 p.m. Reynaud sent a telephone message to Weygand. 'The reports received here from the Front indicate that the offensive from the North cannot succeed.... I think that it would seem very desirable that you should inform General Blanchard at once that you authorize him formally to order a withdrawal towards the ports.' This message failed tragically in its purpose. Weygand, believing the Germans should still be opposed, delayed issuing orders to Blanchard for the evacuation of the French First Army: not until 29 May did the executive orders arrive. And although the French Navy was intended to cooperate to save the French force, Weygand only ordered Admiral Darlan to study a scheme for evacuation, rather than to prepare and execute a definite plan.

Ministers met informally at the Admiralty soon after Reynaud had left London – no record was kept of the first fifteen minutes because the Secretary arrived late. The question of an approach to Italy was again discussed; the French were strongly in favour, but Churchill thought it best to decide nothing 'until we see how much of the Army we can embark from France. The operation might be a great failure. On the other hand, our troops might well fight magnificently, and we might save a considerable portion of the force.' He commented: 'If France cannot defend herself, it is better that she should get out of the war rather than that she should drag us into a settlement which involved intolerable terms.'[40]

The same evening Hitler rescinded his order to delay the advance upon Dunkirk. And, at 6.57 p.m., a signal flashed from the Admiralty in Whitehall: 'Operation Dynamo', the evacuation from Dunkirk, was to begin.

Another telegram left London at about the same time. Between Dunkirk and the main German thrust from the West stood Calais, battered and encircled yet still a stumbling block for the enemy advance. Now the commander at Calais, Brigadier Nicholson, was told his small force would not be withdrawn and must fight to the death. 'The decision affected us all very deeply,' wrote Ismay, 'especially perhaps Churchill. He was unusually silent during dinner that evening, and he ate and drank with evident distaste. As we rose from the table, he said, "I feel physically sick".'[41]

Reynaud was now convinced that the only hope of salvation lay in an approach to Italy. 'The only one who understands is Halifax,' he said on his return to Paris, 'who is clearly worried about the future, and realizes that some European solution must be decided. Churchill is always hectoring and Chamberlain undecided.'[42] This appeal to Mussolini was discussed by the War Cabinet next day, Monday the 27th, the day when Britain's fortunes reached their lowest ebb and when the BEF was desperately trying to disentangle itself and withdraw to the coast between Gravelines and Dunkirk. Churchill told the Cabinet meeting, which began at 4.30 p.m., 'I am increasingly oppressed with the futility of the suggested approach to Signor Mussolini, which he would certainly regard with contempt.' The Prime Minister continued: 'At the moment our prestige in Europe is very low. The only way we can get it back is by showing the world that Germany has not beaten us.... Let us therefore avoid being dragged down the slippery slope with France.' Sir Archibald Sinclair suggested Churchill might go to France to discuss the idea further. 'France,' retorted Churchill, 'has got to settle this matter for herself. It is a question of her word and her army's honour.' He added, in his most belligerent mood: 'If the worst comes to the worst, it would not be a bad thing for this country to go down fighting for the other countries which have been overcome by the Nazi tyranny.' A clash broke out between Churchill on the one side, and Chamberlain and Lord Halifax, the ex-appeasers, on the other, with the latter two believing the French should at least be free to pursue the idea if they wished to; and despite vigorous objections from Churchill, the War Cabinet agreed a non-committal message of vague support should be sent to Reynaud.[43]

The War Cabinet considered the Chiefs of Staff report, first prepared on 19 May, on Britain's situation should France collapse. Asked whether Britain could continue alone, they told Churchill 'The crux of the matter is air superiority.... Germany has most of the cards, but the real test is whether the morale of our fighting personnel and civil population will counter-balance the numerical and material advantage which Germany enjoys. We believe it will.' Earlier, Ministers had heard the latest report on the BEF situation. 'The troops are in good heart,' said Ironside, 'and feel themselves a match for the enemy.... Withdrawal in Dunkirk will, however, take two or three days, and those days will be extremely critical. The gap through which we can withdraw is very narrow, and only two roads are available.' 'Naval vessels are standing by to cover re-embarkation,' said the Chief of Naval Staff.[44] During the day Ironside received a new appointment: he succeeded Sir Walter Kirke to the critical post of C-in-C Home Forces, and Dill became the new CIGS.

Late in the afternoon of the twenty-seventh came more terrible news from Sir Roger Keyes, who was in France. The Belgians, on whom the BEF relied to block the German advance from the East, were about to surrender. The War Cabinet was hurriedly summoned at 10 p.m., and Churchill told them that in spite of this General Weygand had ordered Blanchard and Gort to continue to fight, and he had telephoned the British agreement. 'The collapse of the Belgians will undoubtedly place the BEF in the most serious peril,' warned the CIGS. 'Lord Gort has no troops with which to close the gap and prevent the Germans breaking through to Dunkirk.'

Ministers discussed this frightening news, and Churchill wondered if he himself might have been partly responsible for the Belgian decision. 'I telegraphed Sir Roger Keyes in the early hours of this morning,' he explained, 'that the BEF was withdrawing towards the ports, and that we should do our best to evacuate such of the Belgian Army as could get back to the coast.... This message should not have affected the King's determination to continue the struggle, although, perhaps, he cannot altogether be blamed for the action he is taking.... Nevertheless, he [King Leopold] has been very precipitate in seeking an armistice.... Any grounds for recrimination lie rather in the Belgian action on the outbreak of war than in the more immediate past.' Churchill stressed the serious consequences of the surrender for the BEF, but added: 'Our formations are practically intact and the troops are in excellent heart. They do not realize the plight in which they have been placed.'[45]

The night of 27/28 May marked the climax of the BEF retreat. Calais had finally fallen during the day. Much depended on whether General Montgomery's 3rd Division could pull away from its dangerously exposed position in front of Roubaix – Montgomery was almost 50 miles from Dunkirk and in the heart of the German Sixth Army. Unless his division could shift back before daybreak along roads jammed with refugees, to its new position 25 miles to the north beyond Ypres, the Germans would be able to sweep through the gap on the left of the 5th and 50th Divisions to sever the road to Dunkirk. The night was lit by flashing guns, soaring flares, and flames from ruined vehicles and buildings; the darkness came alive with screeching shells, the sound of labouring, overloaded vehicles, the sobs of refugees and the cursing of the troops as they struggled back amidst the confusion. Montgomery made it; and over the black waters of the English Channel came the British Armada to snatch up troops from Dunkirk: the first men now began to leave.

'The Belgian Army ceased to fire at 4.00 this morning,' Churchill told the Cabinet on 28 May. Keyes, now returned from the Continent, said the Belgian Government were to blame for precipitately fleeing the country. King Leopold would probably be a puppet for the

Germans, Churchill thought. 'No doubt history will criticize the King for having involved us and the French in Belgium's ruin. But it is not for us to pass judgement on him.' The other side of the Belgian coin was revealed by Lieutenant-Colonel Davy, just back from the area of fighting, who gave details of the behaviour of the Belgian Army, especially the loyalty shown to the BEF and the astounding bravery of the Belgian troops. 'For the last three days they have been subjected to incessant low-flying bombing and machine-gunning. They had virtually no air support of their own, and the British fighters were unable to get through to them, as they had to expend all their ammunition dealing with German aircraft further to the seaward.... In one counter-attack, which had been staged by the Belgians after an hour's artillery bombardment north-west of Ghent, the whole of the artillery was destroyed by dive-bombers about half an hour after the bombardment had begun.... A Belgian battalion which had been sent down to try and fill the gap between the Belgians and the British to the east of Ypres, was wiped out by a wave of 60 bombers.'

Keyes had seen Gort on the 26 May, the War Cabinet was told, 'but was unable to get in touch with him on the twenty-seventh. Lord Gort's HQ had been at Cassel, but had later been shelled out of the town. Lord Gort, who is in very good heart, has said that any attack to the southward is out of the question. Although Lord Gort has not said so, Sir Roger Keyes does not think he rated very high the chances of extricating the BEF.' But the First Sea Lord reported that 11,400 men had arrived at Dover from France the previous night, and 2,500 more were on their way. 'A later message from Captain Tennant at Dunkirk reports that "there are 2,000 troops on the beaches and 7,000 among the sand dunes. All these are very badly in need of water, which the Army cannot supply...." Dunkirk itself is covered with a pall of smoke, and the Vice-Admiral, Dover, has been instructed to use smoke from ships to add to this if needed.'

The Minister of Information read a message from Sir Walter Monckton, which pressed for a frank statement 'of the desperate situation of the BEF'. '... He fears that unless this is given out, public confidence will be badly shaken and the civil population will not be ready to accept the assurances of the Government of the chances of our ultimate victory.' Churchill said he would make a statement in the House that afternoon, 'to the effect that the BEF is fighting its way back to the coast under the protection of the RAF, and the Navy is embarking the troops.'[46] He made the statement as planned, and included in it the news of the Belgian surrender. 'The House should prepare itself for hard and heavy tidings,' he warned. But the same day, British forces had one success: Narvik was finally taken. The port which at one time had seemed so important, would be held for just 11 days.

The French are still seeking a way to safety via Mussolini, and appealed for greater British cooperation. The War Cabinet was therefore called again at 4 p.m., but Churchill repeated his objections. 'The French are trying to get us on to the slippery slope. The position will be entirely different when Germany has made an unsuccessful attempt to invade this country.... Nations which go down fighting rise again, but those which surrender tamely are finished.' 'It is important to understand the French position,' intervened Chamberlain; and other members also thought Churchill too harsh; Chamberlain and Halifax were authorized to draft a message to the French. 'We are convinced that at this moment, when Hitler is flushed with victory and certainly counts on early and complete collapse of Allied resistance, it would be impossible for Sr. Mussolini to put forward proposals for a conference with any success ... without excluding the possibility of an approach to Sr. Mussolini at some time, we cannot feel that this would be the right moment.' Ministers also considered a suggestion from Reynaud that the two countries should appeal to America for help, but the War Cabinet decided 'an appeal on the lines contemplated would tend to confirm American fears as to our weakness, and would not produce the desired effect'. French despair was plunged still deeper.[47]

'The fate of the French Army in Artois is sealed,' declared a German communiqué next day, 29 May. 'The British Army, which has been compressed into the territory ... around Dunkirk, is also going to its destruction before our concentric attack.'[48] When the Cabinet met that Wednesday morning, Eden read out a long telegram from Gort.

'PERSONAL. C-in-C to CIGS. Have just arrived La Panne to implement orders of HMG. Advanced parties and staffs have been working for past 36 hours and sit. reported as follows. Impossible use Dunkirk docks or to unload any ships there and supplies cannot be got out and only few wounded can be evacuated owing to damage to town. No water supply in Dunkirk area and elsewhere it is very limited. Food must be landed on beaches and about 20,000 men in dunes now awaiting embarkation. Troops manning portion of the perimeter are in flooded area and impossible to get adequate cover. Quantities of refugees French troops and transport also Belgian troops in area. Given immunity from air attack troops could gradually be evacuated provided food and boats could be made available in sufficient quantity. There can be no doubt that if air attacks continue at present intensities area must become a shambles and such a situation might easily arise in next 48 hours. Strongly urge HMG should consider their policy to meet the coming crisis.'

Eden had telephoned Gort, and formed the impression that he 'wanted some more definite guidance as to the action he should take in the last resort. He had sounded quite calm, but was worried about his flanks, where the pressure was greatest.' A message had been sent: 'HMG fully aprove your withdrawal to extricate your force in order to embark maximum number possible of BEF. We have every confidence that you and the gallant troops under your command will continue to the uttermost the grim struggle for our country's safety in which you are engaged. All possible assistance is being rendered by Royal Navy, and RAF will give maximum cover in their power during these critical days.' But when this telegram was read to the War Cabinet, both Lord Halifax and Chamberlain believed the wording could be interpreted as meaning Gort should continue to resist to the last man. 'A breakdown in communications might prevent him from appealing to the Government for final instructions,' Chamberlain pointed out, in which case, he might continue fighting to the end. Churchill stressed that this 'last man' inference was certainly not intended, and the War Cabinet agreed a further message should be sent. 'The latest information from the Admiralty,' Churchill reported, 'is that 40,000 troops from the BEF have so far been landed in this country, and evacuation is now taking place at the rate of about 2,000 an hour.' Finally, Halifax drew attention to a telegram from Rome, which detailed a talk between Loraine and Ciano. Halifax commented '[Ciano] makes it clear that Italy's entry into the war is now a certainty; there remains only doubt about the date.'[49]

The corridor of safety leading to the coast gradually shrank; British and French troops crammed into the defended perimeter enclosing Dunkirk and 17 miles of beach to the east. From east and west German Army groups increased the pressure. But, by midday on 30 May, nearly all the BEF personnel were within the perimeter, where conditions were made hellish by the bomber attacks and the sporadic artillery and mortar fire, and by lack of basic necessities – water, food, medical equipment. Incredibly, the men filed out in quiet organized lines from the midst of the noise, smoke and confusion, across the beaches and out to the boats. 'The latest information is that 77,000 officers and men, withdrawn from the BEF, have reached this country,' Churchill told Ministers on 30 May. 'Another 4,000 men are *en route*. Withdrawal is proceeding all the time, but the conditions are difficult.... It is thought that not more than 60,000 British troops are now left behind the line of perimeter defence, which runs from a point between Gravelines and Dunkirk to Nieuport. Practically all our troops are now behind this line; small rearguards might have been cut off, but it is not thought many troops have been lost in this way.... It is thought that the perimeter line might be held for, say, another two or three days.'

Chamberlain mentioned that some newspapers that morning claimed Calais was still holding out. He was told there was no justification for that belief. Churchill also told the Cabinet he had sent a telegram to Reynaud the previous night, giving the latest details of the evacuation. 'Front may be beaten in at any time,' he had said, 'or piers, beaches and shipping rendered unusable by air attack and also artillery fire from the south-west. . . . As soon as we have reorganized our evacuated troops, and prepared forces necessary to safeguard our life against threatened and perhaps imminent invasion, we shall build up a new BEF.' The Cabinet approved an additional message for Gort, giving clear instructions that he should not consider sacrificing himself at Dunkirk:

'Continue to defend the present perimeter to the utmost in order to cover maximum evacuation now proceeding well. Report every three hours through La Panne. If we can still communicate we shall send you an order to return to England with such officers as you may choose at the moment when we deem your command so reduced that it can be handed over to a Corps Commander. You should now nominate this Commander. If communications are broken you are to hand over and return as specified when your effective fighting force does not exceed the equivalent of three divisions. This is in accordance with correct military procedure and no personal discretion is left you in the matter. . . .'[50]

Gort held a final conference on 30 May at his HQ on the La Panne seafront. Brooke had just handed over his command of II Corps to Montgomery, after receiving orders to return to England. The other Corps Commander, Lieutenant-General Barker, who had taken over I Corps from Dill back in April, was clearly exhausted and near to collapse, and Gort eventually nominated Major-General H. R. L. G. Alexander, commander of the 1st Division in Barker's Corps, to take over the remains of the BEF. Gort telephoned Eden early in the morning next day, Friday, 31 May, and told him the remaining British force was equivalent in number to one corps. Eden told the Cabinet that Gort expected a major German attack – 'today or tomorrow morning' – and had given orders for the greater part of remaining personnel to be embarked that night. Gort had asked 'whether he ought to hold on as long as possible, in order to evacuate as many French as possible, or whether, when he judged that it was not safe to delay any longer, he should order the withdrawal of the remaining British troops.' Eden had told him 'the second was the course we wished him to pursue'.

'A total of 222 naval vessels and 665 ships and boats have been employed in the operations,' said the First Sea Lord. Three British and one French destroyer had been sunk, and twelve damaged. At the end of the meeting Eden said he had just told Gort on the telephone 'that a boat will leave Dover at 4.00 and will be ready to take him off about six this evening'.[51]

While the War Cabinet met, Churchill and Attlee were on their way to France, for a session of the Supreme War Council. The meeting, held in an atmosphere of complete gloom, considered a number of topics: Norway (the French agreed that Narvik should be evacuated), the French position, the Dunkirk operation, and Italy. Paul Baudouin, Secretary to the French War Cabinet, wrote: 'This meeting was affecting, for Mr Churchill twice had tears in his eyes when he was describing the martyrdom of the armies of the north, the terrible suffering of the men, and the loss of material which were saddening England. His voice broke down when he told us that in order to form a new army, he had given the order to embark the wounded last.'[52] The meeting ended with an impassioned declaration by Churchill: Britain would fight to the finish and would not accept slavery; if one of the two comrades fell the other should not lay down arms until that comrade was on his feet again.

The night of 31 May/1 June saw a larger number of troops taken from Dunkirk than at any other time during the embarkation – about 68,000 men. Throughout the darkness hours they waded out to the boats, and by dawn found themselves in a different world: a perfect English spring morning, with soft sunlight, and clean countryside awakening from winter. Behind them lay roads still crammed with pitiful refugees, the horizons shrouded with oily black smoke, the rubble of war, dead cattle, dead comrades, broken trees, shattered houses, and everywhere the sickly stench of defeat.

'The French expect a further attack on the French armies in the west very shortly,' Churchill told the Cabinet on 1 June, 'and have made an urgent plea that we should despatch reinforcements of land and air forces as early as possible.... My own view is that now we have got off such a large proportion of the BEF we should send some additional troops to France.' Eden told Ministers: 'Lord Gort arrived in England this morning, and has reported that the shelling and bombing of the beaches has been extremely severe, and that the Front has been contracted.' Gort was disturbed by the French belief that the position could be held for several more days and thought, said Eden, 'we should impress upon the French that this is impossible, and that the maximum efforts must be made to get as many troops off as possible tonight. Yesterday, owing to the shelling of the beaches allocated to the British, more French troops than British were evacuated.' Churchill pointed out that at the Supreme War Council the previous day the French had been told the Germans could not be held off for more than 24 hours, or at the very most 48. And the Chief of the Naval Staff commented: 'On naval grounds, it is essential to complete the evacuation tonight. Nearly all the destroyers engaged in these operations have now suffered damage. Many of the smaller craft have also been sunk or wrecked, and the Germans are now in a position to shell the only channel by which shipping can approach Dunkirk in daytime.' The War Cabinet decided the CIGS should send a telegram to the French High Command, warning them of this.

Gort entered the meeting room later amidst loud congratulations. Obviously tired, but as usual very cheerful, he gave an account of the events, from the time when the move into Belgium had started to go awry because the defences on the Dyle were found incomplete. He stressed the lack of Anglo-French coordination throughout most of the campaign; and of Dunkirk, he said: 'I think it will probably be possible to hold the line until tonight, but it might be a near thing.'[53]

The line held. During that night, 64,429 troops – the second highest total – were evacuated. Up to noon that day, 215,369 British soldiers had been saved. Sailings had been interrupted by the heavy artillery fire and the vicious Luftwaffe attacks – on 1 June both the RAF and the Luftwaffe had each lost 30 aircraft. But, Ministers were told on 2 June, 'the evacuation, which has had to be discontinued during the day, will start again at 9 p.m. this evening. The enemy are still being held at the walls of Dunkirk. The French have taken over the defence of the perimeter.'[54] Only about 6,000 British troops remained, but owing to the late orders for embarkation and an understandable reluctance to quit French soil, about 100,000 French troops were still at the mercy of the Germans. Yet miraculously, the battered, bloodied, thin perimeter line withstood German attacks for another night. Over half the remaining French troops were taken off.

The Cabinet Minutes for the meeting at 11.30 a.m., Monday, 3 June – the 153rd meeting of the War Cabinet – recorded: 'The Prime Minister informed the War Cabinet that the personnel of the BEF had now been withdrawn to this country practically intact.'[55] As Churchill spoke, the last British soldiers were on their way to Dover. A total of 338,226 British troops and 139,097 allied troops had been saved.

All the clinging remains of appeasement had been burnt away by the fire of war. Final payment had been made for unpreparedness, delays, failure of confidence between allies, failure to gain the initiative, and over-optimistic pursuit of peace. Now the war could be won.

Sources

Note. Books referred to in these chapter lists are detailed in the bibliography. The Cabinet Papers are given the abbreviations under which they are to be found in the Public Record Office; the main categories are as following:—

Cabinet Minutes: 1938: CAB 23/92 to 96; 1939 (to 3 September): CAB 23/97, 98, 99, 100

War Cabinet Minutes: 1939: CAB 65/1, 2; 1940: CAB 65/5, 6, 7

Foreign Policy Committee: CAB 27/624, 625, 627

Confidential Annexes to War Cabinet Minutes: 1939: CAB 65/3, 4; 1940: CAB 65/11, 12, 13

Cabinet Memoranda: 1939: CAB 24/282 to 288

War Cabinet Memoranda: 1939: CAB 66/1, 2, 3; CAB 67/1, 2, 3; CAB 68/1, 2, 3; 1940: CAB 66/4 to 8; CAB 67/4, 5, 6; CAB 68/4 to 7

Defence Committee: CAB 69.

Chiefs of Staff Committee: Minutes, CAB 79; Memoranda, CAB 80

Foreign Office: 1939: Sir Alexander Cadogan's Correspondence, FO 800/294; Viscount Halifax's Correspondence, FO 80/311, 313, 314 315, 316, 317, 319; 1940: General Correspondence (Political), FO 371; Halifax Papers, FO 800.

Other abbreviations used are DGFP (*Documents on German Foreign Policy*); DBFP (*Documents on British Foreign Policy*); HMSO (1) and HMSO (2) which refer to the official British war histories, respectively *Grand Strategy* (Volume II) and *The War at Sea* (Volume I); NCA (*Nazi Conspiracy and Aggression*); NN and ND (*Nuremberg Documents*).

CHAPTER 1   BLACK WEDNESDAY

1 CHURCHILL, *The Gathering Storm*, 283, 284
2 FEILING, *Life of Neville Chamberlain*, 375, 376
3 *Ibid*, 376

CHAPTER 2   ANSCHLUSS AND AFTER

1   MINNEY, *The Private Papers of Hore-Belisha*, 139
2   HENDERSON, *Failure of a Mission*, 35
3   FEILING, *Life of Neville Chamberlain*, 364
4   CAB 23/92, Cabinet 13 (38)
5   FEILING, *op. cit.*, 367
6   CAB 23/92, Cabinet 12 (38)
7   DBFP, i, 97, 120, 129
8   GARDNER, *Churchill in his Time*, 6, 7
9   CAB 23/92, Cabinets 12, 13, 14, 15 (38)
10 *Ibid*, Cabinet 13 (38)
11 CHURCHILL, *op. cit.*, 232
12 HALIFAX, *Fulness of Days*, 195
13 HENDERSON, *op. cit.*, 325
14 FEILING, *op. cit.*, 319
15 *Ibid*, 321
16 DGFP, ii, 107
17 CAB 23/98, Cabinet 21 (38)
18 DBFP, i, 148
19 *Ibid*, 164
20 DGFP, ii, 149
21 *Ibid*, 151
22 DBFP, i, 450
23 DBFP, i, 266
24 DGFP, ii, 221
25 BULLOCK, *Hitler*, 450
26 DBFP, ii, 45, 58, 59, 63
27 WHEELER-BENNETT, *Nemesis of Power*, 413
28 DBFP, ii, 686
29 DBFP, ii, 126
30 DBFP, ii, 134
31 DBFP, ii, 154
32 SHIRER, *Rise and Fall*, 462
33 DGFP, ii, 401
34 DBFP, ii, 198, 199
35 DBFP, ii, 195
36 DGFP, ii, 424, 448
37 DBFP, ii, 215
38 CHURCHILL, *op. cit.*, 264-266
39 DBFP, ii, 226, 227
40 BULLOCK, *op. cit.*, 451
41 DBFP, ii, 265
42 DBFP, ii, 257

43   DBFP, ii, 278
44   CAB 23/95, Cabinet 37 (38)
45   DBFP, ii, 280
46   DBFP, ii, 649
47   FEILING, *op. cit.*, 360
48   DBFP, ii, 291
49   DBFP, ii, 303
50   GAMELIN, *Servir*, ii, 351, 352
51   CAB 23/95, Cabinet 37 (38)
52   BAYNES, *Hitler's Speeches*, ii, 487-499
53   DBFP, ii, 304
54   DBFP, ii, 305
55   DBFP, ii, 305, 306, 312
56   MINNEY, *op. cit.*, 139
57   ISMAY, *Memoirs*, 90
58   DBFP, ii, 310
59   DBFP, ii, 311, 312
60   DBFP, 314

CHAPTER 3   MUNICH

1   CHURCHILL, *The Gathering Storm*, 270
2   DBFP, ii, 314
3   CAB 23/95, Cabinet 38 (38)
4   CAB 23/94, p. 285
5   FEILING, *Life of Neville Chamberlain*, 357
6   CADOGAN, *Diary*
7   HOARE, *Nine Troubled Years*, 300
8   DBFP, ii, 318
9   DBFP, ii, 325
10   FEILING, *op. cit.*, 363
11   SHIRER, *Berlin Diary*, 108
12   CIANO, *Diary*, 14 September, 1938
13   DBFP, ii, 335
14   FEILING, *op. cit.*, 366
15   HENDERSON, *Failure of a Mission*, 150
16   DBFP, ii, 338
17   CAB 23/95, Cabinet 39 (38)
18   MINNEY, *Private Papers of Hore-Belisha*, 141
19   DBFP, ii, 362
20   DBFP, ii, 370
21   DGFP, ii, 550
22   DBFP, ii, 387-397
23   DBFP, ii, 397-399
24   DBFP, ii, 405

25 MINNEY, *op. cit.*, 142; CAB 23/95, Cabinet 40 (38)

26 SHIRER, *op. cit.*, 111

27 DBFP, ii, 416

28 FEILING, *op. cit.*, 368

29 CHURCHILL, *op. cit.*, 273

30 DGFP, ii, 554

31 DBFP, ii, 424, 425

32 DBFP, ii, 425

33 THORNE, *Approach of War*, 75

34 DBFP, ii, 436

35 WHEELER-BENNETT, *Munich*; BONNET, *De Washington à la Quai d'Orsay*, 250

36 DBFP, ii, 437, 438

37 DBFP, ii, 438, 439

38 DBFP, ii, 439

39 CHURCHILL, *op. cit.*, 274

40 DBFP, ii, 444, 445

41 CAB 23/95, Cabinet 41 (38)

42 DBFP, ii, 454, 455

43 NICOLSON, *Diaries and Letters, 1930-1939*, 357

44 SHIRER, *op. cit.*, 112, 113

45 NICOLSON, *op. cit.*, 358

46 MACLEOD and KELLY, *Ironside Diaries*, 22 September, 1938

47 DBFP, ii, 457, 458

48 DBFP, ii, 459

49 DBFP, ii, 462

50 DBFP, ii, 477

51 DBFP, ii, 467; CAB 23/95, Cabinet 42 (38); HENDERSON, *op. cit.*, 152

52 KIRKPATRICK, *The Inner Circle*, 119

53 DBFP, ii, 480

54 DBFP, ii, 481

55 CAB 23/95, Cabinet 42 (38)

56 DBFP, ii, 483

57 CAB 23/95, Cabinet 42 (38)

58 CAB 23/95, Cabinet 42 (38); DBFP, ii, 499 ff; HENDERSON, *op. cit.*, 156 ff; DGFP, ii, 895 ff; SCHMIDT, *Hitler's Interpreter*, 95-102

59 SHIRER, *Rise and Fall*, 484

60 HENDERSON, *op. cit.*, 158

61 KIRKPATRICK, *op. cit.*, 122

62 DBFP, ii, 497, 498

63 CAB 23/95, Cabinet 42 (38); DBFP, ii, 510

64 DBFP, ii, 511

65 *Ibid*

66 MINNEY, *op. cit.*, 146

67 HOARE, *op. cit.*, 311

68 CAB 23/95, Cabinet 43 (38)
69 CIANO, *Diary*, 25 September, 1938
70 CAB 23/95, Cabinet 43 (38)
71 DBFP, ii, 518, 419
72 CAB 23/95, Cabinet 44 (38)
73 DBFP, ii, 536
74 DBFP, ii, 541, 542
75 DBFP, ii, 536-541
76 CAB 23/95, Cabinet 45 (38)
77 *Ibid*
78 DBFP, ii, 547
79 CHURCHILL, *op. cit.*, 279
80 DBFP, ii, 575
81 SCHMIDT, *op. cit.*, 102, 103
82 KIRKPATRICK, *op. cit.*, 123
83 DBFP, ii, 552, 553
84 DBFP, ii, 553
85 DBFP, ii, 554 ff
86 BAYNES, *Hitler's Speeches*, ii, 1, 508-527
87 SHIRER, *op. cit.*, 486
88 DBFP, ii, 559
89 DBFP, ii, 564 ff
90 ND 388 – PS
91 DBFP, ii, 561
92 DBFP, ii, 561, 570
93 DBFP, ii, 576 ff
94 DBFP, ii, 572, 573
95 DBFP, ii, 585
96 DBFP, ii, 587
97 DBFP, ii, 587, 588
98 HENDERSON, *op. cit.*, 164
99 *Ibid*, 165
100 DBFP, ii, 590
101 DBFP, ii, 592, 593
102 DBFP, ii, 593, 594
103 WISKEMANN, *Rome-Berlin Axis*, 160
104 CIANO, *op. cit.*, 166
105 FEILING, *op. cit.*, 376
106 *Ibid*
107 KIRKPATRICK, *op. cit.*, 128, 129
108 DBFP, ii, 630, 631
109 DBFP, ii, 604
110 CAB 23/95, Cabinet 47 (38)
111 DBFP, ii, 632, 633, 634
112 SHIRER, *op. cit.*, 510, 511

113 CAB 23/95, Cabinet 47 (38)
114 FEILING, *op. cit.*, 376
115 DBFP, ii, 635 ff
116 DBFP, ii, 640
117 SHIRER, *Berlin Diary*, 119
118 FEILING, *op. cit.*, 377
119 HALIFAX, *Fulness of Days*, 199
120 FEILING, *op. cit.*, 377
121 *Ibid*, 382

CHAPTER 4   CONSEQUENCES

1 DBFP, ii, 641
2 EDEN, *The Reckoning*, 36
3 WRIGHT, *Dowding and the Battle of Britain*, 70, 71
4 *Ibid*, 70
5 ND: *Trial of the Major War Criminals*, x, 509
6 EDEN, *op. cit.*, 37, 38
7 HOARE, *Nine Troubled Years*, 323
8 FEILING, *Life of Neville Chamberlain*, 378, 379, 380; HOARE, *op. cit.*, 326
9 HALIFAX, *Fulness of Days*, 199, 200

CHAPTER 5   REACTION AND REPRIEVE

1 DBFP, iii, 382
2 DBFP, iii, 61
3 *Ibid*
4 DBFP, iii, 63, 64
5 JENKINS, *Chequers*
6 CAB 33/95, Cabinet 48 (38)
7 NICOLSON, *Diaries and Letters, 1930-1939*, 368
8 IRVING, *Breach of Security*, 49
9 HOARE, *Nine Troubled Years*, 322
10 NICOLSON, *op. cit.*, 368
11 *Ibid*, 369
12 IRVING, *op. cit.*, 50
13 GARDNER, *Churchill in his Time*, 11
14 DBFP, iii, 67
15 CAB 23/96, Cabinet 49 (38)
16 DBFP, iii, 615
17 DGFP, iv, 46
18 BAYNES, *Hitler's Speeches*, ii, 1, 532
19 ND 388, PS – 4
20 *Ibid*

378

21 DBFP, iii, 156, 158
22 DBFP, iii, 616
23 FEILING, *Life of Neville Chamberlain*, 385, 386
24 DBFP, iii, 167
25 CAB 23/96, Cabinet 49 (38)
26 MINNEY, *Private Papers of Hore-Belisha*, 158, 159
27 ND. C – 136
28 MINNEY, *op. cit.*, 159, 160
29 DGFP, vi, 104-107
30 CP – 231 (38)
31 DBFP, iii, 342
32 CP – 234 (38)
33 CAB 23/96, Cabinet 50 (38)
34 CIANO, *Diplomatic Papers*, 242, 246
35 CAB 23/96, Cabinet 51 (38)
36 CP – 243 (38)
37 CP – 240 (38)
38 CAB 23/96, Cabinet 51 (38)
39 MINNEY, *op. cit.*, 152, 153
40 CP – 247 (38)
41 CP – 218 (38)
42 CAB 23/96, Cabinet 53 (38)
43 FEILING, *op. cit.*, 389
44 KIRKPATRICK, *The Inner Circle*, 135
45 DBFP, iii, 261
46 HOHNE, *Order of the Death's Head*, 339, 340
47 CAB 23/96, Cabinet 54 (38)
48 DBFP, iii, 264
49 SHIRER, *Rise and Fall*, 526
50 DBFP, iii, 266
51 DBFP, iii, 270
52 DBFP, iii, 269
53 DBFP, iii, 330
54 CAB 23/96, Cabinet 56 (38)
55 *Ibid*
56 DBFP, iii, 362
57 DBFP, iii, 458, 459
58 CHURCHILL, *The Gathering Storm*, 299, 300
59 DBFP, iii, 278
60 NICOLSON, *op. cit.*, 374
61 *Ibid*
62 SHIRER, *op. cit.*, 556
63 CAB 23/96, Cabinet 57 (38)
64 DBFP, iii, 369 ff
65 DBFP, iii, 463

66 DBFP, iii, 464
67 DBFP, iii, 391
68 DBFP, iii, 420
69 DBFP, iii, 390
70 CAB 23/96, Cabinet 58 (38)
71 DBFP, iii, 398, 399
72 DBFP, iii, 414, 415
73 DBFP, iii, 387, 388
74 FEILING, *op. cit.*, 392
75 CAB 23/96, Cabinet 59 (38)
76 IRVING, *op. cit.*, 50, 51
77 DGFP, iv, 82, 83
78 MINNEY, *op. cit.*, 163
79 CAB 23/96, Cabinet 60 (38)
80 DBFP, iii, 546
81 KIRKPATRICK, *op. cit.*, 137-139
82 DBFP, iii, 557

CHAPTER 6   IDES OF MARCH

1   NICOLSON, *Diaries and Letters, 1930-1939*, 377
2   FEILING, *Life of Neville Chamberlain*, 319
3   DBFP, iii, 562
4   DBFP, iii, 568
5   DBFP, iii, 573
6   DBFP, iii, 580
7   DBFP, iii, 581
8   *Ibid*
9   CAB 27/624
10 DBFP, iii, 159-161
11 DBFP, iii, 513
12 HALIFAX, *Fulness of Days*, 201
13 SHIRER, *Berlin Diary*, 126
14 HALIFAX, *op. cit.*, 201
15 DBFP, iii, 537
16 FEILING, *op. cit.*, 393
17 CIANO, *Diary*
18 CAB 23/97, Cabinet 1 (39)
19 HALIFAX, *op. cit.*, 202
20 CAB 23/97, Cabinet 1 (39)
21 MINNEY, *Private Papers of Hore-Belisha*, 170, 171
22 DBFP, iv, 19-22
23 DBFP, iii, 610
24 DGFP, iv, 190-202
25 DBFP, iv, 7, 8

26 CAB 27/624
27 *Ibid*
28 MINNEY, *op. cit.*, 171
29 DBFP, iv, 18
30 DBFP, iv, 23
31 DBFP, iv, 30
32 DBFP, iv, 27
33 DBFP, iv, 32
34 DBFP, iv, 34
35 DBFP, iv, 35
36 DBFP, iv, 37, 44
37 DBFP, iv, 41
38 DBFP, iv, 50
39 DBFP, iv, 52
40 CAB 23/97, Cabinet 3 (39)
41 CAB 23/97, Cabinet 5 (39)
42 DBFP, iv, 307
43 NICOLSON, *op. cit.*, 383
44 FEILING, *op. cit.*, 395
45 DGFP, iv, 207, 208
46 CAB 23/97, Cabinet 6 (39)
47 FEILING, *op. cit.*, 396
48 DGFP, iv, 209-213
49 HENDERSON, *Failure of a Mission*, 183
50 CAB 23/97, Cabinet 7 (39)
51 DBFP, iv, 110, 111
52 DBFP, iv, 121
53 FEILING, *op. cit.*, 396
54 DBFP, iv, 592
55 DBFP, iv, 592, 593
56 CAB 23/97, Cabinet 9 (39)
57 DBFP, iv, 162
58 DBFP, iv, 164, 165
59 HENDERSON, *op. cit.*, 200, 201
60 CAB CP – 48 (39)
61 CAB 23/97, Cabinet 9 (39)
62 DBFP, iv, 157
63 DBFP, iv, 173
64 DBFP, iv, 183
65 CAB 23/97, Cabinet 10 (39)
66 MINNEY, *op. cit.*, 173 ff
67 DBFP, iv, 207
68 DBFP, iv, 210-215
69 HOARE, *Nine Troubled Years*, 328
70 FEILING, *op. cit.*, 396, 397

71 HALIFAX, *op. cit.*, 232
72 DBFP, iv, 217
73 DBFP, iv, 218
74 DBFP, iv, 229
75 DBFP, iv, 230
76 HENDERSON, *op. cit.*, 203
77 *Ibid*, 205
78 DBFP, iv, 232
79 DGFP, iv, 271
80 DGFP, iv, 69-72
81 DBFP, iv, 267
82 DBFP, iv, 250
83 HENDERSON, *op. cit.*, 205
84 SCHMIDT, *Hitler's Interpreter*, 124; DGFP, iv, 263-269; HENDERSON, *op. cit.*, 208, 209

CHAPTER 7 CROSSING THE STREAM

1 DBFP, iv, 255
2 HENDERSON, *Failure of a Mission*, 205
3 DBFP, iv, 595
4 CAB 23/98, Cabinet 11 (39)
5 HOARE, *Nine Troubled Years*, 329
6 DBFP, iv, 270
7 DBFP, iv, 284
8 DBFP, iv, 279
9 NICOLSON, *Diaries and Letters, 1930-1939*, 386
10 HENDERSON, *op. cit.*, 215
11 DBFP, iv, 366, 367
12 DBFP, iv, 596
13 DBFP, iv, 364-366
14 DBFP, iv, 291
15 DBFP, iv, 361
16 DBFP, iv, 360, 361
17 DBFP, iv, 369
18 *Ibid*
19 CAB 23/98, Cabinet 12 (39)
20 DBFP, iv, 372
21 DGFP, vi, 39
22 IRVING, *Breach of Security*, 57
23 DBFP, iv, 385
24 DBFP, iv, 392
25 CAB 23/98, Cabinet 13 (39)
26 CIANO, *Diary*, 21 March, 17 March; WISKEMANN, *Rome-Berlin Axis*, 171, 172

27   DGFP, v, 524-526
28   DBFP, iv, 400
29   DBFP, iv, 434-436
30   DGFP, vi, 70-72
31   DBFP, iv, 431
32   CAB 23/98, Cabinet 14 (39)
33   DBFP, iv, 458 ff
34   DBFP, iv, 463
35   DBFP, iv, 467
36   DBFP, iv, 468
37   HOARE, op. cit., 337
38   DBFP, iv, 417, 419
39   DBFP, iv, 497
40   ND. R – 100
41   FEILING, Life of Neville Chamberlain, 403, 408
42   CAB 27/624
43   DGFP, vi, 135, 136
44   DBFP, iv, 515, 516
45   DBFP, iv, 525
46   CAB 23/98, Cabinet 15 (39)
47   DBFP, iv, 627
48   CAB 23/96, Cabinet 17 (39)
49   DBFP, iv, 548
50   DBFP, iv, 549
51   CAB 23/98, Cabinet 17 (39)
52   Ibid
53   DBFP, iv, 557
54   CHURCHILL, The Gathering Storm, 310, 311

CHAPTER 8   EASTERN ENTANGLEMENTS

1   WRIGHT, Dowding and the Battle of Britain, 75, 76
2   DBFP, iv, 573, 574
3   BAYNES, Hitler's Speeches, ii, 1, 590-1, 602
4   DBFP, iv, 574
5   DBFP, iv, 582
6   HMSO (1), 20, 71
7   CHURCHILL, The Gathering Storm, 314
8   DBFP, v, 1-9
9   DBFP, v, 9 ff
10 DBFP, v, 36, 37
11 CAB 23/98, Cabinet 18 (39)
12 DBFP, v, 45
13 DBFP, v, 53, 54
14 DBFP, v, 176

15 DBFP, V, 129
16 DBFP, V, 130
17 DBFP, V, 140
18 CHURCHILL, *op. cit.*, 315
19 DBFP, V, 145
20 DBFP, V, 155
21 DBFP, V, 151, 152
22 CAB 23/98, Cabinet 19 (39)
23 CAB 23/98
24 NICOLSON, *Diaries and Letters, 1930-1939*, 390
25 MINNEY, *Private Papers of Hore-Belisha*, 190
26 DBFP, V, 184
27 CAB 23/98, Cabinet 21 (39)
28 DBFP, V, 105
29 DBFP, V, 106
30 DBFP, V, 107
31 CHURCHILL, *op. cit.*, 317
32 DBFP, V, 209, 210
33 DBFP, V, 199
34 DBFP, V, 205, 206
35 MINNEY, *op. cit.*, 193, 194
36 DBFP, V, 218
37 CIANO, *Diary*, 16 April
38 DBFP, V, 215
39 DGFP, vi, 211
40 DBFP, V, 228, 229
41 DGFP, vi, 266, 267
42 DBFP, V, 222
43 MINNEY, *op. cit.*, 195
44 *Ibid*
45 CAB 23/98, Cabinet 21 (39)
46 NICOLSON, *op. cit.*, 392
47 MINNEY, *op. cit.*, 199
48 CIANO, *Diary*, 20 April
49 DBFP, V, 244, 245
50 DBFP, V, 310
51 DBFP, V, 286
52 CP. 91 (39)
53 CAB 23/99, Cabinet 22, 23 (39)
54 DBFP, V, 320, 321
55 HENDERSON, *Failure of a Mission*, 221
56 CAB 23/99, Cabinet 24 (39)
57 HOARE, *Nine Troubled Years*, 338
58 NICOLSON, *op. cit.*, 393
59 CHURCHILL, *op. cit.*, 319

60   HENDERSON, *op. cit.*, 78
61   DBFP, v, 357, 358
62   DBFP, v, 382, 389
63   DBFP, v, 390, 391
64   CHURCHILL, *op. cit.*, 327
65   CAB 23/99, Cabinet 26 (39)
66   DBFP, v, 571, 572
67   BOOTHBY, *I Fight to Live*, 189
68   DBFP, v, 422
69   DBFP, v, 429; DGFP, vi, 529
70   DGFP, vi, 334
71   DBFP, v, 443, 448-450
72   DBFP, v, 469-471
73   CAB 23/99, Cabinet 27 (39)
74   IRVING, *Breach of Security*, 80; DBFP, v, 478
75   HMSO (1) 80
76   WISKEMANN, *Rome-Berlin Axis*, 179
77   DBFP, v, 558, 559, 567, 568
78   CAB 27/624
79   CAB 23/99, Cabinet 28 (39)
80   DGFP, vi, 535, 536
81   DBFP, v, 594
82   EDEN, *The Reckoning*, 55
83   DBFP, v, 595
84   DBFP, v, 584-586, 620, 621
85   DBFP, v, 609
86   DGFP, vi, 547
87   DBFP, v, 634
88   DBFP, v, 656
89   DGFP, vi, 574 ff
90   CAB 23/99, Cabinet 30 (39)
91   DBFP, v, 668, 669
92   ND. R – 100
93   DBFP, v, 724
94   DBFP, v, 688
95   DBFP, v, 678, 701, 710
96   DGFP, vi, 597, 598
97   DBFP, v, 719, 720
98   DBFP, v, 722
99   DGFP, 616, 617, 624-626
100 DGFP, vi, 547
101 French Yellow Book, 180, 181
102 CAB 27/624
103 DBFP, v, 776, 777
104 DBFP, vi, 96

105 DBFP, vi, 6
106 DBFP, vi, 22
107 CAB 23/99, Cabinet 32 (39)

CHAPTER 9   EASTERN APPROACHES

1 NICOLSON, *Diaries and Letters, 1930-1939*, 393, 397
2 DBFP, vi, 79
3 DBFP, vi, 77
4 ND. C – 142; ND. 2327 – PS
5 NICOLSON, *op. cit.*, 397
6 DBFP, vi, 87
7 DBFP, vi, 89
8 DBFP, vi, 37
9 DBFP, vi, 103, 104
10 CAB 23/100, Cabinet 33 (39)
11 DBFP, vi, 140-142
12 DBFP, vi, 143
13 DBFP, vi, 144, 145
14 ND. C – 126
15 ND. 3787 – PS
16 DBFP, vi, 152, 153
17 CAB 23/100, Cabinet 34 (39)
18 DGFP, vi, 810
19 DBFP, vi, 173, 174
20 CAB 23/100, Cabinet 34 (39)
21 DGFP, vi, 790, 791
22 DGFP, vi, 803
23 DBFP, vi, 201, 202
24 DBFP, vi, 216
25 DGFP, vi, 810
26 DBFP, vi, 230-232
27 DBFP, vi, 251
28 DBFP, vi, 249, 250
29 DBFP, vi, 257, 258
30 DAVIES, *Mission to Moscow*, 450
31 CAB 23/100, Cabinet 36 (39)
32 DBFP, vi, 279, 280
33 SHIRER, *Rise and Fall*, 617
34 DBFP, vi, 288, 289
35 DBFP, vi, 310
36 DBFP, vi, 310-313
37 DBFP, vi, 375-377
38 DGFP, vi, 936-938
39 CAB 23/100, Cabinet 38 (39)

40 IRVING, *Breach of Security*, 71

41 DBFP, vi, 422-426

42 DBFP, vi, 447

43 DGFP, vi, 955, 956

44 DBFP, vi, 531

45 DBFP, vi, 450, 451

46 DBFP, vi, 456

47 DBFP, vi, 456, 460

48 DBFP, vi, 460, 461

49 DBFP, vi, 478

50 CAB 23/100, Cabinet 39 (39)

51 DGFP, vi, 1,106, 1,109

52 DGFP, vi, 1,010, 1,011

53 DBFP, vi, 527, 528

54 CAB 27/625

55 DGFP, vi, 1,015

56 HENDERSON, *Failure of a Mission*, 240, 241

57 FEILING, *Life of Neville Chamberlain*, 409

58 DGFP, vi, 1,022, 1,023

59 DBFP, vi, 578

60 STRONG, *Intelligence at the Top*, 51, 52

61 DBFP, vi, 719

62 CAB 23/100, Cabinet 40 (39)

63 DBFP, vi, 570-574

64 CAB 23/100, Cabinet 40 (39)

65 DBFP, vi, 714

CHAPTER 10 ACCOUNT PRESENTED

1 DBFP, vi, 560

2 DBFP, vi, 575

3 DGFP, vi, 1,047

4 DGFP, vi, 1,048

5 DBFP, vi, 606-608

6 DBFP, vi, 586

7 DBFP, vi, 597

8 DBFP, vi, 592

9 DBFP, vi, 610, 611, 614

10 DBFP, vi, 620, 621

11 DGFP, vi, 864, 865

12 DBFP, vi, 635

13 DBFP, vi, 645, 644

14 DBFP, vi, 645, 646

15 DBFP, vi, 657

16 ND. – 2, 751 – PS

17   DBFP, vi, 759
18   DGFP, vii, 43
19   DBFP, vi, 691, 696; THORNE, *Approach of War 1938-1939*, 155
20   DBFP, vi, 674
21   DGFP, vii, 58, 59
22   ND. 1871 – PS
23   CIANO, *Diary*, 12 August, 13 August
24   DBFP, vi, 763
25   DBFP, vii, 451
26   DBFP, vii, 682
27   DGFP, vii, 58, 59
28   SHIRER, *Rise and Fall*, 625, 626
29   DBFP, vi, 700, 701
30   DBFP, vi, 684
31   HMSO (I) 34
32   CHURCHILL, *The Gathering Storm*, 341, 342
33   DBFP, vii, 8, 25, 26
34   DBFP, vii, 29-32
35   DBFP, vii, 76, 77
36   DGFP, vii, 84, 85
37   DBFP, vii, 22, 23
38   DBFP, vii, 37, 38
39   HÖHNE, *Order of the Death's Head*, 260
40   DBFP, vii, 41
41   DGFP, vii, 84, 85
42   DBFP, vii, 42
43   DBFP, vii, 41, 42
44   DBFP, vii, 53
45   DBFP, vii, 52
46   DBFP, vii, 68
47   DBFP, vii, 53, 54
48   DGFP, vii, 121, 123
49   DBFP, vii, 80-82
50   DBFP, vii, 69, 70
51   DGFP, vii, 132, 133
52   DGFP, vii, 149, 150
53   HÖHNE, *op. cit.*, 262
54   CIANO, *Diary*, 20 August
55   DGFP, vii, 156, 157
56   HALIFAX, *Fulness of Days*, 209
57   DGFP, vii, 161, 162
58   CHAPMAN, *Why France Collapsed*, 53
59   DGFP, vii, 164
60   DBFP, vii, 106, 108
61   DBFP, vii, 114, 115

62 DGFP, vii, 168
63 MINNEY, *Private Papers of Hore-Belisha*, 216
64 DBFP, vii, 101
65 DBFP, vii, 121, 122
66 DBFP, vii, 122
67 DBFP, vii, 125
68 DBFP, vii, 138
69 ND – 798. PS; NN – 1014 PS; DBFP, vii, 258, 259
70 CAB 23/100, Cabinet 41 (39)
71 DBFP, vii, 142, 385
72 DBFP, vii, 145
73 DBFP, vii, 127, 128
74 DBFP, vii, 162, 163, 416
75 DBFP, vii, 147
76 DBFP, vii, 157
77 DBFP, vii, 201, 202, 177-179; HENDERSON, *Failure of a Mission*, 257
78 DBFP, vii, 150
79 ISMAY, *Memoirs*, 97
80 NICOLSON, *Diaries and Letters, 1930-1939*, 405
81 DBFP, vii, 184
82 DBFP, vii, 184, 212, 213
83 CAB 23/100, Cabinet 42 (39); MINNEY, *op. cit.*, 219, 220
84 DBFP, vii, 186
85 DBFP, vii, 187
86 DBFP, vii, 189
87 DBFP, vii, 216, 217
88 DGFP, vii, 281-283
89 DBFP, vii, 255
90 DBFP, vii, 224
91 DBFP, vii, 239
92 DBFP, vii, 225
93 DBFP, vii, 224
94 DBFP, vii, 249
95 DBFP, vii, 239
96 HENDERSON, *op. cit.*, 259
97 DGFP, vii, 289
98 DBFP, vii, 283
99 DGFP, vii, 309, 310; CIANO, *Diary*, 26 August
100 DGFP, vii, 565
101 DGFP, vii, 313, 314
102 CAB 23/100, Cabinet 43 (39)
103 DGFP, vii, 323
104 DGFP, vii, 346, 347
105 DBFP, vii, 282-285
106 CHURCHILL, *op. cit.*, 356

107 NICOLSON, *op. cit.*, 408, 409
108 DBFP, vii, 319
109 DBFP, vii, 302
110 MINNEY, *op. cit.*, 222
111 DGFP, vii, 353, 354
112 DGFP, vii, 357
113 DBFP, vii, 311
114 DBFP, vii, 319, 320
115 CAB 23/100, Cabinet 45 (39); MINNEY, *op.cit.*, 222
116 DBFP, vii, 323
117 NICOLSON, *op. cit.*, 407

CHAPTER 11 THE LAST DAYS OF PEACE

1   DBFP, vii, 331
2   HENDERSON, *Failure of a Mission*, 260
3   DBFP, vii, 351-354
4   DBFP, vii, 356, 357
5   DBFP, vii, 354, 355
6   DBFP, vii, 367
7   DBFP, vii, 364
8   DBFP, vii, 368
9   DBFP, vii, 388-390
10 DBFP, vii, 393, 426, 427; HENDERSON, *op. cit.*, 265, 266
11 DBFP, vii, 377, 378
12 DBFP, vii, 392
13 DBFP, vii, 391; IRVING, *Breach of Security*, 100
14 DBFP, vii, 400
15 CAB 23/100, Cabinet 46 (39)
16 IRVING, *op. cit.*, 103
17 DBFP, vii, 406
18 DBFP, vii, 413, 414
19 HENDERSON, *op. cit.*, 269
20 DBFP, vii, 430, 432, 433; HENDERSON, *op. cit.*, 270, 271
21 HENDERSON, *op. cit.*, 273
22 DBFP, vii, 434
23 IRVING, *op. cit.*, 31, 32
24 DBFP, vii, 434
25 French Yellow Book, 366, 367 (French Edition)
26 DBFP, vii, 446
27 DBFP, vii, 442, 443
28 DBFP, vii, 436, 437
29 TREVOR-ROPER, *Hitler's War Directives*, 38-40
30 HÖHNE, *Order of the Death's Head*, 264, 265
390

31   HENDERSON, *op. cit.*, 275
32   DBFP, vii, 468
33   HÖHNE, *op. cit.*, 264, 265
34   DBFP, vii, 459; CIANO, *Diary*
35   DBFP, vii, 469
36   DBFP, vii, 473, 474
37   HÖHNE, *op. cit.*, 265
38   DBFP, vii, 474
39   DBFP, vii, 474, 475
40   DBFP, vii, 476, 477
41   CIANO, *Diary*; DGFP, vii, 483
42   SHIRER, *Berlin Diary*, 156
43   DBFP, vii, 517
44   *Ibid*
45   CAB 23/100, Cabinet 47 (39)
46   French Yellow Book, 377, 378 (French Edition)
47   DBFP, vii, 477
48   DBFP, vii, 480
49   DBFP, vii, 488
50   French Yellow Book, 379 (French Edition)
51   DBFP, vii, 493, 494
52   CAB 65/1, War Cabinet 26 (39)
53   DGFP, vii, 509
54   DBFP, vii, 501
55   DGFP, vii, 509
56   CAB 23/100, Cabinet 48 (39)
57   DBFP, vii, 514
58   CAB 23/100, Cabinet 49 (39)
59   ELLETSON, *The Chamberlains*, 279, 280
60   NICOLSON, *Diaries and Letters, 1930-1939*, 412
61   DBFP, vii, 525
62   CAB 23/100, Cabinet 49 (39)
63   KIRKPATRICK, *The Inner Circle*, 144
64   CIANO, *Diary*, 3 September
65   DBFP, vii, 535, 534
66   SCHMIDT, *Hitler's Interpreter*, 157, 158
67   DBFP, vii, 537
68   DBFP, vii, 539
69   HENDERSON, *op. cit.*, 285
70   CHURCHILL, *The Gathering Storm*, 361
71   WRIGHT, *Dowding and the Battle of Britain*, 81
72   CHURCHILL, *op. cit.*, 362; MINNEY, *op. cit.*, 228
73   CHURCHILL, *op. cit.*, 362
74   EDEN, *The Reckoning*, 63
75   WRIGHT, *op. cit.*, 81

CHAPTER 12 WAR

1 FEILING, *Life of Neville Chamberlain*, 417
2 CAB 23/100, Cabinet 47 (39)
3 FEILING, *op. cit.*, 421
4 EDEN, *The Reckoning*, 73
5 CAB 66/1; CID Paper No. DP (P) 64; HMSO (I) 9
6 CAB 66/1; DP (P) 50, DP (P) 67
7 HMSO (I) 10, 11
8 WRIGHT, *Dowding and the Battle of Britain*, 87
9 HMSO (I) 33
10 FEILING, *op. cit.*, 424
11 FULLER, *The Second World War*, 55
12 GAMELIN, *Servir*, ii, 410-429; NAMIER, *Diplomatic Prelude*, 246; HMSO (I) 54-57

CHAPTER 13 DEATH OF AN ALLY

1 HMSO (I) 27
2 CAB 65/1, War Cabinet 1 (39); MINNEY, *Private Papers of Hore-Belisha*, 230
3 CAB 65/1, War Cabinet 1 (39)
4 MINNEY, *op. cit.*, 230
5 CHURCHILL, *The Gathering Storm*, 344
6 CAB 65/1, War Cabinet 2 (39)
7 CAB 66/1; COS (39) 5
8 CAB 65/1, War Cabinet 2 (39)
9 HENDERSON, *Failure of a Mission*, 290, 291
10 FEILING, *Life of Neville Chamberlain*, 419
11 CAB 65/1, War Cabinet 3 (39)
12 HENDERSON, *op. cit.*, 291
13 CAB 65/1, War Cabinet 4 (39); HMSO (I) 60
14 CHURCHILL, *op. cit.*, 379, 380
15 CAB 66/1, WP (39) 8
16 CAB 65/1, War Cabinet 7 (39)
17 *Ibid*
18 HENDERSON, *op. cit.*, 292
19 CAB 66/1, WP (39) 15
20 CAB 65/1, War Cabinet 8 (39)
21 DGFP, vii, 24
22 CHAPMAN, *Why France Collapsed*, 59
23 DGFP, vi, 33, 34

24 CAB 65/1, War Cabinet 9 (39)
25 SHIRER, *Berlin Diary*, 164
26 TREVOR-ROPER, *Hitler's War Directives*, 43
27 SHIRER, *Berlin Diary*, 164
28 CAB 65/1, War Cabinet 10 (39)
29 CHURCHILL, *op. cit.*, 402
30 *Ibid*, 404
31 HMSO (1) 36
32 DGFP, vii, 35
33 CAB 65/1, War Cabinet 11 (39)
34 CAB 66/1, WP (39) 19
35 CAB 65/1, War Cabinet 12 (39)
36 SHIRER, *Berlin Diary*, 165
37 HÖHNE, *Order of the Death's Head*, 298; ND. 3047 – PS
38 CAB 65/1, War Cabinet 13 (39)
39 CAB 65/1, War Cabinet 15 (39)
40 DGFP, viii, 60, 61
41 CHURCHILL, *op. cit.*, 38
42 *Ibid*, 404-406
43 *Ibid*, 406
44 CAB 65/1, War Cabinet 16 (39)
45 DGFP, viii, 68-70
46 CAB 65/1, War Cabinet 17 (39)
47 DGFP, viii, 76, 77
48 *Ibid*, 79
49 CHURCHILL, *op. cit.*, 384
50 *Ibid*, 384
51 DGFP, vii, 910
52 WP (G) (39) 12
53 CAB 65/1, War Cabinet 20 (39)
54 CHURCHILL, *op. cit.*, 473, 474
55 MINNEY, *op. cit.*, 241
56 *Ibid*, 243
57 CAB 65/1, War Cabinet 23 (39)
58 WP (39) 43
59 CAB 65/1, War Cabinet 24 (39)
60 FEILING, *op. cit.*, 424

CHAPTER 14   WAR TWILIGHT

1 CALDER, *People's War*, 71
2 NICOLSON, *Diaries and Letters, 1939-1945*, 31
3 *Ibid*, 32
4 CAB 66/2, WP (39) 65

5   CAB 65/1, War Cabinet 26 (39)
6   CAB 66/2
7   NICOLSON, op. cit., 32
8   GARDNER, Churchill in his Time, 22, 23
9   MINNEY, Private Papers of Hore-Belisha, 245
10 CAB 65/1, War Cabinet 29 (39)
11 SHIRER, Rise and Fall, 769
12 CAB 66/2
13 DGFP, viii, 164, 168
14 CAB 66/2, WP (39) 57
15 CAB 65/1, War Cabinet 31 (39)
16 SHIRER, op. cit., 769, 770
17 BRYANT, Turn of the Tide, 51, 52
18 MINNEY, op. cit., 246, 247
19 CAB 65/1, War Cabinet 34 (39)
20 CHURCHILL, The Gathering Storm, 454
21 CAB 65/1, War Cabinet 35 (39)
22 CAB 65/2, WP (39) 65, COS (39) 61; CHURCHILL, op. cit., 426-428; CAB
    65/1, War Cabinet 36 (39)
23 WP (39) 57
24 CAB 65/1, War Cabinet 38 (39)
25 CHURCHILL, op. cit., 477
26 CAB 65/1, War Cabinet 40 (39)
27 ND 2329 – PS
28 SHIRER, op. cit., 773, 774
29 CAB 65/1, War Cabinet 41 (39)
30 CAB 66/2, COS (39) 69
31 TREVOR-ROPER, Hitler's War Directives, 50, 51
32 FEILING, Life of Neville Chamberlain, 424
33 CAB 65/1, War Cabinet 42 (39)
34 SHIRER, op. cit., 774, 776
35 HMSO (1) 176
36 CAB 65/1, War Cabinet 45 (39)
37 WP (39) 87
38 CAB 65/1, War Cabinet 46 (39)
39 HOARE, Nine Troubled Years, 409, 410
40 FEILING, op. cit., 420
41 CAB 65/1, War Cabinet 47 (39)
42 BRYANT, op. cit., 63
43 CAB 65/1, War Cabinet 48 (39)
44 CAB 65/1, War Cabinet 49 (39)
45 BRYANT, op. cit., 63, 64
46 CAB 65/1, War Cabinet 50 (39)
47 CAB 65/1, War Cabinet 56 (39)
48 CAB 65/1, War Cabinet 57 (39)

49 CAB 65/1, War Cabinet 58 (39)
50 BRYANT, *op. cit.*, 64; SHIRER, *op. cit.*, 778
51 MINNEY, *op. cit.*, 252
52 BRYANT, *op. cit.*, 70, 71, 72
53 NICOLSON, *op. cit.*, 41
54 CAB 65/1, War Cabinet 66 (39)
55 MINNEY, *op. cit.*, 252, 253
56 CHURCHILL, *op. cit.*, 408
57 CAB 65/1, War Cabinet 66 (39)
58 ISMAY, *Memoirs*, 109
59 SHIRER, *op. cit.*, 781
60 CAB 65/2, War Cabinet 69 (39)
61 SHIRER, *op. cit.*, 781, 782
62 CAB 65/2, War Cabinet 72 (39)
63 ROTHFELS, *German Opposition to Hitler.*
64 ND. C – 72
65 CAB 65/2, War Cabinet 77 (39); HMSO (I) 161, 162
66 CAB 65/2, War Cabinet 82 (39)
67 CAB 65/2, War Cabinet 84 (39)
68 CAB 65/2, War Cabinet 85 (39)
69 CHURCHILL, *op. cit.*, 428
70 MINNEY, *op. cit.*, 257, 258
71 CAB 65/2, War Cabinet 87 (39)
72 CHURCHILL, *op. cit.*, 450, 451
73 CAB 65/2, War Cabinet 90 (39)
74 MINNEY, *op. cit.*, 259
75 EDEN, *The Reckoning*, 82
76 WP (39) 133
77 CAB 65/2, War Cabinet 91 (39)
78 MINNEY, *op. cit.*, 263
79 CHURCHILL, *op. cit.*, 441
80 CAB 65/2, War Cabinet 94 (39)
81 CHURCHILL, *op. cit.*, 662
82 CAB 65/2, War Cabinet 99 (39)
83 CAB 65/2, War Cabinet 96 (39)
84 CAB 65/2, War Cabinet 97 (39)
85 CAB 65/2, War Cabinet 98 (39)
86 CAB 65/2, War Cabinet 99 (39)
87 MAISKY, *Memoirs of a Soviet Ambassador*, 20
88 CAB 65/2, War Cabinet 99 (39)
89 CAB 65/2, War Cabinet 101 (39)
90 MINNEY, *op. cit.*, 263
91 CAB 65/2, War Cabinet 103 (39)
92 CAB 65/2, War Cabinet 104 (39)
93 CAB 65/2, War Cabinet 109 (39)

94   CAB 65/2, War Cabinet 111 (39)
95   CAB 65/2, War Cabinet 114 (39)
96   HMSO (1) 105
97   WP (39) 162
98   CAB 65/2, War Cabinet 117 (39)
99   MONTGOMERY, *Memoirs*, 58
100 WISKEMANN, *Rome-Berlin Axis*, 227
101 CAB 65/2, War Cabinet 118 (39)
102 CAB 65/2, War Cabinet 120 (39)
103 MINNEY, *op. cit.*, 267, 268
104 CAB 66/4
105 CAB 65/2, War Cabinet 122 (39)
106 FEILING, *op. cit.*, 430
107 WP (39) 173
108 CAB 65/2, War Cabinet 123 (39)
109 HMSO (1) 84

CHAPTER 15   A QUESTION OF ORE

1   CAB 66/4; WP (39) 179
2   CAB 66/4; WP (39) 180
3   CAB 66/4; WP (40) 3
4   CAB 65/5, War Cabinet 1 (40); CAB 65/11
5   CAB 65/5, War Cabinet 2 (40); CAB 65/11
6   MINNEY, *The Private Papers of Hore-Belisha*, 269 ff; CHURCHILL, *The Gathering Storm*, 490; HMSO (1) 152; FEILING, *The Life of Neville Chamberlain*, 434
7   EDEN, *The Reckoning*, 82, 83
8   CAB 65/5, War Cabinet 5 (40); CAB 65/11
9   CAB 65/5, War Cabinet 6 (40); CAB 65/11
10   CAB 65/5, War Cabinet 30 (40)
11   WP (40) 10
12   CAB 65/5, War Cabinet 8 (40); CAB 65/11
13   WP (40) 14
14   CAB 65/5, War Cabinet 10 (40); CAB 65/11
15   CAB 65/5, War Cabinet 11 (40); CAB 65/11
16   CAB 65/5, War Cabinet 12 (40); CAB 65/11
17   CAB 65/5, War Cabinet 13 (40); CAB 65/11
18   CAB 65/5, War Cabinet 14 (40); CAB 65/15
19   CHURCHILL, *op. cit.*, 491, 492
20   *Ibid*, 488
21   GARDNER, *Churchill in his Time*, 29
22   CAB 65/5, War Cabinet 16 (40); CAB 65/11
23   CAB 65/5, War Cabinet 18 (40); CAB 65/11

24 WP (40) 24
25 CAB 65/5, War Cabinet 18 (40)
26 NCA, vi, 883
27 BRYANT, *The Turn of the Tide*, 78
28 CAB 65/5, War Cabinet 26 (40)
29 WP (40) 41
30 CAB 65/6, War Cabinet 31 (40); CAB 65/5, 66/5, WP (40) 41
31 CAB 65/5, War Cabinet 32 (40); CAB 65/11
32 CAB 65/5; WP (40) 35
33 HMSO (1), 107, 108
34 CAB 65/5, War Cabinet 38 (40); CAB 65/11
35 CAB 66/5; WP (40) 39
36 IRVING, *Breach of Security*, 167
37 CAB 65/5, War Cabinet 44 (40); CHURCHILL, *op. cit.*, 498
38 IRVING, *op. cit.*, 168
39 CAB 65/5, War Cabinet 44 (40)
40 WP (40) 59
41 CAB 65/5, War Cabinet 46 (40); CAB 65/11
42 CAB 65/11
43 SHIRER, *Rise and Fall*, 816
44 CAB 65/5, War Cabinet 49 (50); CAB 65/11
45 MAISKY, *Memoirs of a Soviet Ambassador*, 48, 49
46 CAB 65/5, War Cabinet 50 (40)
47 CAB 65/5, War Cabinet 49 (40); CAB 65/11
48 BRYANT, *op. cit.*, 78, 79, 81
49 CAB 66/5; WP (40) 67; CAB 65/5, War Cabinet 53 (40)
50 CAB 65/5, War Cabinet 55 (40); CAB 65/11
51 ROPER, *Hitler's War Directives*, 61 ff.
52 CAB 65/6, War Cabinet 57 (40); CAB 65/12
53 CAB 65/6, War Cabinet 58 (40); CAB 65/12
54 MAISKY, *op. cit.*, 50
55 CAB 65/6, War Cabinet 59 (40); CAB 65/12
56 CAB 65/6, War Cabinet 60 (40); CAB 65/12
57 CAB 65/6, War Cabinet 61 (40); CAB 65/12
58 CAB 65/6, War Cabinet 61 (40); CAB 65/12; WP (40) 84
59 CAB 65/6, War Cabinet 62 (40); CAB 65/12
60 CAB 65/6, War Cabinet 63 (40); CAB 65/12; COS (40) 260 (S)
61 CAB 65/6, War Cabinet 65 (40); CAB 65/12
62 CAB 65/6, War Cabinet 66 (40); CAB 65/12; COS (40) 264 (S)

CHAPTER 16 NORWAY

1 ND. 1809 – PS
2 CAB 65/6, War Cabinet 66 (40); CAB 65/12

3   CAB 65/6, War Cabinet 67 (40); CAB 65/12
4   WP (40) 96
5   CAB 65/6, War Cabinet 68 (40)
6   IRVING, *Breach of Security*, 168, 169
7   CAB 65/6, War Cabinet 70 (40)
8   CAB 65/6, War Cabinet 72 (40)
9   CAB 65/6, War Cabinet 74 (40)
10 WP (40) 111
11 CAB 65/6, War Cabinet 76 (40)
12 CAB 65/6, War Cabinet 78 (40); CAB 65/12; HMSO (1) 121, 122
13 CHURCHILL, *The Gathering Storm*, 514
14 CAB 65/6, War Cabinet 78 (40)
15 EDEN, *The Reckoning*, 84
16 HOARE, *Nine Troubled Years*, 427
17 EDEN, *op. cit.*, 90
18 DGFP, ix, 66-68
19 CAB 65/6, War Cabinet 80 (40); CAB 65/12
20 ND. 1809 – PS
21 ISMAY, *Memoirs*, 110
22 *Daily Express*, 5 April 1940
23 CAB 65/6, War Cabinet 82 (40)
24 CAB 65/6, War Cabinet 83 (40)
25 CAB 65/6, War Cabinet 84 (40); CAB 16/12
26 MACLEOD and KELLY, *The Ironside Diaries*, 247
27 HMSO (1) 126; HMSO (2), Chapter X
28 CAB 65/6, War Cabinet 85 (40)
29 CAB 65/6, War Cabinet 86 (40)
30 CHURCHILL, *op. cit.*, 527
31 HMSO (1) 129
32 EDEN, *op. cit.*, 96
33 CAB 65/6, War Cabinet 87 (40); CAB 65/12
34 CAB 65/6, War Cabinet 88 (40); CAB 65/12
35 CAB 65/12, War Cabinet 89 (40)
36 CHURCHILL, *op. cit.*, 531, 532; NICOLSON, *Diaries and Letters, 1939-1945*, 65, 66
37 CHURCHILL, *op. cit.*, 537
38 CAB 65/6, War Cabinet 89 (40); CAB 65/12
39 REYNAUD, *La France a sauvé l'Europe*, ii, 22-43; GAMELIN, *Servir*, iii, prt. iii, ch. ii
40 WP (40) 126
41 CAB 65/6, War Cabinet 90 (40); CAB 65/12
42 CHURCHILL, *op. cit.*, 533
43 CAB 65/6, War Cabinet 92 (40); CAB 65/12
44 HMSO (1) 135
45 CHURCHILL, *op. cit.*, 541

46 MACLEOD and KELLY, *op. cit.*, 260
47 CHURCHILL, *op. cit.*, 520
48 CAB 65/6, War Cabinet 93 (40); CAB 65/12
49 CAB 65/6, War Cabinet 95 (40); CAB 65/12
50 CAB 65/6, War Cabinet 96 (40); CAB 65/12
51 CAB 65/6, War Cabinet 95 (40)
52 CAB 65/6, War Cabinet 96, 97 (40)
53 CAB 65/6, War Cabinet 98 (40); CAB 83/5
54 CHURCHILL, *op. cit.*, 561
55 FEILING, *Life of Neville Chamberlain*, 437
56 CHURCHILL, *op. cit.*, 562
57 CAB 83/5
58 *Ibid*
59 CAB 65/6, War Cabinet 100 (40); CAB 65/12
60 CHURCHILL, *op. cit.*, 562, 563; CAB 83/3
61 HMSO (I) 138, 164, 165; CHURCHILL, *op. cit.*, 563-565
62 CAB 65/6, War Cabinet 101 (40); CAB 65/12
63 CAB 65/6, War Cabinet 102 (40); CAB 65/12
64 CHURCHILL, *op. cit.*, 566
65 MACLEOD and KELLY, *op. cit.*, 282; CAB 65/6, War Cabinet 103 (40)
66 CAB 83/3
67 CAB 65/6, War Cabinet 104 (40); CAB 65/12
68 CAB 65/6, War Cabinet 105 (40); CAB 65/12
69 ISMAY, *op. cit.*, 112, 113
70 NICOLSON, *op. cit.*, 70
71 CAB 65/7, War Cabinet 109 (40); CAB 65/13
72 CAB 65/7, War Cabinet 110 (40)
73 CAB 65/7, War Cabinet 109 (40); CAB 65/13; EDEN, *op. cit.*, 96
74 CHURCHILL, *op. cit.*, 572
75 CAB 65/7, War Cabinet 111 (40)
76 JENKINS, *Chequers*; FEILING, *op. cit.*, 438
77 CAB 65/7, War Cabinet 113 (40)
78 CAB 65/7, War Cabinet 114 (40)
79 CAB 65/7, War Cabinet 115 (40)
80 CAB 65/7, War Cabinet 115 (40); CAB 65/13
81 FEILING, *op. cit.*, 439, 440; ELLETSON, *The Chamberlains*, 284, 285; CHURCHILL, *op. cit.*, 582; NICOLSON, *op. cit.*, 73-76
82 FEILING, *op. cit.*, 440
83 HOARE, *op. cit.*, 430, 431
84 CHURCHILL, *op. cit.*, 534
85 WP (40) 145
86 HALIFAX, *Fulness of Days*, 220
87 FEILING, *op. cit.*, 442
88 CHAPMAN, *Why France Collapsed*, 93

CHAPTER 17   FINAL PAYMENT

1   HOARE, *Nine Troubled Years*, 432
2   CAB 65/7, War Cabinet 117 (40)
3   CAB 65/7, War Cabinet 118 (40)
4   CAB 65/7, War Cabinet 119 (40)
5   WHEELER-BENNET, *King George VI*, 443
6   NICOLSON, *Diaries and Letters, 1939-1945*, 80
7   FEILING, *Life of Neville Chamberlain*, 440
8   EDEN, *The Reckoning*, 98
9   CAB 65/7, WM (40) 119A
10 SHIRER, *Berlin Diary*, 262
11 CAB 65/7, WM (40) 119C
12 CAB 65/7, WM (40) 120
13 CAB 65/7, WM (40) 121
14 CAB 65/7, WM (40) 122
15 WRIGHT, *Dowding and the Battle of Britain*, 104, 107
16 CAB 65/7, War Cabinet 123 (40); CAB 65/13
17 BRYANT, *Turn of the Tide*, 102
18 CAB 65/7, War Cabinet 125 (40); CAB 65/13
19 CAB 65/7, War Cabinet 126 (40)
20 *Ibid*
21 *Rommel Papers*, 19
22 CAB 65/7, War Cabinet 127 (40)
23 BRYANT, *op. cit.*, 108
24 DO (40) 4th meeting
25 FEILING, *op. cit.*, 444
26 CAB 65/7, War Cabinet 131 (40); CAB 65/13
27 CAB 65/7, War Cabinet 132 (40)
28 CAB 65/7, War Cabinet 133 (40)
29 HMSO (1) 145; CAB 65/7, War Cabinet 134 (40); CAB 65/13
30 BRYANT, *op. cit.*, 116
31 CAB 65/7, War Cabinet 135 (40)
32 CAB 65/7, War Cabinet 136 (40); CAB 65/13
33 BRYANT, *op. cit.*, 117
34 CAB 65/7, War Cabinet 137 (40)
35 CAB 65/7, War Cabinet 138 (40)
36 CAB 65/7, War Cabinet 139 (40); CAB 65/13
37 FEILING, *op. cit.*, 444; CAB 65/7, War Cabinet 139 (40); CAB 65/13
38 FEILING, *op. cit.*, 444
39 CAB 65/7, War Cabinet 140 (40); CAB 65/13
40 *Ibid*
41 ISMAY, *Memoirs*, 131
42 PETRIE, *Private Diaries of Baudouin*, 57

43 CAB 65/7, War Cabinet 142 (40); CAB 65/13
44 CAB 65/7, War Cabinet 141 (40); CAB 65/13
45 CAB 65/7, War Cabinet 143 (40)
46 CAB 65/7, War Cabinet 144 (40)
47 CAB 65/7, War Cabinet 145 (40)
48 SHIRER, *Rise and Fall*, 882, 883
49 CAB 65/7, War Cabinet 146 (40); CAB 65/13
50 CAB 65/7, War Cabinet 147 (40)
51 CAB 65/7, War Cabinet 149 (40)
52 PETRIE, *op. cit.*, 69
53 CAB 65/7, War Cabinet 151 (40)
54 CAB 65/7, War Cabinet 152 (40)
55 CAB 65/7, War Cabinet 153 (40)

Bibliography

AVON, EARL OF, *The Reckoning*, London, 1965
BAYNES, NORMAN, H., ed., *The Speeches of Adolf Hitler*, London, 1942
BIRKENHEAD, EARL OF, *The Life of Lord Halifax*, London, 1965
BOOTHBY, LORD, *I Fight to Live*, London, 1947
BRYANT, ARTHUR, *The Turn of the Tide*, London, 1957
BULLOCK, ALAN, *Hitler: a study in tyranny*, London, 1969 (Penguin edition)
BUTLER, J. R. M., *Grand Strategy*, Vol. II, Official History of the Second World War, HMSO, 1957
CALDER, NIGEL, *People's War*, London, 1969
CHAPMAN, GUY, *Why France Collapsed*, London, 1968
CHATFIELD, LORD, *It Might Happen Again*, London, 1947
CHURCHILL, *The Gathering Storm*, London, 1960 (Penguin edition)
CIANO, *Diary*, ed. Malcolm Muggeridge, London, 1945
——, *Diplomatic Papers*, ed. Malcolm Muggeridge, London, 1948
COLVIN, IAN, *Vansittart in Office*, London, 1965
COOPER, ALFRED DUFF, *Old Men Forget*, London, 1953
COOPER, LADY DIANA, *Trumpets From the Sleep*, London, 1960
Documents on British Foreign Policy, 1919-1939, Series 3, ed. Sir Llewellyn Woodward, vols. II-VII, HMSO, 1947
Documents on German Foreign Policy, 1918-1945, Series D, US State Department
EDEN, *see* AVON
ELLETSON, D. H., *The Chamberlains*, London, 1966
ELLIS, MAJOR F. F., *France and Flanders Campaign*, Official History of the Second World War, HMSO, 1953
FEILING, K., *The Life of Neville Chamberlain*, London, 1946
FRANÇOIS-PONCET, ANDRÉ, *The Fateful Years*, London, 1949
French Yellow Book, *see* Le Livre Jaune
FULLER, MAJOR-GENERAL, J. F. C., *The Second World War*, London, 1948
GAMELIN, GENERAL MAURICE GUSTAVE, *Servir*, 3 vols., Paris, 1949
GARDNER, BRIAN, *Churchill in his Time*, London, 1968
HALIFAX, LORD, *Fulness of Days*, London, 1957
HARVEY, OLIVER, *Diplomatic Diaries*, 1937-1940, London, 1970
HENDERSON, SIR NEVILE, *Failure of a Mission*, London, 1940
HOARE, SIR SAMUEL, *Nine Troubled Years*, London, 1954
HÖHNE, HEINZ, *The Order of the Death's Head*, London, 1969
IRVING, DAVID, ed., *Breach of Security*, London, 1968

ISMAY, GENERAL LORD, *Memoirs*, London, 1960

JENKINS, J. GILBERT, *Chequers*, London, 1957

KIRKPATRICK, SIR IVONE, *The Inner Circle*, London, 1959

LE LIVRE JAUNE FRANCAIS, Documents diplomatiques, 1938-1939, Paris, French Foreign Ministry

LIDDELL-HART, B. H., ed., *The Rommel Papers*, London, 1953

MACLEOD, R. and KELLY, D., *The Ironside Diaries*, London, 1962

MAISKY, IVAN, *Memoirs of a Soviet Ambassador*, trans. Andrew Rothstein, London, 1967

MONTGOMERY, FIELD-MARSHAL, *Memoirs*, London, 1960 (Fontana edition)

NAMIER, SIR LEWIS B., *Diplomatic Prelude, 1938-1939*, London, 1948

Nazi Conspiracy and Aggression (NCA), 10 vols., Washington, US Government, 1946

Nuremberg Documents: Proceedings of the International Military Tribunal, HMSO, 1946; *Trial of the Major War Criminals*, 42 vols.; *Trial of War Criminals*, 15 vols., Washington, US Government, 1951-1952

NICOLSON, NIGEL, ed., *Diaries and Letters, 1930-1939*, London, 1969 (Fontana edition)

——, *Diaries and Letters, 1939-1945*, London, 1969 (Fontana Edition)

PETRIE, SIR C., *Private Papers of Baudouin*, London, 1943

ROSKILL, CAPTAIN S. W., *The War at Sea, 1*, Official History of the Second World War, London, HMSO

ROTHFELS, HANS, *The German Opposition to Hitler*, Hinsdale, Ill., 1948

SCHACHT, DR. H., *Account Settled*, London, 1949

SCHMIDT, PAUL, *Hitler's Interpreter*, London, 1951

SHIRER, WILLIAM L., *Berlin Diary, 1934-1941*, London, 1970 (Sphere Edition)

——, *The Rise and Fall of the Third Reich*, London, 1960 (Pan edition, 1964)

SIMON, VISCOUNT, *Retrospect*, London, 1952

SWINTON, EARL OF, *I Remember*, London, 1952

THORNE, CHRISTOPHER, *The Approach of War, 1938-1939*, London, 1967

TREVOR-ROPER, H. R., *Hitler's War Directives, 1939-1945*, London, 1964 (Pan Edition, 1966)

WHEELER-BENNET, J. W., *King George VI*, London, 1958

——, *Munich, Prologue to Tragedy*, London, 1948

——, *Nemesis of Power*, London, 1953

——, *John Anderson*, London, 1962

WISKEMANN, ELIZABETH, *The Rome-Berlin Axis*, London, 1969 (Fontana Edition)

——, *Europe of the Dictators, 1919-1945*, London, 1967

WRIGHT, ROBERT, *Dowding and the Battle of Britain*, London, 1969

Index